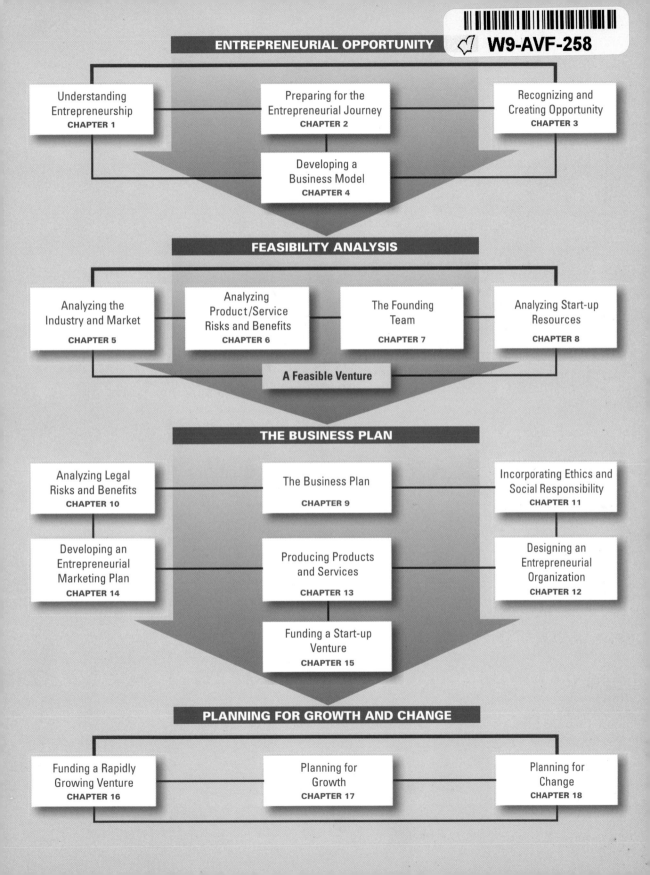

ENTREPRENEURIAL OPPORTUNITY

Understanding
Entrepreneurship
CHAPTER 1

Preparing for the
Entrepreneurial Journey
CHAPTER 2

Recognizing and
Creating Opportunity
CHAPTER 3

Developing a
Business Model
CHAPTER 4

FEASIBILITY ANALYSIS

Analyzing the
Industry and Market
CHAPTER 5

Analyzing
Product/Service
Risks and Benefits
CHAPTER 6

The Founding
Team
CHAPTER 7

Analyzing Start-up
Resources
CHAPTER 8

A Feasible Venture

THE BUSINESS PLAN

Analyzing Legal
Risks and Benefits
CHAPTER 10

The Business Plan
CHAPTER 9

Incorporating Ethics and
Social Responsibility
CHAPTER 11

Developing an
Entrepreneurial
Marketing Plan
CHAPTER 14

Producing Products
and Services
CHAPTER 13

Designing an
Entrepreneurial
Organization
CHAPTER 12

Funding a Start-up
Venture
CHAPTER 15

PLANNING FOR GROWTH AND CHANGE

Funding a Rapidly
Growing Venture
CHAPTER 16

Planning for
Growth
CHAPTER 17

Planning for
Change
CHAPTER 18

LAUNCHING NEW VENTURES

AN ENTREPRENEURIAL APPROACH

FOURTH EDITION

KATHLEEN R. ALLEN
UNIVERSITY OF SOUTHERN CALIFORNIA

Houghton Mifflin Company   Boston   New York

To the students and alumni of the Lloyd Greif Center for Entrepreneurial Studies at the University of Southern California, where the entrepreneurial spirit and the Trojan network continue to grow.

Editor-in-Chief: George Hoffman
Development Manager: Susan M. Kahn
Associate Editor: Julia Perez
Senior Project Editor: Carol Merrigan
Editorial Assistant: Eric Moore
Manufacturing Coordinator: Chuck Dutton
Executive Marketing Manager: Steven W. Mikels
Marketing Associate: Lisa Boden

Cover image: © Tyler Stableford/Getty Images

Text/art credits: p. 8: (Fig. 1.3): Reprinted from Databases for the Study of Entrepreneurship, Vol. 4, No. 1, by Paul D. Reynolds, "National Panel of U.S. Business Start-Ups: Background and Methodology," pp. 153–227. Copyright © 2000, with permission from Elsevier; **p. 11:** (Fig. 1.4): From H. Neck, A.L. Zacharakis, W. Bygrave, and P. Reynolds. (2003). Global Entrepreneurship Monitor: United States 2003 Report. Babson College and the Kauffman Foundation; **p. 39:** (Screenshot 2.1): Reprinted with permission of Lanny Goodman; **p. 72:** (Screenshot 4.1): Copyright Edmunds.com, Inc. Used with permission; **p. 98:** (Screenshot 5.1): Reprinted with permission of NAICS Association; **p. 119:** (Fig. 6.2): Based on the research of Greg A. Stevens and James Burley in "Piloting the Rocket of Radical Innovation," Research Technology Management, March/April 2003. Reprinted with permission of Industrial Research Institute; **p. 120:** (Fig. 6.3): From Kathleen R. Allen, *Bringing New Technology to Market,* 1st edition, copyright 2003. Electronically reproduced by permission of Pearson Education, Inc., Upper Saddle River, New Jersey; **p. 187:** (Screenshot 9.1): Reprinted with permission of SAS Group; **p. 211:** (Screenshot 10.1): Reprinted with permission of Mycorporation.com; **p. 234:** (Distributed.net): Reprinted with permission; (ebay): These materials have been reproduced with the permission of eBay Inc. Copyright © eBay Inc. All rights reserved; and (leadertoleader): Reprinted with permission of Leader to Leader Institute; **p. 259:** (Screenshot 12.1): Reprinted with permission of PEO.com LLC, Rodney B. Diekema; **p. 316:** (Fig. 15.2): From M. Minniti and W.D. Bygrave (2004). Global Entrepreneurship Monitor: United States 2003 Executive Report. Babson College and the Kauffman Foundation, www.gemconsortium.org. Reprinted with permission; **p. 337:** (Fig. 16.1): Money Tree Survey by PricewaterhouseCoopers. Thomson Venture Economics and the National Venture Capital Association. Reprinted with permission; **p. 338:** (Fig. 16.2): Money Tree Survey by PricewaterhouseCoopers. Thomson Venture Economics and the National Venture Capital Association. Reprinted with permission; **p. 340:** (Screenshot 16.1): MAVA represents the collective interests and leverages of success of venture capitalists investing in DC, Maryland and Virginia. Founded in 1986, MAVA provides a wide range of programs, information and forums designed to facilitate quality deal flow, encourage collaboration, and foster solid relationships with key service providers. Membership includes 375 venture capital professionals at 126 firms with over $10 billion in capital under management. In addition, over 265 key service providers from the legal, financial, executive search and consulting fields are also MAVA members. For more information on MAVA, please visit www.mava.org; **p. 388:** (Screenshot 18.1): Reprinted by permission of Pro2Serve® Professional Project Services, Inc., www.p2s.com, Oak Ridge, Tennessee.

Printed in the U.S.A.

Library of Congress Control Number: 2005925806

ISBN: 0-618-52807-5

23456789-DOC-09 08 07 06 05

Brief Contents

Contents

All chapters include Learning Objectives, a New Venture Checklist, Issues to Consider, Experiencing Entrepreneurship, Additional Sources of Information, and Relevant Case Studies.

Preface

L ife is about choices. You can choose to follow the path that everyone expects you to follow, or you can figure out what you're really passionate about and pursue that. You can be at the mercy of someone for whom you work, or you can ensure that you have the skills and attitude to take care of yourself in any situation.

Life is also about change. It is impossible to predict what you will be doing five or ten years from today, let alone twenty years from now. Entrepreneurs realize that they can't predict the future, so they use what they have, who they are, what they know, and whom they know to craft a future of their choosing. They believe that if you can control the future, there is no need to predict it. How do they control the future? By seizing opportunities, building social networks, and becoming resource gatherers. Whether you start a new venture, join an entrepreneurial venture, acquire a business, or create a new venture inside a large organization, you will need entrepreneurial skills to navigate an increasingly complex world and to differentiate yourself from competitors in whatever field of endeavor you choose. One of the major goals of *Launching New Ventures* is to help you acquire those skills.

Entrepreneurship is about the creation of new ventures. But it is much more than a set of skills for starting a business. Just as important, it is a mindset—an approach to the world and to business. To compete successfully in a rapidly changing environment, you must understand and develop this entrepreneurial mindset and constantly scan the environment to be prepared to adapt to change. This book is designed to immerse the reader in the entrepreneurial mindset and provide the "critical thinking" skills required to recognize and effectively evaluate an opportunity.

Entrepreneurship is also about passion, and you can't teach passion. You can only show the results of it. The passion of the entrepreneur is like energy. It can change, but it can never be destroyed—it simply takes another form. When an entrepreneur's business venture fails, the passion doesn't die with it; rather, it sustains the entrepreneur in an effort to start again. Passion is something that happens when a person discovers what he or she was *meant* to do. No one has a monopoly on passion. Some of the most successful entrepreneurs have been teachers, engineers, psychologists, musicians, and filmmakers. Many have had no college education at all, but in every case they were lifelong learners and they believed in themselves. As Will Rogers once said, "Know what you are doing. Love what you are doing. Believe in what you are doing." That is the spirit of the entrepreneur. And that is the spirit of *Launching New Ventures*.

Today, aspects of entrepreneurship are incorporated into many different kinds of academic courses and into a variety of business situations. Even large corporations are spinning off entrepreneurial ventures and encouraging the entrepreneurial mindset in their environments. For example, executive education programs are using *Launching New Ventures* to introduce and teach the entrepreneurial mindset to middle-level managers and CEOs of large companies.

Launching New Ventures, Fourth Edition, represents the most current thought, ideas, and practices in the field of entrepreneurship. In fact, ever since its first edition, *Launching New Ventures* has endeavored to extend the boundaries of what we know about entrepreneurship.

Content, Organization, and Unique Coverage

Launching New Ventures is organized around the process of creating a new venture, from the recognition of an opportunity to the launch of the business. It is designed to help the reader organize and plan for venture creation by mentally (and sometimes physically) engaging in the various activities that entrepreneurs typically undertake. Because the book focuses on the pre-start-up phase of venture creation, it explores these pre-launch activities, such as opportunity creation and feasibility analysis, in more depth than the average book on entrepreneurship.

Part One introduces the foundations of entrepreneurship that are important to understanding the decisions that entrepreneurs make, the environment in which they make those decisions, and the tasks they must undertake before launching a new company. In Chapter 1, students will learn the entrepreneurial mindset and understand the nature of entrepreneurial ventures and how they are distinct from other types of businesses. Chapter 2 dispels many myths about entrepreneurs and helps readers understand the characteristics and behaviors that work for and against entrepreneurs. Chapter 3 introduces the subject of opportunity and how entrepreneurs recognize and create opportunities for themselves. Part One closes with Chapter 4, "Developing a Business Model," where readers will learn how to define and develop a business concept, position it in the value chain, and evaluate it.

Part Two addresses the heart of entrepreneurial activity, the testing of a new business concept through feasibility analysis. Chapter 5 begins with a discussion of how to analyze an industry, which is the environment in which the new business will operate, and follows that with a discussion of the role of the primary customer for a new business and how to research the customer. Chapter 6 explores the way entrepreneurs develop products and services; it considers product development, prototyping, and intellectual property. Chapter 7 analyzes the founding team and discusses how to determine what gaps in experience and expertise may exist in the team and how to compensate for them with such solutions as strategic alliances and independent contractors. Part Two closes with Chapter 8, which considers entrepreneurial resource gathering and prepares the reader to calculate how much capital and other resources will be required to launch the venture.

Part Three focuses on the business plan, which is the document that explains the strategy for executing a feasible business concept and building a company. It begins with Chapter 9, which describes how to move from a feasible concept to a business plan and how to organize and present the plan effectively. Chapter 10 looks at the legal form of the business and discusses the advantages and disadvantages of sole proprietorships, partnerships, and corporate forms. Chapter 11 explores the increasingly important topics of vision, ethics, and social responsibility. The value system of a new business shapes the culture of the business and the image it will have to live up to as it builds its reputation. Students will be challenged to define a vision for a new venture based on the values they believe to be important. They will also gain a greater understanding of the need for ethics and social responsibility in any business. Chapter 12 considers how entrepreneurial businesses are organized, how they determine the best business site, and how they develop their start-up team. Chapter 13 focuses on how products and services are produced and addresses issues related to manufacturing, quality control, and customer service. Chapter 14 deals with the role and implementation of the marketing plan and how to promote new products and services effectively with limited resources. Chapter 15 considers the entrepreneur's resource strategy, how to construct a resource plan, and how to finance a start-up venture with equity and debt.

Part Four looks at planning for growth and change in the new organization. It begins with Chapter 16, which considers how to fund a rapidly growing venture. Chapter 17 deals with growth strategies for entrepreneurial ventures, and Chapter 18 discusses how to plan for change and for exit or harvest.

Special Features in the Fourth Edition

The fourth edition contains a variety of features of value to both instructors and students.

- *Learning Objectives* highlight the key topics for each of the chapters.
- Entrepreneur *Profiles* that begin each chapter provide real-life examples to illustrate the application of chapter concepts and to inspire students. Smaller-scale profiles are also scattered throughout the chapters to maintain the real-life tone of the book.
- *"Global Insights" and "Socially Responsible Entrepreneurship" boxed inserts* highlight additional examples, companies, and organizations that have taken a global or a socially responsible approach to entrepreneurship.
- *Sidebar* features offer quick tips and interesting anecdotes.
- The *New Venture Checklist* serves as a reminder of the tasks that need to be completed at particular stages of the entrepreneurial process.
- *Issues to Consider* are questions at the end of each chapter that provoke interesting discussions in class.
- *Experiencing Entrepreneurship* is a series of activities at the end of each chapter that give students a chance to learn about entrepreneurship by getting involved in entrepreneurial activities and interacting with entrepreneurs and others in an industry of special interest to the student.
- *Additional Sources of Information* lists books and Internet sources that will give the student more in-depth information about a topic.
- Several new *Case Studies* have been added to the fourth edition to reflect a wider variety of businesses and types of entrepreneurs. The companies and products discussed include Craigslist (the Internet "marketplace" phenomenon), Finagle a Bagel (a start-up bagel boutique), and iRobot (the first robot for the domestic market). The cases are followed by discussion questions.

Supplemental Materials

An *Instructor's Resource Manual with Test Items* features suggestions for planning the course; instructional tips; learning objectives; lecture outlines; answers to end-of-chapter questions; a test bank with true/false, multiple-choice, and essay questions; and notes for the instructor's use with the case studies. The test bank is also offered in an electronic, editable, and downloadable format on the HMTesting CD.

The *website* contains resources for both students and instructors. For students it provides links to other useful sites on the web, ACE self-test questions, and examples of feasibility studies and business plans. For instructors it includes sample syllabi, PowerPoint slides for classroom presentation, and downloadable files from the *Instructor's Resource Manual* so that instructors can edit and adapt the material for their particular course needs.

New to this edition, a *video program,* along with a video guide, will be offered to supplement in-class discussions.

Acknowledgments

Many people helped make this fourth edition of *Launching New Ventures* happen — entrepreneurs, university students, professors, and, of course, the publishing staff at Houghton Mifflin. In particular, I would like to thank associate sponsoring editor Susan Kahn, whose patience and humor got me through a tough production schedule. In addition, appreciation is due to Julia Perez, associate editor, who kept me on the straight and narrow, and to Carol Merrigan, senior project editor.

I want to thank the instructors who used the third edition and gave me feedback, as well as my students at the Lloyd Greif Center for Entrepreneurial Studies at the University of Southern California, who willingly share their ideas and comments with me. I also want to thank those instructors who provided formal manuscript reviews at various stages of the revision process for this and previous editions:

Donna Albano
Atlantic Cape Community College

Joseph S. Anderson
Northern Arizona University

Richard Benedetto
Merrimack College

Edward Bewayo
Montclair State University

Bruce Dickinson
Southeast Technical Institute

Janice Feldbauer
Austin Community College

Todd Finkle
University of Akron

Susan Fox-Wolfgramm
San Francisco State University

Frederick D. Greene
Manhattan College

Jeffry Haber
Iona College

Jo Hamilton
Franklin University

Steven C. Harper
University of North Carolina at Wilmington

Timothy Hill
Central Oregon Community College

Sandra Honig-Haftel
Wichita State University

Lilly Lancaster
University of South Carolina–Spartanburg

Tom Lumpkin
University of Illinois at Chicago

Clare Lyons
Hagerstown Community College

Steven Maranville
University of Houston–Downtown

Ivan J. Miestchovich, Jr.
University of New Orleans

Stephen Mueller
Texas Christian University

Eugene Muscat
University of San Francisco

Terry Noel
Wichita State University

Robert Novota
Lincoln University

Fred B. Pugh
Kirksville College of Osteopathic Medicine

Juan A. Seda
Florida Metropolitan University

Randy Swangard
University of Oregon

Charles N. Toftoy
The George Washington University

Lynn Trzynka
Western Washington University

Barry L. Van Hook
Arizona State University

John Volker
Austin Peay State University

Gene Yelle
SUNY Institute of Technology

Mark Weaver
University of Alabama

Dennis Williams
Pennsylvania College of Technology

David Wilemon
Syracuse University

And finally, I would like to thank my husband, John; and my children, Rob, Jaime (a writer herself), and Greg for their love and support.

K.R.A.

About the Author

Kathleen Allen, Ph.D., is a professor in the Lloyd Greif Center for Entrepreneurial Studies in the Marshall School of Business at the University of Southern California, where she is also director of the Center for Technology Commercialization, which focuses on helping faculty and students commercialize the technologies they develop at USC. At a national level, Allen leads the National Network for Technology Entrepreneurship and Commercialization (N2TEC), a partnership of universities, industry, and government formed to raise the level of innovation and technology commercialization in the United States. In addition to *Launching New Ventures,* Allen is the author of *Entrepreneurship and Small Business Management,* 2nd ed., *Bringing New Technology to Market,* and *Growing and Managing an Entrepreneurial Business,* as well as several trade books. As an entrepreneur, Allen co-founded a real estate development company, a real estate brokerage firm that she eventually sold, and two technology ventures, and she is a director of a company listed on the NYSE. In addition to a Ph.D. with an emphasis in entrepreneurship, Allen holds an M.B.A. and an M.A. in Romance languages.

Part One

Entrepreneurial
Opportunity

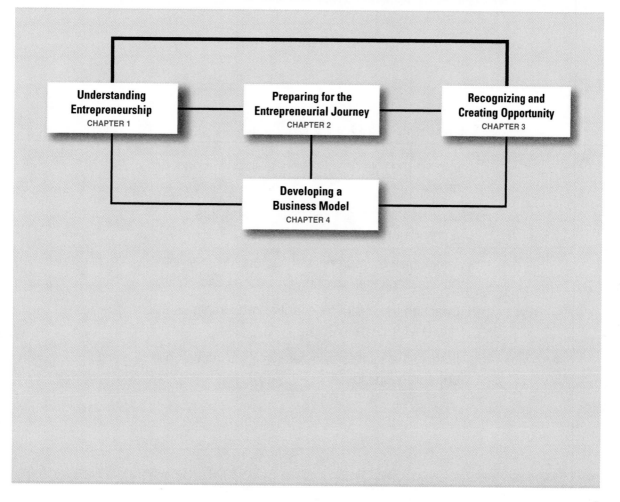

Understanding Entrepreneurship
CHAPTER 1

Preparing for the Entrepreneurial Journey
CHAPTER 2

Recognizing and Creating Opportunity
CHAPTER 3

Developing a Business Model
CHAPTER 4

1

Understanding Entrepreneurship

"We cannot direct the wind, but we can adjust the sails."

Bertha Calloway, founder, Great Plains Black Museum

LEARNING OBJECTIVES

- Explain the role of entrepreneurship in economic growth.

- Discuss the characteristics and behaviors of entrepreneurs.

- Distinguish entrepreneurial ventures from small businesses in terms of their purpose and goals.

- Describe the evolution of entrepreneurship as a field of study since the 1960s.

- Identify the three broad categories of research in entrepreneurship.

Profile 1.1 DAVID CAN STILL BEAT GOLIATH

How do you succeed in a tumultuous industry that can't seem to do anything right and that regularly sues its customers? Meet Mike Boyder and Marc Weinstein, co-founders of Amoeba Music, a three-store California retailer that is the self-proclaimed "largest independent record store on the planet." They have succeeded where industry giants Tower Records, Sam Goody, and even Target are struggling. They have succeeded despite a recording industry dominated by major labels that no longer produce huge wins. On the afternoon of the 2002 World Series between San Francisco and Anaheim, you could find hundreds of music lovers perusing the racks at the Market Street Megastore, because there they can find the largest collection of music anywhere and an environment that supports their love of music.

In 1992, Boyder and Weinstein opened their first store, a tiny outlet in Berkeley, California, that was jammed to the ceilings with more than 11,000 new and used CDs. In entrepreneurship, timing is usually critical, but these two couldn't have picked a worse time to launch their business. The major record labels were turning out megahits in record numbers. On the retail side of the equation, national chains were quickly acquiring the independents and positioning themselves as giants to take advantage of consumers' love of popular music.

Boyder and Weinstein knew that they had to come up with a very clever strategy to have a chance of surviving in that kind of market. The first part of the strategy was to recognize that independents don't have to be small, so one of the first goals was to outgrow their first location. In 1997, Amoeba moved into its 25,000-square-foot location in San Francisco that houses 250,000 titles. By comparison, Wal-Mart carries on average 350 titles and Tower Records carries 60,000 titles, mostly current hits. Diversity and superior merchandising were also important to differentiate Amoeba from the superstores. Amoeba carries an enormously diverse collection of music genres and subgenres and uses every square foot of space for selling merchandise, rather than promoting merchandise as the competitors do. By contrast, the large retail chains tend to push a more homogeneous collection of music on consumers.

The second part of Amoeba's strategy described how customers would view the store not as a music store but rather as a music exchange where they could buy and sell used CDs. This trading concept proved to be a significant piece of their business model and afforded Amoeba margins as high as 70 percent on used CDs (margins are typically 20 percent on new CDs). Whereas the major labels and retailers saw music as a consumable, Amoeba saw it as a commodity for trade with long-term value.

The third component of Amoeba's strategy was to put people first, to make shopping for music a social experience. To make that happen, Amoeba hired people with music and communication skills, people who were obsessed with music. They created an environment exploding with art, live music, and people—and then stood back to watch the show.

The success of a business concept is measured in many ways, but certainly by the more traditional metrics of revenues and growth. In 2002, Amoeba's three-store revenues exceeded $40 million, with year-over-year growth of 75 percent helped by the successful launch of its Los Angeles outlet. Although they have a successful concept now, Boyder and Weinstein understand that it must continue to evolve as the industry changes. They don't want to make the same mistake that their superstore competitors did.

Sources: B. Breen, "What's Selling in America," *Fast Company* (January 2003), p. 86; S. Kang, "CDs a Tough Sell? Music Stores Try Toys," *Wall Street Journal* (June 20, 2003), p. B.1; and N. Wingfield and A.W. Mathews, "Behind the Missing Music: Huge Gaps in Offerings Plague Online Song Sites," *Wall Street Journal* (July 2, 2003), p. D1.

E ntrepreneurship is a phenomenon that continues to excite the imagination of students interested in entering careers in which they must adapt to rapidly changing environments, inventors looking for ways to commercialize their discoveries, government leaders attempting to undertake economic development, and CEOs of large firms seeking to remain competitive in a global marketplace. Since the early 1980s when entrepreneurship was identified as a driver of economic growth, both the term and the field of study have rapidly evolved. From the legendary solo entrepreneur of the 1970s and 1980s to the high-tech entrepreneurial teams and corporate venturers of the 1990s and beyond, entrepreneurs and the entrepreneurial mindset have become ubiquitous and essential elements of this new world.

What is entrepreneurship? Entrepreneurship is a mindset or way of thinking that is opportunity-focused, innovative, and growth-oriented. Although entrepreneurship is most commonly thought of in conjunction with starting a business, the entrepreneurial mindset can be found within large corporations, in socially responsible nonprofit organizations, and anywhere where individuals and teams are desiring to differentiate themselves from the crowd and apply their passion and drive to executing a business opportunity. Entrepreneurs recognize opportunity, gather the resources required to act on the opportunity, and drive the opportunity to completion. At its core, entrepreneurship is about a new entry into new or established markets, and exploiting new or existing products and services.[1]

Entrepreneurship is not the unique domain of any country, gender, race, age, or socioeconomic sector. It can be found in some form in every country, in every age group, and (increasingly) in women as often as in men. The entrepreneurial fever does not distinguish between the rich and the poor; in fact, it touches anyone who has the passion to work for herself or himself, anyone who is determined to be independent and to take charge of his or her life. The mindset of the entrepreneur can be understood and practiced, and the skills and behaviors of the entrepreneur can be learned and applied. The only characteristic of entrepreneurs that is arguably intrinsic is passion, or the drive to achieve something. Passion cannot be taught or practiced; it simply exists when the right elements come together—for example, when an entrepreneur recognizes a business opportunity and devotes his or her full attention and resources to bringing it to life. Passion is found in successful people in all disciplines—great musicians, artists, writers, scientists, and teachers. Passion is what drives a person to go beyond expectations and be the best that person can be.

This chapter explores entrepreneurship as a phenomenon and lays the groundwork for the skills and behaviors that form the basis for the remainder of the text.

The Promise of Entrepreneurship

Early economists recognized that technology is the primary force behind rising standards of living[2] and that technological innovation will determine the success of many nations in the future. **Technological innovation** is the engine of growth for the U.S. economy, yet for a long time economic growth was explained solely in terms of inputs of labor and capital. However, in the 1980s—referred to by many as the Decade of

Entrepreneurship—the work of Paul Romer and others identified technological change as a critical element of a growth model that responds to market incentives.[3] Romer asserted that technological change happens when an entrepreneur identifies new customer segments that appear to be emerging, new customer needs, existing customer needs that have not been satisfied, or new ways of manufacturing and distributing products and services.[4] (See Figure 1.1.) Technological change was the precipitator of the record growth that companies such as Genentech and Netscape achieved. And technology was responsible for the biggest productivity gain achieved in the United States in 19 years, posted in the first quarter of 2002.[5]

Innovation and invention have also played important roles in entrepreneurship. From inventors like Ben Franklin, Thomas Edison, and Gordon Gould to innovators like Bill Gates (Microsoft), Jeff Hawkins (Palm), and Jeff Bezos (Amazon), inventing new technologies and innovating or improving on existing technologies have been key drivers of entrepreneurial opportunity. **Platform technologies** such as the laser, discovered by Gordon Gould in 1957, serve as fertile ground for start-up ventures that license the technology and apply it in a number of different ways. Countless examples throughout history illustrate how economic prosperity can result from invention and innovation, even as industries decline.

Technological change has also facilitated globalization and a new form of creative destruction by moving lower-skilled jobs out of the United States to countries where labor costs are substantially less. Although globalization has produced huge economic benefits, it has also resulted in lower costs of information and transportation, allowing for a broader range of goods and services to be traded over greater distances. Today very few markets enjoy freedom from competition in the global arena.[6] Where local markets in Florida and California once dominated the market for fresh fruits, today consumers are frequently unaware that much of their fresh

FIGURE 1.1   Entrepreneurship and Technological Change

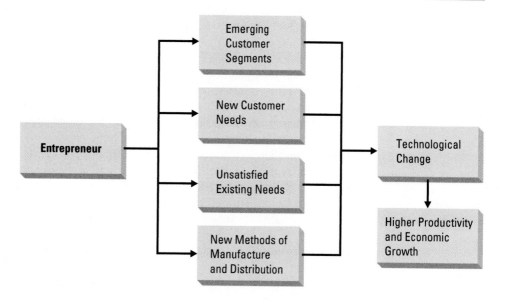

produce comes from Chile, New Zealand, and other parts of the world. Even service companies cannot escape the impact of the global economy. India, for example, has become a dominant player in the software programming industry by transmitting its services electronically and economically to anywhere in the world.

Economic growth comes about through technological change, investment, and trade, and all interact and are facilitated by entrepreneurship.[7] For example, an inventor may develop a robotic mechanism for performing routine tasks in the manufacture of printed circuit boards. Implementing the invention requires an investment in plant and equipment, not to mention people. If the new technology is to be sold in another country, trade regulations, tariffs, and international investment or strategic partnerships may be required.

Those who, out of fear, would encourage a more protectionist or closed economy should consider the lessons of history. In the year 1000, China was far more technologically advanced than Western Europe, but then it closed itself off from the rest of the world and resisted change. By 1977, China had become a third-world country, one of the poorest in the world. Today, after reopening its economy, China is growing faster than any modern economy.[8] The bottom line is that entrepreneurship brings about economic growth.

Industry Formation

New industry formation is another important outcome of entrepreneurship and technological change. New industries are born when technological change produces a new opportunity that an enterprising entrepreneur seizes. (See Figure 1.2.) In the earliest stages of an industry, a few firms enter. As they achieve noticeable levels of success, more and more firms enter the industry, "growing it" to a size that offers an opportunity to consolidate the now fragmented industry, producing a few dominant firms. At that point, the number of firms in the industry begins to stabilize, and if innovation ceases to occur, the industry output may actually begin to decline. But as the gross domestic product (GDP) curve in Figure 1.2 depicts, the industry itself may not decline when the number of firms declines. In fact, the remaining successful companies often grow at a rate that keeps the industry, as a whole, growing for some time.

Disruptive or metamorphic technologies that destroy previous technologies and create new industries generally display a different pattern. The formation phase is characterized by a long period of development, perhaps 10 to 20 years, during which many new firms working in the same area enter the field, more firms than can possibly survive over the long term. This period is followed by either a consolidation period or a shakeout period, lasting from 10 to 30 years, during which most of the firms disappear and a dominant design is adopted. In technological industries, the pattern of growth, shakeout, stabilization, and decline can be interrupted at any point by the entry of another disruptive technology. Why are so many more firms created than an industry can support? The answer lies in the uncertainty of not knowing which new firms will be successful in implementing their breakthrough technologies. In the case of **incremental innovations,** or improvements on existing technologies, research has shown that incumbent firms are generally more successful than new firms, but with

FIGURE 1.2   The Industry Life Cycle

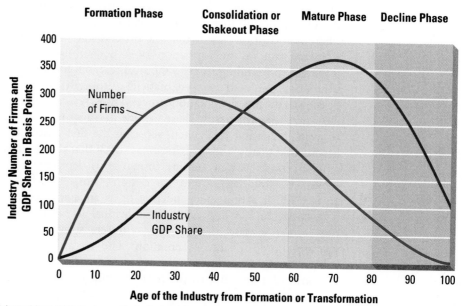

Adapted from M.R. Darby and L.G. Zucker, "Growing by Leaps and Inches: Creative Destruction, Real Cost Reduction, and Inching Up," *Economic Inquiry* (January 2003), pp. 1–19.

paradigm-shifting technologies, it is anyone's guess who the survivors will be.[9] Take the classic case of the rivalry between VHS and Sony Betamax to establish the standard for video tape recording. Sony was unwilling to license its technology to others, whereas VHS made it easy for people to use its format. As a consequence, customers flocked to VHS and made it the standard, even though Betamax was arguably the better technology.

Job Creation

Entrepreneurial ventures are responsible for significant job creation. The Small Business Administration defines a small business as one with fewer than 500 employees, which by many standards is not very small and includes both high-growth technology ventures and small "mom and pops"—quite a range indeed. Still, businesses classified as small by this SBA definition represent 99.7 percent of all employers and pay 44 percent of the total U.S. private payroll.[10] Furthermore, small businesses generate on average 60 to 80 percent of net new jobs annually in the United States. From 1999 to 2000, the most recent years for which data are available, small businesses created 2.5 million new jobs, or three-quarters of all net new jobs.[11] The SBA estimates that in 2002 there were 22.9 million businesses of all forms in the United States. For example, the census data indicate that in 2000, 5.7 million firms had employees, whereas about 16.5 million did not, but those sole proprietorships increased at a rate of 2.7 percent in 2002.

New Business Formation

Entrepreneurs engage in a number of activities in the process of creating a new venture. Although there is not universal agreement on where the process starts and where it ends, one view is that the process starts when one or more people decide to participate in the formation of a new business and devote their time and resources to founding it.[12,13] Empirical research has shown that the process is iterative, nonlinear, and nonsystematic.[14] Although entrepreneurs may go in many directions during the creation process, they typically use identifiable milestones to measure their progress.[15] These include deciding to start a business, researching the concept, preparing for launch, securing the first customer, obtaining the business license, and many other activities that signal that the business is in operation.[16]

The process of new venture formation is depicted in Figure 1.3 and is characterized by four stages and three transitions. The first transition occurs when an individual, acting independently or as an employee of a firm, decides to start a business. In the first case, the individual is called a **nascent entrepreneur;** in the second a nascent corporate venturer, someone who starts entrepreneurial ventures inside a large corporation. The second transition comes about during the gestation of a new venture and includes all the start-up processes that lead to the birth of a firm and to the resulting infant firm. At this point, the new venture does one of three things: It grows at a rate higher than normal, it persists or survives to move into the adolescent (fourth) stage, or it is abandoned. Figure 1.3 also depicts three question marks that represent aspects of the entrepreneurial process about which very little is known. The label ?a stands for the question "How many entrepreneurs in the nascent stage actually complete the process and launch an infant firm?" The label ?b stands for "How many start-ups never

| FIGURE 1.3 | Social, Political, and Economic Context of the Entrepreneurial Process |

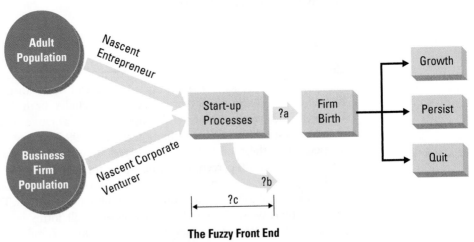

The Fuzzy Front End

Source: Paul D. Reynolds. (2000) National Panel of U.S. Business Start-ups: Background and Methodology. *Databases for the Study of Entrepreneurship,* Amsterdam: JAI/Elsevier Inc. Vol. 4, pp. 153–227.

complete the process? And ?c stands for "What are the tasks and timeline involved in actually completing the start-up process and giving birth to a new firm?"

Borrowing a term from product development, we can call the period of time prior to firm birth the *fuzzy front end*. The fuzzy front end has been modeled in economic terms. Simply put, the amount of investment an individual is willing to make in a new product—or, in this case, in a new venture—is a function of the probability of its success, the value of that success, and the cost of failure. A change in any one of these values will alter the economics of the bet.[17] In terms of the model in Figure 1.3, the nascent entrepreneur uses the time spent in the fuzzy front end to calculate the probability of success as an entrepreneur, what that success will mean in terms of return on investment, and what the risk or cost of failure might be. Those probability estimates are highly subjective. But if the nascent entrepreneur uses the time to gather information about the industry and market, tests the business concept through feasibility analysis, and determines the conditions under which he or she is willing to move forward and start the business, much of the subjectivity will be eliminated. In addition, the risk of start-up will be reduced, and the probability associated with the three outcomes will be more accurate.

It is not entirely clear what actually prompts an individual to move from the status of actor, simulating the role of entrepreneur, to nascent entrepreneur. Even with evaluations of risk involved in a start-up through the fuzzy front end, there appears to be no uniform mechanism that consistently results in efforts to launch a business. One individual may choose to enter the nascent stage in spite of a high level of risk. Another may choose to reject the nascent phase even under conditions where the risk involved is low. Nascents appear to emerge from the population through push or pull factors. *Push* is the mechanism that drives an individual to become a nascent entrepreneur because all other opportunities for income appear to be absent or unsatisfactory. *Pull* is the mechanism that attracts an individual to an opportunity and creates a "burning desire" to launch a business and capture a market.

Business Failure

The intent to start a business is not enough to make it happen. Many potential entrepreneurs drop out of the process as they move from intention to preparation. And a very high number give up before the new business makes the transition to an established firm.[18]

The Small Business Administration Office of Advocacy reports that in 2003, employer firms rose 0.3 percent to 5.7 million; the unincorporated self-employed rose by 3.7 percent to 10.7 million; and the number of sole proprietors (nonfarm) rose 1.9 percent to 18.7 million. Business failures declined 2.3 percent in 2003 to 554,800. In fact, the number of business bankruptcies has been declining for two decades.[19] The Office of Advocacy also reports that about 66 percent of all new businesses survive at least two years, 49.6 percent survive at least four years, and 39.5 percent survive at least six years.[20]

Survival rates of new businesses vary by industry and demographics. In the period 1992–1996, firms in the oil and gas extraction industry had an 82 percent survival rate over four years. In the legal services industry, businesses owned

| TABLE 1.1 | Starts and Closures of Employer Firms, 1990–2002 |

CATEGORY	1990	1995	2000	2001	2002
New Firms	584,892	594,369	574,300	545,400e	550,100e
Firm Closures	531,892	497,246	542,831	568,300e	584,500e
Bankruptcies	63,912	50,516	35,472	39,719	38,155

e = Estimate using percentage changes in similar data provided by the U.S. Department of Labor, Employment and Training Administration

Sources: U.S. Bureau of the Census; Administrative Office of the U.S. Courts; and U.S. Department of Labor, Employment and Training Administration.

by African Americans had a 79 percent survival rate, while Hispanic and Asian American–owned businesses in the health services industry enjoyed 66 percent and 76 percent survival rates, respectively.[21]

One body of research views failure as a liability of newness; that is, the firms that are most likely to survive over the long term are those that display superior levels of reliability and accountability in performance, processes, and structure. Because these factors tend to increase with age, failure rates tend to decline with age.[22] Young firms have a higher chance of failure because they have to divert their scarce resources away from the critical operations of the company in order to train employees, develop systems and controls, and establish strategic partnerships. Another body of research sees failure as a liability of adolescence, claiming that start-ups survive in the early years by relying on their original resources, but that as those resources are depleted, the company's chances of failing increase.

The vital issue for entrepreneurs is not avoiding failure but minimizing the cost of a possible failure. That comes from starting with a robust business model and testing it in the marketplace prior to starting the business.

Minority-Owned and Women-Owned Businesses (MOBWOBs)

Data from 1997 indicate that women then owned 5.4 million businesses and generated $819 billion in revenues. They employed more than 7 million workers and produced $150 billion in payroll. Three-quarters of these businesses were sole proprietorships with receipts under $50,000, but as is typical of businesses in all sectors, high-growth ventures generated the bulk of revenues and new jobs. By 1999, women-owned businesses were generating $3.6 trillion, an increase of 200 percent over 1987 (adjusted for inflation). Nearly 27.5 percent of employees worked for women-owned firms, about 35–40 percent more than the Fortune 500 employed.[23] It is expected that by 2005, 4.7 million women will be self-employed.[24] The 2002 Global Entrepreneurship Monitor found that 12.9 percent of men are involved in entrepreneurial activities, compared to 8.1 percent of women.[25] But breaking these rates out by age categories, it is clear that more women start businesses later in life, where their prevalence rises to 10 percent. (See Figure 1.4.) In general, this growth can be attributed to women's dissatisfaction with corporate life, which is still male dominated; to their desire to balance work and personal life; and to their being determined, like their male counterparts, to seek independence or seize a business opportunity.

FIGURE 1.4 Entrepreneurship in the United States by Gender, Age, and Education

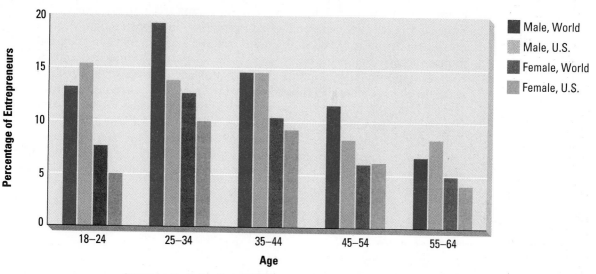

Source: H. Neck, A.L. Zacharakis, W. Bygrave, and P. Reynolds (Eds.). *Global Entrepreneurship Monitor 2003 Executive Report,* p. 14.

The size of women-owned businesses is a factor in the impact that they have on the economy. Research has found that the smaller size of women-owned businesses is explained by the different motivations of women to start businesses and by how they define success.[26] Specifically, they tend to redefine how business is done rather than attempt to make a huge impact on the economy. Size differences are also explained by the industries women choose to enter. More than 55 percent of all women-owned businesses are in services, and such businesses tend to be smaller in size.[27] Also, their businesses tend to be younger on average, which is one reason why from 1992 to 1997, women-owned businesses grew at three times the rate of all businesses.[28]

In 1997, 5.8 percent of all businesses were owned by Hispanic Americans, 4.4 percent by Asian Americans, 4.0 percent by African Americans, and 0.9 percent by American Indians. In 2000, the Office of Advocacy of the SBA reported that minority-owned businesses now account for 15 percent of all U.S. businesses. Asian American–owned businesses earned more than 51 percent of all business revenues in the minority-owned sector, with Hispanic Americans following at 31 percent; African Americans at 12 percent; and American Indians at 6 percent.[29]

African American entrepreneurs find that their biggest challenges are the lack of access to credit and capital and lingering discrimination.[30] As a result, the SBA, in collaboration with the commercial banking community, has provided special funding for minority entrepreneurs, as well as for women entrepreneurs.

Although they constitute a minority, Asian Americans have been very successful as entrepreneurs, owning about one-third of the high-tech firms in Silicon Valley by the early 1990s and 500 companies in the San Gabriel Valley of California by the late 1990s.[31] The highest rate of self-employment is found in the Korean American community; more than 1 in 10 Korean Americans are business owners. Hispanic-owned firms tend to be strong in transportation and construction. Among all of the Hispanic groups, Mexican Americans own the largest number of companies. The increasing tide of Hispanic businesses can be attributed to immigrant entrepreneurs who see opportunity where others do not. Rolando Herrera wanted to be a wine-maker in Napa, California. To accomplish that goal, he washed dishes, broke rocks, and often slept in his car. He also recognized that the Latino market was untapped when it came to wine, which presented an opportunity for him to capture a niche and satisfy an unmet need. Building on this opportunity, Herrera founded his winery and realized his dream. Today his wine, Mi Sueño, is well known and was even chosen to be served at President Bush's first state dinner with Mexican president Vicente Fox.[32]

The Nature of Entrepreneurs

Many of the characteristics normally associated with entrepreneurs also exist in some managers and, in fact, in anyone who is highly successful in his or her career. What characteristics are typically found in entrepreneurs and in people who have the entrepreneurial mindset? Research points to the ability to take calculated risks, an achievement orientation or intense drive to succeed, a sense of independence, an internal locus of control, and a tolerance for ambiguity.

Entrepreneurial Characteristics

The typical characteristics found in most entrepreneurs are useful for dealing with the entrepreneurial process, whether as the founder of a start-up venture or a corporate venturer associated with a large company. While some people come by these characteristics naturally, others must find ways to develop them to increase their chances of being a successful entrepreneur.

Risk-Taking

The consensus of the research on risk-taking in entrepreneurs is that they are not big risk-takers.[33] Instead, they are moderate, calculated risk-takers who define the risks inherent in any venture and attempt to minimize them or manage them while remaining focused on opportunity. Not being a big risk-taker is certainly not a deterrent to entrepreneurship. As discussed in the previous section, entrepreneurs tend to be highly optimistic about their potential for success. It seems likely that this optimism is closely related to their determination to reduce risk as much as possible. Entrepreneurs see challenges as opportunities and regard roadblocks as simply temporary pauses in their journey.

Need for Achievement

Entrepreneurs tend to have a high desire to be personally responsible for solving problems and setting and reaching goals—in other words, they have a need for achievement,[34,35] often referred to as "the burning gut," "fire in the belly," or simply "passion." Entrepreneurs are innately driven to make things happen. They are not generally daunted by failure but tend to keep trying until they succeed. The exploitation of opportunity provides a stimulating environment for achievement.

A Sense of Independence

Entrepreneurs also seem to seek independence purposefully—to be their own boss in situations that allow them to assume a higher degree of personal responsibility for their decisions and achievements and to be self-directed in their pursuit of opportunity.[36] This need for independence, however, often makes it difficult for entrepreneurs to delegate authority. The inability to delegate has often been referred to as the dark side of the entrepreneur.

Internal Locus of Control

Locus of control describes the source to which individuals attribute the things that happen to them. Those who believe they have control over aspects of their environment and destiny are said to have an internal locus of control, whereas those who feel controlled by their environment are said to have an external locus of control. Many studies have shown that entrepreneurs have a strong internal locus of control, which gives them a high level of confidence in their ability to manage the entrepreneurial process.[37]

Tolerance for Ambiguity

The start-up process is by its very nature dynamic, uncertain, complex, and ambiguous. Entrepreneurs, however, seem to work well in this type of environment, possibly because it is challenging and exciting and offers more opportunity than a structured environment. Researchers have found that entrepreneurs have a greater tolerance than others for ambiguity[38] and that those who have a tolerance for ambiguity are more likely to start new ventures.[39]

Entrepreneurial Behavior

The origin of the word *entrepreneur* is found in the French literature on economics, where an entrepreneur is described as someone who embarks on a significant project or activity—a behavior. Therefore, the entrepreneur is also distinguished by what he or she does. Much research suggests that it is the behaviors of entrepreneurs that set them apart from others who might have the same characteristics or traits.[40] The act of creating a business—perceiving an opportunity, assessing the opportunity and risking resources to exploit it, managing the process of building a venture from an idea, and creating value—is the entrepreneurial act. Those who have the passion to build innovative businesses from the idea stage and who continue to act entrepreneurially, making strategic decisions that engage the business in risk-oriented activity, growth, and consequent high performance, are considered entrepreneurs.

In line with the behavioral approach, recent research has proposed that entrepreneurship is about the process of organizing,[41] which includes but is not limited to:

- Committing resources to an opportunity
- Establishing procedures for the use of resources
- Identifying, assembling, and configuring resources
- Interacting with people
- Coordinating and establishing routines

Why Entrepreneurs Start Businesses

Entrepreneurs start businesses for a variety of reasons. Sometimes their progress is blocked at the company for which they work, or they see a better way to do something, or they just want to see whether an idea will work. Marc Maiffret was someone who just wanted to see whether an idea would work. He had accomplished a lot by the tender age of 21, having cofounded a security software business, developed new products, and changed the direction of the computer security industry. Maiffret had a unique understanding of the mind of the computer hacker because he had been one at the age of 15. He did it for the usual reasons, to escape reality and just to see if he could do it. But before he finished high school, and under the guidance of Firas Bushnaq, CEO of eCompany Inc., a software firm, he began using his hacking talent to design software that would thwart hackers and recognize hacking as it happened. Today eCompany has 50 employees and four software programs on the market, and Marc Maiffret, although he is still writing code, finds himself in the more traditional managerial role.[42]

Some entrepreneurs have started their businesses after taking a course in entrepreneurship at a community college or university. Todd Stennett studied entrepreneurship in the MBA program at the University of Southern California. There he completed a feasibility study and business plan on a concept for doing 3D mapping of terrain using technology he could license from a federal government agency, NOAH. Learning the process of developing a business concept, testing it in the market, talking with more than 450 people about his concept, and then using the business plan process to build a plan for execution gave him the confidence to actually start Airborne 1.

Others start businesses for very personal reasons. This was the case with Sandy Gooch, who suffered from toxic reactions to artificial additives in food. Learning that many others also suffered in this way, Gooch decided to become an expert on natural foods, and in 1977 she founded Mrs. Gooch's Natural Foods Market in the Los Angeles area. By 1993 the company had seven stores, was doing about $80 million in annual revenues, and had over 800 employees. In 1996 Gooch sold her company to Whole Foods and went on to start up several other companies. She is credited with founding the natural foods industry.

Still others simply want to own their own businesses. After World War II, Masaru Ibuka started a company in a rented room of a bombed-out department store in Tokyo with $1,600 of his own savings and seven employees—but with no idea what the business should be! After weeks of brainstorming, he and his workers decided to produce a rice cooker. Unfortunately, it didn't work the way it was supposed to. However, Ibuka and his team persisted in spite of failure. Their company is known today as Sony Corporation.

Types of Entrepreneurs

Entrepreneurs are as varied as the kinds of businesses they start. For every characteristic or behavior that defines one successful entrepreneur, another successful entrepreneur who displays completely different characteristics and behaviors can be found. There are many paths to entrepreneurship, and in the following sections we look at four broad categories: the home-based entrepreneur, the cyber entrepreneur, the serial entrepreneur, and the traditional entrepreneur.

The Home-Based Entrepreneur

More than 24 million people operate home-based businesses.[43] Many of these are hobby businesses, consulting, and freelance type businesses, but many others are entrepreneurial ventures that compete in the same arena as brand-name businesses with large facilities. Technology has made it possible to do business from virtually anywhere, so entrepreneurs don't have to work in traditional office spaces to start or run businesses. Moreover, home-based business owners can tap into more resources than ever from their desktops to locate help for any problem they may be facing, from finding business forms to seeking legal advice to learning how to start and run a business. In addition, U.S. tax laws have become friendlier to home-based business owners, who can take a deduction for their home office space and appropriate business expenses.

Many entrepreneurs with aspirations to grow start from home to save on overhead and reduce the risk of start-up. Once the concept has proved itself, they often move out to acquire facilities that will support the growth of the company and the addition of employees. Some entrepreneurs choose never to have office space but rather to enjoy the ability to move around. Such is often the case for the next type of entrepreneur—the Internet entrepreneur.

The Cyber Entrepreneur

The birth of the commercial Internet gave rise to the cyber entrepreneur, who takes pride in the fact that he or she does not have a bricks-and-mortar operation. Cyber entrepreneurs transact all their business with customers, suppliers, strategic partners, and others on the Internet and deal in digital products and services that do not require bricks-and-mortar infrastructure (such as warehousing and physical distribution).

Laura Ricci was tired of being a road warrior, traveling all over the country helping engineers and scientists win government grants. In 1996, she decided to do an experiment and launch her grant-writing consulting firm on the Internet. She knew that her customers used the Internet a lot; in fact, when it came time to design her site, she used a designer in Albany, New York, whom she had never met face-to-face. She absolutely refused to print brochures, opting instead for a total cyber mentality. This gave her company the advantage of looking bigger than it really was. The strategy worked, and now Ricci can claim clients like Lockheed Martin and Radian International.[44]

The Serial Entrepreneur

Many entrepreneurs enjoy the pre-launch and start-up phases so much that when those activities are over and running the business takes center stage, they become impatient to move on to the next start-up. It's the thrill of starting a business that keeps them going; they prefer to leave the management issues to someone else.

Consummate entrepreneur Wayne Huizenga is a classic serial entrepreneur. He started with a single garbage truck and grew his company truck by truck to become Waste Management Inc., the largest garbage hauler and waste management service in the world. Huizenga then went on to tackle the video rental business with Blockbuster Entertainment and the used-car industry with Auto Nation.

The Traditional Entrepreneur

If there really is such a thing as a "traditional entrepreneur," it would probably be that entrepreneur who starts a bricks-and-mortar business and builds it to a point where the wealth created can be harvested. Anthony Arnold reversed the traditional bricks-and-mortar business to Web business path and began his company as an Internet business. Arnold's experience was in Web marketing, and in 1999 he was poised to capture his next big job at Lucent Technologies. While waiting for his employment to start, he and his wife launched an Internet consulting firm to sell their Web marketing expertise — nothing unique; there are thousands of them. To demonstrate their credentials to potential clients, they spent $2,000 to build an e-commerce demo for a company they called PremiumKnives.com, because Arnold's hobby was collecting knives. To their surprise, within three months they had sold $50,000 worth of knives, while the consulting service languished. In February 2000, the division of Lucent that Arnold was supposed to work for was cut and he was out of a job. Arnold and his wife decided to go for it and expand the growing knife business. They moved the business from the Internet to a historic neighborhood in Omaha and began diversifying into kitchen gadgets and the like. They dubbed their store Premium Home and Garden. Their 2003 revenues were about $1 million, and they project earnings of $10 million by 2005 with the addition of two more outlets. But like most entrepreneurs, Arnold envisions things on a grand scale and foresees his company growing to the size of Crate and Barrel or Williams-Sonoma.[45]

Traditional entrepreneurs will not disappear as long as there is a need to build sustainable companies, especially in sectors such as food services, manufacturing, and retail.

The Nonprofit Entrepreneur

Today many enterprising people are turning to nonprofit types of ventures to realize their entrepreneurial dreams. Nonprofit, socially responsible businesses typically focus on educational, religious, or charitable goals. They generally seek tax-exempt status so that they can attract donations from companies and individuals who believe in their mission. Contrary to popular belief, nonprofit businesses can make a profit, but that profit must stay within the company rather than be distributed to the owners. Chapter 10 explores these types of ventures in more depth. For an example of a socially responsible business, see the accompanying box.

Socially Responsible Entrepreneurship

CyberAngels Protecting Cyberspace

Chat rooms attract the young and the young at heart. It is as easy as the click of a mouse button to strike up a conversation with someone anywhere in the world who shares your interests. But it's also easy for criminals to use these sites to prey on unsuspecting young people. One group of socially responsible entrepreneurs saw an opportunity in this problem. Building on their experience with the Guardian Angels, a group that works to keep community streets safe, they started an organization known as CyberAngels, a nonprofit group of volunteers who patrol websites and chat rooms looking for signs of predators. They also work with schools to develop curricula to teach students what to watch out for, and they work with the U.S. Customs' Cyber-Smuggling Unit and the FBI to find and arrest perpetrators. Their Net-Ed division teaches online classes that provide training for parents, teachers, and librarians. They also hold classes for the public in general Internet safety and navigation. Connect-Ed provides Internet safety information to the public through online classes and through published materials and speakers for schools and public libraries.

CyberAngels makes social responsibility its mission.

Source: http://www.cyberangels.org.

The Corporate Venturer

Entrepreneurs can choose to start a new venture from scratch, buy an existing business and build it, or start a venture inside a large existing organization. The choice is a function of the type of business, the opportunity, and the support for such a venture inside the existing organization if such a firm is involved.[46] For example, when capital markets make it difficult to find funding, entrepreneurs are less likely to start new ventures from scratch. By contrast, they are more likely to start new ventures on their own when the incentives inside large organizations are weak or nonexistent, when the opportunity requires individual effort, and when the normal scale advantages and learning curves do not provide advantages to the large organization.[47] Entrepreneurs also choose the start-up process when industry entry barriers are low, when the environment is more uncertain, and when the opportunity they seek to exploit involves a breakthrough or disruptive technology that will make previous technology obsolete.

Increasingly, large organizations are finding it necessary to provide for entrepreneurial activity to remain competitive. In the 1980s, as they saw themselves lagging behind small, young companies in finding great opportunities, they began to look for ways to restructure their organizations to allow creative employees to search for new opportunities the company could exploit. Recognizing that it is nearly impossible to re-engineer and redesign an entire organization, many companies have chosen the "skunk works" route (named for Lockheed's unit that developed the Stealth fighter jet). The term *skunk works* refers to an autonomous group that is given the mandate to find and develop new products for the company that may even be outside the company's core competencies. Other companies attempt to encourage corporate venturing or entrepreneurship inside the structures of their existing organization. This approach has been difficult at best to achieve because the bureaucratic structures of most large organizations—deep organizational charts, their inherent avoidance of risk, and strict budgets—all challenge even the most enthusiastic corporate entrepreneur.

For an entrepreneurial mindset to succeed inside a large corporation, the following are required:

- *Senior management commitment.* Without the support of senior management, it will be difficult to move any entrepreneurial project forward fast enough and far enough to be successful.

- *Corporate interoperability.* The environment must encourage collaboration and give the entrepreneur access to the knowledge and resources of all the company's functional areas.

- *Clearly defined stages and metrics.* Entrepreneurial ventures inside large organizations need a timeline with stages at which decisions can be made about whether to proceed and whether additional or different resources are required. They also need a way to measure progress and success that is not based on the corporation's benchmarks but rather on benchmarks appropriate to start-up ventures with limited resources.

- *A superior team.* Only the best people should be put in corporate venture situations, because by definition these ventures are riskier than projects based on the company's core skills and products. The new venture team also calls for a champion among the top management who will secure help for the team when the project reaches the inevitable roadblock.

- *Spirit of entrepreneurship.* Entrepreneurship is about opportunity—recognizing it, seizing it, and exploiting it—but it's also about failing sometimes. A company that encourages corporate venturing must not penalize its entrepreneurs for failure but must support them as they take what they have learned to a new project.

This book is not intended to address the specific needs of corporate venturers, but recognizing opportunities, conducting feasibility analyses, and business planning are certainly relevant in the corporate environment.

The Nature of Entrepreneurial Start-ups

It is important to make a clear distinction between entrepreneurial ventures and small lifestyle businesses because their visions and goals differ, so their decisions, resources, and strategies will differ as well.

In general, entrepreneurial ventures have three primary characteristics. They are

1. Innovative
2. Value-creating
3. Growth-oriented

An entrepreneurial venture brings something new to the marketplace, whether it be a new product or service (the fax machine or an executive leasing service), a new marketing strategy (viral marketing on the Internet), or a new way to deliver products and services to consumers (*The Wall Street Journal Interactive Edition*). The entrepreneurial venture creates new value through innovation, through bringing to the economy new jobs that don't merely draw from existing businesses, and through finding unserved niches in the market. Entrepreneurs typically have a vision of where they want their businesses to go, and generally that vision is on a regional, national, or (more often) global level.

By contrast, small lifestyle businesses are generally started to generate an income and a lifestyle for the owner or the family. Often referred to as mom-and-pop businesses, they tend to remain relatively small and geographically bound, most often because of a conscious decision on the part of the founder to keep the firm a small, lifestyle business. When Ken Finster started Micro/Sys, now a $4 million electronics manufacturer with 30 employees in Southern California, his goal was simply to provide an income for his family that would allow him to send his children to private schools and eventually college. Doing business in the highly competitive embedded systems industry, he knew that the only way to survive was to think of his business as a service company that provided customized solutions in small lots, something large manufacturers couldn't afford to do.

Choosing what kind of business to start is very important, because that choice influences all subsequent decisions and determines what kinds of goals the entrepreneur is able to achieve. For example, if the intent is to grow a business to a national level, the entrepreneur will make different decisions along the way than if the intent is to own and operate a thriving restaurant that competes only in the local community. Generally, running a small business requires good management skills on the part of the owner, who must perform all tasks associated with the business as it grows. By contrast, entrepreneurs typically do not have the skills to handle the management aspects of the business and often prefer to hire experts to carry out that function, leaving the entrepreneur and the founding team free to innovate, raise capital, and promote the business.

A Brief History of the Entrepreneurial Revolution

The term *entrepreneur* has existed for more than 250 years. The United States was founded on the principle of free enterprise, which encouraged entrepreneurs to assume the risk of developing businesses that would make the economy strong. However, it was not until the 1980s that the word *entrepreneur* came into popular use in the United States, and an almost folkloric aura began to grow around men and women who started rapidly growing businesses. These formerly quiet, low-profile people suddenly became legends in their own time, with the appeal and publicity typically associated with movie stars or rock musicians. From the founding of this country, individuals with an entrepreneurial spirit have started the businesses that are the basis of the free enterprise system. With a careful eye on trends and consumer needs, they have supplied us with new technology and new products and services of every conceivable type, while also creating new jobs. In fact, the most successful entrepreneurs affect our lives, the way we do things, and the choices we make.

Marc Andressen, young entrepreneur and cofounder of Netscape Communications, was responsible for bringing the wealth of information on the Internet to the average

---

FIGURE 1.5   The Entrepreneurial Evolution

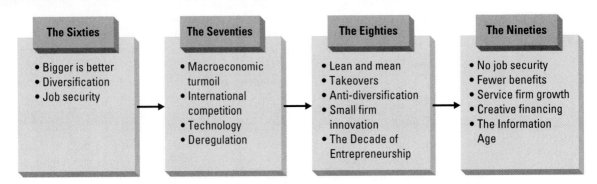

The Sixties	The Seventies	The Eighties	The Nineties
• Bigger is better • Diversification • Job security	• Macroeconomic turmoil • International competition • Technology • Deregulation	• Lean and mean • Takeovers • Anti-diversification • Small firm innovation • The Decade of Entrepreneurship	• No job security • Fewer benefits • Service firm growth • Creative financing • The Information Age

person through a user-friendly graphical interface. Under the leadership of Howard Schultz, Starbucks rekindled the love of coffee and turned coffee drinking into an art form. Entrepreneurs such as these shake up the economy. They look for unsatisfied needs and satisfy them. Figure 1.5 summarizes the entrepreneurial evolution that has taken place since the 1960s.

The Precursors to Entrepreneurship as a Discipline

In the mid-1960s, gigantic companies were the norm. General Motors in the 1960s was so large that it earned as much as the ten biggest companies in Great Britain, France, and West Germany combined.[48] The reason why U.S. companies enjoyed such unrestricted growth at that time was that they lacked competition from Europe and Japan. Therefore, job security for employees was high, and companies tended to diversify by acquiring other kinds of businesses.

The 1970s saw the beginning of three significant trends that would forever change the face of business: macroeconomic turmoil, international competition, and the technological revolution. A volatile economic climate the likes of which had not been seen since World War II pervaded the 1970s. The Vietnam War economy brought inflation, the dollar was devalued, food prices skyrocketed as a consequence of several agricultural disasters, and the formation of OPEC sent gas prices up 50 percent. Furthermore, by the late 1970s the Federal Reserve had let interest rates rise to a prime of 20 percent. The result was no borrowing, no spending, and a recession that spilled into the 1980s, bringing with it an unemployment rate of 10 percent.[49] To compound the effects of the economy on business, by 1980 one-fifth of all U.S. companies faced foreign competitors that had far more favorable cost structures, which included much lower labor costs. Imports, particularly in the automobile and machine tools industries, were suddenly taking a significant share of the market from U.S. businesses.

The third event affecting business was the technological revolution brought about by the introduction of the microprocessor by Intel in 1971, the Mits Altair personal computer in 1975, and the Apple II computer in 1977. Microprocessors succeeded in rendering whole categories of products obsolete—such things as mechanical cash registers and adding machines, for example—and effectively antiquated the skills of the people who made them.

Increasing the pressure on business, the government ushered in a new era of business regulation via the Environmental Protection Agency, the Occupational Safety and Health Agency, and the Consumer Product Safety Commission, all of which increased costs to businesses. On the opposite front, deregulation forced planes, trucks, and railroads to compete, and in general big companies no longer had control of the marketplace.

By the early 1980s, business was in terrible shape. The Fortune 500 saw a record 27 percent drop in profits.[50] Large mills and factories were shutting down; manufacturing employment was declining; and yet, ironically, productivity remained the same or increased. New, smaller manufacturers were still generating jobs—and not only manufacturing jobs, but service jobs as well. How was this possible?

To become competitive, the smaller, more flexible, entrepreneurial manufacturers had hired subcontractors who could perform tasks such as bookkeeping and payroll more efficiently. These service firms developed to support the needs of the product sector, but they inspired the creation of other service firms as well: People who work often need day-care or maid services, so even more jobs were being created.

The Decade of Entrepreneurship

With the creation of all these jobs, it is no wonder that the 1980s has been called the Decade of Entrepreneurship by many, including the dean of management science, Peter Drucker, who was not alone in asserting that the United States was rapidly and by necessity becoming an entrepreneurial economy.[51] On the heels of the emergence of Silicon Valley and its legendary entrepreneurs, the mainstream press began to focus on business activities, creating many popular magazines such as *Inc.* and *Entrepreneur.*

Responding to this entrepreneurial drive, big business in the 1980s found it necessary to downsize and reverse the trend of diversification it had promulgated for so long. If big companies were going to compete with the dynamic, innovative smaller firms and fend off the takeover bids so prevalent in the 1980s, they would have to restructure and reorganize for a new way of doing business. This restructuring and reorganizing actually resulted in improved performance, increased profits, and higher stock prices. It also meant, however, that many jobs would no longer exist, employees would receive fewer benefits, and the only "secure" jobs left would be found in civil service.

Toward the end of the 1980s, researchers observed that young entrepreneurial ventures were internationalizing much earlier than expected and at a much smaller size.[52] A significant number of these ventures were in high-tech industries.[53] Large-sample empirical work revealed that directors and managers with significant international experience played a strong role in the internationalization of entrepreneurial ventures at start-up.[54]

All these events moved this country toward a period that required the vision, the resources, and the motivation of the entrepreneur to seek new opportunities and create new jobs in a vastly different global environment electronically linked via the Internet. The interest in entrepreneurship has not waned since the earliest days of the 1980s. According to recent research, the demand for and supply of entrepreneurship faculty increased dramatically in the period from 1989 to 1998.[55] The number of faculty positions increased 253 percent, while the number of candidates available for these positions increased by 94 percent. This is a direct result of demand from students, which is particularly noteworthy because in most schools, entrepreneurship remains an elective subject offered only when there is sufficient student interest.[56] Still, today there are over 400 U.S. and international schools offering courses in entrepreneurship.

Researching the Entrepreneurial Phenomenon

While entrepreneurs and their ventures became the subject of media attention, they also spawned a new field of research to study the phenomenon. As the instrument by which concepts born in laboratories and in the minds of scientists and engineers are transferred to the private sector in the form of useful products and services, entrepreneurship is the intersection of two phenomena: lucrative opportunities and enterprising individuals.[57] It is worth repeating that neither one nor the other, but the two phenomena interacting, result in entrepreneurship.

In the field of entrepreneurship, researchers study

- Sources of opportunities
- Processes of discovery, evaluation, and exploitation of opportunities
- Individuals and teams who recognize the opportunities, evaluate them, and exploit them[58]

Thus entrepreneurship is not about people and their attributes and behaviors independent of the situations in which they are found.[59] In fact, entrepreneurs represent such a diverse group in their traits and behaviors that it is unrealistic to believe that people are either entrepreneurs or are not entrepreneurs all the time.

Opportunity Recognition

For entrepreneurship to exist and thrive, there must be opportunities to develop new goods and services, means to gather the resources to produce those goods and services, and mechanisms to bring them to market at a price greater than their cost of production. What differentiates entrepreneurial opportunities from other profit-making opportunities is that to exploit entrepreneurial opportunities, one must discover a new means to an end, with unknown outcomes and with resources not yet under the control of the entrepreneur.[60] Exploiting opportunity means that the entrepreneur must assume a risk. Furthermore, there must be differing viewpoints on the value of resources so that the entrepreneur can discover a value that was not previously identified.[61] This scenario is what is commonly termed "finding a niche in the market." In a situation where more than one entrepreneur perceives the same value for a resource (in other words, finds the same niche), competition for profit occurs. The entrepreneur must then seek another source of value, another niche to differentiate himself or herself from the competition.

For entrepreneurs to recognize an opportunity, they have to possess, from experience, prior information that is compatible with the new information they receive from scanning the environment.[62] The new information may be in the form of a customer need, a niche that is not being served, or the juxtaposition of two opposing ideas that triggers an entrepreneurial opportunity. However, an entrepreneurial opportunity will never reach the marketplace if the entrepreneur can't identify a way to make it happen.[63] That is why so many inventions do not become commercialized. Their inventors are unable to visualize their commercial applications, and it often takes teaming with a business entrepreneur to complete the commercialization process.

Opportunity Exploitation

Recognizing an opportunity is only part of the equation; deciding to exploit that opportunity is the other part. Why do entrepreneurs choose to act on an opportunity when others do not? How do entrepreneurs choose the opportunities worthy of exploitation? Not every opportunity has a sufficiently high expected value to warrant action. The return on the investment of time and effort must be large enough to offset the opportunity cost of exploiting another opportunity or doing something else (such as taking a job).[64] Moreover, entrepreneurs must consider their ability to acquire the necessary resources—capital, land and equipment, human resources, and so on. Some research suggests that entrepreneurs who have ready access to capital and strong connections to resource providers are more likely to choose to exploit an opportunity that meets their other criteria.[65]

Another factor that seems to propel entrepreneurs to move forward with an opportunity is information from previous employment and industry experience that serves to reduce the cost of commercializing the opportunity and therefore increases the probability that the opportunity will be exploited.[66] More recent research tells us that entrepreneurs' decisions to exploit an opportunity are influenced by their level of optimism. In fact, entrepreneurs typically perceive their chances of success as much higher than they may actually be. Entrepreneurial optimism tends to minimize the amount of information the entrepreneur requires to make the decision to exploit an opportunity and is reflected in overly optimistic forecasts of sales and profits.[67] Entrepreneurs also display a tendency to act first and analyze at leisure.[68]

The Network Effect

Networking is the exchange of information and resources among individuals, groups, or organizations whose common goals are to mutually benefit and create value for the members. Research in the field of entrepreneurship has revealed much about the positive effects of networking. For instance, entrepreneurship has been found to be a relational process. Entrepreneurs do not act autonomously but, rather, are "embedded in a social context, channeled and facilitated or constrained and inhibited by people's positions in social networks."[69] These social networks consist of strong and weak ties. **Strong ties** are the entrepreneur's close friends and family members whom he or she knows well, whereas **weak ties** are the entrepreneur's acquaintances and business contacts. In general, acquaintances are not socially involved; that is, entrepreneurs do not generally spend their nonbusiness hours with acquaintances.[70] Nevertheless, these weak ties play an important role in the

Profile 1.2 FROM PROFESSOR TO ENTREPRENEUR

Sometimes being a researcher can box you into one thing for the rest of your life—that is, if you let it. Corinna Lathan, a thirty-something Ph.D. in neuroscience from MIT was determined not to let that happen to her. She was interested in too many things. While at MIT, she worked at the Center for Space Research, which gave her the opportunity to see firsthand how technology can improve human performance. Upon finishing her Ph.D., she took a job at Catholic University in Washington, DC, where she taught biomedical engineering and explored medical applications of virtual reality and telecommunications technology. Through a friend who worked with disabled children, she became aware of the lack of toys for these children. It was then that she had the idea for CosmoBot.

CosmoBot is a small, metallic humanoid that can be programmed to speak to the child or respond to the child's voice. When the child wears a glove and cap embedded with hidden sensors, she can raise her arms to make CosmoBot do the same or can wiggle her head and CosmoBot will do likewise. The robot also records the child's movements so that progress can be tracked. Progress reports can then be sent through the Web-based interface, and program adjustments can be made via the Internet as needed.

In 1999, Lathan decided to take a leave of absence from the university to launch Anthro-Tronix, which she based in College Park, MD. After a year, she returned to the university where she was due to get tenure, but after only a month, she left the university, this time for good, to go full-time at AnthroTronix. Instead of becoming the best in one tiny area of research, as an entrepreneur, Lathan could develop real applications in a variety of areas. In fact, her company is now working on developing gesture-controlled devices that let soldiers send wireless communications to each other using only hand motions. Her research and development are funded by government grants.

In May 2002, Lathan was named one of the world's 100 Top Young Innovators by *Technology Review*, MIT's Magazine of Innovation. Lathan is currently testing CosmoBot in clinical and educational settings. She has found that even in industry, there is pressure to specialize, but Lathan is determined to continue to look for new ways to facilitate the interface between humans and technology, and that is the heart of her business concept.

Sources: E. Barker, "The Prodigal Professor," *Inc. Magazine* (September 2002), www.inc.com; AnthroTronix website at www.anthrotronix.com; "Corinna Lathan Named One of the World's Top Young Innovators by *Technology Review*, MIT's Magazine of Innovation" (May 23, 2002).

entrepreneurial process because entrepreneurs typically move forward faster with the help and support of weak ties who are not biased by a prior history with the entrepreneur. Family and close friends, on the other hand, tend to restrict the entrepreneur's potential because they look at the impact on them of the entrepreneur's business activities. Entrepreneurs rely on their weak ties for objective advice.

Entrepreneurs who successfully use their networks to build their businesses generally are committed to the success of the people in their network, are active listeners, and approach every contact with an open mind.[71] In that way, they derive the maximum value from their network ties.

Looking Ahead: The Organization of the Book

Starting a new venture is a process that begins long before the business ever opens its doors. That process is rarely linear. More often it is an iterative—even chaotic—process, but one with a direction and goals. This book is divided into four sections that mirror the entrepreneurial process. Part One focuses on the opportunity. Chapter 1 serves as an introduction to the field of entrepreneurship and the environment in which entrepreneurs start new ventures today. Chapter 2, another foundational chapter, explores the entrepreneurial journey from the entrepreneur's perspective and helps the reader prepare for this journey. At Chapter 3, the process of entrepreneurship begins with the recognition of an opportunity through the development of creativity skills. Chapter 4 covers the development of a business concept and business model.

Part Two (Chapters 5 through 8) explores feasibility analysis by examining the critically important process of testing a new business concept in the market.

Once there is a feasible concept, the business plan is the document that explains the execution of the concept. Part Three focuses on the business plan and what it adds to the feasibility study. Whereas the feasibility process works from the largest area of study—the industry—inward, the business planning process begins with the entrepreneur and a consideration of the purpose, core values, mission, and goals that form the basis for all the decisions that will be made about the company. The business plan documents the creation of a new company—the business model, operating plan, management plan, financial plan, and execution plan. Chapters 9 through 16 deal with the development of the business plan.

Any business undergoes growth and change, so Part Four focuses on those issues. Chapters 17 through 18 consider how to fund and grow the business, plan for unexpected changes, and architect a harvest strategy for the entrepreneur and investors.

In the next decade, entrepreneurial skills will be the key not only to economic independence and success but literally to survival. The marketplace puts a premium on creativity, initiative, independence, and flexibility. Entrepreneurs who develop those behaviors and display those characteristics will be more likely to succeed.

New Venture Checklist

Have you:

☐ Identified which entrepreneurial characteristics you possess?

☐ Determined how current trends will affect your search for a business idea?

☐ Decided whether a small business, an entrepreneurial venture, or corporate venturing is right for you?

Issues to Consider

1. Define the term *entrepreneurship*.
2. Why is it so difficult to assign "typical" descriptive characteristics to entrepreneurs?
3. As the mayor of your community, what incentives would you put into place to encourage entrepreneurship?
4. Describe the current environment for entrepreneurship. How does it differ from the environment pre-1980?
5. What is the role of innovation and invention in the entrepreneurial process?
6. Choose a typical "small business" in the community and discuss how that business could be turned into an entrepreneurial venture.

Experiencing Entrepreneurship

1. Interview an entrepreneur in an industry or business that interests you. Focus on how and why this entrepreneur started his or her business. Be sure to include the following: the entrepreneur's name, address, title, company name, and phone number

   a. Background

   How did you find this person and why did you choose her or him?

   Why is this person an entrepreneur?

   What influenced the entrepreneur to identify and pursue this opportunity?

   How did the entrepreneur's background (family history, prior education and work experience) affect the opportunity discovered?

   b. Describe the opportunity that the entrepreneur decided to pursue and the process the entrepreneur used to evaluate the opportunity.

   How did the entrepreneur evaluate the opportunity?

   What criteria did the entrepreneur use to decide whether to pursue the opportunity?

   What were the perceived risks of this opportunity and how did the entrepreneur expect to manage them?

   c. What did the entrepreneur do to turn the opportunity into a business?

   Identify specific activities the entrepreneur undertook to develop the opportunity into a business.

   Identify when the entrepreneur did these activities (provide dates: month and year).

   Identify important contacts and individuals who were helpful during the start-up process.

   What major problems did the entrepreneur encounter along the way?

   How were these problems solved?

   d. What advice would the entrepreneur give to someone thinking about pursuing an opportunity?

   Why was this entrepreneur successful?

   Analyze how the factors identified in parts (b), (c) and (d) affected this entrepreneur's success.

2. Visit an entrepreneurial venture and a small business. Be sure to interview the owners. Compare and contrast the two businesses in terms of the distinctions discussed in the chapter. Which type of business is better suited to your personality and goals and why?

Additional Sources of Information

Allen, K. (2001). *Entrepreneurship for Dummies.* Chicago: IDG Books.

Catlin, K., and J. Matthews (2001). *Leading at the Speed of Growth: Journey from Entrepreneur to CEO.* Chicago: Hungry Minds.

Drucker, P.F. (1986). *Innovation and Entrepreneurship.* New York: Harper & Row.

Gerber, M.E. (1995). *The E-Myth Revisited.* New York: HarperBusiness.

Koehn, N.F. (2001). *Brand New: How Entrepreneurs Earned Consumers' Trust from Wedgwood to Dell.* Boston: Harvard Business School Press.

Relevant Case Studies

Case 1 Overnite Express, p. 402

Case 2 Craigslist, p. 407

Case 3 Beanos Ice Cream Shoppe, p. 410

Case 4 Wizards of the Coast, p. 423

Preparing for the Entrepreneurial Journey

"Success isn't permanent, and failure isn't fatal."

Mike Ditka, professional football coach

LEARNING OBJECTIVES

- Dispel myths about entrepreneurs.
- Understand the characteristics and behaviors that help, and hurt, entrepreneurs.
- Prepare to become an entrepreneur.
- Understand the nature of entrepreneurial leadership.
- Increase the chances of success.

Profile 2.1 IF AT FIRST YOU DON'T SUCCEED

If you were going to give out an award for entrepreneurial persistence, you might give it to Neil Johnston, who tried and failed three times before he finally had the business of his dreams. Many would-be entrepreneurs would have given up after the second failure, but Johnston believes in learning experiences— entrepreneurship is not an event but a journey, even if the journey is a bit bumpy.

In 1991, Johnston and four partners founded a property management company, Archer Holdings in Carbondale, Illinois. They each contributed about $1,000 to the start-up with hopes of quitting their full-time jobs. They had big plans and big dreams, but Johnston soon learned that partnerships are not always made in heaven, and this one certainly was not. While Johnston spent his weekends painting apartments in the first complex they had been hired to manage, his partners were off enjoying theirs. In the end, they decided that this business and this partnership were not for them and went their separate ways.

Undaunted by the failure of the first partnership, Johnston put together another partnership to capitalize on a new digital press technology and, in 1993, founded ID Label & Systems, a manufacturer of labels for inventory management. For this venture, the partnership borrowed $100,000 for six months, and Johnston quit his day job to start the company although he received no pay from it. Overhead ran about $4,000 a month, and the first sales in months four and five amounted to only $22,000, not enough to repay the debt. Johnston's job was to bring in business, while one of his partners was to find financing. Unfortunately, his partner let him down, and when they were unable to pay back the note, Johnston negotiated a deal with another label company. That company acquired ID Label's press and paid Johnston $22,000 a year for his expertise.

By this time, Johnston had decided that having partners was not the way to go. In 1994, he got his boss at the new business to let him spin off from the business to start a "one-man" label-printing shop. The boss agreed as long as Johnston sold labels to him. He managed to secure $100,000 in investment capital and used $10,000 in credit card debt to fund the new venture. Now on his own with several months of good experience under his belt, Johnston headed to his first trade show and landed a $150,000 account. He found that he liked performing all aspects of the business, from generating the sale to making the labels to packing and shipping. And he liked doing it alone.

The business moved along fine for some time until Johnston realized that he was overworked, trying to run this one-man show. He was working 75–80 hours a week for about $180,000 to $200,000 a year. He wanted to spend more time with his family. It was now 1999, and the company was valued at $1.2 million. Johnston decided to sell a 30 percent interest to a neighbor to raise growth capital. Then, in 2001, the new partners merged with one of their customers, a solo entrepreneur company that sold bar-code labels to libraries. Total investment by the parties to this venture was $383,000, but it added substantially to the company's ability to grow. By 2002, ID Label had made the Inc. 500 fastest-growing private companies in the United States, with revenues at about $2.2 million. Johnston was able to reduce his workload and finally live the kind of life he wanted. Johnston is a prime example of an entrepreneur who did not want the type of business that employed many employees. He realized early on that more employees would not necessarily equal more profits. Furthermore, the challenges of managing all those employees would involve more stress than he wanted to take on. Instead, he kept the business at a manageable size and secured the balanced life he had always wanted.

Source: M. Hofman, "Until You Get It Right," *Inc. Magazine* (October 2002), www.inc.com. http://www.idlabelinc.com/.

Entrepreneurship is a personal journey that begins in the mind of the nascent entrepreneur. It is a personal journey because business is fundamentally about people—how they interact, make decisions, plan for the future, deal with conflict, and so on. In fact, all of entrepreneurship can be reduced to people. From the entrepreneur's motivation to start a business to the decisions made about growth, customers, facilities, employees, and the exit from the business, everything comes down to people and the needs of those people. Entrepreneurs' needs and goals must have the potential to be satisfied by starting a new venture or they will not have the motivation to continue in their efforts. The new venture must also satisfy the needs of customers or they will not be motivated to buy. Kim Camarella understood this. Through the eyes of her overweight best friend, she learned about the difficulty that larger young women have finding fashionable apparel. This motivated Camarella to found Kiyonna Klothing, now a successful line of plus-size apparel that is satisfying a real need in the market.

Finding a market need is a vital step. Another vital step in the entrepreneurial journey is assembling the right team. This can often make the difference between success and failure. Entrepreneur Mike Meek learned this lesson the hard way when he took on a partner for his ISO consulting business and did not take the time to check the man's résumé or references. The partner turned out to be a con artist whose activities cost Meek a great deal of money and compromised his good credit rating.[1]

How large to grow the business is very much a personal decision. Entrepreneurs who want to balance work with a personal life may choose to start a business that generates significant revenues but does not require a great deal of people and physical assets to manage. The profile of Neil Johnston at the beginning of the chapter is a good example of this type of entrepreneur.

The decision about when and how to exit the business is also a very personal one because it is based on the entrepreneur's goals and values. Some entrepreneurs start many ventures in their lives, so they experience the exit multiple times. Others stay with their businesses and choose not to exit. And still other entrepreneurs see their exit strategy change in response to unforeseen circumstances. John Lusk co-founded Platinum Concepts Inc. in July 1999 with some of his classmates from the Wharton School of Business at the University of Pennsylvania. Their core product was the MouseDriver, a computer mouse shaped like a golf-club head. Lusk's goal was to build the company up as fast as he could in two years and then sell it to another business. His plan forecasted the company's revenues skyrocketing to $10 million in 6 months. Unfortunately, this did not happen within his predetermined timeframe. It took approximately 18 months to build any sales for the MouseDriver. As a result, Lusk altered his exit strategy, deciding not to sell the company and instead to spend more time diversifying the product line and getting his products into the mass market.[2]

This chapter explores the personal journey called entrepreneurship, the characteristics and behaviors essential to successful entrepreneurship, and ways to prepare to become an entrepreneur and start a successful new venture.

Saying Goodbye to Stereotypes

Given the widespread public interest in entrepreneurs and the frequency with which they are discussed in the media, it is not surprising that stereotypes have developed around them. Not all of those stereotypes are flattering and most are simply false. This section attempts to dispel some of the myths surrounding entrepreneurs.

Myth 1: Entrepreneurs Start Businesses Solely to Make Money

Entrepreneurs start businesses for many reasons, but the number-one reason is their need for independence. They don't want to work for someone else. This does not suggest that entrepreneurs don't want to make money; they do. They simply figure that if they start and build a great business, the money will follow. In 1984 Suzanne Pogell launched Womanship as an all-woman sailing school whose goal was to do much more than just teach women how to sail. Pogell uses the discipline of sailing to help women learn how to become leaders and chart a course for their careers. Her reason for starting the business had little to do with money; it was based on a desire to help others.

Myth 2: It Takes a Lot of Money to Start a Business

Another false assumption about entrepreneurship is that it takes a lot of money to start a business. Nothing could be further from the truth. Every year *Inc. Magazine* profiles entrepreneurs who started their businesses on $1,000 or less. For example, Lori Bonn Gallagher parlayed her love of travel and of finding unique jewelry into a $2.8-million business. Starting with $1,000 worth of samples of handblown glass jewelry that she discovered in France and a successful selling strategy, Gallagher secured a deal with Nordstrom to begin selling her imported jewelry in the United States. Today her jewelry is designed at her headquarters in Oakland, California, manufactured in Bali, and sold in retail outlets such as Nordstrom, Discovery Store, and Boston's Museum of Fine Arts museum shop.[3] Another example is Multimedia Live, a web site design company that Ken Burke founded in 1995 with just $500 and a lot of promotion of the value of the Internet. In 1999 a major printing company invested $3.4 million in Multimedia, and now the company's revenues exceed $25 million.

Myth 3: It Takes a Great Idea

Jim Collins's research, which was documented in the bestseller *Built to Last,* dispelled the myth that it takes a great idea to start a business. In fact, most of the great businesses that have been successful for at least 50 years—companies such as Walt Disney, Sony, and Merck—didn't start with a great idea. They started with a great team who simply wanted to create an enduring company. Venture capitalists say that they will take a great team over a great idea any day, because it takes a superior team to execute a successful business concept.

Myth 4: Entrepreneurship Is a Zero-Sum Game

Many people believe that if someone is winning, someone has to be losing; in other words, success is a zero-sum game. Fortunately, entrepreneurs don't think like that. They tend to look for ways for everyone to come out with more than they started with. It is to an entrepreneur's advantage if the people on the other side of the negotiation table win too, because they will then support the entrepreneur's efforts. And entrepreneurs need all the support they can get!

Myth 5: The Bigger the Risk, the Bigger the Reward

Students of entrepreneurship often hear that risk is correlated with reward—the greater the risk taken, the greater the reward expected. Certainly, it appears that investors hold that point of view. But *risk* is a relative term, and the goal of most entrepreneurs is to reduce the level of risk in any venture. In fact, money people expect entrepreneurs to do things to reduce the risk for them, such as testing the market, writing a business plan, and so forth. And no one expects the business to be worth less because risk was reduced. It is actually to the entrepreneur's advantage to reduce risk for investors so that the entrepreneur can retain the majority of the equity. Sometimes reward is greater, not because risk is greater, but because the entrepreneur has brought to the business proposition new value that cannot be replicated easily.

Myth 6: A Business Plan Is Required for Success

There is no question that lenders, investors, and others want to see a business plan before agreeing to deal with an entrepreneur. They have a lot to lose if the company fails, so they need to satisfy themselves that the entrepreneur knows what she or he is doing. But many entrepreneurs have started highly successful businesses without having a formal plan in place—including recognizable companies such as Pizza Hut and Crate and Barrel that have survived for decades. Other entrepreneurs have put up websites and been "in business" within a day, making money within a couple of weeks. The truth is that research has not yielded agreement on the value of business planning or even on what components of business planning are correlated with success. In the earliest stages of start-up, what may be more important than the business plan itself is spending time and resources testing the market for the feasibility of the business concept in terms of actual sales. Once such feasibility is determined, a business plan helps the entrepreneur work through the building of a company.

Myth 7: Entrepreneurship Is for the Young and Reckless

Many people believe that if they haven't started their first business by the time they are 30, it is too late. They think that the energy, drive, resources, and risk involved are suitable only for the young. But many great businesses have been started by older entrepreneurs who had the passion to do something original. Ray Kroc started McDonald's at age 52, and Colonel Harland Sanders was over 60 when he started Kentucky Fried Chicken. Research supports the conclusion that being older can be an asset when starting a business. The Global Entrepreneurship Monitor Report found that men and women in the 45–64 age bracket are responsible for 36 percent of all the entrepreneurial activity in the United States and for 22 percent of the activity globally. Fifty percent of entrepreneurial activity is accomplished by men and women between the ages of 25 and 44.[4] Entrepreneurship is for anyone, regardless of age, who wants to experience the thrill of building something from scratch and making it a success.

Myth 8: Entrepreneurship Cannot Be Taught

This myth is a corollary to "Entrepreneurs are born, not made." Both are wrong. There is a lot about entrepreneurship that can be taught, including specific skills and behaviors. People who don't naturally have the skills of a successful entrepreneur can certainly learn and apply them. What cannot be taught is the passion to achieve. Some have called it the "fire in the belly." And indeed, what motivates someone to leave Harvard University to start a business (like Bill Gates of Microsoft) or to start by driving a garbage truck (like Wayne Huizenga, who founded Waste Management) cannot be learned. It is simply part of a person's makeup. Sometimes passion grows as an entrepreneur moves through the feasibility analysis. As questions begin to be answered and possibilities seem more feasible, passion is sparked.

The Good, the Bad, and the Ugly About Entrepreneurs

Interestingly, most entrepreneurs have the intense desire to start a business long before they know what that business will be. It is that internal need to be independent and create something, "the burning gut," that drives entrepreneurs. The reason why passion is so important is that starting a business is hard work that doesn't always go smoothly. The drive to succeed sustains the entrepreneur through the difficult times.

Entrepreneurs display many other behaviors, not all of which are attractive. Here we look at the good, the bad, and the ugly.

The Good

The following are some of the positive qualities of successful entrepreneurs. People who exhibit these behaviors tend to make good entrepreneurs.

Creativity

Entrepreneurship is more art than science. No two start-ups experience exactly the same things. No two entrepreneurs approach a venture in exactly the same way. This is what makes entrepreneurship at once so exciting and so difficult. There are no hard and fast rules for going through the process; there are only examples from which to choose those techniques that seem most appropriate for a given situation. Crafting a start-up strategy successfully requires creativity—the ability to juxtapose things that are normally not found together. For example, the drive-through bank was the result of combining banking and the fast-food model. Chapter 3 explores creativity and the role it plays in recognizing opportunities.

Business Knowledge

One of the best ways to prepare for entrepreneurship is to learn as much about it as possible by reading magazine articles, books, and newspapers and—most importantly—by talking to entrepreneurs. Studying the environment for a business and looking for trends and patterns of change is an important part of the preparation to become an entrepreneur. These activities increase entrepreneurial knowledge, thereby reducing some of the risk and enhancing the chances of success.

Critical Thinking

Because entrepreneurs operate in a world of uncertainty, the ability to analyze a situation, extract the important and ignore the superfluous, compare potential outcomes, and extrapolate from other experiences to the current one is vital. Entrepreneurs also regularly have to weigh options in complex situations. Critical thinking skills can be improved through practice and by observing how others with well-developed skills work through a problem-solving situation.

Integrity

When all is said and done, business is about relationships—with partners, with customers, and with suppliers. Successfully building relationships requires honesty and integrity. It requires giving value and delivering on promises. An entrepreneur's core values are the foundation for the business and are always reflected in the business and in the way customers are treated. Their integrity is something that entrepreneurs guard more carefully than anything else because they cannot afford to taint or lose it.

Self-Discipline and Perseverance

To succeed at anything requires a higher-than-average amount of self-discipline and perseverance. Entrepreneurs don't give up easily, and they tend to stick doggedly to a concept until something or someone convinces them that it's time to move on to something else. For example, Todd Stennett spoke with over 450 people before he found the right person to guide him to the perfect model for his now successful laser mapping business, Airborne 1. If entrepreneurs didn't have this tenacity, there would be no great businesses, because every entrepreneur faces the doubters and nay-sayers when a business concept is in its earliest stages. The ability to stick to the task and persevere against all odds is what wins the day for the entrepreneur.

Thriving on Uncertainty and Chaos

One of the biggest problems that scientists and engineers face when they decide to consider entrepreneurship is the lack of formulas and of right and wrong answers—in short, they face ambiguity and uncertainty. People who wish there were no surprises in life and who want an environment that is predictable and stable will find it very difficult to survive in the world of the entrepreneur. One of the reasons why entrepreneurship is such an interesting and exciting field is that it is constantly changing. It is well known that the greatest, most innovative ideas come about at the edge of chaos when things that don't normally connect are brought together in new ways. Opportunity is rarely found in stable, predictable settings.

The Bad

Certain behaviors prove to be detrimental to entrepreneurs. These behaviors are often found in less successful entrepreneurs and should be avoided.

Greed

Entrepreneurs who display greed rarely share the business's successes with others, including employees. They tend to hold out for the highest price, even at the cost of losing a deal, because they believe that there is someone out there who will pay more. They cut costs in areas that adversely affect customers and impair employees' ability to do their jobs, all just to chalk up more profit in the bottom line. In general, these entrepreneurs are among the minority who often start businesses to create wealth rather than to provide value.

Dishonesty and Lack of Ethics

An unfortunate sentiment expressed by some dishonest and unethical entrepreneurs to justify dishonorable behavior is "I can do it because everyone else in the business is doing it." These entrepreneurs don't pay their suppliers or partners on time, and when they do pay, they usually try to pay less than was originally agreed upon. They are not honest with their bankers about the status of the business; some even keep two sets of books, one to show the banker and one that contains the real numbers. Tactics like these always spell doom for the entrepreneurs who practice them. Every day, the news exposes corporate scandals wherein unethical leaders are being held accountable for their improprieties.

Poor Judgment

People who have a difficult time making decisions or who regularly find that they make poor decisions will probably not be successful as entrepreneurs. Making effective decisions is a critical part of the everyday life of an entrepreneur and is a skill that must be developed and exercised carefully. Poor decisions about hiring, business location, investors, and strategic partners can cost a company a great deal of money and prevent it from achieving its goals. Wise decisions, even in times of crisis, can provide an opportunity for growth. See the profile on Maxons Restorations for a good example.

Not Detail-Oriented

The saying "the devil is in the details" could not be more true in business. Entrepreneurs who proudly claim that they leave the details to others while they focus on the vision are telling the world that they don't participate in the inner workings of their business. Details matter, and although entrepreneurs should not be micromanagers as the business grows, they should be well aware of the status of critical numbers in their business, and they should make their presence known among employees on a regular basis. It is vitally important to the success of the business that the entrepreneur be detail-oriented.

Profile 2.2   **MAXONS RESTORATIONS, INC.: A DIFFERENT KIND OF IMPACT FROM SEPTEMBER 11**

How does an entrepreneur prepare to make wise decisions in the event of disaster? If you are Damon Gersh and your business is a disaster restoration company in the heart of Manhattan, you know that just like the fire department, you have to prepare for every possible scenario so that your employees and equipment are ready at a moment's notice. Maxons Restorations, like its competitors, subcontracts all of its labor, which ranges from 100 people for normal activity to 400 people for a major disaster. Outsourcing labor helps to balance the overhead during slow times. Gersh learned the importance of finding the "choke point" in his business—that is, the part of a business that falls apart when a crisis occurs. Gersh identified his company's choke point as the shared pool of labor. He and his competitors frequently dipped into the same pool of laborers when they needed to increase their labor forces. This particular choke point was severely tested on September 11, 2001.

The day after the September 11 disaster proved to be the busiest day for Gersh's company, which was deluged with calls in a way it had never been before. Gersh immediately got on the phone and contacted all of the subcontractors in the labor pool to secure their work commitments before his competitors had a chance. To achieve that kind of loyalty from his subcontractors in a time of crisis, Gersh had made a decision early on to pay his subcontractors more than his competitors and to pay on time, a practice that was not typical in this industry. Gersh's quick thinking and leadership on that day enabled his company to respond more quickly and effectively to the crisis of September 11. Gersh believes that the most important attribute he brings to his company is leadership. His ability to identify what is important and to set the company's direction for action has kept his company at the top of its industry.

Sources: J. Matthews and J. Dennis, with P. Economy, *Lessons from the Edge* (New York: Oxford University Press, 2003); and D. Gersh, "Care," *Fast Company* (2001) http://www.fastcompany.com/fast50/profile/?gersh1020.

The Ugly

It is sad but true that some entrepreneurs will do just about anything to succeed, even if it means lying, cheating, and stealing. Others will start businesses that are morally and ethically on the edge simply because there is a lot of money to be made in them. Fortunately, this group of entrepreneurs represents a minute proportion of all the entrepreneurs in existence, but they are often the ones that appear in newspapers and on television. The most successful entrepreneurs are successful because they conduct their business activities in accordance with the highest ethical standards and with the goal of creating and giving value to those they deal with.

Preparing to Become an Entrepreneur

Because people invest in *people,* it is important for potential entrepreneurs to assess whether their personality and beliefs are compatible with entrepreneurship. Spending some time in the introspection stage is a good exercise and can help to minimize the odds of choosing the wrong type of business. This section explores some critical issues that anyone contemplating a career as an entrepreneur should consider.

Reasons for Wanting to Own a Business

Anyone looking at entrepreneurship solely as a way to make money should understand that there are easier, less risky ways to do so. Recall that most entrepreneurs start businesses for reasons other than money. Although entrepreneurship is still the primary way to create wealth, it happens only when there is a viable and compelling business concept and a team that knows how to execute that concept. Starting a business is a great deal of work, so the reasons for taking on this challenge must grow out of genuine conviction.

Physical and Emotional Condition of the Entrepreneur

Launching a new business requires tremendous amounts of time and energy, as well as a great deal of support from family and friends. During the early stages of a new venture, resources are limited and the entrepreneur must wear many hats. This is immensely stressful, so it is important that the entrepreneur be in good health and optimal physical and emotional condition. It is often said that entrepreneurs start businesses to be in charge of their lives. The reality is that after they start their own business, they find themselves working more than they ever did for someone else. The major difference is that because they are building something they own, it doesn't feel like the work they are accustomed to. They are bringing to life a new business that reflects *their* goals and values.

Lifestyle Choice

It is important for potential entrepreneurs to think about the kind of lifestyle they are striving to achieve. Not all businesses support the kind of lifestyle that some entrepreneurs want to lead. Is travel important? Is having a large home and all the things that go with it a requirement? Is achieving a balanced life with plenty of time for family and friends important? If so, starting a business that requires a lot of travel or puts the entrepreneur at the mercy of demanding clients probably won't provide that balanced lifestyle.

The Business Environment

Most people spend the majority of the day at their work; therefore, it is certainly important that the work environment be an enjoyable place to be. Entrepreneurs who love the outdoors should probably not start businesses that require them to sit at a desk all day. Entrepreneurs who don't enjoy working with people should probably not start a business that is labor-intensive or involves numerous daily interactions with the public. It is a good idea for a future entrepreneur to take a step back and contemplate his or her ideal work environment. What does this environment look like or "feel" like? What would spending a day in this environment entail?

Global Insights

When New Businesses Go Global

Recent research has made a strong case for acceleration in the rate at which companies are internationalizing their business efforts even at the earliest stages. New ventures, which already suffer from the liabilities of size and newness, must now add the risk of entering a foreign market with its unique political, legal, economic, and sociocultural complexities. K.D. Miller's work in this area has provided a framework for managing the risks of internationalization.[5] Young businesses can increase their chances of international success by (1) imitation, or entering the same countries as others in the industry have; (2) avoidance, or refusing to enter a country where the risk is unacceptably high; (3) flexibility in the design of the company so that it can adapt quickly and effectively when things change; (4) cooperation, or entering into strategic alliances to reduce uncertainty; and (5) control, or attempting to influence the behavior of others. This last area is most difficult for a new firm, but the possibility of influencing customer behavior exists. For example, in China, entrepreneurs have found funding for mainstream Internet portals such as Sina.com, Netease.com, and Sohu.com because the portal industry is large and demand is great. But entrepreneurs with business concepts that are less mainstream will probably not find a ready market at the outset. Entrepreneurs looking to expand their markets into China (or any other international location) need a very clear strategy, strong financial backing, and an effective team—very much as they do in the United States.

Entrepreneurial Leadership

Leadership is one of the most revered topics in business schools today. Hardly any subject has received more research attention. Certainly, poor or unethical leadership has been the target of media attention recently with the downfall of companies such as Arthur Anderson and Enron. Leadership demands a lot of those who assume the role. They are expected to inspire the entire organization to achieve its goals, yet most leaders of larger companies cannot personally interact with all their employees. So those company leaders who do attain legendary status generally do so because of the context in which they assumed leadership rather than as a result of their charisma.[6] Bill Gates and Jack Welch are not known as charismatic leaders, yet when they served as CEOs of their companies, their ability to inspire thousands of workers to adopt the corporate goals was legendary.

Leadership in the earliest stages of a new venture is another matter entirely. Whereas the leader of a large, established organization must deal with the issue of what type of leadership is best for the company, the entrepreneur/leader of a private company is more of a creator. Because the entrepreneur is not shaped by the demands of shareholder value as the CEO of a public company is, the entrepreneur/leader is the creator of the vision, the culture, and the outcomes of the business. This is a different kind of leadership from that espoused in the management textbooks. The next sections explore the nature of entrepreneurial leadership.

To Thine Own Self Be True

Entrepreneurs must understand that the reason why their business exists in the first place is to satisfy their personal needs. Entrepreneurs start businesses for many reasons—independence, to do meaningful work, to achieve a goal, to create wealth—but all of these reasons reflect personal needs of the entrepreneur. If the founder of the company is not satisfying his or her personal needs with the business, the business is not likely to be successful. Lanny Goodman, founder of Management Technologies Inc. and a serial entrepreneur, believes that entrepreneurs should ask themselves four important questions:[7]

1. What do I need and want out of life?
2. How can my company help me accomplish that?
3. What would such a company look like?
4. What would it take to get there?

One of the most exciting aspects of entrepreneurship is the ability to create a company precisely the way the entrepreneur has always dreamed it to be. Designing

---

SCREENSHOT 2.1   **Lanny Goodman of Management Technologies Incorporated**

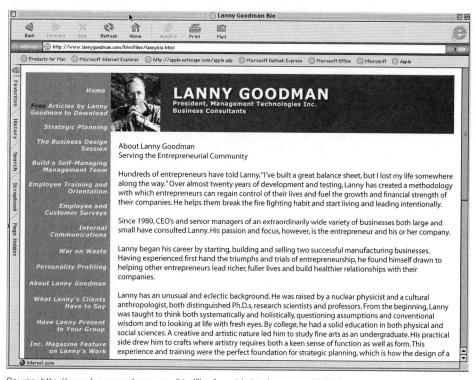

Source: http://www.lannygoodman.com/htmlfiles/lannybio.html, accessed 2/25/05.

a company is not the time to compromise on wants and needs. Effective entrepreneurial leadership demands that a company first meet the needs of the founders, and then everything else will begin to fall into place.

To Be or Not to Be

One of the biggest mistakes that entrepreneurs make when they are in the start-up phase is to assume that they must be "the one" to make the business happen and that everything falls on their shoulders. Because business environments today are immensely complex and fast-moving, no one person has all the know-how to launch a new business. In fact, this misconception is very limiting and has caused more than one aspiring entrepreneur to become overwhelmed and eventually to give up. Instead, it is far more liberating for entrepreneurs to take themselves out of the picture for a moment and figure out *whom* they need to involve in order to make the business a success. That kind of mentality opens up possibilities that would have never been considered if the entrepreneur had relied solely on his or her own knowledge and experience. When entrepreneurs welcome the idea that they *alone* are not the company, they free themselves to invite others to join in the creation and development of the company.

Team as Hero

Entrepreneurial leaders have a distinct advantage over charismatic or heroic leaders. Being a hero is lonely; there are no peers to confide in or teammates with whom to share the load. Today, more than ever before, entrepreneurs see themselves as part of a team, from the founding of the venture throughout all the various stages in the life of that venture. The days of the gun-slinging solo entrepreneur are gone. Today it takes a team to succeed and a leader who can inspire others to motivate and lead as well.

Entrepreneurial leadership, like any effective leadership, is a balance of passion and pragmatism. It is the entrepreneur's passion that launches the business and keeps it going through the early days when survival is often in doubt. But a different kind of leadership is often required once the business has survived and has entered a growth mode. A more pragmatic style of leadership that can deliver the right systems and controls to keep the venture on course is not often found in the same person who founded the venture. Unfortunately, in private companies it is often the entrepreneur/founder who is left to decide when it is time for him or her to hand the reins to a different type of leader, and only the rare entrepreneur recognizes when that moment is at hand. Sometimes, however, the entrepreneur remains as the visionary leader of the company but brings on a CEO with professional management skills. This topic is explored in more depth in Chapter 17.

Increasing the Chances of Success

Starting any business, large or small, requires a tremendous amount of time, effort, and resources. It makes sense to start a business that has the potential to grow large and provide a good return on that investment, rather than spending the same amount of effort on a very small business that yields only a single job. In fact, research supports that notion.[8,9] The probability of success and survival tends to go up with larger businesses or businesses with more potential. Unfortunately, the vast majority of people who start businesses do not think like entrepreneurs. They think like small business owners wanting to keep everything under control, to grow slowly, and simply to provide a job for the owner. Although there is nothing inherently wrong with looking at business from this perspective, it does, regrettably, expose the entrepreneur to significantly more risk. Because these small businesses do not create new value, innovate, or have a plan for growth, they tend to be undercapitalized, poorly managed, and unable to differentiate themselves from competitors.

How, then, does an entrepreneur increase the chances for success? Figure 2.1 presents a model for the entrepreneurial process from the point of view of the entrepreneur/founder. Within each component of the model are opportunities for the entrepreneur to plant the seeds of success. The entrepreneur or founder of the venture is at the heart of the new business concept. Even when a venture is started by a team—and most are—one person is typically the lead entrepreneur who began with the vision and concept for the business. In general, all of the components of the process are the result of decisions based on the values, desires, and goals of the founder. The team that supports the founder will generally possess a similar value system, which makes for a team that is well-rounded, covers all the basic functional needs of the business, enhances the founder's financial statement, and increases the scope of contacts.

One very specific task that an entrepreneur can undertake is to find a **mentor**—that is, someone who is leading the type of life that the entrepreneur

---

FIGURE 2.1   The Entrepreneurial Process from the Entrepreneur's Perspective

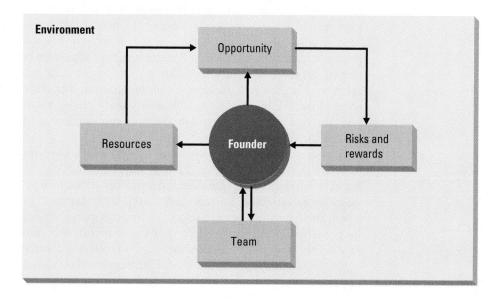

envisions for his or her own future. The mentor can be the entrepreneur's guide and sounding board. The issues of team formation and the founder's role are discussed in more detail in Chapter 7.

The next essential component of the process is the **business opportunity,** which is generally expressed in the form of a **concept statement.** The business concept identifies the customer, the value proposition, the product and/or service to be offered, and the method for delivering the value proposition, or benefit, to the customer. It is a critical element of the process because it serves as the foundation for the development of a business model, or way to make money. It also provides a way to test the business opportunity in the market to determine acceptance and level of demand before actually starting the business. Business concepts are the subject of Chapter 4.

The next element of the process is resources, which include people, physical assets, intangible assets or intellectual property, and financial assets. In general, most entrepreneurs operate in bootstrapping mode, which means that they beg, borrow, outsource, and lease as much as possible in the start-up phase. **Bootstrapping** is not a liability for a new company but rather a competitive advantage, because more of the early revenues go to the profit line instead of supporting costly overhead that does not generate revenues for the company. It is important for entrepreneurs to minimize the number of resources they need to own to start the business. That includes people, which are the single biggest expense of any business. Chapters 8, 15, and 16 explore ways to secure resources in an entrepreneurially sound manner.

Every opportunity has risks and rewards associated with it. Those risks can be financial, personal, or reputational. Risks are also associated with resources, opportunity costs, investors, and strategic partners. However, before entrepreneurs ever risk the time and money of investors and strategic partners, they risk their own finances, their time and effort, and their reputations. As stated earlier in the text, a common misconception is that risk is directly correlated with reward, such that the higher the risk, the higher the reward. But in reality, the more risky the venture, the more of the company an investor will want to own to ensure that outcomes can be controlled to the investor's benefit. Reward is a function of how much value is created by the new venture, and value is often created as risk is *reduced*. For example, one of the most precarious points of entry for an investor is the concept stage before feasibility has been proved. An investor coming in at that stage will want more control of the business and therefore a larger equity stake, or ownership position. But if the founding team reduces some of the risk by conducting a feasibility study, testing the market, and securing the first customer, the investor will probably require somewhat less control and a smaller stake in the venture.

All businesses operate within the context of an environment that includes the industry in which they operate, legal requirements, cultural dynamics, economic impacts, government regulation, and sources of incentives and assistance, among many other variables. Entrepreneurs need to understand fully the environment in which their business operates so that they can devise strategies that allow them to be proactive in that environment rather than reactive. Environmental effects on new ventures related to the industry and market are discussed in Chapter 5.

The next chapter explores how entrepreneurs cultivate ideas into business opportunities.

New Venture Checklist

Have you:

☐ Decided whether or not you have what it takes to be an entrepreneur?

☐ Determined why you want to start a business?

☐ Considered what type of business might be a good fit for you?

Issues to Consider

1. Why do myths emerge around phenomena such as entrepreneurship?
2. What are the steps you should take to prepare yourself for entrepreneurship?
3. How are entrepreneurial leaders different from leaders of large, publicly held companies?
4. What negative characteristics can prevent an entrepreneur from being unsuccessful?
5. Why are more ventures started by teams than by solo entrepreneurs?

Experiencing Entrepreneurship

1. Identify an entrepreneur who is leading the kind of personal and business life that you aspire to lead. Interview that person to find out more about how she or he achieved that lifestyle. During the interview, and only if the two of you have a rapport, approach the entrepreneur about becoming your mentor.

2. Entrepreneurship is a journey, and many people contribute to that journey. Begin a contact portfolio that will contain all the people you meet as you network. Record their contact information, how you met them, and what they contributed to your journey. Strive to meet three to five strangers a week.

Additional Sources of Information

Stephenson, James (2001). *Entrepreneur's Ultimate Start-up Directory: Includes 1,350 Great Business Ideas.* Irvine, CA: Entrepreneur Media Inc.

Boogaert, John F. (2000). *No Feet in Concrete: Leadership in an Entrepreneurial World.* Fresno, CA: Panagraph, Inc.

Krass, Peter (Ed.) (1999). *The Book of Entrepreneurs' Wisdom: Classic Writings by Legendary Entrepreneurs.* New York: Wiley.

Relevant Case Studies

Case 1 Overnite Express, p. 402
Case 2 Craigslist, p. 407
Case 3 Beanos Ice Cream Shoppe, p. 410

Case 5 iRobot, p. 432
Case 6 The Crowne Inn, p. 435

Recognizing and Creating Opportunity

"The greater danger for most of us lies not in setting our aim too high and falling short; but in setting our aim too low, and achieving our mark."

Michelangelo

■ Explain the nature of creativity.

■ Identify the challenges to creativity.

■ Discuss how to remove the roadblocks to creative thought.

■ Name some sources of new product/service ideas.

Profile 3.1 A GENIUS INVENTOR WITH A PASSION FOR LIFE

Dr. Yoshiro Nakamatsu is truly the essence of a creative, innovative person. He holds more than 3,218 patents, three times as many as the great American inventor Thomas Edison. For example, Nakamatsu is responsible for the floppy disk, which he licensed to IBM (and he does get a royalty on the millions of disks sold every year), the compact disk and disk player, the digital watch, and the water-powered engine. So prolific is he that his offices in Tokyo are located just a short walk from the patent office.

At the tender age of 5, he invented an automatic gravity controller for a model plane that he claims made autopilot possible. The patent on that invention has long since expired, and he earns no royalties from autopilot systems. At the age of 14, he invented a plastic kerosene pump on which he still holds the patent. That device can now be found in any hardware store.

Nakamatsu credits his genius to his parent's constant encouragement to be creative and not focus solely on learning. This is contrary to the traditional Japanese upbringing, where children are typically made to memorize great quantities of information and are not allowed to associate freely until their twenties. These factors, along with his discipline and belief that trying too hard stifles creativity, led to Nakamatsu's stellar career as an inventor.

Nakamatsu believes that successful innovation comes from "freedom of intelligence." By that he means that you have to work with no strings attached. Consequently, Nakamatsu has never sought funding from anyone and uses his own resources to develop and invent. The only licensing of his technologies that he has ever done was to IBM in the 1970s for computer-related patents. He prefers to hold on to his intellectual property and to make his unique products himself.

Nakamatsu has a very idiosyncratic way of generating ideas. He starts the creative process by sitting calmly in a room in his home that he calls the "static room" because it has only natural things in it, much like the meditation gardens in Kyoto, Japan. Here he opens his mind to the creative flow of new ideas—he free-associates, letting his mind go wherever it wants to. He then moves to the "dynamic room," a dark room with the latest audio/video equipment. Here he listens to jazz, easy-listening music, and Beethoven's Fifth Symphony—one of his favorites. In this room, new ideas begin to form. Following a period of time in the dynamic room, he heads for the swimming pool, where he swims underwater for extraordinarily long periods of time. It is underwater that he finishes the process of "soft thinking," or playing with the idea, and becomes ready to move on to the more practical phase of considering how to implement the idea. He even records his ideas under water on a special Plexiglas writing pad.

Nakamatsu, by the way, also swears by the brain food he eats, which he dubbed "Yummy Nutri Brain Food": dried shrimp, seaweed, cheese, yogurt, eel, eggs, beef, and chicken livers! He has consumed only his own food for the past 30 years and lives on 4 hours of sleep a night. For Nakamatsu, invention is an act of love. When faced with a choice between the easiest path and the most difficult path, he always chooses the most difficult because there he can find what no one else has found.

Sources: L. Betti, "Yoshiro Nakamatsu: Inventing Genius." *Evolution*, #3 (September 15, 2002), http://evolution.skf.com/gb/article.asp?articleID 425; Linda Naiman and Chic Thompson, "Dr. Yoshiro Nakamatsu," http://www.creativityatwork.com/articlesContent/Nakamats1.html.

What does **creativity** have to do with entrepreneurship? Everything! Creativity is what enables entrepreneurs to differentiate their businesses from competitors so that customers will notice them. Creativity is also the basis for invention, which is discovering something that did not exist previously, and innovation, which is finding a new way to do something. Today, entrepreneurs face a rapidly changing environment brought about in large part by the speed of technological change. The combination of rapid change and the resulting uncertainty about what the future holds presents a fertile ground for new opportunities. Creativity is a critical skill for recognizing or creating opportunity in a dynamic environment.

Dean Kamen embodies this creative zeal. His human transporter, dubbed the Segway, provides an innovative way for people to get around that is not dependent on gasoline. At $5,000, it is just now beginning to find a market. MedExpress Ambulance Service in Louisiana uses Segways to transport its medics through traffic-congested roadways. Some retailers are using them in promotions. For example, one enterprising entrepreneur in San Diego charges $20 for a 45-minute Segway ride rental. The Segway is the result of creative thinking about transportation and the environment.

The American Management Association conducted a survey of 500 CEOs, asking them what companies would have to do to survive in the twenty-first century. The most common answer was "practice creativity and innovation." It seems that the creativity deficit may be the most dangerous threat to businesses today.[1] Companies such as 3M, Bell Laboratories, Xerox, and Hallmark practice creativity by looking at ideas on the fringes of their industries, instead of where everyone else is looking. Future opportunities lie in deviations from what is "common practice."

Before going further, it is important to distinguish among four concepts that are critical to this chapter: (1) idea, (2) business opportunity, (3) **opportunity recognition,** and (4) **opportunity creation.** Everyone has *ideas,* hundreds of them every day. However, a *business opportunity* is an idea that involves a product or service with commercial potential. This idea must create new value for customers and must be able to be attached to a business model; in other words, there must be a way to make money from the opportunity. In fact, the very act of developing a business concept and successfully testing it in the marketplace with potential customers — a process known as feasibility analysis — is what turns an idea into an opportunity.

Some entrepreneurs use their creativity to improve on what they currently do or on what their competitors are doing. This is the process of *opportunity recognition,* or innovation based on a product or service already in existence. Other entrepreneurs do things that no one else is doing by participating in the process of *opportunity creation,* or "starting from scratch." The highest level of creativity and innovation, called radical innovation, involves doing things that seemingly cannot be done.

No matter what the environment throws at entrepreneurs, if they put their creative talents to work, they can find ways to succeed. Opportunity recognition and creation begin with a creative mindset. Some people have an easier time generating ideas than others, but only because they possess better-developed awareness and creativity skills. This is good news, because it means that everyone has the ability to become more creative. The next section explores how entrepreneurs hone their natural creativity to cultivate skills that will put them in a better position to recognize or create a business opportunity.

The Nature of Creativity

Creative people are curious and strongly aware of their surroundings. They ask questions and aren't afraid to do things differently. They are open to all ideas, believing that every one is worthy of at least initial consideration, and they seem to have a high tolerance for ambiguity. However, some people resist creativity and ambiguity; they are uncomfortable in uncertain environments and don't know how to use their creative skills to survive. This is not surprising when one considers that many schools do not challenge students to be creative, encouraging them instead to follow a structured plan laid out by the professor that includes coming up with only the expected correct answers. That is the antithesis of creativity.

Entrepreneurship is a creative, not a scientific, process. From generation of the business idea to development of the marketing plan to management of the growing business, it is creativity in all aspects of the venture that sets the most successful new businesses apart from those that merely survive.

What Is Known About Creativity

Creativity has been defined from both a functional and an outcome perspective. The functionalist perspective dominates the literature and proposes that creativity is the production of novel and useful ideas.[2] The outcome perspective is a more applied approach that emphasizes the generation of valuable, useful products and services, procedures, and processes.[3] The earliest research on creativity focused on the individual, in much the same way that early research on entrepreneurship focused on the entrepreneur. Researchers looked at personality factors and cognitive skills such as language, thinking processes, and intelligence.[4] Then they examined the context in which people are creative and found that a number of environmental settings are conducive to creativity, among them absence of constraints, presence of rewards or incentives, and team effectiveness.[5] The newer models of creativity incorporate organizational variables, including policies, structures, culture, and training. However, little is really known about the specific conditions that promote creativity in individuals within organizations.[6] Furthermore, research reveals that creativity occurs at both an individual and a group level and is a matter of choice on the part of the person involved.[7]

Creativity as a Process

As discussed in the previous section, most researchers have looked at creativity more as an outcome than as a process, so the models they describe are static. However, one group of researchers has proposed that time is an important variable in the creative process and that creativity is not a linear process but an iterative, chaotic one.[8] This view is compatible with research on the new venture process.

The creative process is not formulaic. Indeed, research suggests that certain definable patterns and activities occur in any creative process. These patterns are

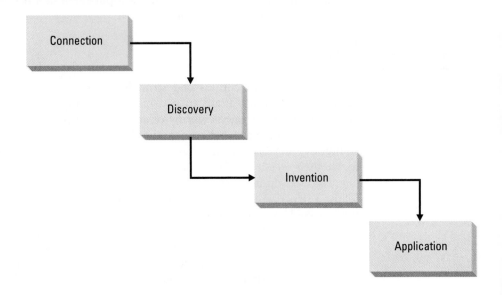

FIGURE 3.1   The Invention Process

connection, discovery, invention, and application as depicted in Figure 3.1.[9] The example of Leonardo da Vinci, one of the greatest inventors of all time, is a good way to investigate the creative process in more depth.[10]

Connection

A connection occurs when two ideas are brought together using such devices as metaphor, analogy, symbol, and hypothesis. Da Vinci saw a connection between the branches of trees and the canal system he was designing for the city of Florence, Italy. He verbalized this connection as a metaphor: canals are tree branches. It is interesting to note that nature has been the metaphor for many an invention, including Velcro® (inspired by the sticky burr) and the entire field of nanotechnology, which has brought about the development of microscopic machines and processes whose functions are based on processes often found in nature.

Discovery

Once a connection has been established, the inventor explores it in depth. Da Vinci did this by drawing tree branches, examining them closely, and conducting experiments. Through his exhaustive research, he learned how trees manage the flow of nutrients and water through their systems. This gave him a better understanding of how water flows through canals. Discovery frequently occurs when we look at something that already exists from a different perspective.

Invention

Inventions are the product of effort once a discovery has occurred. They usually arise out of needs in the market, but they can be serendipitous as well. Da Vinci's insight into the inner workings of tree branches enhanced the development of hydraulic devices to control water levels so a boat could cross a bridge. His other inventions led to a means to create a waterway from Florence to the sea.

Application

Going beyond the initial invention to other applications, da Vinci came up with ideas for mills powered by wind and water. It is interesting that many inventors never see beyond their initial inventions. The highest levels of creativity can occur only when an inventor considers all other possible applications for the invention in a variety of industries and situations.

Profile 3.2 CREATIVITY ON A ROLL

Imagine being so creative that you are regarded as the father of a whole branch of science. That is where Stanford Ovshinsky finds himself after securing more than 275 patents, mostly in the arcane area of "disordered-materials physics." He uses unstructured elements such as cesium to achieve superconductivity. His company is the Michigan-based Energy Conversion Devices, and it has been patenting inventions since the end of World War II. He has focused on coming up with marketable energy-saving products, including rewritable compact disks. Ovshinsky is known at his company for thinking not only in three dimensions but also in a variety of colors.

What is interesting about Ovshinsky is that he actually bypassed college to become a tool maker and machinist. Rather than being stifled by the restrictions of a college education, he, like Yoshiro Nakamatsu (see Profile 3.1), believes in intellectual freedom. Ovshinsky was the son of a Lithuanian scrap metal dealer, and his knowledge of machines led him to his first patented invention, the high-speed machine tool. From there he went on to design intelligent machines. After studying neurophysiology and disordered-materials physics, he was driven to develop a number of fossil-fuel-saving inventions.

Ovshinsky's focus in the 1970s and 1980s was amorphous semiconductor materials, on which he earned many patents. These materials became essential ingredients in optoelectronic copying and fax machines, as well as flat-panel liquid crystal displays.

The biggest achievement came in 1982, when Ovshinsky invented small, powerful batteries made from alloys called nickel metal hydrides. Japanese electronics giants embraced the technology and in 2001, 780 million NiMH batteries were made for computers, cell phones, and other electronic devices, most through licenses on Ovshinsky's patents.

Like most inventors, Ovshinsky was not driven by money, and, in fact, his company is still not consistently profitable. Nevertheless, he claims, "This has been a wonderful life, to have creative ideas and build things." At 81, he is far from finished with his work.

Sources: J. Rosenbloom, "The Lifetime Achiever," *Inc. Magazine* (September 2002), www.inc.com; M. Hornblower, "Listen, Detroit: You'll Get a Charge Out of This," Time .com (March 1999), http://www.time.com/time/reports/environment/heroes/heroesgallery/0,2967,ovshinsky,00.html; and "Inventor of the Week: Stanford Ovshinsky: Amorphous Semi-conductor Materials," Lemelson-MIT Program (March 2000).

Challenges to Creativity

Creativity tends to occur naturally, but entrepreneurs often unintentionally erect roadblocks that prevent them from following the creative path. Some of these road-blocks are discussed in the following sections.

No Time for Creativity

Entrepreneurs are often so busy that there is no time to think and contemplate, and this can keep them from exercising their creative skills. Most people rely on routines to keep their lives organized and under control. But relying on routines too heavily can prevent an individual from taking the time to generate new ideas in response to a changing environment.

No Confidence

Taking the familiar path out of fear of being criticized will keep entrepreneurs from fully realizing their potential. They will be continually held back by the need for their ideas to seem acceptable and rational to others. Rationality is not a prerequisite either for innovative ways to seize opportunities or for receiving a patent on an invention! The inventor of patent number 2,608,083 probably thought he was being rational when he invented the Travel Washing Machine, a portable, mobile appliance that is mounted on the wheel of a vehicle and washes the driver's clothes as he or she motors down the road. Unfortunately, the motorist has to jack up the car first to install the device and, for optimum results, cannot travel faster than 25 miles an hour. Ludicrously irrational inventions notwithstanding, many of the products in use every day—the fax machine and the personal computer, to name two—would not have come about if the people who invented them hadn't had the courage to go against the general thinking at the time.

No Creative Skills

All of the aforementioned roadblocks can stifle creativity, but individuals who believe they are not creative are doing themselves the greatest disservice. They are dismissing ideas before even trying them out. Anyone can learn to become more creative and develop creative skills. The next section examines some ways to prepare for creative success.

Removing the Roadblocks

The creative journey begins with keeping a journal of one's thoughts and ideas. Many entrepreneurs keep this type of journal with them at all times to record whatever pops into their heads. They may not be ready to work on a particular idea at that very moment, but they still jot it down so that they can return to it in the future.

There are a number of things that can be done immediately to remove the road-blocks in the path to more creative thinking. The process starts with preparing an environment that makes it easier to think imaginatively and then moves to some techniques for enhancing creative skills. This chapter cannot present all the creativity tools and skills available, so some additional resources are suggested at the end of the chapter.

Preparing for Innovation

Great inventors and highly creative companies owe their success to having provided an environment that simulated high levels of innovation. Thomas Edison's greatest invention was arguably not the light bulb but rather the concept of a research and development laboratory that served as an incubator for radical innovation. Likewise, Disneyland was not the greatest invention of the Walt Disney Company. Disney Imagineering, its Edison-like laboratory, is the source of its celebrated ideas.

The environment in which a person works can either stimulate or discourage creativity. For example, suppose a business has a very rigid and hierarchical structure with many layers of management. For this type of environment to be effective, its operations must be standardized so that everyone does things in the same way. That kind of environment is not conducive to thinking "out of the box." Here is another example. Picture an advertising and public relations firm that has to meet many deadlines. A fast-paced environment like this leaves little time for contemplation, which is essential to higher levels of creative thought.

Even in environments like these, however, there are ways to make the setting more conducive to creativity and innovation. Here are a few suggestions:

Minimize distractions. Close the door or shut off the phone to prepare to do some creative thinking.

Devote some time each day to quiet contemplation. Doing this on a regular basis trains the mind to shift quickly into the creative mode. It also helps make creative thinking a habit.

Pay attention to the places that inspire the most creative thinking and spend more time there.

Develop a creative culture so that employees contribute to the company's ability to innovate. For example, Premiere Radio Networks, a Los Angeles–based producer and distributor of radio broadcasts, lets its creative writers design their own office space to reflect their personalities. Comedy writer Jaime Case has adopted an eclectic blend of random souvenirs and toys collected during her travels. She refers to her office theme as "F.A.O. Schwartz on steroids," but it provides just the right type of surroundings to suit her particular style of creativity.

Mix people up. It is possible to achieve a more stimulating environment by mixing people up—that is, taking them out of their familiar surroundings and putting them in a new setting that forces them to think outside their normal mode. For example, a company might put a technology person in the marketing group for a month and place a marketing person in the technology group. The cultures of the two groups are typically very different, so the marketing person will bring a new perspective to technology issues and the techie to marketing. One entrepreneur looks for unusual places to locate his businesses because he believes that truly creative ideas can't be generated in a typical office setting. Accordingly, he located one of his businesses in a Victorian mansion and another in an old Army building in the Presidio in San Francisco.

Profile 3.3   ACTOR TURNED ENTREPRENEUR

A number of American actors have become political leaders, so it is not surprising that an actor might also become a successful entrepreneur. Robert Redford, the Sundance Kid, understands the essence of entrepreneurship and its chaotic nature:

> "Do you think the world was created by an accountant?" "No! The universe was created by the combustion of a creative explosion. Fire and chaos started everything. Then order came on top of that."

At the very young age of 24, Redford purchased two acres of land in Utah for $500 and built a log cabin there. From that humble beginning sprang a new industry—the independent film industry or *indie,* an international conglomerate, and a nonprofit institute that produces the renowned Sundance Film Festival. The institute has produced more than 85 feature films in 22 years. So widely recognized is it that 4,000 Blockbuster stores devote an entire shelf to its films. And Redford's Sundance Channel on cable television now has 16.7 million subscribers.

Redford attributes the success of Sundance to his unwavering belief that growth is a creative process. In his mind, it is the essence of business. The idea for Sundance came from Redford's distaste at seeing studio after studio churn out a continuous stream of formulaic entertainment. In Sundance, he saw the opportunity to build a sanctuary for artists where creative ideas could flourish. Lacking business savvy, he set out to learn, observe, and apply everything he could about business. Unlike many entrepreneurs, who compromise their vision to satisfy the demands of investors, Redford refused to do that. The story is told that his partners wanted to build a restaurant adjacent to the ski lift to take advantage of traffic. Redford rejected the idea, however, saying that the restaurant needed its own space so that people could discover it. A huge tree stood in the middle of his proposed site, so he built the restaurant around the tree and called it The Tree Room. It is now one of the finest restaurants in Utah. Not long after that, his partners sold their interests, claiming he was too difficult to work with. According to Redford, it's not just revenue that matters, it's the kind of revenue. And the same might be said of investors.

To foster creativity, Redford keeps the conditions at the institute relatively primitive so that artists must be resourceful and experimental. He is seeking not perfection but originality, process not product. Originality is what makes Sundance different; it has a compelling story and a tribal legend that it fosters through its social and community habits, such as the informal gatherings at the Owl Bar to relive the great moments in Sundance's history and to keep the spirit alive. At the Sundance Institute, innovation is a way of life, not just a business strategy. The design and process of the Institute encourage innovation and creativity. It is a journey without an end.

Sources: S.H. Zades, "Creativity Regained." *Inc. Magazine* (September 2003), www.inc.com; and Sundance Institute, http://institute.sundance.org.

Starting with the Familiar

It is a myth that entrepreneurs only build businesses based on concepts that never existed before. Most business concepts derive from existing ideas that the entrepreneur intends to improve on. And most business ideas stem from a problem or opportunity that the entrepreneur sees in his or her immediate environment. The local neighborhood or community is a rich source of opportunity, and as noted in Chapter 1, finding opportunity in things with which the entrepreneur has experience is the most common and effective way to achieve entrepreneurial success. Research supports this notion. One study at the University of Illinois at Chicago identified the sources of new venture ideas shown in Figure 3.2.[11] These are just a few examples of the many familiar sources of creative inspiration. Of course, current newspapers, magazines, and trade journals are another excellent source of ideas and trends.

Note that in this research, prior experience was cited more often than any other source. Entrepreneurs do frequently find new opportunity in the familiar. Howard Schultz, founder of Starbucks, did. He found a new use for coffee as a designer beverage that creates an experience. Johann Gutenberg took two unconnected ideas—the wine press and the coin punch—and came up with the printing press and movable type. The mechanism for the ballpoint pen inspired roll-on deodorant, and playing with a piece of wire while thinking about a debt he had to repay resulted in Walter Hunt's development of the safety pin.

The federal government or state government can also be a great source of new venture ideas. New laws and regulations often require the use of a product or service that didn't previously exist. For example, the establishment of the Occupational Safety and Health Administration (OSHA) provided an opportunity for people who could train businesses in everything from meeting the stringent requirements that OSHA imposed on the workplace to filling out the incredible amount of paperwork associated with those requirements. City ordinances that require certain products, such as glass and plastic, to be recycled have produced many businesses that provide new uses for these materials.

FIGURE 3.2	Sources of New Venture Ideas

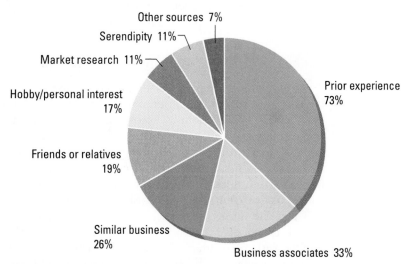

Source: G.E. Hills, "Market Analysis in the Business Plan: Venture Capitalists' Perceptions," *Journal of Small Business Management* (January 1985), pp. 38–46.

Identifying a Problem and Solving It

One of the most effective ways entrepreneurs have of finding opportunity is to see a problem and seek a solution. Most people do this out of habit every day; they just don't realize it. They can't find a particular tool they need (say, a hammer), so they substitute something else (the handle of a screwdriver). That's using creative thinking to solve a problem. Todd Smart saw that small, independent towing companies were having a difficult time surviving and getting new customers in a world of big, brand-name companies. Therefore, he brought many of these little companies together under one umbrella, Absolute Towing and Trucking, which handled customer acquisition and management activities for the owners so that they could do what they do best—tow vehicles.

Problems and needs are everywhere; the trick is to become more observant. One way to practice doing that is to go to some familiar place, such as the airport. Locate a spot where there is a lot of activity, and then carefully observe. Watch what people do and how they do it, and look for sources of stress or ways to make what people are doing easier. There are many needs just waiting to be found. Brainstorming will help identify some ways to satisfy those needs and potentially produce a business opportunity.

Using a Personal Network

The second most commonly cited source of new venture ideas is business associates. A personal **network**—a circle of friends, associates, and acquaintances—not only is a rich source of innovative ideas but also opens the mind to new ways of thinking and new possibilities. Contacts within a personal network can help an individual put together ideas that might not have been considered because the individual was relying solely on her or his personal experiences. Contacts can help refine ideas and can direct an individual to resources to assist in testing the business concept. Personal networks arise not by accident but from the concerted effort of entrepreneurs to go out and meet new people on a daily basis.

Making Time for Creativity and Innovation

When potential entrepreneurs don't see themselves as creative people, it is often because they don't take the time to exercise their latent creative skills. To enhance the chances of successfully becoming an entrepreneur and spotting that great opportunity, it is important for individuals to make time each day for creative thinking and to identify when their minds are relaxed and more open to new thoughts. When is one's mind most open to creativity? Is it while jogging, floating in a pool, lying in a hammock, riding on the subway? Music helps some people become more contemplative (remember Dr. Yoshiro Nakamatsu from Profile 3.1). Writers often find that the music of Mozart is good for clearing mental blocks. The important thing is to schedule at least twenty minutes a day in a place that inspires the mind to wander with no distractions. The best new ideas evolve not because they were forced to happen but because the individual placed himself or herself in an environment where these ideas could flow naturally.

Generating Business Ideas

Here are some exercises you might try to spark some new ideas.

List some geographic areas that are not being reached by a particular product or service.

1. _____
2. _____
3. _____

List some market segments (populations) that are underserved.

1. _____
   _____

2. _____
   _____

3. _____
   _____

List some big or troublesome problems for which the solution could turn into a potential business.

1. _____
2. _____
3. _____

Returning to Childhood

Many creativity and innovation gurus use toys to get their clients to respond more creatively. Legos and K'NEX are great for stimulating creativity because they start with a simple brick or connector piece, and from there the sky's the limit. Take that one step further and play with children to see unfettered imagination in action. Try suspending the adult intellect for a while and become a child again. Creativity guru Doug Hall, whose famed Eureka Mansion near Cincinnati has been the birthplace of thousands of new product ideas, uses games and toys to make people more comfortable doing things they've never done before and coming up with ideas that previously they would have dismissed as strange or unworthy.

Thinking in Opposites

Great ideas often spring from imagining the opposite of what is normal. For example, think about what can be done with a telephone. At one point when AT&T was brainstorming some new marketing tactics, the marketing people asked themselves what a telephone is *not*. It's not something that can be eaten, so they came up with a way to eat telephones—chocolate telephones to be exact, which they sent to their best customers.

Another example can be found in the paradox of **recessions.** Most people regard recessions, or economic downturns, as negative events, but looking for what is good about a recession is a useful creative exercise. A recession brings about many more needs and problems in which to find opportunity. For example, during a recession, many people lose their jobs and go back to school to retrain themselves for new careers. Educational entrepreneurs know this, so they start private schools offering courses and workshops to people who want to take a new direction in their careers or need retraining after losing a job. Publishers know this as well, so they develop books geared toward retraining and refocusing careers.

Sources of New Product/Service Ideas

It is projected that some industries will experience higher levels of wage and employment gain through 2010. Those industries are listed in Table 3.1. The most successful firms in these industries, generally high-tech and high-growth firms, flourish in an environment of change. Let's consider some of the major technological trends that will affect opportunity and every new business concept to some degree into the coming decades.

Technological Trends

Three disruptive technologies (those that render previous technology obsolete) will play a significant role in many business opportunities for the foreseeable future: gene therapy, nanotechnology, and wireless technology.

Gene Therapy

Perhaps the most important scientific finding of the last decade was the mapping of the human genome, first announced in June 2000. Mapping the structure of human genes opens the door to therapies targeted to a person's specific genetic

TABLE 3.1 Industries with the Most Rapid Wage and Salary Employment Growth, 2000–2010

INDUSTRY DESCRIPTION	Thousands of Jobs		Change	Average Annual Rate of Change
	2000	2010	2000–2010	2000–2010
Computer and data processing services	2,095	3,900	1,805	6.4
Residential care	806	1,318	512	5.0
Health services	1,210	1,900	690	4.6
Cable and pay television services	216	325	109	4.2
Personnel supply services	3,887	5,800	1,913	4.1
Warehousing and storage	206	300	94	3.8
Water and sanitation	214	310	96	3.8
Miscellaneous business services	2,301	3,305	1,004	3.7
Miscellaneous equipment rental and leasing	279	397	118	3.6
Management and public relations	1,090	1,550	460	3.6

Source: Bureau of Labor Statistics, U.S. Department of Labor.

makeup and may ultimately make it possible to cure devastating diseases such as cancer. It also makes possible the use of cloning to create duplicate organs and perhaps even to duplicate human beings, a potential outcome that is raising momentous ethical issues.

The Human Genome Project will result in hundreds of business opportunities. For example, companies like PE Biosystems Group make equipment that genomics companies use to sequence and assemble genes. Entrepreneurs with diagnostic laboratories like BioForce Laboratories, a young entrepreneurial firm, will find new opportunities in gene-based diagnostic tests. Entrepreneurs interested in gene therapy will be able to license new technologies for which they can create new applications in the marketplace.

Nanotechnology

Nanotechnology involves processes that occur at the molecular level. (The prefix *nano* stands for one billionth of a metric unit, and 10 nanometers is 1,000 times smaller than the diameter of a human hair.) Scientists and engineers are developing molecular machines, such as microscopic-level diagnostic chips, that a person can swallow so that a doctor can track what's happening in that person's body. The ability to create microscopic machines and robots opens the door to thousands of new products and services that never existed before.

Wireless Technology

The ability to communicate without physical connections will also open up many opportunities to provide new products and services. Today, any manager or sales representative equipped with a web-enabled cell phone or PDA can check on inventory levels and shipping progress for customers and can send and receive e-mail. And that's only the beginning. Many entrepreneurs interested in this area believe that people will become walking Internet portals with wearable wireless technology. They will be able to extend their senses and become an interface for everything they need wherever they go.

The Next Great Idea

Entrepreneurs looking for the next great idea and having trouble finding it should take heart. The most successful businesses—the leaders in any industry—did not start with a great idea but rather with a team that wanted to build a great company. Like Sony's first product (the rice cooker) many ideas fail, but a creative and opportunistic person or team will eventually produce something of value out of industry knowledge, familiar things, the need to solve a problem, or a combination of all three. The entrepreneur in the following story is a good example.

In 1951, a young Bette Nesmith approached a new secretarial position with some trepidation, because she would be working on an electric typewriter for the first time. Her job required that she rapidly create error-free documents, but the electric typewriter seemed destined to keep her from that goal. The slightest touch produced a stream of letters across the page, and the new carbon ribbons made it nearly impossible to erase a mistake.

Recognizing that the key to her survival was to find a solution to the error problem, Nesmith tried putting some white, water-based paint into a nail polish

Socially Responsible Entrepreneurship

Entrepreneurs Teaching the Hungry How to Feed Themselves

People who are born to wealth often choose to work in service to humanity. Free from the need to work to survive, they often start nonprofit ventures designed to target a societal problem that hasn't yet been addressed. Doraja Eberle was born into a wealthy Austrian family. Because she was quite rebellious as a child, her family decided that she might learn to appreciate what she had if she were trained in social work and saw how the less fortunate lived. To their surprise, Eberle loved the work. In 1992, during the Bosnian War, Eberle was overcome with compassion for the suffering of the people there. She had met a young soldier in Zagreb who had no arms and no legs, yet he was thankful that he was alive. From that day forward, Eberle knew that she wanted to devote her life to making the lives of others better. She started an organization called Farmers Helping Farmers to provide food and supplies, as well as to build homes for people displaced by war or some other disaster. In 1998, to the surprise of everyone, she moved 900 tons of food from Germany to the starving Bosnians, something that no other aid organization was able to do. Whereas many organizations seeking to provide such aid are mismanaged, bureaucratic, and ineffective, Eberle's entrepreneurial attitude has enabled her to accomplish things once thought impossible. Instead of simply giving people what they need, she provides them with tools, animals, seeds, and the like, thus empowering them to help themselves.

Sources: Craig Hall, "The Train of Hope," in *The Responsible Entrepreneur* (Franklin Lakes, NJ: Career Press, 2001); and Farmers Helping Farmers, http://www.farmershelpingfarmers.ca/.

bottle and literally painting over her mistakes. For five years she refined and used the concoction she called "Mistake Out," as others in the office began asking her to supply them as well. A business was born.

Nesmith soon changed the name to Liquid Paper, believing it to be a better brand name, and by 1966 she was producing 9,000 bottles a week. In 1979, when Gillette purchased her company for $48 million, it was generating $38 million in annual sales. Nesmith came up with her great idea in an industry she knew, in the context of solving a problem she understood, and in a familiar environment. She was neither an entrepreneur nor an inventor by trade, nor did she consider herself particularly creative, but she discovered her latent creativity and used it to become a successful entrepreneur.

Opportunity is everywhere, and much of it goes unnoticed. Entrepreneurs who make the effort to become more creative and opportunistic will have an unending supply of new ideas available to play with.

New Venture Checklist

Have you:

☐ Identified the roadblocks that keep you from being creative?

☐ Developed a plan for removing those roadblocks?

☐ Started a file to keep track of business ideas?

Issues to Consider

1. Give an example to demonstrate the difference between an idea and an opportunity.
2. Compare the outcome-based approach to creativity with the process approach. Which do you believe is right, and why?
3. Pick a business in the community, and find a creative way to change either the product/service or the way it is delivered to customers. How does your innovation add value to the business?
4. Identify the challenges you face in becoming more creative. What three things will you do to address those challenges?
5. Pick one of the three major trends in technology discussed in this chapter, and identify and discuss a business that has emerged from that trend.

Experiencing Entrepreneurship

1. Spend an afternoon walking around your community or your university or college campus. Don't look for anything in particular. Observe the things that you don't normally pay attention to when you're in a hurry. Watch people—what they do and don't do. At the end of the afternoon, write down all the thoughts that come to you on the basis of your afternoon of observation. Which of these ideas could possibly become a business opportunity and why?

2. Pick one of the trends discussed in the section of this chapter that starts on page 56. Using the Internet or your library, develop a report on the current status of that trend, drawing on articles and sources no more than two years old. What opportunities do you see as a result of your research?

Additional Sources of Information

Crouch, T.D. (1992). "Why Wilbur and Orville? Some Thoughts on the Wright Brothers and the Process of Invention." In *Inventive Minds: Creativity in Technology*, ed. R.J. Weber and D.N. Perkins. New York: Oxford University Press, pp. 80–96.

Gelb, M.J. (2000). *How to Think Like Leonardo da Vinci: Seven Steps to Genius Every Day*. New York: Dell.

Harvard Business Essentials. (2003). *Managing Creativity and Innovation*, Cambridge MA: Harvard Business School Press.

Gladwell, M. (1999). "Six Degrees of Lois Weisberg." *New Yorker* (January 11): 52–63.

Habino, S., and G. Nadler (1990). *Breakthrough Thinking*. Rocklin, CA: Prima Publishing.

Hall, D., and D. Wecker (1995). *Jumpstart Your Brain*. New York: Warner Books.

Pfenninger, K.H., V.R. Shubik, and B. Adolphe (2001). *The Origins of Creativity*. London: Oxford University Press.

van Oech, R. (1990). *A Whack on the Side of the Head*. New York: Warner Books.

Relevant Case Studies

4

Developing a Business Model

"I'd rather have a Class A entrepreneur with a Class B idea than a Class B entrepreneur with a Class A idea."

Gifford Pinchot III

LEARNING OBJECTIVES

- Explain what a business concept is.
- Build a business model for a new concept.
- Position the concept in the value chain.
- Conduct a feasibility analysis.

Profile 4.1 WHY FEASIBILITY MATTERS

It is surprising how many entrepreneurs come up with a great business idea but generate no business model to ensure that they will make money at what they're doing. In the late 1990s, Marc Fleury was working as a sales engineer at Sun Microsystems when he decided that he wanted to develop an application server, which is a software program that manages the applications for a business. At the time, it seemed likely that he could find venture capital. Fleury was very motivated to start his own business, and with a partner, he founded Telkel, Inc. in the fall of 1999. Their business model involved an application hosting business sitting on top of JBoss, the Java application server they had built. They would charge fees for running programs for companies on their server.

To get the business off the ground, they needed funding, but the venture capitalists they approached quickly pointed out that Fleury and his partner had no experience in the hosting business; their expertise was in application development. A more difficult challenge was that their product was ready in the spring of 2000, precisely when the dot com world came crashing down, leaving funders running scared and not interested in tech companies. Unfortunately, whatever money had been gathered quickly ran out, and Fleury and his partner closed Telkel, Inc. in November 2000.

Fleury did not let this failure get him down; in fact, he was more determined than ever to start his own business, and he still believed in JBoss. This time, however, he conducted a feasibility analysis before he invested much time and money in the business. He started by examining all the mistakes he had made the first time around and acknowledged that he had to modify his business model to suit the post-2000 environment. Because he couldn't seek venture capital and had used up all his own money, he realized that the business had to make it on its own from the start.

During this period of feasibility analysis, Fleury began receiving e-mails from users of JBoss who wanted to know whether training was available. Without hesitation, Fleury said that it was and then immediately set out to develop a training course. His first course in Atlanta sold out, grossing him $60,000 for the week. While the training opportunity was taking off, customers also began requesting support, consulting, and documentation, and Fleury soon hired programmers to help him take care of that end of the business. This time he got the business model right. Today JBoss Group employs over 30 people and competes against such major players as IBM. Recently, Fleury has been offering profit sharing and economic interest options to his programmers whether or not they are employees of JBoss. He also achieved his goal of being profitable from day one.

Sources: M. Fleury, "Doing It Wrong, Getting It Right," *Business-Week Online* (September 2, 2003), www.businessweek.com:/print/smallbiz/content/sep2003/sb2003093_8638.htm?sb; www.jbossgroup.com; and Business Editors, "JBoss Group Introduces Annual Compensation Plan: JBoss Developers Receive Profit Sharing and Economic Interest Options in JBoss Group LLC," *Business Wire* (March 25, 2003), http://www.findarticles.com/cf_0/m0EIN/2003_March_25/99150218/p1/article.jhtml?term=JBoss+Group.

In today's chaotic business environment, it is easy to get the impression that business concepts are developed on a napkin during dinner and that the business is funded and operating within a few days. But even for Internet businesses, that exciting scenario is a stretch. Just because an entrepreneur builds a business does not mean that customers will come. In reality, a substantial amount of planning must take place, and a great deal of effort must be put forth, before a company's products or services ever successfully reach the market. That planning includes developing a business concept that can be tested through a process known as feasibility analysis to determine whether a market exists for the business opportunity and to identify the conditions under which the entrepreneur is willing to move forward. Once the entrepreneur has determined that the concept is feasible, a business plan can be prepared to describe the entrepreneur's strategy for executing the concept.

In March of 2003, George Spyrou, CEO of Airship Management Services Inc., which manufactures blimps, was studying the feasibility of expanding his company into the homeland security field. He saw the potential to double or triple annual revenues by selling products to defense and law enforcement agencies. He viewed the blimp as the perfect aerial surveillance platform, because it flies low and slow and the gondola seating/surveillance area has plenty of room. The closest competitor for such a product is the spy satellite, which is far more expensive to build and launch. One of the key challenges to this idea involves the government's willingness to purchase blimps for surveillance. Airship Management Services Inc. will need to ramp up its production capacities in order to deliver far more product than it is delivering now. This takes labor power and money. Spyrou has weighed all of these factors in the feasibility analysis and has determined that Airship Management Services Inc. should move forward with its expansion plan.[1]

Although there are no guarantees, a feasibility study is likely to prevent an entrepreneur from making a costly error by proceeding with a business concept that is not viable. This chapter explains how to develop an effective business concept, consider its position in the value chain, and develop a business model that makes sense. The chapter also includes an overview of the feasibility analysis process and how it evolves over the chapters that follow.

Developing a Business Concept

A **business concept** is a concise description of an opportunity that contains four essential elements: the customer definition; the value proposition (or benefit to the customer) and the compelling story; the product/service; and the distribution channel or means of delivering the benefit to the customer. (See Figure 4.1.) The business concept can be thought of as a type of elevator pitch. *Elevator pitch* is a term that has been applied to the idea that one has only a few seconds—the time it takes to ride an elevator up to the twelfth floor—to get an investor (or other interested party) to "buy into" a business concept. A few seconds is not a lot of time, so having a clear, concise, and compelling statement of the business concept is important. In reality, most people, whether they are potential customers or potential investors, don't have enough time in their busy schedules to give a proposed idea more than a few moments of thought before they decide whether to dismiss it or investigate it further.

| FIGURE 4.1 | The Business Concept |

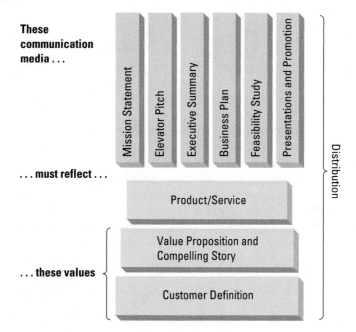

The Customer Definition

Who is the customer? This vital question is deceptively simple. Many entrepreneurs cannot answer it accurately, because they simply assume that their customer is the user of the product. Although it is more common today than ever before for that to be the case, in many industries it is not. When Jordan NeuroScience first considered who the customer was for its ER-EEG technology designed to remotely monitor the brainwaves of trauma patients in emergency rooms, it immediately thought of the patients, the beneficiaries of the technology. But when faced with figuring out how to make money, the company realized that its customers were not the patients, or even the doctors, but rather the hospital administrators who made the purchasing decisions. This revelation changed everything. Jordan NeuroScience had to decide what benefit its product was providing to the hospital administrators, which was something quite different from the benefit to the patients. Its tag line "saving brains" had to be modified in order to speak to its new customer. Although hospital administrators are interested in obtaining technologies to improve patients' quality of life, they are still primarily focused on increasing revenues and reducing costs.

In general, the customer is the one who pays, so, depending on where the company is in the value chain, each customer will be different. As an example, consider Figure 4.2, which depicts a value chain, or distribution channel, for a furniture importer. The importer buys from the furniture manufacturer and sells to the furniture retailer, so the retailer is the entrepreneur's customer, and the consumer

---

FIGURE 4.2   Value Chain for a Furniture Importer

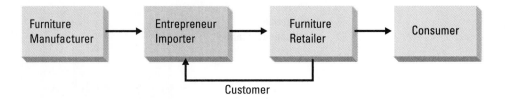

is the beneficiary or end-user of the product and the customer of the retailer. Now, if the entrepreneur were to decide to sell direct through a catalogue or on the Web, the consumer would become the direct customer. Clearly, it is important for entrepreneurs to understand both their customers and their end-users. At the very least, they will need to convince their customer—for example the retailer—that there are plenty of consumers ready to buy.

Defining the customer is a critical part of the business concept, because the customer determines all the other components. A clear and precise customer definition increases the chances that the business concept will be viable.

The Value Proposition and Compelling Story

The **value proposition** is the benefit that the customer derives from the product or service. In other words, "What's in it for the customer?" It is common for entrepreneurs mistakenly to think that they are presenting the benefits to the customer when in fact they are merely describing features of the product or service. Consider the furniture importer discussed earlier. The typical entrepreneur may say that he or she is providing retailers with unique pieces of furniture from many parts of the world. This is certainly true, but uniqueness is a feature or characteristic of the furniture, not necessarily a benefit to the customer. In this example, the entrepreneur is offering the retailer/customer the ability to purchase from a single supplier (the importer), who will supply unique pieces of furniture from many parts of the world. In short, the benefits to the customer are convenience and access. In general, benefits are intangibles such as convenience, better health, speed, or reliability. Table 4.1 offers an example of the distinction between features and benefits for a different type of business. In this business, the product is premium hay for thoroughbred race horses. Note that the benefits for the customer and for the end-user are different.

No value proposition is complete without a compelling story that answers several questions. Why should anyone be interested in this concept? What is the pain that is being eased? Or what problem does this concept solve? In general, if the problem has to be explained, then a real need has not been identified. A simple statement of the problem should elicit a response of "I get that!" or "That makes sense. Why didn't I think of it?" Here is the compelling story for the hay example.

> Imagine spending close to a million dollars on an investment in a horse. This investment has the potential to return millions of dollars to the owner if the horse can make it around the track faster than the competition. If you were the owner, trainer, or breeder of a performance racehorse, wouldn't you be interested in finding a method of ensuring high performance from your animal?

TABLE 4.1	Features versus Benefits for Premium Horse Feed for Thoroughbred Race Horses

FEATURES	BENEFIT TO RETAILER	BENEFIT TO END-USER
2-foot length for hay	Revenue potential — this feature makes the product more attractive to end-users, leading to higher potential sales	Cost savings, because less of it is wastefed than of regular hay
Packaged in plastic bags	Cost savings, because it leads to less waste in inventory	Cost savings, because there is less waste in storage
Flash-baked for greater nutrition and to reduce dust and mold spores	Revenue potential, because this is an attractive feature to customers	Higher revenues, by preventing common ailments which impede racing performance
		Save time and money related to illnesses and medical treatments.
Made with molasses, giving it a good taste for the horse	More reliable revenue potential — this feature leads to more consistent use among horse owners because horses typically do not switch after trying it	Higher revenue — its good taste leads horses to eat this high-nutrition feed, which can improve racing performance

Prepared by Sheryl Sacchitelli, Daniel Wang, and Jason White, MBA class of 2003, University of Southern California.

This statement identifies the challenge for horse owners, trainers, and breeders. Discovering a way to improve the chances of realizing a huge return on this kind of investment is something that would definitely interest this customer.

The Product/Service

Today, most businesses produce both products and services, even if one category predominates. Definition and design of the product or service stem directly from customer needs and the founding team's core competency. Therefore, the concept statement should reflect the customer's perspective on the product or service.

The Distribution Channel

The **distribution** portion of the business concept answers the question *How do you deliver the benefit to the customer?* Many options exist, but in general, the best option is the one that fulfills the customer's expectations about where and how the product or service should be sold. Most services are delivered direct to the customer, but products often go through channel intermediaries such as distributors and retailers. How to reach customers is a critical decision that is discussed in more detail later in this chapter.

Putting the Concept Statement Together

Creating a clear and concise concept statement is not difficult if some questions are answered first. As an example of a concept statement, consider the creation of artificial nerves called BIONS, being developed at the Alfred Mann Institute for Biomedical Research at the University of Southern California. BION's purpose is to re-animate paralyzed muscles through electrical stimulation. In this case the proposed company, BIONNIX, is studying the treatment of pressure ulcers in patients who are bedridden or in a coma.[2] The following questions must be answered in order to create the concept statement:

1. *Who is being helped? Who is the primary customer that the company will be serving?*

   These therapeutic systems will be marketed to health insurance providers, physicians, and patients and sold to hospitals.

   Here the customers for BIONNIX are the hospitals and insurance providers who will write the check to pay for the system. The beneficiary is the patient, and the user is the physician.

2. *What is the market's burning problem, or big pain?*

   Every year there are 3.5 to 5 million people in the United States suffering from pressure ulcers. And an estimated 60,000 persons die annually from ulcer-related complications. Pressure ulcers represent a common but preventable medical problem encountered by primary-care practitioners providing care to older patients, particularly in hospital and nursing home settings.

   This is the problem that must be solved. It must be stated in a way that captures attention and focuses on the "big pain." If the problem must be explained in detail, then the real pain has not been identified.

3. *What emotions does the pain evoke?* It is important to attach emotion to the pain to create a more compelling story. In the BIONNIX case, the primary emotions are probably surprise and outrage that so many people suffer and die from pressure ulcers.

4. *What is the company's tag line?* Remember that Jordan NeuroScience's tag line is "saving brains." It tells the reader exactly what the primary mission of the company is. In the case of BIONNIX, the tagline might be "stimulating possibilities for movement."

By combining the answers to these questions to the business concept developed earlier, it is possible to create a clear and concise concept statement:

   BIONNIX is the leading implantable electrotherapeutic medical device company for hospitals and nursing homes seeking a way to more cost-effectively and conveniently treat pressure ulcers in immobile patients. BIONNIX will manufacture, sell, and support products that provide patients with an effective, easy, and painless solution to pressure ulcers.

Note that in the development of the concept statement, money was not a focal point. Money is always assumed to be the most necessary component of a successful venture. But although money is important, it is only an enabler; its presence does not confirm that the business concept is feasible. In fact, the dot com bust of spring 2000 proved that a large investment in a business idea will not make it feasible if customer demand and an effective business model are not present. Until customers express interest in what is offered and will pay for it, all the money in the world will not make the venture feasible. However, once the concept is judged feasible, it is time to think about how to fund it.

Quick-Testing the Concept

With a preliminary business concept in hand, it is helpful to do a quick test to determine whether a full-blown feasibility study is warranted. Many weak business concepts can be eliminated from further consideration by asking a few simple questions, such as those that follow. Answering these questions does not require any research. The entrepreneur can simply rely on his or her own knowledge and on the advice of people who can provide objective opinions.

1. *Am I really interested in this business opportunity?* If the concept is developed, time and energy will be invested, so it is important that the entrepreneur be passionate about the idea. Many potential entrepreneurs have gone forward with concepts that others suggested, only to discover, after they have spent considerable time, effort, and money, that their hearts weren't in the business.

2. *Is anyone else interested?* A business cannot exist without customers or, in many cases, without investors, so it is important for an entrepreneur to determine whether anyone else is interested in the business concept.

3. *Will people actually pay for what is being offered?* Often when people hear about a new product or service, they express interest—and even excitement. But what are they willing to pay for it? And how much? If they are not willing to pay what it's worth, the idea may need to be revised.

4. *Why me?* The entrepreneur must be convinced that he or she is the right person to execute this concept. What unique capabilities and contacts does the entrepreneur bring to the venture?

5. *Why now?* Why is this a good time to launch this business? Why has no one else done this before? Or, if they have, why did they fail (or succeed)?

Once these questions have been satisfactorily answered, it's time to progress to the next level: the business model.

The Business Model

Once a business concept is identified, entrepreneurs must address the important issue of how to make money from the products and services they offer. More important, they must determine how the company will create value for its shareholders, investors, customers, and value chain partners. Building an effective **business model** addresses all these issues, as well as creating a competitive advantage for the company. One difficulty is that business models tend to change over time as customer needs change, so the challenge is to find a way to sustain the efficacy of the model over time. It should also be protected from imitation, which could turn the company's products and services into commodities.[3]

American Express provides a classic example of a successful business model that was able to change with the times. Imagine a business model wherein the customer pays cash for travelers' checks that they will use sometime in the future. AMEX gets the use of that money until the check is cashed, which can be several months or even *never* (in the case of customers who forget that they have the checks). In other words, it's a riskless business model, or the equivalent of an interest-free loan. This is a unique business model with no receivables and the potential to receive cash without actually supplying a product. The benefits of this business model to consumers are convenience and peace of mind, given that the checks are insured against loss and widely accepted around the world. Merchants that accept travelers' checks are guaranteed the funds, a benefit that makes them more attractive to consumers. For AMEX, the benefit is float (having the customer's money to use until the customer cashes the check) and an occasional windfall when a customer doesn't cash the check at all.

eBay is one of the few really successful business models from the dot com era. It is successful because its model cannot be replicated in the offline world and because the user/customer controls the buying and selling. Union Supply also has a highly successful business model. It sells specialty items to prisons. Demand is high, the government pays up front before receiving the product, and the company has no receivables and no inventory. There aren't too many business models more attractive than that.

The source of the term *business model* is associated with the advent of computer spreadsheets that make possible a more analytic approach to financial projections. Suddenly, every major line item could be analyzed, along with its components and subcomponents. "What if" questions could be posed and **sensitivity analysis** conducted. Of course, the value of spreadsheets is still tied to the assumptions used to create them. When the Walt Disney Company decided to build a theme park in France (Euro Disney), its revenue assumptions proved to be completely wrong. For example, the French, unlike Americans, did not graze at the park's various restaurants throughout the day. Instead, they expected to be seated at a precise hour, as was their tradition. This caused long lines and lots of frustration as the park restaurants struggled to meet demand.[4]

Why Business Models Fail

It is not uncommon for business models to fail when they are not carefully conceived and executed. One of the biggest reasons for failure is lack of a compelling story. During the dot com phase, many misguided entrepreneurs thought that the Internet was the business model, so they developed businesses that had no compelling reason to exist; therefore, customers did not come. Pets.com, for example, was built on the notion that customers would find it easier to buy dog food online. What they didn't realize was that most customers purchase dog food when they purchase their own food, so making online purchases was actually an inconvenience. Funerals.com experienced a similar fate. In times of emotional grief, people did not want to turn to their computers for help; they preferred to deal with someone face-to-face.

Business models also fail when the numbers don't make sense. Online grocers such as Streamline.com and Webvan discovered that they couldn't make the numbers work for home delivery in a commodity industry with very slim margins. In addition, the online merchants incurred new costs for marketing, service, delivery, and technology.[5] Consumers weren't willing to pay more to cover these new costs.

Building a Business Model

It is useful to build a business model in stages. Stage 1: Identify the entrepreneur's place in the value chain. Stage 2: Determine who pays whom, how much, and when. Stage 3: Calculate the impact on the customer in terms of switching costs and learning curve. Stage 4: Identify the revenue streams from the products and services.

Stage 1: Identify the Entrepreneur's Position in the Value Chain

The first step in developing a business model is to identify the entrepreneur's place in the **value chain.** If the entrepreneur's company is a supplier or producer of raw materials, it will generally be at the top of the value chain and upstream from manufacturers. **Intermediaries,** such as distributors and retailers, will be downstream from manufacturers. Where a company is located is normally a function of its capabilities and the desire of the entrepreneur for a particular type of business. Consider Figure 4.3, which depicts a **commitment pyramid.** In very simple terms, it portrays the relationship between the location of a business in the distribution channel and the time commitment, level of risk, and financial capital required. Selling a business concept

| **FIGURE 4.3** | The Commitment Pyramid |

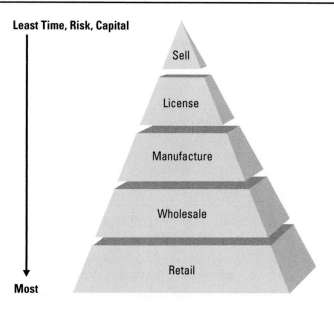

Least Time, Risk, Capital

Sell

License

Manufacture

Wholesale

Retail

Most

FIGURE 4.4 The Value Chain with Markups

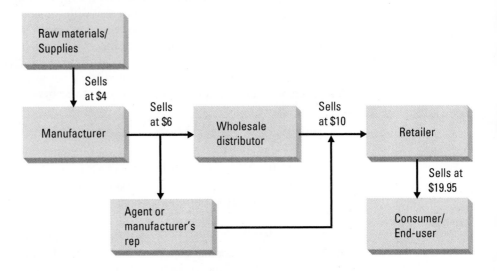

takes the least amount of investment and requires the least time commitment from the entrepreneur. Conversely, starting a retail business requires a huge time commitment, demands substantial capital, and generally carries with it a higher level of risk. A more in-depth discussion of value chain strategy is found later in this chapter.

Stage 2: Determine Who Pays Whom

Once the business is located on the value chain, it is easier to recognize who pays whom and to determine costs and pricing. Figure 4.4 adds this information to a generic example of a complex indirect channel of distribution. The raw materials producer charges the manufacturer $4 per unit; the manufacturer turns the raw material into product and sells it to the distributor for $6. Alternatively, the manufacturer can use an independent sales representative (sales rep), who will find outlets and receive a commission on sales made. Note that the retailer, who buys from the distributor or sales rep, typically at least doubles its cost in setting the price to the consumer. This is known as **keystoning.** Also note that as a rule, **markups** increase as one moves down the channel. This occurs because the cost of doing business increases, as does the risk.

The value chain now illustrates the various markups, which is helpful in determining the lowest price possible for the product. The highest price possible is determined through market research with potential customers. The markups on the original cost reflect profit and overhead for the channel intermediary and are determined by what is typical in the industry. Every product or service has more than one channel option, so it's a good idea to depict distribution options graphically to compare their effectiveness. Graphing the value chain makes it possible to do the following:

Measure the time from manufacturing to customer on the basis of the lead time needed by each channel member.

Determine the ultimate retail price on the basis of the markups required by the intermediaries.

Figure the total costs of marketing the product. For example, manufacturers have to market to distributors, but to support their distributors, they may also market to retailers and even end-users or consumers.

Stage 3: Calculate the Impact on the Customer

It is important to determine whether the proposed business model will force customers to change the way they use or find a particular product or service. Will that change benefit customers in a way that they can readily see? For example, many computer users have not switched to the latest Windows operating system because they can't easily see what benefits it offers over the system they are currently using. In other words, the basic functionality has not changed substantially, but the cost to the customer in terms of time and money is too high to warrant switching. It is also important to determine whether the learning curve for the customer will be steep. If customers see that learning to use the new product or service will take some time and require them to change old habits, they will think twice before purchasing.

Stage 4: Identify Multiple Revenue Streams

One of the most important components of the business model is identifying the revenue streams that will flow from the products and services being offered. A healthy business model always supports revenue streams from multiple types of customers and multiple products and services. Relying on one revenue stream from one type of customer is dangerous. What happens when the market shifts and that customer goes away? In the mid-1990s, Edmund Publications, the 32-year-old publisher of automotive information, saw the Internet as just another marketing vehicle. Today, the Internet *is* the business. Edmunds's website provides independent ratings, reviews, and pricing data for every make and model of car, in addition to a variety of other interactive features. Edmunds.com's basic business model is to make its money through ads placed by manufacturers, parts dealers, and others in the automobile industry. Books now account for less than 1 percent of its revenues. Changing its business model with the changing times, Edmunds.com now has revenue streams from books, from advertising, and from selling and licensing information to other companies.[6]

Sources of Opportunity for Business Models

Many opportunities exist for finding new and innovative business models. Here are three examples:

1. Reposition the company on the value chain. Look for unserved or underserved niches and customer dissatisfaction.
2. Reinvent the value chain. Ignore what currently exists and develop a whole new value chain. This is often accomplished by looking at successful value chains in other industries and extrapolating to the entrepreneur's own value chain.
3. Redefine value-added. Don't do things exactly the way everyone else does. If competitors seek out contracts for work from customers and wait for customers to tell them what to do, try learning what customers want in advance, doing the work, and then approaching the customer with a solution.
4. Redefine distribution. Find out where the customers are and go there. If the channel contains a lot of intermediaries, consider "selling direct" to save the customer money.

SCREENSHOT 4.1 www.edmunds.com

Source: https://www.edmunds.com (Sign In), accessed 3/10/05.

The Value Chain and the Concept

The value chain, or distribution channel, is a central part of the business concept. Today more than ever before, the value chain has the power to make or break a business concept. Three powerful forces are at work changing the very nature of distribution channels. These forces are the Internet, reduced transaction costs, and disintermediation.

The Internet

The Internet was the most disruptive technology to come about in the decade of the 1990s. It has not only affected the way business is transacted but has also reshaped education, entertainment, communication, and even relationships. The Internet has taken on a life of its own and has given Internet businesses a life cycle of their own. Internet years are counted like dog years; that is, an Internet business that is one year old looks and acts like a business that has been around for seven years.[7]

The Internet has the potential to be an extremely efficient channel because it is widely available, relatively inexpensive, and relatively fast. Yet it must often rely on offline intermediaries in channels that move tangible products. For example, software, because of its digital nature, can be produced, warehoused, shipped, purchased, negotiated, warranted, and financed completely in the e-commerce channel with no intermediaries. In fact, software can completely bypass the warehousing and shipping parts of the channel by allowing customers to download from the Internet. On the other hand, apparel cannot be so effectively produced and distributed through the e-commerce channel, because it requires offline manufacture, warehousing, and shipping. Only marketing, purchasing, and the actual transaction (placing the order and paying) take place on the Internet.

Transaction Costs

The Internet has helped to reduce **transaction costs,** in some cases to zero. Consider the example of running out of toner for a printer. Businesses normally keep an inventory of supplies on hand, so someone simply retrieves a new cartridge from the supply room. Businesses track the inventory of products for sale that are on hand, but they often don't consider the cost of carrying supplies on hand. Supplies are carried as a convenience to employees, so they don't have to spend the time to go out and buy them when they run out. Going out to purchase a new cartridge is a cost of using a printer that has been saved.

Of course, this is a very simple example. But extrapolate for a moment to a manufacturer that purchases raw materials from a supplier and must negotiate terms, conditions, and all sorts of legal issues as part of the purchase. These activities carry a much larger transaction cost, and that cost often prompts a manufacturer to **vertically integrate**—to acquire its supplier, thus bringing all those expensive processes in-house and reducing transaction costs.

The Internet has made firms and markets more efficient and thereby reduced transaction costs. The office supply company is now linked electronically to the entrepreneur's supply inventory, so the entrepreneur no longer has to think about stocking printer cartridges. The office supply company knows each customer's usage record and restocks just in time, saving time and money. Of course, much greater savings in transaction costs are possible for the manufacturer who must purchase a wide variety of raw materials. It is no wonder that most companies use the Internet to manage their supply and distribution chains.

Disintermediation

The second major impact of the Internet is to shorten the value chain by getting rid of intermediaries. Most products are part of a distribution channel that includes one or more intermediaries. The function of intermediaries is to reduce the transaction costs for manufacturers in areas that are outside their core competency. They do this by providing added-value services such as warehousing, shipping, and distribution to retail outlets. They are valuable to the manufacturer as long as the cost of using them is less than those services might cost in the open market. And that's where the Internet comes in. The Internet brings buyers and sellers together in a way that makes many of the services of the intermediaries unnecessary. The process is called **disintermediation.** If a manufacturer can easily sell directly to the customer over the Internet and ship directly from the manufacturing plant, it has reduced its transaction costs and made a higher profit on each transaction.

Many industries were not prepared for the disintermediation impact of the Internet. The auto industry never believed that people would make such an expensive purchase online, but companies such as Cars Direct can help consumers make purchase decisions and even route them to a qualified dealer who will provide a binding quote within 24 hours. The banking industry was also slow to react to the Internet effect and watched in disbelief as consumers set up online checking accounts with Internet banks that seemed to appear out of nowhere. In nearly every industry, the Internet has begun to reduce costs, make supply chains more efficient, and generally change the way the industry operates.

Distance does not affect the cost for services or products that can be digitized; online businesses are always open; and web businesses can be operated from anywhere in the world. For this reason, the "Internet effect" has been characterized as a move from marketplace to market space.[8] Businesses that operate in market space differ from conventional businesses in what the buyer purchases, the circumstances in which the purchase occurs, and what the firm needs to do business. The typical Internet business, such as Amazon.com, is selling information as much as it is selling books, through a computer screen from a database housed in a server. This is quite different from selling books off shelves in a bookstore.

But the critical difference between the Internet as a distribution channel and traditional channels is that the Internet is interactive rather than merely a passive conduit for products. Consequently, it has the ability to create virtual marketplaces like eBay (www.ebay.com). However, one interesting effect of the Internet is that it has taken us back to mass marketing and **commoditization** (competing on price), because it reduces the marketer's ability to differentiate on the basis of other product attributes or service. Unfortunately, the more efficient channels become, the more opportunity for commoditization.[9]

What Defines an Effective Channel?

An effective distribution channel has several characteristics, which are discussed briefly in the following paragraphs.[10]

Inventory

At various points along the channel, inventory must be warehoused and ready to be shipped where needed, whether it is raw materials to the manufacturer or finished goods to the consumer. Entrepreneurs need to decide whether they want to hold inventory or outsource that capability to someone else in the channel. Holding the inventory for distribution gives the entrepreneur more control over what happens to products, but warehousing and distribution are competencies that the entrepreneur's team may not have.

Ownership

It is important to distinguish between ownership of the goods and possession of them. As goods move through the channel, ownership typically changes only at the point of purchase, but possession may change at various points. For example, when a fulfillment house agrees to warehouse and ship for a company, it takes possession of the goods but does not purchase them and therefore does not own them. Information, as an intangible product, presents some unique challenges with regard to ownership, and illegitimate channels may even be formed to move the product through the channel. This can be seen, for example, in the pirating of software and music.

Negotiation

Many channels that deal in expensive items, such as automobiles or industrial equipment, function primarily as price negotiators. Prices are set merely as a starting point for negotiation with the final customer, so for these channels to be effective, they must provide the ability to negotiate.

Gathering of Market Information

The Internet has facilitated the gathering of **market intelligence** by companies and industries of all sizes. Because such information is critical to successful product development and business planning, gathering it has become a characteristic of a successful distribution channel.

Financing and Payment

Credit is an essential element of an effective channel because it smoothes out the fluctuations in cash on hand experienced by purchasers. Methods for collecting payments for purchases have been enhanced by technology.

Risk Management

The movement of products through channels entails some level of risk for which third-party insurance is required. Examples of such risk are product loss or breakage during shipping, product liability, and failure of the customer to pay for goods. In addition, manufacturers take on responsibility for risk to the customer via warranty programs and after-sale service agreements.

Member Power

Effective channels often produce channel members who gain the power to control aspects of the channel. A channel member gains power if (1) other members rely on it for their primary needs, (2) it controls financial resources, (3) it plays a critical role in the value chain, (4) it has no substitute, or (5) it has information that reduces uncertainty. For example, Wal-Mart is well known for employing strong-arm tactics to exact the lowest possible prices from its suppliers. Because it is the world's largest retailer, it is well aware that smaller suppliers cannot afford to lose such a huge customer. Strong retailers can also force manufacturers to adopt new systems, as was the case in the 1980s when retailers forced manufacturers to provide UPC symbols on packages so the retailers could scan them for inventory and sales tracking.

In an effective channel, strong members include other members in the decision-making process; they share information and often make concessions when a new policy or technology is costly to a member.[11] One excellent example of channel collaboration

Global Insights

Ireland's Micro-Entrepreneurship Effort

Ireland is very much a rural country with an estimated 42 percent of its population living in villages of fewer than 1,500 people. Its population density is also among the lowest in all of Europe with about 52 people per square kilometer, compared to the European average of 115 people per square kilometer. Ireland is presently short on entrepreneurs. The reasons for this are thought to be massive subsidy programs such as the Common Agricultural Policy (CAP) and the influx of American companies creating new jobs, both of which have removed the incentives for entrepreneurship.

To address this issue, in 1993 Ireland put into place the County Enterprise Boards (CEBs) to support and stimulate rural micro-entrepreneurship. The 35 City/County Enterprise Boards serve as a place where small businesses in their locality can access information and advice about starting and operating a business. Each CEB has a board of 14 people from local businesses, volunteer groups, state agencies, and local elected representatives. Those CEBs that offer financial assistance do so through feasibility study grants, capital grants for the purchase of plants, machinery, or equipment, employment grants, and some equity capital. The efforts of the CEB have also stimulated online resource providers such as Empower.ie, which has positioned itself as the "empowering force" for e-commerce in Ireland. These resource providers help Ireland's micro-businesses find a home on the Internet. Now the Irish government is positioning Ireland as a hub for Internet business, which is a logical next step, given that Ireland is one of the best-connected countries in the world.

Sources: http://www.etradebusinessireland.com/; and Tom McFadden, "The Building of a New Rural Micro Entrepreneurship Model for Ireland—Phase 1," www.ncirl.ie.; http://www.startingabusinessinireland.com/dirceb.htm.

---

comes from the apparel industry, where DuPont, a fiber producer; Milliken & Co., a textile mill; Robinson Mfg., an apparel manufacturer; and JC Penney, a retailer, joined forces to identify customer needs and develop a new line of clothing.

Creating a Distribution Strategy

Distributors, retailers, and other outlets are one means through which manufacturers and other producers communicate with the customer, so they are very much partners with the organization, particularly in a virtual company. Their goal is to gather information from the customer so that the manufacturer or producer can revise and improve its offerings. Finding good, loyal outlets is competitively difficult. In fact, distribution, once a mundane, routine occupation, has become the glamour stock of the business world, and "channel surfer" entrepreneurs constantly seek the most productive channel.

The following examples illustrate just a few innovative distribution strategies.

- Snap-on Tools differentiates itself in its market by stocking mobile trucks with its products and sending them to sites where buyers of tools are likely to be.

- Jet Blast Corporation found its most effective distribution channel in TV shopping channels such as Home Shopping Network and QVC for products like the Pro-Jet 2000, which converts ordinary garden hose pressure into high-velocity water flow. For inventors with single products, TV shopping channels offer a means of competing with major companies.

- McAfee Associates produces and distributes security tools, in particular Virus-Scan, a program that detects and destroys computer viruses. Its initial strategy was to post virus "fixes" (instructions) on computer bulletin boards and ask anyone who downloaded its software to pay what they thought it was worth. That strategy made John McAfee $5 million in his first year. And the company continues to offer many of its products free in the form of computer downloads.

Before choosing a distribution strategy, the wise entrepreneur looks at the various distribution channels that similar companies are using. That provides an indication of customer expectations about time and place of delivery. It also helps reveal opportunity gaps—innovative distribution strategies that might allow the entrepreneur to capture a group of customers that is not currently being served.

Factors Affecting the Choice of Strategy

In very broad terms, the choice of distribution strategy is a function of desirability (Will customers be happy with it?), feasibility (Can the channel do what the entrepreneur wants it to do?), and profitability (Can the entrepreneur make money using this channel?). The following factors should be considered when one attempts to determine the most effective distribution strategy: costs, market coverage, level of control, speed and reliability, and type of intermediary.

Costs

Costs include all the various expenses related to marketing the product and distributing it to the customer or end-user. Consider the situation of a manufacturer producing a consumer product in the sporting goods industry.

At each stage, the channel member adds value to the product by performing a service that increases the chances of the product's reaching its intended customer. The wholesaler seeks appropriate retail outlets, and the retailer advertises and promotes the product to its customers. The value created allows each channel member to increase the price of the product to the next channel member. For example, the manufacturer charges the wholesaler a price that covers the costs of producing the product, plus an amount for overhead and profit. The wholesaler, in turn, adds an amount to cover the cost of the goods purchased and his or her overhead and profit. The retailer does the same and charges the final price to the customer. That price can typically be four to five times what it cost to manufacture the product (labor and materials).

Suppose the manufacturing entrepreneur decides to bypass the wholesaler and sell directly to retailers:

Manufacturer ———➤ Retailer

It appears on the surface that the final retail price could be substantially lower, perhaps even the rate at which the manufacturer sold to the wholesaler in the first example. However, there is a flaw in this reasoning. The wholesaler performed a valuable service. He or she made it possible for the manufacturer to focus on producing the product and not to incur the cost of maintaining a larger marketing department, a sales force, additional warehouses, and a more complex shipping department. All these activities now become a cost to the manufacturer of doing business with retailers and must be factored into the price charged to the customer as well as the decision to choose this distribution channel. This is not to say that it never makes sense for manufacturers to sell direct to retailers. However, it is important for the entrepreneur to consider all the costs, advantages, disadvantages, and consequences of choosing a particular market channel to reach the customer.

Other aspects of starting the new venture can be examined by studying the distribution channel options. For example, the choice of channel affects where the business is located and how products are transported to the customer. Consider the following channel:

$$\text{Manufacturer} \longrightarrow \text{Retailer}$$

In this instance, it may be advantageous to locate the manufacturing plant near major transportation networks to hold down shipping costs. Now consider the following channel:

$$\text{Manufacturer} \longrightarrow \text{Wholesaler} \longrightarrow \text{Retailer} \longrightarrow \text{Customer}$$

Here it is not important for the manufacturer to be located conveniently near the retailer. Having a location that minimizes shipping costs to the wholesaler becomes more relevant.

If the entrepreneur is a retailer (or wholesaler), she or he looks at the distribution channel from both directions. The customer will be reached directly, but looking back down the distribution channel, the retailer must also be concerned with finding a good distributor who represents quality manufacturers. The cost of a distribution channel will directly affect the company's ability to make a profit.

Market Coverage

With a start-up company, it is often advantageous to use intermediaries, because doing so enables the entrepreneur to enter a larger market more quickly. Selling a product to just five distributors can provide access to hundreds of wholesale and retail outlets without increasing marketing efforts or sales staff. This is important because entrepreneurs typically have very limited resources.

Control of Distribution

The choice of distribution strategy affects the level of control an entrepreneur exerts over what happens to the product once it leaves the entrepreneur's hands. If the product requires unique or unusual marketing tactics to entice the customer, an intermediary that is carrying competing lines or a variety of other products may not be a good choice; the entrepreneur's product might not get the attention it requires to achieve the target sales level. In this case, a direct channel may be more appropriate.

Speed and Reliability

The Internet creates the impression that business is moving much faster than before, and in some cases it is. Customers expect products and services to be available more quickly and they want instant access to information. If speed is essential to the successful distribution of a product or service, then any channel under consideration must meet that criterion. Likewise, if a reliable channel is essential to the distribution strategy, then many channels will be screened out of the selection process on that point alone.

Having taken all of these considerations into account, and armed with a clear and compelling concept and business model, entrepreneurs are ready to conduct an effective market feasibility analysis.

The Nature of Feasibility Analysis

Feasibility analysis is unquestionably one of the most important skills individuals can acquire if they want to become entrepreneurs or to use their entrepreneurial mindset inside a large corporation. Feasibility analysis forces the entrepreneur to conduct serious research, to think critically about the business concept, to answer fundamental questions, and to achieve a high level of confidence about their willingness to move forward with the business or project.

In general, the feasibility analysis is performed to answer the following three broad questions:

1. *Is there a customer base and a market of sufficient size to make the concept viable?* Research will provide real numbers that can be converted into sales forecasts. Those forecasts and additional numbers that describe the costs of doing business will help the entrepreneur decide whether the concept can make money—that is, whether it's worth the time and effort. Some market niches are not large enough for an entrepreneur to make a suitable profit once competitors enter the market. Knowing in advance that the market is too small permits the entrepreneur to make adjustments in the concept to broaden the market niche or decide not to go forward with the business before time and money have been wasted.

2. *Do the capital requirements to start, based on estimates of sales and expenses, make sense?* Can this business be started with an amount of capital that the entrepreneur has or will be able to raise?

3. *Can an appropriate start-up or genesis team be put together to execute the concept?* Recall that most successful start-ups involve teams rather than solo entrepreneurs. Based on the entrepreneur's research, what kind of team can be put together to comprise all the skills needed to effectively execute the concept? A team consists of the founders and any strategic partners, which can be people or other businesses with capabilities that the business requires.

Conducting a feasibility analysis is somewhat like zeroing in on a target or peeling away the layers of an onion to get at the core. In this case, the core is the feasible business concept, and the layers are simply the levels of analysis that must be traversed to get to the core. Figure 4.5 depicts this analogy.

When the feasibility analysis is complete, the entrepreneur should be able to determine whether the conditions are right to go forward with the business concept. If conditions are not favorable, the entrepreneur will need to review the areas tested to see whether another approach might make the concept viable. For example, suppose

| FIGURE 4.5 | Feasibility Analysis |

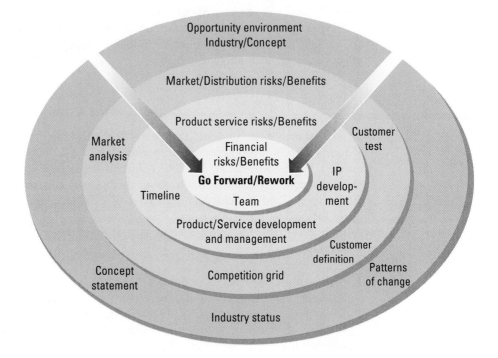

an entrepreneur has a concept for a new type of wheelchair that is better suited to people with active lives. Through the entrepreneur's analysis, she may have determined that the cost to execute the concept (set up a factory, purchase equipment, and so on) is well beyond her means and would probably not be of interest to major investors because this is not a high-technology, high-growth concept. All it may take to make the concept feasible, however, is to consider outsourcing the expensive aspects (such as product development and manufacturing) to an existing company. Immediately, the direct costs are reduced, and the entrepreneur doesn't have to invest in expensive equipment and a manufacturing facility. Alternatively, the entrepreneur may decide that licensing the patent to a wheelchair manufacturer is a low-cost, low-risk way to bring the product to market.

The point is that many concepts can achieve feasibility if the right conditions are in place. The real question is whether the entrepreneur is convinced of the concept's feasibility and is confident enough to put the time, money, and effort into its execution. Has the analysis provided the entrepreneur with enough supporting evidence that he or she is willing to take a calculated risk and begin to plan the launch?

An Overview of the Feasibility Tests

Table 4.2 provides an overview of the feasibility tests, the questions addressed by each test, and the chapter in this book that discusses in detail that aspect of the feasibility analysis and how to accomplish it. A brief discussion of each of the tests follows.

TABLE 4.2	Feasibility Analysis

AREA TO BE ANALYZED AND QUESTIONS TO ASK BUSINESS CONCEPT (CHAPTER 4)

1. Who is the customer?
2. What is the value proposition?
3. What is the product/service being offered?
4. What does your value chain look like?
5. Which distribution channel alternatives are available, and which customers will be served by them?
6. Are there ways to innovate in the distribution channel?

INDUSTRY AND MARKET/CUSTOMER (CHAPTER 5)

7. What are the demographics, trends, patterns of change, and life cycle stage of the industry?
8. Are there any barriers to entry? If so, what are they?
9. What is the status of technology and R&D expenditures?
10. What are typical profit margins in the industry?
11. What are distributors, competitors, retailers, and others saying about the industry?
12. What are the demographics of the target market?
13. What is the customer profile? Who is the customer?
14. Have you talked with customers?
15. Who are your competitors, and how are you differentiated from them?

PRODUCT/SERVICE (CHAPTER 6)

16. What are the features and benefits of the product or service?
17. What product development tasks must be undertaken, and what is the timeline for completion?
18. Is there potential for intellectual property rights?
19. How is the product or service differentiated from others in the market?

FOUNDING TEAM (CHAPTER 7)

20. What experience and expertise does the team have?
21. What are the gaps and how will you fill them?

FINANCIAL NEEDS ASSESSMENT (CHAPTER 8)

22. What are your start-up capital requirements?
23. What are your working capital requirements?
24. What are your fixed cost requirements?
25. How long will it take to achieve a positive cash flow?
26. What is the break-even point for the business?

Developing the Business Concept

This chapter examined the development of the business concept and the business model. An effective feasibility analysis begins with the compelling story (the pain), followed by a clear and concise statement of the business concept, which includes the customer definition, value proposition, product/service, and distribution strategy. Today, more than ever before, businesses can create a competitive advantage by looking at ways to streamline the value chain or bring products and services to customers in new ways. This chapter discussed many of the issues related to the value chain.

TABLE 4.3	Feasibility Analysis Outline

COVER FOR THE FEASIBILITY STUDY

EXECUTIVE SUMMARY
- Include most important points from all sections of the feasibility study. Do not exceed two pages.
- Make sure that the first sentence captures the reader's attention and that the first paragraph presents the business concept in a compelling way.

TITLE PAGE (NAME OF COMPANY, FEASIBILITY STUDY, FOUNDING TEAM MEMBERS' NAMES)

TABLE OF CONTENTS

FEASIBILITY DECISION
- The decision regarding the conditions under which the entrepreneur is willing to go forward with the business concept

THE BUSINESS CONCEPT
- What are the business concept and the compelling story?
- Who is the customer?
- What is the value proposition, or benefit(s), being delivered to the customer?
- How will the benefit be delivered (distribution)?
- What is the potential for growth and spin-offs?

INDUSTRY/MARKET ANALYSIS
- Industry analysis
- Target market analysis
- Niche the entrepreneur is entering
- Competitor analysis and competitive advantages
- Customer profile
- Distribution channels (alternatives and risks/benefits)
- Entry strategies (initial market penetration — first customer)

FOUNDING TEAM
- Qualifications of founding team
- How critical tasks will be accomplished
- Gap analysis — what is missing and how will it be addressed (professional advisers, board of directors, independent contractors)?

PRODUCT/SERVICE DEVELOPMENT PLAN
- Detailed description and unique features of product/service
- Current status of product development
- Tasks and timeline to completion
- Intellectual property acquisition (if relevant)
- Plan for prototyping and testing

TABLE 4.3	**Feasibility Analysis Outline** *(Continued)*

FINANCIAL PLAN
- Summary of key points on which financial feasibility is based
- Narrative assumptions or premises for resource needs assessment
- Cash needs assessment (cash flow statement from start-up to positive cash flow)
- Pro forma income statement (1–3 years) by month or quarter
- Break-even analysis

TIMELINE TO LAUNCH
- Tasks that will need to be accomplished up to the date of launch in the order of their completion

BIBLIOGRAPHY OR ENDNOTES (FOOTNOTES MAY BE SUBSTITUTED.)

APPENDIX (A, B, C, ETC.)
- Questionnaires, maps, forms, résumés, and so on

Identifying Industry and Market Risks and Benefits

The broadest level of analysis is an in-depth understanding of an industry. A well-constructed industry analysis will point up strengths and weaknesses in the industry, provide an understanding of how the industry operates, and identify where the business might fit in. It also gives the entrepreneur clues to viable entry strategies.

Testing the business concept with potential customers is perhaps the most important test of all, because it indicates who the first customer is and whether there is sufficient demand for the product or service. Profile 4.2 provides a good example of a young entrepreneur who knew what her customers wanted. The information gathered from primary and secondary research lets the entrepreneur develop a comprehensive customer profile, which will help with product/service design and marketing. An effective market/customer analysis will demonstrate a demand for the product or service and prove that the customer is willing to purchase from the entrepreneur's company. If that analysis doesn't demonstrate sufficient demand, then the entrepreneur will need to revisit the concept, taking this feedback into account. The industry/market analysis is discussed in Chapter 5.

Analyzing Product/Service Risks and Benefits

In this test, the entrepreneur will be developing the product/service and considering such issues as protection of intellectual property, product development, and prototyping. The goal is to establish the unique features and benefits of the products and services to be offered and to develop a "bundle" of competitive advantages. Creating a bundle of competitive advantages such as intellectual property, efficient and fast product development processes, and relationships with customers ensures that the entrepreneur isn't putting all of his or her eggs in one basket. These issues are considered in detail in Chapter 6.

Profile 4.2   **LET YOUR PRODUCT SPEAK FOR YOU**

In December 1999, Courtney Hennessey was a 22-year-old junior at Saint Louis University in Missouri. It was winter break just before the holidays, and Courtney decided to indulge her passion for making jewelry. At the local bead shop, she found herself overwhelmed by all the possibilities—beads and crystals in every color and shape imaginable. Before she knew what she was doing, she had spent $400 on her father's credit card. Resolved to pay him back out of revenues from the bracelets she intended to make and sell, she put together some of her original creations and began wearing them around town.

When people saw her jewelry, they immediately wanted to buy it. In fact, she took 20 different samples to her great aunt's wake and left with orders worth $800. As more and more people began to wear her jewelry designs, the customers themselves became advertisements for her new business. To brand her jewelry, she came up with the name Codi, which was the first two letters of her first and middle names, Courtney Diane. She also attached a sterling heart on every piece of jewelry as a trademark.

The customer referral marketing strategy eventually led a Neiman Marcus associate to find Courtney and ask her to show her designs. That led to a trunk show and then to sales in upscale boutiques around the United States. Courtney successfully started a business with a product she was passionate about. She tested the feasibility of her concept by letting the customer tell her what to make, and she let customers be her sales staff. She realized that when you have something the customer wants, starting a business is much easier and much more satisfying.

Sources: Codi Jewelry, http://www.codijewelry.com/index .html; and C. Hennessey, "The Key Is Happiness," in *Student Entrepreneurs*, ed. M. McMyre and N. Amare (St. Louis, MO: Premium Press America, 2003).

Evaluating the Founding Team

The founding team is what most investors and other interested parties look at first, because no matter how good the concept is, it won't get anywhere without a founding team that can execute the concept. In many cases, the quality of the founding team becomes the deciding factor in whether the entrepreneur takes the risk associated with the new concept. And where the team lacks either expertise or experience, entrepreneurs must show that they have identified people they can tap to fill the gaps. The founding team is considered further in Chapter 7.

Analyzing Financial Risks and Requirements

In feasibility analysis, money is not considered until after the entrepreneur determines that there is market demand for the concept and a great team to execute it. The financial analysis focuses on the capital requirements for launching the business. Through forecasts of potential sales and expenses, and of requirements for working capital and equipment, the entrepreneur gains a sense of whether it is financially feasible to move forward with the business concept. Issues related to start-up resources are examined in Chapter 8.

New Venture Checklist

Have you:

☐ Developed a clear and concise business concept that contains the product/service, customer, value proposition, and distribution?

☐ Done a quick test of the business concept to see whether it is worthy of a feasibility analysis?

☐ Planned for conducting a full feasibility analysis beginning with a thorough understanding of the industry?

☐ Answered the key questions for every feasibility test?

☐ Determined the conditions under which you are willing to go forward with the concept?

Issues to Consider

1. What is the role of the compelling story in defining the value proposition?
2. Why is it important to identify the real pain that needs to be addressed by the business concept?
3. Are there instances where a feasibility study is not warranted or can be reduced in scope?
4. What is the purpose of the business model, and why do business models typically fail?
5. What are the characteristics of an effective business model?

Experiencing Entrepreneurship

1. Define a concept for a new venture using the four components discussed in the chapter: product/service, customer, benefit, and distribution. Conduct a quick test on some potential customers through a focus group, interviews, or a survey. Did you get enough information to move forward to a feasibility study? Why or why not?

2. Suppose you intend to start a theme restaurant than can be replicated and franchised. Judging on the basis of an analysis of some existing theme restaurants, what revenue streams could this business generate?

Additional Sources of Information

Banfield, Emiko (1999). *Harnessing Value in the Supply Chain: Strategic Sourcing in Action.* New York: Wiley.

Evans, Christopher J. (2000). *Financial Feasibility Studies for Healthcare.* New York: McGraw-Hill.

Fullen, Sharon. (2004). *Opening a Restaurant or Other Food Business Starter Kit: How to Prepare a Restaurant Business Plan and Feasibility Study.* Ocala, FLA: Atlantic Publishing Company (FL); Bk&CD-Rom. edition.

Relevant Case Studies

Part Two

Feasibility Analysis: Testing the Business Concept

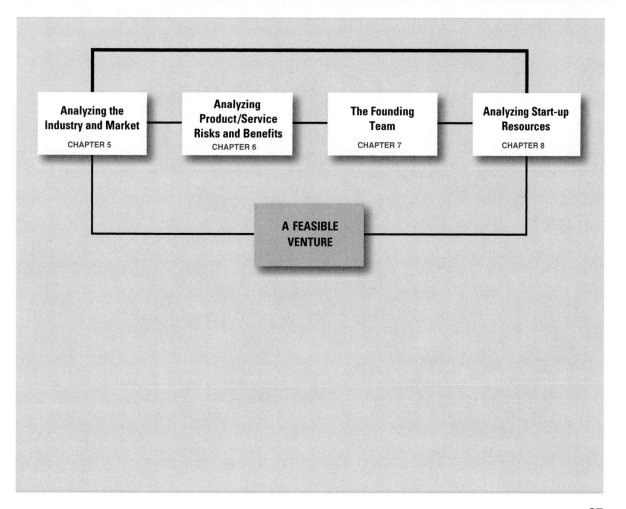

Analyzing the Industry and Market	Analyzing Product/Service Risks and Benefits	The Founding Team	Analyzing Start-up Resources
CHAPTER 5	CHAPTER 6	CHAPTER 7	CHAPTER 8

A FEASIBLE VENTURE

5

Analyzing the Industry and Market

"A moment's insight is sometimes worth a life's experience."

Oliver Wendell Holmes (1809–1894)

LEARNING OBJECTIVES

- ■ Explain the industry life cycle.
- ■ Use frameworks to characterize an industry.
- ■ Conduct an industry analysis.
- ■ Characterize the target market.
- ■ Gather competitive intelligence.
- ■ Forecast demand for the new product or service.

Profile 5.1 JOAQUIM SPLICHAL: REALLY COOKING IN A TOUGH INDUSTRY

If you look at a ranked listing of the industries in which venture capital is most likely to be spent, you'll typically find restaurants and food services at the bottom, right next to retail. That's because the restaurant industry is notorious for its high failure rate. Thus, to succeed in the restaurant business, you have to understand the industry inside out, and you have to find a niche.

Joaquim Splichal came to the United States in 1981 from Spaichingen, a small village in Germany, in his early thirties, having worked in the hotel and culinary businesses from the age of 18. His years in Holland, Switzerland, and France, serving as an apprentice to some of the great chefs, had earned him many culinary awards when he took his first job in the United States as executive chef for the Regency Club in Los Angeles. Later he became part of the launch of the successful Seventh Street Bistro, also in Los Angeles. Then, in 1984, he had his first entrepreneurial opportunity when one of his customers gave him a minority stake in his own restaurant, Max au Triangle. The food he created there was outstanding, but unfortunately, he knew nothing about managing a restaurant, and very soon the restaurant closed. For the next five years, Splichal took consulting jobs until he was ready to try his luck at entrepreneurship again, and he learned some important lessons that would ensure the success of his later ventures: "Control the capital investment, . . . and make sure you're in the right area to open a restaurant." Splichal had a very clear vision of what he wanted to achieve and what a superior restaurant should be when, in 1989, he opened Patina, an upscale French restaurant in Los Angeles, with an investment of $650,000 from people who believed in him. He also took advantage of the expertise of his wife, Christine, who has an MBA in international management and who runs the management and investment end of the business. Joaquim was the visionary, and Christine was the one who executed the concept. This time, their restaurant was a huge success, paying back its investors to the tune of 110 percent in fifteen months.

With investors paid, the Splichals now owned 50 percent of the company. But with typical entrepreneurial vision, Joaquim Splichal determined early on that more restaurants were part of his dream. At Patina, he was the chef and was in the kitchen every night. He wanted to build a company that endured beyond him—that didn't require him to be in the kitchen. Splichal knew that he had no desire to build a brand based on his persona, as his good friend, the renowned chef Wolfgang Puck, had done. He wanted to take a more low-profile approach. In 1992, he had an opportunity to purchase a failed French restaurant in the San Fernando Valley. He turned that site into Pinot Bistro and once again paid back the million dollars in investment capital in less than two years, to retain a 60 percent interest in the restaurant. Splichal's biggest concern with this new restaurant was that he had developed an image for Patina that was upscale and expensive. Pinot was intended to be a different experience: less expensive and not the super-high quality of the original restaurant. Would customers accept the difference? After a short period of confusion, they did and the restaurant succeeded. To achieve his goal of not being at the restaurant all the time, he hired a very talented executive chef who trained all the chefs he would later need in his subsequent restaurants.

Splichal did not take a cookie-cutter approach to new restaurants; instead, he tried to give each its own unique character. He went on to develop four more restaurants, all rooted in classic French cuisine, but with a touch of California whimsy. Restaurants were not the only undertaking of this multi-talented entrepreneur. Catering became one of the most important divisions of his ever-growing company. In 1995 he hired a catering manager, who promptly won the Emmy Awards dinner that next year. The catering business began earning $1 million a year and by 1999 had reached $6.2 million in revenues.

In 1998, the Splichals consolidated all their holdings under The Patina Group (http://www.patinagroup.com), which made the company more attractive to lenders and investors. When they received a lowball offer from Restaurant Associates (RA), who wanted to expand to the West Coast, the Splichals decided it was time to retain the services of an investment bank. Their subsequent association with an investment banking firm almost doubled the value of their business, and in 1999, after careful consideration, the Splichals merged the business with RA in a deal said to be worth about $40 million. Joaquim Splichal and his wife Christine still run The Patina Group of restaurants, which has grown to 22 operations and 2,000 employees.

Splichal was named Bon Appétit/Food Network Restaurateur of the Year for 2002. The Splichals are as busy as ever. With the huge resources of RA behind them, they are expanding at a rapid pace. They are even looking into vineyards in Europe, perhaps to find their next entrepreneurial venture.

Sources: Mary Caldwell, "Joachim Splichal: Patina Group Founder Creates New Concepts, from Fine Dining to Bistros, with Elegant Flair," *Nation's Restaurant News* (January 27, 2003); Restaurant Associates, "Joachim Splichal" and "News: The Patina Group Merges," *Nation's Restaurant News* (January 1997), http://www.restaurantassociates.com; and Arthur Lubow, "Recipe for a $40 Million Score," *Inc. Magazine* (October 2000).

U nquestionably, the analysis of the industry and market in which the business will operate is the most important analysis of the entire feasibility study. Without customers—without an industry and market that are receptive to the business concept—there is no business. From the broadest perspective, the industry is essentially a grouping of similar businesses that interact in a common environment. Recall from Chapter 3 that ideas for new ventures frequently come from understanding and having experience with an industry. Knowing an industry thoroughly opens the door not only to discovering an opportunity but also to finding strategic partners, customers, venture capital, and strategies for success. A strategic position in a growing, dynamic, healthy industry can go a long way toward ensuring a successful venture. For example, a young, growing industry with many new entrants, although it is a highly competitive environment for the new venture, also offers the entrepreneur a chance to become a major player in the industry. By contrast, occupying a weak position in a mature industry may sound a death knell for the business before it ever opens its doors, unless the entrepreneur has identified a niche market not being served by the major players. Understanding how an industry works is fundamental to shaping effective entry and growth strategies.

A market is a grouping of customers that the entrepreneur targets. Identification of the primary market and the primary customer is one of the most important tasks in analyzing the feasibility of a business concept. In broad terms, defining the primary customer begins with an analysis of the segment of the marketplace that is most likely to purchase the product or service.

Entrepreneurs identify their primary customers by recognizing a need, or pain, in the market. Gus Conrades and his partner Bryan Murphy saw a need for a central online place where people and businesses could purchase auto parts and car-care products. In the highly fragmented auto products market, customers had a difficult time finding what they needed. Conrades and Murphy launched Wrenchead.com to remedy that situation, and they now sell millions of auto parts and brand-name accessories around the world to people who love cars and, at the same time, provide e-commerce business solutions to dealers.

Identifying a pain or need in the market is only the first step. Unfortunately, many entrepreneurs don't place enough emphasis on in-depth market analysis to support the need they have recognized. As a result, they tend to overestimate their market forecasts for demand by as much as 60 percent. And that kind of error can be devastating to a start-up venture. This chapter helps the reader learn how to do efficient and effective industry and market research within the constraints of the limited resources that entrepreneurs typically have.

The Industry Life Cycle

Industries do not remain static or stable over time; in fact, they are almost constantly evolving. Like people, industries move through a life cycle that includes birth, growth, maturity, and ultimately decline. The stages of the industry life cycle are identified by the different kinds of activities occurring at each stage. Figure 5.1 displays this life cycle.

1. *Birth:* A new industry emerges, often with the introduction of a disruptive technology such as the Internet that displaces previous technology and creates opportunities that didn't exist before.
2. *Growth and adaptation:* The new industry goes through a volatile stage as companies and their respective technologies jockey for position and the right to determine industry standards.

FIGURE 5.1   Industry Growth Cycle

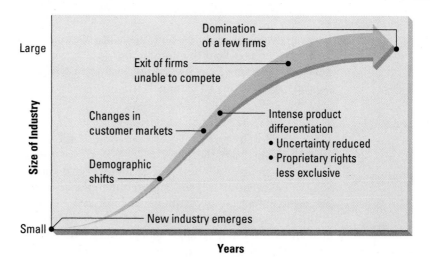

3. *Differentiation and competition:* As more firms enter the industry, intense product differentiation occurs, because the industry's established standards and proprietary rights no longer provide the exclusivity they once did.
4. *Shakeout:* When competition is the most intense, those companies that are unable to compete leave. The remaining firms then grow more rapidly as they pick up the slack.
5. *Maturity and decline:* The industry reaches a mature state in which several major players dominate. If new research and development in the industry do not produce a resurgence of growth, the industry could face decline.

For every industry, these life cycle stages occur at different times and vary in their duration. The video rental industry presents a classic example of an industry in transition. In the early stages it was made up of small independent (mom-and-pop) owners. Wayne Huizenga sought to consolidate the industry by developing Blockbuster Video, a video megastore. In just a few years, independents were disappearing in favor of large-volume chain outlets. In the not-too-distant future, the megastores will probably give way themselves to video on demand, available over cable television and even the Internet.

It is important to look for the five signs listed above to discover which stage of the life cycle an industry is in. Reading the analyses of industry watchers in trade magazines and talking with people who regularly work in that industry are also good ways to learn where an industry is in the life cycle.

Frameworks for Understanding Industries

It is often helpful to put a framework around the concept of an industry. Many frameworks have been proposed, and several have been adapted successfully by entrepreneurs. The following sections discuss the Starbuck framework, the Porter Five Forces model, SWOT analysis, and STEP analysis.

The Starbucks Framework

The early work of Starbucks and others has identified three dimensions of an industry environment that help the entrepreneur grasp the nature of an industry and a new venture's potential for success in that industry. These dimensions are carrying capacity, uncertainty, and complexity.[1]

Carrying Capacity

Carrying capacity, or degree of saturation, is the ability of the industry to support growth, from both the entry of new ventures and the growth of existing ones. Entrepreneurs typically seek out an industry that can support expansion, thus allowing the new venture to grow and to obtain the resources it needs. Difficulty entering a specific industry due to the presence of many competitors, major companies that control needed supply chains, or problems achieving economies of scale suggests that an industry may be approaching saturation. That is, the production capability of the existing firms may equal or exceed customer demand for their products. The only way to enter such an industry is through the introduction of new technology or the discovery of a niche where a need has not been met.

Uncertainty

Uncertainty is the degree of instability and ambiguity in an industry. A dynamic, uncertain environment is one that is difficult to predict because it is in constant flux. Volatile industries like biotech contain higher degrees of uncertainty or risk, so it is important that the potential rewards be higher as well. Dynamic, even chaotic, environments also provide fertile ground for new opportunities and have given rise to many successful companies.

Complexity

Complexity consists of the number and diversity of inputs and outputs facing an organization. Firms that operate in complex industries usually have to deal with more suppliers, customers, and competitors than firms in other industries, and they regularly produce a greater number of dissimilar products for global markets. Industries with a high degree of complexity, such as the electronics industry, are by their very nature difficult for new businesses to enter. They are also extremely competitive; therefore, new ventures often encounter a great deal of hostility rather than collaboration within those industries. Telecommunications and biotechnology are both industries with a high degree of competition and government regulation and in which product life cycles can be very short.

Porter's Five Forces

For years, the work of Michael Porter has provided a way of looking at the structure of an industry. Porter's basic premise is that sustaining high performance levels in an industry requires a well-thought-out strategy and implementation plan based on knowledge of the way the industry works. Porter asserts that there are five forces in any industry that affect the ultimate profit potential of a venture in terms of long-run return on investment. His Five Forces framework is a way to classify the industry structure so that a strategy for entry and sustained growth can be developed.[2] The Five Forces drive competition and affect the long-run profitability of the new venture, as well as of other firms in the industry. By contrast, such things as economic forces, changes in demand, material shortages, and technology shifts affect short-run profitability. Porter's Five Forces are discussed below.

Barriers to Entry

In some industries, barriers to entry are high and will discourage a potential entrepreneur from attempting to enter. These barriers may include the following:

Economies of Scale Many industries have achieved economies of scale in marketing, production, and distribution. This means that their costs to produce have declined relative to the price of their goods and services. A new venture cannot easily achieve these same economies, so it is forced into a "Catch-22" situation. If it enters the industry on a large scale, it risks retaliation from those established firms in the industry. If it enters on a small scale, it may not be able to compete because its costs are high relative to everyone else's. Another version of this dilemma occurs in an industry in which the major players are vertically integrated; that is, they own their suppliers and/or distribution channels, which effectively locks out the new venture. What most new ventures do when they must compete with companies that have achieved economies of scale is try to form alliances with other small firms to share resources and thus compete on a more level playing field. This type of collaboration is occurring more and more often as businesses realize that the marketplace is too complex for any one company to have all the resources and intellectual property required to control a portion of a market. This strategy has been prevalent in the grocery industry, where independent grocers have joined forces to achieve more buying power.

Brand Loyalty New entrants to an industry face existing products and services with loyal customers, so an extensive marketing campaign focused on making the customer aware of the benefits of the new venture's products will be required. The cost of undertaking this strategy can be a significant barrier to entry unless customers are dissatisfied with the competing brands. On the Internet, it has become clear that when they set up shop in cyberspace, companies such as Barnes & Noble and The Gap retain the brand presence they have already established in their bricks-and-mortar stores—they can be profitable immediately. By contrast, it takes a company like Amazon (with the strongest online brand recognition) years to become profitable.

Capital Requirements The cost of entering many industries is prohibitive for a new venture. These costs may include up-front advertising, research and development (R&D), and expenditures for plant and equipment. Entrepreneurs often overcome this barrier by outsourcing to or partnering with established companies to leverage their resources and industry intelligence.

Switching Costs for the Buyer Buyers in most industries don't readily switch from one supplier to another unless there is a compelling reason to do so. Switching costs the buyer money and time. For example, a manufacturing business that has spent a lot of time and money finding the best supplier for the raw materials it needs to produce its product will not easily change suppliers, because that would mean going through the whole process again.

Access to Distribution Channels The new venture must persuade established distribution channel members to accept its new product or service and must prove that it will be beneficial to distributors to do so. This persuasion process can be costly for a new venture. One solution is distributing via the Internet, which is a direct method of reaching the customer.

Proprietary Factors Barriers to entry also include proprietary technology, products, and processes. Where established firms hold patents on products and processes that the new venture requires, they have the ability either to keep the new venture out of the industry or to make it very expensive to enter. Most favorable location is another form of proprietary barrier. Often entrepreneurs will discover that existing firms in the industry own the most advantageous business sites, forcing the new venture to locate elsewhere. The Internet diminishes such location advantages somewhat, but the ability of customers to find a Web address quickly through the major search engines also becomes a location advantage. These proprietary factors are all substantial barriers to entry for a new venture.

Government Regulations The government can prevent a new venture from entering an industry through strict licensing requirements and by limiting access to raw materials via laws or high taxes and to certain locations via zoning restrictions. Food products and biochemicals must obtain FDA approval, which is a significant barrier to entry. Isis Pharmaceuticals, a drug development company located in Carlsbad, California, recognizes that any delay in approvals can result in millions of dollars lost. It invested in a local area network for its company and an Intranet on the Web; now it can manage its FDA-mandated clinical trials on thousands of patients without losing time. By submitting its required forms electronically, it cuts several months off the FDA's normal 15-month review process.

Industry Hostility Some industries are extremely retaliatory toward new businesses that attempt to compete in the industry. This typically occurs where there are many well-established firms that have sufficient resources to spend the time and money going after a new entrant. It is also common in mature industries where growth has slowed, so rivalry for market share intensifies as profits decline. Weaker firms ultimately are forced to exit the industry. But today, retaliatory behavior is also common in technology industries where companies are finding it difficult to maneuver the intellectual property minefields. For example, with the barrage of broadly defined business method and software patents hitting the U.S. Patent and Trademark Office (USPTO), many companies are going to find it difficult to compete without infringing on someone's patent. The USPTO is not set up to find all the bad patent applications, so court battles like the one over Amazon's one-click patent will become more and more common.

Threat from Substitute Products

A new venture must compete not only with products and services in its own industry but also with logical substitutes that other industries bring to the market. Generally, these substitute products and services accomplish the same basic function in a different way or at a different price. For example, movie theaters regularly compete with other forms of entertainment for the consumer's disposable dollars. The threat from substitute products is more likely to occur where firms in other industries are earning high profits at better prices than can be achieved in the new venture's industry.

Threat from Buyers' Bargaining Power

In industries where buyers have bargaining power, it is more difficult for a new entrant to gain a foothold and grow. Examples of buyers that have this type of bargaining power include Price/Costco, Barnes & Noble, and Toys 'R' Us. Buyers like these can force down prices in the industry through volume purchases. This is particularly true where industry products constitute a significant portion of the buyers' requirements—books for Barnes & Noble, toys for Toys 'R' Us. Under this scenario, the buyer is more likely to achieve the lowest possible price.

The largest buyers also pose a threat of backward integration; that is, they may actually purchase their suppliers, thus better controlling costs and affecting price throughout the industry. The more buyers understand the nature of the industry and the more their products are standardized, the greater the likelihood that these buyers will have significant bargaining power.

Threat from Suppliers' Bargaining Power

In some industries, suppliers exert enormous power through the threat of raising prices or changing the quality of the products that they supply to manufacturers and distributors. If the number of these suppliers is few relative to the size of the industry, or the industry is not the primary customer of the suppliers, that power is magnified. A further threat from suppliers is that they will integrate forward—that is, they will purchase the outlets for their goods and services, thus controlling the prices at which their output is ultimately sold.

Rivalry Among Existing Firms

In general, a highly competitive industry will drive down profits and ultimately the rate of return on investment. To position themselves in a competitive market, firms often resort to price wars and advertising skirmishes. Once one firm decides to make such a strategic move in the industry, others will follow. The clearest example is the airline industry; when one airline discounts its prices significantly, most of the others immediately follow.

The problem with this tactic is that it ultimately hurts everyone in the industry and may even force out some smaller firms, because competitive prices drop below costs. Most new ventures can't compete on price and can't afford costly advertising battles to build an image. To compete in an industry that is highly competitive, they must identify a market niche that will allow them to enter quietly and gain a foothold. Many entrepreneurs seeking entry into industries such as software and telecommunications deliberately position themselves to be acquired by the larger rivals rather than trying to compete against them.

SWOT and STEP Analyses

Both SWOT analysis and STEP analysis look at the external macro-environment in which the new venture will operate. The acronym SWOT refers to the strengths, weaknesses, opportunities, and threats that the firm faces. (See Figure 5.2.) Strengths include competitive advantages such as patents and cost superiority. Weaknesses generally reflect the lack of strength in a particular area. Opportunities

---

| **FIGURE 5.2** | SWOT Analysis |

	Strengths	**Weaknesses**
Opportunities	Opportunities that fit with core strengths	Opportunities that do not fail within core competencies
Threats	Strengths that reduce vulnerability to threats	Overcome weaknesses that make the company vulnerable

| FIGURE 5.3 | Step Analysis |

Social and Cultural Factors (e.g., changing demographics)	**Opportunities:** Increasing demand for assisted-living facilities
	Threats: Increasing market will attract more new ventures
Technological Advances (e.g., more information available more rapidly)	**Opportunities:** Can meet specific needs of customers
	Threats: Mass marketing is no longer effective
Economic Trends (e.g., the economy is pulling out of a recession)	**Opportunities:** Customer spending is increasing
	Threats: Government may act to curtail spending and associated inflation
Political and Regulatory (e.g., government is seeking to reduce its costs)	**Opportunities:** Provide new products and services
	Threats: Business must take more responsibility and incur increased costs

are the potential the business faces for growth, and threats are those things in the environment that could adversely affect the business, such as shifts in consumer preferences. The matrix in Figure 5.2 offers a way to analyze which opportunities fall within the new venture's core competencies or strengths and which do not (the upper two quadrants). The bottom two quadrants deal with ways in which the company can use its strengths to avoid vulnerability to threats and to overcome the weaknesses that may make it more vulnerable.

By contrast, STEP analysis (Figure 5.3) examines specific aspects of the macro-environment: its social, technological, economic, and political facets. Social factors involve demographic and cultural aspects, such as age distribution and health consciousness. Technological factors include such things as R&D activity and rate of technological change. Economic factors deal with the firm's cost of capital and customers' purchasing power. Political factors involve government regulation and the various legal issues that affect the business's operations.

Frameworks are a way to organize an analysis of an industry so that characteristics, trends, and anomalies can be exposed. Competitors certainly play an important role in the industry/market analysis, and competitive analysis is discussed next.

Conducting Industry Analysis

Any good analysis needs a plan to ensure that the industry is clearly defined and the right kind of information is gathered. Such analysis typically begins with the classification system that the United States, Canada, and Mexico developed to identify industries and allow for common standards and statistics across North America. The North American Industry Classification System (NAICS) is replacing the traditional U.S. Standard Industrial Classification system (SIC) and will soon change the way we view the economy. NAICS covers 350 new industries that have never been coded before. Some of these industries reflect high-tech developments such as fiber optic cable manufacturing, satellite communications, and the reproduction of computer software. However, far more of these new categories are not technology-based: bed and breakfast inns, environmental consulting, warehouse clubs, pet supply stores, credit card issuing, diet and weight reduction centers, to name only a few.

NAICS industries are identified by a six-digit code, in contrast to the four-digit SIC code. The longer code accommodates the larger number of sectors and allows more flexibility in designating subsectors. It also provides for additional detail not necessarily appropriate for all three NAICS countries. NAICS is organized in a hierarchical structure much like the existing SIC. The first two digits designate a major

SCREENSHOT 5.1　　**NAICS**

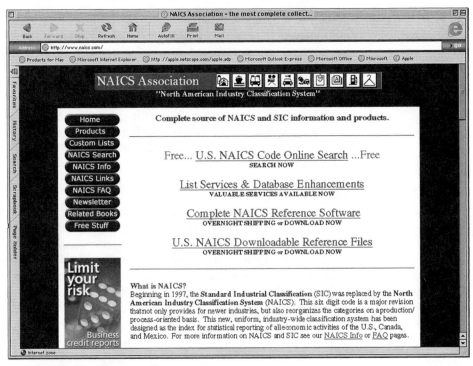

Source: http://www.naics.com/, accessed 3/10/05.

Economic Sector (formerly Division), such as Agriculture or Manufacturing. The third digit designates an Economic Subsector (formerly Major Group), such as Crop Production or Apparel Manufacturing. The fourth digit designates an Industry Group, such as Grain and Oil Seed Farming or Fiber, Yarn, and Thread Mills. The fifth digit designates the NAICS Industry, such as Wheat Farming or Broadwoven Fabric Mills. The international NAICS agreement fixes only the first five digits of the code. The sixth digit is used for industrial classifications in other countries where necessary. With the NAICS code, one can find statistics about size of the industry, sales, number of employees, and so forth.

Secondary Sources of Industry Information

A search of secondary sources of information will include journals, trade magazines, reference books, government publications, and annual reports of public corporations—normally available in a university or community library and on the Internet. Historical data, such as annual reports over a 10- to 15-year period, can often help analysts spot trends, cycles, and seasonal variations in the industry. Trade magazines provide a good sense of key firms and of the directions the industry may be taking.

The data collected should answer the following questions:

1. *Is the industry growing?* Growth is measured by sales volume, number of employees, units produced, number of new companies entering the industry, and so forth.
2. *Where are the opportunities?* Does the industry provide opportunities for new businesses with strategies involving new products and/or processes, innovative distribution, or new marketing strategies?
3. *What is the status of any new technology?* How quickly does the industry adopt new technology, and does technology play a significant role in the competitive strategy of firms in the industry?
4. *How much does the industry spend on research and development?* Expenditures on R&D indicate how important technology is, how much needs to be spent, and how rapid the product development cycle is.
5. *Who are the major competitors?* Which firms dominate the industry?
6. *Are there young, successful firms in the industry?* This information will provide an indicator of how formidable the entry barriers are and whether the industry is growing rapidly.
7. *What does the future look like?* What appears likely to happen over the next five years? What are the trends and patterns of change?
8. *Are there any threats to the industry?* Is there any chance that new technology will render obsolete either the industry or that segment of the industry in which the entrepreneur is doing business?
9. *What are the typical margins in the industry?* Looking at gross margins in the industry provides an indication of how much room there is to make mistakes. A gross margin is derived by dividing gross profit by sales. It indicates how much money is left to pay overhead and make a profit. If the industry typically has 2 percent margins or less, as the grocery industry does, making a profit will require selling in large volumes and keeping overhead costs to a minimum.

Where margins run at 70 percent or higher, there is a lot more room to play, but generally these industries (such as the software industry) have relatively short product life cycles, so R&D costs are high.

The Importance of Primary Data

Secondary research paints a broad picture of the industry, but given the lead-time from data gathering to print, it rarely yields the most current information available. Therefore, to access the timeliest information, it is extremely important to gather primary field data on the industry. In other words, entrepreneurs need to talk with people in the industry. Some of the sources to tap are

Industry observers, who study particular industries and regularly report on them in newspapers or newsletters or through the media.

Suppliers and distributors, who are in an excellent position to comment on the health of the industry in terms of demand for products and services, as well as on the financial strength and market practices of major firms.

Customers, who can be a clue to satisfaction with the industry and the product or service supplied.

Employees of key firms in the industry, who are a good source of information about potential competitors.

Professionals from service organizations, such as lawyers and accountants, who regularly work with a particular industry.

Trade shows, which give a good indication of who the biggest competitors are and who has the strongest market strategy.

Characterizing the Target Market

No matter what the size of the target market, it is crucial that the entrepreneur know as much as possible about the customer. Ashbury Images, a San Francisco screen printer that serves as a transition job for the homeless, had always viewed its primary customers as small nonprofits. The problem was that these businesses were not profitable customers for Ashbury. As the company looked closer at its customers, it discovered that its best customers, the ones whose needs were actually being served, were larger corporate clients. These clients understood Ashbury's value proposition: a high-quality product and a social mission. Ashbury has now refocused its efforts to put more emphasis on its best customers.[3]

In the beginning stages of market analysis, the customer definition may be fairly loose and may even change fairly substantially as field research is conducted. It is easy to become overwhelmed by the amount of information available about the target market, so it's important to keep in mind the key questions that should be answered:

Who is most likely to purchase the product or service at market introduction?

What do these customers typically buy, how do they buy it, and how do they hear about it?

How often do they buy? What is their buying pattern?

How can the new venture meet the customers' needs?

Socially Responsible Entrepreneurship

Having It All

Imagine an entrepreneurial venture competing against the likes of AT&T and Verizon. Sound impossible? Not at all. Working Assets is a long-distance, wireless, credit card and broadcasting company that was started in 1985 to "build a better world." It donates 1 percent of its revenues to "progressive" nonprofits nominated by its customers. Customers can also round up their bills to the next dollar amount, and the difference is contributed to charity. Working Assets has funded nonprofits such as Greenpeace, Planned Parenthood, Oxfam America, and the Children's Defense Fund. It works with socially responsible companies such as Ben & Jerry's Ice Cream to create joint promotions and is internally consistent in its environmental message. It uses recycled paper for billing and recycled plastic for its calling card. And in an industry that is not known for customer loyalty, Working Assets has a loyal customer base. The company also enhances its customers' ability to speak out on important issues by allowing them to place free calls to decision makers on critical issues of the month. Since its inception, the company has raised $35 million by helping its customers make a difference in the world through philanthropy and political activism, while still succeeding as an entrepreneurial venture.

Sources: www.workingassets.com; and J.G. Dees, J. Emerson, and P. Economy, *Enterprising Nonprofits* (New York: Wiley, 2001), p. 224.

Researching the Target Market

Target market research provides some of the most important data that one needs to decide whether the new venture is feasible. But data are only as good as the research methods used to collect them. To ensure that useful and correct conclusions can be drawn from the data collected, sound research methods must be employed. Table 5.1 depicts a four-step process for ensuring that the right information is gathered and that it is used correctly.

The Internet is a good starting point for gathering secondary data. Many of the traditional resources found in libraries are now available in online versions; for example, U.S. census data can be found at www.census.gov. Using census data, entrepreneurs can determine whether the geographic area they have defined is growing or declining, whether its population is aging or getting younger, or whether the available work force is mostly skilled or unskilled, along with many other trends.

Some demographic data (data on age, income, race, occupation, and education) help identify the likelihood that a person will choose to buy a product.[4] Demographic data also make it possible to segment the target market into subgroups that are different from one another. For example, if the target market is retired people over age 60, their buying habits (such as product requirements and quantity or frequency of purchase) may vary by geographic region or by income level.

Finally, census data can be used to arrive at an estimate of how many target customers live within the geographic boundaries of the target market. Then, within any geographic area, those who meet the particular demographic requirements of the product or service can be segmented out.

TABLE 5.1	Steps in Market Research
Assess your information needs.	• How will the data be used? • What data need to be collected? • What methods of analysis will be used?
Research secondary sources first.	• What are the demographics of the customer? • What are the psychographics of the customer (i.e., buying habits)? • How large is the market? • Is the market growing? • Is the market affected by geography? • How can you reach your market? • How do you competitors reach the market? • What market strategies have been successful with these customers?
Measure the target market with primary research.	• What are the demographics of your customer? • Would they purchase your product or service? Why? • How much would they purchase? • When would they purchase? • How would they like to find the product or service? • What do they like about your competitors' products and services?
Forecast demand for the product or service.	• What do substitute products/services tell you about demand for your product/service? • What do customers, end-users, and intermediaries predict the demand will be? • Can you do a limited production or test market for your product or service?

It is not only consumer markets that are described by demographic data. Business markets can also be described in terms of their size, revenue levels, number of employees, and so forth. Information about business demographics is found at such sites as Economy.com's "The Dismal Scientist" at http://www.economy.com/dismal/and the Census Bureau at http://www.census.gov.

Online sources are not the only sources of secondary market data. Most communities have economic development departments or Chambers of Commerce that keep statistics on local population trends and other economic issues. Some communities have Small Business Development Centers (SBDCs), branches of the Small Business Administration that offer a wealth of useful information, as well as services, for small and growing businesses. Other sources available in the library include reference books and trade journals on all types of industries (many of these are also available online). Apart from the library, useful information can be obtained from trade associations such as the National Association of Manufacturers, commercial research firms, and financial institutions.

Measuring the Market with Primary Data

The most important data that entrepreneurs can collect on potential customers are primary data derived from observation, mail surveys, phone surveys, interviews, and focus groups. Each data collection technique has advantages and disadvantages, and the decision which one(s) to use is generally based on time and money. The first three techniques require drawing a representative sample from the population of customers that the entrepreneur is interested in. The sample should be selected with great care, for it will determine the validity of the results. In general, in order to avoid bias, a sample should be random—that is, one in which the entrepreneur has as little control as possible over who participates. Most entrepreneurs, because of limitations on cost and time, use what is called a convenience sample. This means that not everyone in the defined target market has a chance of being chosen to participate. Instead, the entrepreneur may, for example, choose to select the sample from people who happen to be at the airport on a particular day. Clearly, the entrepreneur will not be reaching all possible customers at the airport, but if the target customer is typically found at airports, there's a good chance of obtaining at least a representative sample from which results can be derived fairly confidently.

Even if a convenience sample is used, there are ways to ensure the randomness of selection of the participants. Using the airport example, the entrepreneur can decide in advance to survey every fifth person who walks by. Thus the respondents are not chosen on the basis of attractiveness or lack of it—or for any other reason, for that matter. A random-number generator on a computer can select names from a telephone book. Whatever system is employed, the key point is to make an effort not to bias the selection.

Primary Research Techniques

Many techniques are available for gathering primary information from potential customers. Each has advantages and disadvantages. In general, mail surveys have a response rate of only 2 percent, and several follow-ups are required to get a sufficient sample. Phone surveys are ineffective because in the past few years, people have been bombarded by telemarketers and now resist responding to a telephone survey. With limited resources, entrepreneurs tend to use interviews, focus groups, the Internet, and immediate-response surveys.

Structured Interviews

Although personal interviews are more costly and time-consuming than mail or phone surveys, they have many advantages:

They provide more opportunity for clarification and discussion.

The interviewer has an opportunity to observe nonverbal communication and hence assess the veracity of what the interviewee is saying.

The response rate is high.

Interviews permit open-ended questions that can lead to more in-depth information.

They provide an opportunity to network and develop valuable contacts in the industry.

Where time and money permit, structured interviews are probably the best source of valuable information from customers, suppliers, distributors, and anyone else who can help the new venture.

Focus Groups

One more efficient way to gain valuable information before investing substantial capital in production and marketing is to conduct a **focus group,** in which a representative sample of potential customers is brought together for a presentation and discussion session.

It is important to ensure that the person leading the focus group has some knowledge of group dynamics and is able to keep the group on track. Often these focus group sessions are videotaped so that the entrepreneur can spend more time later analyzing the nuances of what occurred. Thus, in many ways, focus groups can prevent the entrepreneur from making the costly error of offering a product or service in which there is little or no interest.

Internet and Immediate-Response Surveys

Doing a survey entails designing a survey instrument, usually a questionnaire that, once filled out, provides the desired information. Questionnaire design is not a simple matter of putting some questions on a piece of paper. There are, in fact, proven methods of constructing questionnaires to help ensure unbiased responses. It is not within the scope of this text to present all the techniques for questionnaire construction; however, a few key points should be remembered:

Keep the questionnaire short, with lots of white space, so that the respondent is not intimidated by the task.

Be careful not to ask leading or biased questions.

Ask easy questions first, progressing gradually to the more complex ones.

Ask demographic questions (questions about age, sex, income, and the like) last, when the respondent's attention may have waned. These questions can be answered very quickly.

The Internet has made it easy for small businesses to conduct valuable data without having to enlist the help of expensive market research firms.[5] Internet surveys are less expensive than traditional surveys, and the response time is greatly reduced. It's easier to include global respondents seamlessly. Posting surveys on the Internet is a convenient way to conduct research if the primary customer is an Internet user. The survey can be posted in user groups, sent via e-mail to target customers, or placed on a website (as long as the people who need to respond to the survey have a way of knowing that it's there).

The Customer Grid

One useful way to look at various customer segments to determine which should be the primary customer is to construct a customer grid that lays out the benefits, distribution, and product/service for each of the customer segments. The grid in Table 5.2 highlights three potential customers for Rhino Records, a producer and distributor of

| **TABLE 5.2** | **Customer Grid for Rhino Records** |

CUSTOMER	BENEFIT	DISTRIBUTION
Baby-boomers	Convenience and economy: Can find compilations of their favorite songs without having to buy multiple one-artist albums.	Retail outlet
Record stores	Provides unique compilations of hard-to-find great hits of the past to satisfy the baby-boomer segment of their market.	Wholesale to record store
Busy professionals	Convenience: Can shop any time of the day or night and have all the information at their fingertips.	Internet store for online purchasing

music compilations. Once the customer segments are identified, the entrepreneur has to make a choice. Which of these three customers should the entrepreneur go after first? The decision where to go first is affected by size of the market, customer demand, and resources, but the most important consideration is which customer is most likely to buy. Market research with customers may suggest, for instance, that the quickest early sales will come from music enthusiasts who like to peruse a retail outlet. Note also that the different benefits and distribution strategies for each customer actually produce three different businesses: a retail outlet, a wholesale distributorship, and an Internet business. The type of business the entrepreneur wants to own will then influence the decision on first customer.

The Customer Profile

Out of the primary research will come a complete profile of the customer. Entrepreneurs need to be able to describe the primary customer, be it a consumer or a business, in great detail. The profile is critically important to the marketing strategy, because it provides information vital to everything from product/service design to distribution channels and the marketing plan. Here is a list of some of the information that goes into the customer profile of a consumer or a business:

- Age
- Income level
- Education
- Buying habits—when, where, how much
- Where customers typically find these types of products and services
- How they would like to purchase

The list will contain other data as well, depending on whether the customer is a consumer or a business. Sandy Gooch is one of the leaders in the health food industry. When she was preparing to open her first store, she had a complete picture of her target customer: a 45- to 50-year-old professional woman who was well educated, was a life-long learner, valued physical fitness, and read labels when she shopped. She would also be a regular shopper who stopped into the store several times a week on her way home from work. Certainly, not everyone who shopped at Mrs. Gooch's was a 45- to 50-year-old professional woman, but that was the customer most likely to purchase when Gooch started the business: her primary customer. Knowing that much about her customer enabled Gooch to tailor her advertising. Mrs. Gooch's ads always contained a lot of information, for instance, because she knew her customers wanted to learn something from each ad.

If the customer is a business, it can be described in essentially the same way—for example, as a small to mid-sized construction company with annual revenues of $5 million that makes purchases quarterly, buys primarily over the Internet, and pays within sixty days. The customer profile will also be an important piece in the marketing plan, as we will see in Chapter 14.

Gathering Competitive Intelligence

One of the weakest portions of any feasibility analysis or business plan is the competitive analysis. This is because the entrepreneur typically looks only at what can easily be seen on the surface rather than digging for what is not so obvious. It is important for entrepreneurs to study competitors' strengths, weaknesses, opportunities, and threats as thoroughly as they study their own. The idea is not to benchmark against a competitor but rather to find ways to create new and innovative value.

Identifying the Competition

There are generally three types of competitors for a product or service: direct, indirect or substitute, and emerging. Identifying exactly who these companies are, including their strengths, weaknesses, and market share, will put the new venture in a better position to be a contender in the industry—and particularly in the target market.

Direct competitors are those businesses that supply similar products or services. Indirect competitors may not even be in the same industry as the new venture but do compete alongside it for customer dollars. For example, consumers may choose to spend their limited dollars at the movies rather than on an expensive restaurant. Or a business looking for videoconferencing capability may choose an Internet-based system delivered through an application service provider (ASP) rather than purchasing and maintaining equipment. Therefore, it is important to look outside the immediate industry and market for alternatives. An entrepreneur also needs to look beyond existing competition to emerging competitors. In many industries today, technology and information are changing at such a rapid pace that the window of opportunity for successfully starting a new venture closes early and fast. Consequently, the entrepreneur must be vigilant in observing new trends and new technology, both in the industry in general and in the specific target market.

Finding Information About Competitors

Collecting information on competitors is one of the most difficult parts of researching the industry. It is easy to gain superficial information from the competitor's advertising, website, or facility, but the less obvious types of information, such as

Profile 5.2   EVEN MICRO-BUSINESSES REQUIRE MARKET RESEARCH

It was fairly easy for Michael Cain to parlay his love of building things into a successful micro-business concept when he began college at the University of Nebraska in 2000. However, what he learned along the way was that even the tiniest of businesses require some market research to ensure that money and time are not wasted. Dorm rooms are small at best, and students often find creative ways to overcome the space limitations. One solution was the loft bed—that is, a bed on stilts under which a desk or bureau could be placed, thereby providing several feet of usable space in the room. Using the metal bed frame provided by the university, Cain spent 10 hours one weekend constructing his loft bed. While he was installing it, four students in the dorm approached him about building beds for them. Cain immediately spied an opportunity to generate some cash flow. The first task was to find out how to make a company out of this new concept, which he dubbed "Loft in Space."

Cain began talking to every university office he could find, and most were supportive. His one nemesis was a housing director who had been renting loft beds to students. Cain knew he could build his loft beds cheaper than the cost of renting them from the university for four years. Cain had a conversation with the housing director, in which the director explained why he thought Cain's idea would never work:

1. The university didn't allow students to operate businesses out their dorm rooms.

2. Cain could not use the university phone in his room or his university e-mail address to conduct business.

3. If he worked for the university to build his lofts, he would need a million-dollar liability insurance policy and another million-dollar policy on any vehicle he brought onto campus.

This news did not deter Cain in the least; in fact, it told him exactly what he needed to do to create the business. He quickly shifted into entrepreneurial gear and went out to acquire a post office box, a new e-mail address, and an insurance agent.

Then Cain had to figure out how to reach his primary customer over the summer so that he could have the lofts built by the start of the fall semester. He developed a brochure and began attending orientation sessions for new students during the summer months to secure orders. In his first year, he secured 55 orders, which required him to create and implement templates for the design and assembly plan. Working with a couple of friends, he successfully completed the first year of his micro-business with satisfied customers and referrals that kept him in business throughout his career at the university.

Sources: http://www.loft-in-space.com; and M. Cain, "Reaching Lofty Goals with Hard Work and Persistence," in *Student Entrepreneurs,* ed. M. McMyne and N. Amare. Premium Press America, 2003.

revenues and long-term strategies, are another matter. Information on publicly held competitors can be found in annual reports and other filings required by the Securities and Exchange Commission (SEC). Unfortunately, however, most start-up companies are competing against other private companies that will not be willing to divulge these sensitive data.

Here are some of the data that it is helpful to gather:

- Current market strategies
- Management style and culture

- Pricing strategy
- Customer mix
- Promotional mix

The following are some suggestions on where to look for this information. Other resources are listed at the end of the chapter.

- Visit competitors' websites or the outlets where their products are sold. Evaluate appearance, number of customers coming and going, what they buy, how much, and how often. Talk to customers and employees.
- Buy competitors' products to understand the differences in features and benefits and to learn much about how they treat their customers.
- Use Internet search engines such as Google.com.
- Find information on public companies to serve as benchmarks for the industry. Public companies can be investigated through Hoover's Online (www.hoovers .com), the U.S. Securities and Exchange Commission (www.sec.gov), and One Source (www.onesource.com).
- Search government websites. Some of these sites are found in the Additional Sources of Information section at the end of this chapter.
- Seek out trade associations and other industry organizations.

Looking for the Less Obvious

Sometimes the most threatening aspect of a competitor is not readily visible in the typical facts that are reported, and often competitors come from outside the entrepreneur's industry and market. For example, understanding a competitor's real core competency helps to determine whether that competency can ever be shifted to the entrepreneur's niche market. Suppose the entrepreneur's business concept is a company that trains unskilled workers for well-paying jobs in industry. The entrepreneur looks at all the competitors in the training industry and decides that he can compete because he has created a unique niche in the market. What the entrepreneur has failed to do is look outside his industry to companies that might have the same core competency and might have the resources to shift to his niche very rapidly. Those companies are not always obvious. For example, one of Marriott's core competencies is training unskilled workers in the language and work skills they need to perform the various jobs in Marriott's hotel chain. It certainly has the resources to take this competency into any niche it desires. To make sure that they are not missing a potential threat, entrepreneurs should

- Determine what the competitor has to do to be successful in its own core business. Are there any core competencies that it must acquire?
- Determine which of the competitor's core competencies are transferable to the entrepreneur's business.
- Determine whether the competitor has a competency in the same area as the entrepreneur.

If the competitor is a large company, the entrepreneur may strategically position his company to be acquired, because most large companies acquire core competencies rather than developing them.

Employing a Niche Strategy to Compete

Entrepreneurs typically use a niche strategy to compete in their industry and market. What this means is that the new venture focuses on a particular customer group, an unserved need, or a specific geographic region not currently served effectively by other players in the industry. By selecting a segment of a market, niche entrepreneurs attempt to insulate themselves from market forces such as competitors and the barriers to entry in an industry. Niches can be created by focusing on any of the key elements of the business: customer, product design, price, service, packaging, geographic focus, and distribution.

Many a new venture has entered an established industry via a niche by finding a gap in the market that enables the company to compete without going head-to-head with major companies. Where competition is weak and exposure to substitute products is a minor issue, the niche strategy offers a safer route to establishing a foothold in the industry. Tim Bernard, the owner of a drive-line transmission repair service in Boise, Idaho, is an avid on- and off-road motorcycle rider. Some of his rider group approached him about designing and making heavy-duty luggage racks for their bikes. Because he had the skills and the machinery from his business, he decided to give it a try. He created another company, Happy Trails Products, and began selling accessories to riders nationwide, primarily through word-of-mouth. He claims that his biggest successes have been creating products that his customers asked him to make. He now enjoys a niche in the market and a loyal list of customers.[6]

The important thing to remember about niche creation is that it gives a new venture time to define and "own" a segment of the market. Working in a niche gives the company time to develop, to become stronger and better able to compete against companies in the mainstream market. However, niche strategies can fail when the costs to serve the niche exceed the size of the market, so it is important to choose an appropriate niche. Niches, by their very nature, are small and usually serve to provide only an entry strategy, not a sustainable strategy for long-term viability.

Forecasting New Product/Service Demand

One of the most difficult tasks facing the entrepreneur is forecasting the demand for the new product or service, particularly if that product or service has never existed previously in the marketplace. Much of this difficulty is due to the lack of historical data and to issues of seasonality and price discounts. Because entrepreneurs often overestimate the level of sales they will achieve in the early stages of the company, it is important to triangulate demand from three different points of view: historical analogy, prospective end-users and intermediaries, and the entrepreneur's own perspective, gleaned from going into limited production or doing a formal test market. A number of different techniques can help entrepreneurs arrive at a realistic forecast of demand.

Use Historical Analogy or Substitute Products

If the new product is an extension of a previously existing product, it may be possible to extrapolate from that product's adoption rate and demand to the new product. For example, the demand and adoption rate for compact disks were derived from the historical demand for cassette tapes and records. In other cases, it may be possible to turn to another product in the same industry for an indication of demand potential and the rate at which customers will purchase, assuming that the target markets are the same.

Interview Prospective End-Users and Intermediaries

No one knows the market better than the men and women who work in it every day. They are typically very astute at predicting trends and patterns of buyer behavior. Spending time in the field talking with customers, intermediaries (distributors or wholesalers, sometimes referred to as "middlemen"), retailers, and the like can provide a fairly good estimate of demand.

Go into Limited Production

Sometimes the only way to test the reaction of potential customers is to produce a small number of products and put them in the hands of people to test. This is also an appropriate next step if the first two techniques have produced positive results. Not only will limited testing of the product gauge customer satisfaction; it may also suggest possible modifications to improve the product. These samples of the product are called prototypes. Prototypes are generally associated with product companies, but service businesses must also develop a prototype of the operation or procedures involved in delivering the service. Prototyping permits the testing of a product or service in the actual environment in which it will be used. It is difficult to conduct meaningful market research without a working prototype, because most potential customers need to see and use the actual product before they can become enthusiastic about it. Construction of a prototype will also facilitate estimating the costs to produce the product for distribution later on. Prototyping is discussed in more depth in Chapter 6, which focuses on product development.

Do a Formal Test Market

When a product is fairly complex and expensive to produce, a formal test market in a selected geographic area can provide valuable information about demand for and acceptance of the product before substantial capital is spent for a major product roll-out. The movie industry regularly introduces new movies with a "limited release" in a few strategic theaters. In this way, film companies can gauge audiences' reactions and make changes based on them before releasing the film nationwide. Major product companies such as Procter & Gamble often put a new product into certain geographic test markets, such as Denver, Colorado, to get feedback from customers. (Many a new product has met an early death as a result of these test market studies.)

In addition to all the benefits discussed in this chapter, completing an in-depth industry and market analysis will prepare an entrepreneur to make more effective decisions about product/service design, which is the subject of the next chapter.

New Venture Checklist

Have you:

☐ Identified the NAICS code for the industry in which the new venture will operate?

☐ Collected secondary data on the industry?

☐ Conducted field research by interviewing suppliers, distributors, customers, and others?

☐ Developed an industry profile that will indicate whether the industry is growing, who the major competitors are, and what the profit potential is?

☐ Defined the target market for the product or service?

☐ Listed the information needed to do the market analysis?

☐ Researched secondary data sources such as census data on demographics?

☐ Determined the most effective method for gathering primary data on the target market?

☐ Estimated demand for the product or service?

Issues to Consider

1. Which primary and secondary information will tell you whether the industry is growing and favorable to new entrants?
2. What kind of information can suppliers and distributors provide?
3. How should an entry strategy be determined? What factors should be considered?
4. What is the value of defining a market niche?
5. Suppose you are introducing a new type of exercise equipment to the fitness industry. What types of research methods would you use to forecast demand, and why?

Experiencing Entrepreneurship

1. Choose an industry that interests you. Create a status report using the Internet, Lexis/Nexis, current periodicals, and interviews with people in the industry. In your estimation, is this an industry that has a great potential for new business opportunities? If so, where do those opportunities lie?

2. Pick a product or service, and formulate a plan for researching the customer. Identify what information needs to be collected and how to collect it. Justify the plan.

Additional Sources of Information

Day, G.S. (1999). *Market Driven Strategy: Processes for Creating Value*. New York: Free Press.

Gilad, B. (2003). *Early Warning: Using Competitive Intelligence to Anticipate Market Shifts, Control Risk, and Create Powerful Strategies*. New York: AMACOM.

Hague, P., and P. Jackson (1999). *Market Research: A Guide to Planning, Methodology and Research*. London: Kogen Page.

Miller, J.P. (2000). *Millennium Intelligence: Understanding and Conducting Competitive Intelligence in the Digital Age*. Medford, NJ: CyberAge Books.

Porter, M. (1980). *Competitive Strategy: Techniques for Analyzing Industries and Competitors*. New York: Free Press.

Porter, M. (1985). *Competitive Advantage*. New York: Free Press.

Relevant Case Studies

Case 1 Overnite Express, p. 402

Case 2 Craigslist, p. 407

Case 4 Beanos Ice Cream Shoppe, p. 423

Case 5 iRobot, p. 432

Case 8 Finagle a Bagel, p. 450

Analyzing Product/Service Risks and Benefits

"When each thing is unique in itself, there can be no comparison made."

D.H. Lawrence, British author

LEARNING OBJECTIVES

- Discuss the nature of product/process development.

- Differentiate the way entrepreneurs develop products from the way they develop services.

- Describe the product development cycle.

- Explain the process of intellectual-property development.

Profile 6.1   WHEN PROPRIETARY RIGHTS BITE

Johnny's Selected Seeds has been in business in Winslow, Maine, since 1973. In 1995, when the Internet was just catching the attention of retailers, Rob Johnston, Johnny's CEO, hired a Web developer to build an e-commerce site to promote and sell his seeds to gardening enthusiasts and commercial customers. Much to his surprise, his company was hit with a lawsuit for patent infringement by Divine Inc., a Chicago-based software and technology services company that claimed ownership of the shopping-cart technology that Johnny's was using. Divine Inc. wanted a one-time licensing fee of $20,000 or 1 percent of Johnny's Internet sales. Although Johnston didn't believe that the claim would hold up in court, at revenues of $10 million annually he couldn't afford to spend approximately $1 million to defend his rights. In January 2003 he negotiated a settlement with Divine—unfortunately, one month too soon. In late February 2003, because a number of its acquisitions had gone bad, Divine Inc. voluntarily filed for bankruptcy protection under Chapter 11 reorganization. An auction in May 2003 saw its assets divided by four bidders.

Johnston's case is not unique. PanIP, a San Diego technology development company, has sued 51 companies for activities like having a website that gathers financial data such as credit card information. PanIP claims that it is not in the business of filing lawsuits; it is simply trying to protect its intellectual property. Still, for small business owners, one lawsuit can be a devastating financial blow. To fight back, a group of 15 defendants in the PanIP case have banded together to create a joint legal defense. However, most of the small businesses being sued are settling because, even after banding together, they still can't afford the high litigation costs. You can find more information about this case and others at www.youmaybenext.com.

Other entrepreneurs are being proactive about the situation, recognizing that intellectual-property rights in the form of patents and trademarks have become bargaining chips for those that hold them. Scott Jordan founded Scott eVest LLC in 2002 to demonstrate the feasibility of technology-enabled clothing. He filed a patent on his 17-pocket vest that holds every kind of electronic gadget imaginable. His goal is to license his technology to clothing manufacturers, and he is prepared to spend whatever it takes to defend his patent should he receive it. Today, more than ever before, it is important for entrepreneurs to be aware of intellectual property, to secure as much protection as possible, and to make certain they are not infringing on someone else's intellectual-property rights.

Sources: Elaine Pofeldt, "Small e-Tailers Get Squeezed by Questionable IP Claims," *Fortune Small Business* (March 4, 2003), www.fortune.com; Barbara Rose, "Filipowski Not Among Bidders at Divine's Auction," *Chicago Tribune Online* (May 2003), www.chicagotribune.com; and Jef Bailey, "How Some Small Firms Are Fighting Off Giants," *Wall Street Journal—Startup Journal* (July 2002), www.startupjournal.com.

Putting the customer at the center of the business is a persistent theme throughout this book, particularly when a new product or service is being developed. Every business—large or small, product or service—is involved in product/service development at every stage of its life cycle. Each time a new product or service or an improvement on an existing product or service is introduced, it will have gone through a design and development process. Moreover, new products and services create assets for a business that need to be protected, so it is essential that entrepreneurs understand the process of protecting those assets. Every business has intellectual property, or protectable assets, that can be leveraged to compete in the marketplace and generate new sources of revenue.

On a sleepless night in 1957, Gordon Gould conceived the idea for the laser. He wrote down all his thoughts, sketched the design and its components, and forecasted future uses. He had a notary witness, sign, and date his notebook in anticipation of applying for intellectual-property protection in the form of a patent. But then he made a critical mistake. Thinking that he had to build a working model of the laser before filing for a patent, he went to work for Technical Research Group Inc. (TRG) to begin the development of laser applications. In the meantime, a pair of scientists, Charles Townes and Arthur Schawlow, had filed for a patent on the optical maser (it used microwave energy instead of light, as Gould's did), and it would be considered the true laser patent for many years. Gould spent the next 30 years of his life battling the Patent and Trademark Office before he could finally lay claim to one of the most important inventions of all time. His laser applications are used in 80 percent of the industrial, commercial, and medical applications of lasers. Had Gordon Gould understood the patent process, he might have saved himself years of struggle.

Product development and intellectual-property development are closely intertwined. This chapter describes the product/service development process from an entrepreneur's perspective and discusses how to protect the various assets created from the process: patents, copyrights, trademarks, and trade secrets.

The Nature of Product/Process Development

International Competition

Since the 1980s, the number of companies competing in the global marketplace has increased enormously. Coupled with the fact that most new products are derivatives of something that already exists, this means that an intensely competitive arena for product development has emerged. Moreover, United States companies find they are no longer competing only with U.S. firms; now, they must also compete with companies from diverse regions of the world who put their own stamp on processes and products. This volatile environment actually is good news for entrepreneurs who realize that the most innovative new products emerge when uncertainty, risk, and ambiguity are high.[1] In these environments, small companies often shine because of their high degree of flexibility and ability to respond quickly.

Sophisticated Customers in Fragmented Markets

Today's customers can differentiate products on a very subtle level; therefore, they demand products that reflect their individual lifestyles and value systems. Thus product developers must create offerings that distinguish themselves on many levels in the marketplace. Whereas product performance and price were the main competitive measures in the past, today these two factors are givens. A company must offer superior performance and value-based pricing to even begin to be competitive. This means that a manufacturing company can never stop improving its design and manufacturing processes, and a service company must continually find ways to improve its delivery methods and customer service.

The Impact of Technology

Technology is essential to product/service development, and today the marginal cost of added technological capability is small. Yet a growing business cannot build its competitive advantage around technology alone. Customers are primarily interested in a product that will meet a need or desire; they are not necessarily interested in the technological processes that produced it. Often a customer is not willing to pay for extra technology just because it's readily available.

A company operating in a technology-based industry such as electronics must keep up with changing consumer demand as well as with the technological innovations of its competitors. A competitive advantage can be built around a line of market-differentiated products, but it must be enhanced by proprietary processes. A new product not only must create value for the customer but also must be difficult for someone else to produce at the same quality level and for the same cost.

Technology has also shortened product life cycles. Whereas 50 years ago a new tool product had a life cycle of 18 years and a new game or toy a life cycle of 16 years, today those life cycles have shrunk to 5 years.[2] Consequently, companies must always be researching and developing new products and improving existing ones to stay ahead of the competition. The same can be said of service companies. New products often create the need for new services to support them. Even fundamental services such as advertising, consulting, and food services are affected by shrinking development life cycles. Customers expect service entrepreneurs to provide new and innovative services more rapidly and at lower costs. As a result, the fast-food industry continues to grow; even grocery stores have gotten into the game with an increasing number of convenience food offerings, such as packaged salads and reheatable fresh meals. In addition, with e-mail and the Internet ubiquitous throughout the professional services industry, customers now expect much shorter response times on correspondence and document preparation.

How Entrepreneurs Develop Products and Services

A 2003 study of The Conference Board found that large companies had an increasing interest in innovation strategies. This study of 104 companies with sales over $1 billion in the United States and Europe found that 90 percent of the companies considered innovation "integral to current strategic goals," and 83 percent expected it to spur strong top-line growth for their companies. This is not innovation solely for innovation's sake, but innovation to produce new sources of revenues for the company.[3] What does this mean for these company's smaller entrepreneurial counterparts? Entrepreneurial ventures typically don't like to play by other companies' rules, but if they are operating in a business environment where the major players are spending a great deal on new product development, they will need to have a product development strategy in place in order to compete successfully in their own niches.

Most large corporations have separate departments responsible for research and development, engineering, and testing. In many cases, the budgets for these departments are astronomical, because new product development and the continual improvement of existing products and processes are among the most important and challenging tasks of high-performing, world-class businesses.

In the case of start-up ventures, the task is equally challenging; however, most new ventures, unlike large corporations, have very limited or nonexistent budgets for product development. Investors frequently consider research and development, engineering, and testing to be the highest-risk stages for new companies, so funding for these activities is difficult, if not impossible, to secure. Entrepreneurs are left with a dilemma: how to perform the research and development (R&D) that will result in a high-quality, engineered prototype as quickly and as inexpensively as possible. A lack of sufficient new product development (NPD) resources has many unintended consequences, which are discussed in the next section.

The Impact of Insufficient Resources

Whether in large, established companies or in small entrepreneurial ventures, new product development typically suffers from severe resource deficiencies that result in too much time to market, poor project performance, and meager value creation. One of the biggest sources of insufficient resources is, surprisingly, too many projects—in other words, a lack of focus. Typically, this happens when the entrepreneur throws a lot of projects into a market, hoping that one will stick. Then the entrepreneur doesn't want to let go of the project because money has already been spent (even though these monies represent sunk costs). There is no mechanism for stopping or killing projects in place, so old, useless projects carry on. As illustrated in Figure 6.1, a lack of resources focused on NPD results in six common problems.[4]

1. *Poor execution.* The critical due diligence and market analysis required to ensure a successful product launch are often shortened or bypassed in favor of speed. Approximately 75 percent of NPD projects don't include vital market research.[5]

2. *Time-to-market increases.* When a new venture lacks sufficient resources, bottlenecks and backups tend to occur because people aren't getting around to doing the work, and when the work *is* done, it must often be redone because it was done in haste. Overall execution is generally poor.

FIGURE 6.1   The Consequences of Resource Shortfalls for New Product Development

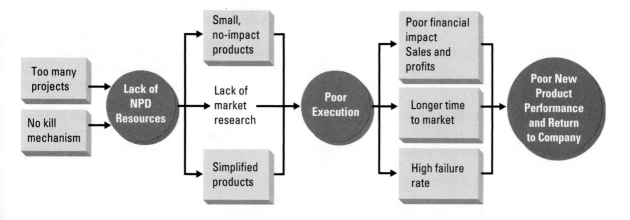

3. *First-to-market opportunities are missed.* Poor execution results in missed opportunities to enter the market at a quiet time without immediate competition. Also, because these "game changer" opportunities often require more resources than less risky initiatives, they are often bypassed in favor of incremental opportunities that are easier and can be done quickly at a much lower cost. Unfortunately, these kinds of opportunities provide little value or return to the company, and in fact, the returns continue to diminish until the company finally decides to change the game with a truly innovative project.

4. *Projects are made simpler so that more can be done with less.* The dumbing-down of projects is another consequence of resource scarcity. Where resources are limited, product features and benefits are often sacrificed in order to get more products out.

5. *Team morale declines.* The combination of a lack of resources and increasing time pressure causes morale problems on product development teams and a sense that the team must accomplish the impossible.[6] Although members of the team are often willing to get the job done, more frequently the stressful environment saps their morale.

Entrepreneurs can avoid a shortage of resources by carefully planning their product development strategy so as to focus on projects that are closest to the company's core competency and will bring the company closer to its primary goal. Entrepreneurs also have to learn how to say no to opportunity when it threatens to stretch the company's resources too thin and endanger other activities. Some resources should be dedicated to new product development to keep the company competitive, but the mantra should be "fewer but better new product projects."

New Product Failure

Despite all the benefits that have accrued to new product development through the advent of information and systems technologies, the probability of success at launch is still about 60 percent.[7] Figure 6.2 depicts the classic new product development process and illustrates the high failure rate of new product ideas as they move through the process.

A significant body of research has revealed that the principal reason for new product failure is lack of good market analysis. Entrepreneurs with a "build it and they will come" attitude fail to consider that the only way to know what customers really want is to talk with them. The second biggest cause of new product failure is technical problems. The path from laboratory to production is fraught with challenges and obstacles, often because the company has moved too rapidly through the design and early prototyping phase. Some recent research suggests that one overlooked cause of new product failure is the human factor.[8] The very early stages of the NPD process typically involve one person with an idea. If that person's level of creative thought, tolerance for risk, and commitment to doing thorough market research is not sufficient, a viable project may be doomed to failure. It is only in the later stages of development that teams typically form around new product projects that seem feasible.

| FIGURE 6.2 | The New Product Development Success Curve |

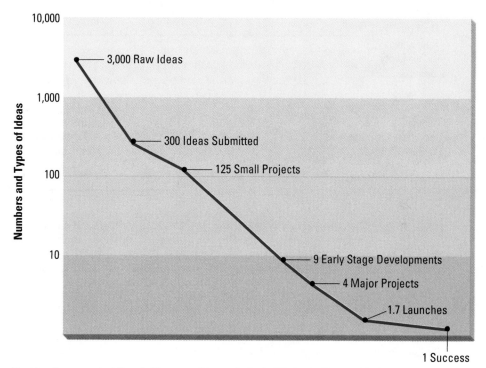

Based on the research of Greg A. Stevens and James Burley in "Piloting the Rocket of Radical Innovation," *Research Technology Management,* 46(2):16–26.

Competing Effectively in Product Development

There are ways for entrepreneurial firms to compete effectively in the area of product development. In fact, the new environment for product development is uniquely suited to smaller companies, which are often better able to adapt to change and move quickly in new directions. Three fundamental strategies should be incorporated into any entrepreneur's product development program to enhance the chances of competing effectively: (1) design products right the first time, (2) shorten the time-to-market, and (3) outsource some product development tasks. These strategies will be discussed in the next section.

The Product Development Cycle

Entrepreneurs who develop products usually go through a process much like that shown in Figure 6.3. The **product development cycle** consists of a series of tasks leading to introduction of the product in the marketplace. Although it appears to be a linear process, it is actually quite iterative with multiple feedback loops. A summary of the components of this process follows.

FIGURE 6.3   From Idea to Market

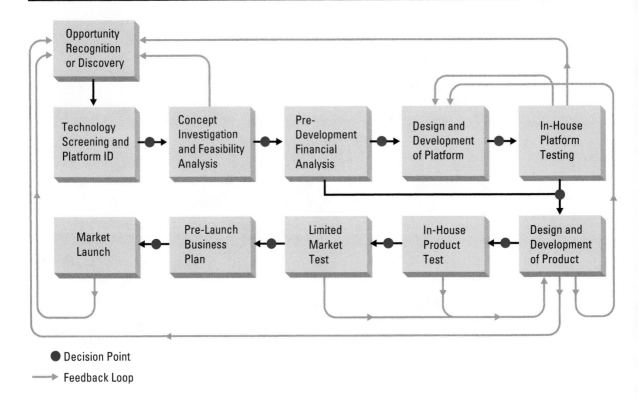

● Decision Point

→ Feedback Loop

Opportunity Recognition: Recall from Chapter 3 that the first stage in the development of a business concept is opportunity recognition: identifying a niche that has not been served, detecting a potential improvement in an existing product, or seeing an opportunity for a breakthrough product. Often inventors (who are not always entrepreneurs) have an idea for a product or a technology without any thought to who might use the invention and in what manner.

Concept Investigation and Feasibility Analysis: **Concept investigation** is simply doing some preliminary research to determine whether the product or service idea currently exists, whether there is a potential market, how much it will cost to produce the product, and how much time it will take.

Design and Development of Platform: The first stages of design preparation go hand in hand with concept investigation, because planners normally need some preliminary working drawings of the product in order to estimate costs and manufacturing processes. These preliminary drawings are also used to apply for a patent if the product is patentable. The **platform** is the core product or technology from which other products or applications can be developed.

Prototype Building and Field Testing: From the initial engineered drawings will come the **prototype** or model of the product. Often the first prototype does not closely resemble the final product in appearance, but it usually does in function. Physical prototypes are helpful in the following ways:

Communicating the form, fit, and function of the device

Providing an example to a vendor for quotation

Facilitating quick changes in a design

Designing the correct tooling (devices that hold a product component in place during manufacturing and assembly)

Small engineering firms or solo engineers who support entrepreneurs and inventors; small job shops; and machine shops or model builders may be used to complete the prototype. These sources are normally quicker and less expensive than the larger, better-known firms. When seeking an engineer or a model builder, one must use caution and check out their qualifications, experience, and references relative to the task required of them. A major university engineering department is a good source of referrals, as are other engineers.

Businesses that do not manufacture products—service, retail, wholesale, and so forth—still need to design a prototype, but the prototype in this case will not always be physical. Instead it will be a design or flowchart for how the business will provide a service or product to its customer. For example, a restaurant entrepreneur will design the layout of the restaurant and kitchen with an eye to how customers and servers move through the restaurant. The food preparation area will need to be laid out efficiently so that the chef and cooks can work quickly and do not have to move great distances to retrieve cooking utensils and food items. Every activity the restaurant undertakes should be prototyped to ensure that there is no duplication of effort and that each task is performed as efficiently and effectively as possible.

Initial Market Tests: With a working prototype of near production quality, it is possible to field-test it with potential users in environments where the product will typically be used. For example, it would be important to put a new construction tool in the hands of construction workers on real jobs in the field. In this way, the company can collect feedback based on actual use in real-life situations.

The number of prototypes used in the field-testing stage is normally limited, because the cost per unit is much higher (as much as ten times higher) than it will be when the company is in normal production. This is because the company will not yet be meeting its suppliers' volume levels for discounts. After conducting a small initial test production run in a limited market, the entrepreneur can go back and fine-tune the product to completion and market-ready status. This is also the first opportunity to test the manufacturing and assembly processes and determine accurate costs of production at varying levels of volume.

Product Market Introduction and Ramp-Up: The achievement of a production-quality prototype—one that has specifications that can be replicated in a manufacturing and assembly process—is a major milestone in the product development process, because the company now has a product that can be sold in the marketplace. During the final phases of developing this production-quality product, other aspects of the feasibility analysis have been completed.

TABLE 6.1	New Product Checklist

	YES	NO	PERHAPS
THE MARKET			
Is there an existing need for this product in the marketplace?	_____	_____	_____
Will I be first in the marketplace with this product?	_____	_____	_____
Can the product be protected legally?	_____	_____	_____
Can entry barriers be erected?	_____	_____	_____
SWOT ANALYSIS (STRENGTHS, WEAKNESSES, OPPORTUNITIES, AND THREATS)			
Do the strengths of this product exceed any weaknesses?	_____	_____	_____
Are there various opportunities for commercializing this product?	_____	_____	_____
Do any significant threats exist to the development of this product?	_____	_____	_____
DESIGN/DEVELOPMENT/MANUFACTURING			
Is the product innovative?	_____	_____	_____
Can it be developed quickly to market-ready state?	_____	_____	_____
Can it be easily manufactured?	_____	_____	_____
Do I have the resources to manufacture the product?	_____	_____	_____
Is it more practical to subcontract the manufacturing?	_____	_____	_____
Is there a possibility for spin-off products?	_____	_____	_____
FINANCIAL			
Is the return on this investment sufficient to justify the effort?	_____	_____	_____
Are the development costs within reason?	_____	_____	_____
Will it be possible to minimize the manufacturing investment through outsourcing, while still maintaining quality and control?	_____	_____	_____
Is the money needed to produce the product available?	_____	_____	_____

Now it will be important to consider manufacturing and assembly needs and whether to manufacture in-house or outsource. Table 6.1 gives a checklist for assessing the feasibility of new products.

Outsourcing Product Development

It is becoming more and more common for entrepreneurs with both large and small companies to outsource all or part of their product development to third parties. The decision is due in large part to today's requirements for fast-paced innovation with shorter windows of opportunity. Most start-up companies don't have the resources to do adequate product development in-house. And there is no reason why it should be done this way when it is possible to reduce risk, lower costs, and decrease cycle times by factors of 60–90 percent by **outsourcing product development.**[9] Outsourcing provides a young firm with a network of expertise that it couldn't afford to hire in-house.

Some of the areas of product development that require engineering analysis, design, and expertise and are suitable for outsourcing are component design,

Six Elements Crucial to Successful Product Realization

Going from an idea to a commercial product is not easy. Here are the top six elements you must have in place to be successful:

1. A multidisciplinary team that works well together
2. Excellent communication skills that help you communicate ideas, information, and data both verbally and in written form
3. The ability to design for manufacture effectively by reducing the number of parts needed, developing modular designs, and designing multi-functional parts
4. Computer-aided design systems (CAD) that enable you to design product specifications by creating images and then assigning mass, kinematics, material, geometry, and many other properties to the product
5. Ethical standards of conduct on the part of both the industry and the team
6. Creative thinking that lets the team make new connections and expand the scope of opportunities

Based on a presentation at the 1996 National Design Engineering Conference by three members of the PRP Project: Donovan G. Evans, Hug R. Mackenzie, and Christian Przirembel, http://www.prosci .com/prp1.htm.

materials specifications, machinery to process, ergonomic design, packaging design, assembly drawings and specifications, parts and material sourcing (suppliers), and operator's and owner's manuals.

When using other companies to do part or all of the product development, it is important to understand that they work with many other companies, so no single company will be a high priority for them. That's why it's important to plan well in advance and allow extra time for delays that strategic partners might cause in the time-to-market plan. If time-to-market is the most critical factor in a business's success, it may want to consider doing tasks that could delay the process in-house rather than outsourcing them and being dependent on someone else's time schedule. It is also a good idea to help suppliers and **original equipment manufacturers (OEMs)** understand that the partnership will be a win-win relationship, so they have a vested interest in seeing it succeed. Contracts should be drawn up with every consultant, original equipment manufacturer, or vendor with whom the company does business so that there will be no confusion about what is expected and needed. During the process, it is vital to stay in touch with outsource vendors and to be available to answer questions as they arise.

Intellectual Property

Developing a new product creates an asset that must be protected. If the product is a unique device, a unique process or service, or another type of proprietary item, it may qualify for **intellectual property rights.** These are the group of legal rights associated with patents, trademarks, copyrights, and trade secrets. Every business, no matter how small, has intellectual property rights associated with it: a trademark on the name of the business or a product name, copyrights on advertising design, patents on a device the entrepreneur has invented, or trade secrets such as the company's customer list.

In the growing knowledge economy, where intellectual assets are often more valuable than physical assets, the recognition and protection of intellectual-property rights are gaining increasing importance. Any entrepreneur needs to understand what those rights are, not only to protect his or her property but also to avoid infringing on the rights of others. The rest of this section provides an overview of the various rights under intellectual-property law and how they can be used to gain a competitive advantage.

Patents

If a new venture opportunity relies on a product or device of some sort, it is especially important that the entrepreneur investigate applying for a **patent,** which is the primary means of protecting an original invention. A patent gives the patent holder the right to defend the patent against others who would attempt to manufacture, use, or sell the invention during the period of the patent. At the end of the patent life, the invention is placed in public domain, which means that anyone can use any aspect of the device the inventor created without paying royalties to the inventor.

The U.S. patent system was designed 200 years ago by Thomas Jefferson. Its purpose was to provide a brief legal monopoly to give the inventor an opportunity to get the invention into the market and recoup development costs before competitors entered the market. Since the first patent was issued in 1790, more than five million U.S. patents have been granted.

Today, although most inventors work in the research departments of large corporations and 80 percent of all patents come from large companies, the basic legal tenets of patent law still protect the interests of the independent inventor. And in cases where large corporations have infringed on those interests, the courts have generally sided with the independent inventor. In a further effort to support the small inventor, the Patent Office recently created the Office of the Independent Inventor to handle the 20 percent of patents submitted by independent inventors. (See the Additional Sources of Information section at the end of this chapter.)

Is the Invention Patentable?

Before filing for a patent on an invention that the entrepreneur believes to be unique, he or she should consider the USPTO's four basic criteria that the invention must meet before it can be patented.

The invention must fit into one of the five classes established by Congress:

1. Machine or something with moving parts or circuitry (fax, rocket, photocopier, laser, electronic circuit)
2. Process or method for producing a useful and tangible result (chemical reaction, method for producing products, business method)
3. Article of manufacture (furniture, transistor, diskette, toy)
4. Composition of matter (gasoline, food additive, drug, genetically altered lifeform)
5. A new use or improvement for one of the above that does not infringe on the patents associated with them

Many inventions can be classified into more than one category. That does not present a problem, however, because the inventor does not have to decide into which category the invention fits. In fact, the Supreme Court of the United States has stated that "anything under the sun that is made by man" falls into the statutory subject matter (*Diamond v. Chakrabarty*, 1980).[10]

With this definition, it may appear that anything can receive a patent, but in fact, there are some exclusions. Laws and phenomena of nature, naturally occurring substances, abstract mathematical formulas, and mere ideas are not eligible to be patented. However, alterations to something found in nature, such as genetically enhanced corn, can be considered for a patent. In *Diamond v. Chakrabarty*, Chakrabarty engineered a bacterium that broke down components of crude oil. No such bacterium existed in nature; thus the Court ruled that this bacterium was the product of human ingenuity and could be patented.

*The invention must have **utility**; in other words, it must be useful.* This is not usually a problem unless the invention is something like an unsafe drug or something purely "whimsical," although the USPTO has been known to issue patents on some fairly strange inventions, such as a laser beam to motivate cats to exercise (Patent No. 5,443,036, Aug. 22, 1995). The utility must be a reality, not merely speculation, and must be described in the patent application.

*The invention must not contain **prior art**; that is, it must be new or novel in some important way.* Prior art is knowledge that is publicly available or was published prior to the date of the invention—that is, before the filing of the patent application. This means that an invention can't be patented if it was known or used by others, patented, or described in a printed publication before a patent was applied for. Accordingly, it is important to document everything that is done during the creation of the invention. Also, the invention must not have become public or available for sale more than one year prior to the inventor's filing the patent application. This rule is meant to ensure that the invention is still novel at the time of application. Novelty consists of physical differences, new combinations of components, or new uses. There are two levels of challenge to novelty: statutory and anticipatory. If the invention is published or used in an unconcealed manner either in the United States or in another country, the inventor is statutorily barred from seeking a patent. Furthermore, if the patent is substantially similar to an existing patent, the inventor may not seek a patent because in this case, the patent was anticipated.

The invention must not be obvious to someone with ordinary skills in the field. This is a tricky criterion, but it has been further explained by the USPTO as meaning that the invention must contain "new and unexpected results." That is, the invention should not be the next logical step for someone knowledgeable in the field. Obviousness is one of the most common reasons why patent applications are rejected.

If all the requirements for patentability have been met, then the type of patent most appropriate for the invention should be considered. There are two major categories of patents: utility patents and design patents.

Utility Patents

Utility patents are the most common type of patent. They protect the functional part of machines or processes. Some examples are toys, film processing, protective coatings, tools, and cleaning implements. Software qualifies for patent protection if it produces a useful and tangible result. For example, the USPTO will not issue a utility patent on a mathematical formula used in space navigation, but it may on software that translates equations and makes a rocket take off.[11] (Copyrights, discussed in a later section, are commonly used for software programs that don't qualify for a patent.) A utility patent is valid for 20 years from the date of application.

Design Patents

Design patents protect new, original ornamental designs for manufactured articles. A design patent protects only the appearance of an article, not its structure or utilitarian features.[12] The design must be nonfunctional and part of the tangible item for which it is designed. It cannot be hidden or offensive or simulate a well-known or naturally occurring object or person. Some examples of items that can receive design patents are gilding, an item of apparel, and jewelry. Inventors should be aware that although design patents are relatively easy to obtain, they are very hard to protect. It is not difficult to modify a design patent without infringing on the original patent. Design patents are valid for 14 years from date of issuance.

Business Method Patents

The 1990s saw the advent of the **business method patent,** which arose out of the need of Internet companies to protect their ways of doing business. The rush to patent business methods all started with one click—that is, the single click of a mouse that enables a user to order a book from Amazon.com. That one click tells Amazon to charge the purchase, take the book from its warehouse shelves, and send it to the purchaser. Jeff Bezos, Amazon's founder, thought the concept was so original that he decided to patent it. And in September 1999, the PTO granted him U.S. Patent No. 5,960,411, "method and system for placing a purchase order via a communications network." Bezos followed that success with a lawsuit in U.S. District Court in Seattle for patent infringement against Barnes & Noble (*Amazon.com v. Barnesandnoble.com,* 73F. Supp. 2 1228 [W.D. Wash. 1999]). In December 1999, a federal judge issued an injunction against Barnes & Noble to stop it from using its version of the "One-Click" process, but in February 2001, a federal appeals court overturned the lower court's ruling because it "raised substantial questions as to the validity" of Amazon.com's patent.[13] In fact, the prior art discovered suggests that both Barnesandnoble.com and Amazon.com may be entangled in litigation for some time to come.

Although the Amazon case opened the floodgates for business method patents, it was actually the ruling in *State Street Bank & Trust Co. v. Signature Financial Group,* 149 F.3d 1360, that first allowed patents for business models in 1998. Priceline.com quickly followed in the wake of Amazon, filing a patent for its reverse-auction process. Since that time, much controversy has surrounded the method patent. *Business method* is actually a generic term to describe a variety of process claims, and as of this writing, the courts have not yet defined what differentiates a business method claim from a process claim. Thus business method claims are treated like any other process claim.[14] On March 29, 2000, the Patent Office issued a statement that the business method patent will cover only fundamentally different ways of doing business and that the embedded process must produce a useful, tangible, and concrete result.[15]

The process for applying for any of these patents is well defined by the USPTO and is discussed in the next section.

The Patent Process

Although the USPTO has described the process clearly on its website (www.uspto .gov), it is always a good idea to seek the counsel of an intellectual-property attorney. An attorney who specializes in intellectual property can increase the chances of moving successfully through the USPTO application process. The following sections outline that process as an introduction and guide.

File a Disclosure Document

One very important way in which inventors protect their inventions at the earliest stages of conceptualization is to take advantage of the USPTO's **Disclosure Document Program.** The purpose of a disclosure document is to serve as evidence of the date of conception of an invention. This statement is crucial if it turns out that two inventors are working on the same idea at the same time. The one who files the disclosure document first has the right to file for a patent. However, filing a disclosure statement does not in any way "diminish the value of the conventional, witnessed, permanently bound, and page-numbered laboratory notebook or notarized records as evidence of conception of an invention."[16] Furthermore, a disclosure document is not a patent application, so the date of its receipt at the USPTO will not be the effective filing date of any patent application an inventor might subsequently file.[17]

The disclosure document contains a detailed description of the invention and its uses and may include sketches and photos such that a person of "ordinary knowledge in the field of the invention" could make and use the invention.[18] The USPTO will keep the document in confidence for two years, and the inventor has that two-year period in which to file a patent application. Even so, she or he must demonstrate diligence in completing the invention and filing the application to maintain the right to first filing for a patent.

Many people are under the mistaken impression that mailing a dated description of the invention to themselves by certified mail is as good as filing a disclosure document. Do not use this tactic because it has no value to the Patent Office.

File a Provisional Patent

A **provisional patent** is a way for inventors to undertake a first patent filing in the United States at a lower cost than a formal patent application. It is legally more powerful than a disclosure document, allows the inventor to use the term *patent pending,* and is designed to protect the small inventor while he or she speaks with manufacturers about producing the invention. A provisional patent also puts U.S. applicants on a par with foreign applicants under the General Agreement on Tariffs and Trade (GATT) Uruguay Round Agreements (see the discussion in the section on foreign patents). The provisional patent does not, however, take the place of a formal patent application, which is discussed in the next section.

The term of the provisional patent is 12 months from the date of filing, and it cannot be extended. This means that the inventor must file a nonprovisional (formal) patent application during that period. The 12-month period does not count toward the 20-year term for a nonprovisional patent. Because the 20-year clock starts with the filing of the formal patent application, the provisional patent effectively extends patent protection by 1 year.

The invention disclosure in the provisional patent application should clearly and completely describe the invention so that someone with knowledge of invention could make and use it. If a nonprovisional application is not filed within the 12-month period, the provisional application is considered abandoned, and the entrepreneur loses the ability to claim the nonprovisional date of application as the date of invention.

File a Nonprovisional Patent Application

The **nonprovisional patent** application is required for any patent, whether or not the entrepreneur previously filed a provisional patent application, and it extends for 20 years from the date of filing. The patent application contains a complete description of the invention, what it does, how it is uniquely different from anything currently existing (including prior art), and its scope. It also includes detailed drawings, explanations, and engineering specifications such that a person of ordinary skill in the same field could build the invention from the information provided.

The **claims** section of the application specifies the parts of the invention on which the inventor wants patents and must include at least one claim that attests to its novelty, utility, and nonobviousness. The claim serves to define the scope of patent protection; whether the USPTO grants the patent is largely determined by the wording of the claims. The claims must be specific enough to demonstrate the invention's uniqueness but broad enough to make it difficult for others to circumvent the patent—that is, to modify the invention slightly without violating the patent and then duplicate the product.

For example, suppose an entrepreneur attempts to patent a new type of rapid prototyping device. If the patent application defines the invention for use in prototyping of machine components, that would be a narrow definition. Another inventor could conceivably patent the invention for a new use, such as creating artificial bone, for example. That's why it is important to define the claims as broadly as possible to include as many potential applications as can be identified. Drafting a claim is an art, so it's a good idea to hire an intellectual-property attorney to draft the patent application.

Once it has received the application, the USPTO will conduct a search of its patent records for prior art. The Patent Office then contacts the inventor to either accept or deny the application claims and, in the case of denial, gives the inventor a period of time to appeal or modify the claim. It is not uncommon for the original claims to be rejected in their entirety by the USPTO, usually due to the existence of prior art, but often because of lack of nonobviousness. It will then be the job of the inventor's attorney to rewrite the claims and resubmit the revised application for another review.

If and when the Patent Office accepts the modified claims, the invention enters the patent-pending stage; that is, it awaits the issuance of the patent. The inventor may market and sell the product during this period but must clearly label it "patent pending." Most patent applications filed on or after November 29, 2000, will be published 18 months after the filing date of the application. The USPTO maintains all patent applications in the strictest confidence until the patent is issued or the application is published. Once the patent has been issued, the original application and the patent itself become public record.

If the patent examiner rejects the modified claims again, the inventor has the right to appeal to a Board of Patent Appeals within the Patent Office. Failing to find agreement at this point, the inventor may appeal to the U.S. Court of Appeals for the Federal Circuit. This appeals process may take years.

One thing that many inventors fail to realize is that there are maintenance fees on utility patents that occur at $3\frac{1}{2}$, $7\frac{1}{2}$, and $11\frac{1}{2}$ years from the date the patent is granted. Failure to pay these fees can result in expiration of the patent.

Patent Infringement

Once issued, a patent is a powerful document that gives the holder the right to enforce the patent, in federal court, against infringement. If such a lawsuit is successful, the court may issue an injunction preventing the infringer from making any further use of the invention and award the patent holder a reasonable royalty from the infringer; if the infringer refuses to pay, the patent holder can enjoin or close down the operation of the infringer. Alternatively, the court may mediate an agreement between the parties under which the infringing party will pay royalties to the patent holder in exchange for permission to use the patented invention.

Infringement of patent rights occurs when someone other than the inventor (patent holder) or licensee makes and sells a product that contains every one of the elements of a claim. The Patent Office also protects inventors from infringers who would violate a patent by making small, insignificant changes in the claims. This policy is called the doctrine of equivalents. If, for example, an entrepreneur had a patent on a three-legged wooden chair, and the infringer made the exact same chair but gave it three metal legs, that person would be violating the entrepreneur's patent under the doctrine of equivalents.

Patent infringement actions are costly and difficult to prosecute. Many times, the alleged infringer will defend himself or herself by attempting to prove that the patent is invalid—that is, that the USPTO mistakenly issued the patent. Today, unfortunately, a number of companies regularly challenge their competitors' patents in the courts as a business strategy, as Profile 6.1 illustrates.

Foreign Patents

It is important to remember that the patent rights granted to an individual extend only to the borders of the United States. They have no effect in any foreign country. Because every country has different laws regarding intellectual property, patent attorneys face a real challenge when helping their clients apply for or defend foreign patents.

Two important differences exist between international and U.S. procedures in the areas of first-to-file and novelty.[19] First, the European Patent Convention (EPC) grants patent rights to the first person to file for the patent, whether or not that person is the original inventor. By contrast, in the United States, only the original inventor has the first right to file an application. Second, in the United States, an inventor can sell an invention up to one year before filing a patent application. That is not true in other countries, where publication of any kind before the date of filing will bar the right to a patent. Furthermore, most countries require that the invention be manufactured in the country within three years of the issuance of the foreign patent.

When considering foreign patents, be sure to consult an intellectual-property attorney who specializes in this area. Because of the high cost and effort involved in obtaining foreign patents, it is important to determine whether a reasonable profit can be made from them. Often, it's more valuable to seek solid strategic alliances in other countries, thus obtaining good distribution channels through which to export products, than to spend the time and money seeking patents in every country in which the entrepreneur will do business. Advice from a knowledgeable attorney can make this decision easier.

Trademarks

Trademarks have become nearly as popular as patents as intellectual-property assets. A **trademark** is a symbol, logo, word, sound, color, design, or other device that is used to identify a business or a product in commerce. The term *trademark* is regularly used to refer to both trademarks and service marks, which identify services or intangible activities "performed by one person for the benefit of a person or persons other than himself, either for pay or otherwise."[20] Other, less commonly used types of trademarks can be found at the USPTO website.

Here are some examples of trademarked items:

Logo: McDonald's double arches

http://www.mcdonalds.com/

Slogans: Xerox's "The Document Company"

http://www.xerox.com/

Container shape: Coca-Cola's classic beverage bottle

http://www.coca-cola.com/

Colors can even be trademarked. In the 1995 Supreme Court case *Qualitex Co. v. Jacobson Products Co.,* 115 S.Ct. 1300 (1995), the Court held that the green-gold color of a dry cleaning press pad can be trademarked. To do so, the applicant must be able to demonstrate that the color has a secondary meaning—that is, that people associate the color with the product. For example, pink has been associated with insulation, even though the color has nothing to do with the insulation's function. Colors that are functional in nature cannot be trademarked.

A trademark—with certain conditions—has a longer life than a patent. A business has the exclusive right to a trademark for as long as it is actively using it. However, if a trademark becomes part of the generic language, as have *aspirin* and *thermos,* it can no longer be trademarked. Furthermore, a trademark cannot be registered until it is actually in use. The symbol ® means **"registered trademark."** Before a trademark is registered, the holder of the trademark should file an **intent-to-use application** and place ™ (or ᔆᴹ for services) after the name until the trademark has been registered. This is an important point, because trademarks cannot be stockpiled and then sold to potential users. They must be in use in the market to be protected.

Global Insights

East Meets West in Product Pioneering

It is often helpful to be first to market, but when the market is a global one, is this still the case? There are high costs, both in time and money, associated with penetrating global markets. Being first to a global market is much more difficult than being first to a domestic market. A study conducted at Temple University concluded that product managers from both the East and the West believe that pioneering is a good thing, but for different reasons. Managers in the United States and Western Europe view pioneering as creating a cost advantage, whereas their Asian counterparts see it as facilitating long-term relationships in the distribution channel. That means that being first to the market gives the pioneer an opportunity to establish and cement value chain relationships, something that generally takes a great deal of time. Within both Eastern and Western groups, manufacturing firms see more benefit in higher market share and return on investment than do service firms. The difference may be explained by the fact that it is very difficult to protect a service concept, so the risk of someone copying the concept is higher. Also, operating a service company is less costly than operating a manufacturing business. There appear to be four pioneering advantages that service companies can enjoy: (1) economies of scale and learning curve effects, (2) holding proprietary technical information, (3) locking in the best suppliers, the best market niche, and the best processes, and (4) brand loyalty. In general, studies have shown that a short-term view and an individualistic approach are typical of Western countries and that a long-term view and collectivist approach are typical in the East.

Source: Anthony DiBenedetto, "Comparing How Product Managers in the East and West Look at Product Pioneering," *Visions Magazine* (October 2002), www.pdma.org/visions/.

Registering a Trademark

To register a trademark, one of three methods can be used:

1. If the mark has already been in use, the entrepreneur can file a use application requesting registration and ownership of the mark. Three specimens showing actual use of the mark must also be submitted.
2. If the mark has not yet been in use, an intent-to-use application can be filed. After the mark has been used, the entrepreneur must submit three specimens showing actual use before receiving registration.
3. Depending on international agreements with a specific country, the entrepreneur can file on the basis of having a trademark in another country.

The USPTO does not require a search for potentially conflicting marks prior to filing the application. However, it is probably wise to do a search; doing so is not difficult and can save time and effort later. A search can be conducted in the USPTO public search library at www.uspto.gov or in a patent and depository library, or a specialist can be hired to conduct the search. In any case, after application the USPTO determines whether the mark may be registered and notifies the entrepreneur. If the USPTO rejects the application, the entrepreneur has six months to respond.

Marks that cannot be trademarked include:

Anything immoral or deceptive

Anything that uses official symbols of the United States or any state or municipality, such as the flag

Anything that uses a person's name or likeness without permission

Trademark Infringement, Counterfeiting, and Dilution

Like patents, trademarks can suffer from infringement, counterfeiting, or misappropriation. Infringement is found if a mark is likely to cause confusion with a trademark already existing in the marketplace. The deliberate copying of a mark (counterfeiting) is subject to civil and criminal penalties.

Trademarks are also subject to dilution, which occurs when the value of the mark is substantially reduced through competition or through the likelihood of confusion from another mark. For example, American Express was able to prove that it suffered dilution when a limousine service used the American Express trademark for its business, even though the two companies were in different industries.[21]

Copyrights

It has been said over and over again that we live in an information economy. Certainly, information-based products and services have been growing at a breathless pace, propelled by technology and the Internet. But with the proliferation of digital works comes the difficult task of finding ways to protect all the intellectual property that is being accessed, duplicated, transmitted, and published in digital form. Copyrights are the form of protection that comes into play here.

Copyrights protect original works of authors, composers, screenwriters, and computer programmers. A copyright does not protect the idea itself but only the form in which it appears, which cannot be copied without the express permission of the copyright holder. For example, a computer programmer can copyright the written program for a particular type of word processing software but cannot copyright the idea of word processing. This is why several companies can produce word processing software without violating a copyright. What they really are protecting is the unique programming code of their software.

A copyright lasts for the life of the holder plus 70 years, after which the copyrighted material goes into public domain. However, under the Sonny Bono Copyright Extension Act of 1998, no expired copyrights will enter the public domain until 2019. Works for hire and works published anonymously now have copyrights of 95 years from the date of publication.

The first copyright statute was enacted in 1793, but it has been successfully adapted for over 200 years. The courts have said, "the purpose of the copyright law is to create the most efficient and productive balance between protection (incentive) and dissemination of information, to promote learning, culture, and development."[22] There is no question that copyright law is undergoing its most strenuous test in the information economy.

The Digital Millennium Copyright Act

One of the problems associated with delivering products over the Internet is the ease with which a person can infringe on another's rights. In October 1998, President Clinton signed into law the Digital Millennium Copyright Act (DMCA), which prohibits the falsification, alteration, or removal of copyright management data on digital copies. The law contains a safe harbor clause to protect service providers from monetary damages if they unknowingly infringe on someone's rights, either by transmitting or storing infringing material or by linking users to websites containing infringing material. This law clears the way to licensing intellectual property for a fee over the Internet.

The Special Case of Software

For entrepreneurs who publish software, federal copyright protection (absent the ability to patent) is the most important legal protection available. But just as with patents, if someone infringes on the copyright, it is the entrepreneur's job to file a lawsuit and plead her case against the infringer. And a lawsuit cannot be filed unless the entrepreneur has registered her copyright, so it's a good idea to register the copyright when the product is ready to go to market. Another benefit of registering early (before facing infringement) is that if the entrepreneur wins a lawsuit against an infringer, she may be entitled to recover attorney fees, court costs, and statutory damages up to $100,000 without having to establish the actual amount of damages, which is not easy to do.

Obtaining Copyright Protection

To qualify for federal copyright protection, the work must be in a fixed and tangible form—that is, someone must be able to see or hear it. It should contain a copyright notice (although this is no longer required by law) so that a potential violator cannot claim innocence because there was no notice. The notice should use the word *copyright* or the symbol © and should provide the year and the complete name of the person responsible for the work, as in © 2004 Stephen Barry.

Though not required, registration at the Copyright Office at the Library of Congress in Washington, DC, is important in order to obtain full protection under the law.

International Protection

Fortunately, copyright protection laws are fairly consistent across countries because of a number of international copyright treaties, the most important of which is the Berne Convention. Under this treaty, which includes more than one hundred nations, a country must give copyright protection to authors who are nationals of any member country for at least the life of the author plus 50 years.

Trade Secrets

A **trade secret** consists of a formula, device, idea, process, pattern, or compilation of information that gives the owner a competitive advantage in the marketplace, is novel in the sense that it is not common knowledge, and is kept in a confidential state. Some examples of trade secrets are the recipe for Mrs. Field's cookies, survey methods used by professional pollsters, customer lists, source codes for computer chips, customer discounts, and inventions for which no patent will be applied.

Many companies, such as Hewlett-Packard (HP), choose not to patent some of their inventions but rather keep them for internal use only as trade secrets. The reason is that once a patent has been issued, anyone can look up the patent on the USPTO website and see how the device is made. Some of HP's inventions are devices used in the manufacture of its computers and peripherals, and they give the firm a significant competitive advantage that it would lose if they got into the hands of competitors. With the patent in hand, the competitor could build that device and use it to improve its own manufacturing processes. As long as the competitor is not selling the device in the market, it would require a court to decide whether the firm is actually infringing on HP's patent.

There are no legal means under patent and trademark law to protect trade secrets. The only way to protect them is to have all employees sign an employment contract that specifically details what is considered trade secret information, both at the time the employee is hired and during his or her tenure as an employee. Then, should a current or former employee use or reveal a specified trade secret, the company can pursue legal remedies, such as an injunction or suing for damages.

Some Final Words on Intellectual Property

This chapter discussed how important it is to an entrepreneur's business strategy to protect the assets created. The key point to remember about intellectual-property rights is that they can't stop someone from infringing on the entrepreneur's rights. What they can do is provide the entrepreneur with offensive rights—that is, the right to sue in a court of law, a long and costly process (remember the story of Gordon Gould at the beginning of this chapter). Consequently, intellectual-property rights should never be the sole competitive advantage a business possesses, but rather one of a bundle of strategies that includes customer relationships and organizational culture.

There are risks and benefits associated with the products and services that entrepreneurs develop. Part of the goal of feasibility analysis is to address those risks and benefits so that informed decisions can be made about whether to go forward with a new business concept.

New Venture Checklist

Have you:

☐ Found ways to incorporate customer input into the design of your products, processes, and services?

☐ Found independent contractors who can build a prototype?

☐ Identified intellectual-property rights appropriate to the business concept?

Issues to Consider

business.college.hmco.com/students

ACE

Self-tests

1. How has the environment for product development changed in the last decade, and what does this mean to entrepreneurs starting new businesses?
2. What are the principal reasons why new products fail?
3. Suppose you are going to develop and market a new device for tracking calories consumed during the day. What will your product development strategy be, and why?
4. In what ways should you protect an invention from the time of its earliest conception?

Experiencing Entrepreneurship

1. Visit an entrepreneurial company that is developing new products. What is the company's product development strategy, and how effective is that strategy? You may need to use outside sources to confirm what the company tells you.

2. Visit your local patent office or the U.S. Patent Office on the Internet, http://www.uspto.gov. Pick a patented product that interests you, and do a search to find the patent for the product. How many patents have been filed for products that closely match your product?

Additional Sources of Information

Cooper, R.G. (2000). *Product Leadership: Creating and Launching Superior New Products.* Cambridge, MA: Perseus Publishing.

Kahn, K.B. (2004) *The PDMA Handbook of New Product Development,* 2nd Ed. New York: John Wiley & Sons.

Maskus, K.E., and C.F. Bergsten (2000). *Intellectual Property Rights in the Global*

Economy. Washington, DC: Institute for International Economics.

Spinello, R.A. (2004). *Intellectual Property Rights in a Networked World: Theory and Practice.* Information Science Publishing.

Ulrich, K.T., and S.D. Eppinger (2003). *Product Design and Development.* New York: McGraw-Hill.

Relevant Case Studies

Case 2 Craigslist, p. 407
Case 5 iRobot, p. 432

Case 7 Linksys, p. 446

The Founding Team

"The people who get on in this world are the people who get up and look for the circumstances they want, and, if they can't find them, make them."

George Bernard Shaw

LEARNING OBJECTIVES

- ■ Explain how to build a founding team effectively.
- ■ Understand how to work with professional advisers.
- ■ Discuss when to add a board of directors.
- ■ Compare and contrast outsourcing with independent contractors and hiring employees.

Profile 7.1   GOT MILK?

Entrepreneurial opportunity often presents itself in the most unlikely of places; in this case, it was the emerging market for soy milk, and the unlikely entrepreneurs were global giants DuPont and General Mills. But this tale is not about a big company launching a new product; it's about entrepreneur Scott Lutz, who, as a "rising star" at General Mills, convinced the two companies to complete a 50/50 joint venture partnership to support his founding of 8th Continent.

DuPont had developed a proprietary soy bean that it wanted to put into its first consumer food product in 200 years. At the same time, General Mills was interested in DuPont's bean in the hope that it would help General Mills make a better soy-milk beverage and overtake the market leader, Silk. Thus General Mills needed DuPont's soy bean, and DuPont needed General Mills' marketing expertise and distribution channels. It was a perfect match. Lutz believed it was important for the new company to be autonomous and entrepreneurial in spirit, and the corporate parents agreed. He secured a small office in a building four miles from General Mills headquarters, bootstrapped furniture and equipment, and began recruiting entrepreneurial types from both General Mills and DuPont to join him.

He succeeded in attracting a founding team of 20 and began to build a culture that would give the team a sense that they were partaking in something monumental. One of the first things he did was take his team into the field to test every aspect of their business plan, including the name of the company, 8th Continent, which signifies "a better place of wellness." Three months after the new product was launched in July 2001, it became the second-leading brand (right behind the market leader, Silk). 8th Continent rolled out nationally in July 2003 with a lot of room for growth. Forecasters predict that the soy-milk products market will reach $1 billion by 2005. This market has bigger margins than most food items, enjoys a market base of educated consumers, and offers products that can bear premium prices.

In building the team for 8th Continent, Lutz learned many lessons. The relationship of a start-up to its corporate parent is much like a traditional parent–offspring relationship. At some point, the offspring has to leave the nest and develop its own rituals and practices, but offspring can always call home when they need help. There is a constant emotional connection between the two, so the parents' pictures sit on the entrepreneur's desk, and the entrepreneur shows the parents his or her stellar report card. They remain a team even though the offspring has taken flight. In the same way, 8th Continent will continue to have a close working connection with DuPont and General Mills.

Sources: Linda Tischler, "Deep Pockets, Open Mind," *Fast Company* (May 2002), p. 32; 8th Continent website, http://www.8thcontinent.com/; "8th Continent Soymilk Goes National, Delivering the Promise of Great Taste and Good Nutrition to People Across the Country," *Business Wire* (July 10, 2003).

In the past, entrepreneurs in their quest for independence often attempted a new venture as soloists. In this way they could retain sole ownership, make all the key decisions, and would not have to share the profits. This approach to starting a business is still common in small firms and among craftspeople and artisans. However, in today's global, complex, and fast-changing environment, most entrepreneurs find it necessary to start their ventures with a team. In fact, a growing body of research supports a team approach to entrepreneurial events.[1] Teams have a much greater chance for success than solo efforts for a variety of reasons:[2]

- The intense effort required of a start-up can be shared.
- Should any one team member leave, it is less likely to result in the abandonment of the start-up.
- With a founding team whose expertise covers major functional areas—marketing, finance, operations—the new venture can proceed further before it will need to hire additional personnel.
- A skilled founding team lends credibility to the new venture in the eyes of lenders, investors, and others.

The entrepreneur's ability to analyze information and make decisions is improved because he or she benefits from the varied expertise of the team, and ideas may be viewed from several perspectives. When the start-up effort is collective, with a team that displays diverse capabilities, the new venture is more likely to be innovative and to carve out a unique niche for itself.[3] Yet another body of empirical research has provided evidence that firms founded by heterogeneous teams are generally more successful than those founded by individuals.[4]

Although new ventures today are typically started by teams, there is evidence to support the notion of a lead entrepreneur—that is, a person who displays a higher level of entrepreneurial vision and self-efficacy than other members of the team.[5] Lead entrepreneurs drive the development of new ventures and serve as the guardians of their vision. They have the ability to see what others cannot see and to identify ways to change the marketplace rather than simply recognize an opportunity.

The reality is that entrepreneurs never start businesses all on their own. Recall, from Profile 7.1, the start-up team of 8th Continent. Researchers have learned that entrepreneurs are "embedded in a social context, channeled and facilitated, or constrained and inhibited, by their positions in social networks."[6] Successful ventures take advantage of **social networks** to grow and maintain loyal customers. For example, building a community was online auction company eBay's goal from the start, and its success in doing so has been one of the most important reasons why eBay has survived where others have failed. Its customers manage the site— rating the quality of trading experiences with buyers and sellers, forming neighborhood watch groups to protect users against fraud and abuse, and providing input to the company on website design. eBay has become the place where people go to network with others who share their interests. eBay's CEO describes eBay as "of the people, by the people, for the people."[7]

Although the founding team is at the core of the new venture, the teambuilding reaches far beyond the founders to strategic partnerships with professional advisers, industry players, and others who help devise and execute an effective business strategy. The **extended networks** of entrepreneurs are critical to the entire entrepreneurial process.[8] Extended networks consist of "the relations between owners, managers, and employees, and they are structured by patterns of coordination and control."[9] Furthermore, when the entrepreneurial firm interacts with other firms in its industry, it creates additional extended networks. At the hub of this network (or **agile web,** as it is often called) is the founding team that has the vision and dedication to coordinate the efforts of all the partners toward a common goal. See Figure 7.1 for an overview of the entrepreneurial team and the agile web formed by its various networks.

| FIGURE 7.1 | The Entrepreneur's Team |

Professional Advisers
- Attorneys
- Accountants
- Bankers
- Insurance agents
- Board of directors
- Advisory board

Consultants
- Management
- Sales
- Market research
- Training

Service Agency Buying Office

The Entrepreneur's Team

Governmental Agencies

Manufacturing Support
- Subcontractors
- Design engineers

Sales Support
- Manufacturer reps
- Sales agencies
- Distributors
- Foreign reps

The Founding Team

Choosing partners to start a new venture is one of the most critically important tasks that the entrepreneur must undertake. And it is a difficult task because it is often not possible to understand a person's character until that person has spent some time working in the company. The stressful environment of a start-up may bring out traits and responses that were not apparent when the person was selected. Everyone from investors to bankers to potential customers looks at the founding team of the new venture to determine whether its members have the ability to execute their plans. Thus it is vital to choose partners who have complementary skills and experience and who do not have a history that might be detrimental to the company.

Finding partners with complementary skills means making sure that the team is not overloaded with people who all have the same expertise. A team of three engineers or three finance analysts is generally less attractive than a team with more diverse skills. Research has suggested that teams with diverse skills make better strategic choices that lead to higher performance.[10] In fact, some research has found team heterogeneity to be a significant predictor of long-term performance.[11] In terms of skill sets, heterogeneous teams also tend to handle the complexity of new ventures better than homogeneous teams.[12] Table 7.1 highlights five mechanisms of team composition.

TABLE 7.1	Mechanisms for Founding Team Composition
Homophily	The extent to which the characteristics of founding team members, such as gender, race, age, values, and beliefs, are similar.
	A high degree of similarity predisposes the team toward interpersonal attraction, trust, and understanding.
Functionality	The degree of diversity among team members with respect to leadership skills and task expertise.
	Diversity of work experience and occupational background has been found to be linked to functional performance[13] and to communication and innovation.[14]
Status Expectations	Widely held cultural biases regarding status (such as men having higher status than women) frequently affect the process of task group formation (although, in the case of gender, less so today).
	Those who perceive themselves to be in a higher-status group will tend to choose team members of the same status, however they define that status. Therefore, the entrepreneur who has lower status typically starts a venture as a soloist.
Network Constraint	The ability to choose members of a team is constrained by structural opportunities for social contact. For example, starting a business with only family members makes it more difficult to create a diverse team, because family members tend to be linked by strong ties and are in many respects an undesirably homogeneous group.[15]
Ecological Constraint	The research literature recognizes the importance of the size of the population of potential team members and of their geographic proximity in the formation of founding teams.[16] Thus the likelihood that different group members will associate is a function of their relative proportions in the population and their degree of segregation.[17]

Based on Martin Ruef, Howard E. Aldrich, and Nancy M. Carter, "The Structure of Founding Teams: Homophily, Strong Ties, and Isolation Among U.S. Entrepreneurs," *American Sociological Review,* 68(2) (2003): 195.

There is also another advantage to forming a multifunctional team. Because members of an entrepreneurial team often invest not only their time but also their money, the burden of gathering resources is shared. The lead entrepreneur also gains access to the network of contacts of the other members. This vastly increases the information and resources available to the new venture and enables it to grow more rapidly.

Of course, it isn't always possible or necessary to put together the "perfect" team from the start. The right person to fill a particular need may not have been determined, or the right person may be too expensive to bring on board during start-up. In the latter situation, it is important to talk to that person about joining the team at a later date and to keep him or her apprised of the company's progress. Many an aggressive start-up company has eventually wooed an experienced person away from a major corporation.

A Benchmark for an Effective Team

Although there are no perfect founding teams and no fail-safe rules for forming them, effective founding teams have the following characteristics:

- The lead entrepreneur and the team share the same vision for the new venture.
- The team members are passionate about the business concept and will work as hard as the lead entrepreneur to make it happen.
- One or more members of the founding team have experience in the industry in which the venture is being launched.
- The team has solid industry contacts with sources of capital.
- The team's expertise covers the key functional areas of the business: finance, marketing, and operations.
- The team members have good credit ratings; this will be important when the team seeks financing.
- The team is free to spend the time a start-up demands and can endure the financial constraints of a typical start-up.

Special Issues for High-Tech Teams

New ventures in the high-tech arena are frequently funded by "angel," or venture, capital, and these start-ups face different issues in the formation of their founding teams. Very often, the founding team consists of scientists and engineers with little market experience. Investors understand clearly that these kinds of teams are not the most effective for overseeing the rapid and successful execution of the business strategy. A high-tech venture with significant up-front funding and the potential for exponential growth early on requires a professional management team with experience and an excellent track record in the industry. Usually, the investors will help the entrepreneurs locate the right people for the job. Bringing on professional management at start-up ensures that there will be no glitches when rapid growth begins, and it also leaves the creative founders the time they need to continue to develop the product and/or service.

Unique Issues Surrounding Virtual Teams

Technology has made it possible for geographically dispersed teams to form and collaborate through **synchronous** and/or **asynchronous communication** media, relieving team members of the need to juggle global and local priorities.[18] **Virtual teams** are distinctly different from face-to-face teams in both spatial distance and communication. It is not the actual distance that matters but the effect that this distance has on how the team interacts. For example, suppose a start-up team is located in Los Angeles and one team member lives in Pasadena, approximately 10 miles away. The spatial distance is not great, but given traffic and other challenges, the time distance may be 40 minutes or more. Therefore, technologies such

Profile 7.2 **COLLABORATING IN A VIRTUAL WINE COMPANY: MORE POSITIVES THAN NEGATIVES**

Rob Bevis, president of Winspeer International Group Ltd., a Vancouver, Canada–based wine importer, has faced the challenges and advantages of working in a virtual environment. His company spreads from Vancouver to Edmonton to Calgary and all the roads in between. It is impossible for him to run his business in any other manner. In a rapidly growing global marketplace that is easily accessible via the Internet, an entrepreneur needs to expand into new markets. These new markets may not be geographically local, and this may create significant personnel challenges. This virtual work arrangement also further complicates the task of getting people to work together.

Winspeer was founded by Bob Harkness in 1994 to focus on sales and distribution of imported wines in Alberta, Canada's fourth largest province. Over the years since, the company has grown to take on British Columbia, Manitoba, and Saskatchewan. In 1998, Harkness sold his minority interest in the company during a financial and management restructuring in preparation for continued growth. In 2001, Winspeer joined the Trialto Wine Group, which comprised two other fine wine marketing companies: Liquid Art Fine Wines Ltd. and Calibrium International Ltd. Liquid Art works with small-production, family-owned properties or boutique wineries selling ultra-premium wines in the $25 to $500 range. Calibrium was spun off from the other two companies to meet the needs of larger wineries with world-class brands that require fully integrated, year-long marketing programs. The three companies operate independently in their sales and marketing, but they share accounting, finance, and computer systems.

In his role as president of Winspeer, Bevis soon realized that he needed to be able to coordinate the activities of his employees, who were scattered throughout western Canada. One of his major duties was to ensure that when an employee left the company, the incoming replacement would not need to reconstruct all of the previous work. His needs fell into three areas: (1) tactical collaboration to reach employees at their desks or on the road through e-mail, instant messaging, and cell phone; (2) strategic collaboration that involved information sharing, file sharing, and message boards; and (3) task management using public calendars and checklists. His ultimate concern was that it was vital for all employees to know what was going on at any given time. This required a central database, a virtual private network (VPN), and a common calendar. Today, with these collaboration tools in place, Bevis and his team can respond quickly to a marketplace that changes daily, and this has made all the difference for his winning team.

Sources: Matthew Friedman, "Create the Virtual Company," *Canadian Business and Current Affairs* (2002). Accessed via LexisNexis on 9/30/2003; Trialto Wine Group Ltd., www.trialto.com; and Winspeer International, Ltd., www.winspeer.com.

as videoconferencing, phone, and e-mail are used to mediate the distance. In addition, appropriate routines keep everyone connected and on track.[19]

Despite any disadvantages caused by distance, virtual teams have several advantages. They enable the entrepreneur to access the most qualified individuals for a particular position, regardless of location, and to create a more flexible organization. Of course, the entrepreneur will need to find partners who will evolve into a coherent, seamless, and well-integrated team.[20] Trust, therefore, is a critical component of an effective virtual team.

Founding Teams for International Ventures

Traditionally, entrepreneurial venturers were advised to establish themselves in the domestic market before taking on the enormous challenge of a global market. Increasingly, however, we are seeing more and more firms going international from start-up. And these international start-ups are generally being founded by teams.[21] Research indicates that whether these small firms succeed in the international market depends on the skills and knowledge of the entrepreneurial team.[22] The characteristics found to predict success in international ventures include the extent to which members of the founding team have traveled and/or worked abroad and the number of languages spoken.[23]

Experienced founding teams are also more likely to form partnerships to facilitate their entering a foreign market.[24] Because international start-ups are relatively vulnerable, they usually seek partnerships to provide financial, political, and cultural resources and the contacts they will need to be successful.

Rules for Friends and Families

Turning to friends and family members is certainly the easiest and quickest way to find partners to start a new venture, but it may not be the best decision for the business. If a small business has no intentions of seeking outside financing, having a founding team that consists entirely of family members may not be a problem if they are all compatible. But if the plan is to grow the venture significantly, seek outside investors, or potentially do a public offering, a founding team of family members may not be an attractive asset. Here are some things to think about before making the decision to take on a family member or close friend as a partner:

- Friends or family members should possess real skills and expertise that the business needs to be successful.
- They should have the same work ethic as the entrepreneur. If the entrepreneur is a workaholic and loves it, and a family member is a slacker, there will be problems.
- If there are family members on the start-up team, there should be outsiders on the advisory board and/or board of directors so that the company will have the benefit of objective input to the business.
- The relationship with family and friends should be treated as a business relationship. The responsibilities and duties of all should be clearly spelled out, and everyone should understand how disagreements will be settled. As much as possible, the business should not be brought home at night.

Professional Advisers

When a new venture is in its infancy, it generally doesn't have the resources to hire in-house professional help such as an attorney or accountant. Instead, it must rely on building relationships with professionals on an "as-needed" basis. These professionals provide information and services not normally within the scope of expertise of most entrepreneurs, and they can play devil's advocate for the entrepreneur, pointing out potential flaws in the business concept. They provide the new venture—and the entrepreneurial team in love with its own concept—a reality check that is invaluable. There are a number of these professional advisers that entrepreneurs rely on at various times in their venture's life.

Attorneys

There is hardly any aspect of starting a new venture that is not touched by the law. Unfortunately, entrepreneurs who have never had any education in the legal aspects of business often don't recognize that they need legal help until their business gets into trouble. Attorneys are professionals who typically specialize in one area of the law (such as taxes, real estate, business, or intellectual property) and can provide a wealth of support for the new venture. Within their particular area of expertise, attorneys can

- Advise the entrepreneur in selecting the correct organizational structure: sole proprietorship, partnership, LLC, or corporation.
- Advise about and prepare documents for acquisition of intellectual-property rights and for licensing agreements.
- Negotiate and prepare contracts for the entrepreneur, who may be buying, selling, contracting, or leasing.
- Advise the entrepreneur on compliance with regulations related to financing and credit.
- Keep the entrepreneur apprised of the latest tax reform legislation and help to minimize the venture's tax burden.
- Assist the entrepreneur in complying with federal, state, or local laws.
- Represent the entrepreneur in any legal actions as advocates.

Choosing a good attorney is a time-consuming but vital task that should be accomplished prior to start-up. Decisions about such things as the legal form of the business or contracts made at inception may affect the venture for years to come—hence the need for good legal advice. To find the best attorney for the situation, entrepreneurs should

- Ask accountants, bankers, and other business people to recommend attorneys who are familiar with the challenges facing start-ups, particularly those in the entrepreneur's industry.
- Look for an attorney who is willing to listen, has time, and will be flexible about fees while the business is in the start-up phase.
- Check out the firm by phone first. One can learn a lot about a law firm by noting who answers the phone and with what tone of voice. If the attorney answers his or her office phone directly, this may be a very small firm with limited resources. Does the person answering the phone sound genuinely interested in being helpful?
- Confirm that the attorney carries malpractice insurance.

Accountants

A lawyer is an advocate, but an accountant is bound by rules and ethics that do not permit advocacy. Whereas an attorney is bound to represent his or her client no matter what the client does, an accountant cannot defend a client who does something that violates the accounting industry's Generally Accepted Accounting Principles (GAAP).

Accounting is a fairly complex field that the entrepreneur needs to understand at least at a basic level in order to communicate with accountants, auditors, lenders, bankers, and investors, in addition to internal and external stakeholders. In the beginning, the accountant may set up the company's books and maintain them on a periodic basis, or, as is often the case, the entrepreneur may hire a bookkeeper to perform the day-to-day recording of transactions. The accountant will also set up control systems for operations, as well as payroll. The entrepreneur then goes to the accountant during the tax season. Once the new venture is beyond the start-up phase and is growing consistently, it's a good idea to do an annual audit to determine whether the company's accounting and control procedures are adequate. The auditors may also require a physical inventory. If everything is in order, they will issue a certified statement, which is important should the entrepreneur ever decide to take the company public.

Accountants are also a rich networking source in the entrepreneur's search for additional members of the new venture team. Like attorneys, accountants tend to specialize, so it is wise to find one who is used to working with young, growing businesses. Indeed, the accountant who takes a business through start-up and early growth will probably not be the best person to take care of the company's needs when it reaches the next level of growth. As the financial and record-keeping needs of the business increase and become more complex, the entrepreneur may have to consider a larger firm with expertise in several areas.

Bankers

There is a saying that all banks are alike until you need a loan. Today this is truer than ever, so having a qualified banker on the advisory team will put the new venture in a better position to seek a line of credit for operating capital or a loan to purchase equipment. The firm's banker should be thought of as a business partner who can be a source of information and networking, help make decisions regarding capital needs, assist in preparing pro forma operations and cash flow analyses and evaluate projections, and assist in all facets of financing.

To narrow the search for a banker, entrepreneurs should prepare a list of criteria that define the banking needs of the new venture. They should also talk with other entrepreneurs in the same industry to identify a bank that works well with the type of venture they plan to launch. Another approach is to ask an accountant or attorney to suggest the best bank for the new venture.

When choosing a banker, seek out an officer with a rank of assistant vice president or higher, because these officers are trained to work with new and growing businesses and have enough authority to make decisions quickly. In particular, it is important to ensure that the lending officer can approve loans and lines of credit in the amounts needed. Today many of the largest banks have moved their lending facilities to a central location, so it is difficult to establish a relationship with the person who has responsibility for approving a request. That's why many entrepreneurs seek out community banks that have a vested interest in supporting local businesses.

Insurance Agents

Many entrepreneurs overlook the value of a relationship with a competent insurance agent, but a growing venture will require several types of insurance:

- Property and casualty
- Medical
- Errors and omissions
- Life (on key managers)
- Workers' compensation
- Directors and officers
- Unemployment
- Auto (on the firm's vehicles)
- Liability (product and personal)
- Bonding

Major insurance firms often can handle all types of insurance vehicles, but specialists will be required for certain kinds of protection, such as bonding (which is common in the construction industry to protect against a contractor's not completing a project), product liability insurance, and errors and omissions (which protects the business against liability from unintentional mistakes in advertising). The new venture's insurance needs will change over its life, and a good insurance agent will help the entrepreneur determine the needed coverage at the appropriate times.

Board of Directors

The decision to have a **board of directors** is influenced by the legal form of the business. If the new venture is a corporation, a board of directors is required and is elected by the shareholders. If the business needs venture capital, a board will be necessary, and the venture capitalist will probably demand a seat on it. Boards of directors serve a valuable purpose; if chosen correctly, they provide expertise that will benefit the new venture. In that capacity they act as advisers. They also assist in establishing corporate strategy and philosophy. They do not have the power to sign contracts or commit the corporation legally. Instead, they elect the officers of the corporation, who are responsible for its day-to-day operations.

It is important to distinguish between boards of privately owned corporations and those of publicly owned corporations. In a privately owned corporation, the entrepreneurial team owns all or the majority of the stock, so directors serve at the pleasure of the entrepreneur, who has effective control of the company. On the other hand, directors of publicly traded companies have legitimate power to control the activities of the company and liability for what they do or fail to do. They are elected by the shareholders and represent the shareholders' interests in the company.

Boards can be comprised of inside or outside members or a combination of the two. An inside board member is one who is a founder, employee, family member, or retired manager of the firm, whereas an outside board member is someone with no direct connection to the business. Which type of board member is better is a matter of opinion and circumstance; research has not provided any clear results on this issue. In general, however, outside directors are beneficial for succession planning and for raising capital. They can often bring a fresh point of view to the strategic planning process, along with expertise that the founders may not possess.

Insiders have the advantage of complete knowledge about the business; they are generally more available and have demonstrated their effectiveness in the particular positions they occupy in the business. Often the company chief executive officer (CEO), chief financial officer (CFO), and in-house attorney sit on the board. But there are political ramifications when the board members report to the CEO; insiders may not always be objective and independent. They also may not have the broad expertise from outside the company that is necessary to guide the growth of the business effectively.

Consider carefully whether the new venture requires a working board—that is, one that directs the strategy of the business. Most working boards are used for their expertise, for strategic planning, for auditing the actions of the firm, and for arbitrating differences. These activities are not as crucial in the start-up phase, when the entrepreneurial team is gathering resources and raising capital. However, a board of directors can assist the entrepreneurial team in those functions and can network with key people who can help the new venture. At this juncture, some potential directors will ask to be included on the board so that they can monitor their investment in the company. This is common among large private investors, bankers, and even accountants. To be sure of getting only the best people on the board, entrepreneurs should set standards for membership in advance and should strictly adhere to them.

The size and complexity of the entrepreneur's business, as well as the legal requirements of the state in which the company operates, will determine how many directors serve on the board. There is no research consensus on the relationship between the size of the board and the performance of the company, although some research has found that a large board encourages laziness on the part of some members[25] and thus may undermine the board's ability to initiate strategic actions.[26] Moreover, larger boards tend to develop factions and coalitions that often lead to conflict. The general recommendation is to have no fewer than 5 and no more than 15 board members. In the earliest stages of a new venture, the board will often consist of the founders, though that should quickly change as the company begins to grow and needs to tap the expertise of people who have managed growth in their own companies.

When choosing people to serve on the board of directors, entrepreneurs should consider those who have

- The necessary technical skill related to the business
- Significant, successful experience in the industry
- Experience running a company at the level the entrepreneur wants to grow to next
- Important contacts in the industry

- Expertise in finance, capital acquisition, and possibly IPOs
- A personality compatible with the rest of the board
- Good problem-solving skills
- Honesty and integrity, to engender a sense of mutual trust

If the entrepreneurial team is not careful, it may learn too late that a director it has appointed to the board considers the position an appointment for life, much like being appointed to the Supreme Court. To prevent such a misunderstanding, and to bring a fresh point of view to the board, directors should be asked to serve on a rotating basis for a specified period of time.

The board is headed by the chairperson, who, in a new, private venture, is typically the lead entrepreneur. The entrepreneur is also likely to be the president and CEO. The current trend is for the CEO and perhaps the chief operating officer (COO) to be the only inside members on the board.

Depending on the type of business, boards normally meet face-to-face an average of five times a year and through teleconferences as necessary. How often the board meets will be largely a function of how active it is at any given time. Directors typically spend about nine to ten days a year on duties related to the business and are usually paid a retainer plus a per-meeting fee. Their expenses are also reimbursed. The compensation can take the form of cash, stock, or other perquisites.

Today it is more difficult to get people to serve as directors because in some cases they can be held personally liable for the actions of the firm, and the frequency with which boards are being sued is increasing. For this reason, potential directors often require that the business carry directors' and officers' (D&O) liability insurance to indemnify them.

The expense of this insurance is often prohibitive for a growing company, but it is essential in getting good people to serve. Additional expenses related to the development of a board of directors include meeting rooms, travel, and food. Because of the expense of maintaining a formal board of directors, many entrepreneurs with new ventures maintain a small insider board of directors and rely heavily on their informal advisory board for a more objective perspective.

Advisory Board

The advisory board is an informal panel of experts and other people who are interested in seeing the new venture succeed. They are a useful and less costly alternative to a formal board of directors. Advisory boards can range from those that meet once or twice a year and do not get paid, to those that meet more regularly and are provided honoraria of anywhere from $500 to $1,000 per meeting.

Advisory boards are often used when a board of directors is not required or in the start-up phase when the board of directors consists of the founders only. An effective advisory board can provide the new venture with needed expertise, without the significant costs and loss of control associated with a board of directors. In a wholly owned or closely held corporation (in which the entrepreneur or team holds all the stock), there really is no distinction between the functions of a board of directors and those of a board of advisers, because in either case, control remains in the hands of the entrepreneurial team. The advisory board is not subject to the same scrutiny as the board of directors, because its actions are not binding on the company.

Entrepreneurs tend to resist the idea of having outside advisers because of the founders' intense desire to be independent and to maintain some secrecy about the business. Entrepreneurs also tend to believe that an outsider could never understand the business.[27] Although many business owners may reject a formal board, they risk developing "tunnel vision" unless they consider using an advisory board. An advisory board is a step in the direction of creating a more professional organization that exhibits

1. Shareholder harmony, achieved through shareholder agreements and buy–sell agreements
2. Effective management that has a vision and goals for the company
3. Efficient internal communication, achieved through shareholder meetings, advisory board meetings, and management meetings.[28]

Mistakes to Avoid with Teams and Boards

Assembling the extended founding team is a serious undertaking, and failure to put the team together successfully could have severe ramifications for the future of the business. Here are several common mistakes that should be avoided:

- Forming the team casually or by chance—that is, without careful consideration of the experience and qualifications each person brings to the team.
- Putting together a team whose members have different goals, which could impede the growth of the company.
- Using only insiders for the board of directors—that is, appointing only friends and family members instead of the people most qualified to advise the business.
- Using family members or friends as attorney and accountant for the business. Because these professional advisers must remain objective at all times to best represent and assist the entrepreneur, choosing relatives can cause unnecessary problems.
- Giving the founding team stock in lieu of salary. The lead entrepreneur does not want significant shares of stock in the hands of people who may later leave the company if things don't work out. The use of a buy–sell agreement, which specifies how shares in the business are to be transferred in the case of a co-owner's death, will prevent this problem.

The Mentor Board

Entrepreneurs should have a personal board of mentors who serve as a sounding board for ideas and act as coaches to raise their spirits and warn them when they're heading down a wrong path. The members of a personal board usually are role models, people who have businesses and lifestyles like the one the entrepreneur wants to create. Mentors also provide a safe place for entrepreneurs to air their fears and concerns and express their hopes and dreams. Jennifer Lawton benefited from

Socially Responsible Entrepreneurship

Survival of the Fittest

Survival is a skill that is critical to entrepreneurs, and no one understands survival better than Rabbi Arthur Schneier, who lost his father and grandparents to the Nazis when he was six years old. Surviving that ordeal and making it to America, he, like many other survivors, felt compelled to dedicate their lives to public service. Schneier trained to become a rabbi in honor of his grandfather, and in 1962, he became the senior rabbi at Park East Synagogue. There he was determined to develop a new school dedicated to young children, which at the time was a fairly radical vision. His entrepreneurial spirit drove him to find the land, raise money, design the building, and do everything possible to achieve his goal. By 1966 he had put all the property pieces together, and by 1973 he had finally raised enough money to begin construction. In 1977, his ultimate dream of building a school was realized in an eight-story facility. And today, more than 25 years later, the school serves 320 children.

But Schneier didn't stop there. He had a simultaneous dream to end human oppression. He founded the Appeal of Conscience Foundation to fight against social injustices and promote religious freedom in Russia and other countries where people could not freely practice their religious beliefs. Since then he has served presidents, won medals for his contributions to society, and continued to display the best attributes of successful entrepreneurs giving back to their communities.

Sources: C. Hall, "It's All About Freedom," in *The Responsible Entrepreneur* (Franklin Lakes, NJ: Career Press, 2001), The Appeal of Conscience Foundation, http://www.appealofconscience.org/.

several important career mentors when she founded her Boston-based computer networking consulting firm, but she maintains that the lessons that lasted a lifetime came from role models who had nothing to do with her chosen career path. Lawton credits her grandmother and mother with instilling a strong belief system, and her grandfather, a survivor of the Great Depression, with teaching her that laughter is the best medicine.[29] Clearly, it is important to have both personal and professional mentors in the entrepreneurial journey.

Outsourcing with Independent Contractors

A new business typically does not have the resources to pay for all the management staff that may be necessary to keep it running. In fact, most entrepreneurs try to avoid hiring employees as long as possible, because employees are the single biggest expense in the business. But how does a new venture survive with as few employees as possible and still grow?

The solution lies in **outsourcing,** which means using independent contractors. **Independent contractors (ICs)** own their own businesses and are hired by the entrepreneur to do a specific job. They are under the control of the entrepreneur only for the results of the work they do, not for the means by which those results are accomplished. The independent contractors that entrepreneurs use on a regular basis include consultants, manufacturers, distributors, and employee leasing firms (note that professional advisers are also independent contractors). The popularity of outsourcing can be seen in the fact that companies outsource about one-third of their information technology, human resources, and marketing and sales, and one-fifth of their financial activities.[30] One area most often outsourced is information technology because of its expense. It is hard for most companies to keep up with changes in technology, and the vendors to which they outsource can provide the same service and better performance at a lower cost.

Entrepreneurs seek out independent contractors for their expertise in specific areas. Using an independent contractor means that the new venture doesn't have to supply medical and retirement benefits, provide unemployment insurance, or withhold income and social security tax. These are costly benefits that can amount to more than 32 percent of an employee's base salary.

But there are hidden costs to outsourcing that entrepreneurs should be aware of:[31]

- *The cost of searching for and contracting with an independent contractor.* The best way to reduce this cost is for entrepreneurs to get referrals from people they know who have had a successful experience with the IC.
- *Transferring activities to the IC.* Getting the IC "up to speed" on the business takes time and human resources. Transfer costs can be reduced if entrepreneurs identify up front what they want the IC to handle.
- *Managing the independent contractor.* This is one of those cases where experience counts. The first IC contract takes the longest and costs the most. The best IC relationships occur when communication is an ongoing process so that the IC becomes a real part of the business.
- *Bringing the activity in-house.* Many companies eventually bring in-house activities that they once outsourced. This may occur because the company has grown to the point where it needs and can afford in-house staff for the activity or because the company wants more control over the activity. One way to reduce the transition cost is to have the person who manages the IC relationship learn enough about the activity to be able to ease the company through the transition.

Here are some ways to reduce the hidden costs of using independent contractors:

- Avoid outsourcing critical activities or those that are idiosyncratic or unique to the business.
- Research vendors carefully and get referrals.
- Work with legal advisors who have experience in independent contractor law to draft well-written contracts.

The IRS and Independent Contractors

The IRS has very strict rules for the use of independent contractors. The Law of Agency defines the terms *employee* and *independent contractor.*[32] It states, "While an employee acts under the direction and control of the employer, an independent contractor contracts to produce a certain result and has full control over the means and methods that shall be used in producing the result." If an employer doesn't follow the rules regulating classification of workers as independent contractors, they can be considered employees for tax purposes, and the employer can be held liable for all back taxes plus penalties and interest, which can amount to a substantial sum.

To ensure compliance with IRS regulations, entrepreneurs who use independent contractors should

- Consult an attorney.
- Draw up a contract with each independent contractor, specifying that the contractor will not be treated as an employee for state and federal tax purposes.
- Be careful not to indicate the means or methods of accomplishing the work only the desired result.
- Verify that the independent contractor carries workers' compensation insurance.
- Verify that the independent contractor possesses the necessary licenses.

More specifically, the IRS uses a 20-point test for classifying workers. (See Table 7.2.) Even if an employer follows all the IRS rules, however, there is no guarantee that the IRS won't challenge its position. Therefore, it is important to document the relationship with an independent contractor through a legal agreement that explicitly demonstrates that the independent contractor owns his or her own business. The IRS can decide that a worker is an employee even if only one of the 20 points is true!

On the positive side, independent contractors can make the very small start-up venture look like an established corporation to anyone on the outside. A large corporation will generally have vice presidents for departments of operations, sales,

TABLE 7.2	The 20-Point Test for Independent Contractors

A worker is an employee if he or she

1. Must follow the employer's instructions about how to do the work.
2. Receives training from the employer.
3. Provides services that are integrated into the business.
4. Provides services that must be rendered personally.
5. Cannot hire, supervise, and pay his or her own assistants.
6. Has a continuing relationship with the employer.
7. Must follow set hours of work.
8. Works full-time for an employer.
9. Does the work on the employer's premises.
10. Must do the work in a sequence set by the employer.
11. Must submit regular reports to the employer.
12. Is paid regularly for time worked.
13. Receives reimbursements for expenses.
14. Relies on the tools and materials of the employer.
15. Has no major investment in facilities to perform the service.
16. Cannot make a profit or suffer a loss.
17. Works for one employer at a time.
18. Does not offer his or her services to the general public.
19. Can be fired at will by the employer.
20. May quit work at any time without incurring liability.

marketing, and finance. It is possible to replicate these functions by using independent contractors, thereby lowering costs and remaining more flexible. Figure 7.2 shows how a growing entrepreneurial venture can imitate the strength, stability, and expertise of a much larger, more established company through the use of independent contractors. The concept is called the "virtual company" and will be discussed at length in Chapter 12.

Types of Independent Contractors

Many types of independent contractors operate behind the scenes of the new venture but make a valuable contribution nonetheless. Various independent contractors make up the entrepreneur's extended team.

Consultants

The consulting industry is one of the fastest-growing industries in the United States, and it can provide a variety of services for the new venture. Consultants can

- Train the sales staff and/or management
- Conduct market research
- Prepare policy manuals
- Solve problems

FIGURE 7.2 A Virtual Company

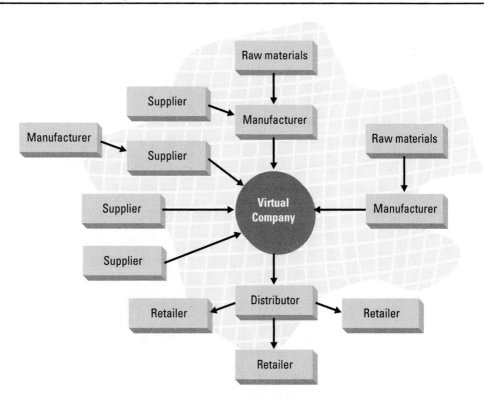

- Act as temporary key management
- Recommend market strategy
- Design and engineer products
- Design a plant layout and equipment
- Conduct research and development
- Recommend operational and financial controls

Because they tend to be fairly expensive, consultants are best used for critical one-time advising or problem-solving assignments. In that capacity, they are typically more cost-effective than employees because they are accustomed to working quickly within the constraints of a fixed budget.

Consultants are generally paid in one of three different ways: monthly retainer, which pays for a specified amount of time per month; hourly rate; or project fee. More recently, consultants have also been known to ask for some form of equity stake in the companies for which they consult. Some entrepreneurs have chosen to go this route when cash is in short supply. However, entrepreneurs should consult an attorney before giving up any equity in their company.

Staff

Leasing the staff is a way for a new business to enjoy the advantages of major corporations without incurring the expense. A leasing company assumes the payroll and human resource functions for the business for a fee that generally ranges from 3 to 5 percent of gross payroll. Each pay period, the new venture pays the leasing company a lump sum to cover payroll plus the fee. The National Staff Leasing Association reports that there are about one million leased employees in the United States and that the industry is growing at an annual rate of 30 percent.

Manufacturing Support

Even those new ventures that involve manufacturing a product can avail themselves of the benefits of independent contractors. Because the cost of building and equipping a new manufacturing plant is immense by any standard, many entrepreneurs choose to subcontract the work to an established manufacturer domestically or in another country. In fact, it is possible for the entrepreneur who has a new product idea to subcontract the design of the product to an engineering firm, the production of components to various manufacturing firms, the assembly of the product to another firm, and the distribution to yet another.

Sales Support

Hiring sales staff can be an expensive proposition for any new venture, not only from the standpoint of benefits but also because salespeople must be trained. As new high-growth ventures seek a geographically broad market, even a global one, it is vital to consider enlisting the aid of manufacturer's representatives (reps) and foreign reps who know those markets. Using distributors allows the entrepreneur to reach the target market without having to deal with the complex retail market. In addition, sales agencies can provide the new venture with fully trained salespeople in much the same manner as temporary services supply clerical help. Some can also provide advertising and public relations.

Service Agencies

With many established firms downsizing and contracting out for services, some entrepreneurs have seen an opportunity to provide those services and have built highly successful, high-growth businesses. As a result, it is now possible for a new venture to subcontract for payroll services, technology support, temporary help, and other services. The service firm employs the individual and provides the benefits while the entrepreneur pays a fee for the services.

Governmental Agencies

Many agencies at the federal, state, and local levels offer various services to new ventures. Notable among them are the Small Business Administration, which provides education, loans, and grants to small businesses; the Department of Commerce, which can assist the entrepreneur on issues of trade; and state and local economic development corporations.

By taking advantage of the many services available, an entrepreneur can literally start a business from home to reduce start-up capital requirements, yet still operate like a major corporation. This is not to suggest that a company can always avoid hiring employees and still grow. That will depend on the type of business. However, it does suggest that in the start-up phase of a new venture, the use of independent contractors can help ensure that the business survives long enough and generates enough revenues to hire employees.

A carefully conceived founding team, combined with an extended team of expert advisers and outsourced capability providers, can make the uncertain life of a start-up venture much easier. Entrepreneurs should form teams to reduce the risk inherent in starting new ventures in a dynamic and uncertain global marketplace.

New Venture Checklist

Have you:

☐ Identified the members of the founding team or at least the expertise needed to start the venture?

☐ Determined what expertise is missing from the management team and how you will supply it?

☐ Begun asking questions about potential professional advisers, such as an attorney or accountant?

☐ Determined whether you will need a board of directors, an advisory board, or both?

☐ Identified at least one type of independent contractor that the new venture could use?

Issues to Consider

1. For what kinds of businesses is starting as a solo entrepreneur sufficient? Are there advantages to starting even these types of businesses with a team?
2. What strategy should an entrepreneur employ when selecting a personal board, an advisory board, or a board of directors?
3. Attorneys are considered advocates; accountants are not. Why is it important for an entrepreneur to understand this distinction?
4. How can you ensure that you are using independent contractors correctly and in accordance with the law?
5. Suppose you are starting an apparel company where you will design and manufacture a unique line of clothing. What kinds of independent contractors can help you start this venture?

Experiencing Entrepreneurship

1. Interview an entrepreneur who started a venture as a soloist, and then visit an entrepreneurial venture started by a team (two or more people). Based on your interviews, what are the advantages and disadvantages of each approach?

2. Choose a lawyer, accountant, or banker to interview as a potential professional adviser to your business. What information will you need to get from him or her to make your decision?

Additional Sources of Information

Dimma, W.A. (2002). *Excellence in the Boardroom: Best Practices in Corporate Directorship.* New York: Wiley, 2002.

Gibson, C.B., and S.G. Cohen (2003). *Virtual Teams That Work: Creating Conditions for Virtual Team Effectiveness.* New York: Jossey Bass.

Lipnack, J., and J. Stamps (2000). *Virtual Teams: Reaching People Working Across Boundaries with Technology.* New York: Wiley.

Robbins, H., and M. Finley (2000). *Why Teams Don't Work: What Goes Wrong and How to Make It Right.* San Francisco: Berrett-Koehler.

Relevant Case Studies

Case 1 Overnite Express, p. 402
Case 3 Beanos Ice Cream Shoppe, p. 410

Case 6 The Crowne Inn, p. 435

Analyzing Start-up Resources

"Finance is the art of passing currency from hand to hand until it finally disappears."

Robert W. Sarnoff, former president of NBC/RCA

LEARNING OBJECTIVES

- Demonstrate an understanding of entrepreneurial resource gathering.
- Explain how to find the right numbers.
- Estimate sales and expenditures for the new venture.
- Prepare the pro forma income statement.
- Forecast start-up cash needs.

Profile 8.1 FUELING THE FUTURE: A MATTER OF TIMING

If you are in a position to capitalize on a great opportunity, it can mean all the difference in your company's chances of success. Larry Bawden knows what it's like to capitalize on an opportunity because twice he has been at the right place at the right time. In 1995 Bawden was working as director of fuel cell products at Aerojet in Sacramento, California, when his unit was sold and he found himself with a golden parachute. While on an around-the-world cruise to sooth his spirits, he was contacted by some friends who insisted that he return to become a vice president at PowerTek, a fuel cell company they were founding. Fuel cells operate in much the same way as a battery, turning oxygen and hydrogen into electricity. Although they have been around a long time, their high price and large size have prevented their adoption into the mainstream market.

Unfortunately, PowerTek's first customer was the fabled Enron, which was just about to crumble. The good news was that PowerTek's contact at Enron, Jon Berger, was ready to leave Enron anyway to go back to school to earn his MBA, and Bawden and his colleagues enticed him to come on board to launch a new company, Jadoo (the Hindi word for "magic") in November 2001. Jadoo would provide batteries that were about half the size of those currently in use and would last longer and cost only slightly more. Berger helped Bawden and his team write a business plan, and then a classmate of Berger's invested $200,000 in the company. They were well on their way when the co-founders and four other employees added another $100,000 to the pool. That initial investment enabled Jadoo to attract the attention of opinion leaders such as Sinclair Broadcasting Group, the parent for 62 local news stations in the United States. Sinclair invested $5 million in 2002.

That was one opportunity. The second came when President George W. Bush referred to hydrogen as an alternative to foreign oil during his State of the Union address in January 2003. Jadoo had been invited, along with 22 other fuel cell companies, to make a presentation at the White House. Besting such competition as Ford and Motorola, Jadoo was invited to do a one-on-one presentation to President Bush. The icing on the cake came when the President held a video camera, containing one of Jadoo's lightweight fuel cells, on his shoulder. Word of Jadoo's coup spread quickly. Jadoo is now selling those batteries to the broadcast market and to Boeing, the CIA, the Secret Service, the U.S. Army, and several other government agencies.

Timing is everything in launching a new venture. That is why it is so important to gather sufficient resources to be able to seize an opportunity when it presents itself.

Sources: R. Turner, "MBA Showdown: Third Place: Jadoo Power Systems," *Fortune Small Business* (October 30, 2003), www.fortune.com/fortune/smallbusiness/articles/; "Jadoo Power Systems Presents Fuel Cell Products to President Bush," *PRNewswire* (February 6, 2003), www.findarticles.com; and Jadoo, www.jadoopower.com.

Every business requires resources to start and grow. Resource gathering is one area where entrepreneurs demonstrate their unique capabilities to maximize the use of minimal resources, whether in the form of people, equipment, inventory, or cash. Up to this point, feasibility analysis has focused on testing the concept in the market to ensure that there are customers and sufficient demand. With a positive response from the market, it now becomes important to consider the financial conditions under which an entrepreneur would be willing to go forward—that is, what in the way of resources will be needed to start the business and sustain it until it generates a positive cash flow. No matter how many financial tools entrepreneurs use or how many complex analyses they construct, the bottom line for any new venture is cash. Income statements and balance sheets can make a company look good on paper—

these are accounting measures—but cash pays the bills and allows the company to grow. A new venture's health is measured by its cash flow.

This chapter examines entrepreneurial finance at start-up and provides a plan for conducting an assessment of resource needs so that the entrepreneur will have a clearer picture of the financial feasibility of the new venture concept. Once the entrepreneur decides to execute the business concept, a business plan with a full set of pro forma financial statements will be developed. The business plan is discussed in Chapter 9, and financial statements are discussed in Chapter 15.

Gathering Entrepreneurial Resources

Determining what resources are needed, when they are needed, and how to acquire them is a critical piece of the feasibility puzzle. Start-up resources include (1) people, such as the founding team, advisors, and independent contractors; (2) physical assets, such as equipment, inventory, and office or plant space; (3) and financial resources, such as cash, equity, and debt. The goal is to create a mix of resources that will allow the new venture to start and operate until the income of the business produces a positive cash flow—that is, until income exceeds expenses.

One of the secrets to success in constructing this resource mix is to maintain flexibility by owning only those resources that cannot be obtained by any other means. Owning a resource reduces the entrepreneur's flexibility and mobility. A dynamic marketplace, coupled with the inherent chaos of a start-up venture, requires that a new venture remain lean so that its products, services, and strategies can be tested and modified quickly in response to customers' feedback. Consider the case of the software management entrepreneur who let his ego get the better of him. After signing a long-term lease on prime office space in an expensive section of Los Angeles, he expected customers to be impressed by his success and want to do business with him. Instead, he discovered that his customers wanted to meet at their sites or in restaurants, not in his office. Moreover, his programmers did not require offices; they could work from home. As a result, this entrepreneur soon found himself saddled with expensive overhead that neither his customers nor his programmers needed.

Bootstrapping is the term often applied to the minimizing of resources. It simply means that entrepreneurs beg, borrow, or lease resources whenever they can so that they can keep their overhead, or fixed costs, as low as possible. Some bootstrapping techniques will be discussed in Chapter 15 on funding a start-up venture. New venture start-up teams typically have no previous history, no track record with customers, and no evidence of performance, so their resource decision making is based solely on current information and advice from others.[1] Consequently, many new ventures fail because of poor decisions about resources and their management. To succeed, entrepreneurs must create innovative combinations of resources that will generate a competitive advantage and lead to the creation of wealth.[2] Research has also concluded that innovative entrepreneurial ventures require different types of resources from their small business counterparts.[3]

Two Examples of Resource Building

The path to success for a new venture starts with the initial resources, and those early resources are generally a function of the entrepreneurial team's circumstances

When to Raise Money

Knowing when to raise money for your business is as important as knowing how much to raise and from whom to raise it. Timing really is everything. Here are three critical pieces of information you must have to make sure your timing is perfect.

1. When must you have the money in your business accounts? Normally your business needs money because of some milestone or event that is imminent.
2. How confident are you that your sales and cash flow will take you to that critical date? In other words, make sure that the date by which the money must be there is not at a time when you risk having no money in the business's accounts.
3. Are you seeking money from sources that can provide it quickly, or will it take time? Generally, it takes many months to obtain funding from professional investors such as venture capitalists. Funding from private sources like friends and family is the quickest to secure.

at the time of start-up. The researchers Brush, Greene, Hart, and Haller looked at entrepreneur Jeff Hawkins, who founded Palm Computing in 1992 and Handspring in 1998 under completely different circumstances.[4] Hawkins was a highly intelligent technology expert with a good reputation, but he had no financial resources, no business plan, and no experience starting and running a business. While a Ph.D. candidate in neurobiology at Berkeley, Hawkins had developed a handwriting algorithm, for which he later secured a patent. He licensed that technology to his former employer Grid Systems and, with them, developed the GRIDPAD, a handheld handwriting-recognition device that salespeople used to track deliveries. Hawkins's frequent contact with customers led him to think about a more consumer-oriented product. He wanted to start his own venture but lacked the resources to do so, so he began capitalizing on his expertise and reputation by speaking at conferences and trade shows. By networking, he raised nearly $2 million from two venture capitalists, licensed his technology back from his employer, and recruited engineers to begin product development. He now had one key resource, the product development people, in place. He next decided to tackle his lack of business expertise by hiring Donna Dubinsky, an experienced executive, as CEO and president. By 1995, they had a product ready to go to market, but no marketing resources. As a result, they sold Palm Computing to US Robotics Corporation for approximately $44 million in stock, plus the capital necessary to bring the product to market.

Neither Hawkins nor Dubinsky enjoyed working in a large corporation, and in July 1998, they resigned to start another company, Handspring, in the handheld-computing space. This time, however, their resource issues were different. They began with an experienced management team and several employees from Palm. Because they had all worked together before, the team had acquired a high level of knowledge about the technology and the customer, as well as each other. Their shared knowledge and social capital enabled them to secure more complex resources and to create a unique competitive advantage that was not easily imitated. They also had their pick of venture capitalists because their need for the money was not urgent; they ultimately chose two leading Silicon Valley venture capital firms.

Figure 8.1 depicts the resource pathways for Palm and Handspring. In general, resources can be divided into six categories: human, social, financial, physical, technological, and organizational.[5] In this figure, each resource is characterized in terms of how complex it is. For example, **simple resources** include financial resources and physical resources such as machinery and vehicles, which are tangible and property-based. These two simple resources are typically applied to create more complex, proprietary resources either directly in the production process (utilitarian) or in obtaining other critical resources (instrumental). Similarly, **complex resources,** which may be the output of simple resources, can be either utilitarian, as in the case of patents that protect an intellectual-property asset, or instrumental, as in the case of industry contacts used to create other intangible assets, such as tacit knowledge and organizational culture. When Hawkins started Palm, the assets he controlled, in addition to technology, were human resources—industry knowledge, contacts, and a good reputation. He used these assets to secure venture financing, which enabled him to develop the product and the organization. When he started Handspring, by contrast, he had a much more diverse set of resources, and although the venture was new, it was able to leverage complex organizational resources from Palm. Furthermore, the founders at that time had enough capital to fund the "seed round" and were therefore in a much stronger negotiating position when they sought venture capital.

From these examples we learn that, in general, entrepreneurs begin with complex resources in the form of human and social capital that can be used to acquire financial and physical resources and to hire skilled workers. It is also clear, however, that the resource pathway is unique for each venture and depends to a great extent on the quality of the initial resources that the entrepreneur brings to the venture. In many respects, the entrepreneur will also have to choose between buying a particular resource and making it. If the resource is not readily available or costs too much, the entrepreneur may choose to make it. On the other hand, if time to market is critical, he or she may pay the price for the resource so as to not lose the opportunity.

Identifying Resource Needs

To identify accurately the resources required to start the venture, it's important to understand all the activities and processes in the business—in other words, to know exactly how the business works. This is best accomplished by creating a **process map** that details how information flows through the business. Having such a map at hand makes it much easier to define the operations, information flow, and resource requirements of the business. To create a process map, take an imaginary tour of the business during a single day, listing all the functions, people, equipment, supplies, and space required to run the business. Begin at the front door of the business and ask the following questions:

1. Who does the work in this business?
2. Where do these people work?
3. What do they need to do the work (equipment, major supplies, space, etc.)?

| FIGURE 8.1 | Resource Pathways for Palm and Handspring |

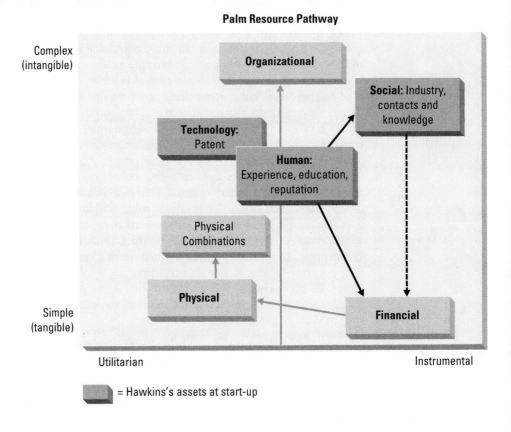

4. What information is being generated (work orders, invoices, customer lists, etc)?
5. Where does that information go?

Then begin making lists of tasks, equipment, and people needed to complete a particular process or activity. This information will be useful for figuring expenses for financial projections and for determining what kind of personnel will have to be hired to perform those tasks.

In a packaging solutions business, for example, what is the first thing a customer sees when he or she approaches the site? The sign for the business? A display window? When customers enter, is there a counter attended by someone who will answer their questions? What equipment does that person use to do his or her job? Note that without going beyond the customer's entry through the door of the business, a significant list of resources has been amassed. The imaginary tour is one of the best ways to begin to detail the processes in the business. Figure 8.2 traces one such imaginary tour of a service business. Understanding how the business works should help to clarify whether the entrepreneur can employ a virtual organizational structure or whether a traditional organizational structure is more appropriate.

FIGURE 8.1 (cont.)   Resource Pathways for Palm and Handspring

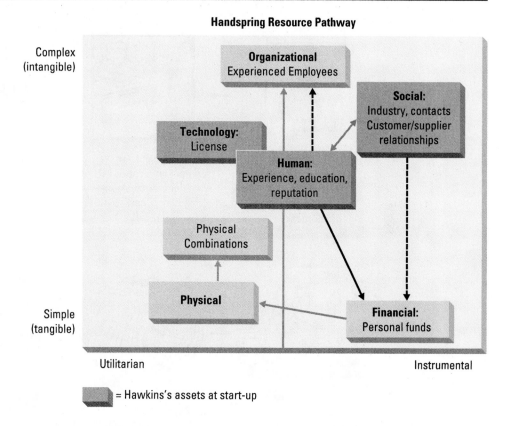

Handspring Resource Pathway

All of these decisions regarding resources come into play in the calculation of how much start-up capital is needed to start the business and operate it until it begins to generate a positive cash flow, which is the subject of the next section.

Finding the Right Numbers

Estimating revenues, expenses, and start-up costs at the feasibility stage is a daunting task at best for an entrepreneur with a new business concept. At this stage the concept is still fluid, so many of the numbers collected may change when the business plan is complete. Even the numbers in the business plan's pro forma statements will change when the business is in operation and the real world throws unexpected curves at the new venture. There are many reasons why feasibility estimates of sales, expenses, and start-up costs will probably change by the time the business plan is written.

1. If the entrepreneur's business is manufacturing or outsourcing to a manufacturer, it will be nearly impossible to estimate parts and manufacturing costs accurately without a production-quality product in place. For this reason, it is important to get to a physical prototype stage early, so as to have a better idea of the parts, components, and types of materials that will be needed, as well as what provision to make for labor.

| FIGURE 8.2 | A Virtual Tour of a Service Business |

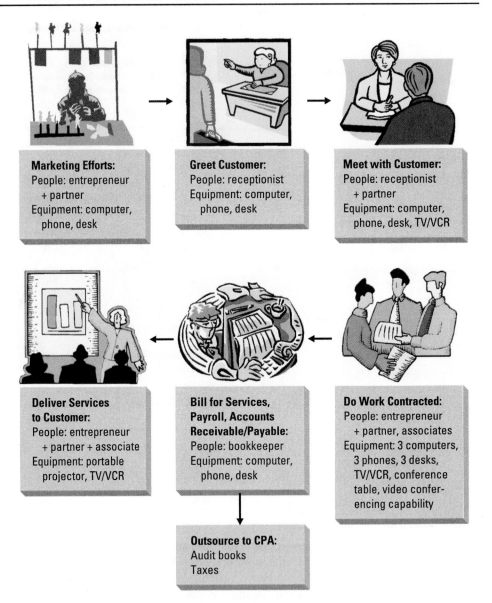

Marketing Efforts:
People: entrepreneur
 + partner
Equipment: computer,
 phone, desk

Greet Customer:
People: receptionist
Equipment: computer,
 phone, desk

Meet with Customer:
People: receptionist
 + partner
Equipment: computer,
 phone, desk, TV/VCR

**Deliver Services
to Customer:**
People: entrepreneur
 + partner + associate
Equipment: portable
 projector, TV/VCR

**Bill for Services,
Payroll, Accounts
Receivable/Payable:**
People: bookkeeper
Equipment: computer,
 phone, desk

Do Work Contracted:
People: entrepreneur
 + partner, associates
Equipment: 3 computers,
 3 phones, 3 desks,
 TV/VCR, conference
 table, video confer-
 encing capability

Outsource to CPA:
Audit books
Taxes

2. For many new product companies, product development may take several months to several years, depending on the nature of the product—and the costs for prototyping are always substantially higher than the ultimate production costs will be. Therefore, it is difficult to determine true feasibility from an economic perspective before there is a physical prototype.

3. For service companies, the actual costs to deliver a service must be based initially on information gathered from other companies in the industry. This is tricky to

achieve without "inside information"—that is, without knowing someone who works in that type of company. Estimates for the cost of delivery of the service will be more accurate if the service is prototyped under a variety of the most common scenarios. For example, a restaurant owner might want to calculate how long it takes to completely serve a customer, from arrival to departure. The owner needs to look at the number of tables planned, hours of operation, and the number of servers and cooks needed. Peak and slow periods and other aspects of serving customers are also factored in. The more variables that can be accounted for, the better the estimates will be.

4. As entrepreneurs grow in knowledge of their industry, they naturally gather better information because they know whom to talk with and where to find the best industry intelligence. Because getting inside an industry is difficult and time-consuming, many entrepreneurs choose to start ventures in industries with which they're familiar or in which they have experience.

Armed with an understanding of the difficulties inherent in forecasting numbers for a potential new business, it's important to have an overall strategy that will at least offer a higher probability of arriving at some numbers that make sense. In a process called **triangulation,** the problem is attacked from three angles: the entrepreneur's own knowledge, the industry, and the market/customer.

The Entrepreneur's Knowledge and Experience

The knowledge and experience an entrepreneur brings to the business will be helpful in forecasting sales, particularly if the entrepreneur has worked in the industry in which the business will be operating. Nevertheless, the entrepreneur's experience is anecdotal and should always be confirmed by other sources.

The Industry

The importance of understanding how an industry works cannot be stressed enough. A solid understanding of typical margins, sales patterns, and purchase cycles will provide valuable benchmarks for the entrepreneur's forecasts, although these numbers will need to be adjusted to reflect the new venture's inexperience in the industry. See Chapter 5 for information on how to research the industry and market.

The Market/Customer

Another critical source of information is the customer. Customers are far more likely than a competing business to provide useful information. Talking to customers and observing them in their "buying habitat" is an important way to gain insights into patterns and cycles of buying that can be applied to the entrepreneur's forecast.

With three sources of information—the entrepreneur's own knowledge, the industry, and the market/customer—the entrepreneur's estimates should be closer to reality. It is important to remember that forecasting is more art than science in new ventures, so the more information the entrepreneur has, the better.

Global Insights

Born Global

It appears that the old adage about our shrinking planet may be true, at least as it pertains to entrepreneurial ventures. More and more start-ups are "born global." This is quite a change from a time when companies went global gradually, in stages. Recent research conducted in Denmark and Australia has uncovered some commonalities among start-ups that are born global. For example, founders don't always have intentions to start an international company, but they typically recognize quite early that the product or service they are offering must compete in a global market. In all cases, the research found that such businesses are started because the founders want the independence of owning their own business. But their products and services dictate the need to go global, whether they are producing expensive furniture in Denmark or developing software for Web design in Australia. The research also revealed that entrepreneurs with international experience are more likely to found born-global companies.

Sources: P.D. Harveston, B.L. Kedia, and P.S. Davis, "Internationalization of Born Global and Gradual Globalizing Firms: The Impact of the Manager," *Advances in Competitiveness Research*, 8(1) (2000): 92–100; and E.S. Rasmussan, T.K. Madsen, and F. Evangelista, "The Founding of the Born Global Company in Denmark and Australia: Sensemaking and Networking," *Asia Pacific Journal of Marketing and Logistics,* 13(3) (2001): 75–108.

Estimating Sales and Expenditures

The sales forecast should be calculated first because sales affect the expenditures of the business.

The forecast should start with a timeline that depicts the seasonal patterns in the industry and the key events that might cause a change in the level of sales. Figure 8.3 depicts a timeline for the first ten months of a new venture. Note that two key events are identified that will affect sales volume: the acquisition of a lead customer and the off season typical in this industry. New sales from a lead customer will not occur immediately; rather, they will typically be delayed by a few months as the customer goes through its purchasing process. Then and only then will the new venture begin to see an upturn in its sales figures. Similarly, month 8, the start of the off season, begins a downturn in demand, which bottoms out in months 9 and 10.

Having created a timeline for the new venture, the entrepreneur should next

1. Identify events that could trigger a change in the estimate at any point in time.
2. Calculate the impact of the change on the estimate. Will it cause sales to go up? Will it cause sales to go down? Or are sales likely to remain stable?
3. Figure the probability that the event will occur. Is there a 50 percent chance that it will occur? A 20 percent chance? The percentage chosen is based on the information gathered during the triangulation process.

Sales figures will come from estimates of demand based on primary research with the customer, analysis of adoption patterns for similar products, and estimates from value chain partners such as distributors and retailers. One word of caution: When choosing competing companies for comparison purposes, be aware that if the

FIGURE 8.3	Sales Forecast Timeline

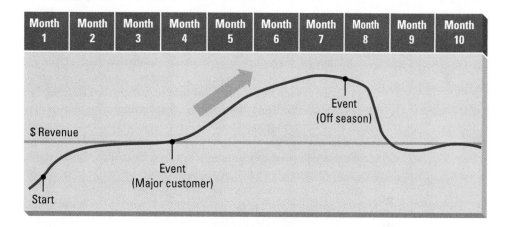

company is publicly held or well established, the new venture probably will not achieve the same level of sales for some time. Therefore, the sales figures gathered from these companies serve merely as an upper limit. The entrepreneur determines how much below that figure actual sales will be. The percentage increase in sales over a three- to five-year period will depend on the following factors:

- Growth rates in the market segment of the product or service
- The innovations offered that will make the product/service more attractive to the consumer, even at a higher price
- The technological innovations employed that enable the entrepreneur to produce the product or service at a lower cost than competitors, thus making it more accessible and enticing to the consumer

Demand can be estimated from primary research with the customer. For example, suppose that 7 out of 10 potential customers would purchase the entrepreneur's product. Given that these responses might be optimistic, the entrepreneur should consider reducing the ratio. The amount of reduction is purely arbitrary and is based on how confident the entrepreneur is in the responses received from research with the customer. Suppose the entrepreneur decides to reduce the estimate of demand to 6 out of 10, or 60 percent. Applying this percentage to the size of the niche market that the entrepreneur intends to enter can give a rough estimate of how many customers might purchase. Then comparing these results with feedback from value chain partners might confirm the numbers or cause the entrepreneur to modify the estimate. Results of research on adoption patterns for similar products or services would then be applied to determine sales on a month-by-month basis.

Forecasting Expenditures

Once sales have been forecast, predicting expenditures becomes much easier, particularly if expenditures vary with sales, as in the case of the cost of goods sold and commissions. In wholesale businesses, for example, after the sales forecast has been determined, the figures for inventory purchases can be applied as a percentage of sales and forecast from that. Thus, if inventory cost is 25 percent of sales, one can apply that percentage to sales, as they increase, to forecast increases in the volume of inventory. Be aware, however, that in some industries, volume discounts on raw materials or inventory may actually reduce costs over time and should be factored into the expenditure forecast. Whether volume discounts will be available is an important piece of information that is gathered during field research.

In manufacturing businesses, forecasting expenditures is a bit more complex because **cost of goods sold (COGS)** must be derived first. COGS consists of direct labor, cost of materials, and direct factory overhead. Applying COGS as a percentage of sales will probably suffice for purposes of pro forma statements for the feasibility stage. Month-by-month analysis of outcomes and use of a cost accounting model that considers raw materials inventory, work-in-process inventory, finished-goods inventory, total inventory, factory overhead, work-in-process flow in units, and weighted-average cost per unit will give a more accurate estimate as the business grows.

In service businesses, the COGS is equivalent to the time expended for the service. The rate at which the service is billed, say $100 an hour, comprises the actual expenses incurred in providing the service, a contribution to overhead, and a reasonable profit. The actual expenses incurred are equivalent to the cost of goods sold.

Selling, General, and Administrative Expenses

The expenses of running the business, or **selling, general, and administrative (S,G&A) expenses,** are considered fixed because they do not vary with the volume of sales. They should be forecast separately in a detailed breakout statement. This is because some of these items may vary over a 12-month period, whereas others remain stable. For example, rent is normally fixed during a 12-month period, but utilities costs will vary with use, and commissions will vary with sales. Therefore, a percentage-of-sales figure should not be used for S,G&A expenses. To make the financial statements clearer and more concise, one should use only the totals of S,G&A expenses for each month in the financial statements, with a footnote directing the reader to the S,G&A breakout statement. Selling expenses, which include advertising costs, travel expenses, sales salaries, commissions, and the cost of promotional supplies, should be handled in the same manner, in a breakout statement, with only totals appearing in the financial statements. Table 8.1 presents some sample expenditures for various types of businesses.

Taxes

The last item to forecast is taxes, which include such things as payroll taxes and federal, state, and local income taxes. The various rates for those taxes and when they must be paid can be found by consulting the IRS website at http://www.irs.gov/ and any state franchise tax board or local governmental agency. To calculate the business tax liability, a pro forma income statement will need to be developed. This is discussed in a later section.

Developing Narrative Assumptions

Assumptions explain the way numbers in the financial statements were derived. These narrative line-item assumptions are more important than the financial statements

| **TABLE 8.1** | **Expenditures for Various Types of Businesses** |

SAMPLE MANUFACTURING OR CONSTRUCTION EXPENSES LIST

Manager's Salary	Paid Employees' Salaries
Payroll Taxes	Vehicle Lease and Maintenance
Related Travel	Packaging Costs
Supplies	Depreciation on Owned Equipment

SAMPLE DISTRIBUTION AND WAREHOUSE EXPENSES LIST

Manager's Salary	Employees' Salaries
Drivers' Salaries	Payroll Taxes
Vehicle Lease and Maintenance	Warehouse Loading Vehicles
Lease/Maintenance	Depreciation on Owned Equipment
Freight Expenses	Supplies

SAMPLE LIST OF SELLING EXPENSES

Sales Manager's Salary	Inside Sales Salaries
Inside Sales Commissions	Telephone Sales Salaries
Telephone Sales Commissions	Field Sales Salaries
Field Sales Commissions	Payroll Taxes for Sales Employees
Sales Vehicles Lease and Maintenance	Sales-Related Travel
Advertising and Promotion	Depreciation on Owned Equipment

SAMPLE LIST OF GENERAL, SELLING, AND ADMINISTRATIVE EXPENSES

Advertising	Rent
Salaries and Wages	Utilities
Office Supplies	Insurance
Office Equipment	Business Taxes
Payroll Taxes	

themselves, because they make clear the reasoning behind the numbers and demonstrate that the entrepreneur didn't simply pull them out of the air. For example, assumptions would explain how the sales forecast was derived and why two employees were added in month 6. Without narrative assumptions accompanying the financials, it is difficult to put much faith in the numbers.

Preparing the Pro Forma Income Statement

The **income statement,** also known as a **profit and loss statement,** gives information about the projected profit or loss status of the business for a specified period of time. *Profit* and *loss* are accounting terms that refer to how much the business earned or lost after all the expenses were deducted. Figure 8.4 displays an income statement for a software company. The income statement is normally the first financial statement prepared so that the business's **income tax liability** can be calculated.

The taxes owed—the income tax liability—are based on the profit made by the company, and they appear in the cash flow statement (which records the business's cash inflows and outflows) in the month in which they are forecast to be paid. Because income taxes vary from state to state, the financial statements presented here are not indicative of tax rates in every state. Furthermore, whether a company pays the taxes or the entrepreneur pays the taxes at his or her personal rate is a function of the type of legal entity chosen for the business. Choice of the legal form of organization, discussed in Chapter 10, is a significant decision made during the development of the business plan.

It is important to note that revenues and expenses are recorded in the income statement when the transaction occurs in the case of sales, and when the debt is incurred in the case of expenses, whether or not money has been received or expended. If a sale occurs in March, it is recorded as a sale in March even if the money is not received until May. In the interim, that money becomes an account receivable.

The first section of the income statement details the revenues coming into the business from a variety of sources, but typically from sales. A product-oriented business will show a cost of goods produced or sold, which is a calculation of all the costs directly related to making the product or purchasing the goods to be sold. Refer to the discussion of cost of goods sold in the previous section. A service business does not typically calculate a COGS.

The difference between COGS and revenues is gross profit. This is an important figure because **gross profit** divided by sales gives the gross margin, a figure often used to describe the room that businesses have to make financial mistakes. For example, suppose a company sees revenues of $500,000 in year 1 and the COGS equals $350,000. Subtracting the COGS from revenues gives a gross profit of $150,000. Then the gross margin is 30 percent, which means that out of every dollar the company earns, it has 30 cents left to pay its general, administrative, and selling expenses.

Revenue	$500,000
COGS	($350,000)
Gross Profit	$150,000
Gross Margin = $150,000/$500,000 or 30%	

The next major section of the income statement is **operating expenses,** which details all the expenditures of the business. A typical income statement might include the following expenses:

Selling expenses

Advertising and promotion

Salaries and wages

Office supplies

Rent

Utilities

Insurance

Payroll taxes

FIGURE 8.4 Sudden Presence — Pro Forma Income Statement, Year 1

INCOME STATEMENT PROJECTIONS	Jan-06	Feb-06	Mar-06	Apr-06	May-06	Jun-06	Jul-06	Aug-06	Sep-06	Oct-06	Nov-06	Dec-06	FYE 2006
Military/Engineering	24,375	24,375	24,375	28,031	28,031	28,031	32,236	32,236	32,236	37,071	37,071	37,071	365,141
Educational/Entertainment	-	-	-	-	-	9,375	9,375	9,375	9,844	10,336	11,370	12,506	72,181
Total Consulting	24,375	24,375	24,375	28,031	28,031	37,406	41,611	41,611	42,080	47,407	48,441	49,578	437,321
Up-Front Revenue	-	-	-	-	-	-	-	-	-	50,000	-	50,000	50,000
Royalty Revenue	-	-	-	-	-	-	-	-	-	346,667	346,667	346,667	1,040,000
Total Development Income	-	-	-	-	-	-	-	-	-	396,667	346,667	346,667	1,090,000
Total Revenue	**24,375**	**24,375**	**24,375**	**28,031**	**28,031**	**37,406**	**41,611**	**41,611**	**42,080**	**444,074**	**395,108**	**396,244**	**1,527,321**
Consulting Group Expenses	16,486	16,486	16,486	17,053	17,053	18,788	19,439	19,439	19,526	20,367	20,558	20,768	222,450
Game Development Expenses	12,292	12,292	12,292	12,292	12,292	12,292	12,292	12,292	12,292	12,292	12,292	12,292	147,500
Gross Profit	**(4,403)**	**(4,403)**	**(4,403)**	**(1,314)**	**(1,314)**	**6,327**	**9,880**	**9,880**	**10,262**	**411,416**	**362,258**	**363,185**	**1,157,371**
General and Administrative	3,000	1,650	12,150	1,650	2,650	4,400	1,900	1,900	4,400	1,900	1,900	4,900	42,400
Total Expenses	**(7,403)**	**(6,053)**	**(16,553)**	**(2,964)**	**(3,964)**	**1,927**	**7,980**	**7,980**	**5,862**	**409,516**	**360,358**	**358,285**	**1,114,971**
Depreciation and Amortization	583	583	583	583	583	583	583	583	583	583	583	583	7,000
Net Income	**(7,986)**	**(6,636)**	**(17,136)**	**(3,547)**	**(4,547)**	**1,344**	**7,397**	**7,397**	**5,279**	**408,932**	**359,775**	**357,701**	**1,107,971**

Interest on loans

Depreciation

Miscellaneous

Subtracting expenses from gross profit gives net profit before taxes (income taxes). This is the business's **taxable income.** Subtracting the company's tax liability gives net profit. Most entrepreneurs project profit and loss out three years. The farther out the projections go, the less reliable they are, so it's better to stay within three to five years. The income statement should contain footnotes for each item to refer the reader to supporting material in the "Notes to Financial Statements" or "Assumptions." Any unusual major expenses, such as the cost of participating in a trade show, should be explained in a footnote.

The income statement depicts when the new venture will cover its costs and begin to make a profit. However, the expenses of the business are paid not with profit but with cash. Therefore, during feasibility analysis, the most important financial statement is the cash flow statement or cash budget.

Forecasting a Start-up's Cash Needs

One of the key things to be determined during feasibility analysis is how much money will be needed to start the business and keep it operating until a positive cash flow has been achieved from the revenues of the business. The bulk of expenses in the first year of a new business are probably incurred prior to the business's opening its doors for the first time. The costs of purchasing furniture, equipment, start-up inventory, and supplies can quickly add up to a substantial amount—and that doesn't include deposits for leases and utilities. A manufacturing start-up might also include product development costs, a deposit on the lease for a plant, and raw materials costs. Start-ups with new products typically accrue heavy pre–start-up development costs that include engineering, prototyping, and patent assessment and application. These are one-time expenses to get the business started.

For accounting purposes, some of these initial costs, such as those for equipment, must be depreciated, or discounted over a period of time, on the income statement; others, such as organizational and formation expenses, must be amortized, or spread out over time, as start-up costs. It is important to check with a good accountant to learn the correct method for depreciating and amortizing certain expenses. For determining start-up funding requirements, however, these costs will be treated as a lump sum.

The estimated sales, expenses, and taxes calculated in the income statement can now be placed in a **cash flow statement** as the first step in arriving at start-up cash needs. Figure 8.5 shows a cash flow statement for a software company. As in all financial statements, each item on the statement should be footnoted in the "Notes to Financial Statements" to explain what the assumptions were and how the figures were derived.

The first section of the statement, cash inflows or receipts, records all the inflows of cash into the business *when they are received*. It is important to remember that the cash flow statement records cash inflows and outflows when they occur. Therefore, if a sale is made in March, for example, but payment is not received until April, the sale is counted in April on the statement. The income statement differs from

| FIGURE 8.5 | Sudden Presence — Pro Forma Cash Flow Statement, Year 1 |

CASH FLOW PROJECTIONS	Start-up	Jan-06	Feb-06	Mar-06	Apr-06	May-06	Jun-06	Jul-06	Aug-06	Sep-06	Oct-06	Nov-06	Dec-06	FYE 2006
CASH INFLOWS														
Revenues Collected	-		24,375	24,375	24,375	28,031	28,031	37,406	41,611	41,611	42,080	444,074	395,108	1,131,077
Consulting Group														
Business Development								2,083	2,083	2,083	2,083	2,083	2,083	12,500
Sales Expense		4,289	4,289	4,289	4,307	4,307	4,354	5,208	5,208	5,210	5,237	5,242	5,248	57,187
Web								208	208	208	208	208	208	1,250
Artist								833	833	833	833	833	833	5,000
Art Director								417	417	417	417	417	417	2,500
Project Manager								4,167	4,167	4,167	4,167	4,167	4,167	25,000
Independent Contractor			3,656	3,656	3,656	4,205	4,205	5,892	6,523	6,523	6,607	7,421	7,607	59,952
Game Development														
Lead Designer								2,083	2,083	2,083	2,083	2,083	2,083	12,500
Business Development								1,042	1,042	1,042	1,042	1,042	1,042	6,250
Sales Expense														
Art Director								1,667	1,667	1,667	1,667	1,667	1,667	10,000
3-D Animator								3,333	3,333	3,333	3,333	3,333	3,333	20,000
Project Manager								4,167	4,167	4,167	4,167	4,167	4,167	25,000
Sound Effects														
CASH OUTFLOWS														
General and Administrative														
CPA				500			500			500			500	2,000
Accounting														
Travel				8,000		1,000	250	250	250	250	250	250	250	10,750
Advertising				1,500			1,500			1,500			1,500	6,000
Legal		1,000		500			500			500			1,000	3,500
Equipment Leases/Supplies		500	500	500	500	500	500	500	500	500	500	500	500	6,000
Computer Lease														
Utilities														
Phone		500	500	500	500	500	500	500	500	500	500	500	500	6,000
Office Space														
Web Hosting		350												350
Insurance		500	500	500	500	500	500	500	500	500	500	500	500	6,000
Other		150	150	150	150	150	150	150	150	150	150	150	150	1,800
Administrative Assistant														
Executive Salaries														
Benefits														
Equipment Acquisition	15,000													15,000
Software Acquisition	10,000													10,000
Total Cash Outflow	-	7,289	9,595	20,095	9,613	11,162	12,958	33,000	33,631	36,133	33,744	34,563	37,755	304,538
Total Start-up Expenses	25,000				1,534 Break-even									
Tax Distributions													498,587	498,587
Net Cash Flow	(32,289)		14,780	4,280	14,762	16,870	15,073	4,406	7,980	5,478	8,335	409,511	(141,235)	327,951
Cumulative Cash Flow	(32,289)		(17,508)	(13,228)	1,534	18,404	33,476	37,882	45,862	51,340	59,675	469,186	327,951	327,951

the cash flow statement in this regard. That is why the cash flow statement is so valuable; it lets the entrepreneur see the patterns of cash inflow to the business.

The next section records **cash outflows** or **disbursements.** Normally, a business incurs a number of expenses at launch, before the business is in operation. These start-up costs can be reflected in a Month Zero or Start-up column at the beginning of the cash flow statement. The final section gives the entrepreneur crucial information: the net change in cash flow—in other words, whether the business had a positive or a negative cash flow in that month. Note that in each month, the net cash flow reflects only the cash inflows and outflows for that month, assuming no start-up capital. An additional line, the cumulative cash flow, will provide a critical piece of the cash needs: the highest negative. This figure ($32,289 in Figure 8.5) plus start-up costs is the minimum amount the entrepreneur needs to survive until a positive cash flow is achieved. Because this figure is an estimate based on a whole series of estimates, there is a very good chance that it is not entirely accurate, so it is important to add a safety or contingency factor. The safety factor is often based on the sales and collection cycle of the business. If, for example, customers typically pay on a 60-day cycle, it will be important to be able to cover at least 60 days of fixed costs.

Table 8.2 presents a breakout of the start-up capital requirements for the software company. Note that the cash needs are separated into types of money: start-up (which includes capital expenditures broken out), working capital (the highest cumulative negative cash flow), and the safety factor, which is a contingency amount based on the probability that their estimates might be off. This is important information that the entrepreneur can use when the time comes to fund the business. For example, rather than purchasing equipment (an outlay of several thousand dollars in the example), the entrepreneur could choose to lease it and thus reduce start-up expenditures significantly. In fact, the entrepreneurs in this example did choose to lease their more expensive computer equipment.

From this cash needs assessment, it is clear that the entrepreneur will need a minimum of $82,289, including the safety factor, to start and operate this business until it generates a positive cash flow. The company will break even on a cash basis in month 4.

Assessing Risk

Many entrepreneurs make the mistake of thinking they have done a complete analysis of their start-up financial requirements because they have generated pages of spreadsheets with numbers that, on the surface, appear to work. And if they have developed assumptions that justify their numbers, it is not irrational on their part to believe their work is done. But this would be a mistake. The true test of financial feasibility is whether the key financial figures are in line with the company's goals. Chapter 15 focuses on matching the financial plan to the company's goals. Here are some questions that must be considered: What would be the effect on the financials of a change in price, a decline in sales, or unexpected demand? What would be the effect on cash flow if the company grew at a more rapid pace than a certain percentage a year? What if it grew more slowly? How sensitive to change are the cash flow numbers and net income? And how will the company deal with these changes?

TABLE 8.2	Cash Needs Assessment

START-UP EXPENSES	
Equipment	$15,000
Software	$10,000
Working Capital	$ 7,289
Highest Cumulative Negative CF	$32,289
Safety Factor	<u>$50,000</u>
	$82,289

At the feasibility stage, it is important to consider the changes with the highest probability of occurring and to factor in how the impact of these changes will be dealt with. Analyzing the financial risks and benefits of a new venture is a difficult and challenging exercise, but it must be done so that two fundamental questions can be answered: (1) Do the start-up capital requirements make sense? In other words, is the business financially feasible? And (2) looking at the capital investment and the profit possibilities, is there enough money in this opportunity to make the effort worthwhile?

Unfortunately, many businesses are feasible—they can be made to work financially—but the return on the initial investment is so low that the entrepreneur would be better off putting that investment in real estate or some other vehicle. New businesses take an extraordinary amount of work, which entrepreneurs often fail to put a value on. All too often, the business is running and making a profit, but the entrepreneur is making less than he or she would have made working for someone else. The feasibility stage, when the investment has still been minimal, is the time to look seriously at financial feasibility and quantify the risks and potential benefits. Once the venture has been deemed feasible, a business plan with a full set of financial statements can be developed. That process will further reduce the uncertainty inherent in the start-up process. The financial plan for a start-up venture is discussed in Chapter 15.

New Venture Checklist

Have you:

☐ Gathered the numbers you need for performing your financial analysis?

☐ Gathered sales forecast data through triangulation?

☐ Prepared a pro forma income statement?

☐ Created a cash flow statement from start-up until a positive cash flow is achieved?

☐ Performed a cash needs assessment to determine how much capital you will need to start the business?

☐ Determined whether this venture is financially feasible?

Issues to Consider

1. What are the types of resources that entrepreneurs need to gather to start a new venture?
2. Why is the cash flow statement the most important statement for the entrepreneur?
3. What are the primary differences between an income statement and a cash flow statement or cash budget?
4. What are some ways to forecast sales effectively for a retail business? For a manufacturer? For a service business?
5. What are the three categories of funds in the cash needs assessment, and how are they used to calculate how much money is needed to start the business?

Experiencing Entrepreneurship

1. Interview a banker and an accountant about the key financial statements that entrepreneurs need to understand to run their businesses. Ask about the biggest mistakes business owners make in preparing their financial statements. Compare and contrast the responses of the banker and the accountant. Are their views of the financials different? Why?

2. Interview an entrepreneur who has been in business no longer than five years to find out how he or she calculated how much money was needed to start the venture. Did it turn out to be enough? Why or why not? What would you have advised the entrepreneur to do differently?

Additional Sources of Information

Adelman, P.J., and A.M. Marks (2004). *Entrepreneurial Finance: Finance for Small Business.* Upper Saddle River, NJ: Pearson/Prentice-Hall.

Burton, E.J., and S.M. Bragg (2000). *Accounting and Finance for Your Small Business.* New York: Wiley.

Stancill, J. (2003). *Entrepreneurial Finance: For New and Emerging Businesses.* Mason, OH: Southwestern College Publishing.

Relevant Case Studies

Case 3 Beanos Ice Cream Shoppe, p. 410
Case 5 iRobot, p. 432

Case 7 Linksys, p. 446

Part Three

The Business Plan: Building a Company

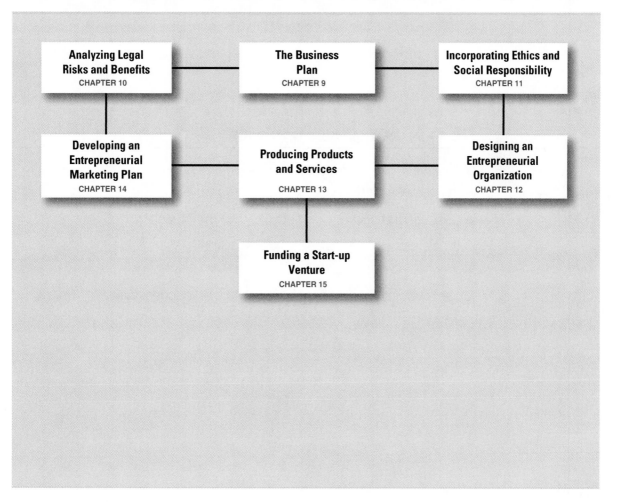

Analyzing Legal Risks and Benefits CHAPTER 10	**The Business Plan** CHAPTER 9	**Incorporating Ethics and Social Responsibility** CHAPTER 11
Developing an Entrepreneurial Marketing Plan CHAPTER 14	**Producing Products and Services** CHAPTER 13	**Designing an Entrepreneurial Organization** CHAPTER 12
	Funding a Start-up Venture CHAPTER 15	

The Business Plan

"When all is said and done, the journey is the reward. There is nothing else."

Randy Komisar, The Monk and the Riddle

LEARNING OBJECTIVES

- Describe how to move from a feasible concept to a business plan.

- Discuss the strategy and structure of the business plan.

- Explain how to organize a business plan effectively.

- Describe how to present a business plan successfully.

Profile 9.1   ANATOMY OF A NEW BUSINESS FAILURE

Stories of great successes can be inspiring, but entrepreneurs often learn much more and avoid fatal mistakes by doing a postmortem on a failed business. A good example of a business that seemed to have everything going for it and yet could not succeed is Future Beef, an Arkansas-based business founded in 2001.

The Opportunity

In a new world where genetics is used to improve the quality, shelf life, and size of the foods we eat, Future Beef saw an opportunity to use genetic data and high-tech equipment to produce enormous amounts of superior meat. That was its primary product, but its plan also included providing its workers with the highest wages and benefits in the industry, as well as apartments and day-care centers as an additional benefit. To accomplish these ambitious goals would require a lot of investor capital. By late 1997, Future Beef had its first round of capital, enough to allow the founders to quit their day jobs and recruit an experienced CEO (H. Russell Cross, former director of the Institute of Food Science and Engineering at Texas A&M) and two financial officers. The deal with Safeway included a $15-million infusion of capital, and with the over $200 million total raised, the company was able to begin building plants.

Experience of the Founders

Rod Bowling and Rob Streight were the brains behind Future Beef. Bowling had a Ph.D. in meat and muscle biology from Texas A&M, and he had held the highest positions at some of the biggest plants in the industry. In 1996, frustrated by his inability to implement his innovative ideas in a very traditional industry, Bowling sought the help of Streight in designing a very different kind of beef-producing company, one that integrated the value chain. Streight's role was to build the business's technology infrastructure.

How the Business Makes Money

Not only did Future Beef want to control the entire value chain from the ranch to the packinghouse; it also wanted to use every bit of the cow to create value-added products and deliver those products through one grocery retailer, Safeway. Unfortunately, at that time the cattle market was depressed, and the September 11 terrorist attacks only served to worsen the situation. Future Beef was already in trouble, with huge cost overruns, malfunctioning equipment, and even some lawsuits. It was losing money on every steer because it had purchased its cattle at market high prices and at lower weights than normal. Future Beef also kept cattle in the grow yards longer than normal to control their nutrition, but this only served to increase the company's holding costs. Only one month after it opened its 450,000-square-foot plant, its exclusive retail partner, Safeway, was also in trouble. Three months later, Future Beef was forced to declare Chapter 11 bankruptcy. Then it laid off all its workers five months after the bankruptcy and, in August 2002, liquidated its holdings. The postmortem revealed that the company was trying to implement too many expensive new systems, largely because there was a lot of industry knowledge in the company but no business experience. It appears that the founders were visionaries and not execution people—a fatal flaw in many business plans.

Epilogue: In May 2003, just nine months after Future Beef closed its operations, the plant resumed cattle slaughter operations as Creekstone Farms Premium Beef. It is estimated that 80 percent of Creekstone's employees are former Future Beef employees. Creekstone purchased the plant at a bankruptcy auction.

Sources: J. McCuan, "Failure of Genius," *Inc. Magazine* (August 2003); "New Owners of Defunct Future Beef Plant Begin Operations," DodgeGlobe.com, accessed January 15, 2004; and Wes Ishmael, "Why Future Beef Went Under," 11/1/02, http://beef-mag.com/mag/beef_why_future_beef/, accessed 6/24/04.

I t is an unfortunate fact that universities and institutions everywhere are perpetuating the myth that entrepreneurs must have business plans before they start businesses. Potential entrepreneurs are spending up to 200 hours of their valuable time in pursuit of the perfect plan to present to an investor, only to discover that the investor is more interested in the founding team and in whether the business is up and running.

When Jennifer Lawton started Net Daemons Associates in 1992, she didn't have a plan. At that time the economy was in recession, so as an independent contractor providing computer networking services to companies without in-house staff, she had plenty of business opportunity. She didn't have to prove the market; it was knocking down her door. Not until they had been in business for several years in more competitive times and had fifteen associates did Lawton and her management team realize that it would be easier to concentrate on strategy and explain where the business was going if they had a plan.[1] Given an existing track record, her business plan would be real, not a work of fiction like the plans of ventures that are in the feasibility analysis stage.

Recall that feasibility analysis tests the business concept in the market to determine the conditions under which the entrepreneur is willing to move forward and start the business. Going through the process of feasibility analysis helps the entrepreneur learn about the business and prepare to launch. The business plan depends on a feasible concept that has been market-tested, because the business plan is about building a company and executing that feasible concept.

There is another reason why business plans have had to be based on reality. The post–dot-com era and the crash of technology stocks have resulted in a much cooler investment climate. Investors are taking a far more conservative approach to both formal and informal investing. Still, there is money available for great business concepts, particularly in some areas of technology, such as biotech, security, robotics, and nanotech if they convey a compelling story and deliver a management team that can execute the plan effectively.

For years, the traditional model of business planning involved carefully crafting a business plan and then sending it out to potential funders for consideration. Of course, much like a slush pile of manuscripts at a publishing house, these business plans sat stacked on the investor's desk, rarely seeing the light of day. Today, submitting a professionally crafted business plan is less important than making it clear what the entrepreneur has accomplished in the way of starting the business.[2] Investors want to see that the venture has customers and a track record, however brief. They want to see that the business model actually works.

The new environment for business planning actually makes the case for the importance of the feasibility study to prove the concept and enable the founding team to launch the venture and test it before completing the formal business plan and seeking outside investment capital.

From Feasible Concept to Business Plan

Chapters 1 through 8 dealt with analyzing the feasibility of a new venture concept. Simply stated, feasibility is about the business idea and testing the business concept. The **business plan** is about the execution strategy that will bring that idea to market. The business plan serves three purposes: (1) it serves as a reality check for the entrepreneur, who will need to think very carefully about all aspects of the business; (2) it is a living guide to the business, a complete and comprehensive picture; and (3) it is a statement of intent for interested third parties such as investors, bankers, and strategic partners. Each of these potential stakeholders in the new venture will view the business plan from a different perspective.

Investors' Interests

Anyone investing in the new venture has four principal concerns: rate of growth, return on investment, degree of risk, and protection. Investors are generally betting that the value of their ownership interest in the business will increase over time at a rate greater than that of another type of investment or of a bank account. They want to know how fast the business is projected to grow, when that growth will take place, and what will ensure that the growth actually occurs as predicted. For this reason, they tend to look for market-driven companies rather than product- or technology-driven companies, because they're interested in such things as short payback periods for customers.[3] They expect that predictions will be based on solid evidence in the marketplace and on thorough knowledge of the target market.[4] Investors are naturally concerned about when and how the principal portion of their investment will be repaid and how much gain on that investment will accrue over the time they are invested in the company. The answers to these concerns are largely a function of the structure of the investment deal: whether it involves a limited or general partnership, or preferred or common stock, and so forth. Investors want to understand thoroughly the risks they face in investing in the new venture; principally, they want to know how their original equity will be protected. They expect the entrepreneur to present the potential dangers facing the new venture, along with a plan for mitigating or dealing with them to protect the investors against loss. Finally, investors want to know how their equity will be protected if the business fails and how the business will protect its assets from seizure by creditors.

Although the business plan is vital to investment decision making, it is not the only piece of information considered. In one survey of 42 venture capitalists, 43 percent claimed to having invested in a venture in the previous three years without the benefit of a business plan.[5] Only 36 percent reported that the business plan was "very important" in their evaluation. And perhaps the most revealing statistic of all was that 96 percent preferred to learn about a potential investment through a referral from someone they trusted. Furthermore, investors found that the primary flaws in most business plans were overly optimistic financial projections, too much hype, poor explanation of the business model, and no demonstration of customer demand.

Bankers'/Lenders' Interests

Bankers/lenders are primarily interested in the company's margins and cash flow projections, because they are concerned about how their loans or credit lines to the business will be repaid. The margins indicate how much room there is for error between the cost to produce the product (or deliver the service) and the selling price. If margins are tight and the business has to lower prices to compete, the firm may not be able to pay off its loans as consistently and quickly as the bank would like. Similarly, bankers look at cash flow projections to see whether the business can pay all its expenses and still have money left over at the end of each month. Bankers also look at the qualifications and track record of the management team and may require personal guarantees of the principals. Like investors, bankers or lenders want to know they are going to get their money back. When considering a business plan and an entrepreneur for a loan, lenders have several concerns:

- *The amount of money the entrepreneur needs.* Lenders are looking for a specific amount that can be justified with accurate calculations and data.

- *The kind of positive impact the loan will have on the business.* Lenders would like to know that the money they are lending is not going to pay off old debt or to pay salaries, but rather will improve the business's financial position, particularly with regard to cash flow.

- *The kinds of assets the business has for collateral.* Not all assets are created equal. Some assets have no value outside the business, because they are custom-made or specific to that business and therefore cannot be sold on the open market. Lenders prefer to see industry-standard equipment and facilities that can easily be converted to another use.

- *How the business will repay the loan.* Lenders are interested in the earnings potential of the business over the life of the loan, but even more important, they want to know that the business generates sufficient cash flow to service the debt. Fixed expenses are fairly easy to predict, but variable expenses—those related to the production of the product or service—present a more difficult problem. In an attempt to avoid any long-term issues, lenders pay close attention to the market research section of the business plan, which highlights the demand for the product/service. They also focus on the marketing plan, which tells them how the entrepreneur intends to reach the customer.

- *How the bank will be protected if the business doesn't meet its projections.* Lenders want to know that the entrepreneur has a contingency plan for situations where major assumptions prove to be wrong. They want to ensure that they are paid out of cash flow, not by liquidating the assets of the business, which generally would only give them a small percent of the value of the assets.

- *The entrepreneur's stake in the business.* Like investors, lenders feel more confident about lending to a business in which the entrepreneur has a substantial monetary investment. Such an investment reduces the likelihood that the entrepreneur will walk away from the business, leaving the lender stranded.

Strategic Partners

Some entrepreneurs, particularly those who intend to manufacture a product, choose to form a **strategic alliance** with a larger company so that they don't have to incur the tremendous costs of purchasing equipment for a manufacturing plant. They may, for example, license another firm to manufacture and assemble the product and supply it to the entrepreneur to market and distribute. Alternatively, an entrepreneur may enter into an agreement with a supplier to provide necessary raw materials in exchange for an equity interest in the start-up venture.

Strategic alliances may take the form of formal partnership agreements with major corporations or may consist simply of an informal agreement such as a large purchase contract. In either case, the larger company that is allying itself with the new venture is usually looking for new products, processes, or technologies that complement its current line of products or services. Accordingly, it will seek a new venture management team that has some previous corporate experience so that the relationship will be smoother. Larger companies are also interested in strategic issues such as the marketing and growth strategies of the new venture. Tim Welu, CEO of Minnesota-based Paisley Consulting, finds that strategic alliances are essential to the success of his business accountability software product. His premiere product, AutoAudit, enables businesses to document internal audit results. Its benefits led to Paisley gaining a Big Five accounting firm as a partner, which gave it distribution to 80 countries. The only problem was that strategic partner was Arthur Andersen, the accounting firm that went bankrupt as a result of its association with Enron as its auditor. Fortunately, however, many of Andersen's employees went to Ernst & Young, which became Paisley's next strategic partner. Although there are risks associated with partnering with a larger firm, the benefits of broader distribution and access to deeper resources make the positives outweigh the negatives.

Knowing in advance what these third parties are looking for will help an entrepreneur address their specific needs in the business plan, enhancing the partnership's ability to achieve the goals of the business.

Starting the Process with a Presentation

Spending hours and days writing a business plan may not be as valuable as understanding the business and conveying that understanding in a compelling way. Given the new investor environment discussed previously, a more constructive first step is to prepare an extended version of the "elevator pitch." The **elevator pitch** is a brief but convincing statement of the business concept: the ever-important issues of why you, why now, how you will change the world. The exercise of putting together a presentation (typically in PowerPoint) forces the founding team to focus on the critical success factors for the business. In other words, what must be in place for the business to succeed? With a very focused presentation in hand, it will be easier to develop the full business plan without deviating from the essentials. Later in the chapter, we will address the matter of how to present the business plan effectively. Several fundamental questions must be answered before the presentation.

What Need Is Being Served?

In other words, is there really an opportunity here? Support for the answer to this question will come from the market research with potential customers and should demonstrate a real market for the opportunity. The answer should also convey that the company is customer-driven, in that it is solving a real need that customers have.[6] In addition, a detailed profile of the most likely customer should be included.

Can the Founding Team Serve That Need?

Why is this founding team the best team to execute this concept? Can it be demonstrated that the founding team has the experience and skills required by the various

Socially Responsible Entrepreneurship

The Little Schoolhouse That Could

Gifford Pinchot is best known for his classic 1985 book on intrapreneuring; but largely thanks to the influence of his grandfather, who founded the forest service in 1905, Pinchot has become an avid conservationist. In this capacity, he founded the Bainbridge Island Graduate Institute (BGI) near Seattle, Washington, in 2002. There students are immersed in studies of environmental sustainability and social responsibility in the context of entrepreneurship and innovation.

BGI was launched in just six months with $120,000 of Pinchot's own money. Thereafter, he raised another $300,000 from Ben Cohen (Ben and Jerry's co-founder) and Wayne Silby (founder of the Calvert Fund). He recruited a president and they worked to gain state authorization to award an MBA. The first class of 18 students enrolled in the fall of 2002. BGI is one of the first graduate schools in the United States to focus on sustainable business, to "create profit in ways that contribute to taking care of people and the planet." Pinchot is determined to make a mark on society by educating more people in how to be entrepreneurial while also being socially responsible.

Sources: BGI, http://www.bgiedu.org/index.htm; and E. Winninghoff, "The Little Green Schoolhouse," *Inc. Magazine* (July 2003), www.inc.com.

areas of the business? Do the founders have their own money invested in this concept? It is easy to spend other people's money or to consider "sweat" equity as equivalent to cash—but it isn't equivalent in the eyes of investors, who figure that the founding team won't give up easily if they have invested their own money in the deal. Does the team have passion and the drive to make this business a success? Passion and drive are difficult to measure but are reflected in the level of work that was put into the market research. How many people did the team talk to—industry experts, customers, and so forth?

Why Is Now the Right Time to Launch This Venture?

What makes this concept so valuable right now? If this business is the only one of its kind, why is that so? Has anyone tried this before and failed? If so, why? What makes the current environment right for this venture? Timing is critical in the launch of any new venture, so it is important to explain why *now* is the right time.

What Is This Venture's Competitive Advantage?

No venture can succeed in the long term without a **sustainable competitive advantage**—not a single competitive advantage, but a bundle of them in every aspect of the business. The presentation needs to address what advantages will enable this venture to create a unique unserved niche and to enter the market and secure customers with little or no competition in the beginning.

Can This Venture Make Money?

Most business plans do not adequately address the business model. How will the business make money over the long term? How will value be created at various points in the business's life? In general, value is created when the business is adequately capitalized and has highly regarded investors, an experienced management team, a unique technology or service, the ability to continually innovate, and a rapidly expanding market.[7] Once the new venture has passed the start-up stage, additional value is created by its position in the market, significant customers, effective operating systems, a strong gross margin, positive cash flow, and a high return on equity.

Because business plans are most often used to raise capital, the questions they answer are frequently of great interest to an investor or lender. Here are some of the questions that the business plan should answer: How much money is needed to address this opportunity? How will capital be allocated (i.e., to increase sales, to boost profits, or to enhance the value of the company)? How will the business provide a superior return on investment (ROI)? Which exit strategies are possible?

Profile 9.1 provides an example of one business plan that failed because it didn't answer all these questions.

Starting the Process with a Website

Today when people hear about a new business or a new product or service, the first place they go for more information is the Internet. This makes sense, because the Internet is the perfect place to communicate a new venture's message. However, many new businesses make the mistake of simply slapping up a single page marked "under construction" or "coming soon," until they finish their business plan and start the business. On the Internet, a new business can look as successful and established as any large company for relatively few dollars invested in development of the site. A quick online demonstration can communicate to the visitor what the business does, who its customers are, and what its value proposition is. The site should discuss the founding team, state the company's goals or mission, and tell potential investors, customers, and other interested parties how to contact the business.

One word of caution about the website: Proprietary information that is not protected by patents or trademarks should not be put on the site, because companies regularly peruse the Internet for information on their competitors. In fact, entrepreneurs should definitely study the websites of their competitors for important clues about what features they should build into their own sites and how they might improve on what their competitors are doing. As with every promotional or informational piece about the business, differentiation is critical. The following are a few important points to consider when developing a website.

- *The site should speak to potential customers.* They are the most important visitors, and investors appreciate that entrepreneurs recognize that fact.
- *Identify the pain for the customer, and then show how it can be cured.* Identifying the pain or problem that customers are experiencing is an effective way to get their attention. Immediately following up with the solution assures them that they have come to the right place.
- *Clearly describe the business model.* Customers should understand what they are paying for, how much, and in what manner. Free items should be clearly distinguished from those that carry a price. If customers are not certain what they are getting for their money, they will resist purchasing.

- *Make sure that customers take something of value from the site.* That something of value could be free information, an article, or a coupon. If the visit to the site was worthwhile, customers will return again and again.

It is not within the scope of this text to discuss website development. Information on building an effective website is ubiquitous on the Web and in every bookstore. Some examples can be found in the Additional Sources of Information section of this chapter.

The Business Plan: Strategy and Structure

Writing a business plan is a huge undertaking that should be planned in terms of tasks and timeline. If the new venture has already been launched as suggested in previous sections—via a presentation, a website, or an actual start-up based on a successful feasibility analysis—the writing of the business plan must now be sandwiched in among all the day-to-day activities associated with an operating business. Even if the new venture has not yet been launched, an action plan for completing a business plan in a relatively short period of time will help accelerate the process. The following tasks are a guide to preparing to write the business plan.

- *Identify who is responsible for what.* A lot of updated information must be gathered about industry, market, customer, and costs. Even though all of these data were gathered when the feasibility study was conducted, some time may have elapsed before the writing of the business plan, so it is important to make sure that all information is current. Make a list of everything that must be collected and how it needs to be collected (secondary research, talking to customers, etc.). Decide who will do what and by when it must be accomplished.
- *Develop a timeline based on tasks identified.* It is important to be realistic about how much time it will take to complete all the tasks associated with the business plan. The timeline is very likely to be too long, especially if the work is being done on evenings and weekends, so the next job will be to determine whether all of the tasks are critical to the business plan and to prune any that are not.
- *Hold the team to the timeline and work diligently to get the plan done.* Once the business plan is complete, it's a good idea to get a trusted third party to review the plan to catch anything the team may have missed.

Components of the Business Plan

All business plans have some major sections in common. The following sections and the outline in the appendix at the end of the book are merely guides. It is important that entrepreneurs customize their business plan to meet their specific needs and the needs of those who will read it.

Executive Summary

The **executive summary,** the most important part of the business plan, is a standalone piece and is the primary means of stimulating an investor, banker, or other interested party to read the full business plan. Typically, the executive summary should be no more than two pages and should contain the most important points from all the sections of the business plan.

It is vital that the executive summary capture the reader's attention instantly in the first sentence. This is often best accomplished by hitting the reader with a one-two punch: a strong and compelling statement about the pain in the market, followed by a clear and concise statement of how the entrepreneur intends to cure that pain. This concept statement spells out the product/service, customer, value proposition, and distribution channel by which the benefit to the customer will be delivered. The business concept was discussed in depth in Chapter 4. The business model should also be emphasized, along with the profitability potential of the company and its potential for growth. See Figure 9.1 for an outline of a typical business plan.

See Figure 9.2 for an example of what an actual executive summary looks like.

Business Concept

The **business concept**—product/service, customer, value proposition, and distribution—should be stated clearly and concisely. The statement should be followed by some elaboration on each of the components so that the reader will have a clear understanding of the opportunity. The business model—how the business will make money—should be discussed in enough detail to ensure that the

---

SCREENSHOT 9.1   SAS Business Concept

Source: https://www.scandinavian.net/EC/Appl/Home/FrontDoor/0,3479,SO%253DF49DD4A4A82E4E02
_A9680BF2F448262E%2526MKT%253DGB,00.html, accessed 3/10/05.

| FIGURE 9.1 | Business Plan Outline |

Executive Summary

Include the most important points from all sections of the business plan.

Keep the summary to two or three pages max.

Make sure that the first sentence captures the reader's attention and the first paragraph presents the business concept in a compelling way.

Table of Contents

The Business Concept

What is the business?

Who is the customer?

What is the value proposition or benefit(s) being delivered to the customer?

How will the benefit be delivered (distribution)?

What is your differentiation strategy?

What is your business model?

What are the spin-offs from your original products/services, and what is the company's potential for growth?

Founding or Management Team

Qualifications of founding team

How critical tasks will be covered

Gap analysis, or what's missing (professional advisors, board of directors, independent contractors)

Industry/Market Analysis

Industry analysis
   Demographics, major players, trends, etc. . .
Target market analysis
   Demographics, customer grid or market
      segmentation, etc. . .
   Customer profile (based on primary research)
Competitor analysis and competitive advantages
   (competitive grid)
Distribution channels (alternatives and risk/benefit)
Entry strategy (initial market penetration, first customer)

Product/Service Development Plan

Detailed description and unique features of product/service

Technology assessment (if applicable)

Plan for prototyping and testing (all businesses require this)

Tasks and timeline to completion of products or service prototype (all businesses)

Acquisition of intellectual property

Operations Plan

Facilities
Business processes
Plan for outsourcing
Manufacturing and distribution

Organization Plan

Philosophy of management and company culture
Legal structure of the company
Organizational chart
Key management
Duties and responsibilities

Marketing Plan

Purpose of marketing plan
Target market
Unique market niche
Business identity
Plan to reach first customer

Financial Plan

Summary of key points and capital requirements
Risk factors and mediation
Break-even analysis and payback period
Narrative assumptions for financial statements
Full set of pro forma financial statements (cash flow, income, balance sheet) for three years
Plan for funding

Growth Plan

Strategy for growth
Resources required
Infrastructure changes

Contingency Plan and Harvest Strategy

Strategies for dealing with deviations from the plan
Strategies for harvesting the wealth created from the business

Timeline to Launch

Graphic: Tasks that will need to be accomplished up to the date of launch of the business in the order of their completion. Also includes milestones of first customer, multiple customer, and multiple products.

Bibliography or Endnotes (footnotes may be substituted)

Appendices (A, B, C, etc.)

Questionnaires, maps, forms, résumés, and the like

| FIGURE 9.2 | SWEst Executive Summary |

Introduction

One serious issue that arises during software development is the inability to estimate accurately the cost, resources, and schedule associated with developing software. Traditional intuitive estimation methods consistently produce overly optimistic results that contribute to cost overruns and schedule slips. Furthermore, the rapid advancement of software development tools and processes and the increasing complexity of software packages have made accurately estimating the cost and schedule of software projects more important than ever. In fact, a recent study on software development projects revealed that[10]

- 16 of projects are completed on time and on budget
- 53 of projects are challenged from a scope, schedule, or cost perspective
- 31 of projects are cancelled
- 189 is the average cost overrun of software over original estimates

Insufficient software estimation has played a significant role in these alarming industry statistics. Although current software cost estimation tools use mathematically sophisticated methods, their algorithms for cost calculation are highly sensitive to unclear and undefined input parameters. SWEst proposes to add value by helping to eliminate these issues with a requirements analysis engine and a knowledge database that will lead to more accurate estimates. With better estimation of the resources required to complete a software project, companies can better analyze the financial viability of pursued projects and ultimately improve their bottom line.

Business Concept

SWEst is a software supplier to software development companies that rely heavily on cost estimation for their internal software development. SWEst's novel software estimation interface will provide managers with more reliable and accurate software cost estimates, resulting in lower risk and more profitable business opportunities. Specifically, SWEst will initially provide two modules:

1. A **Requirements Analysis Engine** that supplements commercial estimation tools. This module will help the company estimate the key input parameters (such as source lines of code and function points) of existing commercial software tools, thereby eliminating the undefined and unclear cost drivers that lead to improper estimation.
2. A **Knowledge Databas**e that taps into a company's business system and integrates back into a software estimation tool. SWEst will build the common interfaces that will "plug" into the individual company's cost collection databases and software estimation tools to develop better software estimates.

The SWEst software package gives managers and cost analysts increased confidence in their estimates because critical input parameters are estimated with better reliability. The program's single, intuitive environment for defining input parameters and exporting them to their cost estimation tool of choice also results in savings of time and money. Managers and analysts can now spend their time triangulating on realistic cost estimates by running several estimation tools instead of repeatedly inputting parameters in the archaic formats that the various codes require. More reliable cost estimates, provided sooner and at less cost, offer software developers and planners a competitive advantage. Less time dedicated to manual data entry also means a more relaxed work environment, where more time is dedicated to results rather than to set-up.

Industry Analysis

In 2002, the top five companies in the PC Business Software market spent a combined $10.4 billion on research and development. This amount spent by just a few companies provides evidence that the software development is robust. There are roughly 50 commercial software cost estimation tools available in the United States. Internally developed spreadsheet cost models are also used extensively, although they are losing favor because of their limited feature sets. Surveys suggest that 42 percent of estimators use commercial software packages, 48 percent use spreadsheets, and the remainder rely on hand calculations.[11] SWEst combines these three potential beneficiaries into two target groups for software estimation: software package users and spreadsheet users.

FIGURE 9.2(cont.)   SWEst Executive Summary

Market Analysis

Initial demand was calculated using market research, surveys, and interviews. A company's positive response to questions regarding beta testing and the possibility of purchasing SWEst's software determined whether there was sufficient demand. Survey results show that over 80 percent of respondents answered these questions positively, signifying strong demand for SWEst's product. Specifically, key companies such as AOL, Mindspeed, and Denso expressed interest in beta-testing a tool that could achieve better software estimating capability. Furthermore, Boeing has allocated time to further define the feasibility of launching this project in partnership with SWEst.

Product and Service Development Plan

SWEst will initially provide two software cost estimation interface modules: the "Requirements Analysis Engine," which aides in defining input parameters, and the "Knowledge Database Collector," which compiles actual company costs into a "Knowledge Database". SWEst will work closely with potential customers to help design and develop final products. SWEst will also provide fee-based service support and educational training to make its product effective for customers.

Founding Team

SWEst's founding team is made up of four partners: Bruno Bachinger, Justin Jessee, Gregory Wood, and Thomas Obkircher. Justin Jessee will take the lead in financial activities, and Thomas Obkircher will assume the role of technical director and head SWEst's initial product development team. Bruno Bachinger will run marketing and sales, while Gregory Wood will oversee product development and customer technical support.

Financial Plan

On the basis of conservative sales assumptions, SWEst expects to achieve positive cash flow 11 months after launching the business. This turnaround corresponds to a maximum negative cash flow of $374,000. Thus, with a safety margin of $125,000, the business needs $500,000 in initial start-up capital. SWEst will break even after 19 months of operation.

Timeline to Launch

SWEst will achieve key milestones in a timely manner. The first sale of a "Front-End Requirements Analysis Engine" module is anticipated in month 6 after launch. "Knowledge Database" sales will begin the next month. Positive cash flow is anticipated in month 11 after product launch, and break even is expected in month 19.

reader understands the sources of revenue to the new venture and the sustainability of the business model. This section can conclude with a brief discussion of the growth possibilities and any potential for spin-off products and services. Refer to Chapter 4 for a more in-depth discussion of how a business concept is developed.

Founding Team

This section needs to provide evidence that the **founding team** has the necessary skills and experience to execute the business plan successfully. Everything depends on a great team. Investors typically look at the components of the business plan in the following order of importance: team, market, technology, and product/service. If the founding team is lacking in some area of expertise or experience, that gap needs to be closed by a member of the board of directors, by additional managers hired, or by a strategic partner. Chapter 7 explores building a founding team. This section also elaborates on the general management plan for the company—how the company will be structured. It includes such things as the philosophy of management and company culture, the legal structure, key management, compensation, and key policies. The issues that need to be addressed in the organization plan are dealt with in Chapter 12.

Industry/Market Analysis

This section discusses the nature of the industry in which the company will do business. Does the industry support a new entrant? Where is the industry in its life cycle? What are the defining characteristics of the industry; in other words, how does it work? Who are the industry opinion leaders? A more detailed discussion of performing an industry analysis is found in Chapter 5.

The market is defined by a set of customers, so this section addresses the size of the market, the customer profile, and the level of demand expected. This crucial section of the business plan provides the most persuasive argument to convince investors that there is a market of sufficient size and demand to interest them. An in-depth discussion of market research can be found in Chapter 5.

Product/Service Plan

This section provides more detail about the product or service being offered by the business. It also discusses the plan for prototyping the product/service and its associated tasks and timeline. Block and Macmillan suggest milestone planning.[8] This process includes ten milestones, or performance points at which the entrepreneur must make choices that will have a significant impact on the success of the company. See Table 9.1 for these milestones. If a new technology is being offered, then a technology assessment included in this section describes the nature of the technology, the status of the development, associated costs, and the status of the acquisition of intellectual property such as patents. The product/service plan is detailed in Chapter 6.

TABLE 9.1   **Product Development Milestones**

1. Completion of concept and product testing to determine whether there is a market
2. Completion of physical prototype
3. First financing from outside sources (investors and/or bank financing), normally to fund taking the initial prototype to market-ready product
4. Completion of initial plant tests (pilot or beta test): testing the manufacturing capability and producing a run of the product. This is true even if the manufacturing activity is outsourced.
5. Market testing: conducting a limited sale of the product to potential customers to gauge response and refine demand
6. Production start-up for product launch
7. Bellwether sale (first substantial sale to the primary customer)
8. First competitive action in the form of a response to the new product
9. First redesign or redirection in response to the market
10. First significant price change in response to the market

Operations Plan

This section of the business plan includes a detailed description of the business operations, including those processes that the new venture will own, such as facilities, and those that will be outsourced to a strategic partner, such as manufacturing. A major portion of this section explains how the business will operate, where it will get its raw materials, how the product will be manufactured and/or assembled, and what type and quantity of labor will be required to operate the business. Producing products and services is discussed in detail in Chapter 13.

Marketing Plan

The **marketing plan** is something quite distinct from market analysis. Market analysis gives the entrepreneur the information about the customer and market that will be used to create a marketing plan. The marketing plan, by contrast, is the strategy for developing awareness on the part of the customer and enticing the customer to purchase. The marketing plan includes a discussion of the plan's purpose, the market niche, the business's identity, the tools that will be used to reach the customer, a media plan for specific marketing tools, and a marketing budget. The marketing plan is discussed in Chapter 14.

Financial Plan

The **financial plan** begins with a definition of the legal form of the organization so that the reader will have a basis for understanding the tax treatment in the financials. Legal forms are discussed in Chapter 10. The plan then presents the entrepreneur's forecasts for the future of the business. Generally, these forecasts are in the form of a complete set of pro forma financial statements broken out by month in the first year or two, and then annually for the next two to five years. This section demonstrates the financial viability of the venture and indicates the assumptions made by the entrepreneur in doing the forecasts. It is designed to show that all the claims about the product, sales, marketing strategy, and operational strategy can work financially to create a business that can survive and grow over the long term. This section also includes a cash needs assessment of the capital required to start the business.

The dynamic nature of markets today makes it almost impossible to project out three to five years with any degree of certainty; hence the need and importance of having detailed financial assumptions that explain the rationale for the numbers. Also important is sensitivity analysis to identify triggers that may change the financial forecasts and affect the business negatively. A complete discussion of the financial plan appears in Chapter 8.

Growth Plan

The **growth plan** discusses how the entrepreneur plans to take the business from start-up through various stages of growth. It outlines the strategy that will be used to ensure that the business continues to grow over its life. This may mean looking at new products and services or acquiring other businesses. It is important that this section reassure an investor or lender that the company has a future. Growth is covered in Chapter 17.

Contingency Plan and Harvest Strategy

The **contingency plan** is simply a way of recognizing that sometimes, even the "best laid plans" don't work the way they were intended to work. It presents potential risk scenarios, usually dealing with situations such as unexpected high or low growth or changing economic conditions, and then, for each situation, suggests a plan to minimize the impact on the new business. The harvest strategy is the plan for capturing the wealth of the business for the entrepreneur and any investors. That strategy may include an initial public offering, a merger, or a sale, among other options. The contingency plan and harvest strategy are discussed in Chapter 18.

It is not normally a good idea to discuss **deal structure** in the business plan. Entrepreneurs rarely value their businesses correctly—typically, they are too optimistic. Putting such optimistic statements into the business plan only alerts an investor or other interested party that the entrepreneur is naïve. Deal structure will evolve over many meetings with potential investors and will ultimately be reflected in a term sheet. Deal structure is discussed further in Chapter 16.

Timeline to Launch

The business plan should contain a graphic that depicts the **timeline to launch** and should include critical milestones that take the business from its present status to first customer, multiple customers, and multiple products.

Appendices

Appendices are the appropriate place to put items that support statements in the main body of the report—things like résumés, calculations, surveys, and so forth. A good rule of thumb is not to put in the appendix anything that it is vital for a reader to see. Refer to appendix entries at the points in the body of the report where they are relevant.

Effectively Organizing the Business Plan

Mistakes in Developing the Business Plan

The following are some errors that entrepreneurs commonly make when developing the business plan, particularly when the audience is made up of investors.

- *Projecting rapid growth beyond the capabilities of the founding team.* This is a common problem. The new venture shows potential for rapidly increasing demand, sales doubling or tripling on an annual basis in the first few years. The entrepreneur believes this will be very attractive to investors. What he or she doesn't realize is that there is no evidence in the business plan that the founding team can manage and control this type of growth, and this can cause great concern on the part of the investors. Too often they have seen a business fail during rapid growth because management didn't have the systems in place to deal with it. It is far better to project controlled growth and have a plan for bringing on the necessary personnel when the company is ready for more rapid growth. The other danger in projecting too high a level of success is that doing so increases the chances that the new venture will not live up to the projections. It is better to project more conservatively and try to exceed those projections.

■ *Envisioning a three-ring circus with only one ringleader.* Many entrepreneurs pride themselves on being generalists. They claim to have expertise in all the functional areas of the new venture. What they really have is general knowledge of all the functional areas and maybe a real expertise in only one. Investors are very nervous about relying on solo entrepreneurs to lead world-class ventures. They much prefer a team of founders with at least one person specializing in each of the functional areas.[9]

■ *Reporting performance in some or all areas that exceeds industry averages.* Although it is possible for a new venture to exceed industry averages in a particular area, it is not likely. Most averages, such as those for receivables turnover and bad debt losses, have come about as a result of economies of scale, which the new venture is not likely to achieve for some time. It is better for the business plan initially to indicate performance measures at or slightly below industry averages, with a credible plan for exceeding those averages at some time in the future.

■ *Underestimating the venture's need for capital.* Investors need to know that the business plan projects sufficient capital infusion to (1) grow the company until internal cash flows can carry the load and then (2) provide an additional infusion of capital when the company is ready for rapid expansion. If the entrepreneur underestimates the amount of capital needed, most savvy investors will recognize this and attribute the error to naïveté on the part of the entrepreneur, or, conversely, they will rely on the figures presented in the plan and ultimately suffer the potential loss of their investment as a result. Every estimate of capital should contain an additional amount for contingencies.

■ *Mistaking tactics for strategy.* It is much easier to develop tactics than to develop strategies. Strategies define the overall focus of the business; tactics are the methods by which those strategies will be achieved. When an investor asks what the entrepreneur's strategy is for achieving a projected market share by year 3, and the entrepreneur responds with "attending trade shows and advertising in trade journals," the entrepreneur loses the confidence of the investor by citing tactics rather than strategy. This is a common mistake, because many entrepreneurs focus on tactics to the exclusion of identifying the overall strategy those tactics will support. An entrepreneur's strategy for achieving the market share might be to become the first mover in a market niche.

■ *Using price as a market strategy for a product or service.* Using price as a strategy is similar to projecting performance above industry averages. It is rarely possible for a new venture with a product or service that currently exists in the marketplace to enter on the basis of a lower price than that of its competitors. Established companies have achieved economies of scale that the new venture usually cannot duplicate, and they will no doubt easily match the price set by a new entrant into the market. Furthermore, this strategy does not impress investors. They are more interested in how the new venture will differentiate itself in terms of product, process, distribution, or service.

■ *Not investing in the business.* Investors are more comfortable investing in a new venture where the entrepreneur has contributed a substantial amount of the start-up capital. That signals to the investors a level of commitment necessary to achieve the goals of the company.

The Look of the Business Plan

Considering the appearance of the business plan is the first step in getting the plan read. The trick is to have the plan look professional but not too slick. For instance, a hard-bound, full-color, textbook-style format would look too polished and suggest that the plan is not subject to change, which is not an impression the entrepreneur wants to convey. Some ways to make the business plan stand out from the crowd are to ensure that the plan is bound in such a way that it lies flat when read (a spiral-type binding or binder works well), use index tabs to separate major sections and make it easier for readers to find their way around, choose a readable 12-point type font (such as Times Roman), employ bold subheadings and bullets generously, include the new venture logo on the top of every page, and make sure the writing is focused and concise. The plan should be written and revised several times, and several people should serve as editors. All claims should be supported by solid evidence. Note that computer boilerplate programs should not be used to write the plan; the result will not reflect the personality of the business. Each copy of the business plan should be numbered and should include a **Statement of Confidentiality** that each reader should sign. The venturer must always keep track of who has which copy of the plan. Finally, a clear statement that prohibits copying of the plan should be included.

Physically Organizing the Business Plan

Although there are no hard and fast rules about all the items to include in a business plan and where to put them, most business plans contain the items discussed below.

The Cover Page for the Bound Document

Like any other document designed to sell something, the business plan is attempting to convince various third parties—as well as the entrepreneur—of the viability of the new venture. Therefore, the cover page should convey, in an attractive, professional manner, the confidence and creativity of the entrepreneur. Dozens of business plans cross the desks of most venture capitalists and lenders every day, so it is important to make the plan stand out. Appearance may be only skin deep, but positive first impressions go a long way toward attracting the attention of a potential financial source. The information that appears on the cover page typically includes the name of the company, the words *Business Plan,* the name of the contact person for the new venture, and the address and phone number of the business. Some ways to make the business plan stand out are to use color on the cover, include the business's logo with the name, and create a consistent design that reflects the personality of the business.

Between the executive summary and the table of contents for the business plan, it is useful to put another cover page containing the name of the business and the words *Business Plan* to separate the executive summary from the body of the business plan. Consider the executive summary as a standalone document that is not part of the main business plan. In this way, it can be handed out to interested parties, especially in situations where the entrepreneur doesn't want to release the complete business plan.

The Body of the Business Plan

The body of the business plan contains all the major sections that were discussed earlier in this chapter: business concept, industry/market analysis, management team, product/service plan, marketing plan, operations plan, growth plan, and contingency plan.

Supporting Documents—The Appendices

Many items that might be important to the reader but would clutter the body of the business plan and make it more difficult to read quickly can be placed in appendices after the body of the plan. Some items that typically go in an appendix are complete financial statements (a summary goes in the body of the plan), a media plan, résumés of the founding team, job descriptions, lease agreements, license agreements, contracts, letters of intent, incorporation agreements or partnership agreements, evidence of patents, architectural or product designs, and a personal financial statement (only where required, typically by a lender or investor).

Successfully Presenting the Business Plan

It is not uncommon, particularly if the plan is being used to seek capital, for the entrepreneur to be asked to do a presentation of the business concept, highlighting the key points of the business plan. Usually this occurs after the potential funders have read the executive summary and perhaps done a cursory reading of the complete business plan. In any case, they feel it is worth their time to hear from the entrepreneur and the founding team to judge whether they measure up to expectations.

Presentation Do and Don'ts

The presentation of the business plan should answer the fundamental questions discussed in the section on components of the business plan. The presentation itself should take less than half an hour, though questions and discussion will probably follow. It should catch the audience's attention in the first 30 seconds. This is usually accomplished by the compelling story of the pain in the market that the new venture will cure. The presenter should stand without using a podium. This allows for better command of the situation, enhances rapport, and makes it easier to use gestures and visual aids. The presenter should feel free to move around (but no pacing). Moving helps reduce stress and livens up the presentation. The presenter should maintain eye contact with everyone and talk to the audience but not over their heads. Visual aids, such as color PowerPoint slides or overheads, keep the presentation on track and focused on key points. Be careful, however, not to dazzle

TABLE 9.2	**Business Plan Checklist**

1. Does the executive summary grab the reader's attention and highlight the major points of the business plan?
2. Does the business concept section clearly describe the purpose of the business, the customer, the value proposition, and the distribution channel and convey a compelling story?
3. Do the industry and market analyses support acceptance and demand for the business concept in the marketplace and define a first customer in depth?
4. Does the management team plan persuade the reader that the team could successfully implement the business concept? Does it assure the reader that an effective infrastructure is in place to facilitate the goals and operations of the company?
5. Does the product/service plan clearly provide details on the status of the product, the timeline for completion, and the intellectual property that will be acquired?
6. Does the operations plan prove that the product or service could be produced and distributed efficiently and effectively?
7. Does the marketing plan successfully demonstrate how the company will create customer awareness in the target market and deliver the benefit to the customer?
8. Does the financial plan convince the reader that the business model is sustainable — that it will provide a superior return on investment for the investor and sufficient cash flow to repay loans to potential lenders?
9. Does the growth plan convince the reader that the company has long-term growth potential and spin-off products and services?
10. Does the contingency and exit strategy plan convince the reader that the risk associated with this venture can be mediated? Is there an exit strategy in place for investors?

the audience with too many overheads, or listeners may find themselves more interested in the rhythm of the slides' motion. Keep the slides simple (no more than five lines per slide), big enough to read, and professional-looking. The technology (overhead projector, PowerPoint projector, or the like) should be tested *before* the presentation to be sure it's working correctly. All key members of the founding team should be involved in the presentation. If there is a service or product involved, a live demonstration helps to generate excitement about the concept. Most important, the presenters should practice the presentation in advance for a small group of friends or colleagues who will critique it. Alternatively, a practice session can be videotaped so that the founding team can critique themselves.

Answering Questions

When the founding team has successfully made it through the presentation, it has cleared the first hurdle. The second hurdle, however, is harder: answering questions from investors. One thing to remember about investors is that they generally like to ask questions to which they already know the answers; this is a test to see whether the founding team knows what it's talking about. Furthermore, investors often ask questions that either require an impossibly precise answer or are so broad that it's hard to tell what the questioner is looking for.

Another type of question typically asked is "What are the implications of . . . ?" With this question, investors are looking for an answer that addresses their needs and concerns relative to the request for capital. Finally, the type of question that poses the most problems for the founding team is the inordinately complex one that contains several underlying assumptions. For example, "If I were to analyze your new venture in terms of its market share before and after this potential investment, how would the market strategy have changed and how much of the budget should be allotted to changing that strategy?"

The first thing an entrepreneur should do when faced with such a complicated question is to ask that it be repeated, to ensure that she hasn't missed anything or made an incorrect assumption. Alternatively, the entrepreneur can restate the question and confirm that she has understood it correctly. She can then ask for a few minutes to formulate an answer. The entrepreneur may feel comfortable answering only part of it; for example, the entrepreneur may have evidence that could be presented to support a change in market share as a result of the capital infusion. On the other hand, it is critical not to commit the venture to any course of action or any budget amount without having had time to consider it further and gather more facts. Saying this in response to the question will no doubt gain the entrepreneur a measure of respect, for having demonstrated that she doesn't make important decisions precipitously, without considering all the facts.

If investors ask a factual question to which the entrepreneur does not know the answer (usually, such queries are tangential to the business plan and are asked to see how the entrepreneur will respond), the entrepreneur should admit that he doesn't have that answer off the top of his head but will be happy to find it after the meeting is over and get back to the questioner. If the presentation or anything the team has proposed is criticized (a likely possibility), the entrepreneur should be careful not to be defensive or to turn the criticism in any way on the audience.

Preparing and presenting the business plan is the culmination of months of work. The business plan represents the heart and soul of the new venture, and if it has been researched thoroughly and written well, it can enhance the chances of starting a successful high-growth venture. Entrepreneurs should understand, however, that a business plan is not just for those starting new businesses, but for the growing company as well. The business plan allows for benchmarking progress toward company goals. It establishes the purpose, values, and goals of the company that will guide its decision making throughout its life. No entrepreneur plans to fail, but many fail to plan and thus end up reacting to situations in the environment instead of proactively dealing with a changing environment.

Undertaking a business plan is certainly a daunting task, but it is an important exercise that helps an entrepreneur understand more clearly every aspect of the new venture and how all the pieces fit together. Even successful entrepreneurs who have started businesses without a written plan have had to write business plans when they needed growth capital or a credit line from the bank. Those starting high-growth global ventures often find that they need outside capital and resources fairly quickly, so a business plan is essential. A sample business plan can be found in the appendix, and additional plans are located on the student website.

New Venture Checklist

Have you:

☐ Determined the conditions under which you are willing to go forward?

☐ Gathered all the information necessary to complete the business plan?

☐ Determined the focus of the plan and who the potential readers are?

☐ Developed a set of tasks and a timeline for completing the business plan?

☐ Decided on the presentation format for the business plan?

Issues to Consider

1. Why is the business planning process an excellent exercise for any entrepreneur contemplating the start-up of a new venture?
2. What is the difference between a feasibility study and a business plan?
3. Why might it be better to start the business after completing the feasibility study and before completing a business plan?
4. How might the business plan change if the reader were an investor versus a potential management hire?
5. What are three key elements of a successful business plan presentation?

Experiencing Entrepreneurship

1. Interview someone who invests in small businesses about what she or he looks for in a business plan. On the basis of your discussion, what will you need to remember when you write your business plan?

2. Go to http://www.bplans.com/and select a business plan to review. Using the guidelines for an effective plan given in this chapter, evaluate the plan in three to five pages. What are its strengths and weaknesses?

Additional Sources of Information

Esposito, J.E. (2000). *In the Spotlight: Overcome Your Fear of Public Speaking and Performing.* Strong Books.

Gumpert, D.E. (2003). *How to Really Create a Successful Business Plan.* Needham, MA: Lauson Publishing.

Horan, J., and T. Peters (2004). *The One-Page Business Plan.* Berkeley, CA: The One-Page Business Plan Company.

Relevant Case Studies

Case 1 Overnite Express, p. 402

Case 3 Beanos Ice Cream Shoppe, p. 410

10

Analyzing Legal Risks and Benefits

"It will not injure you to know enough of law to keep out of it."

The Old Farmer's Almanac (1851)

LEARNING OBJECTIVES

- Distinguish between sole proprietorships and partnerships.

- Discuss the corporation.

- Explain the limited liability company.

- Define the nonprofit corporation.

- Make a decision about legal form.

- Discuss how a business entity can evolve from one legal form to another.

Profile 10.1 **WHICH FORM IS BEST?**

Making a decision about the best legal form for your business is no longer a simple task; there are more choices than ever before. Yet many new business owners are making the decision without adequate expert advice. Mark Kalish is the co-owner and vice president of EnviroTech Coating Systems, Inc. of Eau Claire, Wisconsin. His company paints products ranging from motorcycles to musical instruments, using an electrostatic process known as powder coating. In trying to determine which legal form made sense, Kalish and his business partner John Berthold focused on three key issues: legal liability, tax ramifications, and cost of creation. Kalish and his partner didn't want (and couldn't afford) the personal liability for any potential losses or problems arising from the operation of the business. This meant that they could not consider the sole proprietor and partnership forms, both of which entail personal liability for the owner.

The next consideration was the owners' desire to minimize tax liability. Corporations have more options in this regard but are also subject to "double taxation"; that is, income is taxed first at the corporate level and again when dividends are distributed. However, Kalish learned that his company might benefit from the limited liability company (LLC) form of organization, which passes profits and losses through to the owner to be taxed at the personal income tax rate. In addition, the losses that businesses typically face in the early years can be used to reduce the owners' personal tax liability.

The next issue to consider was the cost of forming and maintaining the chosen form. Kalish learned about the high cost, in time and money, of record keeping and paperwork associated with a corporation, as well as the higher initial costs of incorporating.

His conclusion was that the sole proprietorship was the best option in terms of cost, assuming that he had a substantial umbrella insurance policy for protection against liability. But for several reasons, Kalish could not avail himself of that option. He had intentions of growing the business by issuing and selling additional shares of stock. The corporate form makes this relatively easy to do, as does the LLC with its membership interests. He also wanted to ensure that the business survived his death, and both the corporation and the LLC would do that. Kalish finally settled on the corporate form.

Sources: Laura Tiffany, "Choose Your Business Structure," Entrepreneur.com, March 19, 2001; Envirotech Coating Systems, Inc. website, 2005: http://www.envirotechcoating.com.

The choice of legal structure is one of the most important decisions to be made about the business, because it will affect every aspect of the business, including tax planning and the cost of maintaining the structure. For example, if a business entails any degree of risk, such as product liability, then choosing a legal form that protects the entrepreneur's personal assets from being attached as the result of a lawsuit is just as important as carrying the appropriate insurance. The decision about the legal form of the business should reflect careful consideration about the type of business and the entrepreneur's personal goals for that business, and it should always be made under the guidance of a qualified attorney. In order to make an informed decision about the legal form of the business, it is important to understand all the risks and benefits associated with the chosen form. Profile 10.1 explains how one business made its choice.

Sole Proprietorships and Partnerships

All businesses operate under one of four broad legal structures—sole proprietorship, partnership, limited liability company, or corporation. Because the legal structure of a new venture has both legal and tax ramifications for the entrepreneur and any investors, entrepreneurs must carefully consider the advantages and disadvantages of each form. It is also quite possible that a business may decide to change its legal form sometime during its lifetime, usually for financial, tax, or liability reasons. These situations are discussed as each legal form is examined. Table 10.1 presents a summary comparison chart of all the structures.

TABLE 10.1 Comparison of Legal Forms

BUSINESS FORM ISSUES	SOLE PROPRIETORSHIP	PARTNERSHIP	LIMITED LIABILITY COMPANY	C-CORPORATION	SUBCHAPTER S-CORPORATION
NUMBER OF OWNERS	One	No limit	No limit. Most states require a minimum of two members.	No limit on shareholders	75 shareholders or fewer
START-UP COSTS	Filing fees for DBA and business license	Filing fees for DBA; attorney fees for partnership agreement	Attorney fees for organization, documents; filing fees	Attorney fees for incorporation documents; filing fees	Attorney fees for incorporation; filing fees
LIABILITY	Owner liable for all claims against business, but with insurance can overcome liability	General partners liable for all claims; limited partners liable only to amount of investment	Members liable as in partnerships	Shareholders liable to amount invested; officers may be personally liable	Shareholders liable to amount invested
TAXATION	Pass-through; taxed at individual level	Pass-through; taxed at individual level	Pass-through; taxed at individual level	Tax-paying entity; taxed on corporate income	Pass-through; taxed at individual level
CONTINUITY OF LIFE OF BUSINESS	Dissolution on the death of the owner	Dissolution on the death or separation of a partner, unless otherwise specified in the agreement; not so in the case of limited partners	Most states allow perpetual existence. Unless otherwise stated in the Articles of Organization, existence terminates on death or withdrawal of any member.	Continuity of Life	Perpetual existence

TABLE 10.1	Comparison of Legal Forms *(Continued)*				
BUSINESS FORM / ISSUES	SOLE PROPRIETORSHIP	PARTNERSHIP	LIMITED LIABILITY COMPANY	C-CORPORATION	SUBCHAPTER S-CORPORATION
TRANSFER-ABILITY OF INTEREST	Owner free to sell; assets transferred to estate upon death with valid will	General partner requires consent of other generals to sell interest; limited partners' ability to transfer is subject to agreement	Permission of majority of members is required for any member to transfer interest	Shareholders free to sell unless restricted by agreement	
DISTRIBUTION OF PROFITS	Profits go to owner	Profits shared based on partnership agreement	Profits shared based on member agreement	Paid to share-holders as divi-dends according to agreement and shareholder status	
MANAGEMENT CONTROL	Owner has full control	Absent an agreement to the contrary, partners have equal voting rights	Rests with management committee	Rests with the board of directors appointed by the shareholders	

Sole Proprietorship

Nearly 76 percent of all businesses in the United States are **sole proprietorships,** probably because the sole proprietorship is the easiest form to create.[1] In a sole proprietorship, the owner is the only person responsible for the activities of the business and, therefore, is the only one to enjoy the profits and suffer the losses.

To operate as a sole proprietor requires very little—only a DBA (see below), and not even that if the entrepreneur uses his or her name as the name for the business. In other words, a sole proprietorship called Jennifer Brooks Corporate Consultants does not require a DBA if the entrepreneur's name is Jennifer Brooks, but a sole proprietorship called Corporate Consultants does. A DBA, or Certificate of Doing Business Under an Assumed Name, can be obtained by filing an application with the appropriate local government agency. The certificate, sometimes referred to as a "fictitious business name statement," ensures that this is the only business in the area (usually a county) that is using the name the entrepreneur has chosen and provides a public record of business ownership for liability purposes.

Advantages

A sole proprietorship has several advantages. First, it is easy and inexpensive to create. It gives the owner 100 percent of the company and 100 percent of the profits. It also gives the owner complete authority to make decisions about the direction of the business. In addition, the income from the business is taxed only once, at the owner's personal income tax rate, and there are no major reporting requirements such as those imposed on corporations.

Disadvantages

There are, however, some distinct disadvantages that deserve serious consideration. The sole proprietor has unlimited liability for all claims against the business; that is, any debts incurred must be paid from the owner's assets. Therefore, the sole proprietor puts at risk his or her home, bank accounts, and any other assets. In today's litigious environment, exposure to lawsuits is substantial. To help mitigate this liability, a sole proprietor should obtain business liability insurance, including "errors and omissions coverage," which protects against unintentional negligence such as disseminating incorrect information in a company advertisement. Another disadvantage is that it is more difficult for a sole proprietorship to raise debt capital, because often the owner's financial statement does not qualify for the amount needed. The sole proprietor usually needs to rely on his or her skills alone to manage the business. Of course, employees with specific skills can be hired to complement the skills of the owner. Another complication associated with a sole proprietorship is that the business's ability to survive is dependent on the owner; therefore, the death or incapacitation of the owner can be catastrophic for the business.

Often small businesses such as restaurants, boutiques, and consulting businesses are run as sole proprietorships. This is not to say that a high-growth venture cannot be started as a sole proprietorship—many are—but it will in all likelihood not remain a sole proprietorship for long, because the entrepreneur will typically want the protections and prestige that organizing as a corporation affords.

Patti Glick knew that most of all she wanted to be a mom and raise her kids right. A nurse by trade, she discovered that she had great interest in feet and a desire to help people in her Silicon Valley community take better care of theirs. She envisioned starting a business that would enable her to be home when her children arrived from school. With the full support of her family, Glick started Foot Nurse (www.footnurse.com), a business dedicated to helping people understand foot care, protection, safety, and health. In her first year as a sole proprietor, she conducted 24 presentations for major companies such as Cisco. Demand grew, and in her second year she did 46 presentations. Now she is finding ways to leverage her new-found celebrity with foot-care products and a website. She prefers the life of a soloist, saying that she would rather charge more than have to hire someone to do what she does.[2]

Partnership

When two or more people agree to share the assets, liabilities, and profits of a business, the legal structure is termed a **partnership.** The partnership form is an improvement over the sole proprietorship from the standpoint that the business can draw on the skills, knowledge, and financial resources of more than one person. This is an advantage not only in operating the business but also in seeking bank loans. Like the sole proprietorship, however, the partnership requires a DBA when the last names of the partners are not used in naming the business. Professionals such as lawyers, doctors, and accountants frequently employ this legal structure.

In terms of its advantages and its treatment of income, expenses, and taxes, a partnership is essentially a sole proprietorship consisting of more than one person. However, where liability is concerned, there is a significant difference. In a partnership, each partner is liable for the obligations that any other partner incurs in the course of doing business. For example, if one partner signs a contract with a supplier in the name of the partnership, the other partners are also bound by the terms of the contract. This is known as the doctrine of ostensible authority. Creditors of an individual partner, on the other hand, can attach only the assets of that individual partner, including his or her interest in the partnership.

Partners also have specific property rights. For example, unless otherwise stated in the partnership agreement, each partner owns and has use of the property acquired by the partnership. Each partner has a right to share in the profits and losses, and each may participate in the management of the partnership. Furthermore, all choices related to elections such as depreciation and accounting method are made at the partnership level and apply to all partners.

Advantages

Partnerships have all the advantages of sole proprietorships, in addition to others. Partners have the added advantage of sharing the risk of doing business. Partnerships have the clout of more than one partner and, therefore, more than one financial statement. Partners can also share ideas, expertise, and decision making. Financially, partnerships enjoy pass-through earnings and losses to the individual partners, to be taxed at their personal tax rates.

Disadvantages

Partnerships have several disadvantages that entrepreneurs should consider carefully before using this form. Partners are personally liable for all business debts and obligations of the partnership. Individual partners can bind the partnership to a contract or other business deal. Unless a buy–sell agreement is included in the partnership agreement, the partnership dissolves when a partner either leaves or dies. And finally, individual partners can be sued for the full amount of any partnership debt. If that happens, the partner who is sued, and loses, must then sue the other partners to recover their shares of the debt.[3]

Partnership Agreement

Although the law does not require it, it is extremely wise for a partnership to draw up a written **partnership agreement,** based on the Uniform Partnership Act, that spells out business responsibilities, profit sharing, and transfer of interest. This is advisable because partnerships are inherently fraught with problems that arise from the different personalities and goals of the people involved. A written document executed at the beginning of the partnership will mitigate eventual disagreements and provide for an orderly dissolution should irreconcilable differences arise. Many partnerships have minimized conflict by assigning specific responsibilities to each of the partners and detailing them in the partnership agreement. Additional issues arise when one or more of the partners in a partnership leave, either voluntarily or through death. To protect the remaining partners, the partnership should have in place a buy–sell agreement and "key-person" life insurance.

A **buy–sell agreement** is a binding contract between the partners. It contains three primary clauses that govern[4] the following issues:

1. Who is entitled to purchase a departing partner's share of the business? May only another partner do so, or is an outsider permitted to buy in.
2. What events can trigger a buyout? Typically, those events include a death, disability, or other form of incapacity; a divorce; or an offer from the outside to buy the partner out.
3. What price will be paid for the partner's interest?

Having this formula in place from the beginning prevents disagreements and legal battles with the departing partner or with the estate of a deceased partner.

It is unfortunate that many entrepreneurs fail to take the precaution of creating a partnership agreement with a buy–sell clause. The consequences can be critical for the business. For example, say one partner dies, and the partnership, absent a buy–sell agreement, is forced to work with the spouse or family member of the deceased, who may not be qualified to run the business. Furthermore, with no partnership agreement, one partner can sell his or her interest to a stranger without the consent of the other partners, so it is critically important to have such an agreement.

"Key-person" life insurance is a policy on the life of principal members of the partnership, usually the senior partners. Upon the death of a partner, the insurance proceeds can be used to keep the business going or to buy out the deceased partner's interest under a buy–sell agreement.

For more protection from liability than a partnership affords, organizing the business as a corporation or a limited liability company should be considered.

Types of Partnerships

There are two types of partnerships: general and limited. In a **general partnership**, all the partners assume unlimited personal liability and responsibility for management of the business. In a **limited partnership**, by contrast, the general partners have unlimited liability, and they seek investors whose liability is limited to their monetary investment; that is, if such a limited partner invests $25,000 in the business, the most he or she can lose if the business fails is $25,000. It is important to note, however, that limited partners have no say in the management of the business.

TABLE 10.2	Structuring an Effective Partnership Agreement

CRITICAL ISSUES TO ADDRESS WITH AN ATTORNEY PRESENT
- The legal name of the partnership
- The nature of the business
- The duration of the partnership
- Contributions of the partners
- Sales, loans, and leases to the partnership
- Withdrawals and salaries
- Responsibility and authority of the partners
- Dissolution of the partnership
- Arbitration

Global Insights

China Espousing New Forms of Business Ownership

Since the 1970s, the Chinese economy has experienced exceptional growth, despite the fact that its transition from a centrally directed to an open market economy has been relatively slow. China made a conscious decision to reform its state-owned enterprises gradually at the same time as it encouraged the development and growth of other forms of ownership, such as private, cooperative, and joint ventures. Today much of the success that China has experienced in the marketplace has been due to the rapid growth of entrepreneurial firms that were privately owned and market-driven.

Now China must move toward making its state-owned firms independent and autonomous and must allow them to work under a profit and efficiency maximization model. Obstacles that the government has placed in the path of entrepreneurial ventures will need to be removed. These enterprises must be free to make production and business decisions, to set prices, market products, purchase materials, export and import, make investments, form partnerships, and set wages and bonuses, among many other activities common in a free enterprise system. In addition, the government must encourage foreign investment and increase the availability of low-cost borrowing and venture capital.

There is a long road ahead for China to become an efficient market economy where private ownership in the form of entrepreneurial firms drives technological change and economic growth and productivity. But the potential for positive effects domestically—and for the rest of the world—is there.

Source: A.M. Zapalska and W. Edwards, "Chinese Entrepreneurship in a Cultural and Economic Perspective," *Journal of Small Business Management,* 39(3) (2001): 286.

In fact, they are restricted by law from imposing their will on the business. The penalty for participating in the management of the business is the loss of their limited liability status.

Corporation

Only about 17 percent of all U.S. businesses are corporations, but they account for 87 percent of all sales transactions. A **corporation** is different from the preceding two forms in that it is a legal entity in and of itself. The U.S. Supreme Court has defined the corporation as "an artificial being, invisible, intangible, and existing only in contemplation of the law." It is chartered or registered by a state and can survive the death of the owner(s) or their separation from the business. Therefore, it can sue, be sued, acquire and sell real property, and lend money. The owners of the corporation are its stockholders, who invest capital in the corporation in exchange for shares of ownership. Like limited partners, stockholders are not liable for the debts of the corporation and can lose only the money they have invested.

Most new businesses form what is known as a closely held corporation; that is, the corporate stock is owned privately by a few individuals and is not traded publicly on a securities exchange such as the New York Stock Exchange. This chapter will focus on such private corporations. The issue of "going public" typically arises after the business is established and the entrepreneur wants to raise substantial capital for growth by issuing stock (shares of ownership in the corporation) through an **initial public offering (IPO).** The IPO and public corporations in general are the subject of Chapter 16.

A corporation is created by filing a certificate of incorporation with the state in which the company will do business and issue stock. This is called a domestic corporation. A foreign corporation, by contrast, is one that is chartered in a state other than in the one in which it will do business. A corporation requires the establishment of a board of directors, which meets periodically to make strategic policy decisions for the business. The regular documentation of these meetings is crucial to maintaining the corporation's limited liability status. The board also hires the officers who will run the business on a day-to-day basis.

There are two corporate forms from which to choose: the C-corporation and the S-corporation. Their purpose and advantages and disadvantages are discussed in the next sections.

C-Corporation

It would be difficult to claim that the Pennsylvania Railroad Corporation of the 1950s resembles in any way the General Electric Corporation of today, let alone the Business.com Corporation operating on the Internet. Even the most traditional of legal forms has evolved over time. Yet the corporation remains the most commonly chosen legal structure for a growing company that seeks outside capital in the form of equity or debt.

Advantages

The **C-corporation** offers several important advantages. It enjoys limited liability in that its owners are liable for its debts and obligations only to the limit of their investment. The only exception to this protection is payroll taxes that may have been withheld from employees' paychecks but not paid to the Internal Revenue Service.

Capital can be raised through the sale of stock up to the amount authorized in the corporate charter; however, be aware that the sale of stock is heavily regulated by federal and state governments. A corporation can create different classes of stock to meet the various needs of its investors. For example, it may issue nonvoting preferred stock to conservative investors who, in the event that the corporation must liquidate its assets, will be first in line to recoup their investment. Common stock is more risky, because its holders are paid only after the preferred stockholders. Common stockholders are, however, entitled to vote at stockholders' meetings and to divide the profits remaining after the preferred holders are paid their dividends, assuming that these profits are not retained by the corporation to fund growth.

Ownership is easily transferred. This is at once an advantage and a disadvantage, because the entrepreneur will want to be careful, particularly in the start-up phase, to ensure that stock does not land in the hands of undesirable parties such as competitors. This problem is normally handled through a buy–sell clause in the stockholders' agreement that states that stock must first be offered to the corporation at a specified price before being offered to someone outside the corporation.

Because it is a legal entity, the corporation can enter into contracts, sue, and be sued without the signature of the owners. In a start-up or young company, bankers, creditors, and the like generally require that majority shareholders or officers personally guarantee loans to ensure that the lender is protected against the potential failure of the corporation by having the ability to pursue the assets of the owners.

Corporations typically enjoy more status and deference in business circles than do other legal forms, principally because they are a legal entity that cannot be destroyed by the death of one—or even all—of the principal shareholders. Moreover, to enter the public equity markets, a business must be incorporated, so it will be subjected to greater scrutiny from governmental agencies. The reason for this scrutiny is the fact that the assets of the corporation are separate from the assets of the individual owner/shareholders. Therefore, the owners may take risks that they wouldn't take with their personal assets.

Corporations can take advantage of the benefits of retirement funds, Keogh and defined-contribution plans, profit-sharing arrangements, and stock option plans for their employees. These fringe benefits are deductible to the corporation as an expense and not taxable to the employee.

Finally, the entrepreneur can hold certain assets (such as real estate) in his or her own name, lease the use of the assets to the corporation, and collect a lease fee.

Disadvantages

Corporations do, however, have disadvantages that must be carefully considered. They are certainly more complex to organize, are subject to more governmental regulation, and cost more to create than sole proprietorships or partnerships. Although it is possible to incorporate without the aid of an attorney, doing so is not recommended. In too many cases, businesses have failed or endured significant financial hardship because they did not incorporate properly at the start of the business.

A more cumbersome disadvantage derives from the fact that the corporation is literally a person for tax purposes. Consequently, if it makes a profit, it must pay a tax, whether or not those profits were distributed as dividends to the stockholders. And, unlike partners or sole proprietors, shareholders of C-corporations do not receive the benefit of losses (the S-corporation does enjoy these benefits). In a C-corporation if losses can't be applied in the year they are incurred, they must be saved to be applied against future profits. Accordingly, C-corporations pay taxes on the profits they earn, and their owners (shareholders) pay taxes on the dividends they receive; hence the drawback of "double taxation." It is principally for this reason that many entrepreneurs who operate alone or with a partner do not employ this form. However, if the entrepreneur draws a salary from the corporation, that salary is expensed by the corporation, effectively reducing the company's net income subject to taxes. The entrepreneur will be taxed at his or her personal income tax rate.

By creating a corporation and issuing stock, the entrepreneur is giving up a measure of control to the board of directors. But for privately held corporations, the entrepreneur largely determines who will be on the board. Entrepreneurs who seek outside venture funding in the early stages of their venture may find that they have to give up the majority of the stock to the investors. The choice is either to hang on to the equity and watch the business stall because funding can't be secured or to give up control so that the founder can own a smaller piece of something successful. It is not always necessary, however, that the founder retain 51 percent of the stock to maintain effective control. As long as the founder's skills and vision are vital to the success of the venture, and as long as most of the shareholders share that vision, the entrepreneur will have effective control of the organization, no matter how much stock she or he has given up. With a corporate form, unlike the sole proprietorship or partnership, the entrepreneur is accountable principally to the stockholders and secondarily to anyone else. If the corporation is privately held, the board usually serves at the pleasure of the entrepreneur, who is accountable to himself or herself and to any investors.

A corporation must endeavor in all ways to act as an entity separate from its owners. It must keep personal finances completely separate from corporate finances, hold directors' meetings, maintain minutes, and not take on any financial liability without having sufficient resources to back it up. Failing to do any of these things can result in what is known as "piercing the corporate veil," which leaves the officers and owners open to personal liability.

Where to Incorporate

Apart from legal considerations, where to incorporate is also an important issue. It is normally advantageous to incorporate in the state in which the entrepreneur intends to locate the business, so that it will not be under the regulatory powers of two states (the state in which it is incorporated and the state in which it must file an application to do business as an out-of-state corporation).

Normally, however, a corporation will not have to qualify as a "foreign" corporation doing business in another state if it is simply holding directors'/shareholders' meetings in the state, or holding bank accounts, using independent contractors, or marketing to potential customers whose transactions will be completed in the corporation's home state. It has often been said that incorporating in Delaware is wise because that state has laws favorable toward corporations. If neither seeking venture capital nor doing a substantial amount of business in Delaware is a goal of the company, however, the cost and hassle of qualifying in another state as well may outweigh the benefits of incorporating in Delaware. Entrepreneurs should also consider the favorableness of the tax laws governing corporations in the state chosen. Some states, such as California, levy a required, minimum annual corporate income tax, whether the business has a taxable income or not.

S-Corporation

An **S-corporation,** unlike the C-corporation, is not a tax-paying entity. It is merely a financial vehicle that passes the profits and losses of the corporation to the shareholders. It is treated much like a sole proprietorship or a partnership in the sense that if the business earns a profit, that profit becomes the income of the owners/stockholders, and it is the owners who pay the tax on that profit at their individual tax rates.

Some of the key rules for election of the S-corporation option include the following: The S-Corporation may have no more than 100 shareholders. These shareholders must be U.S. citizens or residents (partnerships and corporations cannot

SCREENSHOT 10.1   **mycorporation.com**

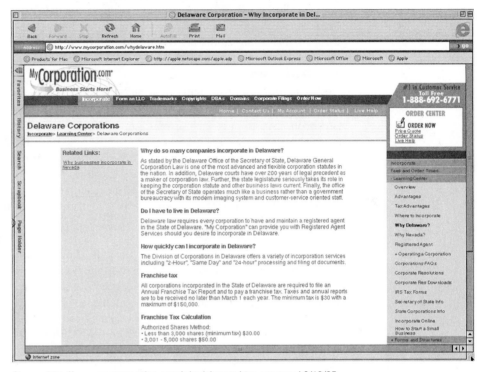

Source: http://www.mycorporation.com/whydelaware.htm, accessed 3/10/05.

be shareholders). Profits and losses must be allocated in proportion to each shareholder's interest. An S-corporation shareholder may not deduct losses in an amount greater than the original investment. In addition, it is always wise to check with an attorney to make certain that the election of S-corporation status is valid. If a C-corporation elects to become an S-corporation and then reverts to C-corporation status, it cannot re-elect S-corporation status for five years.

Advantages

The S-corporation permits business losses to be passed through to be taxed at the entrepreneur's personal tax rate. This offers a significant benefit to people who need to offset income from other sources. The businesses that benefit most from an S-corporation structure are those that don't have a need to retain earnings. In an S-corporation, if the entrepreneur decides to retain, say, $100,000 of profit to invest in new equipment, the stockholders must still pay taxes on that profit as though it had been distributed.

The S-corporation is a valuable financial tool when personal tax rates are significantly lower than corporate rates. However, as top personal rates increase, a C-corporation might be preferable at higher profit levels. For some small businesses, however, the S-corporation may still be less costly in the long run because it avoids double taxation of income. A good tax attorney or certified public accountant (CPA) should advise the entrepreneur on the best course of action. Ventures that typically benefit from S-corporation status include service businesses with low capital asset requirements, real estate investment firms during times when property values are increasing, and start-ups that are projecting a loss in the early years.

Disadvantages

Entrepreneurs should probably not elect the S-corporation option if they want to retain earnings for expansion or diversification, or if there are significant passive losses from investments such as real estate. Furthermore, although most deductions and expenses are allowed, S-corporations cannot take advantage of deductions based on medical reimbursements or health insurance plans. Another consideration is that unless the business has regular positive cash flow, it could face a situation in which profit is passed through to the owners to be taxed at their personal rate, but the firm has generated insufficient cash to pay those taxes, so they must come out of the pockets of the shareholders.

One young entrepreneur from Massachusetts finally realized her dream of opening a restaurant catering to people who dined as much for the atmosphere and service as for the great food she served. She wanted the protection of the corporate form but didn't want the double taxation of a corporation. She also knew that restaurants generate a lot of cash, so her attorney advised her to consider the S-corporation. That way her company's earnings would be taxed at her personal tax rate, and her restaurant would generate enough cash to pay the tax liability on the profits. She could also have as many as 75 investors if she wanted.

Professional Corporations

State laws permit certain professionals, such as health care professionals, engineers, accountants, and lawyers, to form corporations called **professional service corporations.** Anyone who holds shares in the corporation must be licensed to provide the service it offers.

The limited liability company (LLC) structure is also available to professionals, but in a special form known as a professional limited liability company (PLLC). Under this form, the member is liable only for his or her own malpractice, not that of other members. Some states also offer the limited liability partnership (LLP), which protects the owner from the malpractice claims of its partners but not from other partnership debts.

Legal forms of organization evolve over time to meet the changing needs of business. In the next section, the most recent structure, the limited liability company, is discussed.

Limited Liability Company

The **limited liability company (LLC),** like the S-corporation, enjoys the pass-through tax benefits of partnerships in addition to the limited liability of a C-corporation. It is, however, far more flexible in its treatment of certain ownership issues. Only privately held companies can become LLCs, and they must be formed in accordance with very strict guidelines. LLC statutes vary from state to state, so in addition to meeting the partnership requirements of the Internal Revenue Code, applicants must file with the state in which they intend to do business and follow its requirements as well.

An LLC is formed by filing articles of organization, which resemble articles of incorporation. Today an LLC can be formed with only one person in every state that allows this form except for Massachusetts and the District of Columbia, which require two people. The owners of an LLC are called members, and their shares of ownership are known as interests. The members can undertake the management of the company or hire other people to manage it. Managers, officers, and members are not personally liable for the company's debts or liabilities, except when they have personally guaranteed these debts or liabilities. The members create an "operating agreement," which is very similar to a partnership agreement that spells out rights and obligations of the members.

Advantages

Most LLCs will be organized for tax purposes like partnerships, so that income tax benefits and liabilities will pass through to the members. In New York and California, however, the LLCs will also be subject to state franchise taxes or fees. Under the Internal Revenue Code, an LLC exhibits all four characteristics of a corporation—limited liability, continuity of life, centralized management, and free transferability of interests—and still can be treated as a partnership for tax purposes without fear of being reclassified as a corporation. This enhances the attractiveness of the LLC, already the most rapidly growing legal form.

The LLC is often thought of as a combination of a limited partnership and an S-corporation. However, there are differences. In a limited partnership, one or more people (the general partners) agree to assume personal liability for the actions of the partnership, whereas the limited partners may not take part in the management of the partnership without losing their limited liability status. In an LLC, by contrast, a member does not have to forfeit the right to participate in the management of the organization in order to retain his or her limited liability status.

Moreover, in an LLC, unlike in an S-corporation, there are no limitations on the number of members or on their status. Corporations, pension plans, and nonresident aliens can be members. Also, whereas S-corporations can't own 80 percent or more of the stock of another corporation, an LLC may actually possess wholly owned subsidiary corporations. LLCs are not limited to one class of stock, and in some ways they receive more favorable tax treatment. For example, unlike an S-corporation shareholder, the LLC member can deduct losses in amounts that reflect the member's allocable share of the debt of the company.

If at a later date the entrepreneur decides to go public, the LLC can become a C-corporation by transferring the LLC assets to the new corporation. It is, however, a bit more difficult to go in the other direction, and capital gains tax must be paid on the appreciation.

Disadvantages

Clearly, the LLC offers more flexibility than other forms, but it does have a few disadvantages that should be considered. In contrast to the creation of a partnership or sole proprietorship, a filing fee must be paid when the LLC is formed. It is probably not a good form if there will be a large number of members, because it will be difficult to reach consensus among the owners, who might also be the managers of the LLC. It is not a separate tax-paying entity. Earnings and losses are passed through to the members to be taxed at their individual tax rate, so members must make quarterly estimated tax payments to the IRS. If all the members do not elect to actively manage the LLC, the LLC ownership interests may be treated like securities by the state and the Securities and Exchange Commission (SEC). This means that if the company does not qualify for an exemption (most small LLCs do), it must register the sale of its member interests with the SEC.

LLCs are becoming a popular vehicle for companies that may have global investors, because the S-corporation does not permit foreign ownership. An attorney should be consulted to find out whether this form is available in a particular state.

One ambitious entrepreneur knew that she wanted her furniture-importing business to be global in all respects. She even intended to bring in investors from among her business acquaintances around the world, because that would help her find the important contacts she needed to be successful. As an importer, she needed liability protection but did not want the high tax rates she would have with a corporation. Friends had told her that the S-corporation would solve the tax problem, but her attorney advised her to consider the LLC as her choice of legal form because it would allow her to have foreign investors.

Profile 10.2 GROWING WITH AN LLC

Choosing the right legal form is also critical if your goal is to build an empire. Lea Marquez-Peterson and her husband, Dan, founded American Retail Corp. in 1996. The company owns and operates several gas stations and mini-marts in Tucson, Arizona, but the founders have a vision of growing the company to 30 stations around the state. They used investor capital to grow the company to $15 million in sales, but with the weaker economy and falling gasoline prices, they needed to change their strategy to attract investors. They decided to make each station a separate limited liability corporation (LLC) to entice investors that were nervous about investing in groups of stations. The LLC is easier and cheaper to form than a corporation but provides the same liability protection, and it is flexible in terms of the types of members it can have.

In 2001, recognizing another niche in the market, the Petersons created a spin-off company, American Retail Management Services. This company focused on managing corporate service stations. Today the American Retail Corp. is well on its way to reaching its goal.

Source: K.E. Klein, "Imperial Forces: The Truly Ambitious Entrepreneur Has But One Goal, One Drive, One Prime Motivating Factor—the Desire for Empire, *Entrepreneur* (March 2002), accessed at www.findarticles.com on January 4, 2004.

The Nonprofit Corporation

It is not outside the realm of possibility for a nonprofit corporation to be a high-growth, world-class company; however, it is not generally started with that goal in mind. A nonprofit corporation is a corporation established for charitable, public (scientific, literary, or educational), or religious purposes, or for mutual benefit (such as trade associations, tennis clubs), as recognized by federal and state laws. Some additional examples of nonprofits are child-care centers, schools, religious organizations, hospitals, museums, shelters, and community health care facilities. Like the C-corporation, the nonprofit corporation is a legal entity and offers its shareholders and officers the benefit of limited liability. There is a common misconception that nonprofit corporations are not allowed to make a profit. As long as the business is not set up to benefit a single person and is organized for a nonprofit purpose, it can make a profit on which it is not taxed if it has also met the IRS test for tax-exempt status. However, income derived from for-profit activities is subject to income tax.

There are two distinct hurdles that a business must overcome if it wants to operate as a nonprofit corporation and enjoy tax-exempt status: The first is to meet the state requirements for being designated a nonprofit corporation and operating as such in a given state. The second is to meet the federal and state requirements for exemption from paying taxes [IRS 501(c)(3)] by forming a corporation that falls within the IRS's narrowly defined categories.

Advantages

Nonprofit organizations offer many advantages to entrepreneurs seeking to be socially responsible or just to start a business doing something they love that helps others. The nonprofit with tax-exempt status is attractive to corporate donors, who can deduct their donations as a business expense. The nonprofit can seek cash and in-kind contributions of equipment, supplies, and personnel. It can apply for grants from government agencies and private foundations. The nonprofit may qualify for tax-exempt status, which means that it is free from paying taxes on income generated from nonprofit activities.

In forming the nonprofit corporation, the entrepreneur gives up proprietary interest in the corporation and dedicates all the assets and resources of the corporation to tax-exempt activities. If a nonprofit corporation is ever dissolved, its assets must be distributed to another tax-exempt organization.

Disadvantages

There are a few disadvantages to a nonprofit organization. For example, profits earned by the corporation cannot be distributed as dividends. Corporate money cannot be contributed to political campaigns or used to engage in lobbying. Nonprofits do not have shareholders or owners but simply members. The entrepreneur does not own the nonprofit, so it can't be sold. If the directors decide to dissolve it, then after paying all debts, they must distribute the remaining assets to another tax-exempt nonprofit. Finally, the nonprofit cannot make substantial profits from unrelated activities, and it must pay taxes on the profits it does make.

It is not uncommon for tax-exempt organizations to engage in activities (also known as UBI activities) that generate unrelated business income—that is, income that is not related to the nonprofit's exempt purpose. For example, if a research institute were to operate a café on a regular basis, this would be considered a UBI activity. The institute would have to report it to the IRS and pay taxes on the income. If and when their UBI activities start to become significant, nonprofits often establish for-profit entities to run their UBI activities to protect the tax-exempt status of the parent organization.

Musical theatre companies are not the first type of company one thinks of when looking for examples of nonprofit organizations, but James Blackman had no doubt that this was the form of choice for the Civic Light Opera of South Bay Cities in California, one of the leading musical theatre companies on the West Coast. The nonprofit form would allow Blackman to receive donations from corporations and grants from foundations to support his efforts in the community with the physically challenged. It would also allow him to sell tickets to performances and make a profit, as long as that profit was not distributed but remained in the company. More important, he would meet the requirements for tax exemption, and that would enable him to keep more money in the business to help it grow.

Making the Decision About Legal Form

Prior to making the decision on which type of legal form to choose, several very important questions should be asked.

Asking the Right Questions

There are seven integral questions that an entrepreneur should ask. They include the following:

1. Does the founding team have all the skills needed to run this venture?
2. Do the founders have the capital required to start the business alone or must they raise it through cash or credit?
3. Will the founders be able to run the business and cover living expenses for the first year?
4. Are the founders willing and able to assume personal liability for any claims against the business?
5. Do the founders wish to have complete control over the operation of the business?
6. Do the founders expect to have initial losses or will it be profitable almost from the beginning?
7. Do the founders expect to sell the business some day?

The answers to these questions will narrow the choices. Then it's always wise to get the advice of an attorney and/or accountant. For example, if the new venture is expected to have initial losses in the first year due to product development or other large start-up costs (question 6), a form that allows those losses to pass through to be taxed at owner's personal income rate. Since the company is not yet generating income, by doing this the entrepreneur will be able to shelter other personal income from a tax liability. Sole proprietorships, partnerships, S-corporations, and limited liability companies all permit pass-through earnings and losses.

Choosing the Right Form at Each Milestone

It's also good to know the strategic plan for the venture going forward because choosing either a form that won't have to be changed or one that can easily be shifted to when the time is right would be important. For example, suppose an entrepreneur plans to offer shares of stock in the company at some point in the future to raise additional capital. To accomplish that, the company will need to become a corporation or LLC, so if it began as a sole proprietorship, it would need to file incorporation or LLC papers in the state in which it would be doing business. The next section considers the issues of evolving from one form to another.

As is clear from the previous sections, growing businesses often move from one legal form to another as their needs change. Consider the following example of a married entrepreneur, Cheryl Kastner. Kastner's spouse is a highly paid executive for a major corporation, making it possible for her to devote herself full time to developing a tech product she has been designing for some time. Kastner decides to set up a small business with a shop near their home. She is not worried about medical insurance because she is already covered by her spouse's company. However, she needs to limit liability, because they have acquired a number of valuable assets and don't want those to be in danger should things go badly. She realizes that in any business dealing with products, some liability issues crop up and she wants to make sure they're covered.

In the beginning, it is typical to experience losses as equipment is purchased, and prototypes are built and tested in the market. Once the product is launched, there probably will be continuing losses from promoting the business, finding space outside the home to lease, and hiring new employees. Kastner has big plans for her business; in fact, within a year of introducing the product, she expects to need venture capital to be able to grow as fast as the market demands. She also sees an IPO in the future when that market returns. The IPO will be the liquidity event when investors need to cash out. Given these circumstances, she considers which organization form is best at each milestone.

In the beginning, during product development, it often doesn't make sense to use a more formal form such as a corporation. A simple sole proprietorship or partnership (if there's more than one person involved) will suffice. At this stage, the liability to family assets is small. But the minute Kastner's business grows out of the home environment and takes on the responsibilities of a lease and employees, she must consider either being heavily insured or moving to a legal form with limited liability. Kastner plans to move the business to a leased location and hire employees. Since there would still be losses from product development and she would want to use them to shelter other income, she is also advised to consider either the S-corporation or the LLC, depending on the degree of flexibility she needs. She was also advised that at the point at which she decides to seek venture capital and/or an IPO, she will need to convert to a C-corporation.

It is clear from this example that the legal form of an organization is not a static decision, but rather one based on the needs of the company at the time of formation and into the future. Choosing the legal structure of the new venture is one of the most important decisions an entrepreneur can make, because it affects the tax strategy of the company for years to come. The correct selection depends on the type of venture the entrepreneur is starting, the profits the venture generates, the personal tax bracket of the entrepreneur, the assets used by the business, its potential for growth, and state laws. Again, particularly in the case of corporations and LLCs, it is important that an attorney review the documents to ensure that all the rules have been followed and that the entrepreneur will receive all of the benefits to which the business is entitled.

Other Legal Considerations

There is hardly any aspect of a new business that isn't touched by the law, from contracts with employees and suppliers to regulations on workplace safety and laws related to privacy.

The Health Insurance Portability and Accountability Act of 1996

As of April 14, 2004, tough new privacy regulations enacted under the **Health Insurance Portability and Accountability Act of 1996** or **HIPAA** went into effect for small companies that provide health insurance to their employees.[5] There are huge fines for companies not in compliance, including $50,000 fines and up to one year in prison. The cost of compliance with regulations like these must be factored into the financials to figure the real cost of starting the business. Some of the regulations related to the workplace and human resources are discussed in their respective chapters; however, it is not within the scope of this book to discuss all the legal aspects of starting and running a business. Additional resources are provided at the end of the chapter, and, certainly, a competent attorney can assist an entrepreneur in learning which laws and regulations apply to a particular business.

New Venture Checklist

Have you:

☐ Answered the questions on page 216 before considering which legal form to choose?

☐ Consulted with an appropriately qualified attorney to determine the best form to meet your business goals?

☐ Completed the necessary agreements for the legal form you have chosen (partnership agreement, articles of incorporation, and so forth)?

☐ Met the test for tax exemptions under IRC 501(c)(3) if you are founding a nonprofit corporation?

☐ Met with a qualified attorney to determine what other legal issues might arise with your particular type of business?

Issues to Consider

1. Assuming that you were running a successful consulting practice as a sole proprietorship, what would induce you to change the legal form to a corporation?
2. Why would you choose an LLC form over a partnership or an S-corporation?
3. What kinds of businesses are well suited to the nonprofit legal structure?
4. What key factors determine the strategic plan for the legal organization of the business?

Experiencing Entrepreneurship

1. Using this text and additional research on the Internet, acquire a basic understanding of the different legal forms of organization. Then, using a business that you are considering launching, discuss your initial strategic plan for the business with a qualified attorney to get his or her advice about the best form to use for that type of business. Write a two-page summary of your findings to justify the choice of legal form.

2. Visit an entrepreneur whose business is set up as a partnership. How do the partners describe the experience of setting up the business? How have they divided up the duties and responsibilities? What key issues have they covered in their partnership agreement? Summarize your findings in a two- or three-page paper.

Additional Sources of Information

Bagley, C.E., and C.E. Dauchy (1998). *The Entrepreneur's Guide to Business Law.* Mason, OH: Southwestern Publishing.

Clifford, D., and R.E. Warner (2001). *The Partnership Book: How to Write a Partnership Agreement.* 5th ed. Berkeley, CA: Nolo Press.

Diamond, M.R., and J.L. Williams (2000). *How to Incorporate: A Handbook for Entrepreneurs and Professionals.* New York: Wiley.

Hopkins, B. (2001). *Starting and Managing a Nonprofit Organization: A Legal Guide.* New York: Wiley.

Mancuso, A. (2002). *How to Form a Nonprofit Corporation.* 5th ed. Berkeley, CA: Nolo Press.

Steingold, F.S. and Bray, I.M. (2003). *Legal Guide for Starting and Running a Small Business.* 7th ed. Berkeley, CA: Nolo Press.

Relevant Case Studies

Case 3 Beanos Ice Cream Shoppe, p. 410

Case 6 The Crowne Inn, p. 435

Chapter

11

Incorporating Ethics and Social Responsibility

". . . An ethic is not an ethic, and a value not a value without some sacrifice to it. Something given up, something not taken, something not gained."

Jerome Kohlberg, Jr., Kohlberg Kravis Roberts & Co., May 18, 1987

LEARNING OBJECTIVES

- Explain the role of ethics in entrepreneurship.
- Discuss how entrepreneurs can demonstrate social responsibility.
- Describe how an entrepreneur's vision and values contribute to the culture of the new venture.
- Discuss the relationship of core values to success.

Profile 11.1 PROMOTING WOMEN ENTREPRENEURS IN BANGLADESH

It is fairly commonplace for women to have financial power in developed countries, but it's the last thing you might expect to find in a third-world country like Bangladesh. Nevertheless, thanks largely to one man's entrepreneurial genius, women are now gaining financial power in this impoverished country. In the 1980s, Muhammad Yunus decided that traditional economic development programs would not bring about economic improvement fast enough in his home country of Bangladesh. A Fulbright scholar in classical economics, Yunus studied the challenges that the poorest people faced in attempting to secure capital to start even the smallest of businesses. They had no collateral and were generally illiterate, so he concluded that a traditional banking model was not appropriate for them. Instead, he began to work on the concept of social collateral, which comes about from a small group of people working together. He called it his "peer lending" model, wherein small groups of borrowers in the same village would take responsibility for repaying the loans of anyone in the group.

Founded in 1983, the Grameen Bank began lending to the poorest of the poor on a group liability basis with no collateral. Borrowers repay the loans in small weekly installments over one year. Because of peer pressure from the group to repay, the collection rate is about 98 percent, far higher than for traditional banking institutions. But what is most unusual about this entrepreneurial bank is that 95 percent of its borrowers are women. Bangladeshi women have traditionally had no employment opportunities and thus have lived far below the poverty line. With no other options, the women are predisposed to try the Grameen loan system, which allows them to start micro-businesses such as making bamboo stools, weaving floor mats, and raising poultry. Borrowers are also required to save some of their money against potential natural disasters or sickness.

From Grameen Bank's point of view, the return to them is infinite because, for example, a $100 donation to the nonprofit bank can be lent and repaid over and over again. The Grameen Foundation accepts donations, and the bank administers the loans.

Yunus built on the success of the micro credit effort by making mobile phone ownership possible as a business opportunity to Bangladeshis. Women have purchased phones and then provided services to other villagers who can't afford to own their own phones. Grameen Phone is a subsidiary of Grameen Bank and now has well over 100,000 subscribers. Today communication between villages across Bangladesh is growing and is succeeding in reducing the gap between rich and poor.

Sources: "Motley Fool Selects Grameen Foundation USA for 2002 Foolanthropy Charity Drive," *PR Newswire* (December 3, 2002); "From Small Acorns," www.findarticles.com, August 2000; and Abu Wahid, "The Grameen Bank and Women in Bangladesh," *Challenge* (September-October 1999).

Never have entrepreneurial businesses needed ethics policies more than they do today. The lessons of Enron, Worldcom, and many other companies that resorted to unscrupulous tactics to create phantom company wealth should serve as a potent reminder to entrepreneurs that ethics in business practices is vital to business survival. In a dynamic, global marketplace that places a premium on speed and quick returns, shareholder value is often considered more important than basic human values. The pressure to achieve unachievable goals and survive in such a chaotic environment causes stress; and when people suffer stress, they don't always make wise decisions. Moreover, the global economy, made more accessible than ever through the Internet, has juxtaposed U.S. businesses with cultures that may define morality in terms of very different contexts, values, and codes of ethics. Yes, it's a challenging environment, but those entrepreneurs who understand their value systems and create a code of ethics for their businesses can successfully maneuver through these challenges without forsaking their principles.

This chapter looks at three key issues for entrepreneurial companies, issues that will become increasingly important as companies interact more frequently in the global marketplace: vision and values, ethics, and social responsibility. Profile 11.1 on Grameen Bank clearly demonstrates that every industry is looking for ways to reinvent itself and become more socially responsible. The chapter closes with a discussion of the components of success and how to make sure that a company's success is congruent with its vision and values.

Ethics

Ethics, or the moral code by which we live and conduct business—essentially the concept of right and wrong—derives from the cultural, social, political, and ethnic norms with which we were raised as children. People don't often sit down to think about their value system; they merely act instinctively on the basis of it. It's only when they are faced with a dilemma that raises moral or ethical issues that they may consciously ask themselves what is the correct thing to do. Harvard Business School conducted a survey of its alumni to find out what it needed to teach future business leaders. The top responses included leadership, technology, entrepreneurship, and globalization. But the response cited most often overall was ethics, morals, and values.

Many people believe that if they follow the Golden Rule (Do unto others as you would have them do unto you), they're safe from ethical dilemmas. Unfortunately, most ethical dilemmas in the business environment are complex and offer "gray areas" that are troubling when one attempts to apply an ethical principle. One Oregon construction company hired a subcontractor to do a $15,000 concrete job. That particular subcontractor did not have solid bookkeeping practices and never submitted an invoice to the construction company for the work it did. The construction company could have kept quiet, but instead it sent the subcontractor a copy of the plans, specifications, and names of workers on the job, and told the subcontractor how much to bill it. The gray area here is the decision point—whether to notify the subcontractor of its failure to invoice. The construction company demonstrated its ethical values by contacting the subcontractor to ask for the invoice.

Another ethical decision had to be made by a marketing company that received two checks from a client for the same $50,000 project. There was no way the client would have discovered it, yet the marketing firm immediately sent the second check back. These kinds of ethical dilemmas occur every day in business. Although these two entrepreneurs did what they believed to be ethically correct, not everyone operates under the same standards of ethics. The employee who steals notepads, pens, and computer disks because "the employer won't miss them," the executive who abuses his or her expense account, and the business owner who evades taxes by not reporting employee income demonstrate their lack of clear ethical standards. This kind of behavior is accepted too widely and costs entrepreneurs both time and money. Entrepreneurs face special problems when it comes to ethical issues. Their small companies generally are more informal and lack systems and controls. They often don't have the time or resources to focus on ethics during their attempts to keep their businesses alive, and they often take for granted that everyone in their organization and everyone with whom they do business shares their values. This is a mistake, because unethical behavior left undetected can contaminate a business for as long as it exists.

Another very practical reason why small firms should pay attention to the ethics of employees concerns their ability to defend themselves against criminal action in a court of law. The U.S. Sentencing Commission's guidelines assert that an effective ethics program can serve to protect a company from criminal penalties, or at least in lessening their impact, if an employee violates federal law.[1]

In general, ethical dilemmas in business are found in four areas: conflicts of interest, survival tactics, stakeholder pressure, and pushing the legal limit.

Conflicts of Interest

Conflict of interest is one of the most universal problems in business today. A conflict of interest occurs when a person's private or personal interests clash with her or his professional obligations. Business owners have vested interests in many areas of their lives: careers, a business, family, community, and their investments, to name just a few. It is rare for all these interests to be in complete harmony with one another. A potential conflict of interest occurs when there is a discrepancy between an individual's private interests and his or her professional obligations such that an independent observer might reasonably question whether the individual's professional actions or decisions are influenced by personal gain, financial or otherwise. For example, a company may want to continue an important manufacturing process that provides many jobs and profit, even when the community claims that this same process is not good for the environment.

Conflict of interest has also found its way into e-commerce. Today an online company can use its website to gather information about customers, profile them, and send the right message to the customer at the right moment. Through "cookie" technology, a company can track customers' movements online. Over time, the company will have compiled an enormous amount of data that it can use to better target its marketing messages. A company that uses cookie technology will usually offer a notice of privacy to its customers, promising not to sell the information it gathers to other companies. Unfortunately, many an Internet company has gone back on its promise to protect customers' privacy. When Internet ad company DoubleClick (DCLK) was exposed for matching online and offline databases (essentially matching cookie data to real names, addresses, and phone numbers), it was hit with a Federal Trade Commission inquiry, investigations by the states of New York and Michigan, six lawsuits, and a lot of bad press.[2] The Electronic Privacy Information Center (EPIC) wants to require companies to obtain customer consent before creating a profile. Proponents of profiling claim that advertising is the "lifeblood" of the Internet and that if it is too heavily regulated, content may no longer be free. This conflict of interest is one that will not go away for a long time because there is so much potential marketing benefit in consumer profiling.

The issue of privacy, however, is big enough to warrant a watchdog, and that watchdog is TRUSTe, a nonprofit organization dedicated to auditing and approving online privacy policies. Designed to reassure customers that the business they're dealing with online is sticking to its promises, the TRUSTe seal of approval is the most displayed banner on the Internet, but even so, it has its critics. More than one famous Internet company, while sporting the TRUSTe seal, has been caught violating its privacy clause. As a result, TRUSTe has competitors such as The Council of Better Business Bureaus and most of the major accounting firms.

Survival Tactics

Many are the stories of entrepreneurs who did whatever it took to survive, even violating their own standards. Survival is the area where most people's ethics really face a test. It's easy to be ethical when things are going your way, but what about the entrepreneur who is facing bankruptcy or can't make payroll? What do that entrepreneur's ethics look like then? Small firms, especially in the early years, are vulnerable to setbacks that would not significantly affect a large organization. The loss of a major customer or supplier could put a small business out of business. In these types of life-or-death situations, a small business owner's commitment to ethical practices can force the company to make some difficult decisions. Again, the importance of sticking to an ethical code is critical, because what an entrepreneur does today out of desperation will follow him for the rest of his business career.

One entrepreneur, whose company, Haven Corporation—a manufacturer of products for the mail-order industry—had a history of cash flow problems, finally reached the point where it was time to close the doors. It was a tough decision because the entrepreneur felt a profound sense of duty to his fanatically loyal employees and to customers who would be stranded by his decision. But, as he said in the e-mail he sent out to his customers and suppliers, the company could not pay its bills, and he was personally $100,000 in debt. Little did this entrepreneur know but his e-mail notice would turn out to be a survival tactic. Over 400 customers began communicating with each other to seek technical help, to bemoan the loss of the company, and to begin to generate some ideas for how to resurrect it. Out of the rush of communications came the person who would ultimately raise the money to breathe life back into the company![3]

Stakeholder Pressure

There are many stakeholders in a business, and they all want what is owed them when it's owed them. Stakeholders include any person or organization that has an interest in seeing the company succeed—investors, shareholders, suppliers, customers, and employees, to name a few.[4] Every business, no matter how small, has stakeholders.

One area of research has focused on what the business ought to do in terms of the "ends it pursues and the means it utilizes."[5] For many entrepreneurs, there are times when managing the demands of stakeholders becomes a real juggling act. For example, to grow the company to the next level, the entrepreneur may decide to consider an IPO. Once that issue is raised, the entrepreneur will find lots of stakeholders pressuring him to move forward, even when he is not sure it's the best thing to do. These stakeholders include investment bankers who get a fee for doing the deal, business partners who may be able to cash out of some of their holdings in the company, and lawyers who want the additional business. All these stakeholders want to be served, but research has revealed that the most healthy outcome is for the entrepreneur to hold to his or her code of ethics and base decisions on it, not on the personal agendas of stakeholders who may not have the best interests of the company at heart.

Pushing the Legal Limit

Some entrepreneurs look for ways to bend the law as much as possible without actually breaking it. Entrepreneurs who regularly play too close to the edge of legality eventually get caught, and the price is often their businesses and their reputations. Ethical entrepreneurs don't play those games, but they're always on the alert for companies that might use quasi-legal practices against them to gain an edge in the market. These types of tactics must be dealt with decisively. For example, a large water-meter repair company that operated within the law was attacked by a competitor in collusion with a newspaper reporter. The competitor entrepreneur accused the company of bribing public officials. It was a false accusation, clearly unethical, but perhaps not illegal. It caused the innocent utility company a great many problems and cost it a lot of money defending itself, but the company had no choice because its reputation was at stake.

Learning from Real-Life Dilemmas

There is no better way to understand the role of ethics in any business than to encounter real-world dilemmas and determine how they might be resolved. Here are some examples of real-life ethical dilemmas. Think about how they might be resolved.

- A struggling Internet company is not producing revenues at the rate originally projected. At the same time, the burn rate (the rate at which cash is spent) is increasing as the company continually seeks new customers. The site claims to protect the privacy of visitors who purchase its products and services, and this is something the company takes pride in. However, the entrepreneur is concerned that if she doesn't find a quick source of income, the company may not survive. The entrepreneur learns that she can sell customer information lists to companies that will pay a lot of money for them. She has also heard that if she starts tracking which websites her customers visit, she can sell that information to major advertising firms for use in targeted advertising, another source of revenue. These tactics will violate customers' privacy, but if she doesn't do something quickly, she may have no business to offer them. What should she do?

- One of a company's best customers has asked for a specific product. After telling the customer the price, the company learns from the customer that a competitor is selling the same item at the company's cost. It is well known that this competitor engages in unethical business practices. Should the company tell its customer about the competitor's practices or let the customer purchase where he can get the best price?

■ An employee confides to an entrepreneur that another employee is planning to leave the company in two months to start her own company as a competitor. Armed with this knowledge, the entrepreneur is tempted to fire this employee immediately, but she is in the middle of a major project that is critical to the company, and it will be completed within two weeks. What should the entrepreneur do?

■ A company has hired an engineering design firm as an independent contractor to design and build an e-commerce site. It paid a large portion of the fee, $25,000, up front to begin the work. The owner assures the company that the work is on schedule to be completed on time, but as of a week before the due date, the company has yet to see any designs. A meeting is scheduled at the engineer's office to check on the status of the project. While waiting at the office, the entrepreneur overhears employees talking about the impending closure of the business. She also hears that the programmer assigned to the project has not been paid and there is no money to pay him. The owner of the engineering firm says nothing about this during the meeting and instead assures the entrepreneur that the project will be completed as planned. The entrepreneur suspects that he is not being truthful and worries that if the business closes and she has not received the designs and software for the project, her company will be out $25,000 and will have to file a lawsuit. Should the entrepreneur talk to the programmer and reveal what she has heard? Should she confront the owner? Should she approach his disgruntled employees to find a way to gather the data she needs to win a lawsuit?

■ A company is about to begin doing business in another country where it is well known that paying cash to officials makes business transactions move more quickly. The entrepreneur knows that paying bribes is illegal in the United States, the home base for the business, but this contract will ensure that the company establishes a foothold in the global market before its competitors do. What should the entrepreneur do?

These are all difficult choices when often the very survival of the business is at stake. Small businesses are as guilty as multinational corporations when it comes to ethical missteps. Paying personal expenses out of business funds and writing them off, not reporting all cash receipts, cheating customers on price, using misleading advertising, failing to pay bills on time, and lying to customers, employees, and suppliers are all examples of poor ethics. Aristotle, the Greek philosopher, said that courage is the first of the human virtues because without it, the others are not possible. How we make these difficult and courageous choices is the subject of the next section.

The Importance of Developing a Code of Ethics

Most of the research on ethics has been conducted in large organizations, so we have very little information about small businesses. However, work done by Longenecker and others found that small-business owners in particular have more stringent ethical views on such things as favoritism in promotion, acquiescence to a dangerous design flaw, misleading financial reporting, and misleading advertising. Surprisingly, they view with much greater tolerance padded expense accounts,

Profile 11.2 PERSONAL RESPONSIBILITY IN A POST-ENRON ERA

Corporate Ethics was rarely a topic of conversation during the 1980s and 1990s when business was booming. The general attitude was that it was a Darwinian world where, as Andy Grove, Intel's famous CEO, often put it, "only the paranoid" could survive. Any management strategies that ultimately led to profits and higher stock prices were, by definition, good for business. But one voice has been heard consistently through the cacophony of less-than-responsible corporate growth strategies, that of Jeffrey Seglin, who writes the monthly business ethics column in the *New York Times*. Seglin pulls no punches when he asks hard questions that CEOs and top management often deal with when the stakes are high. One good example of how businesses lose credibility when they don't take responsibility is his analysis of the fallout from the 2000 recall of 6.5 million Firestone tires on Ford Explorers following numerous blowouts and vehicle rollovers. Ford and Firestone, instead of immediately trying to solve the problem, spent valuable time pointing fingers of blame at one another, which only succeeded in costing them their reputation with customers.

Often irresponsible decisions come from denial of problems, nostalgia, and arrogance. Certainly, that was the case with Enron. Kenneth Lay, Enron's CEO, believed that he had found the mother of all business models, one that would work in any market. It is true that Enron created markets in gas, power, and telecommunications when none had existed previously, but its model was quickly copied as new companies entered Enron's markets, hoping to take advantage of the feeding frenzy. As a result, Enron constantly had to come up with new business opportunities capitalizing on the hottest trends in the industry. This bred a corporate culture that encouraged backstabbing, lying, cheating, and stealing. Employees would go to any lengths to discover the next big deal, claim it as their own, and become millionaires almost overnight. Lay and his top management continually denied any problems with the company in public as they scrambled to keep things going in private. But ultimately, their arrogance played itself out in financial fraud and misrepresentation and sent the company into a death spiral. Enron "succeeded" only in proving that integrity once lost can never be regained.

Sources: J.A. Fraser, "Book Review: The Right Thing—Conscience, Profit and Personal Responsibility in Today's Business," *Inc. Magazine* (2003), www.inc.com; J. Seglin, *The Right Thing: Conscience, Profit and Personal Responsibility in Today's Business* (New Greenham Park, Newbury, UK : Spiro Press, 2003); and S. Watkins, *Power Failure: The Inside Story of the Collapse of Enron* (New York: Doubleday, 2003).

tax evasion, collusion in bidding, insider trading, discrimination against women, and the copying of computer software.[6] Research has also found that the ethical behavior of employees is very much influenced by the **code of ethics** of the company.[7] When a code of ethics is spelled out and written down, people in the organization take it more seriously. Thus it would seem to be important for a business owner to develop a formal code of ethics for the business. After all, the best way to handle ethical dilemmas is to have in place a mechanism for avoiding them to begin with. Profile 11.2 provides a good example of an entrepreneurial company, Enron, that did not subscribe to a code of ethics, which ultimately caused its downfall.

Socially Responsible Entrepreneurship

Setting Standards in the Jewelry Industry

Trust is a significant issue in the jewelry business. Customers must rely on the integrity of the jeweler because they usually aren't able to judge quality with any degree of success. But the jewelry industry is highly competitive, and that attracts unscrupulous retailers. The Jewelers of America (JA) tried to address that issue by establishing a set of standards for all its members. It also wanted to recognize members who upheld the standards by awarding a special designation that they could place in the windows of their stores. In this way, customers would feel more comfortable shopping there.

It began by developing a Code of Ethics and Rules of Professional Conduct and Business Practices. Basically, the code spells out the need for all jewelry dealers to (1) act in a professional manner in all their dealings; (2) continue to improve their expertise; (3) keep promises and commitments; and (4) deal honestly with customers. The Rules of Professional Conduct then explain how the jeweler can achieve these goals. The ERC (Ethics Resource Center, www.ethics.org) helped JA to develop the procedures for monitoring compliance and dealing with customer complaints.

To get members to buy into its effort, the JA chose to use a positive approach, presenting the code to its regional affiliates as the new standard for the industry. It is now the largest trade association in the industry, with more than 10,000 members who sign on to the Code of Ethics. You can visit the site at http://www.jewelers.org/.

The Process of Developing a Code of Ethics

The process of developing a code of ethics begins with a company self-examination to identify values held by individuals and alert everyone to inconsistencies in how people deal with particular issues. For a new company, this means getting the founding team together to discuss how certain issues should be dealt with. For a larger company, forming a committee to oversee the process may be appropriate.

The Josephson Institute of Ethics developed a list of ethical values that should be considered in any code of ethics:[8,9]

Trustworthiness: loyalty, honesty, integrity

Respect: privacy, dignity, courtesy

Responsibility: accountability, pursuit of excellence

Caring: compassion, kindness, giving, consideration

Justice and fairness: impartiality, consistency, equity, due process, equality

Civic virtue and citizenship: abiding by laws, community service, protection of environment

A code of ethics should also outline behaviors that would allow the business to display these characteristics. This can be accomplished by asking four questions about any ethical decision to be made:[10]

1. Will the actions taken result in the "greatest good for all parties involved"?
2. Will the actions respect the rights of all parties?

3. Are the actions just? Will anyone be hurt by the actions?
4. Would I be proud if my actions were announced in my local newspaper?

The last question gets to the heart of how one determines what is ethical in any situation, and most people can immediately and intuitively answer it.

Characteristics of an Effective Code

The most effective code of ethics will have the following characteristics. The code and its attendant policies will be clear and easy to understand. Details about special situations that need further explanation will be included (for example, political factors in certain countries). In cases where employee judgment may be required, descriptions and examples will make it easier for the employee to make the decision.

Entrepreneurs should make sure that all employees are aware of and understand the code as well as the values and culture of the company. The following are some guidelines for ensuring that the code of ethics is implemented and maintained over time.

An Ethical Dilemma

Superior Machine Works had developed a new type of generator that was environmentally friendly and could be controlled from a distance. Superior's research had determined that the market was quite large and had the potential to be very profitable.

Superior was marketing two models: a small, lightweight version for people who would use it to power small tools, and a bigger, heavier version used generally as backup power for an office or home, in addition to supplying power for a variety of electrical tools. The smaller version retailed for $895, and the larger version sold for $1,500. The larger version had a patented noise reduction feature that significantly reduced the sound the machine produced. Studies on similar equipment had shown that over a long period of time, the noise level of the small machine could produce hearing loss.

Meanwhile, Superior's main competitor was also developing a generator very much like Superior's small version, and that company was also aware of the noise problem and the potential for deafness over time. Still, it was going ahead with the product. Superior was faced with a real dilemma. If it didn't move quickly to get its smaller version to market, it would lose its first-mover advantage to its competitor. At the same time, did Superior want to market a product that was known to cause deafness over time? If it marketed only the larger machine, it would quickly lose market share to its competitor's smaller, lighter machine. If Superior could not introduce a successful product quickly, it would have to lay off many of its workers. Considering the downward trend in its current sales, the company might fail if it couldn't introduce its product quickly.

1. What options does Superior have and what are the consequences of each?
2. What should Superior do and why?

1. Entrepreneurs should model the behavior expected of others in the company. In some companies, the ethical behavior exhibited by managers and employees in tough situations can become legendary—a part of the company culture that people remember and speak about with pride over and over again.

2. Employees should be educated about ethics through workshops that put employees in hypothetical situations. For example, "What would you do if you found out that your best customer was harassing your administrative assistant?"

3. Entrepreneurs should demonstrate commitment to the ethics program by mentioning it on a regular basis and providing examples of appropriate behavior that employees display during the course of their work.

The code of ethics should be shared with customers so that they all understand the company's commitment and are assured of its integrity. A clear channel for reporting and dealing with unethical behavior should exist, and there should be a means of rewarding ethical behavior through recognition, bonuses, raises, and so forth. An example of a fairly extensive code of ethics for data management provider Sybase can be found at http://www.sybase.com/.

Once a sound code of ethics and business practices has been developed, some steps must be taken to ensure that the established standards become part of the company culture, and as the leader of the company, the owner needs to be the role model for ethical behavior.

There is no way to avoid the ethical problems that business brings. But developing a strong ethical code and enlisting the cooperation of everyone in the business will go a long way toward making those problems easier to deal with.

Social Responsibility

Today it's not enough to have a successful business and make a profit. The business must hold itself to a higher standard of **social responsibility** by giving something back to the community or communities in which it does business and, through them, to society as a whole. According to Business for Social Responsibility (http://www.bsr.org/), a nonprofit organization dedicated to helping companies become socially responsible, social responsibility is "operating a business in a manner that meets or exceeds the ethical, legal, commercial and public expectations that society has of business." This means obeying the law, respecting the environment, and being mindful of the impact the business has on its stakeholders, the industry, and the community in general. Socially responsible entrepreneurs, then, are distinct from other entrepreneurs in a number of ways. First and foremost, they start their businesses with a social mission, and they are faced with different challenges as they seek the resources to fund and sustain the business.[11] Their rewards derive not so much from profits as from the social value they create by being change agents for the betterment of society. There are many types of social ventures serving a variety of purposes. For example, Rubicon programs, Inc., based in Richmond, California, has the objective of providing job training for people who typically cannot find jobs. It does this through its several ventures, including a bakery, home care, and a buildings and grounds maintenance business. A different example is The Nature Conservancy, which is a global organization based in Arlington, Virginia. With a mission of preserving plants, animals, and natural communities, it operates the largest private system of nature sanctuaries in the world.[12] The benefits to businesses that seek to become socially responsible are many.[13] They include improved financial performance, reduced operating costs by cutting waste and inefficiencies, enhanced brand image and reputation, increased sales and customer loyalty, increased productivity and quality, increased ability to attract and retain employees, and reduced regulatory oversight.

Some business owners have chosen to define their businesses publicly as "socially responsible businesses." But when their goals are too ambitious, their businesses do not always succeed. In 1989, Ben & Jerry's co-founder Ben Cohen launched Community Products Inc. (CPI), whose purpose was to save the rainforest and contribute to a number of worthy causes by donating an astronomical 60 percent of its profits to these causes. But things didn't turn out the way Cohen intended. The idea was to import nuts for the company's ice cream products (namely, Rainforest Crunch) from the local economies in the region of the rainforests. This vision was newsworthy, so Ben & Jerry's received a lot of free publicity, helping to generate revenues of $3 million within the first year.

CPI then partnered with Cultural Survival Enterprises, a nonprofit organization dedicated to finding markets for products from developing countries, but soon found that this organization's goals were not compatible with CPI's. Cultural Survival was charging high prices for its nuts and was not controlling quality. But more important, the products received from Cultural Survival contained a number of foreign substances—everything from glass and rocks to insects. Then there were CPI's operating problems, poor working conditions, and constraints on its ability to pay workers because of the requirement that 60 percent of its profits had to go to charity.

By 1993, CPI was losing money and the glow on the "save the rainforest" vision was merely a glimmer. By 1997, the company was in bankruptcy. Although Ben Cohen's goal was certainly lofty, it was highly unlikely that one corporation could do what entire nations had been unable to accomplish. In other words, for all practical purposes, CPI was setting itself up for failure. Furthermore, because a company such as this puts its social goals into all its publicity and advertising, it is held to impossibly high standards by the public and the media, who are ready and willing to remind it of its failure to achieve its goals. Although CPI gave away half a million dollars to save the rainforest, it ultimately crashed, leaving its creditors hanging.

Stories like this should never discourage a company from being socially responsible. But they should warn entrepreneurs of the importance of choosing a mission that is achievable. Paul Brainerd founded a company, the Brainerd Foundation, in Seattle, Washington, for the purpose of helping entrepreneurs "give back" strategically. He suggests that entrepreneurs follow two rules:

1. Don't wait until later in life to begin giving back. Start when you and the business are young.
2. Don't go for something huge. Start at the grassroots level, where help is needed the most.

Effective Ways to Become Socially Responsible

A company does not have to be a large, multimillion-dollar firm to begin to give something back to society. Even a very small company can have an impact on its community if it does a few things by way of preparation. First, the company needs to set goals. What does it want to achieve with its social responsibility efforts? The company should also pick a single cause to focus on, rather than trying to support many different causes. It should also consider partnering with a nonprofit organization. The nonprofit contributes its expertise in the social issue. The entrepreneurial company contributes its expertise and the time of its employees to the nonprofit. Next, it is vital that everyone in the organization get involved. There really is strength in numbers. In addition to getting employees involved, the entrepreneurial company should also get its customers involved. With goals in place and a cause that fits the company's core values, the new venture can do a number of things to establish positive relationships in the community.

Donate Products or Services

One of the least expensive ways to do good is to donate the products or services the company produces. Saint Louis Bread Company gives bread, muffins, and so forth to the homeless to the annual tune of $700,000 retail. Stanford Coaching Inc. serves wealthy clients who need academic test tutoring, but it has found a way to give back by giving away its services to needy students via scholarships. Volunteers drawn from Stanford's employees, who are never in short supply, provide those services.[14]

Get Other Companies Involved

In the spirit of networking, consider putting together a group of small businesses, whose combined efforts will produce results with more impact. Just Desserts, a San Francisco bakery, put together a group of thirty-five businesses to "adopt" an elementary school. With its combined financial strength, the group planted trees on the school grounds, painted the school, and refurbished the classrooms, creating a positive environment for students.

Offer the Company's Expertise Free of Charge

Some organizations in the community need the expertise a company has developed. Abby Margalith, who owns Starving Students of San Diego, a moving company, has relocated more than 100 women and children from abusive homes. Her crews volunteer to do the work, and she collaborates with the local YWCA.[15] Jay Backstrand used his technology expertise to develop a website, Volunteer America, which merged with Impact Online in October 1996, to match nonprofit organizations with people looking for opportunities to volunteer (http://www.volunteermatch.org/).[16]

Contribute to the Community

Many entrepreneurs have found cost-effective ways to give back to their communities without breaking the bank. In fact, they have made social responsibility a regular part of their businesses. Each store of a bagel chain in New Hampshire adopts a local nonprofit organization for a year. Customers vote for their favorite charity, and the winning choice receives a cash donation, bagels, meeting space, and a place to advertise its services in the store. They also get volunteer help from the bagel employees, who do their good deeds on company time.

Another entrepreneur shares the benefits of his success with his community by providing ski trips for underprivileged children, food drives for the hungry, highway cleanups, and the Easter Seals poster-child campaign, among many other things.

There are numerous ways to demonstrate social responsibility through a business. It doesn't have to cost much time or money to make a significant difference as long as efforts are focused where they will count the most.

Vision and Values

Every great company begins with the entrepreneur's vision of what that company will become. Just as top professional athletes envision every play of an upcoming game before they ever set foot on the playing field, so do entrepreneurs envision the kind of company they want to build. The company's "true north" acts like a beacon, guiding it in the right direction.

Although it is possible for a company to be successful without a vision, it is difficult, if not impossible, to become a *great* company without a vision. Researchers Jim Collins and Jerry Porras, authors of *Built to Last: Successful Habits of Visionary Companies,* back up this assertion.[17] Collins and Porras found that the number-one company in every industry outperformed its number-two competitor by a significant amount in terms of revenues, profits, and return on investment. The primary reason was that each number-one company each had a strong vision based on core values that it regarded as inviolable. Vision is made up of core values, purpose, and mission. The following sections on these three topics are based on the work of Collins and Porras.

Core Values

Core values are the fundamental beliefs that a company holds about what is important in business and in life in general. They are based on the personal values and beliefs of the founder; therefore, they are not something that can be created or invented for the company out of thin air. A company's core values tell the world who it is and what it stands for. Because they are so fundamental to the existence of the company, core values rarely change over time, and they endure beyond the tenure of the founder. For example, Nortel Networks' core values are as follows:[18]

Customers are the driving force.

People are our strength.

Quality is in every aspect.

Innovation fuels our future.

Accountability brings clarity.

Integrity underpins everything.

One way to test whether a value (for example, "The customer is always right") is a core value or not is to ask whether it would ever be relinquished if there were a penalty for holding it. If a company is willing to let go of the value, then it is not a core value.

Purpose

Purpose is the company's fundamental reason to be in business. It is the answer to the question "Why does the business exist?" It is not necessarily a unique characteristic of the business; in fact, more than one business may share the same purpose. What is crucial is that the purpose be authentic; that is, it must mean what it says.

"We are in the business of helping people" might be the purpose of a socially responsible business. Jordan Neuroscience is in the business of "saving brains." A properly conceived purpose will be broad, enduring, and inspiring, and it will allow the company to grow and diversify.[19]

Mission

A company's mission is what brings everyone together to achieve a common objective and is closely related to the company's purpose. According to Collins and Porras, a mission is a "Big Hairy Audacious Goal" designed to stimulate progress. All companies have goals, but a mission, or BHAG, is a daunting challenge, an overriding objective that mobilizes everyone to achieve it. The natural metaphor for a mission is mountain climbing. The mission is *to scale Mt. Everest,* a major challenge to be sure. To get there, however, will require smaller goals, such as *reaching base camp in one week*. The smaller wins motivate the team to achieve the more bold and compelling mission.

A company's mission is communicated through a **mission statement.** A mission statement precisely identifies the environment in which the company operates and communicates the company's fundamental philosophy.[20] Peter Drucker asserts that a company's mission should "fit on a T-shirt."[21] The best mission statements are simple, are precise, and use clear words.

Here are three examples of mission statements:

Distributed.net believes in the capability and potential of distributed computing. Our mission consists of three interdependent goals: development, deployment, and advocacy, to be pursued in the advancement of distributed computing. (Source: http://www.distributed.net/mission/php/php)

eBay's mission is to provide a global trading platform where practically anyone can trade practically anything. (Source: http://pages.ebay.com/aboutebay/thecompany/companyoverview.html)

Leader to Leader Institute: To strengthen the leadership of the social sector. (Sources: http://leadertoleader.org/leaderbooks/sat/mission.html and http://www.pfdf.org/about/index.html)

The mission statement should convey what the company wants to be remembered for. In writing a mission statement, it's important to gather the thoughts of everyone in the organization. The initial drafts should be evaluated against a set of criteria. The Leader to Leader Institute suggests that a mission statement should be short, sharply focused, clear, and easily understood. It should explain why the organization exists, indicate what the company wants to be remembered for, and be sufficiently broad in its scope. It should not prescribe means but should provide direction for doing the right things. Finally, the mission statement should address the company's opportunities, match the company's competence, and inspire the company's commitment.

Strategies and Tactics

Figure 11.1 presents a broad view of the components of vision and their relationship to each other. To review, the vision for the company stems from the founder's core value system. It becomes the guideline for all the decisions made by the company as it grows and operates. The company needs a compelling mission that is congruent with its core valued—a BHAG to propel it forward—and goals or operating objectives, which are milestones along the way to achieving the mission.

FIGURE 11.1   **The Components of Vision**

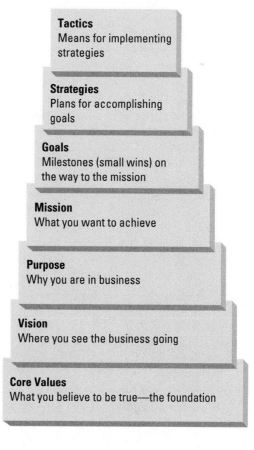

Tactics
Means for implementing strategies

Strategies
Plans for accomplishing goals

Goals
Milestones (small wins) on the way to the mission

Mission
What you want to achieve

Purpose
Why you are in business

Vision
Where you see the business going

Core Values
What you believe to be true—the foundation

Once goals have been set, **strategies** should be developed. These are the plans for achieving those goals and, ultimately, accomplishing the mission.

Tactics, which are the means to execute the strategies, should also be put in place. An example will make these points clearer. Suppose a company's mission is *to be number one in its industry*. Two goals or milestones it might set to help it accomplish the mission might be (1) to create an Internet presence and (2) to achieve brand recognition. Strategies for achieving these goals are needed, such as building a website to meet goal 1 and developing a marketing campaign to build the brand (goal 2). Then there must be a variety of tactics, or ways to implement the strategies. For example, to implement the strategy of building a website, a company might employ the following tactics: determine the purpose and focus of the website, hire a Web designer and developer, purchase a server, and plan the content.

Merely setting a goal is not enough. A plan for achieving the goal must be in place, and that is the role of strategy. But even strategy is not enough to achieve a company's goals; tactics, or action plans, will also be required.

Core Values and Success

Why are we talking about success in a chapter on ethics and social responsibility? Because an entrepreneur's personal definition of success—what it means to be successful—is really a function of the core values and vision that entrepreneur has for his or her life. A business's success is easily measured in terms of total revenues, earnings, return on investment, and so forth, but entrepreneurs don't typically measure their personal success solely in these terms. In fact, research has shown that the personal rewards that motivate entrepreneurs to start businesses are independence and freedom.[22] Entrepreneurs are goal-oriented and tend to cite being one's own boss, being in control of one's destiny, and having ultimate control of the success of the venture as reasons for going into business.[23] They measure their personal success by their achievement of those goals.

Wally Amos of Uncle Noname Cookies believes that success is "turning lemons into lemonade." For Sue Szymczak of Safeway Sling in Milwaukee, success is "being happy with what you're doing and feeling as though you're accomplishing something." One group of entrepreneurs decided that measuring the financial performance of the business did not totally reflect their definition of success, even at the company level. These are the entrepreneurs who started many of the "socially responsible" businesses that we discussed earlier. They intend to take their personal definitions of success to the company level. This is possible if, at the same time, the business is conducted effectively so that it can achieve its financial goals and give the entrepreneur a vehicle for his or her social responsibility efforts.

Constants of Success

No matter how success is defined, there are some constants that seem to permeate everyone's definition. These constants are purpose, failure, a sense of satisfaction with what was accomplished, and having to pay for, or earn, success.

- *Purpose.* To feel successful, entrepreneurs need to know that what they are doing is taking them in the direction of a goal they wish to achieve. True success is a journey, not a destination—even the achievement of a goal will be just a step on the way to the achievement of yet another goal.

- *Failure.* The second constant is that life has its ups and downs. *Failure* is the other half of success, and most entrepreneurs have experienced several failures of one sort or another along the way. Still, they do not fear failure, because they know intuitively that those who obsessively avoid failure are doomed to mediocrity. To avoid failing, one has to virtually retreat from life, to never try anything that has any risk attached to it. Most entrepreneurs are calculated risk-takers, so they make sure that every time they come up to bat they give it their best; then, win or lose, they strive to learn from the experience and go on. Entrepreneurs are generally optimists who believe that failure is a normal part of the entrepreneurial process.

- *Sense of satisfaction with work.* The most successful entrepreneurs are doing what they love, so their satisfaction level is usually very high. Does satisfaction with the work result in success, or does success bring satisfaction? Probably a little of both, so it's important to know what kinds of tasks and activities will return satisfaction in business.

- *No free lunch.* Success rarely comes without work. Entrepreneurs do not have the luxury of a nine-to-five workday; they usually are married to their businesses twenty-four hours a day. It is not just the number of hours of work that distinguishes entrepreneurs, of course, but also the way they use their time. Entrepreneurs make productive use of odd moments in their day—while they're driving, on hold on the telephone, in the shower, or walking to a meeting. Because they love what they're doing, it doesn't feel like work, and that's probably why, wherever entrepreneurs are, they're always working on their businesses in one way or another.

Firm core values and ethics plus a socially responsible business can lead to the kind of success that is most meaningful to most entrepreneurs: satisfaction in creating something and seeing it thrive. Today, more than ever before, the world is watching the way entrepreneurs run their businesses, so it is more critical than ever to design a new business on the basis of sound values and ethical practices.

New Venture Checklist

Have you:

☐ Identified the core values held by the founding team?

☐ Developed a code of ethics for the business?

☐ Listed possible ways in which your business can be socially responsible?

☐ Defined what success means to you?

Issues to Consider

1. Do you believe that your code of ethics should remain firm in any situation? Why or why not?
2. Suppose you are doing business in a country where paying fees (bribes) to get through the process more quickly is standard practice. In the United States, bribery is against the law. How will you deal with this conflict in ethical standards when you're doing business in that country?
3. In addition to the suggestions given in the chapter, name two ways in which your company can demonstrate its social responsibility.
4. Would you require your employees to give back to the community as part of their work contract with your company? Why or why not? If yes, how could you implement this policy?
5. How do you define your personal success? How can your definition be applied to your business?

Experiencing Entrepreneurship

1. Choose an industry that interests you and interview a manufacturer, a distributor, and a retailer about the code of ethics in that industry. Does the industry have ethical problems? If so, what are they and how are people responding? If not, how are they avoided?

2. Choose two companies in different industries. Interview a manager in each company about its code of ethics and its stance on ethical standards. In a two-page paper, compare these managers' answers and account for any basic differences.

Additional Sources of Information

Cohen, B., and J. Greenfield (1997). *Ben & Jerry's Double-Dip: Lead with Your Values and Make Money Too.* New York: Simon & Schuster.

Houck, J.W., and O.F. Williams (Eds.) (1996). *Is the Good Corporation Dead? Social Responsibility in a Global Economy.* Lanham, MD: Rowman & Littlefield.

Murphy, P.E. (1998). *Eighty Exemplary Ethics Statements.* Notre Dame, IN: Notre Dame Press.

Reder, A. (1995). *75 Best Business Practices for Socially Responsible Companies.* New York: J.P. Tarcher/ Putnam.

Rushworth, M.K. (1995). *How Good People Make Tough Choices.* New York: William Morrow.

Seglin, J. (2000). *Good, the Bad, and Your Business: Choosing Right When Ethical Dilemmas Pull You Apart.* New York: Wiley.

Solomon, R.C. (1999). *A Better Way to Think About Business: How Personal Integrity Leads to Corporate Success.* London: Oxford University Press.

Trevino, L.K., and K.A. Nelson (1999). *Managing Business Ethics: Straight Talk About How to Do It Right.* 2d ed. New York: Wiley.

Relevant Case Studies

Case 2 Craigslist, p. 407
Case 6 The Crowne Inn, p. 435

Case 8 Finagle a Bagel, p. 450

12

Designing an Entrepreneurial Organization

"Until someone has a small business, they have no comprehension of how hard it is. People who start businesses from scratch, if they survive, are the toughest people on the face of the earth."

Sue Szymczak, Safeway Sling

LEARNING OBJECTIVES

- Describe how businesses are organized.

- Explain how to identify the appropriate business site.

- Discuss issues related to forming a founding team.

Profile 12.1 YOU WON'T FIND THIS FENDER ON A CAR

If your company and its products achieve the enviable position of being the leading brand in the industry, be prepared for an uproar if you ever make major changes. Fender Musical Instruments can attest to that. Its clients, who range from Bruce Springsteen to Eric Clapton and Travis Tritt, love their Fender guitars because "they're as close to perfection as anything gets." And that has been true for fifty years. Actually, in the 1950s Leo Fender revolutionized the music industry when he introduced his solid-body electric guitars—the Telecaster and the Stratocaster—to the music industry in a market niche and soon set the standard.

In the late 1970s, however, a recession hit, interest rates soared, and Fender's famous quality began a precipitous slide. William Schultz, then an executive for CBS, organized a buyout and in 1985 acquired the name and distribution, taking the company private. At that point Fender was manufacturing only 12 guitars a day, as musicians were becoming entranced with music synthesizers. Schultz, however, succeeded in implementing a total quality management plan that would make Fender profitable every year from 1985 on. Fender now produces more than 335,000 guitars annually, all presold.

Schultz's plan revisited the organization of his business and focused on five areas that needed improvement:

1. **The management team.** Schultz put together a group of people who had musical backgrounds and were as passionate about Fender as he. As a team, they would carry the vision.
2. **Location.** He moved the guitar factory from Orange County, California, eastward to less pricey Corona in Riverside County. This enabled the company to focus its resources on production and quality.
3. **Quality.** Schultz invested in state-of-the-art woodworking machines so that quality would be consistent. He also trained every worker in quality control procedures and efficiency, and incorporated inspecting for quality into the manufacturing process, so that every guitar would be defect-free.
4. **Customization.** Schultz created a separate custom shop to meet the needs of customers requesting guitars designed and hand-built to their exact specifications. These customers have a wait of up to one year and pay between $1,500 and $50,000.
5. **Core competency.** One of the outstanding things Schultz did was return Fender to what it had been doing best when it was the industry leader in the late 1950s and 1960s. To win back loyal customers, he reissued some of the original designs and updated 1940s low-tech vacuum-tube amps that were preferred by professional musicians.

Today, Fender Musical Instruments has come of age and is creating the best guitars possible; blending science, music, and computer technology; and reducing time-to-market and material costs. Fender partnered with the Experience Music Project (EMP), Seattle's interactive music museum, to create regional and national educational programming. One example of this educational programming is a guitar lease/loan program, which is dedicated to serving underprivileged music students who might not have access to guitars or guitar lessons. They will be able to learn to play in exchange for giving back to the community by volunteering their time at music-related events.

This company has successfully reinvented itself. The lesson for entrepreneurs is to maintain the vision at all costs, make sure that employees hold the vision as well, choose the business location carefully, focus on what you do best, and do it the best way you can.

Sources: "Fender Musical Instruments Corp. Partners with Experience Music Project," *Business Wire* (August 28, 2002); Bob Spitz, "And on the Lead Guitar . . .," *Sky* (August 1996), p. 55; and Fender Musical Instruments Corporation, "SiliconWorks Success Stories" (http://www.sgi.com/Works/SuccessStories/fender.html); http://www.fender.com.

Organizational design is a critical component of any business plan because it represents the infrastructure, processes, and systems by which the business will move from idea to reality. Therefore, it is important to consider how to organize the business effectively and profitably and in a way that reflects the culture of the organization. Superior organizational design begins with an understanding of how the business works—how information flows through the business. This understanding is critical to making decisions about business location, number of employees, management expertise required, and technology needed to facilitate business goals.

Three broad components make up the entrepreneurial organization: formal processes, people, and culture. Formal processes include the planning system, control mechanisms, compensation and reward policies, and other processes that make the organization run more efficiently and effectively. These processes are not independent but, rather, are linked to all functions of the organization that require them. For example, quality control mechanisms are not solely the purview of a single department, but flow from product development through manufacturing, to distribution, and throughout all the support functions needed to get a product to the customer.

Team building is a common phenomenon in entrepreneurial ventures. People who work in entrepreneurial companies must have team-building skills as well as the ability to make decisions and implement them with very little input from top management or the CEO. In new ventures those teams often consist of independent contractors whose skills are "rented" on an as-needed basis. Informal networks create flexibility and speed up operations. They also facilitate management of personal issues not easily handled through policies and structure.

Culture is the glue that binds people, processes, and structure. Culture is fundamentally the personality of the organization—the reflection of the company's vision and goals. It forms the basis for all the activities that the company undertakes. It is also the view of the company that customers see. An effective company culture enhances customer relationships, reduces employee turnover, and serves as a formidable competitive advantage for a company.

This chapter focuses on strategies for organizing the business and its many processes, finding a superior location, and putting together a team that will implement the company's processes.

Organization: Understanding the Way the Business Works

There probably is no single best organizational structure for all types of ventures in all situations. Rather, the entrepreneur must find the best fit, given the existing contextual factors (environment, technology, market), design factors (strategy and models), and structural factors (complexity, formalization).[1] A misalignment or misfit among these factors could result in an organizational structure that does not suit the particular market the company wishes to serve. For example, if a firm chose a low-cost strategy but did not implement tight control systems, minimize overhead, and focus on achieving economies of scale, it would be unlikely to succeed.

Firms in different industries tend to also differ in their administrative mechanisms and structures.[2] Several studies have found that the design of the organizational structure—how business activities are grouped, divided, and coordinated—is a critical factor in business performance and that a growing entrepreneurial firm must continually modify its structure to meet the demands of growth.[3] These findings reinforce the argument presented in Chapter 5 on the importance of conducting thorough industry and market analyses to understand the external conditions that will affect the business.

Ambiguity is a significant force in most entrepreneurial ventures. It derives from conflicting constituencies with different goals and needs, and from lack of immediate control over resources. As a result, ambiguity often manifests itself in pressures on the new business for legitimacy and commitment.[4] Legitimacy is validation of the business by external constituencies such as suppliers, customers, distributors, and others in the value chain. Commitment is the binding of an individual to the goals of the business. Commitment and legitimacy are interdependent; in particular, legitimacy cannot exist without commitment. The success of an entrepreneurial organization is a function of its ability to secure commitment and legitimacy while operating in an ambiguous context. Suppliers and others in the value chain expect the firm to demonstrate legitimacy through formalized systems and controls, something that entrepreneurial ventures in the earliest stages typically don't have because the dynamic environment in which they operate predisposes them to develop structures that are flexible and loosely defined with informal and minimal management systems.[5]

Information systems technology has facilitated new kinds of structures that enable new businesses to compete more effectively in rapidly changing environments.[6] The move from centralized structures to more decentralized or distributed structures is highly compatible with the mindset of the entrepreneur.

Because of limited resources and a creative and opportunistic mindset, entrepreneurs are naturals at improvisation—they are the jazz musicians of the business world—and can find ways to work around even the most rigid structure of a traditional bricks-and-mortar business model. Because entrepreneurial organizations reflect a fine balance between structure and chaos, they are innovative and creative. In that environment, entrepreneurs give free rein to new ideas and space to allow them to grow. Entrepreneurs in dynamic environments need to retain internally what the company does best and outsource the rest. In other words, focus on its core competencies until the company has established itself in the market. Then begin to look outside core competencies for new opportunities. Entrepreneurs also need to look for ways to keep overhead (non–revenue-producing plant and equipment) to a minimum. Again, outsourcing will facilitate this.

Identifying Business Processes

One of the most eye-opening experiences an entrepreneur can have is identifying all the processes (activities, tasks, etc.) that occur in the business. Even more revealing of how the business works is a process map or flowchart that traces how information flows through the business. The reason for this is that designing the way the business will work is often not the entrepreneur's area of expertise. Entrepreneurs are usually good at generating business ideas, testing concepts, and gathering resources to give the new business traction. Designing the operations and organization of the business is not always within their competence. Nevertheless, considering how the business will operate is crucial to figuring out how many people to hire, how much equipment to purchase, and what kind of facility will be needed. To create such a map of the business processes, take an imaginary tour of the business during a single day, listing all the tasks, people, equipment, supplies, and space required to run the business. For example, if customers entered the door of this business, what would they see? Who does the work in this business? Where do they work? What do they need to do the work? What information is being generated? Where does that information go?

The information gathered during this "fantasy tour" will also be useful when figuring expenses for financial projections later on and when determining what kind of personnel need to be hired to perform those tasks. Chapter 8 included an example of how to do this process analysis.

Another benefit of understanding how the business works is that such familiarity makes it easier to determine whether to employ a traditional organizational structure or a virtual organizational structure, which is discussed in the next section.

The Virtual Organization: Getting Traction Quickly

In the early 1990s, the virtual organization was a relatively new concept and certainly had yet to benefit from the Internet, which didn't affect the business sector in any significant way until 1995. The term **virtual enterprise** was borrowed from the science of virtual reality, which enables a person to become an integral part of a computer-generated, three-dimensional world. In business, a "virtual enterprise" has much the same purpose. The entrepreneur builds a company that to the rest of the world looks like any other company, but it is a business without walls where the entrepreneur does not incur the risk of acquiring employees, costly equipment, and enormous overhead. A virtual company makes it possible to operate the business from practically anywhere—a home, car, or vacation cabin. The goal of the virtual enterprise is to deliver to the customer the highest-quality product at the lowest possible cost in a timely manner. To do this requires the participation and management of the entire distribution channel, from producer to customer, through a series of strategic alliances. Traditionally, this was accomplished by building the business to the point where it could afford to buy out its suppliers and/or distributors, giving the company more control over quality and delivery. This strategy is known as vertical integration. Today that same goal can be accomplished through strategic partnerships with other companies in the value chain. Verifone, a leader in point-of-sale (POS) solutions, was one of the first companies to employ the virtual organization. In 1982, when it launched its first credit authorization box, it had five people in four different locations, few resources, and huge competitors such as AT&T and GTE. Verifone quickly discovered that the very bigness and centralization of these companies worked in its favor, because Verifone was agile and flexible and could

| FIGURE 12.1 | The Virtual Entrepreneurial Organization |

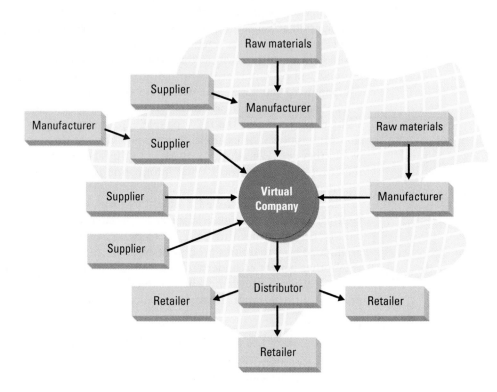

make changes rapidly. That virtual strategy turned out to be the secret of its success as Verifone garnered 70 percent of its market.

Outsourcing in a Virtual World

Today it is much more difficult for a new venture to achieve total in-house control of its value chain. The global marketplace is more complex, time-to-market has decreased, and it is difficult for any one company to have the broad expertise necessary to master all the functions of the distribution channel. Today a growing company is more likely to increase its flexibility by choosing one function to concentrate on—its core competency—and subcontracting functions it does not want to handle. The general rule is that if the resources to manufacture, assemble, and distribute the product already exist efficiently in the market in which the entrepreneur wishes to do business, the process should be outsourced.

Often a business whose competitive advantage lies in proprietary rights to its product will choose to maintain control of strategic functions and outsource such things as warehousing, transportation, and some aspects of marketing. A retailer may outsource administrative functions such as payroll, accounting, and inventory management and may even lease its employees from an employee-leasing company while operating the company in the virtual world of the Internet. Becoming a virtual company lets the new venture be more innovative, stay closer to the customer, and respond more rapidly to the market. Today many companies outsource aspects of their business processes, but virtual organizations outsource everything except their core management function. To their customers, they look like any other company, but behind the public image lies a very different kind of organization—one where the entrepreneur is basically a ringmaster in a three-ring circus.

Forming a Network of Strategic Alliances

Another way in which virtual companies become more flexible and responsive is by forming strategic alliances, or teams of businesses, to share resources and reduce costs. These alliances are more than sources of capability for the entrepreneurial venture; they are the glue that holds the venture together. Strategic alliances are more like true partnerships. They may purchase major equipment jointly or share the costs of research and development and of training. Particularly in the area of R&D, it is very difficult for any one small company to manage the expense alone. Networking and business alliances enable smaller businesses to bid successfully against large companies. They offer the convenience and savings of access to one source for everything, shared quality standards, and coordination of vendors. The key to managing a small-business alliance successfully is being willing to share internal information such as manufacturing processes, quality control practices, and product information for the good of all.

Building a virtual company and dealing with strategic alliances is not without problems. For the entrepreneurial team that wants to maintain control of every aspect of the growing venture, it is frustrating to have to give up some of that control to other companies. Getting virtual partners to meet entrepreneurs' demands for quality, timeliness, and efficiency can also be a long and difficult process. Consequently, it is important that the entrepreneur and the virtual partner come to written agreement on their duties and responsibilities and that they both enjoy the benefits of the relationship. Many entrepreneurs have found that the benefits of virtual partners far outweigh the problems and that the virtual corporation is the most efficient and effective way to give the venture traction.

However, there are management issues unique to this type of business, and they must be thoroughly understood. The next section describes what these management challenges are and how to solve them.

Keeping Virtual Employees and Strategic Partners Linked

One of the important challenges that virtual organizations face is keeping everyone connected and in touch even though they are geographically separated. A virtual company may be a great way to keep overhead down and flexibility up, but it is no substitute for human contact and face-to-face communication. Even in a virtual environment, it's important to conduct a face-to-face meeting at least once every three to six months. Arrange for employees and partners in specific geographic regions to meet regularly in between company-wide meetings. It is also important to create a discussion area on the company's Intranet and to encourage everyone to share important information and discussion points. A regular conference call should be

Global Insights

A Rock Solid Global Business

Richard Rhodes is a rock star, but his industry is not the music industry. Rather, his company, Rhodes Architectural Stone, a Seattle-based company, seeks out the most extraordinary building materials available around the world. Whether it's 500-year-old stone in China or two-century-old dolomitic limestone from an Indonesian military barracks about to be destroyed, Rhodes will find it. The Internet has made his business possible. Without the ability to contact customers in the United States quickly with digital photos of his finds, he couldn't do what he does. Using 14 scouts who travel the world taking pictures of potential materials and then displaying them on his company website, Rhodes can offer customers materials they can find nowhere else.

Sources: www.rhodes.org; and Lee Buchanan, "Rock Star," *Inc. Magazine* (December 2002).

set up once a week to stay in touch. In addition, it's a good idea to investigate video-conferencing. There are companies (Kinko's is one) that rent video time to companies and individuals.

Online Help for Virtual Companies

With virtual companies growing by leaps and bounds, online companies have sprung up to provide services and products that these businesses may need. Here are some examples:

Management team: Many websites aggregate independent professionals and help small businesses find experienced financial management on a limited budget.

Marketing: At several online sites, a company can accomplish its public relations, marketing, direct mail, and even market research for far less than it would cost to hire a marketing firm.

Supply chain management: Online companies will do everything from order management to assembly, configuration, packaging, and e-commerce fulfillment and collaboration.

Location: Finding the Appropriate Business Site

If the new venture cannot be operated as a virtual organization (and very few can't), a significant part of the organizing process is finding an appropriate site for doing business. Most people are familiar with the three key factors for determining value in home sites: "location, location, location." Similarly, the location of the business has a serious impact on its success. Location determines who will see the business, how easily they can find it and access it (Is the business at ground-floor level and easily seen? Or is it out of sight in a multistory building?), and whether or not they will want to access it (Is the neighborhood safe? Is parking available?). Even businesses such as manufacturing, where the customer doesn't come to the site, benefit from a location near major sources of transportation. Because many business owners view their business site as permanent, selecting the best site becomes a crucial decision that will need to be justified to investors, lenders, and others. Site decisions generally begin at a macro level, considering first the state or region of the country, next the city, and then the parcel on which the facility will be located.

Choosing the Region, State, and Community

Locating a site for a new business normally begins with identifying the area of the country that seems best suited to the type of business being started. "Best suited" may mean that firms in a particular industry tend to congregate in a particular region, such as the high-tech firms that gravitate to Route 128 in Massachusetts or to the Silicon Valley in California. For some businesses, "best suited" may mean that a state is offering special financial and other incentives for businesses to locate there. In other cases, "best suited" means located near major suppliers. Often an entrepreneur starts a business in a particular region because that's where he or she happens to live. This may be fine during the incubation period, but soon, what the area contributes to the potential success of the business over the long term must be considered.

Economic Base

The **economic base** of a region or community is simply the major source of income for the area. Communities are viewed as primarily industrial, agricultural, or service-oriented. In general, industrial communities export more goods than they import. For example, suppose the community's principal income is derived from farming and the associated products that it ships to other communities. This activity brings money into the community. Now suppose the citizens of the community must travel to another community to do major shopping. This activity takes money out of the community. An important thing to learn about any community being considered as the home base for the business is whether the money brought in from farming exceeds the money that leaves through shopping. If it does, the community appears to have a growing economic base, which is a favorable factor for new businesses.

Entrepreneurs can learn more about the economic base of any community by contacting the state or regional economic development agency in the area. These organizations exist to bring new business into the region, so they have to stay on top of what is going on. They can provide all the statistics on the economic condition of the region, as well as estimate the cost of doing business there. Also check the U.S. Department of Commerce website (www.doc.gov).

Financial Incentives

Most community governments are faced with cash needs that go well beyond the tax tolerance level of their citizens; consequently, they work diligently with economic development agencies to attract new businesses—and the accompanying tax revenues—into the community. One of the ways they attract businesses is by offering incentives such as lower taxes, cheaper land, and employee training programs. Some communities have enterprise zones, which give the businesses that locate in them favorable tax treatment from the state, on the basis of the number of jobs created, as well as lower land costs and rental rates. They also expedite permit processes and help in any way they can to make the move easier.

Look carefully, however, at communities that offer up-front cash in compensation for the community's lack of up-to-date infrastructure. They may be hiding a high corporate tax rate or some other disincentive that could hurt the new business's chances of success. In general, the larger the incentives, the more exacting the entrepreneur's homework must be.

Demographics

In addition to studying the economic base and the community's attitude toward new business, look carefully at the population base. Is it growing or shrinking? Is it aging or getting younger? Is it culturally diverse? The level and quantity of disposable income in the community will indicate whether there is enough money to purchase what a new company is offering.

Demographic information is usually based on the U.S. census, which tracks changes in population size and characteristics. The United States is divided into **Standard Metropolitan Statistical Areas (SMSAs),** which are geographic areas that include a major metropolitan area such as Los Angeles or Houston. These are further divided into census tracts, which contain approximately 4,000–5,000 people, and into neighborhood blocks. With this information, it is possible to determine, for example, whether the city in which an entrepreneur wants to locate a new software development firm has enough people with sufficient technical and educational skills to support it. Population data also indicate the number of people available to work. Demographic data are easily obtained from the economic development agency, the public library, the Internet, or the Post Office, which tracks populations by zip code.

Choosing a Retail Site

With a retail business, the entrepreneur is dealing directly with the consumer, so naturally, one of the first considerations is locating near consumers. Because a retail business is unlikely to survive if not enough consumers have access to the business, it is important to locate where there are suitable concentrations of consumers. Understanding a trade area is one way to calculate the potential demand from consumers.

The Trade Area

The **trade area** is the region from which the entrepreneur expects to draw customers. The type of business will largely determine the size of the trade area. For example, if a business sells general merchandise that can be found almost anywhere, the trade area is much smaller; customers will not travel great distances to purchase common goods. Yet a specialty outlet—for example, a clothing boutique with unusual apparel—may draw people from other communities as well.

FIGURE 12.2   Sample of a Trade Area

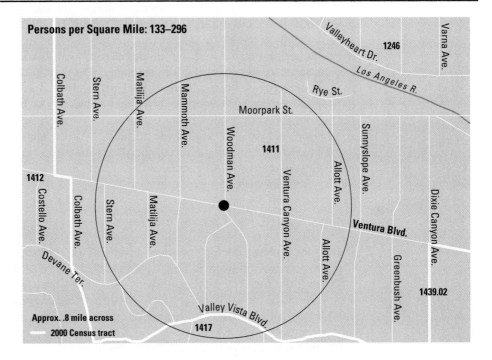

Once the location within the community is identified, the trade area can be calculated. With a map of the community, designate the site for the business, and place the point of a compass on the proposed site and draw a circle whose radius represents the distance people are expected to be willing to drive to reach the site. Within the circle is the trade area, which can now be studied in more detail. Using a census tract map, identify census tracts within the trade area, and look at the census data to determine how many people reside within the boundaries of the trade area. (See Figure 12.2.) The demographic information will also describe these people in terms of level of education, income level, average number of children, and so forth.

Competition and Character

Once the trade area is established, the competition can also be identified. One way to do this is to drive or walk through the area (assuming it is not too large) and spot competing businesses. Note their size and number, and gauge how busy they are at various times of the day by observing their parking lots or actually entering the business. If competitors are located in shopping malls or strip centers, look for clusters of stores that are similar to the new venture and have low vacancy rates. Then look at the stores near the proposed site to check for compatibility. Often, locating near a competitor is a wise choice because it encourages comparison shopping. Observe the character of the area. Does it appear to be successful and well maintained? Remember that the character of the area will have an important impact on the business.

Accessibility

It is important to identify the routes customers might take to reach a proposed site: highways, streets, and public transportation routes. If a site is difficult to locate and hard to reach, potential customers will not expend the effort to find it. Also check the parking situation. Most communities require provision of a sufficient amount of parking space for new construction, through either parking lots or garages; however, in some older areas, street parking is the only available option. If parking is hard to find or too expensive, customers will avoid going to the business. A foot and car traffic count for the proposed site will determine how busy the area is. Remember, retail businesses typically rely heavily on traffic for customers. A traffic count is easily accomplished by observing and tallying the customers going by and into the business. City planning departments and transportation departments maintain auto traffic counts for major arterials in the city.

Choosing the Service/Wholesale Site

If a service or wholesale business has customers who come to the place of business, the entrepreneur will need to find a site that offers some of the same attributes that a retailer looks for. Accessibility, attractiveness, and a trade area of sufficient size are all key factors in the selection of a site. The entrepreneur does not, however, need to choose from among the more expensive commercial sites, because customer expectations are not as great for a wholesale outlet that sells to the public, for example. Customers who patronize these types of businesses usually want to save money, so they don't expect the Cadillac version of a business site. Some service businesses, on the other hand, require attractive office space that is easily accessible. These are usually professional businesses—lawyers, accountants, consultants, and so forth. The image they present through the location and appearance of their offices is crucial to the success of the business.

Choosing the Manufacturing Site

For the manufacturer, the location choices narrow significantly. Communities have zoning laws that limit manufacturing companies to certain designated areas away from residential, retail, and office commercial sites to reduce the chance of noise, odor, and pollutants affecting the citizens. Often these areas are known as industrial parks, and they usually are equipped with electrical power and sewage plants appropriate to manufacturing. By locating in one of these parks, the new business may also benefit from the presence of other manufacturing nearby. Opportunities for networking and sharing resources and costs are enhanced.

Another common location for manufacturing is **enterprise zones,** which are public–private partnerships designed to bring jobs to inner cities, downtown areas, and rural areas suffering from the shift of jobs and population to the suburbs. The draw for businesses is tax incentives, regulatory relief, and employee training programs. Empowerment zones in any state can be found by going to the U.S. Housing and Urban Development Agency website (www.hud.gov/ezec/locator/).

Entrepreneurs seeking manufacturing sites are concerned with four key factors: access to suppliers, cost of labor, access to transportation, and cost of utilities. These factors may not be weighted equally. Depending on the type of manufacturer, one or more factors may have greater importance in evaluating a site.

Access to Suppliers

Manufacturers and processors usually try to locate within a reasonable distance of their major suppliers to cut shipping time and save transportation costs. Thus a food processor attempts to set up business near the growing fields, so that the food is as fresh as possible when it arrives at the processing plant. Similarly, a manufacturer that uses steel as one of its main raw materials might want to locate in the same region of the country as the steel mills to save the high costs of trucking heavy steel great distances.

Cost of Labor

Today many manufacturers choose a location on the basis of the cost of labor, rather than proximity to suppliers, because labor is generally the single greatest cost in the production of goods. Wages and laws related to workers, such as workers' compensation, vary from state to state—and sometimes from city to city. For example, California laws and cost of living tend to make it a more expensive place to hire employees than, say, Missouri. Some labor-intensive businesses have found that the only way they can compete is by having plants in Mexico or China, where labor costs are a fraction of those in the United States, and where laborers are not protected by as many laws. Mattel Toy Company, for example, has a plant in China to produce the hundreds of different toys it markets every year. The bottom line is that the entrepreneur must carefully weigh the cost of labor when considering a particular location for a manufacturing plant.

Access to Transportation

Most manufacturers prefer to locate near major transportation networks: railways, major highways, airports, and ports of call. The reasoning is obvious: The greater the distance between the plant and a major transportation network, the higher the cost to the company and, ultimately, to the customer. Also, the more transportation people who handle the product, the greater the cost. Thus, in terms of simple economics, to remain competitive, manufacturers must conduct a cost-benefit analysis on any proposal to locate away from a major transportation network. Higher transportation costs will result in a smaller profit margin for the company or in higher costs for the customers. Either way, the company loses.

Cost of Utilities

Utility rates vary from state to state, and usually from city to city within a given state. If the new venture is heavily dependent on electricity, gas, or coal, this factor could be a significant variable in the cost of producing a product and therefore should be carefully examined.

The land and location are only part of the equation. If the site contains an existing building, the question becomes whether to lease or to buy. If the site is bare land, building a facility is the only option. Because the facility accounts for a significant portion of a new venture's start-up costs, it is important to consider these scenarios in more detail. Also see Table 12.1 for an overview of the broad criteria for the lease-build-buy decision.

TABLE 12.1	The Lease–Build–Buy Decision			
STAGE OF BUSINESS	LEASE	BUILD	BUY	TEMPORARY SPACE
QUESTIONS TO ASK	1. Also ask the "buy" questions 2. Do you need to conserve capital for growth? 3. Do you expect the company to grow rapidly and need to move? 4. Can you include clauses that permit the option to renew the lease? 5. Can you remodel to suit your needs? 6. Which type of lease works best for the business: gross, net, or percentage? Do you have a choice?	1. Do you have the time to build? 2. Is it important to show an asset on your balance sheet? 3. Are your facility needs unique? 4. Do you intend to remain in the facility for a long time?	1. Is the building of sufficient size to meet future needs? 2. Is there sufficient parking? 3. Is there space for customers, storage, inventory, offices, and rest rooms? 4. Curbside appeal and compatibility with surroundings? 5. Sufficient lighting fixtures and outlets, and power to run equipment?	1. Do you need to keep overhead costs very low? 2. Are you willing to share space? 3. Is your product or service suitable to a mobile location such as a kiosk or push cart? 4. Do you need to test the product on customers in a real situation before committing to a building? 5. Do you have a product that can be demonstrated?
START-UP	A short-term lease gives the business the option to move and to gauge its long-term requirements.	At start-up, use this approach only when there is no facility available to meet the needs of the business. It requires large amounts of capital and time.	Not recommended at start-up unless it is the only option and the company is sufficiently capitalized.	Excellent for testing new products, services, and locations on customers. Low overhead.
RAPID GROWTH	A short-term lease will enable the business to move to larger facilities to meet growing demand without tying up a lot of precious capital.	Resist building during rapid growth as it will use up limited cash needed for growth. It is also a time-consuming process, and time is precious during rapid growth.	Rapid growth is not the time to buy a facility unless the company has received, from investors, a large infusion of cash that more than meets its operational needs.	During rapid growth, temporary locations make sense. This approach keeps the overhead low so that more cash can be directed toward satisfying demand.

TABLE 12.1	The Lease–Build–Buy Decision *(Continued)*			
STAGE OF BUSINESS	LEASE	BUILD	BUY	TEMPORARY SPACE
STABLE GROWTH	If the location is appropriate to the growth needs of the company, a long-term lease will provide more stability in cash flows.	With stable growth and positive cash flow, the company can afford to spend the time, effort, and capital to build a facility that specifically meets its needs.	Buying a building that allows for expansion is appropriate when company growth stabilizes and the company has a loyal customer base. It is also appropriate when the company needs to show a sizable asset on its balance sheet. If the company subsequently needs cash for a new period of growth, it can sell the building to an investor and lease it back, providing an instant infusion of capital.	Temporary space will typically be used to test new products and services before making a commitment.

Alternatives to Conventional Facilities

Today business owners have a variety of alternatives to conventional business locations. These alternatives lower the cost of overhead and make it easier for a business to change its mind should the location not work out. We'll consider four of these alternative sites: incubators, shared space, mobile locations, and temporary tenant agreements.

Incubators

Some entrepreneurs find it helpful to start their new venture's life in a business incubator, which has the same purpose as an incubator for an infant—to create a controlled environment that will enhance the chances that the business will survive the start-up phase. Private and state-sponsored incubators can be found in nearly every region of the country for almost any type of business. Incubators offer space at a lower-than-market rate to several businesses, which may then share common support functions, such as receptionist, copy machine, and conference room. The incubator may even offer business courses and training to help new entrepreneurs with the myriad details involved in running the business. After about three to five years, depending on the incubator, the young business is helped to move into its own site elsewhere in the community.

Some incubators cater only to high-tech firms or to service firms. Others, such as the Entrepreneur Partnership Program at the Mall of America in Bloomington, Minnesota, help entrepreneurs determine whether their retail or service businesses are suited to the demands of a major mall. This particular program helps the entrepreneur formulate a business plan and open a store. It also provides such incentives as waiving the costs of improving the store space and consulting in marketing and operations.

When considering an incubator, look at its track record and make sure it provides critical higher-order needs, such as like a network of contacts, access to expertise and capital, professional resources, and access to customers.

Shared Space

Another choice is to locate the company within the facilities of a larger company. As the largest of the chain stores continue to downsize, opportunities to take excess space arise. A variation on this theme is to lease a location that has enough space to sublet to a complementary business. For example, a copy service might lease excess space to a new computer graphics company or one that is seeking a new location. A shared arrangement is an effective way to secure the best location at a reasonable price.

Mobile Locations

One of the more interesting ways to introduce new businesses and new products/ services to the marketplace is through the use of pushcarts and kiosks. Pushcarts and their more fixed alternative, the kiosk (a small booth), also enable a company to expand to many new locations without the high overhead of a conventional retail storefront. Mobile locations like these are often found in airports, malls, and other areas where consumers gather.

Temporary Tenant Agreements

Some landlords have found that, rather than sitting on an empty space until the new tenant moves in, they can rent the space on a temporary basis so that their cash flow is not interrupted. In fact, the concept of the temporary tenant has grown so rapidly that there are now leasing agents who specialize in that area. The most successful of these temporary tenants possess the following characteristics that seem to draw customers to them: personalized merchandise, opportunities to sample the product, products that can be demonstrated, and products that can be used for entertaining the customers.

For the temporary concept to work, significant foot traffic and high customer turnover are required. This is an excellent alternative for retail businesses that want to test a location before making a major commitment.

People: Organizing the Start-up Team

The organization of the business processes and the site for the business are critical aspects of the management and operational plan, but it is people who implement those processes and use the company facility on a daily basis. The roles and responsibilities of people in the organization are typically depicted in an organizational chart. See Figure 12.3 to compare the traditional organizational chart, which tends to have layers or a hierarchy, with the distinctive virtual entrepreneurial start-up depicted in Figure 12.1. The entrepreneur and the founding team often perform all the functions when the business is just starting, and much of the work is accomplished through an informal organization or network of relationships. Informal networks of people consist of those who tend to gravitate toward each other in an effort to accomplish tasks in a more efficient and effective manner than may

| **FIGURE 12.3** | Traditional Line and Staff Organizational Chart for a Simple Manufacturing Plant |

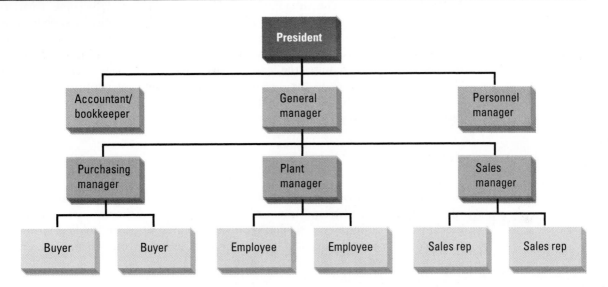

be dictated by the organizational chart. These networks form the "shadow" organizational structure that often brings the business through an unexpected crisis, an impossible deadline, or a formidable impasse. They are social links that constitute the real power base in the organization. Metaphorically speaking, the organizational chart is the skeleton of the body, while the informal network consists of the arteries and veins that push information and activity throughout the organization—in other words, it is the lifeblood of the organization.

Entrepreneurs seem to have recognized intuitively the value of informal networks in the organizational structure, and often the most successful new ventures adopt a team-based approach with a flatter structure. The lead entrepreneur is the driving force for the entrepreneurial team, which normally consists of people with expertise in at least one of the three functional areas of a new venture: marketing, operations, and finance. The organization consists of interactive, integrated teams. In the new venture, these are rarely "departments" in the traditional sense, but rather functions, tasks, or activities.

What is the explanation for this? For one thing, entrepreneurs are usually too creative and flexible to be bound by the strictures of a formal organizational structure. They are more comfortable bringing together resources and people as a team and making decisions on the spot without having to go through layers of management. Another reason is that new, growing ventures must be able to adapt quickly as they muscle their way into the market. Uncertainty and instability are a way of life for young ventures, and a rigid, formalized, bureaucratic structure would unduly burden a new venture both financially and operationally.

What makes the entrepreneur's situation unique is that—at least when the venture is in the start-up phase or the initial growing phase and capital resources are limited—the team the entrepreneur develops will probably include several people from outside the organization: independent contractors. For example, an entrepreneur may decide to subcontract the manufacturing of a product to an established company. The subcontractor will then, of necessity, become a part of that company's team in the production of the product. Marketing, sales, operations, and finance people must also be able to work with the manufacturing subcontractor to ensure that the goals of the new venture are met with the timeliness and level of quality desired. This requires the team to have skills not normally learned in school, skills such as diplomacy in the management of intra- and inter-team relationships, problem-solving skills, and the ability to take responsibility for innovative changes on the spot, often without direct approval.

Hiring the Right Team

Today, with ever more employees suing their bosses for wrongful discharge, sexual harassment, and racial/gender/age discrimination, it is increasingly important that the entrepreneur understand how to hire. Hiring is not a simple matter of placing a help-wanted ad in the newspaper, receiving résumés, and then holding interviews to select the best candidate. The bulk of the work of hiring comes before the person is actually needed.

Functions to Fill

Part of organizing the business is determining what positions are needed for the required tasks of the business. This is a wise practice, because employees are generally the largest expense of the business and therefore should be hired only when necessary. Nevertheless, it is important to develop job descriptions to prepare for the eventuality of hiring employees. Typically, when entrepreneurs (and managers) develop job descriptions, they focus entirely on the duties and responsibilities of a particular job. Although this is important, it is equally important to develop behavioral profiles of these jobs. Even though a job candidate may have the education and experience required by the job description and may display some of the behavioral traits necessary for success in the position, the candidate's personality and values may not fit in well with the culture of the organization. This is an important distinction, because education and experience can be acquired and behaviors can in most cases be taught, but the right values—which enable the new hire to fit in with the company culture—must already be present. In today's business environment, a company's culture is a competitive advantage, so hiring people whose attitudes and values are consistent with it becomes a most important goal in hiring.

The Employee Search

The first and best place to look for an employee is among current employees, subcontractors, or professional advisers. Referrals from trusted people who know the business have a greater likelihood of yielding a successful hire. Even during start-up, it is important to be constantly on the lookout for good people who might come on board as the business grows.

Executive search firms are good sources for management positions, and online resources have become an effective starting place for hiring, particularly with technically oriented positions. Companies such as Monster.com (www.monster.com), Guru.com (www.guru.com), and MSN Job Hunt (http://content.jobhunt.careers.msn.com/) are places where qualified people post their résumés, and it's easy for an employer to search for the particular skills required.

Interviews

Most entrepreneurs dread interviewing job candidates, primarily because they don't know what to say and don't understand that their questions should be designed to reveal the individual's personality and behavior—how he or she might react in certain situations. This can be accomplished in part by asking open-ended questions, questions that call for more than "yes-no" answers. For example, ask, "What is your greatest strength?" or "How would you handle the following hypothetical situation?" While the person is answering the questions, be careful to note the nonverbal communication being expressed through body language.

Entrepreneurs must be aware that certain questions should never be asked in an interview situation because they are illegal and leave the entrepreneur open to potential lawsuits. Under the laws administered by the **Equal Employment Opportunity Commission (EEOC),** before the point of hire a person may *not* be asked about religion or religious background, nation of origin, living arrangements or lifestyle choices, plans for pregnancy, age (to avoid discrimination against people over 40 or under 21), criminal arrest record ("Have you ever been convicted of a crime?" may be asked), or military record.

Human Resource Leasing

Entrepreneurs who are not ready to hire permanent employees or who need to remain flexible because the business environment is volatile and unpredictable may want to consider leasing employees or employing temporary services. A leased employee is not legally the entrepreneur's employee but is, rather, the employee of the lessor organization. That firm is responsible for all employment taxes and benefits. The entrepreneur simply receives a bill for the person's services.

Employee leasing is a rapidly growing industry now known as the **professional employer organization (PEO)** industry (www.peo.com/peo/). More and more business owners are finding it advantageous to have a third party manage their human resources. In effect, the PEO becomes a co-employer, taking on the responsibility of payroll, taxes, benefits, workers' compensation insurance, labor law compliance, and risk management.

Managing Employee Risk

Risk management is a set of policies and their associated decision-making processes that reduce or eliminate risks associated with having employees. For example, one entrepreneurial service company with 120 employees was suffering from a high turnover rate of new hires during the first 90 days of employment. Although the company's overall turnover rate was in line with the industry average, its turnover rate for new hires was about double that of its competitors. This turnover was costing the company over $10,000 per employee. This was a significant financial risk for

TABLE 12.2   Important Employment Laws

LAW	TYPE OF BUSINESS IT APPLIES TO
Age Discrimination in Employment Act Prohibits discrimination against people aged 40 to 70, including discrimination in advertising for jobs	All companies with 20 or more employees
Americans with Disabilities Act Prohibits discrimination on the basis of disability	All companies with 20 or more employees
Civil Rights Act Guarantees the rights of all citizens to freedom from discrimination on the basis of race, religion, color, national origin, and sex	All companies with 20 or more employees
Equal Pay Act Requires equal pay for equal work	All companies with 20 or more employees
Family and Medical Leave Act Provides for up to 12 weeks of unpaid leave for employees who are dealing with family issues	Companies with 50 or more employees
Immigration Reform and Control Act and the Immigration Act of 1990 Designed to prevent undocumented aliens from working in the United States. Companies must complete an Employment Eligibility Verification Form (I-9) for each employee.	All companies of any size
National Labor Relations Act and Taft-Hartley Act Requires employers to bargain in good faith with union representatives and forbids unfair labor practices by unions	All companies of any size
Occupational Safety and Health Act (OSHA) Designed to ensure safety and health in the work environment	All companies of any size
Title VII of the Civil Rights Act The original was amended to include discrimination again pregnant women; people with AIDS, cancer, or physical and mental disabilities; and people who are recovering from, or being treated for, substance abuse. Victims of discrimination may sue for punitive damages and back pay.	Companies with 15 or more employees for 20 weeks in the current or preceding year
Worker's Compensation Each state has enacted a law to compensate employees for medical costs and lost wages due to job-related injuries.	Requirements vary by state

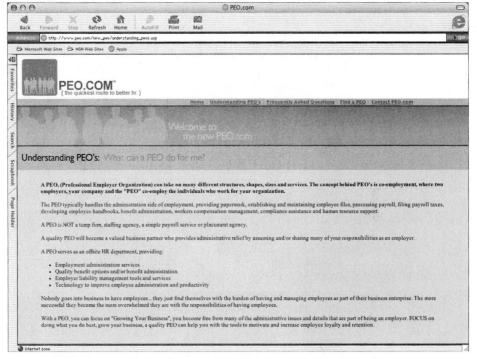

Source: http://www.peo.com/new_peo/, accessed 2/25/05.

the company and raised its cost of doing business substantially. To solve the problem and reduce the risk, the company improved its interviewing skills and instituted an orientation program for new employees.

Financial risks are one type of employee risk. In Chapter 10 the legal issues related to the formation of the business were discussed, but the law affects every aspect of business operations as well, especially the way employees are treated. The federal government and state governments have enacted a number of laws and regulations to protect employees from unhygienic or dangerous work environments, discrimination during hiring, and payment of substandard wages. One of the critical tasks of the person in charge of human resources is to make certain that the business is obeying all the laws and regulations to which it is subject. Failure to do so could result in severe penalties for the business and its owners. It is not within the scope of this text to address these laws in depth; however, Table 12.2 presents some of the major employment laws that affect small businesses. More information can be found on the Internet and through the federal and stage agencies associated with these laws.

Planning for Ownership and Compensation

Two of the most perplexing management issues faced by an entrepreneur heading a new corporation are how much of the company to sell to potential stockholders and how much to pay key managers. Whatever method is ultimately chosen, it should reflect the goals of the company and reward the contributions of the participants.

There is a tendency on the part of small, privately held companies to use minority shares as an incentive to entice investors and to pay key managers, primarily because new companies do not have the cash flow to provide attractive compensation packages. The prevailing wisdom is that providing stock in the new company will increase commitment, cause management to be more cost-conscious, reduce cash outlay for salaries, and induce loyalty to the company in the long term. But studies have found that this is not always the case.[7] More often than not, the person who has been given stock in good faith will ultimately leave the company, possibly taking the stock with her or him (absent an agreement prohibiting this), and this action creates the potential for future harm to the business. During the dot com craze of the late 1990s and into 2000, stock options were the most attractive benefit to potential employees, and many candidates would forgo large salaries in favor of more stock options. But after the dot com crash in April 2000 and the subsequent decline in valuation of technology stocks in general, stock options took second place to salaries.

In the initial growth stage of a new venture, it is difficult to determine with any degree of accuracy what long-term role a particular person may play in the organization. As a consequence of their limited resources, entrepreneurs typically are not able to attract the best person to take the company beyond the start-up phase, so they often hire a person with lesser qualifications for little salary plus a minority ownership in the company. In this scenario, the entrepreneur is literally betting on the potential contribution of this person—and it is a gamble that frequently doesn't pay off. Later, when the company can afford to hire the person it needs, it will have to deal with a minority shareholder who has developed territorial "rights." Therefore, when minority ownership is an important issue to a potential employee, it is imperative to make clear to that person exactly what it means. There are few legal and managerial rights associated with a minority position; thus, for all practical purposes, minority ownership is simply the unmarketable right to appreciated stock value that has no defined payoff period and certainly no guarantee of value. Using a stock-vesting agreement is one way to make sure that only stock that has been earned will be distributed. With a stock-vesting agreement, stock purchased by the team is placed in escrow and released over a three- to five-year period. A buyback provision in the stockholders agreement is another way to ensure that stock remains in the company even if a member of the team leaves in the early days of the new venture.

Compensating with Stock

Giving someone ownership rights in the company is a serious decision that should receive very careful consideration. There are several things to contemplate before taking on an equity partner, be it an investor or key manager. For example, anyone brought in as an investor/shareholder or partner with the entrepreneur does not have to be an equal partner. An investor can hold whatever share of stock is warranted on the basis of what that partner will contribute to the business. In general, one should never bring someone in as a partner/investor if that person can be hired to provide the same service, no matter how urgent the situation. The most advantageous way to hire someone for a new venture is to hire the person as an independent contractor. In addition, do not lock the company into future compensation promises such as stock options. Use cash for bonuses whenever possible. The company should be established as the founder's before any partners are taken on — unless, of course, the company has been founded by a team. Finally, consider having employees work for the company at least two years before they are given stock or stock options.

Founder's Stock

Founder's stock (144 stock) is stock issued to the first shareholders of the corporation or assigned to key managers as part of a compensation package. The payoff on this stock comes when the company goes public or is sold. Assuming that the company is successful, founder's stock at issuance is valued at probably the lowest it will ever be, relative to an investor's stock value. Consequently, a tax problem can arise when private investors provide seed capital to the new venture. Often the value of the stock the investors hold makes it very obvious that the founder's stock was a bargain and that its price did not represent the true value of the stock. According to Internal Revenue Code (IRC) §83, the amount of the difference between the founder's price and the investor's price is taxable as compensation income.

One way to avoid this problem is to issue common stock to founders and key managers and to issue convertible preferred stock to investors. The preference upon liquidation should be high enough to cover the book value of the corporation, so the common stockholders would receive nothing. This action would effectively decrease the value of the common stock so that it would no longer appear to be a bargain for tax purposes and subject the founders to an immediate tax liability.

Founder's stock is restricted, and the SEC rules (Rule 144) state that the restriction refers to stock that has not been registered with the SEC (private placement) and stock owned by the controlling officers and shareholders of the company (those with at least 10 percent ownership). If a stockholder has owned the stock for at least three years and public information about the company exists, Rule 144 can be avoided in the sale of the stock. If the stockholder has held the stock for less than three years, the rules must be strictly complied with. It is not the intent of this chapter to discuss the details of Rule 144. Suffice it to say that the rule is complex and that the appropriate attorney or tax specialist should be consulted.

Issuing Stock When the Company Is Capitalized

The number of shares authorized when a corporation is formed is purely arbitrary. Suppose a new venture, NewCorp, authorizes one million shares of stock. This means that NewCorp has one million shares available to be issued to potential stockholders. If each share of stock is valued at $1 and $100,000 is capitalized, the company will have 100,000 **issued shares;** if each share is valued at $10, the company will have 10,000 issued shares. The value placed on each share is arbitrary. For psychological reasons, however, it is customary to value a share at $1, so a shareholder who contributes $10,000 to the business can say that he or she owns 10,000 shares of stock (as opposed to 1,000 shares at $10/share). In short, the number of shares issued depends on the initial capitalization and the price per share.

Now suppose that the founder of NewCorp will initially be contributing $250,000 in cash and $300,000 in assets (equipment, furniture, etc.) to fund the company. At $1 a share, the company issues the founder 550,000 shares of stock; this constitutes a 100 percent interest in the company, because only 550,000 shares have been issued. At a later date, the company issues 29,000 additional shares at $5 a share to an investor. This minority shareholder has therefore contributed $145,000 (29,000 shares × $5/share) to the company and owns a 5 percent (29,000/579,000) interest in the company (that is, 29,000 of the 579,000 shares of stock that have been issued). The investor will require that the current value or future additional income of the company be sufficient to justify the increase in price per share. As additional shares are issued, the original investor's percentage ownership in the company declines. However, the founder's shares will not go below 55 percent (550,000/1,000,000) unless the company authorizes additional shares and issues a portion or all of those additional shares.

The type of stock issued is **common stock,** which is a basic ownership interest in the company. This means that holders of common stock share in both the successes and the failures of the business and benefit through dividends and the appreciating value of the company. Once common stock is issued, a company can then issue **preferred stock,** whose holders are paid first if the company is liquidated. Preferred stockholders must accept a fixed dividend amount, no matter how much profit the company makes. Recall that if the company were a sub-chapter S-corporation, it could issue only one class of stock.

Alternatives to Equity Incentives

There are other ways to compensate key managers that do not require the founder to give up equity in the company. The following are a few of these alternatives. In choosing among them, consider the advice of an accountant, who can recommend the most appropriate structure for the business.

Deferred Compensation Plans In a **deferred compensation plan,** the entrepreneur can specify that awards and bonuses be linked to profits and performance of both the individual and the company, with the lion's share depending on the individual's performance. The employee does not pay taxes on this award until it is actually paid out at some specified date.

Bonus Plans With a bonus plan, a series of goals are set by the company with input from the employee, and as the employee reaches each goal, the bonus is given. This method is often used with sales personnel and others who have a direct impact on the profitability of the company. The key to success with bonus plans is to specify measurable objectives.

Capital Appreciation Rights Capital appreciation rights give employees the right to participate in the profits of the company at a specified percentage, even though they are not full shareholders with voting rights. Capital appreciation rights, or "phantom stock," provide long-term compensation incentives whose value is based on the increase in the value of the business. The phantom stock will look, act, and reward like real stock, but it will have no voting rights and will limit the employee's obligation should the business fail. Typically, the employee has to be with the company for a period of three to five years to be considered vested in capital appreciation rights, but otherwise employees do not have to pay for these rights.

Profit-Sharing Plans **Profit-sharing plans** are distinct from the previously discussed plans in that they are subject to the ERISA rules for employee retirement programs. These plans must include all employees, without regard to individual contribution to profit or performance. They are different from pensions in that owners are not required to contribute in any year and employees are not "entitled" to them.

Organizing business processes, location, and people is an important and difficult task that requires thought and planning. Decisions made in the earliest stages of the new venture can seriously—and often negatively—affect the new firm's ability to grow and be successful in the future. This chapter highlighted many critical organizational considerations and offered suggestions for addressing them. However, it is important to consult with people who specialize in these functions to be sure that the right decisions are made.

New Venture Checklist

Have you:

☐ Identified the processes and information flow in your business?

☐ Identified ways to operate like a virtual enterprise or at least to outsource some aspects of the business?

☐ Located a site for the business?

☐ Decided whether to lease, buy, or build the facility?

☐ Determined the personnel required to run the business at start-up and over the next three to five years?

☐ Created job profiles for positions in the business?

☐ Determined the ownership and compensation requirements of the business?

☐ Formulated a plan to find the best candidates for positions in the company?

Issues to Consider

1. What are the advantages and the disadvantages of a virtual company?
2. What is the purpose of the imaginary tour of the business?
3. Which factors that are important in choosing a retail site would not be relevant to a manufacturing site—and vice versa?
4. What are the advantages and disadvantages of using stock as compensation and incentives?
5. How can the entrepreneur improve the chances of choosing the best job candidate?
6. List three alternatives to equity incentives for key managers.

Experiencing Entrepreneurship

1. Choose an industry in which you have an interest. Find a business in that industry, arrange to visit the site and talk with key personnel, and do a flowchart of the business process that reflects what you learned about it on your visit. Did you find any inefficiencies that if corrected could improve the process flow?

2. Interview an entrepreneur about his or her hiring practices. How successful have those practices been in getting and retaining good employees?

Additional Sources of Information

Berger, L.A., and D.R. Berger (1999). *The Compensation Handbook*. New York: McGraw-Hill.

Heneman, R.L., D.B. Greenberger, and P.B. Innis (2002). *Human Resource Management in Virtual Organizations*. Greenwich, CT: Information Age Publishing.

Lipnack, J., and J. Stamps (2000). *Virtual Teams: People Working across Boundaries with Technology*. New York: Wiley.

Small Business Association. *Using Census Data to Select a Store Site*. SBA Pub. No. MA2.023. Washington, DC.

Yate, M. (1997). *Hiring the Best: A Manager's Guide to Effective Interviewing*. Avon, MA: Adams Media Corporation.

Zankel, M.I. (2000). *Negotiating Commercial Real Estate Leases*. Fort Worth, TX: Mesa House Publishing.

Relevant Case Studies

Case 7 Linksys, p. 446

Case 8 Finagle a Bagel, p. 450

13

Producing Products and Services

"One way to increase productivity is to do whatever we are doing now, but faster. . . . There is a second way. We can change the nature of the work we do, not how fast we do it."

Andrew S. Grove, CEO, Intel Corporation

LEARNING OBJECTIVES

- Identify the components of production.

- Discuss how to prepare to produce products and services.

- Explain production cost issues.

- Understand how to maintain and warrant production processes.

Profile 13.1 CAPITALIZING ON GE'S LEAVINGS

Imagine generating $40 million in revenues from someone else's garbage. That's exactly what Thomas Mackie and Paul Reckwerdt did when, in 1997, GE Medical, which had been funding their research, decided that it wouldn't amount to a substantial business. Mackie and Reckwerdt were working on a machine that would make a radiation beam lock onto a tumor so that a doctor could clearly see it and, at the same time, zap it with radiation with amazing accuracy. GE Medical had been providing the duo with approximately $700,000 annually, so losing that funding was a major crisis. But since both men had lost close relatives to cancer, they were not about to give up.

Using $1.5 million that they had received for selling a medical software program, they launched TomoTherapy to develop and market the Hi-Art, a combination CT scan and radiation gun. They received FDA approval in 2002 and began installing eight of the $3.2 million machines. Since then, more than 26 additional machines have been ordered. With over 7,500 traditional radiation machines in operation around the world and hundreds being replaced annually, the market appears to be about $1.6 billion. With cancer increasing as a cause of death, the need for these machines will increase as well.

Yet as positive as all this might seem, there is danger on the horizon. Large medical device companies such as Siemens Medical Solutions and Varian Medical Systems have also recognized the opportunity and are hastening to bring their own versions of the Hi-Art to market. It is not easy for a small, entrepreneurial company spun out from a university lab to compete with the manufacturing and marketing resources of a public company. But Mackie and Reckwerdt are innovators who are able to look at a problem from hundreds of angles. They also knew that they didn't possess the business smarts to compete in the volatile medical device industry. So they brought on John Barni, a 28-year veteran of Marconi Medical, who was experienced in both manufacturing and marketing. Still, the road ahead may be rocky. Despite patents on aspects of its machine, TomoTherapy can't prevent competitors from building machines that also combine high-quality imaging with radiation treatment. Varian and Elektra are both introducing machines that compete directly with TomoTherapy, but Barni is convinced that Tomo can preserve its advantage by constantly innovating at a faster pace than its much larger competitors. At the same time, he will have to work to keep manufacturing costs and operational costs down, because as more competitors enter the field, the price point will inevitably decline.

Sources: TomoTherapy, www.tomotherapy.com; J. Martin, "Finding Gold in GE's Garbage," *Fortune Small Business* (April 25, 2004), www.fortune.com; and "TomoTherapy Inc. Gains FDA 510(k) Clearance for New Radiation Therapy System," eReleases, http://www.ereleases.com/pr/2002-02-01b.html, accessed on 7/20/04.

One of the topics that is rarely covered in texts on entrepreneurship is the manufacturing process, yet today, most new ventures produce a product of some sort, even if they define themselves as service businesses, and product businesses typically offer services as well. In other words, the boundaries between these two types of businesses have blurred if not disappeared altogether. Consequently, every entrepreneur should understand production processes and apply those concepts to his or her venture.

In simple terms, production is about managing the flow of material and information from raw materials to finished goods.[1] Think of manufacturing equipment as hardware, and of the people and information needed to run the machines as software, and it's easy to see why it's possible for two companies to have the same equipment and yet produce significantly different outcomes. The difference lies in the software driving the machinery—in other words, information and people.

Many high-growth ventures market innovative new products. The operational plan for the business consists of a fairly complex analysis that includes product development, prototyping, production processes, and inventory control mechanisms. The depth of analysis is a function of the type of product offered, the technological newness of the product, and the number of different ways the product can be produced. The more complex the product, the deeper the analysis. Thomas Mackie and Paul Reckwerdt were facing a complex problem when they decided to produce a technology that GE Medical had abandoned. (See Profile 13.1)

This chapter will look at the way products and services are produced. Recall that the product development aspect of the production process was discussed in Chapter 6.

The Components of Production

Production consists of four primary components: the customer, state-of-the-art technology, superior resources and processes, and continuous improvement. The absence of any one of these will result in a decline in overall productivity and in the company's effectiveness.

The Customer

The customer is considered the driving force and the foundation on which all the other functions are based. Superior performance as a manufacturer or producer can be achieved only when the customer is involved in the process. Today, at a time when customers expect superior levels of quality, service, and response time, manufacturers and producers cannot afford to be rigidly structured, cumbersome in size, and bureaucratic in their decision making. Instead, they must be small, flexible, fast, organizationally flat, and simple in design. This is good news for entrepreneurs, whose businesses generally reflect these characteristics.

Technology

Probably no single factor has had more of an impact on manufacturing processes for entrepreneurs than technology. Technology has made it possible for entrepreneurs to focus on their core competencies—what they do best—and outsource to other manufacturers those tasks that the other manufacturers do best. Network technology enables entrepreneurs to stay in touch with the companies to which they outsource and to decrease their set-up and wait times. In fact, in some industries, small companies are elaborately linked to provide a type of "one-stop shopping" experience for a much larger company. Certainly this is the case in the film industry, where many smaller companies (special-effects artists, graphics artists, sound editors, and so on) work together on a single project for a much larger film production and distribution company. In addition to private networks, the Internet has added a new dimension to manufacturing processes by causing manufacturers to rethink their relationships with suppliers and customers.[2] To accomplish this, manufacturers need to agree on business practices and be willing to share information. Accenture, a supply-chain management enabler, has identified six processes that benefit from collaborative manufacturing: (1) planning and scheduling, (2) product design, (3) new product introduction, (4) sourcing, and (5) order management.[3]

Superior Resources and Processes

Manufacturing is a process that uses the inputs supplied by procedures, people, and information to produce something tangible. Thus the job of manufacturing is to keep the process moving along by coordinating all the activities and keeping records of procedures to ensure quality control. Manufacturing also includes resource planning and demand flow.

Total quality management (TQM) is a framework or system for integrating superior quality into all aspects of a business. For manufacturers, this means designing processes that include continuous improvement, total quality control, self-directed teams, automation, computer-integrated manufacturing, and just-in-time production and inventory control. For service providers, it means designing processes that include continuous improvement, total quality control, and self-directed teams, in addition to methods for acquiring feedback from customers on additional services and potential products that might satisfy their needs. Here we consider those TQM activities that product and service businesses have in common.

Continuous Improvement

Under the principle of **continuous improvement,** everything a company does is a process, and every element of that process is scrutinized under a microscope to see whether it can be improved upon. Continuous improvement can be accomplished through a process known as PDCA, which stands for plan, do, check, act. It is a way of analyzing a process problem (for example, a problem in judging quality against a standard) and then planning for a change in the current process and monitoring the results of that change. PDCA begins with a *plan* for how to evaluate the process, identify problem areas, and decide on a solution. In general, it is important to choose areas of improvement that yield the greatest return for the effort. *Do* stands for execution of the plan to solve the problem, often on a small scale first. This is followed by *check,* which represents evaluating the success of the solution. What went right? What went wrong? *Act* signifies the decision whether the change should be adopted, abandoned, or reinstituted with modifications.

Total Quality Control

The goal of **total quality control (TQC)** is to eliminate all defects at all stages of the process—in other words, to achieve perfection. The basic principles of TQC include (1) customer satisfaction as the fundamental goal of any organization;

Profile 13.2 MANUFACTURING CAN STILL BE A SUCCESSFUL STRATEGY

With Vince Lombardi's mantra "no substitute for victory" firmly implanted in his brain, Richard E. Dauch has done an end run around the prevailing wisdom that you must outsource your manufacturing to China to compete in a price-competitive industry. His American Axle & Manufacturing (AAM), based in Detroit, has grown to $4 billion since he founded it in 1994. Years of experience in the auto industry prepared him to recognize a niche in the market. Dauch was concerned about a number of problems in the auto industry: lack of quality, artificial restrictions in union contracts that impaired productivity, and poor treatment of factory workers.

Through two decades, Dauch worked his way up the ladder at companies such as Chevrolet and Chrysler. In every position, he introduced innovations, modernized plants, and improved quality. Before his competitors, he introduced flexible manufacturing and assembly systems, which made it possible to change models quickly and run more than one type of vehicle down the same line. In 1991 he left Chrysler, which at that time was experiencing turmoil in the upper echelons of management, and began looking for new manufacturing opportunities. Also at that time, General Motors, in an effort to avoid bankruptcy, was selling off five axle and drivetrain plants in Detroit. With a group of investors, Dauch raised $300 million over two years and purchased the plants. Although many people thought he had lost his sanity, Dauch knew that GM would ultimately need these plants to produce the drivetrain systems for the burgeoning truck and SUV markets. Having secured contracts with GM to purchase most of the plants' output, Dauch began improving the plants and raising the level of quality.

He searched the world for the best equipment and was even able to reduce the amount of equipment he needed by using more efficient machines. He implemented the latest computer tools to save time and money—for example, a road-load simulator that enables workers to test and validate products before building them. Using a factory information system, management can view in real time the status of various assembly lines at any of the five plants.

This kind of dedication to quality, lean manufacturing, and superior work conditions for employees has made his company profitable every year. Recognizing that it is never wise to rely on one customer alone, Dauch has been diversifying, adding customers from other U.S., Japanese, and European manufacturers.

Today, AAM is a true entrepreneurial success story in manufacturing, with 17 plants and 12,000 workers around the world. Dauch has also proved that he can manufacture in Detroit and compete with Chinese manufacturers by providing higher-quality parts and more advanced technology. Bucking a trend, Dauch has no plans to "outsource America."

Sources: G. Bylinsky, "Heroes of Manufacturing: Richard E. Dauch: Pumping Up a Weak Auto Supplier," *Fortune* (February 23, 2004), www.fortune.com; American Axle & Manufacturing, http://www.aam.com/; and http://www.nyse.com/listed/axl.html.

(2) the use of quality circles or some process by which employees are assembled frequently to discuss issues and plans; (3) policy deployment, or a planning and review tool that consists of annual objectives and strategies; and (4) foolproof solutions to problems so that they don't occur again. TQC is discussed in more detail on page 278.

Self-Managed Teams

Like quality circles, **self-managed teams (SMTs)** give employees more input into what they do for the company and result in higher levels of productivity and quality. They also improve flexibility and responsiveness to changing market conditions, because decisions are made more quickly and changes are implemented with fewer problems. In manufacturing, this may mean putting a team in charge of the production of a particular product or a particular portion of a more complex product. SMTs have responsibility and authority to make decisions related to quality issues. Similarly, in a service company, it may mean putting associates in charge of projects and making them accountable for the outcomes.

Preparing to Produce Products and Services

Building a complex production system while the company is in start-up or later when it is rapidly growing is a recipe for disaster. Entrepreneurs who are fortunate enough to have a product that enjoys mass-market acceptance early on must be prepared in advance to meet market demand. Many a company has lost customer loyalty and significant revenues because it lacked the effective systems and controls necessary to produce and deliver products to customers in a timely fashion. Once

Profile 13.3 WHY NOT BE AN OEM?

Staying in the background as an original equipment manufacturer can sometimes be more lucrative and less stressful than having your name clearly in the public eye. From 1997 to 2001, Ogio, a Bluffdale, Utah, sports bag manufacturer, grew 500 percent because of a lucrative niche in the market. "Ogio Engineered" can be found in such big-name companies' products as Callaway golf bags. Ogio's niche is looking for ways to "ogioize" "sleeper" product categories. The term *ogioize* was coined by Ogio's founder, Michael Pratt, to refer to its multipatented gear-bag technology. Ogio innovates on product features that others might overlook, including how a bag's sling rests on your back and how golf balls pop out of their dispenser when you pinch the neoprene sleeve.

Ogio's goal is simply to make its strategic partner, Callaway, stand out from the crowd.

The trend of small, innovative product developers and manufacturers supplying big powerhouse companies is unlikely to reverse itself. The smaller company is freer to think out-of-the-box about new ideas, unencumbered by the overhead and inertia that plague most large companies. Large companies can't afford to look at the smaller profits that would sustain an entrepreneurial company, so it makes more sense for them to use the smaller company in a variety of interesting ways. It is a truly symbiotic relationship.

At the moment, Ogio has no intention of being acquired by Callaway or anyone else. This dynamic team of sports enthusiasts simply wants to go on having fun innovating its own products and those that it produces for others.

Sources: http://www.ogio.com/index.cfm; and E.A. Grant, "Creation Nation: Innovation: Part II," *Inc. Magazine* (October 2002).

lost, that customer base is nearly impossible to regain in time to fend off competing firms and save the company from failure.

One of the best ways to understand how the production process touches customers and affects the bottom line is to follow an order through the company and document where the order flow gets bogged down, is duplicated, or is hindered in some manner. Any slowdown or duplication of effort means higher production costs and slower response to the customer. Consider a market research firm that provides customized reports to companies to enable them to judge their markets for new products and services. This is an example of what would typically be called a service firm, yet note that this service firm produces a product—a market research report. Now suppose that in the process of gathering the research and analyzing it, there is no plan for who should do a particular aspect of the research. Duplication of effort could easily occur, and it's possible that something important, such as an emerging competitor, might be overlooked. Both duplication of effort and the need to go back and cover something that has been overlooked are costly and retard the production process, potentially causing the company to miss a customer deadline.

For any product or project, it's important to track all the components, raw materials (parts), or data. Some things to look for are the costs to purchase from the supplier and inspect for quality; how long raw materials or supplies sit in the company's inventory before they are used in the production process; how many people handle the parts or data before they become part of the product or project; how many set-ups (adjustments of machinery to do a particular task) before the product can be assembled; how much time a product or project spends in production; how many times errors occur during the process; and how effective the delivery process is.

Each one of these points in the process can be a source of delay and cost for the company, so the production process needs to make each one as efficient and effective as possible. One of the best ways to do that is to inspect for quality in product and process at *every* point of activity along the production line and to keep the tolerance levels for error or variance very low. This approach minimizes failures in the product after it is in the hands of the customer. Pelco Inc., a leader in the video surveillance industry, has designed quality control into every process in its company. Any worker can stop production for a defect, so by the time the product reaches the end of the production line, it is defect-free. Pelco would rather take the time to look for errors before the product reaches the customer than have the customer find defects. Contrast this approach with that of the software industry, which regularly launches products with "bugs" that they expect their customers to find and report.

The Production Process

A typical manufacturing plant has five functional areas—(1) purchasing, (2) materials management and production scheduling, (3) production and assembly, (4) quality control, and (5) maintenance—as depicted in Figure 13.1. Each has measurable components that should be tested for effectiveness; that is, there are ways to measure the efficiency and effectiveness of every aspect of the production process. In general, manufacturing and production firms are organized as product-focused or process-focused organizations. Product- or project-focused organizations generally

| **FIGURE 13.1** | The Production Process |

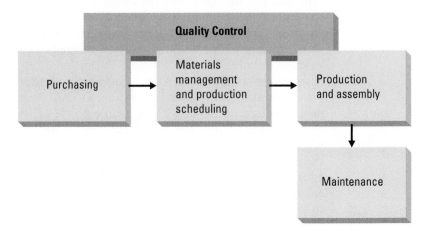

are highly decentralized so that they can respond better to market demands. Each product or project group acts essentially as a separate company, a profit center. This type of organization is well suited to products or projects that don't require huge economies of scale or capital-intensive technologies. Process-focused organizations, on the other hand, are common among manufacturers with capital-intensive processes (such as those in the semiconductor industry) and among service companies (such as advertising firms). These organizations are highly centralized in order to control all the functions of the organization. Whether the company is product- or process-focused, it must be able to extend its control beyond the five functional areas so that it will not be at the mercy of its suppliers at one end and its distributors at the other. This control is usually accomplished through strategic alliances.

As noted in Chapter 12, the virtual enterprise, consisting of strategic alliances among all links in the value chain, is one way to achieve control of the entire process from raw materials to distribution, while still keeping the firm small and flexible enough to meet changing needs and demands. This model is similar to the Japanese *keiretsu* in the automobile industry, which links banks, suppliers, electronics, and auto firms through a series of cross-ownerships. The United States model leaves ownership in the hands of the individual owners but links the organizations into a virtual entity that acts as a team with a common goal. Wal-Mart is probably the best example of this type of partnership and integration in the United States. It has established point-of-sale linkups with its suppliers and has given its manufacturers the responsibility for handling inventory. The ultimate goal is to construct one organization with a common purpose that encompasses the entire supply chain from raw materials supplier to retailer, with each link along the chain performing the task that it does best. Establishing this type of network takes time. A start-up company can't expect to achieve quickly the level of integration and control that a Wal-Mart has taken years to accomplish. Instead, start-up companies need to build relationships slowly, beginning with key independent contractors to whom they may be outsourcing some tasks.

Don't Forget Packaging as a Cost of Production

Entrepreneurs producing consumer products, in particular, need to recognize that effective packaging of a product is an essential component of a successful strategy to build a brand. Often a product's package will determine whether a customer picks it off the shelf or walks by without noticing it. Here are some tips for making packaging a cost-efficient and effective tool.

1. Packaging is not the place to cut corners. Use a cross-functional team to generate ideas, and consider bringing in a packaging consultant with experience in the industry.
2. Identify the objectives for the packaging strategy, which should include both graphic and structural design. These objectives should be congruent with the marketing objectives.
3. Do some market research on packaging ideas and packaging technology. Things like flip-top closures and resealable packaging can make a difference.
4. Outsource packaging to a reliable vendor and build a long-term relationship. This will save the company a lot of money.

The Internet has been a valuable tool for streamlining distribution and supply channels in many industries, and even small, growing businesses can take advantage of its power. For example, suppose a company is sourcing parts for a product it is building; that is, it is trying to find out where to find the best parts at the best prices. Before the Internet, it could have taken months of phone calls and faxes to find the best vendors. Now this new company can quickly compare vendors and products online in the same way that large companies do.

The next sections will explore more closely the five functions of production.

Purchasing

Locating vendors to provide raw materials or goods for resale is not difficult, but finding the best vendors is another matter entirely. The issue of vendor relationships has become increasingly important in markets that demand that companies reduce costs and maintain effective relationships. Research has found that these relationships reflect factors such as trust or commitment,[4] uncertainty and dependence[5] and the effect of these on performance.[6]

Furthermore, buyers and sellers are connected in an increasing number of ways: through information sharing that improves the quality of the product produced[7] or brings about new product development[8]; operational linkages such as computerized inventory, order replenishment systems, and just-in-time delivery; legal bonds such as binding contractual agreements; cooperative norms; and relationship adaptations wherein vendors modify their products to meet the needs of the customer.

Given the importance of the vendor–customer relationship,[9] should a company buy from one vendor or from more than one? Obviously, if a single vendor cannot supply all the company's needs, that decision is made. However, there are several advantages to using a single vendor where possible. First, a single vendor will probably offer more individual attention and better service. Second, orders will be consolidated, so a discount based on quantity purchased may be possible. On the other hand, the principal disadvantage of using just one vendor is that if that vendor suffers a catastrophe (say, its facility burns to the ground, like the Japanese company that was the prime supplier of RAM chips several years ago), it may be difficult or impossible to find an alternative source in a short time. To guard against this contingency, it is wise for a company to use one supplier for about 70 to 80 percent of its needs and one or more additional suppliers for the rest.

When considering a specific vendor as a source, ask several questions. Can the vendor deliver enough of what is needed *when* it's needed? What is the cost of transportation using a particular vendor? If the vendor is located far away, costs will be higher, and it may be more difficult to get the service required. What services is the vendor offering? For example, how often will sales representatives call? Is the vendor knowledgeable about the product line? What are the vendor's maintenance and return policies?

It is also important to "shop around" and compare vendors' prices. Check for trade discounts and quantity discounts that may make a particular vendor's deal more enticing.

Computer technology has made materials planning more of a science than ever before. Information systems can now provide the person doing the purchasing with detailed feedback on supplier performance, reliability of delivery, and quality control results. Comparing results across suppliers provides more leverage when it's time to renegotiate the annual contracts with suppliers.

Materials Management

Any business that purchases raw materials or parts for production of goods for resale must carefully consider the quality, quantity, and timing of those purchases. Quality goods are those that meet specific needs. Quality varies considerably among vendors, so if a company has established certain quality standards for its products, it must find vendors who will consistently supply that precise level of quality, because customers will expect it. The quantity of raw materials or parts that are purchased is a function of (1) demand by the customer, (2) manufacturing capability, and (3) a company's storage capability; consequently, timing of purchases is very important. Purchases must be planned so that capital and warehouse space are not tied up any longer than necessary. Because materials account for approximately 50 percent of total production cost, it is crucial to balance these three factors carefully.

Inventory Requirements

Today, businesses that hold inventories of raw materials or goods for resale have found that they must reduce these inventories significantly to remain competitive. Instead of purchasing large quantities and receiving them on a monthly basis, businesses are purchasing daily or weekly in an effort to avoid costly inventories. Of course, some inventory of finished goods must be maintained to meet delivery deadlines; therefore, a delicate balance must be achieved among goods coming into the business, work in progress, and goods leaving the business to be sold.

In the past, inventories were built up on the basis of the state of the economy or in reaction to problems in an inventory control system. If times were good, producers increased stocks of inventory to meet expected demand. Then, when the economy slowed, they usually had shelves of leftover stock. Reductions in inventory succeeded in exposing typical problems: equipment imbalances, paperwork backlogs, excessively long set-ups, vendor problems, and problems with purchase lead time.

Newer systems, such as just-in-time (JIT), help manufacturers and producers maintain better control of their inventories by eliminating production and inventory problems and then reducing inventory to only that which is needed.

Just-in-Time

The **just-in-time system** of materials and inventory management is fundamentally different from other inventory systems. Originating in Japan, JIT rapidly took hold in the United States. The philosophy behind JIT is to produce the minimum number of units in the smallest possible quantities at the latest possible time. A well-devised and implemented JIT system can do many things, such as increasing direct and indirect labor productivity, increasing equipment capacity, reducing manufacturing lead time, reducing the cost of failure, reducing the cost of purchased materials, reducing inventories, and reducing space requirements. In essence, the goal of JIT is to eliminate waste in the manufacturing process. Consequently, to implement JIT, it is necessary to look beyond mere inventory to all other aspects of the manufacturing process as well. Starting with the last operation, which is usually meeting the customer requirement, work backward through the manufacturing process. Customer demand determines how many products are produced. The number of products to be produced determines the production capability requirements, which in turn determine the amount of raw materials needed. In general, a JIT firm maintains an inventory no larger than is needed to support one day of production. To do this, it has to have the cooperation of its suppliers and its distributors, and it must impose severe penalties for not being on time—that is, for being either too early or late. This stringent requirement reduces the number of suppliers a JIT firm typically deals with. JIT also requires strict quality control, because with minimal inventories there is no excess inventory to cover rejects.

A traditional factory is laid out by functional department, usually based on a particular process or technology. The result is that products are produced in batches. This is the antithesis of JIT, which specifies that the plant be laid out by product. With JIT, the equipment is positioned in the order in which it is used to produce a particular product or family of related products. It is also important to plan production in such as way as to produce only enough to meet demand. For example, consider a situation in which a company expects to sell a total of 100 units of product in the next month. Then

$$100/20 \text{ work days} = 5 \text{ units a day}$$
$$5/8 \text{ work hours} = .63 \text{ unit per hour}$$
$$\text{or 1 unit every hour and a half}$$

This calculation must be reworked every month as demand changes.

One way suppliers are meeting the needs of a company using JIT is by involving independent contractors specializing in "time-sensitive" deliveries. For example, one company has installed two-way satellite communication on its trucks so that shipments can be tracked in real time. Other businesses, such as American Cargo Systems, help businesses that need to ship to retailers. They stock merchandise in their warehouses, process orders, make deliveries, and handle billing. In that way, retailers don't incur the costs associated with maintaining a backup supply of items. Avoiding too much inventory is a trend that is expected to continue for the next decade. However, working effectively requires careful coordination and cooperation of all members of the supply chain.

Production and Assembly

The lifeblood of any business is its production function. Decisions made about production directly affect output level, product quality, and costs. Planning for production, therefore, is critical to manufacturing efficiency and effectiveness. Most manufacturers and producers begin by scheduling—that is, by identifying and describing each activity that must be completed to produce the product and indicating the amount of time it takes to complete each activity. Two methods traditionally used in the scheduling process are Gantt Charts and PERT Diagrams.

Gantt Charts

Gantt Charts are a way to depict the tasks to be performed and the time required for each. Consider Figure 13.2. The tasks to be completed (in this case, fulfilling customer orders) are listed in the first column, and the time to completion is traced in horizontal rows. Note that the solid line represents the plan for completion, whereas the dashed line depicts where the product is in the process. Gantt Charts work best for simple projects that are independent of each other.

FIGURE 13.2   Gantt Chart

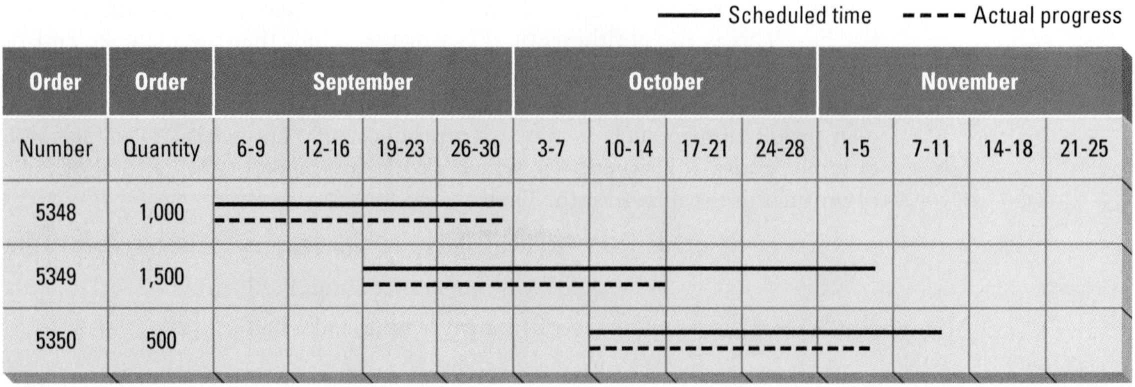

——— Scheduled time   ‑ ‑ ‑ ‑ Actual progress

Order Number	Order Quantity	September 6-9	September 12-16	September 19-23	September 26-30	October 3-7	October 10-14	October 17-21	October 24-28	November 1-5	November 7-11	November 14-18	November 21-25
5348	1,000	----	----	----									
5349	1,500			----	----	----	----						
5350	500						----	----	----	----			

PERT Diagrams

PERT is an acronym for Program Evaluation and Review Technique. This method is helpful when the production being scheduled is more complex and is subject to the interdependence of several activities going on either simultaneously or in sequence. In other words, some tasks cannot be started until others have been completed. To begin, the major activities involved in producing the product must be identified and arranged in the order in which they will occur. Be sure to identify any activities that must occur in sequence—that is, cases where one activity cannot occur until another is finished.

A pictorial network that describes the process is then constructed. The time to complete each activity is estimated and noted on the chart. This is usually done three times, and the answers are given as most optimistic, most likely, and most pessimistic. The statistics of analyzing the network are beyond the scope of this book, but the process consists essentially of (1) identifying the critical path, which is the longest path and is important because a delay in any of the activities along the critical path can delay the entire project; (2) computing slack time on all events and activities (the difference between latest and earliest times); and (3) calculating the probability of completion within the time allotted.

The numbered nodes on Figure 13.3 refer to the start and completion points for each event. The dummy line was placed in the diagram to account for the completion of event **e**'s being preceded by events **b** and **d**. Both must be completed before event **g** can start.

There are several popular software products on the market, such as Micro Planner X-Pert and Microsoft Project that can help entrepreneurs schedule their production capacity. Like any new technique, it takes time to learn the PERT system, but it is time well spent. Tracking production from the outset of the business permits more realistic strategic decisions about growth and expansion.

Identifying all the tasks in the production process makes it easier to determine what equipment and supplies are needed for completing the tasks. If, for example,

---

FIGURE 13.3 PERT Diagram

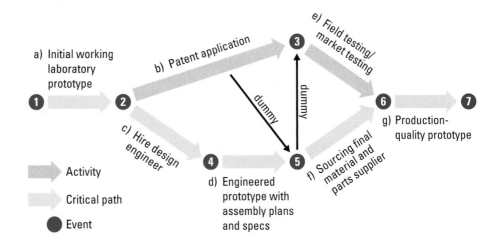

the equipment necessary to produce the product is beyond the company's start-up resources, it may be time to consider outsourcing part or all of production to a manufacturer that has excess capacity with the needed equipment.

After the production tasks have been identified, create a preliminary layout of the plant to estimate floor space requirements for production, offices, and services. It may be beneficial to consult an expert in plant layout to ensure that one makes the most efficient use of limited space.

Quality Control

Quality control is the process of reconciling product or project output with the standards set for that product or project. More specifically, it is "an effective system for integrating the quality-development, quality-maintenance, and quality-improvement efforts of the various groups in an organization so as to enable marketing, engineering, production, and service at the most economical levels, which allow for full customer satisfaction."[10] In this sense, quality does not necessarily mean "best"; rather, it means "best for certain customer requirements," which consist of the features and benefits of the product or service and its selling price.[11] It is said that one thing manufacturers and producers learn from history is that "the primary objective of the company is to put the quality of the product ahead of every other consideration. A profit or loss notwithstanding, the emphasis will always be on quality."[12] Today thousands of manufacturers and producers have embraced the philosophy of quality first but have focused principally on equipment and processes rather than on the human element. Both must be considered in order for total quality control to permeate every aspect of the organization. Over the past twenty years, manufacturers have invested heavily in quality improvements. Concepts such as lean manufacturing and Six Sigma have helped companies lower production costs, produce less scrap, allow fewer defects, and reduce warranty expense.[13]

Producing products for the medical industry is particularly difficult because quality is not simply a desired outcome, but an essential one. When Corinna Lathan decided to produce devices to help disabled children enjoy their physical therapy exercises, she knew her products had to be perfect. Therapeutic devices are costly — nearly ten times the price of a high-tech toy for able-bodied children. Lathan, a Ph.D. in neuroscience and a professor of biomedical engineering, recognized that although she had the ability to take the product through the primitive prototype phase, she needed a major partner to get the product to the projected $2 billion market. To cut the retail price of her JesterBot to $100 *and* ensure consistent quality, she is working on a licensing agreement with Toytech Creations to mass-produce the robot for her.[14]

Quality is a strategic issue that is designed to bring about business profitability and positive cash flow. Effective total quality programs result in "improved levels of customer satisfaction, reduced operating costs, reduced operating losses and field service costs, and improved utilization of resources."[15]

The Inspection Process

One way in which manufacturers and producers control quality is through a regular inspection process that takes place during several stages of the production process.

Often, primarily to reduce cost, a random sample of products or project outcomes is chosen for the inspection. This method catches potential defects early in the process, before the products become finished goods. Whether each item produced is checked or a random sampling is conducted depends on what is being produced, on its cost, and on whether the inspection process will destroy the item. For example, when a company is producing an expensive piece of machinery, it may be prudent to subject each item to the inspection process, because the cost of inspection is more than offset by the price of the item. But compare the situation when a food is being produced. Once such a product is inspected, it cannot be sold, so it is not feasible to inspect more than a representative random sample of each batch.

Entrepreneurs who want to achieve total quality will probably set a no-defect goal for product manufacturing. Chapter 6 discussed the importance of designing right the first time and designing for producibility. Superior design is the first step in achieving defect-free production. Another step is giving work teams the power to stop production in order to resolve a quality issue. Recall the example of Pelco earlier in this chapter.

Six Sigma

Six Sigma is a quality initiative that Motorola introduced in the 1980s. The program identifies quality levels that predict the likelihood that defects will occur—the higher the level, the lower the probability of a defect. Six Sigma relies on statistical tools and specific processes to achieve the measurable goals of fewer defects, increased productivity, reduced waste, and superior products and processes.[16]

Although large companies like GE and Allied Signal are widely known for their Six Sigma programs, small companies like Technically, Inc., a Boston-area provider of contract laboratory services and manufacturing to the chemical industry, have also benefited from the program. Technically, Inc.'s founder, Debra Saez, left Dupont to start the company in 1985 and brought with her the Six Sigma skills that are now a hallmark of her company's rigorous approach to refining industrial processes. For example, the statistical technique ANOVA, or analysis of variance, is used to optimize weak processes so that they can be performed with less labor and raw materials and in about half the time.[17]

Quality Circles

Quality circles are groups of employees who regularly work together on some aspect of the production process. They meet several times a month, usually with the help of an outside facilitator, to discuss problems and ideas related to their work environment. They often come up with new solutions to problems, and these solutions are often put into effect, thus improving the efficiency and effectiveness of the manufacturing process and the product as well. Quality circles give employees a vested interest in what they are producing; consequently, they are more likely to pay close attention to improving the way their task is completed.

The real success or failure of the quality control effort is dependent on the human element in the process: customers, employees, and management. Quality begins with satisfying the needs of the customers, and that cannot be accomplished unless those needs and requirements are communicated to managers and employees. An entrepreneur with a new venture has a unique opportunity to create a philosophy of quality from the very birth of the business, in the way the business is run and in the employees hired. The new venture has the advantage of creating new habits and patterns of behavior instead of having to change old ones.

Using Customers for Quality Control

The philosophy that a company produces what the customer needs, when he or she needs it, is fundamental to quality control. Customers, by their demands for reliability and performance in a highly competitive market, establish the standards that must be met when the product is designed and produced. If customers perceive that the product does not meet their needs or does not meet them as well as another product could, sales are lost.

Using Employees for Quality Control

For employees to buy into the notion of quality control at every level, they must be given the responsibility and authority to make changes that will improve the process and product at every level. If the firm is going to install new technology to improve the process, employees need to be trained not only in how to use it but also in how to look for potential problems that would affect quality. The continual use of awareness and training programs will help employees understand their importance in the whole manufacturing process.

Using Management for Quality Control

For total quality management to work, key managers must be "on the floor," learning every aspect of production and supporting the efforts of employees. It is their job to bring the requirements of customers to the people who will satisfy those requirements. It is also management's job to establish company-wide, measurable quality goals. Too often managers focus more on productivity goals than on quality goals. Ultimately it is quality, not productivity, that will sell the product.

In an increasingly global market, it is not surprising that the need for international quality standards has arisen. ISO 9000, developed by the International Organization for Standardization in Geneva, Switzerland, is a series of international quality standards and certification that makes it easier for a product to enter the export market. Adopted by thousands of companies in over 100 countries, the standards apply to both manufacturing and service businesses and certify quality control procedures. The purpose of ISO is to provide a single set of standards that everyone internationally agrees on. To meet ISO standards, a company must develop a quality management system. That process starts with a gap analysis—comparing where the company is now with the ISO requirements. The ISO standards are too detailed for presentation here, but the broad areas covered include the following requirements: System, Management, Resources, Realization or deliverables, and Remediation. See the resources at the end of the chapter to find an online site with more information about these standards.

Putting effective production processes in place is only half the battle. Maintaining them is equally important, as the next section demonstrates.

Global Insights

Manufacturing "on the Fly"

In Cologne, Germany, you might be surprised to find bright yellow spires alongside the breathtaking spires of ancient cathedrals. They belong to Ignus Inc., a manufacturing plant that produces polymer bearings and power-supply chains, but this is no ordinary manufacturing plant. In fact, this plant has been designed to do business on the fly—to shrink, expand, radically change, or modify any aspect of the business at any time and without disrupting anyone. The building is the size of three football fields, and nothing is permanently installed.

Workers fly around the open space on small scooters as they perform their roles in the production of 28,000 different products in the areas of office products, home and office automation, and telecommunication. Because 90 percent of Ignus's customers have special requirements, the company is organized to exist in a continuous state of innovation and change. Ignus stays flexible by designing the space to accommodate the business needs at any point in time; recruiting employees who can work in this type of environment; working for speed, mindful that practicing speed helps workers learn to be more effective in this type of environment; and inspiring everyone to think creatively.

Sources: Ignus Inc., http://www.ignus.com/; and C. Salter, "This Is One Fast Factory," *FastCompany,* 49: 32.

Production Cost Issues

In Chapter 6, which focuses on product development, we discussed the need to source raw materials and parts for the product prototype. Once this is accomplished and the assembly process is defined, including labor requirements, it is possible to calculate the total investment required to start the business and the per-unit cost of manufacturing the product. Figuring production costs is an important component of production for several reasons. First, it is critical to pricing an item competitively. Second, it makes it possible to see how much of the total cost of operating the company is devoted to producing the product. Third, it provides the information needed to determine how to make the production process more efficient from a cost perspective.

Production costs consist of direct and indirect costs. Direct costs are those directly involved in production of the product, such as materials and labor, and they generally vary with production volume. Indirect costs are company overhead, such as lighting costs, rent, and salaries. These are more difficult to divide and apportion to a single unit being produced. Entrepreneurs should seek the advice of an accountant to apportion indirect costs correctly.

To be sure, the initial units produced will cost significantly more to manufacture and assemble, because the volume will usually not be sufficient to merit industry discounts on raw materials and parts, and the plant and equipment will not be used to full capacity. Consequently, gross margins may be extremely small in the early stages, until a sufficient increase in volume makes possible economies of scale that reduce the per-unit cost. Similarly, the materials, supplies, and labor required to provide the company's service will have to be itemized. Service entrepreneurs often fail to realize that time and materials are the production costs associated with providing a service. They tend to think only in terms of hourly rates. The components of the service process must be itemized in the same manner as those of the manufacturing process.

Outsourcing to Reduce Costs

Calculation of the up-front investment in plant, office, and equipment, coupled with the high per-unit cost of production, has convinced many entrepreneurs to outsource manufacturing to an established manufacturing firm. Some products that consist of off-the-shelf components from original equipment manufacturers (OEMs) can give the entrepreneur the option to set up an assembly operation, which is far less costly than a manufacturing plant. In any case, the process of outlining all the costs of setting up a product company is invaluable in making the final decisions about how the business will operate.

Entrepreneurs who wish to manufacture products have many options today. It is still possible, in most industries, to manufacture domestically and to compete successfully if processes are refined and quality is built into every step. If it is too costly to do all the manufacturing in-house, outsourcing non-core capabilities is one possibility; another is outsourcing everything and playing the role of coordinator until the company is producing a healthy cash flow. The fact is that many successful companies today are outsourcing production. Dell Computer outsources production and simply does assembly, whereas Coca-Cola Company outsources its machinery-intensive bottling work to third parties but often holds an equity stake in those companies to control quality.

Manufacturing Overseas

In some industries, particularly labor-intensive ones, the only way to achieve competitive costs is to manufacture in a country where labor costs are low; Mexico and China are two examples. Entrepreneurs should look at what other firms in their industry are doing. One Tampa, Florida, manufacturing company moved some of its manufacturing operations to China several years ago and achieved real cost savings by doing so. Today, however, it is re-evaluating that decision for several of its products. These are too heavy to ship by air, and shipping by sea is costly because the company loses the advantage it has in schedule flexibility. Schedule flexibility is an example of an opportunity cost—that is, forgoing an important competitive advantage in order to save on production costs.

Not all products are appropriate for offshore manufacturing. For example, a business that uses expensive equipment to produce its products may not achieve enough cost savings to overcome the problems associated with offshore manufacturing, such as difficulties in communication and degradation in quality control. By contrast, a manual-labor-intensive business such as apparel manufacture can often achieve significant cost savings by moving overseas.

The weight of the product is also a factor in the decision whether to manufacture overseas. Heavy products with large "footprints" must be shipped by sea, which typically takes four to six weeks. That represents an inventory issue for the entrepreneur and added cost for the customer.

Some entrepreneurs have calculated that it takes a 15 to 20 percent cost savings to justify manufacturing offshore and to balance the added costs of freight, customs, security, logistics, and inventory carrying cost. It is also important to remember that customers are not always looking for the lowest price; rather, they're looking for the highest quality at a competitive price. If products are innovative and meet the specific needs of target customers, a company may be able to manufacture domestically in a successful way.

Maintaining and Warranting Production Processes

In the production process, maintenance refers both to the maintenance of plant and equipment used to produce a product or project outcome and to the maintenance or servicing of the product or project outcome after it is sold. Maintenance must be taken into account when planning the costs of starting a company. Unfortunately, too often it is forgotten and catches the entrepreneur by surprise.

Process Maintenance

At some point any machine or process will break down, which can mean lost sales and costly repairs and redesign. There are three ways to prevent unexpected breakdowns from disrupting the production process. The process can be organized in such a way that when one machine is down, the work can be shifted to another. Another approach is to build up inventories at each stage of the production process so that machines can keep working as long as the inventory lasts. (This method, of course, will probably not work in a company that has chosen the JIT system of inventory management.) The third, and perhaps the best, approach is to undertake preventive maintenance regularly by checking and fixing the machines before they break down. The advantage of this approach is that the company controls when the downtime occurs.

Service processes can also break down when a key person on a project becomes ill or leaves the company. By analogy to shifting work from one machine to another in a manufacturing process, it is important to cross-train personnel so that someone else can immediately step into the absent person's position and keep the process moving along.

Product Maintenance

The entrepreneur who subscribes to total quality management will probably wish to provide warranties with products and services, both in order to protect the firm from potential liability and to demonstrate that the company stands behind what it produces and the work that it does. Today, product/service warranties have also become a competitive marketing tool. A number of decisions must be made about warranties.

The length of the warranty depends on industry standards. Another decision is what components of the product, or what aspects of the service, to cover. Some components may come from other manufacturers who have their own warranties. In this case, it is important to have use of that component on the product certified by the OEM so that the warranty isn't inadvertently invalidated. Then, if a warranted component from that manufacturer becomes defective, it can be returned to the OEM. However, it is probably good business practice to have customers return the product directly to the entrepreneur's company or its distributors for service, repair, or exchange under the warranty, which covers the whole product. Warranties on services cover satisfaction with work completed. For example, a company may conduct ISO 9000 certification workshops for companies and may warrant that if a client company attends the workshops and implements the suggestions, it will receive certification. If, for some reason, the client does not receive certification, there is no way to "return" a workshop in the way that a product could be returned, but the entrepreneur can offer the client a fact-finding audit to discover what went wrong or can simply refund the client's money (a less satisfactory solution for the client).

The product/process scope should also be considered. Will the warranty cover one or all products in a line or will there be separate warranties? Generally, for services, a warranty covers the service as a whole, unless there are products involved as well. In addition to the product scope, the market scope is a factor. Will the same warranty apply in all markets? This will depend on local laws. Another consideration involves the conditions of the warranty that the customer must fulfill. Is there anything the customer must do to keep the warranty in force, such as servicing or replacing disposable parts? These conditions should not include registering the product via a postcard. Today a product is covered by warranty from the moment it is purchased, whether or not the purchaser returns a postcard stating when and where it was purchased and answering a short, informational questionnaire. What many companies now do is offer update notification and potential discounts on future products in exchange for the information the postcard solicits.

Another consideration is who executes the warranty. The entrepreneur must decide who will handle warranty claims (manufacturer, dealers, distributors, the entrepreneur's company), recognizing that customers do not like to mail products back to the manufacturer. It is also necessary to decide how the public will be educated about the warranty. What are the plans for advertising and promotion relative to the warranty? Finally, the policies for refunds and returns, and who will pay shipping and handling costs, need to be considered. A return policy is a function of the entrepreneur's philosophy about doing business. A customer-oriented company is likely to offer a generous return policy and pay for the cost of returns.

The manufacturer who provides a warranty incurs a cost, but that cost must be weighed against the potential loss of business if no warranty is provided. In the case of a new business with a new product or service, it is difficult to anticipate the number of problems that might occur as the product or service gets into the marketplace. Careful and adequate field testing prior to market entry will go a long way toward eliminating many potential problems and the possibility of a recall (in the case of a product), which is very costly for any firm, let alone a growing new business. Remember the recall of Firestone tires a few years ago and the disastrous financial and public relations impact it had on Firestone and its customer, Ford Motor Company.

Production is a critical component of any business. The fastest way to increase profits is to reduce the cost of production by becoming more efficient—purchasing the right materials and supplies at the right time and in the right quantities, inspecting for quality during the production process to avoid costly returns, and providing warranties that ensure customer loyalty.

New Venture Checklist

Have you:

☐ Outlined the production process for your business?

☐ Found suppliers for your materials and supply requirements?

☐ Determined how inventory will be handled?

☐ Developed quality control measures?

☐ Itemized and calculated your production costs?

☐ Determined the product/process maintenance requirements?

Issues to Consider

1. Why is it important to consider your manufacturing plan in the earliest stages of a new venture?
2. What are three factors that an entrepreneur must take into consideration when choosing vendors to meet materials requirements?
3. Suppose you had a new advertising firm. How could you use just-in-time scheduling to create more efficiencies in your operations.
4. In what ways can the human resources of the business help control quality in all areas of the organization?

Experiencing Entrepreneurship

1. Visit a manufacturing facility that is using technology to facilitate its processes. Develop a flowchart of the manufacturing process. Can you see any ways to improve the process?

2. Interview a manufacturing entrepreneur about his or her views on quality. How is this entrepreneur implementing quality control in his or her organization?

Additional Sources of Information

Conner, G. (2001). *Lean Manufacturing for the Small Shop*. Dearborn, MI: Society of Manufacturing Engineers.

Hobbs, D.P. (2003) *Lean Manufacturing Implementation: A Complete Execution Manual for Any Size Manufacturer*. Boca Raton FL: J Ross Publishing.

Juran, J.M. (1998). *Juran's Quality Handbook*. New York: McGraw-Hill.

Pande, P.S., R.P. Neuman, and R.R. Cavanagh (2000). *The Six Sigma Way: How GE, Motorola, and Other Top Companies Are Honing Their Performance*. New York: McGraw-Hill.

Relevant Case Studies

Case 4 Wizards of the Coast, p. 423
Case 5 iRobot, p. 432

Case 7 Linksys, p. 446

14

Developing an Entrepreneurial Marketing Plan

"Don't forget that it [your product or service] is not differentiated until the customer understands the difference."

Tom Peters, Thriving on Chaos

LEARNING OBJECTIVES

- Understand the importance of relationship marketing in entrepreneurial ventures.

- Discuss the role and implementation of the marketing plan.

- Explain how to promote new products and services effectively with limited resources.

- Discuss the advantages and disadvantages of online marketing.

Profile 14.1 WHAT'S IN A NAME?

Terri Williamson, an MBA from the University of Chicago, knew that a name is everything when trying to brand a product line. She wanted to start a business producing and distributing bath and body products. The image she wanted to create was simple, clean, and catchy. One day the name Glow came to her. After checking the Internet to see whether anyone was using the name and finding nothing, she decided to go forward to build the brand name Glow, Inc.

After achieving more than $1 million in sales to 20 top high-end retailers, Williamson and her partner, Jennifer Levy, opened the Glow boutique on an upscale street in Los Angeles. Williamson and Levy had been branding consultants before starting Glow, so they knew how to create a distinctive brand with a look and feel that carried throughout their product line labeling and into their store design. They also knew the importance of developing strong relationships with their customers on the basis of meeting customer needs. One of the distinguishing characteristics of their products was scent: a unique blend of essential oils that held their fragrance for hours.

Williamson's strategy for success also involved partnering with department stores, because for the same amount of effort as she would put into one specialty store deal, she could gain access to 130 or more stores with a department store deal.

Things were going well until June 2002, when she received a phone call from a woman who owned an upscale apothecary in Florida to ask her whether she was working with Jennifer Lopez. Williamson had no idea what she was talking about. The caller quickly informed her that Lopez was coming out with a Glow perfume. Williamson had a hard time believing this, because J.Lo's manager's office was just a block away from the Glow shop, and his employees had often ordered gift baskets from her. Williamson's lawyer sent a cease and desist letter to the "Glow by J.Lo" group just as their new fragrance was being introduced. They responded that they intended to continue their campaign because *glow* was a generic term that by itself could not be trademarked. Williamson worried that no one would carry her brand because it would be confused with Glow by J.Lo.

On August 7, 2002, Glow Industries filed suit against Jennifer Lopez and Coty, alleging trademark infringement. Glow by J.Lo hit the department stores in September, and stores had a hard time keeping it on the shelves. It was a phenomenal success. Williamson immediately began losing business because department stores didn't want to confuse customers with two "Glows."

Williamson and her lawyers went to court in November 2002. To win an injunction, she would have to convince the judge that she had a protectable trademark, that consumers would be confused by the brands, and that her company might suffer irreparable damage. Because the Patent and Trademark Office had not completed her registration, however, she couldn't win on the first point. Lopez then took advantage of this situation by acquiring an existing patent, Glow Kit, for $40,000. This put Williamson in the awkward situation of infringing on Lopez's patent! Ultimately, the judge denied the request for a preliminary injunction because of insufficient evidence of consumer confusion between the two brands and then set a trial for October of the following year. By October, however, the two companies had reached a settlement that included dismissing the pending claims and counterclaims. The terms of the agreement were not disclosed, but Glow Industries (Williamson's company) was allowed to continue to use the Glow trademark on its bath, body care, and fragrance products during a limited transition period. The lesson from Williamson's experience? Protect your brand and don't make it easy for other companies with more resources to take it from you.

Sources: Coty Beauty Lancaster Group, Company Press Release, October 22, 2003; United States District Court, Central District of California, Case No. CV 02–06167 MMM (PJWx), *Glow Industries, Inc. v. Jennifer Lopez, Coty, Inc.* Order Denying Plaintiff's Motion for Preliminary Injunction; and Bo Burlingham, "Whose Brand Is It, Anyway?" *Inc. Magazine* (May 2003), p. 63.

Marketing includes all the strategies, tactics, and techniques used to raise customer awareness; to promote a product, service, or business; and to build long-term customer relationships. Marketing can be thought of as a bundle of benefits a company is providing to its customers. These benefits reflect the core values of the company that provides them. For example, one of Southwest Airline's core values is that the customer's needs are paramount. How does that translate into customer benefits?

Traditionally, marketing has been described in terms of the "5 P's"—people, product, price, place, and promotion. It often consists of a push strategy, whereby a customer who did not necessarily express a need for or interest in a company's product or service is persuaded to purchase it through selling techniques. In other words, the focus of the traditional marketing effort is on the product, not the customer. Most entrepreneurs, however, understand that a business cannot exist without customers. Thus, rather than pushing a marketing strategy on potential customers—a very costly approach—entrepreneurs, who typically have limited resources in the early stages of their ventures, prefer to invest in relationship marketing. In relationship marketing, the primary focus is on the customer. If the product or service is designed with the customer's needs in mind, much of the "selling" that would otherwise have to be done has been taken care of by giving customers what they want, when they want it, and in the way they want it. Read Profile 14.1 to see what Glow Industries did.

Marketing in times of change means that traditional methods may not work. Given unique products and services with a much shorter competitive life cycle, the challenge is to rise above the crowd and build a competitive brand that is sustainable.[1] Too many entrepreneurs underestimate the strength of their competitors, discount the impact of the global market, and develop products for a general market rather than a specific and unique niche market. This chapter is based on marketing for a changing environment—an approach predicated on the need to reinvent, to acquire technological competence, and to build relationships with customers, strategic partners, and even competitors.

The intent of this chapter is not to review marketing fundamentals but to explore marketing from an entrepreneurial perspective and discuss creating a marketing plan to help a new company build long-term relationships with its customers. This chapter builds on the feasibility analysis and market research strategies and tactics discussed in Chapter 5. The market/customer information gathered during market research can now be applied to the business plan in the form of a marketing plan.

Relationship Marketing for Entrepreneurs

The essence of relationship or one-to-one marketing is building trust, satisfying customers, producing shared customer and company goals, communicating with customers, and making customers part of the team. In 1993, Don Peppers and Martha Rogers, in their book *The One to One Future,* recognized a trend they called "share of customer."[2] To achieve share of customer, a learning environment must be developed where customer and company learn from each other with the goal of

TABLE 14.1	Transaction versus Relationship Marketing

TRANSACTION MARKETING	RELATIONSHIP MARKETING
Concerned with the single sale	Concerned with maintaining a long-term relationship
Focus on product/service features	Focus on benefits to customer
Customer service is an afterthought	Customer service is everything
Limited commitment to customer	Total customer commitment
Moderate customer contact	Continual customer contact
Quality is responsibility of production	Quality is everyone's business

achieving a mutually beneficial lifelong relationship. Relationship marketing is also about providing a bundle of benefits that the customer sees as valuable. In today's Internet environment, where many products and services quickly become commodities (that is, price becomes the key differentiating factor), strong, loyal, lifetime customer relationships can enable a company to break out of the commodity bracket. Table 14.1 displays the differences between traditional transaction marketing and relationship marketing.

Relationship marketing changes not just the company's philosophy but the very way the company does business. Using interactive databases, companies can effectively focus on one customer at a time, with the goal of supplying as many individual needs as possible. However, one-to-one marketing is not just about collecting information from the customer. For example, merely asking customers where and how they bought a product doesn't produce an answer to the question "How do customers want to buy the product?" It only reveals which of the available purchasing methods they chose. It doesn't expose which purchasing method they would prefer. Relationship marketing is about carrying on a dialogue with the customer, over time, in a market niche the entrepreneur has created and defined. Market share per se is no longer a major goal, because in a market niche, there is the potential to serve 100 percent of the market. For example, suppose that through primary market research, an entrepreneur has learned that today many professionals are commuting into major metropolitan areas from other cities or even other states, staying three or four days out of every week at their work, and then flying back to their homes and families. While they are in the major city, they need a regular place to stay that is less costly than a hotel and makes more sense than maintaining an apartment full-time. The entrepreneur decides to satisfy that need with a business concept that lets the entrepreneur enter the very competitive hotel and apartment markets by targeting a group of customers who aren't presently being served. The major concern is not getting a share of the larger market but, rather, attracting all the potential customers in that defined niche and making them loyal customers. Retaining loyal customers and selling more to them is more cost-efficient than constantly striving for more and more customers in a much larger market. Once a new company has established itself in the niche, it is in a better position to expand to new customer segments.

There is an added benefit to building relationships with customers. If a problem occurs, a customer who has a relationship with the company won't automatically shift their loyalty to a competitor. Often their loyalty is actually *strengthened* when a problem-solving session with the company results in a satisfying conclusion. All too often, however, customers have had negative experiences with companies, where the problem has not been resolved satisfactorily. In those situations, the customer never forgets.

Today, customers have a multitude of platforms from which to publicize their grievances, and one problem aired on national television can cause a public relations nightmare from which the company may never recover. A case in point was the Cunard cruise line's public relations disaster during the launch of its expensive Christmas cruise on the renovated Queen Elizabeth II. Despite a ship full of builders still working to complete construction, management decided to sail the ship. Apparently Cunard believed the customers would overlook the mess! This is clearly not the way to build long-term customer relationships.

Perhaps the most important benefit of establishing lifelong customer relationships is that over time, the full value of customers is revealed. Customers no longer are viewed as a series of transactions but as bona fide, contributing members of the team who bring value to the bottom line. The more the company learns from its customers, the better the company becomes, and the more difficult it will be for a competitor to attract these customers.

Identifying and Rewarding the Best Customers

It is not uncommon for a company to find that as few as 24 percent of its customers account for 95 percent of its revenues. That 24 percent are the customers the company needs to know well and to keep happy, because these are the customers who will readily try new products and services and refer the company to others. After a company has been in business for a while, it becomes easier to identify the most valuable customers. One way to do this is to calculate the lifetime customer value as a series of transactions over the life of the relationship.[3] A statistical method for doing this calculates the present value of future purchases, using an appropriate discount rate and period of time for the relationship. Add to that the value of customer referrals, and subtract the cost of maintaining the relationship (advertising, promotions, letters, questionnaires, 800 numbers). The result will be the customer's lifetime value. Another, nonstatistical method is simply to carry on a dialogue with customers about their buying intentions.

Frequency Programs

There are a variety of ways by which companies can provide special programs, incentives, and rewards for their best customers. The airlines have used frequency programs or customer loyalty programs with great success. The people who fly the most frequently with the airlines receive free tickets, VIP service, and upgrades. Rewards increase with use; therefore, the customer has a vested interest in using a particular airline again and again.

Frequency programs have also yielded good results for other businesses. Cosmetics companies, for instance, issue cards that give customers a free product after a certain number of purchases. Similarly, small entertainment centers, such as miniature golf and water parks, often offer discounts on season passes purchased by customers who use the service the most.

Setting up a club or membership makes customers feel special, because they have input into the company and receive special privileges for being a member; examples of these privileges include informational newsletters, discounts, and other special programs. Some companies offer their best customers next-day delivery as well as access to a special unlisted toll-free number. The benefits that accrue to the company from frequency programs are derived from the repeat purchases they inspire. The more a customer buys from a company, the higher the probability that he or she will buy repeatedly, and the lower the cost to the company of each repeat purchase. In establishing one-to-one relationships, of course, it's essential to single out the best customers for special treatment.

Just-in-Time Marketing

Customer wants are often tied to major events or rites of passage, such as birthdays, marriage, purchase of a home, pregnancy, and relocation. Keeping track of dates that are important to customers gives the company an opportunity to contact the customer on a special occasion, such as a birthday, to remind the customer of the need to purchase something, or to notify the customer of an impending sale of an item he or she typically buys. This is known as just-in-time marketing. Amazon.com has made just-in-time marketing a critical component of its overall marketing strategy. Not only does Amazon welcome customers back to its website by showcasing the latest books and gadgets *that reflect their interests,* but it also notifies them by e-mail of new books or videos in areas they have selected.

Complaint Marketing

A dissatisfied customer will probably tell at least nine other people about the problem he or she faced with a company. (And those nine people will tell their friends as well!) It's easy to see how quickly even one unhappy customer can damage a company's reputation. Consequently, complaints should be viewed as opportunities for continual improvement. Making it easy for a customer to register a complaint and carry on a dialogue with a human being who listens and attempts to understand is an important way to learn from the customer. Nothing is more frustrating than to have to leave a complaint on a voice mail message.

Some companies have used bulletin board services on the Internet to let customers communicate complaints, but this method, though effective, attracts more complaints than any other method. Companies using bulletin boards have found, in fact, that this system works almost too well, because customers feel free to vent their frustrations more angrily online than when they are hearing a soothing, caring voice at the other end of a phone line. Moreover, because anyone with access to the Internet can read the angry messages, a strong complaint can build momentum and create more problems than necessary.

One way to stem complaints at the source is to provide satisfaction surveys at every point of contact with the customer so that problems can be coped with quickly, at the outset, before the customer becomes so angry that resolution and satisfaction are nearly impossible. Effective handling of complaints can be accomplished by understanding that the customer is a human being and should be treated as such—never as a number or as someone without a name or feelings. The customer should be allowed to explain the complaint completely, without interruption. Extending this courtesy acknowledges that the complaint is important and worthy of attention. Customers should always be asked the most important question: "What is one thing we can do to make this better?" A customer's anger should be defused by sincerely taking his or her side on the issue; then the customer should be moved from a problem focus to a solution focus. Finally, the customer should be contacted one week after the complaint to find out whether he or she is still satisfied with the solution and to express the company's desire for a continued relationship.

The most important message that can be sent to customers through a company's marketing effort is that the customer is the most important part of the organization and the company will do whatever it takes to keep good customers satisfied. While it's certainly true that a young, growing company needs to build a customer base by continually adding new customers, it will reap the greatest returns from investing in the customers it currently has.

The Marketing Plan

For any company, an effective marketing strategy begins with a marketing plan. The marketing plan for an entrepreneurial company is a living guide to how the company plans to build customer relationships over its life in order to fulfill the mission statement in the business plan. It details the strategies and tactics that will create awareness on the part of the customer and build a loyal customer base. Marketing plans are written at many points in the life of a business. The original business plan will contain a marketing plan for introducing the company and its products and services to the marketplace. Later a marketing plan may be used to introduce new products and services and/or to grow the business, perhaps in a new direction.

A few important steps taken before the actual writing of the marketing plan ensure that the plan is on target and is one the company can live with for a long time. Living with a plan for a long time may sound inconsistent with an entrepreneur's need to remain flexible and adapt to change in the marketplace, but one of the biggest problems with most marketing plans is that they are not followed long enough to achieve the desired results.

Typically, the business owner does not see immediate results from the marketing effort and decides it must not be working—so he or she changes it and starts the cycle all over again. Changing the plan on impulse is the wrong thing to do. It takes time to make customers aware of the product or service. It takes time for a particular marketing strategy to take hold and build confidence in the customer. For example, from the first time a customer sees an ad to the point at which the customer actually buys the product, weeks or even months may pass. In fact, on average, the customer will see an ad 15 to 20 times before actually purchasing the product. Therefore, just like a good stock market investor, the entrepreneur must think of the marketing plan as an investment in the future of the business and must remember that any investment takes time to mature. Reaping the benefits of a well-structured marketing plan requires persistence and unwavering dedication until the plan has an opportunity to perform.

A company's mission and core values will set the tone for the marketing plan. Several steps should be taken prior to writing a marketing plan. First, the approach to the market, or the bridge between strategy and execution, must be defined. The approach to the market includes such things as the message, differentiation tactics, channel strategies, and performance goals. Choosing the wrong approach can result in customers not understanding the benefits being provided. Choosing the same approach for all customers will mean that not everyone will be satisfied. Next, the entrepreneur should make a list of all marketing options. To begin to understand which options should be considered, it is important to talk to other business owners, customers, and suppliers and to read books and articles on marketing strategies for entrepreneurs, such as those suggested at the end of this chapter. This process will generate a list of possibilities to consider, which may range from sponsoring a business conference to advertising in a national trade publication. Determining which strategies are the most effective, or even feasible, can be left for later. Also, the entrepreneur must think like a customer and imagine the business from the customer's point of view. What would entice a customer to enter that store, buy that product, or avail himself or herself of that service? The entrepreneur should study the competition and take a look at competing businesses to determine what makes them successful or unsuccessful. What marketing strategies do competitors seem to employ, and are they effective? What improvements could be made on what competitors are doing? Finally, the entrepreneur must analyze the marketing options and rank them by first eliminating those that either don't meet the needs of the target market or simply are not feasible at this time (usually for budgetary reasons). A ranking of the top ten choices should suffice. Once all these tasks have been completed, it's time to write the marketing plan.

The Marketing Plan in One Paragraph

Many experienced marketers suggest that the first step in creating the marketing plan is to condense all the ideas about marketing strategy into a single paragraph. Impossible? Not at all. Crafting a single well-written paragraph forces the entrepreneur to focus carefully on the central point of the overall marketing strategy. This paragraph should include the purpose of the marketing plan (*What will the marketing plan accomplish?*), the benefits of the product/service (*How will the product/service help the customer or satisfy a need?*), the target market (*Who is the primary buyer or first customer?*), the market niche (*Where does the concept fit in the industry or market? How does the company differentiate itself?*), the marketing tactics to be used (*What specific marketing tools will be employed?*), the company's convictions and identity (*How will the customers define the company?*), and the percentage of sales that the marketing budget will represent (*How much money will be allocated to the marketing plan?*). Here is an example of an effective one-paragraph statement of the marketing plan for a product/service business.

> TradePartners enables qualified importers and exporters from a variety of countries to find trading partners through an Internet-based, business-to-business network. The **purpose** of the marketing plan is to create awareness and name recognition for Trade-Partners in the market space. The **target customer** or **first customer** is the small

exporter who needs to find buyers in another country or to find a buyer for excess inventory; the secondary customer is the importer who wants to find new sources for products to import. Customers will enjoy the **benefits** of reduced time and risk in finding new customers or suppliers. TradePartners has defined a **niche** targeting smaller companies that want access to the same opportunities as large companies worldwide. **Customers will view** TradePartners as a professional, innovative, and customer-focused company. Initial **marketing tactics** include personal selling at industry events, strategic alliances with complementary companies, and providing free workshops on import/export. TradePartners will spend an average of **40 percent of sales** to implement the marketing strategy in the initial stages.

With such a paragraph in hand and the focus established, the entrepreneur is ready to develop a more detailed marketing plan.

Components of the Marketing Plan

Every marketing plan incorporates the traditional 5 P's of marketing: people, product, price, place, and promotion, which are discussed in any marketing text. Once these aspects of the plan have been addressed, it is time to consider the creative aspects, such as the advertising and promotional goals, and to develop a media plan that details what media will be used, when they will be used, and how much they will cost. The next section outlines the major issues that should be addressed in the marketing plan. Refer also to the "Business Plan Outline" in the Appendix for additional items that should be included in the marketing plan.

Marketing Plan Outline

The following suggestions describe sections that should be included in any marketing plan, and they apply to most types of businesses. Depending on the type of business, however, additional sections may need to be included.

One-Paragraph Overview of the Marketing Plan

The complete marketing plan begins with a one-paragraph summary that serves as a concise overview of the marketing plan.

Key Marketing Issues That Will Affect the Success of the Company

After presenting the one-paragraph plan, it is important to identify issues the company faces that will affect the way it can market its products and services to customers. For example, the company may not be located near its customers, so it will have to figure out creative ways to create those important personal relationships. In other words, this section describes the environment in which the marketing plan will be implemented.

Launch Objectives

These are the key objectives for the marketing campaign. What needs to be accomplished and how does the company intend to do it? For a start-up venture, two important objectives are to create awareness for the company and its brand, and to reach target customers to produce sales.

Milestones

Objectives need to be matched to a timeline for achieving them. Marking on a time-line the major milestones for advertising, promotional events, and trade shows gives some direction to the marketing plan.

Strategic Alliances

Many businesses today form partnerships with other companies in compatible markets to promote each other's products and services. It is important to identify which companies and other partners will be used in the marketing campaign.

Assessing Effectiveness

Measuring the effectiveness of marketing efforts is critical to avoid wasting precious company resources. For example, matching sales forecasts to specific marketing tactics and assigning a specific person responsibility for measuring the outcome is important to assessing the effectiveness of the marketing plan. Another way in which entrepreneurs measure success in a marketing effort is to ask customers how they heard about the company or the product/service.

Strategic Alignment

Strategies deal with the needs of the market and what is being offered to satisfy those needs. Tactics are the media, channels, and delivery mechanisms used to reach the customer. Goals, strategies, and tactics must be in alignment. If a business's goal is to emphasize reliability and customer satisfaction, for example, the marketing plan should spell out strategies and tactics—such as customer feedback mechanisms and training in the use of the products—for achieving that goal.

Strategies for Pricing

Pricing a product or service is as much a part of a marketing strategy as of the financial strategy. Pricing is one of the many features associated with a product or service; it becomes the central selling point when the product or service is a commodity—that is, when the only feature differentiating the product or service from those offered by competitors is price. Some examples of commodities are basic food products, such as milk, and most electronics categories that have been in the market for some time, such as desktop computers and printers. Entrepreneurs can price new technology higher because it offers features and benefits not currently in the market, but it quickly becomes a commodity as competitors introduce their versions of the new technology.

How a product or service is priced is a function of a company's goals. If the goal is to *increase sales or market share,* prices may need to be lowered to raise the volume sold. If the goal is to *maximize cash flow,* raising prices and reducing direct costs and overhead may be the answer. *Maximizing profit* can be accomplished by raising prices, lowering prices and increasing volume, or decreasing overhead. If the goal is to *define an image,* setting a higher price based on higher perceived and/or actual quality is one way of establishing a particular image in an industry. To *control demand* when a company doesn't have the resources to meet it may mean setting prices at a level that discourages sales to a particular degree.

Knowing what a pricing strategy is supposed to accomplish in advance of setting a price will ensure compatibility with the company's goals. With a pricing strategy in place, the components of pricing can be considered.

Cost-Based Pricing

In this pricing strategy, the entrepreneur adds the cost of producing the product, the related costs of running the business, and a profit margin to arrive at a market price.

Demand-Based Pricing

Demand pricing is based on finding out what customers are willing to pay for the product and pricing it accordingly. For new products or services with no direct comparison, a combination of this approach and cost-based pricing is often used to arrive at a satisfactory price. In general, customers recognize several prices for any one product: the standard price, which is the price normally paid for the item; the sale price; the price paid for specials; and the relative price, which is the price of the item compared to the price of a substitute product. For some products, customers may have to add the normal cost of shipping, handling, or installation to their comparison with other like products.

Competition-Based Pricing

Where the product has direct competition, it is important to study the competitors' pricing strategy and to price the product or service in line with theirs—higher if it is determined that one's own product has added value or lower if one has decided to compete on price.

Psychological Pricing

Using an odd–even strategy can suggest a pricing position in the market: an odd number ($12.99) to suggest a bargain, an even number ($40.00) to suggest quality, or higher than average pricing to suggest exclusivity.

Distribution Channel Pricing

The channel of distribution through which an entrepreneur chooses to move a product or service affects the ultimate price to the customer, because the costs and profit for each intermediary in the channel must be taken into account. In a channel with many intermediaries (distributors, retailers), it is important to ensure that the final price to the consumer or end user is tolerable, given all the mark-ups along the value chain. That is why it is crucial to compare what the market will bear with the cost of getting a product to market.

Extrapolating from Other Industries

It is essential to look at the pricing strategies of businesses in other industries. The fact that one's own industry does not seem to employ a particular strategy does not mean that the strategy won't work. Staying competitive on price means always looking for new methods of pricing products.

Product/Service Promotion

For many entrepreneurs, putting a great deal of money into advertising and promotion doesn't make sense. They simply don't have the resources and budgets of a General Motors, so their money is better spent on more effective ways of reaching very specific customers. Amilya Antonetti, the founder of SoapWorks, a manufacturer of hypoallergenic soap products, has built a large customer base on a fairly small advertising budget.[4] She does it by interacting constantly with her current and prospective customers. Many of her female customers are tired of all the advertising hype directed at them and gravitate to her all-natural products and more personal approach. She offers online purchasing at her website (www.soapworks.com). Antonetti herself takes many of the calls that come in to her company daily and personally hands out samples of her products at hospitals and women's shelters. Her customers regularly share their problems and needs with her and spread the word about her company. Antonetti has found an effective way to promote her business directly to the people she wants to serve.

Entrepreneurs approach marketing from a point of view distinctly different from that of the traditional marketer. Although they may employ some of the same techniques as a large corporate marketer, they also take advantage of many other marketing opportunities that the corporate marketer may ignore. Jay Conrad Levinson has called the entrepreneurial marketing approach **guerrilla marketing,** an alternative to traditional, expensive marketing tactics.[5] Because entrepreneurs don't have the time or money for elaborate, high-profile marketing strategies, they essentially mimic what the big companies do, but they do it for much less money, in more creative ways, and for a shorter period of time. Guerrilla marketing is a do-it-yourself approach to marketing for entrepreneurs. This chapter profiles many guerrilla-type tactics that can be deployed in a small business to reach and keep customers. For example, the tactics mentioned earlier—just-in-time marketing, frequency programs, and complaint marketing—are big-company tactics with a guerrilla twist to them.

There are many ways to promote a company and its products and services effectively. The next sections consider a variety of entrepreneurial promotional tactics.

Taking Advantage of Publicity

Publicity and word-of-mouth (referrals) are two of the most effective entrepreneurial marketing tools around because they don't cost the company any money. What they do require is a compelling story that will attract attention. James Lindsay, founder of Rap Snacks, wanted to encourage kids to eat his company's popcorn, chips, and cheese curls in 11 flavors. The packaging features popular rap artists, such as Lil' Romeo and Nelly, and the products are distributed to independent businesses in the inner city. The hook? Each bag sells for a quarter, because "every kid has a quarter." It's a great way to develop brand loyalty. In addition, the artists on the label pay a promotional fee to Rap Snacks.[6] Another example is Patricia Tsai, who founded Chocolate de Oaxaca (www. Mexichoco.com). Tsai had no budget for advertising, so she contacted the editor of the Wednesday food pages of the *New York Times* and convinced her to run a small article about the company at the time of Cinco de Maya, the Mexican independence day celebration. That one article brought in hundreds of orders.

Choosing a Name for the Business

There is no formula for choosing the right name for a new business. The name certainly depends on the type of business and on the personality and tastes of the founder. In general, a great name should be distinctive and easy to remember. It should be easy to spell and pronounce, and it should reflect the products and services being offered. Finally, it should distinguish your company from your competitors.

Browsing through trade magazines, surfing the Web, and bouncing ideas off friends and business associates are all ways to begin to develop a list of candidates. Once the list has been narrowed down to 3 to 5 names, it's a good idea to conduct a name and trademark search to make sure that the selected candidates are available. This can be done on the USPTO.gov website, or one can go to www. Nolo.com for instructions on conducting an effective search. When it is time to settle on a name, a qualified attorney can ensure that the name chosen is really available. Google, the highly successful search engine, is now facing a challenge to its catchy name, which it took from a mathematical term. The term *Googol* was coined by a Columbia University professor, Edward Kasner, in the 1930s to stand for 10 to the 100th power, or a 1 with 100 zeros following it. Now Kasner's family is seeking compensation for the term's use.

Getting Publicity

If the business or product is newsworthy, there are several ways to get some publicity. Writing to a newspaper, magazine, or online reporter or editor to tease him or her with an idea, and then following up with a phone call, often works. Whenever possible, it's a good idea to get to know people in the media on a first-name basis. Try taking them to lunch before there is a need for free publicity. When it comes time to seek that publicity, the entrepreneur who already has a contact can simply issue a press release answering the who, what, where, when, and why of the business. The best approach is to include a press kit containing the press release, bios and photos of the key people in the story, any necessary background information, and copies of any other articles written about the company. The idea is to make it as easy as possible for the reporter to write or tell the story. The media are always looking for news and appreciate the effort to give them something newsworthy. When an article is written about the business, reprints can be used in future advertising and brochures, and thus the company gains even more value for the effort.

Constructing an Effective Press Release

An effective news release should contain the date, the name of the person to contact for more information, and a phone number; the release date (for immediate release or for release after a certain date); an appropriate, descriptive headline; the release information typed double-spaced with wide margins; the who, what, where, when, and why at the very beginning of the press release; a photo, if appropriate; and a note explaining briefly why the release was sent. There are also several publishing services that can be used to gather and distribute information about the business. For example, PR Newswire is the leading source for press releases on companies (http://www.prnewswire.com/).

Socially Responsible Entrepreneurship

Making Money While Being Responsible

The food business is a highly competitive one in which streamlining costs is critical to survival. Growing organic products, using alternative power sources, and providing living wages for workers are a costly undertaking for a start-up with limited financial backing. In 1999, enter Paul Dolan, the 54-year-old president of Fetzer Vineyards in California, a standout in the food industry for taking on all three challenges. Dolan has grown Fetzer into the sixth largest premium winery in the United States, with annual revenues of over $220 million. This is no small feat considering that there are over 3,000 wineries in the United States alone, not to mention all the European, Australian, and Chilean labels.

In 1989, Dolan began experimenting with organic grapes and immediately noticed the difference in flavor. It was clear that years of applying chemical pesticides and fertilizers had leached the richness from the soil and produced grapes with no flavor. Fetzer's goal is to be 100 percent organic by 2010. Fetzer also provides employees with housing, preventive immunizations for children, and higher wages. It's not easy being socially responsible in competitive times, but Fetzer is determined to stay the course.

Sources: Allison Overholt, "The Good Earth," *Fast Company* (December 2003), p. 85; and http://www.fetzer.com/, accessed 9/1/04.

Getting Customer Referrals

The best customers are those acquired through referrals from satisfied current customers. Unfortunately, most entrepreneurs don't understand how to get customers to refer others to their business and become their company evangelists. It is important to begin by getting critical information that will clarify customers' motivations for buying and referring. Talking with current customers who have provided referrals is an excellent way to find out what they really like about the company, how they describe it to others, and what they value most about it. Specific ways to gather this information include taking a customer to lunch at least once a week and encouraging him or her to do the talking. Another approach is doing a global Internet search on a search engine like Google.com to find out what is being said about the company. Companies frequently don't know that some customers set up personal websites to either praise or criticize a company they have strong feelings about. Other options include having a qualified third party conduct in-depth interviews with customers, administering an open-ended online survey that's easy to complete, and hosting an online discussion. Finally, another great way to gather customer feedback is to create a customer advisory board to advise the company on everything from what products to carry to how best to market them.[7]

Giving It Away

Although it seems contrary to what is taught in business schools, more and more entrepreneurs are using the tactic that Netscape and Microsoft used when they gave their browsers away in order to grow their markets rapidly. Giving customers something for nothing makes sense in an environment where it's hard to get the customer's attention. But it is important to know whether giving something away will help the business or simply cost money that it can't afford to lose.[8] Entrepreneurs should consider giving away information, consulting, or samples of a product when the customer is likely to return; when the cost for each additional item is low and margins are high; when customers need to try the product or service in order to risk the money to buy it, especially if it's unproven technology (consider offering the product or service to a well-known customer who will testify to his or her satisfaction with it); or when samples of the product or service can be offered at a large event such as a conference or trade show.

On the other hand, don't give away a service such as financial expertise that relies on credibility, because doing so may cause customers to question its quality. Similarly, expensive items and commodity items, which customers buy on the basis of price, should not be given away, especially when the probability of retaining those customers is low.

Print Media Advertising

Advertising is promotion that costs the company money. Advertising media generally fall into two categories: print and broadcast. The following sections examine the various types of media and their uses. It is not the purpose of this book to provide all the information the entrepreneur needs to use each medium presented, but only to create awareness of how and when each is used.

The Newspaper

The purpose of a newspaper is to distribute the news in a direct, to-the-point fashion. Most cities have one or more major newspapers, in addition to business newspapers, shopper newspapers, ethnic newspapers, and national newspapers, which often have regional editions. How does an entrepreneur know which is most appropriate for the product or service being sold? With businesses spending nearly one-third of their advertising dollars on newspaper ads, this question becomes crucial.

Newspaper advertising offers many advantages, including broad coverage in a selected geographic area, flexibility and speed in bringing an ad to print and changing it along the way, quickness in generating sales, and relatively low costs.

Newspapers have disadvantages as well. Broad coverage means the company may be paying to reach people who may not be part of the target market. Furthermore, because newspapers carry hundreds of ads every day, it is not easy (short of taking a full page) to attract the attention of the reader. Also, a newspaper has a very short life. A person may read it with breakfast and throw it out before leaving for work. Even an ad that was noticed at sunrise may be forgotten by the end of the day. Therefore, advertising in a specialized newspaper that will better reach the targeted customer may be advisable.

To use newspaper advertising effectively, try to determine which newspaper is best for the business by placing ads in all the papers in the target region the first time. If appropriate, include in the ad a coupon or toll-free number so that the potential customer will either bring the coupon into the place of business or call on a special line. In either case, it is important to ask the person who responds where he or she heard about the business. Ads in the papers with the highest response rates should be continued and all others dropped. Once this strategy has been executed in one or two geographic regions, it is likely that advertising in a similar type of newspaper in another part of the country will have similar results.

It is important to create a basic design for advertising that reflects the philosophy of the business and to use that design consistently in all advertising. Customers will eventually recognize that the ad is for a particular company before they even read it. The best location for the ad (because it is the most visible) is on a right-hand page, above the fold of the newspaper, but this location is also the most costly.

Magazines

A number of national magazines offer businesses the opportunity to advertise to certain broad-based target markets. Magazines such as *People, Newsweek, Business Week,* and *Time* reach hundreds of thousands of people every week. In addition, such specialty magazines as *Sports Illustrated, Modern Maturity, Rolling Stone,* and *Road & Track* focus on specific interests. These magazines are useful for businesses that are targeting a particular interest, such as sports, music, or cars. There are also a great number of trade magazines that reflect the needs of specific trade organizations; examples include *Advertising Age* and *Variety Magazine.* However, magazine advertising is more costly, and the time lag for printing is generally six to eight weeks, so it lacks the flexibility of newspaper advertising. One issue to consider when contemplating magazine advertising is whether the magazine has a regional edition, as *Time* does. It is a better use of advertising dollars to run the ad in the region being targeted. A media buying service can provide real cost advantages. A buying service purchases a lot of ad space in bulk, acquiring it at rates that a single company cannot get. Another wise idea is to ask the magazine whether a split-run ad is possible—that is, whether it is possible to run one headline in half the magazines that go to one geographic area and another headline in the other half. The ads should be coded to keep track of responses. All ads should also be coded to reflect publication, date, run, and ad size; this will make it easier to determine which is more effective. The aesthetics of the ad are important. Color should be used effectively to take advantage of the fact that more information can be provided in a magazine ad than in a newspaper ad (because the reader generally spends more time with a magazine ad). It is vital to give a phone number, web address, or mail-in coupon in the ad to encourage people to contact the company for a full brochure or a video. Finally, it is a good idea to check on "remnant space," or leftover space that must be filled before the magazine goes to print. If any exists, it will be sold at a fraction of the original cost of an ad.

The Yellow Pages

Many businesses, particularly retail and service businesses, can benefit from placing ads in the Yellow Pages of their telephone directory. There is a good chance that people will look in the Yellow Pages for a particular service. However, advertising in the Yellow Pages is fairly expensive and targets only the local market for a product or service, so it should not be considered a major advertising resource, particularly if a company markets nationally or globally. At the same time, entrepreneurs should check into listing their company in the online Yellow Pages as well.

Signs

Signs are a relatively inexpensive way to expose a lot of people to the business. They also encourage impulse buying of consumer products. Naturally, signs play the most important role in retail businesses where they become part of the total advertising campaign. In other types of businesses, the sign merely helps someone locate the business. Signs for sales or special events do, however, outlive their usefulness rather quickly. When a sale sign is left in a window too long, people tune it out, and as soon as that happens, it has lost its value.

Direct Marketing

Direct marketing includes direct mail, mail order, coupons, telemarketing, door-to-door, and TV shopping networks. The essence of direct marketing is that the entrepreneur attempts to close a sale at the moment the advertising takes place. Direct marketing permits coverage of a wide geographic area, while, at the same time, targeting specific customers; therefore, more sales can be generated with fewer dollars. Much more information can be provided in a direct-response brochure than in other types of advertising. In other words, the brochure can answer all the customer's questions so that he or she can make an immediate decision. Consequently, direct mail has the highest response rate of any type of advertising, and the responses received from a purchased mailing list can become the basis of a business's own direct mailing list. Another way to create a personalized mailing list is to have people who walk into the place of business fill out a database card and suggest other people who may be interested in the product or service.

The average response rate for direct mail is 2 percent. That rate can be increased 50 to 100 percent when the advertising includes a toll-free number; many customers are more likely to call than to fill out an order form. That response rate, in turn, can be increased 100 to 700 percent by following up the mailing with a phone call—a method known as telemarketing—within 72 hours. When telemarketing is used as a tactic, it is important to understand the Telephone Consumer Protection Act (47 USC 227), which requires that a "do-not-call" list be maintained and bans unsolicited advertising via fax machines. More information about this law can be found at http://www.fcc.gov/cgb/consumerfacts/tcpa.html.

It is essential for a small, growing company to consider the staff resources it has available and to restrict mailings to the number it can reasonably follow up on within 72 hours. To get the highest possible response rate, it is necessary to conduct several repeat mailings, as well as to repeat the telemarketing effort. For catalogs, conducting four mailings a year is typical. Also, because most customers have a tendency to throw out unsolicited mail before reading it, it is important to put the central selling point on the envelope as well. Customers must be enticed into opening the envelope.

Not all products are suitable for direct mail, however. Those that do not require repeat orders, are not easily shipped, are readily available in stores, or are seasonal or short-lived (such as fad items) are not good candidates for direct mail.

Broadcast Media

Radio

Radio is an excellent medium for local or regional advertising, because the audience can be targeted geographically and generally by age group. Radio stations keep extensive records on the demographics of their listening audience to help determine whether this audience will be interested in a particular product or service. It is useful to advertise on more than one station to saturate the market. Recently many companies have been able to gain a national presence by sponsoring a national radio program. When considering radio advertising, it is important to understand that the ad can't be a one-shot ad. Because radio listeners are fickle and tend to change stations often, the ad needs to be played several times a day, several days a week to have an impact. It is important to keep track of the responses received from the radio ad in the same manner as suggested for print media to determine which ad, on which station, has the greatest impact. A general rule of thumb is that prime radio time is during commuting hours in the morning and late afternoon. The cost will be higher at those times, but the ad will reach more people.

Television

Many businesses spend one-quarter of their advertising dollars on television; consequently, it is the second most popular form of advertising for consumer products (after newspapers). With television, people can see as well as hear about the product or service, and the audience can be targeted at the national, regional, or even local level (as well as by interest group via cable channels). However, television advertising is expensive, not only in terms of buying the actual on-air time but also in terms of the high cost for the preparation and filming of the commercial.

When using television, entrepreneurs should seek the help of a media buying service. Making use of such services is the equivalent of buying health insurance through group pools. These services can get media time much more inexpensively than an individual because they buy millions of dollars' worth every month.

Miscellaneous Advertising

Many simple advertising tactics have been very successful for new and growing consumer products or service businesses. Offering T-shirts and baseball caps with the company's name emblazoned on them for sale (or as a giveaway) has been a very successful tactic. Using searchlights to attract people to the business site is an attention getter. Couponing has certainly been an advertising staple, and there are many coupon magazines in which a company can buy space. These magazines are distributed to households across the country and have been an excellent source of new customers for businesses. Look for any and all opportunities to demonstrate the product free to potential customers. One southern California entrepreneur who developed a successful, easy-to-use cleaner for silk plants reports that his sales always increase when he does demonstrations in stores. Creating a videotape of the product in action is another useful technique, especially when the product is not easily transported.

Personal Selling

Traditional selling techniques don't always meet the needs of today's customers, who expect a quality product at a fair price with good service. It is clear that a traditional approach will not be effective. Today, a business distinguishes itself in the marketplace by identifying and meeting specific customer needs. Therefore, even if an entrepreneur is selling a commodity, he or she needs to figure out some way to add value to the product.

A good example of a company that adds value to a product is a small manufacturer of molded plastic parts in Massachusetts. Its largest account is a major acoustic speaker manufacturer, also in Massachusetts. The speaker company asked the plastics company to assign a full-time salesperson to its plant, which would help it eliminate some of the costs of buyers and planners and, at the same time, enable the plastics plant to concentrate on service rather than on trying to acquire new accounts. As a result, the plastics company's sales have increased nearly 40 percent per year.

Becoming a value-added company by tailoring products to meet customers' needs requires that everyone in the company become service-oriented, a time-consuming task that necessitates training and educating employees. It also demands an opportunity mindset, rather than a selling mindset. It is a lengthier process, but the returns are potentially greater. Working more closely with customers can translate into reduced selling and marketing costs.

Improving Personal Selling Skills

Personal selling is an important talent that entrepreneurs typically possess and continue to hone throughout their careers. To improve upon personal selling skills, entrepreneurs should do some research before attempting to sell. They need to learn what customers want from the sale and give them what they want. The first meeting with the customer is typically designed to gather as much information as possible about the customer's needs. Then, the entrepreneur should build credibility with the customer before trying to sell anything by doing a lot of listening to understand the customer's needs. Next the entrepreneur must position the company as a solution provider in the mind of the customer, making sure to grab the customer's interest immediately. Whenever possible, the customer should be able to use the product to understand and appreciate it. During demonstrations and conversations, the entrepreneur should stand in front of the customer, not to the side, paying close attention to the customer's facial expressions as the benefits are being explained. Time is of the essence, so the customer's time should not be wasted. The major points should be explained quickly in order to facilitate speedy decision making. If the customer declines the offer, the entrepreneur should maintain a sense of composure, then inquire why, and follow up by repeating the value the company is providing. As a final touch, the entrepreneur could invite the prospect to contact two existing customers. If, despite these efforts, the sale ends up going to a competitor, the entrepreneur should try to determine what he or she could have been done to present a more effective case.

One of the most difficult issues an entrepreneur faces with regard to selling is compensation—what and how to pay sales representatives. The possibilities are endless: Incentives can be tied to profit or gross margins, contract size, the number of new accounts acquired, company goals, and so on. Salespeople can also be paid a straight salary or a salary plus a percentage of the profits.

Another issue in sales involves how to compensate those who provide service to customers. Service is the key to customer retention, and the people who provide that service are becoming increasingly important to a firm's success. Studying the compensation practices in one's own industry, as well as those in other industries, will help determine which method is best for the business.

Trade Shows and Exhibits

For entrepreneurs in many industries—electronics, industrial equipment, and gift items, for example—trade shows, fairs, and exhibits are a primary way to expose their products. Attending trade shows is a good way to find out who the competitors are and what marketing techniques they are using. A trade show is also one of the best places to meet and negotiate with sales representatives and to gather contact information for a mailing list. But the primary reason to display products at a trade show is to eventually sell more product. To accomplish this, the entrepreneur should consider renting booth space and hiring a display designer to produce a quality display booth that will attract attention. Visiting several trade shows before setting up a booth will clarify what works and what doesn't. It may also be possible to work out a deal with a company that has compatible products to share a booth and combine resources. The entrepreneur should hire a professional model or salesperson to distribute an information sheet that invites people to stop by the booth. Save the expensive brochures to hand out to potential customers who actually come to the booth and provide their business cards. It is important to have enough knowledgeable, personable people in the booth so that potential customers are not kept waiting to talk with someone. Breaks should be staggered to keep the booth staffed at all times. Another good idea is to offer something free at the booth, such as a sample or a raffle.

Entrepreneurs should also consider renting a hospitality suite in the hotel where the trade show is located to entertain key people in the industry, after exhibit hours. Finally, it is vital to follow up with letters to anyone whose business card was collected and to call all serious prospects.

Marketing to Industrial Customers

When the target market is other businesses, the marketing strategy is somewhat different in terms of advertising and promotion. With consumer products and services, a considerable amount of high-profile advertising and promotion is necessary to entice customers away from the other possible choices. With industrial products and services, however, the focus is on letting the targeted businesses know that the product or service is available and what it can do for them.

In general, producers of industrial products and services do not use broadcast media or most popular print media. Instead, they rely heavily on direct mail, personal selling, trade shows, and articles and advertisements in trade journals. Because most industrial product manufacturers distribute their products through wholesalers, it becomes the wholesalers' job to locate and market to retail outlets. When dealing with industrial customers, investigate how products and services are marketed in a particular industry. Today, many industries do much of their supply-chain transacting on the Internet, which has saved them time and money and enabled employees to make purchases from their desktops.

Customer Relationship Management (CRM)

One of the newest and most rapidly growing areas of marketing is customer relationship management, or CRM. **Customer relationship management (CRM),** formerly known as database marketing (DBM), is a combination of technology, training, and business strategy that results in a system for gathering and using information on current and prospective customers, with the goal of increasing profitability. This critical component of any successful marketing strategy has long been a mainstay of large corporations, but until only a few years ago it was too costly for smaller companies. Today, however, affordable database software with sample templates makes it easy to set up a CRM system in a relatively short period of time. A good CRM system can generate better sales leads, allow rapid responses to changing customer needs, and ensure that all employees who need customer information have it when they need it in the form they need.

A well-constructed database contains the names, addresses, and attributes of people who are likely to purchase what the company has to offer. It will help the entrepreneur define a trading area, reach new customers in the marketplace, select specific target audiences, and survey current customers.

CRM is not merely a way to reach customers by mail more easily. Today, retaining and maintaining current customers is more important than spending money to find new customers. It has been reported that 65 percent of a company's business comes from current customers. In fact, it costs five to ten times more to go after a new customer than to serve an existing one. Furthermore, with good customer profiles, an entrepreneur can match demographic information about current customers with demographic data in the geographic area of interest to find prospects more effectively. Information contained in the database can be used in advertising, sales promotion, public relations, direct mail, and personal selling.

The competitive advantages of CRM are many. Customer relationship management helps entrepreneurs increase their response rates, enhances the development of new products, aids in the forecasting of sales, and improves decisions about mass marketing. CRM also enables the company to personalize advertising, cross-sell related products, and increase customer loyalty. For example, an entrepreneur with a combination book, video, and CD outlet can begin to track customers by offering a "frequent buyer" card that entitles customers to free items once they have made a specified amount of purchases. To receive the card, the customer fills out an information form. Every time the customer purchases something, the item is recorded in the customer's database record. Over time, the entrepreneur can detect patterns in the kinds of items this customer buys and suggest purchases to the customer that match those patterns.

CRM is really an overall approach to doing business, an approach that requires the total commitment of everyone in the organization. As in any marketing effort, the payoff to this approach takes time, and many frustrated entrepreneurs give up before seeing the results of their efforts.

Online Marketing

The big challenge in online marketing is to give customers what they want instead of what marketers think they want. Although users want the ability to sign up for free samples online, the ability to receive coupons and offers online, and the opportunity to learn about community events, online marketers overwhelmingly tend to give them only product and company information and advertising.

There is a misconception that advertising on the Internet is cheap and/or free. Actually, any method of acquiring new customers on the Internet carries an acquisition cost that can often be quite high. In 2001, AOL claimed to spend about $90 to acquire a customer.[9] It could justify that cost only because the company was selling a subscription, so it was building a relationship with the customer for the long term. By contrast, online payments provider PayPal grew from 10,000 users in early 2000 to more than 10.6 million users in September 2001. During that same period they kept a careful eye on their customer acquisition costs, which they succeeded in dropping from $3.29 per customer to 13 cents per customer. The ability to keep customer acquisition costs low is a primary reason why PayPal was the first successful initial public offering by an Internet company following the dotcom crash.[10]

Any marketing strategy should be anticipated, personal, and relevant. Potential customers don't want to be surprised by marketing tactics. They want to know that marketing is about them, and they want to know that it's about things they're interested in. The reason why most online marketing campaigns (and offline ones as well) are unsuccessful is that they are unanticipated, impersonal, and irrelevant.

Viral Marketing

Viral marketing was born of the Internet's ability to replicate and distribute information quickly and efficiently. Its offline counterparts are "word-of-mouth" and "network marketing." Even though the term *viral marketing* has negative connotations, it is widely used to describe a marketing strategy that entices customers to pass on the marketing message to others. For example, Hotmail.com, the highly successful free e-mail service, provides its users with free e-mail addresses but carefully includes a tagline on each message the user sends: "Get your private, free e-mail at www.hotmail.com." Hotmail is hoping that when users send messages to friends, they will sign up as well, taking its services to an ever-widening audience. If the strategy is well developed, the viral marketing message will spread rapidly, bringing in many more users. Hotmail will be able to translate the increased usage into higher advertising revenues.

Another example is Adobe Acrobat. Adobe, the successful software company, gives away its proprietary software that lets people share documents across multiple platforms in a form called PDF, which retains the original formatting but can't be manipulated. Adobe puts a link in the document that sends the person to the Adobe website to download the required Adobe Reader. That gives Adobe an opportunity to let the user know about its other software products available for sale. The strategy has been so successful that Adobe is now the de facto standard for sending corporate documents.

Although there is no single best way to craft a viral strategy, most successful viral marketers

- **Provide free products and services.** Good marketers know that "free" is the most powerful word in any language, and online marketers know that if they generate enough "eyeballs" through a viral marketing campaign, somewhere down the road, they will also achieve a level of profit.
- **Make it easy to pass on the message.** There is nothing easier than clicking on a button and forwarding an e-mail to someone. For example, online magazines have made it easy to forward an article to someone by simply clicking on a button that brings up an e-mail message into which the person's address is entered.
- **Make sure that the mail server can handle the traffic.** There is nothing worse than starting a viral campaign that ultimately annihilates its host. Remember that viral marketing spreads a message extremely rapidly, so plan ahead for additional server capacity.
- **Take advantage of existing social networks.** Just as in the offline world, people in cyberspace create networks of people and information that they tap into regularly. Place a message into one of those networks, and its diffusion is accelerated exponentially.
- **Use other people's websites.** Find compatible websites and arrange to place a message on them. In that way, the company is tapping into another network and increasing the scope of its own.

Affiliate Programs

One way to increase the traffic on a website is to use **affiliate programs,** which are basically strategic partnerships with other companies that offer complementary products and services. Banner exchange programs are one example of an affiliate program. The banner company posts the entrepreneur's banner on other compatible Internet sites. Costs may be associated with posting a banner, or it may be possible to negotiate a barter exchange if the company's website is compatible with the website on which it wants to place a banner. Getting a banner on a website may be the easiest part of the challenge. Convincing people to click through and buy a product or service is quite another thing. There are many effective ways to attract customers to a website. These include assuring them that their private information will not be sold; giving them something free to entice them to discover more; offering them more, beyond the free information, that they will have to pay for; using electronic gift certificates as a way of getting customers to try products or services; providing a toll-free number for people who need to hear a human voice to overcome resistance; and offering to accept payment for items in as many ways as possible: credit cards, checks, debit cards, and so on.

Privacy Issues

Although companies have collected consumer information for years and used it to target customers and sell more products and services, the advent of e-commerce has made consumers more aware of privacy issues. When Jane Consumer goes online to purchase a handmade doll for her collection, she soon finds that she is inundated with advertisements for gifts, collectibles, and anything else remotely related to her doll collection. This is the power of the Internet at work, as it magnifies anything done in the offline world.[11] The retailer who sold her the doll probably also sold her e-mail address and other information to catalog companies and others looking to target the same customer. Amazon.com ran afoul of the Federal Trade Commission (FTC), which claimed that the company's practices were deceptive. Amazon did not make it clear to customers that it was selling their information to other companies. In fact, an FTC survey estimates that 97 percent of all e-commerce websites collect information that is personally identifiable. Therefore, companies must now do more to ensure that their customers' privacy is respected. Customer-focused companies inform their customers how the information collected will be used. The most successful companies maintain policies against selling customer information. Other firms seek seals of approval from online auditing companies such as TrustE and PricewaterhouseCoopers LLP, but these audits can cost up to tens of thousands of dollars. The best practice is to get a customer's permission before using his or her information for any purpose. Any effective marketing strategy, whether online or offline, should target the appropriate customers and address their specific needs, including their need for privacy.

New Venture Checklist

Have you:

- ☐ Analyzed the marketing options and ranked them?
- ☐ Written a clear, concise, one-paragraph statement of the marketing plan?
- ☐ Developed an advertising, publicity, and promotion strategy?
- ☐ Discovered your business's compelling story?
- ☐ Created some innovative ways to promote your business online?

Issues to Consider

1. What are the differences between an entrepreneurial marketing strategy and a large corporation's marketing strategy?
2. Is it important to stick with your marketing plan even if it isn't returning immediate results? Why or why not?
3. Suppose you have invented a new product and you're trying to determine an appropriate price. What should you consider when setting your initial price?
4. How does the promotion strategy for consumer-oriented businesses differ from that of industrial businesses?

Experiencing Entrepreneurship

1. Compare and contrast the marketing strategies of two companies in the same industry in terms of the points in the marketing plan on pages 292–295.
2. Find an entrepreneurial company that is using a relationship marketing strategy. Interview the entrepreneur or the person in charge of implementing this marketing strategy to discuss how it builds effective customer relationships.

Additional Sources of Information

Hoyer, W.D., and D.J. MacInnis (2003). *Consumer Behavior.* 3d ed. Boston: Houghton Mifflin.

Koehn, N.F. (2001). *Brand New: How Entrepreneurs Earned Consumers' Trust from Wedgwood to Dell.* Boston: Harvard Business School Press.

Kotler, P. (2002). *Marketing Management.* Upper Saddle River, NJ: Prentice-Hall.

Levinson, J.C. (1998). *Guerrilla Marketing: Secrets for Making Big Profits from Your Business.* Boston: Houghton Mifflin.

Seybold, P.B., R.T. Marshak, and J.M. Lewis (2001). *The Customer Revolution.* New York: Crown.

Relevant Case Studies

Case 2 Craigslist, p. 407

Case 8 Finagle a Bagel, p. 450

15

Funding a Start-up Venture

"Money is the seed of money, and the first guinea is sometimes more difficult to acquire than the second million."

Jean Jacques Rousseau

LEARNING OBJECTIVES

- Develop a resource strategy.
- Construct a plan.
- Discuss how to finance start-ups.
- Explain financing with equity.
- Discuss financing with debt.

Profile 15.1 NOTHING HAPPENS UNTIL SOMEONE SELLS SOMETHING

Greg Gianforte's motto "Nothing happens until someone sells something" is the essence of what he believes bootstrapping is—focusing entirely on the customer to figure out whether you have a business that will work. With bootstrapping, if you fail, all you've lost is time, according to Gianforte. After selling a successful venture for over $10 million, Gianforte moved to Bozeman, Montana, at the age of 33 to raise a family. But it wasn't long before he had the urge to start another business. It was 1997, and an Internet software business seemed to make sense. By searching the Internet, he learned that there was no company helping companies respond to e-mail from their customers. To determine whether he could "sell" his fantasy product that didn't yet exist, he began cold-calling companies and talking to them about whether a product like this might be useful if it were available within 90 days. If they said no, he would ask why and then build their response into his product design as long as he could do it within the time he had specified. It took Gianforte only a couple of weeks of cold calls to learn exactly what his potential customers wanted. Then he spent two months developing a rough prototype that potential customers could test and report back to him the features they still needed. Because he wasn't incurring any overhead working out of his house, he decided to give the product away just to get people using it. Within three months he was able to price his RightNow software at a very low license fee. By early 1998, he was bringing in revenues of $30,000 a month and was ready to hire his first three employees, all of them for sales positions. He didn't create sales materials but, rather, prepared a demonstration website built by students at Montana State University that showed customers how their websites would work with the RightNow software loaded.

In late 1998, Gianforte hired his first technical person, which represented his first investment in real overhead. Nevertheless, he stayed in bootstrap mode until he was confident that he understood the business model. By that time, he also had several large competitors, so it was the right moment to seek some outside funding to open offices in Dallas, London, and Sydney, Australia. He knew he could have grown with internal cash flows, but it would have taken a lot longer.

Gianforte is perhaps an extreme example of a bootstrapper. He housed his business in his home, then in a room at the back of a real estate agency, and then in a former elementary school. It was only when he began to hire experienced managers that he decided it was time to think about the company's image. But he stands by bootstrapping, and although his company is now much more traditional, he still makes sure that money is spent to *make* money not just to spend money.

Sources: E. Barker, "Start with Nothing," *Inc. Magazine* (February 2002), www.inc.com; RightNow Technologies, www.rightnow.com; and M. Middlewood, "RightNow Technologies Jumps on the IPO Bandwagon," *TechNews World*, http://www.technewsworld.com/story/33730.html.

"How can I fund my new business?" Probably no question is more on the minds of entrepreneurs with new venture ideas because they often believe that money is the critical driver of successful new ventures. They suppose that if an entrepreneur has enough money, he or she can make any business concept a success. Unfortunately, that reasoning is faulty. In fact, throwing money at a bad idea doesn't change it into a good idea; it just delays the inevitable failure. Putting a lot of money into the hands of an inept team is like throwing it away. Moreover, a team that has more money than it needs often makes poor decisions because there's plenty of money to pay for mistakes.

The first source of money that inexperienced entrepreneurs typically identify is venture capital, but this tendency springs from a misconception about the needs of start-up ventures and the nature of financial markets. Money is only one of the resources an entrepreneur needs to start a successful business, and it may not even be the most important.

Because start-up companies are inherently risky investments, the number of sources of financing for them is somewhat limited. Once a business has survived start-up and achieved a successful track record, however, multiple new sources of financing are available to help the business grow. Still, funding a new venture is a difficult process, mostly because of information asymmetry; that is, entrepreneurs have more information about themselves and their ventures than do the people from whom they seek funding.[1] The entrepreneur understands the value of his or her concept, but can that value be successfully conveyed to the investor market? How does an entrepreneur improve her or his chances of securing venture funding? Research points to the importance of the entrepreneur's social network and reputation in increasing the chances of securing funding. But that is only the beginning. This chapter will look at sources of financing for start-up companies to prepare entrepreneurs for finding the right funding from the right source at the appropriate time. Not all of the sources and strategies discussed in this chapter will be suitable for every business, but it's important to understand all the options in order to make wiser choices.

Resource Strategy

The resources necessary to launch a new venture fall into four broad categories: human capital, social capital, physical capital, and financial capital. Although this chapter focuses on financial capital, it is important to understand its role relative to the other resources. All of these resources have significant implications for the survival and growth of a venture. Determining which activities will require which resources and in what quantities is part of putting together a carefully conceived financial plan. And creating a unique bundle of resources that is rare, valuable, and inimitable becomes a core competency for the business as well as a competitive advantage.[2] The primary resource is the entrepreneur, who brings his or her experience, expertise, personal resources, and vision to the new venture. Many entrepreneurs are in the position of Jeff Hawkins, who founded Palm Computing in 1992. A highly regarded neurobiologist, Hawkins had developed a handwriting algorithm on which he received a patent. He had his reputation and the patent, but no money, no business plan, and no know-how to start a business.[3] Using his social (reputational) capital and his technical skills, he was able to raise $2 million from two venture capitalists whom he had met through one of his work associations. Then he executed a deal with Tandy Computer Corporation, his former employer, for that firm to invest $300,000, sit on the board of directors, and have nonexclusive distribution rights to his new products and cross-license technology.[4] With these pieces in place, he was able to recruit the engineers he needed and an experienced executive to fill the role of president and CEO. Starting with only his social capital and his technical expertise, Hawkins was able to build the beginnings of a complex bundle of resources.

Years later, when Hawkins left Palm to start Handspring, he started off with a strong resource base of personal money, a core management team, supplier relationships, customer know-how, and superior technical skills. This time, he was able to launch without the aid of outside investors.

The work of Brush and associates[5] suggests a process for constructing a resource base. It consists of five steps:

1. Identify and specify required resources at various milestones in the company's growth: Human, social, financial, physical, technological, and organizational.
2. Identify potential suppliers of those resources. Finding the best resources is a long and time-consuming process, so it is important to do this before the venture is launched.
3. Assess the entrepreneur's ability to attract resources. To attract the right resources, entrepreneurs must be out in the industry and market, talking to people and building relationships, so that when a particular resource is needed, the relationship that will produce it is already there.
4. Combine resources to create new, unique resources. One example is using financial resources to acquire rare human capital with unique technical skills
5. Transform individual resources into organizational resources. Most resources are initially individual resources, usually the founder's. If the entrepreneur can transform these into organizational resources, they can become a core competency and competitive advantage for the company.

The remainder of the chapter will focus on the acquisition of financial capital to start the new venture.

Starting with a Plan

In the effort to plan and gather funding, knowing whom to tap for investment capital is only half the battle. The other half is having a strategic plan for funding the start-up and growth of the company with the right kind of money from the right sources. Entrepreneurs should raise only what is actually needed, not whatever is possible in the prevailing economic environment. At the same time, planning carefully will avoid the need to seek financing too often, which can be costly.

The Search for Money

It is important at the outset to approach the search for money armed with accurate information. The fact is that relatively few investment sources for start-up companies exist outside of the 3 F's: friends, family, and fools. When the Kirchhoff Innovation Framework (see Figure 15.1) is used to explain what types of money are available to what types of businesses, it quickly becomes apparent that venture capitalists are interested primarily in "superstar" ventures.[6] *Glamorous firms,* from which the superstars emerge, are firms that grow as a result of high rates of innovation. They tend to attract a lot of media attention and to be based on technology products. E-Bay is one such firm. *Economic core firms* are generally low-innovation, low-growth companies and represent the vast majority of all businesses in the United

| FIGURE 15.1 | Focus of Informal Capital Compared with That of Venture Capital (Based on Kirchhoff Innovation Framework) |

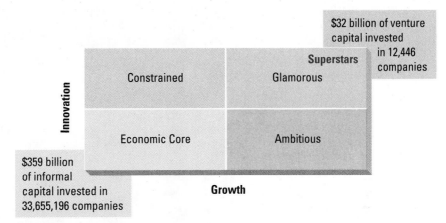

Source: Gem 2003 Global Report Venture Capital, Global Entrepreneurship Monitor 2003, www.gemconsortium.org, accessed September 2004, p. 6.

States. This group also includes those firms that are small temporarily and that will move to other categories as they grow. For example, Wal-Mart founder Sam Walton's first store, Gibson Discount Store, was a typical rural store in the economic core category until he developed the business model that would grow the store into what it is today. Growth in *ambitious firms* is usually based on simple innovations. Dell Computer innovated in distributing and servicing microcomputers through direct mail. For a time, Krispy Kreme Doughnuts grew very rapidly because it was offering something new to the fast-food market and it had innovated with new doughnut-making technology. However, without additional innovations, it will not be able to sustain the rate of growth it saw after it went public in 2000. *Constrained firms* produce most of the glamorous firms. Firms in this category generally have high rates of innovation but are constrained by limited resources, including the inability to attract the capital or personnel required for growth.

As Figure 15.1 explains, $32 billion of venture capital was invested in 12,446 superstar companies in 2002. But a staggering $359 billion of informal capital was invested in over 33 million businesses in the other categories.[7] Thus the informal markets offer a higher probability of success in the search for funding.

Looking at the informal capital market a little more closely reveals that even in that much broader market, there are limitations. Figure 15.2 depicts the breakdown of informal investment according to where it's placed. Clearly, the majority of such informal investment goes to family members and friends, and only about 14 percent goes to colleagues at work and strangers. What this means to the entrepreneur is that it's important for entrepreneurs to elevate their status from strangers to friends in order to increase their chances of getting funded. How do they do this? By networking and developing relationships before it's time to seek funding.

In general, 77 percent of informal investors want their payback within two to five years. This represents a much shorter timeframe than was historically demanded

| FIGURE 15.2 | Where Is Informal Capital Invested? |

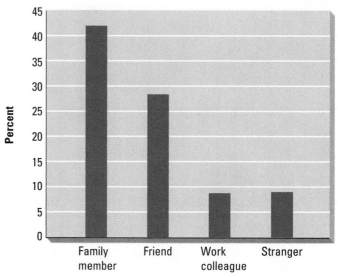

Source: United States Executive Report 2003, Global Entrepreneurship Monitor 2003, www.gemconsortium.org, accessed September 2004, p. 33.

by informal investors. Furthermore, the Global Entrepreneurship Monitor (GEM) found that most informal investors are male, of high net worth, and well educated and that they are four times more likely than others to have been entrepreneurs themselves. Therefore, this research suggests that, apart from the entrepreneur's personal investment and that of friends and family members, the entrepreneur should be seeking investment capital from former entrepreneurs with a high net worth.

Strategic Planning

The starting point for planning is identifying the stages of growth that a business will experience. Every business is different, but in general, each will reach certain milestones that suggest the time has come to grow to the next level. Figure 15.3 indicates the typical funding stages. In the first phase, start-up funds are required. These will typically come from the founders and other sources of "friendly money." Once the company is up and running and has achieved success in a small market, it's time to grow the company to reach a wider audience.

By the second phase, the business is requiring capital to grow on the basis of a proven concept. In fact, customers may have demanded that the company grow, a point that most entrepreneurs look forward to. At this point, the company may be unable to grow rapidly enough using internal cash flows and will require outside capital from a private investor, venture capitalist (VC), or debt source. Taking on outside investment capital requires that the entrepreneur plan for some kind of liquidity event so that investors can cash out of the business and receive a return on their investment. That liquidity event may be in the form of an initial public offering (IPO), which will

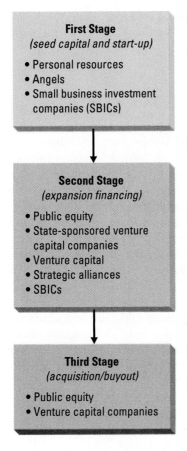

FIGURE 15.3

Stages of
Financing for
Ventures

First Stage
(seed capital and start-up)

• Personal resources
• Angels
• Small business investment
  companies (SBICs)

Second Stage
(expansion financing)

• Public equity
• State-sponsored venture
  capital companies
• Venture capital
• Strategic alliances
• SBICs

Third Stage
(acquisition/buyout)

• Public equity
• Venture capital companies

give the entrepreneur access to the capital markets from which it is easier to raise large amounts of money.

The third phase calls for a different type of money, termed **mezzanine financing** or **bridge financing,** to provide the entrepreneur with the funds the company needs to get through an initial public offering in which millions of dollars may be raised. This phase of rapid growth can come relatively early in the venture's life cycle or very late. For some businesses, particularly lifestyle businesses, rapid growth may never be part of their evolution. They may instead enjoy slow, steady growth. If a business survives over the long term, it will probably reach a mature phase in which it ideally maintains a stable revenue stream with a loyal customer base. In today's dynamic environment, however, stability is rarely an enduring state. To continue to be profitable, a mature business must punctuate its equilibrium with new products and services and new markets so that it can remain competitive. What is clear is that there are different types of money for different stages of the venture. In general, the milestones a business achieves create more value for the business and enable it to seek greater and greater amounts of capital in the form of equity or debt.

Planning for a High-Tech Venture

High-tech ventures that introduce **break-through** or **disruptive technologies,** such as a new drug or a device that changes the way we do things, tend to follow a pattern discussed in the works of Geoffrey Moore.[8] Early seed funding supports a long period of product development. Often this money comes from government grants or foundations. It is a rare venture capital firm that will invest during the earliest product development phase of a high-tech venture, because the risk is too high. Once the technology approaches market readiness, however, it moves into a phase known as the "early adopter" stage wherein technically oriented users, who regularly purchase leading-edge technology, begin to use it. At this point, the company will require marketing and educational dollars to capture enough niches in the market to cause the product to be drawn into what Moore refers to as the "tornado," a period of mass adoption of the new technology wherein it has the potential to become the standard in the industry. During this frenzied period, the business focuses solely on producing and delivering product to meet extraordinary demand. Later, when demand tapers off, money needs to be devoted to building loyal customer relationships and developing new applications for the core technology over the long term. High-technology ventures have longer development times but generally move through the product and business evolution cycle much more rapidly than other types of businesses. Chapter 17 deals with the unique issues of growth in high-technology ventures.

Financing Start-Ups

Most start-up ventures begin with a patchwork of funding sources that include credit cards, savings, friends, family members, borrowing, and bartering or trading products and services. The term **bootstrapping** refers to techniques for getting by on as few resources as possible and using other people's resources whenever feasible. It involves begging, borrowing, or leasing everything needed to start a venture and is the antithesis of the "big-money model" espoused by many when they talk about entrepreneurial ventures.[9] More often than not, boot-strapping is a model for starting a business without money—or at least without any money beyond that provided by the entrepreneur's personal resources. At 38 and having been out of work for two years in 1992, Paul Aldrich decided that his future lay in commercializing his candle-making hobby. Starting in his kitchen in Maine with very limited resources, he began researching glass manufacturers to find containers for his candles. He would call the manufacturers and request samples. Those early samples enabled him to manufacture his creations at a very low cost. He found his first customer on a trip through the Poconos when he stopped at a candle shop. From the trunk of his Dodge Caravan, Aldrich showed the proprietor his candles in apothecary jars and secured a $3,400 order. Family and friends became part of his production crew in the kitchen as his little company grew. Today Village Candle is a $30 million business, grown entirely on internal cash flows.[10]

Global Insights

Highlights from the GEM Study

Some of the results of the 2003 Global Entrepreneurship Monitor Study of 40 countries were presented early in this chapter, but here are some additional highlights to give you an idea of the economic importance of entrepreneurship around the world. Informal capital (angels, friends, and family) represents 1 percent of the U.S. gross domestic product (GDP) and funded 99.963 percent of all companies. If you consider all forms of venture capital as a percent of GDP, China has the highest percentage of GDP contributed by venture capital, about 5.5 percent, whereas the corresponding figure in the United States is a little over 1 percent. Of course, the U.S. GDP is far greater, which explains the smaller percentage. Still, the number demonstrates that entrepreneurship in China is a growing phenomenon. If you look at the number of companies that received classic venture capital in the United States, however, it was just over 5,000, whereas in China it was only a few hundred. In general, countries such as China are putting more dollars into fewer start-up ventures.

Source: www.gemconsortium.org.

The capital structure of start-up ventures includes savings, credit cards, mortgages, stock market accounts, vendor credit, customer financing, and loans. A PricewaterhouseCoopers survey of the fastest growing private companies found that the number of these companies seeking to fund growth through bank loans increased 568 percent since 1999. Still, most firms, about 32 percent of those surveyed, will seek non-traditional means of financing growth.[11] Jeanne Battaglia-Dillon, founder of Managed Care Network, rented out part of the family's house to college students to get the capital to launch the venture.[12] Dean Soll, president of SubZero Constructors, used frequent-flier miles to purchase a first-class ticket to Atlanta where, with a "think big, act big" attitude, he managed to secure a $1 million contract with a client from a previous job.[13] These entrepreneurs are the rule, not the exception; typically, personal resources are the most reliable source of start-up funding. This is because new ventures suffer from the liability of newness. By definition they have no track record, so all their estimates of sales and profits are pure speculation. An enormous number of new ventures fail, so the risk for an outside investor is usually high. Many new ventures have no proprietary rights that would give them a competitive advantage and a temporary monopoly in the market they enter. The founders often do not have a significant track record of success. And too many new ventures are "me too" versions of something that already exists, so they have no competitive advantages.

Consequently, pre-launch preparation in the form of feasibility analysis and business planning is critical to optimizing the firm's use of the options available at start-up. Poor planning can result in less than advantageous financial choices and a poor return on investment.

Some bootstrapping tips for financing the launch of a new venture follow.

Hire as Few Employees as Possible

Normally, the greatest single expense a business has is its payroll (including taxes and benefits). Subcontracting work to other firms, using temporary help, or hiring independent contractors can keep the number of employees and their associated costs down. But it is important to be careful. One California company, a maker of heart catheters, found out the hard way that failing to follow the rules can cost the company a lot. Several of this company's "independent contractors" were working 40 hours a week exclusively for the high-tech company and were being paid by the hour, all of which suggested to the IRS that they were really employees. This misclassification cost the company $25,000 in penalties and interest. The rules for using independent contractors and leasing employees are discussed in Chapter 7.

Lease or Share Everything

At some point, virtually all new ventures need to acquire equipment, furnishings, and facilities. By leasing rather than purchasing major equipment and facilities, a new venture can avoid tying up precious capital at a time when it is badly needed to keep the venture afloat. With a lease, there usually is no down payment, and the payments are spread over time. A word of caution, however. Be careful about leasing new, rapidly changing technology for long periods of time to avoid saddling the company with obsolete equipment.

Some entrepreneurs have shared space with established companies not only to save money on overhead but also to give their fledgling ventures the aura of a successful, established company.

Other People's Money

Another key to bootstrapping success is getting customers to pay quickly and suppliers to allow more time for payment. Entrepreneurs must be willing to stay on top of receivables. Sometimes that means walking an invoice through the channels of a major corporation in person or locating the individual who can adjust the computer code that determines when a government agency pays its bills.

Suppliers are an important asset of the business and should be taken care of. Establishing a good relationship with major suppliers can result in more favorable payment terms. After all, the supplier has an interest in seeing the new venture succeed. Often a young company can't get sufficient credit from one supplier, so it is a good idea to seek smaller amounts of credit from several reputable suppliers. In this way, the firm can establish its creditworthiness, and when it qualifies for a larger credit line, it will know which supplier is the best source.

Where possible, sell wholesale rather than retail. Dealing with wholesale distributors makes life easier because they are the experts at working with customers. They have already set up the consumer and industrial channels needed to expand a company's markets. See the sidebar for a list of other bootstrapping techniques.

Some Great Bootstrapping Techniques

- Use student interns, who will often work free just to get the experience.
- Surf the Internet for a wealth of information on anything related to your business.
- Barter for media time.
- Work on getting referrals from loyal customers.
- Don't hire employees until you absolutely have to.
- Use independent contractors whenever possible.
- Seek ways to motivate employees without money.
- Seek vendor credit.
- Stay on top of receivables.
- Get customers involved in the business.
- Leverage purchasing discounts.
- Keep operating expenses as low as possible.
- Put resources into things that make money rather than using money.
- Use e-mail; it's essentially free.
- Work from home as long as possible.

Bootstrapping Ethics

Ethical issues arise whenever bootstrapping tactics are employed to let a new venture survive long enough to use other sources of financing. When an entrepreneur bootstraps, by definition he or she is making the new venture appear much more successful than it is to gain credibility in the market. But the entrepreneur must be careful not to cultivate that image at all costs, because those costs can be too great. Lying to survive by misrepresenting who the entrepreneur is or by misrepresenting how long the company has been in business, is not an acceptable business practice. Intuit, a very successful software manufacturer, spent several start-up years bootstrapping, during which time it became clear to the company that earning the customer's trust is essential to long-term success. It had been a common practice in the software industry to use promotional schemes to load dealers with excess product in the belief that the dealer would then push that product to get rid of it before taking on a competitor's product. Intuit refused to participate in this behavior scheme and unfailingly communicated expectations for sales honestly to the dealers. Thus the dealers were not burdened with excess inventory, and Intuit kept its manufacturing facilities operating on an even keel rather than experiencing costly boom-and-bust cycles. See Profile 15.1 for a profile of a typical bootstrapper.

Financing with Equity

When someone invests money in a venture, it is normally done to gain an ownership share in the business. This ownership share is termed **equity.** It is distinguished from debt in that the equity investor puts his or her capital at risk; usually there is no guaranteed return and no protection against loss. For this reason, most entrepreneurs with start-up ventures seek investment capital from people they know who believe in them. There are a variety of sources of equity financing, including personal resources, "angels," private placement, and venture capital. This chapter focuses on informal capital.

Friends and Family

Entrepreneurs need to think very carefully about accepting money in the form of loans or equity investment from family members and friends. This is said to be the most expensive money around because the entrepreneur pays for it for the rest of his or her life. Chris Baggott knows that all too well. In 1992, he quit his job and bought a local dry cleaning business, eventually building it to a seven-store chain. To fund the business, Baggott borrowed $45,000 from his father-in-law, who also co-signed on a $600,000 bank loan. Things were going well until the "business casual" trend happened, and people stopped wearing suits and clothes that needed dry cleaning. The unfortunate end to the story was that Baggott had to sell the business, pay his debts, and live with the very uncomfortable knowledge that his father-in-law had lost tens of thousands of dollars on the deal.[14]

Because of the difficulties associated with equity investments from friends and family, many entrepreneurs prefer debt, because it is cheaper and lets the entrepreneur retain control of the business.

Private Investors — Angels

The most popular follow-up source of capital for new ventures is private investors, typically people the entrepreneur knows or has met through business acquaintances. These investors, who are called **angels,** are part of the informal risk-capital market, the largest pool of risk capital in the United States. They can't be found in a phone book, and they don't advertise. In fact, their intentions as investors are often well hidden until they decide to make themselves known. They do, however, have several definable characteristics. Angels normally invest between $10,000 and $500,000 and usually focus on first-stage financing—that is, start-up funding or funding of firms younger than five years. They are generally well educated, are often entrepreneurs themselves, and tend to invest within a relatively short distance from home, because they like to be actively involved in their investment. They tend to prefer manufacturing, energy and resources, and service businesses. Retail ventures are less desirable because of their inordinately high rate of failure, but angels with restaurant experience can be found. Today angels are also investing in high-technology firms. They typically look to reap the rewards of their investment within three to seven years. The risk/reward ratio is a function of the age of the firm at the time of investment. Angels may want to earn as much as ten times their original investment if the venture is a start-up, and as much as five times their investment if the venture has been up and running for a couple of years. They find their deals principally through referrals from business associates and tend to make investment decisions more quickly than other sources of capital. Their requirements in terms of documentation, business plan, and due diligence may be lower.

Today, many angels have joined forces to create larger pools of capital. These "bands" of angels have strict rules about how much their members must invest each year and how much time they must spend in exercising due diligence over other members' deals. In some cases, these angel groups look and act like professional venture capitalists. As venture capital pools have grown in size to the point where the deals they engage in are much larger, angels have stepped in to take the deals formerly funded by VCs.

In general, angels are an excellent source of seed or start-up capital. The secret to finding these elusive investors is networking—getting involved in the business community—to come into contact with sources of private capital or people who know these sources: lawyers, bankers, accountants, and other businesspeople. Developing these contacts takes time, so it is important not to wait until the capital is needed before beginning to look for them. Of course, taking on an investor will mean giving up some of the ownership of the company. Therefore, it is probably wise to plan at the outset for a way to let the investor exit. Including a buyout provision with a no-fault separation agreement in the investment contract will ensure that the entrepreneur doesn't have to wait for a criminal act such as fraud to end the relationship. Structuring the buyout to be paid out of earnings over time will avoid jeopardizing the financial health of the business. Above all, it is vital to avoid using personal assets as collateral to protect an angel's investment.

The bottom line on an angel investment is that the angel is investing in the entrepreneur, and it's a very personal investment. Angels often want to experience again the excitement of starting a new venture, but they want to do it vicariously through the entrepreneur. That is why they often fund young entrepreneurs with a lot of enthusiasm, a great idea, and the energy to make it happen. They want to be involved and to mentor the entrepreneur. Like the venture capitalist, they would like to make money, but the real payback is in doing good and helping a novice entrepreneur get his or her start.

Private Placement

Private placement is a way of raising capital from private investors by selling securities in a private corporation or partnership. Securities include common stock, preferred stock, notes, bonds, debentures, voting-trust certificates, certificates of deposit, warrants, options, subscription rights, limited partnership shares, and undivided oil or gas interests. The investors solicited via a private placement memorandum must be aware of the rules of private placement, which are stated in the Securities and Exchange Commission's **Regulation D.** Regulation D was designed to simplify the private offering process and enable the entrepreneur to seek funding from private investors who meet the rule's requirements. Doing a private placement memorandum requires first completing a business plan and a prospectus detailing the risks of the investment.

Just as in the drafting of any complex legal document, it is crucial that the entrepreneur consult an attorney well versed in the preparation of the private placement memorandum and in the disclosure of information about the company and its principals. Problems don't usually arise if the business is successful; however, if the venture fails and the investors uncover a security violation, the entrepreneur and other principal equity holders may lose their protection under the corporate shield and become personally liable in the event of a lawsuit. Security violations have been dealt with severely by the courts, and there is no statute of limitations on the filing of such a suit.

Private placement is a less costly, less time-consuming process than a public offering, and many states now offer standardized, easy-to-fill-out disclosure statements and offering documents. The advantages of a private offering are many. The growing venture is not required to have a great many assets or credit references, which it would need for bank financing, nor does it need a lengthy track record. The entrepreneurs also don't have to file with the Securities and Exchange Commission (SEC). They do, however, have to qualify under the rules of Federal Regulation D, which makes it easier and less expensive for smaller companies to sell stock. Not all states recognize the exemptions under Regulation D in their "Blue Sky" laws (laws that protect investors from fraud), so the issuer of a private placement memorandum may have to register with the state.

The burden is on the issuer to document that the exemption from registration requirements has been met. Therefore, the "sophistication" of all offerees should be examined closely, and the reasons why they qualify should be carefully documented. A sophisticated investor is one who has a net worth of at least $1 million and has taken investment risk in the past. The issuer should number each private placement memorandum and keep a record of who has looked at the memorandum or discussed the offering with the issuer. The memorandum should include a qualifying statement that the contents must not be copied or disclosed to anyone other than the offeree. If an offeree becomes an investor, the issuer should document when and where the offeree examined the books and records of the company. When the offering is complete, the issuer should place in the offering log a memo stating that only those persons listed in the log have been approached about the offering.

Even if the offering qualifies as exempt from registration, it is still subject to the antifraud and civil liability provisions of federal securities laws and state Blue Sky securities laws. Many states have adopted the Small Corporate Offering Registration Form, also called **SCOR U-7,** which makes the registration process much simpler by providing 50 fill-in-the-blank questions that ask for the basic financial, management, and marketing information for the company. A lawyer should be consulted, because some of the adopting states restrict who can use Form U-7.

Within the structure of the corporate private placement, the entrepreneur can sell preferred and common stock, convertible debentures (debt that can be converted to equity), and debt securities with warrants (similar to convertible debentures). Recall that preferred stock has dividend and liquidation preference over common stock, in addition to antidilution protection and other rights as may be specified in a stockholder agreement. Common stock, on the other hand, carries voting rights and preserves the right of the corporation to elect S-corporation status. Convertible debentures are secured or unsecured debt instruments that can be converted to equity at a later date as specified in the agreement. In its debenture form, however, this instrument provides for a fixed rate of return (interest), which can be used as a tax deduction. Debt securities with warrants give the holder the right to purchase stock at a fixed price for a specified term. Purchasing common stock under this instrument does not invalidate the preferred position of the debt holder as creditor.

Strategic Alliances

A partnership with another business—whether formal or informal—is a strategic alliance. Through strategic alliances, entrepreneurs can structure deals with suppliers or customers that will help reduce expenditures for marketing, raw materials, or research and development (R&D). Reducing expenditures increases cash flow, providing capital that wouldn't otherwise have been available.

One type of strategic alliance is the R&D limited partnership. This vehicle is useful for entrepreneurs starting high-tech ventures that carry significant risk due to the expense of research and development. The limited partnership contracts with the new venture to provide the funding for the R&D to develop a market technology that will ultimately be profitable to the partnership. This is advantageous for both the limited partner and the new venture. Limited partners are able to deduct their investment in the R&D contract and enjoy the tax advantages of losses in the early years on their personal tax returns; they also share in any future profits. In the R&D limited partnership, the new venture acts as a general partner to develop the technology and then structures a license agreement with the R&D partner whereby the venture can use the technology to develop other products. Often the limited partnership's interest becomes stock in a new corporation formed to commercialize the new technology.

An alternative to this arrangement is an agreement to pay royalties to the partnership. Yet another vehicle is the formation of a joint venture, which allows the entrepreneur to purchase the joint venture interest after a specific period of time or when the company reaches a certain volume in sales. As in the private placement, it is important to work through an attorney. The new venture may incur significant costs in creating the partnership, a process that could take up to a year. In addition, giving up sole ownership of the technology may be too high a price to pay if the partnership does not survive.

Strategic alliances are discussed further in Chapter 17, where growing a company is considered.

Small Business Investment Companies

Small business investment companies (SBICs) are actually privately managed venture capital firms licensed by the Small Business Administration. They get financing at very favorable rates, in partnership with the federal government, to invest through equity (generally preferred stock or debt with warrants) and long-term debt in small and growing businesses.

Companies that qualify for SBIC financing should have a net worth under $18 million and average after-tax earnings of less than $6 million during the previous two years. The typical deal involves a loan with options to buy equity, a convertible debenture (debt that can be converted to equity). Preferred stock, which pays the investor back first in the event of a failure, is sometimes used for first-round financing.

Grants

The **Small Business Innovation Development Act of 1982** was designed to stimulate technological innovation by small businesses in the United States. It requires that all federal agencies with research and development budgets in excess of $100 million give a portion of their budgets to technology-based small businesses in the form of Small Business Innovative Research (SBIR) grants. Small businesses find out about these grants by checking the published solicitations by the agencies to see whether they can qualify by providing what the agency needs. Grants have three phases. Phase I is the concept stage and feasibility phase, which provides $50,000 to $100,000 for an initial feasibility study to determine the scientific merit of the proposed idea. This amount is made available for six months. If results are promising, the company is eligible for Phase II funding. Phase II provides up to an additional $200,000 to $750,000 for two years, for the firm to pursue the innovation and develop a well-defined product or process. Phase III brings in private sector funds to commercialize the new technology.

To qualify for an SBIR grant, the company must employ fewer than 500 people, be at least 51 percent independently owned by a U.S. citizen, be technology-based, be organized for profit, and not be dominant in its field. The grant holder must perform two-thirds of the Phase I effort and one-half of the Phase II effort. At least half of the principal investigator's time must be spent working in the small business.

Venture Capital Institutes and Networks

Many areas of the country offer access to venture capital networks through institutes established on the campuses of major universities. The university acts as a conduit through which the entrepreneurs and investors are matched; it neither assumes any liability for nor has any ownership interest in either the new venture or the investor's company. The entrepreneur typically pays a fee, in the range of $200 to $500, and submits a business plan to the institute. The plan is then matched to the needs of private investors in the database who subscribe to the service. If an investor is interested in the business concept, he or she contacts the entrepreneur. In general, venture capital networks are a way for entrepreneurs to gain access to investors whom they may not be able to find through other channels. Furthermore, the investors have chosen to place their names in the database, so they are actively looking for potential investments.

Financing with Debt

When an entrepreneur chooses a debt instrument to finance a portion of start-up expenses, he or she typically provides a business or personal asset as collateral in exchange for a loan bearing a market rate of interest. The asset could be equipment, inventory, real estate, or the entrepreneur's house or car. Although it is best to avoid pledging personal assets as collateral for a loan, it's sometimes unavoidable, because banks generally require first-time entrepreneurs to guarantee loans personally. There are several sources of debt financing.

Commercial Banks

Banks are not normally a readily available source of either working capital or seed capital to fund a start-up venture. Banks are highly regulated; their loan portfolios are scrutinized carefully, and they are told in no uncertain terms not to make loans that have any significant degree of risk. Banks like to see a track record of positive cash flow, because it is out of this cash flow that their loan will be repaid. Unfortunately, new ventures don't *have* a track record, so an unsecured loan is probably not possible.

Generally, banks make loans on the basis of what are termed the five C's: character, capacity, capital, collateral, and condition. In the case of the entrepreneur, the first two—character and capacity—become the leading consideration, because the new business's performance estimates are based purely on forecasts. Therefore, the bank will probably consider the entrepreneur's personal history carefully. However difficult, it is important for the new venture to establish a lending relationship with a bank. This may mean starting with a very small, secured loan and demonstrating the ability to repay in a timely fashion. Bankers also look more favorably on ventures with hard assets that are readily convertible to cash.

Commercial Finance Companies

As banks have tightened their lending requirements, commercial finance companies have stepped in to fill the gap. They are able to do this because they are not so heavily regulated, and they base their decisions on the quality of the assets of the business. Thus they are often termed asset-based lenders or hard asset lenders. They do, however, charge more than banks, as much as 5 percent over prime, at rates more similar to those charged by credit card companies. Therefore, the entrepreneur must weigh the costs and benefits of taking on such an expensive loan. Of course, in cases where starting the business or not starting it, or surviving in the short term or failing to survive, depends on that loan, the cost may not seem so great.

Factoring, one of the oldest forms of banking, accounts for more than $1 trillion a year in credit. Factoring is a particular type of receivable financing wherein the lender, called the factor, takes ownership of a receivable at a discount and then collects against it. When the U.S. military needed machinery to create the infrastructure in Afghanistan after the invasion, it turned to one of its major contractors, IAP Worldwide Services, which specializes in logistics. But IAP had to purchase the goods the government needed and meet payroll before it would be paid from the order. IAP turned to a factor to get the cash it needed to serve its customer.[15]

Factoring has become a popular form of cash management in smaller businesses that sell to big companies. Large companies are notorious for paying extremely slowly, which can wreak havoc with an entrepreneur's cash flow. But a small business that sells to Wal-Mart can't afford not to be patient with the giant, because that account is probably very important to it. Therefore, it sells some of those receivables to a factor in order not to interrupt its cash flow. Factors know that Wal-Mart will eventually pay, so there is little risk to them of taking on the receivable. In fact, Wal-Mart has helped to grow the factor industry significantly.

Entrepreneurs should make sure that any factor they use is a member of the Commercial Finance Association, which is the major trade group for the industry. They should also have an attorney verify the authenticity and background of the factor. In general, taking out a bank loan is less expensive than using a factor.

Small Business Administration Loan

When a traditional commercial bank loan does not appear to be a viable option, the entrepreneur may want to consider an SBA-guaranteed loan. In 2004, the SBA backed more than $12.3 billion in loans to small businesses. With an SBA-guaranteed loan, the entrepreneur applies for a loan of up to $2 million from his or her bank, and the SBA guarantees that it will repay up to 75 percent of the loan to the commercial lender (generally a bank) should the business default. This guarantee increases the borrower's chances of getting a loan. A further incentive to banks is that SBA-funded ventures tend to be growth-oriented and have a higher survival rate than other start-ups. Of course, because the government backs these loans, the documentation and paperwork are extensive, and interest rates are usually no different than those paid on a conventional loan.

The Small Business Administration also has a program called the micro loan that makes it easier for entrepreneurs with limited access to capital to borrow small amounts (up to $35,000). Instead of using banks, as in their guarantee program, the SBA uses nonprofit community development corporations.

State-Funded Venture Capital

Many states provide a range of services to help new and growing ventures. From venture capital funds to tax incentives, states such as Massachusetts, New York, and Oregon are seeing the value of establishing business development programs. New and growing ventures usually receive their funding from the state government, which enables them to seek larger investment amounts from private sources. In states where equity funding is not available, there is typically a loan program aimed at new ventures. In Massachusetts, for example, favorable debt financing is often exchanged for warrants to purchase stock in the new company. Pennsylvania was the first to create a funding program aimed at minority-owned businesses.

Profile 15.2 INTERNET BUSINESSES CAN STILL BE HOT

It seems that in the world of the Internet, things move from one extreme to the other. Before 2000, everyone was proclaiming that the Internet would change the way business was done forever—that if you didn't jump on the bandwagon and start an Internet business, you would be left behind. Then after 2000, you couldn't get money for an Internet venture because, with the e-commerce crash, we learned that fundamental economic principles still hold and you have to solve a real pain to get customers.

Dany Levy, journalist turned entrepreneur, knew that fundamental truth, and in late 1999, when she started her Internet business— DailyCandy—she did it because the market was telling her that busy people wanted to know what was "hip" on any particular day in clothes, restaurant openings, books, and so forth, but they didn't have the time to weed through all the Internet sites. DailyCandy could do that for them. Furthermore, if she could build a subscriber base for her lifestyle e-mails, advertisers would want to have a presence on her site and to be included in the daily e-mails that went out to her subscribers.

It was Levy's experience at *New York* magazine, and later at *Self* magazine, that gave her expertise in style. Combining that with what she loved best about the Internet, its immediacy, and she had a business concept. Levy, like many other entrepreneurs, believed in being frugal and in bootstrapping her way to success. Working from a desk in a friend's office, she began contacting all her journalist friends about DailyCandy and asking them to forward the e-mails to their friends. Before she ever officially launched the business, she had 700 subscribers in hand. It took the business only a year and a half to become profitable.

Levy believes that one reason why she has been successful where other Internet ventures have failed is that she did not spend a lot of money. She actually turned down a venture capital offer because she didn't want to give up control of her company. She also chose wisely among ways to grow her business. At one point, she considered expanding to London until she realized that it would be very difficult to run a company over three time zones—east coast, west coast, and Europe. In addition, no one on the staff had international experience. Instead, she focused on making her customers, the advertisers, succeed. For example, when she wrote about the Silk Day Spa in New York City, it received more than 15,000 visits to its website and 400 bookings in about three days. This kind of power brings with it responsibility, and Levy is mindful of that. She makes sure that everything DailyCandy produces is high-quality.

Sources: B. Gossage. "How I Did It with Dany Levy," *Inc. Magazine* (February 2004), www.inc.com; DailyCandy, www.dailycandy.com; and J. Rosen, "DailyCandy Offers Some Sweet News," *The Heights* (January 22, 2002), www.bcheights.com.

Incubators

There is no doubt that after the dot com debacles and subsequent drop in the value of technology stocks, the incubators that spawned a rash of Internet businesses have fallen on hard times. **Incubators** are places where start-up ventures can get space and support for the early stages of start-up. Because of the dot com implosion, the term *incubator* has developed such a negative connotation that Idealab, one of the first companies to popularize the for-profit incubator concept, has stopped referring to itself as an incubator.[16] And not only is the name under attack, but the very concept of the incubator as well. In the beginning, incubators were nonprofit organizations designed to help nascent businesses get up and running so that their chances of survival in the marketplace would be enhanced. But the new for-profit incubators seem designed to produce concept deals rather than technology deals with real value.

Entrepreneurs starting new businesses—Internet or otherwise—should examine incubators with caution. See Chapter 12 for some suggestions on what to look for in an incubator.

Customers and Suppliers

Many entrepreneurs neglect to consider one of the largest and most accessible sources of funding—their customers and suppliers. The reason why these two groups are more accessible than many other types of financing is that they are colleagues in the same industry; they understand the entrepreneur's business and have a vested interest in seeing the entrepreneur succeed. Suppliers and customers can grant extended payment terms or offer special terms favorable to the business. In return, the entrepreneur's business can provide such things as faster delivery, price breaks, and other benefits.

Starting a business takes preparation, particularly when outside capital is required. But a successful launch can lead to additional sources of funding for growth, the subject of Chapter 16.

New Venture Checklist

Have you:

☐ Considered how many personal resources you have to help fund the new venture?

☐ Determined ways to bootstrap the start-up of the new venture?

☐ Networked to come in contact with potential "angels"?

☐ Identified an attorney who can help structure a private placement agreement if needed?

☐ Investigated the sources of debt financing in the community?

Issues to Consider

ACE

business.college.hmco.com/students

Self-tests

1. How does bootstrap financing fit into the strategic plan of a new venture?
2. What is the role of angels as a source of new venture funding?
3. At what stage of venture development do venture capitalists typically become involved, and why?
4. Why are commercial banks not usually a reliable source of new venture financing?
5. Why should a private offering be used as a capital-raising vehicle before a public offering is used?

Experiencing Entrepreneurship

1. Define a venture concept that interests you. Then develop a timeline and financial strategy for the start-up of the venture.

2. Interview an angel or a banker to learn what his or her expectations are when reviewing business plans for new ventures.

Additional Sources of Information

Amis, D., and H. Stevenson (2001). *Winning Angels: The Seven Fundamentals of Early-Stage Investing.* London: Financial Times/Prentice-Hall.

Kawasaki, G. (2004) *The Art of the Start.* New York: Penguin Group.

Long, M. (2000). *Financing the New Venture.* Holbrook, MA: Adams Media Corporation.

Robinson, R.J., and M. Van Osnabrugge (2000). *Angel Investing: Matching Startup Funds with Startup Companies.* New York: Jossey-Bass.

Relevant Case Studies

Case 1 Overnite Express, p. 402
Case 3 Beanos Ice Cream Shoppe, p. 410

Case 4 Wizards of the Coast, p. 423
Case 7 Linksys, p. 446

Part Four

Planning for Growth and Change

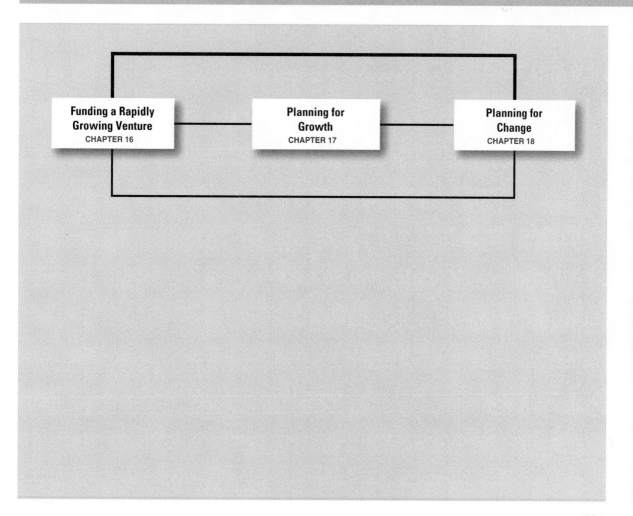

Funding a Rapidly Growing Venture
CHAPTER 16

Planning for Growth
CHAPTER 17

Planning for Change
CHAPTER 18

16

Funding a Rapidly Growing Venture

"Growth is directly proportionate to promises made: profit is inversely proportionate to promise kept."

John Peers, President, Logical Machine Corporation, 1979

LEARNING OBJECTIVES

■ Discuss the cost and process of raising capital.

■ Explain the role of the venture capital market.

■ Describe the process associated with the initial public offering.

■ Discuss how to grow with strategic alliances.

■ Explain ways to value a business.

Profile 16.1 A GROWTH MODEL FOR PONDS

Greg Wittstock may be the only person in the United States to have spent his life in and around ponds and then to have found a way to revolutionize the water garden industry by creating an innovative business model and growth strategy. At the age of twelve, at his Wheaton, Illinois, home, Wittstock built his first pond out of concrete to contain his pet turtles, which had outgrown their aquarium. The pond employed a modified garbage can and cattle trough that served as makeshift pond filters. Unfortunately, the pond leaked and turned green; it eventually sent his turtles scrambling for safer shelter. That first exercise in water gardens became a hobby that turned into a career and a multimillion-dollar business.

Every summer until he reached college age, Wittstock and his father worked on refining and improving their backyard pond, trying different filtration systems, pumps, and construction methods. In the summer of 1990, they thought they had finally built the best pond possible. Wittstock had completed his sophomore year at Ohio State and was working for the summer at a subsidiary of Union Carbide, where his father was an engineer. Wittstock didn't enjoy his job, but what else could he do? And then it hit him. He could start a pond-building business; that was something he knew well and loved doing. For Christmas that year, his parents gave him a wheelbarrow and a shovel, which served as the first investment in his emerging business, Aquascape Designs.

Placing ads in the classifieds and leaving business cards at strategic suppliers, Wittstock managed to secure contracts for more than 17 ponds. In the summer of 1992, when a article about his fledging company appeared on the front page of the *Chicago Tribune*'s Tempo section one Sunday, his phone starting ringing off the hook. That one article generated 81 orders, more than he could handle alone.

By that time, Wittstock's father had left Union Carbide and started a struggling engineering consulting firm. He decided to come on board to help his son manage the demand. With just the two of them doing the work, it was important to create efficiencies immediately so that every order would be filled on schedule. One of these efficiencies was the 20/20 rule—a way to reduce construction time by having all materials at the site before the job began. It was at this time that Wittstock also hired his first employee to implement the one-day pond-building technique without him.

But the full potential to grow this business emerged when Wittstock met an Arthur Andersen consultant who helped him understand how to leverage his hands-on knowledge of pond building to reach the broader consumer market. At first Wittstock tried franchising, but when that failed, he decided that instead of selling his knowledge, he would give it away by teaching landscapers how to make money building water gardens.

Over the next few years, as the business grew, Wittstock and his father quarreled about how to run the business. Although they had worked together for ten years, in the end their views of the business differed significantly. Eventually, Wittstock bought out his father for $184,000, and to Wittstock's chagrin, his father became his first real competitor with a company he founded in 1997 called Pond Supplies of America. But Aquascape was on the fast track, and every year from 1995 to 2003, its revenues doubled. In 2003, Aquascape did $45 million in sales. The focus of the company shifted to the design and marketing of pond-building equipment, and Aquascape invested more money in research and development. One of Aquascape's chief competitive advantages is its no-back-orders policy. Parts are always available when a landscaper needs them. Another is its traveling training program, along with its publishing and video division. In March of 1999, Wittstock completed a 57-city tour of sold-out seminars, and although he no longer does the seminars himself, he is often seen attending them and biting his tongue to resist putting in his two cents.

In January of 2003, Aquascape acquired its major competitor, Water Creations. This surprised everyone, because for years Aquascape had denounced this competitor and its products. But the acquisition was strategic. Wittstock wanted to capture the do-it-yourself market that was Water Creation's focus. With ponds and water gardens now being the fastest-growing segment of the lawn and garden industry, Wittstock has room to grow. Today the company has over 130 employees, serves more than 35,000 customers, and has been on the Inc. 500 list three times.

Too often, companies try to raise money to grow when what they really need to do is figure out how to operate more efficiently. Wittstock lets his employees know where they stand in the business and what they contribute to its profitability. If an employee wants to make a certain salary, that employee is given the amount in new sales that she

or he will have to generate to cover that salary. Wittstock is also adamant about getting estimates right. Often companies will submit a bid to win a contract and never check to see that the contract will actually cover the costs of doing the job. Teaching business financials to landscapers who buy from him is one of the goals of Wittstock's training program. Wittstock's passion for the pond business and his innate understanding of its operations have made it possible for Aquascape to grow substantially. Expectations are that it will outshine its competitors for the foreseeable future.

Sources: B. Burlingham, "Building a Marketing Juggernaut," *Inc. Magazine* (November 2003), p. 58; AquascapeDesigns, "About Us," www.aquascapedesigns.com; and "Aquascape Designs Expands," *Pool & Spa News* (February 28, 2003), www.findarticles.com.

The natural by-product of a successful start-up is growth. But growth is costly and often puts an enormous strain on the already sparse resources of the young venture. Typically, to meet significant demand, the new company will need additional capital beyond any internal cash flows. Growth capital, or second-round financing, consists of those funds needed to take the venture out of the start-up phase and move it toward becoming a market presence. To the extent that the entrepreneur has met the sales and earnings targets estimated in the start-up business plan, available financing choices increase substantially when growth financing, or second-round financing, is sought.

The fact that more choices are available is important because, normally, the amount of money needed to grow the business is significantly greater than that required to start the business. One exception is high-tech companies that incur considerable research and development costs prior to start-up. This type of company may spend millions of dollars and accrue several years of losses before its first sale. It may also go through several rounds of financing and grants before it has something to sell to customers.

Most venture capital today is still going to biotechnology, software, and other high-technology ventures, but in general, the best companies in any industry have the easiest time finding capital from any source. Being one of the "best" companies requires having an excellent track record (however short), a sound management team, a potential for high growth, and a plan for investor exit with an excellent rate of return on the money invested. Investors in growth companies typically will not go into a situation where their new money is paying off old debt or where cash flow is poor. They want to know that the infrastructure is in place, sales are increasing, and the growing venture needs capital only to take it to the next stage.

The Cost and Process of Raising Capital

Make no mistake about it, raising growth capital is a time-consuming and costly process. For this reason, many entrepreneurs choose to grow slowly instead, depending exclusively on internal cash flows to fund growth. They have a basic fear of debt and of giving up, to investors, any control of or equity in the company. Unfortunately, they may act so conservatively that they actually stifle growth.

Raising Money Takes Time

It's important that entrepreneurs understand the nature of raising money so that their expectations will not be unreasonable. The first thing to understand about raising growth capital (or any capital, for that matter) is that it will invariably take at least twice as long as expected before the money is actually in the company's bank account. Consider the task of raising a substantial amount of money—several million dollars, for instance. It can take up to several months to find the financing, several more months for the potential investor or lender to do "due diligence" and say yes, and then up to six more months to receive the money. In other words, if an entrepreneur doesn't look for funding until it's needed, it will be too late. Moreover, because this search for capital takes the entrepreneur away from the business just when he or she is needed most, it is helpful to use financial advisers who have experience in raising money, and it is vital to have a good management team in place.

The second thing to understand about raising growth capital is that the chosen financial source may not complete the deal, even after months of courting and negotiations. It's essential, therefore, to continue to look for backup investors in case the original investor backs out.

Another point about second-round investors is that they often request to buy out the first-round funding sources, who could be friends or family, because they feel the first-round investors have nothing more to contribute to the business and they no longer want to deal with them. This can be a very awkward situation, because the second-round funder has nothing to lose by demanding the buyout and can easily walk away from the deal; there are thousands more out there.

It Takes Money to Make Money

It truly does take money to make money. The costs incurred before investor or bank money is received must be paid by the entrepreneur, whereas the costs of maintaining the capital (accounting and legal expenses) can often be paid from the proceeds of the loan or (in the case of investment capital) from the proceeds of a sale or internally generated cash flow.

If the business plan and financial statements have been kept up-to-date since the start of the business, a lot of money can be saved during the search for growth capital. When large amounts of capital are sought, however, growth capital funding sources prefer that financials have the approval of a financial consultant or investment banker, someone who regularly works with investors. This person is an expert in preparing loan and investment packages that are attractive to potential funding sources. A CPA will prepare the business's financial statements and work closely with

Socially Responsible Entrepreneurship

Venture Capital for Social Responsibility

Lewis Buchner needed to raise money to launch a new product line for his furniture manufacturing company, Vida. Buchner didn't want to take on any debt, however, and equity didn't seem like an option, because his was a very low-tech business and the company would never experience the rapid growth necessary to attract venture capital. Even so, in five months Buchner managed to raise $250,000 from Silicon Valley Community Ventures (SVCV), a firm that focuses on low-income communities in the San Francisco Bay area. SVCV took a 6 percent equity stake in the business.

SVCV is a unique type of firm that looks for both a monetary and an altruistic return on its investment—also known as a "double bottom line." The altruistic return is in the form of a benefit to the local community, such as jobs for unskilled workers and opportunities for women and minorities. What attracted SVCV to Vida was Vida's commitment to training blue-collar workers and to sustainable forestry. In addition to the money, Buchner gained access to SVCV's advisory service, which includes volunteer executives with experience in a variety of business areas. As a result, Buchner's company was able to take on major projects such as the San Francisco Public Library, the San Francisco International Airport, and many Fortune 500 offices.

Community development investment funds are a good way for companies that would otherwise be overlooked by the equity markets to gain access to capital.

Sources: K. O'Sullivan, "Capital: The Bucks in Your Backyard," *Inc. Magazine* (April 2002), www.inc.com; and Center for Environmental Health, www.cehca.org.

the financial consultant. All these activities result in costs to the entrepreneur. In addition, when equity capital is sought, a prospectus or offering document will be required, and preparing it calls for legal expertise and often has significant printing costs. Then there are the expenses of marketing the offering. Such things as advertising, travel, and brochures can become quite costly.

In addition to the up-front costs of seeking growth capital, there are "back-end" costs when the entrepreneur seeks capital by selling securities (shares of stock in the corporation). These costs can include investment banking fees, legal fees, marketing costs, brokerage fees, and various other fees charged by state and federal authorities. The cost of raising equity capital can go as high as 25 percent of the total amount of money sought. Add to that the interest or return on investment paid to the funding source(s), and it's easy to see why it costs money to raise money.

The Venture Capital Market

Private venture capital companies have been the bedrock of many high-growth ventures, particularly in the computer, software, biotechnology, and telecommunications industries. Because venture capitalists rarely invest in start-up ventures outside the high-tech arena, the growth stage of a new venture is where most entrepreneurs consider approaching them. Waiting until this stage is advantageous to the entrepreneur, because using venture capital in the start-up phase can mean giving up significant control.

Venture capital is, quite simply, a pool of money managed by professionals. These professionals usually assume the role of general partner and are paid a management fee plus a percentage of the gain from any investments. The venture capital firm takes an equity position through ownership of stock in the company. It also normally requires a seat on the board of directors and brings its professional management skills to the new venture in an advisory capacity.

The ability of an entrepreneur to secure classic venture capital funding depends not only on what the entrepreneur brings to the table but also on the status of the venture capital industry. PricewaterhouseCoopers, Thomson Venture Economics, and the National Venture Capital Association have joined forces to track total venture capital investing in the United States. They report that at the historical peak in 2000, the height of the dot com/technology boom, VC investing was at $105,785 billion. By the end of 2003, it had plunged to $18,330 billion (Figure 16.1). Although that is certainly a drastic decline in investment activity, it is clear from

---

FIGURE 16.1 **Venture Capital Investment**

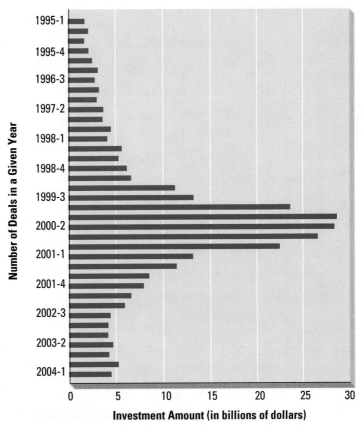

Source: PricewaterhouseCoopers, Thomson Venture Economics, and the National Venture Capital Association, *The Money Tree Survey,* 2004, http://www.pwcmoneytree.com/moneytree/index.jsp.

Figure 16.1 that $18 billion invested in 2,800 deals is closer to the historical norm for venture capital investment, so it may be considered a return to normal from an aberrant period. Many would say that the recent trend is a healthy return to investment rates that prevailed before the dot com boom and bust. Fewer deals are being made, but those that are made are likely to fund well-conceived business concepts with solid business models. In fact, historically, difficult economic times have spawned about great companies such as Compaq Computer in the early 1980s and Palm Computing and Starbucks in the early 1990s. All in all, now is a fairly good time for early-stage investment for growth.

Figure 16.2 presents venture capital investments by industry for the first quarter of 2004. Clearly, software and biomedical technology dominated the investment focus. The next biggest category was computer-related technologies. These results support the general notion that venture capital is narrowly focused on high technology in very specific sectors.

FIGURE 16.2   VC Investment by Industry, Q1 2004

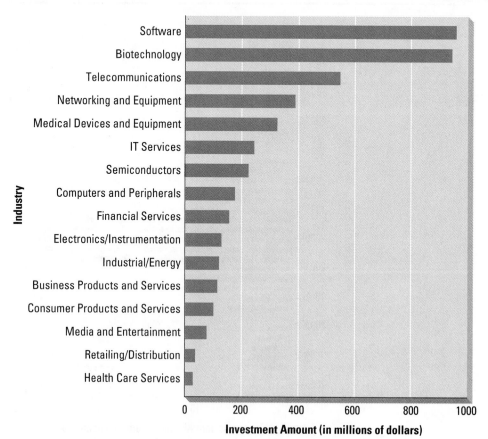

Source: PricewaterhouseCoopers, Thomson Venture Economics, and the National Venture Capital Association, *The Money Tree Survey,* 2004, http://www.pwcmoneytree.com/moneytree/index.jsp.

The Sequence of Events in Securing Venture Capital

To determine whether venture capital is the right type of funding for a growing venture, the entrepreneur must understand the goals and motivations of venture capitalists, for these dictate the potential success or failure of the attempt. The venture capital company invests in a growing business through the use of debt and equity instruments to achieve long-term appreciation on the investment within a specified period of time, typically three to five years. By definition, this goal is often different from that of the entrepreneur, who usually looks at the business in a much longer frame of reference. The venture capitalist also seeks varying rates of return, depending on the risk involved. An early-stage investment, for example, characteristically demands a higher rate of return, as much as a 50 percent or greater annual cash-on-cash return, whereas a later-stage investment demands a lower rate of return, perhaps 30 percent annually. Depending on the timeframe for cash-out, the VC will expect capital gains multiples of 5 to 20 times the initial investment. Very simply, as the level of risk increases, so does the demand for a higher rate of return, as depicted in Figure 16.3. This relationship is not surprising. Older, more established companies have a longer track record on which to base predictions about the future, so normal business cycles and sales patterns have been identified, and the company is usually in a better position to respond through experience to a dynamic environment. Consequently, investing in a mature firm does not command the high rate of return that investing in a high-growth start-up does.

Usually the first thing venture capitalists look at when scrutinizing a potential investment candidate is the management team, to see whether experienced people with a good track record are in place and able to take the company to the next level of growth. In addition to experience, venture capitalists are looking for commitment to the company and to growth, because they recognize that growing a company requires an enormous amount of time and effort on the part of the management team. Once they have determined that the management team is solid, they look at

---

FIGURE 16.3   **Risk versus Rate of Return**

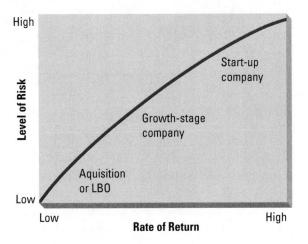

the product and the market to see whether the opportunity is substantial and whether the product enjoys a unique or innovative position in the marketplace. Product uniqueness, especially if protected through intellectual-property rights, helps create entry barriers in the market, commands higher prices, and adds value to the business.

The other major factor is the potential for significant growth and the amount of growth possible, because it is from the consequent appreciation in the value of the business that the venture capitalist will derive the required return on investment. The venture capitalist weighs that potential for growth against the risk of failure and the cost of achieving the growth projected. Therefore, when negotiating with venture capitalists, entrepreneurs should have a good sense of the value of the business, a topic discussed at the end of this chapter.

Armed with an understanding of what venture capitalists are looking for, the entrepreneur is prepared to begin the search for a company that meets his or her needs. Because the venture capital community is fairly close-knit, at least within regions of the country, it is wise not to "shop" the business plan around looking for the best deal. It is important to do some research on the local venture capital firms to determine whether any specialize in the particular industry or type of business that the entrepreneur is growing. Getting recommendations from attorneys and

---

SCREENSHOT 16.1   Mid-Atlantic Venture Association

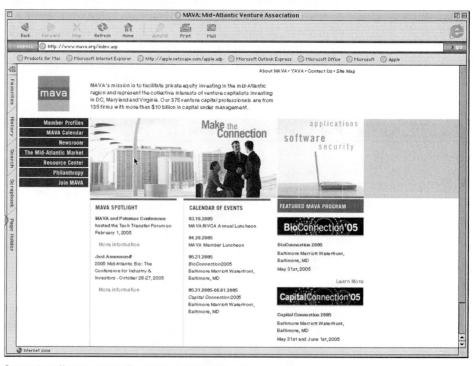

Source: http://www.mava.org/index.asp, accessed 9/2/04.

accountants who regularly deal with business investments is an excellent way to find these VC firms. In fact, the best way to approach venture capitalists is through a referral from someone who knows the VC.

Once a venture capital company has been chosen, stay with that company unless and until it becomes apparent that the deal will not work. Under no circumstances should the entrepreneur be talking with two companies at the same time. The venture capital community is small and negotiating with two VC companies at once may well leave the unwise entrepreneur with no firm wanting to invest.

The venture capital company will no doubt ask for a copy of the business plan with an executive summary. The executive summary is a screening device—if it can't be immediately determined that the entrepreneurial team's qualifications are outstanding, the product concept innovative, and the projections of growth and return on investment realistic, the company officials will not bother to read the rest of the business plan.

On the other hand, if they like what they see in the plan, they will probably request a meeting to determine whether the entrepreneurial team can deliver what they project. This may or may not call for a formal presentation of the business by the entrepreneur. During this meeting, the initial terms of an agreement may be discussed, but the entrepreneur's team should not be too eager to discuss issues such as owner compensation until the venture capitalist indicates that a deal is imminent. It is also very important not to hype the business concept or make claims that can't be substantiated. Venture capitalists have literally seen it all, and they recognize puffery the moment they hear it. Any potential negative aspects, however, should be disclosed and ways to deal with them proposed.

If the meeting goes well, the next step is due diligence—that is, the venture capital firm has its own team of experts check out the entrepreneurial team and the business thoroughly. If the venture capitalists are still sold on the business, they draw up legal documents to detail the nature and terms of the investment and declare that "the check is in the mail." Entrepreneurs should not expect to receive it immediately, however. Some venture capitalists wait until they know they have a satisfactory investment before putting together a partnership to fund the investment. Others just have a lengthy process for releasing money from the firm.

The money is typically released in stages linked to agreed-upon goals. Also realize that the venture capital firm will continue to monitor the progress of the new venture and probably will want a seat or several seats on the board of directors, depending on its equity stake in the company, to ensure that it has a say in the direction the new venture takes.

Capital Structure

It may seem that the entrepreneur is totally at the mercy of the venture capitalist. That, unfortunately, is true if the entrepreneur enters the negotiation from a weak position, desperately needing the money to keep the business alive. A better approach is to go into the negotiation from a position of strength. True, venture capitalists have hundreds of deals presented to them on a regular basis, but most of those deals are not big hits; in other words, the return on the investment is not worth their effort. They are always looking for that one business that will achieve high growth and thus will return enough on their investment to make up for all the average- or mediocre-performing investments in their portfolio. If the entrepreneur enters the negotiation with a business that has a solid record of growth and performance, he or she is in a good position to call many of the shots.

Any investment deal has four components:

1. The amount of money to be invested
2. The timing and use of the investment moneys
3. The return on investment to investors
4. The level of risk involved

The way these components are defined will affect the new venture for a long time, not only in constructing its growth strategy but also in formulating an exit strategy for the investors.

Venture capitalists often want both equity and debt—equity because it gives them an ownership interest in the business, and debt because they will be paid back more quickly. Consequently, they tend to want redeemable preferred stock or debentures so that if the company does well, they can convert to common stock, and if the company does poorly or fails, they will be the first to be repaid their investment. If the entrepreneur has entered the negotiation from a position of strength, he or she is more likely to be able to convince them to take common stock, which makes things much easier. In another scenario, the venture capitalists may want a combination of debentures (debt) and warrants, which allow them to purchase common stock at a nominal rate later on. If this strategy is implemented correctly, they may be able to get their entire investment back when the debt portion is repaid and still enjoy the appreciation in the value of the business as stockholders.

There are several other provisions that venture capitalists often request to protect their investment. One is an antidilution provision, which ensures that the selling of stock at a later date will not decrease the economic value of the venture capitalist's investment. In other words, the price of stock sold at a later date should be equal to or greater than the price at which the venture capitalist could buy the common stock on a conversion from a warrant or debenture.

In addition, to guard against having paid too much for an interest in the company, the VC may request a forfeiture provision. This means that if the company does not achieve its projected performance goals, the founders may be required to give up some of their stock to the VC as a penalty.[1] The forfeited stock increases the VC's equity in the company and may even be given to new management that the VC brings on board to steer the company in a new direction. Entrepreneurs should never accept these terms unless they are confident of their abilities and commitment to the venture. One way to mitigate this situation is for the entrepreneur to request stock bonuses as a reward for meeting or exceeding performance projections.

Venture capital is certainly an important source of funding for the entrepreneur with a high-growth venture. It is, however, only one source, and with the advice of experts, the entrepreneur should consider all other possible avenues. The best choice is one that gives the new venture the chance to reach its potential and the investors or financial backers an excellent return on investment.

The Initial Public Offering (IPO)

Making the **initial public offering,** or "going public," is the goal of many companies because it is an exciting way to raise large amounts of money for growth that probably couldn't be raised from other sources. However, deciding whether to do a public offering is difficult at best, because doing so sets in motion a series of events that will change the business and the relationship of the entrepreneur to the business forever. Moreover, returning to private status once the company has been a public company is an almost insurmountable task.

An initial public offering is just a more complex version of a private offering, in which the founders and equity shareholders of the company agree to sell a portion of the company (via previously unissued stocks and bonds) to the public by filing with the Securities and Exchange Commission and listing their stock on one of the stock exchanges. All the proceeds of the IPO go to the company in a primary offering. If the owners of the company subsequently sell their shares of stock, the proceeds go to the owners in what is termed a secondary distribution. Often the two events occur in combination, but an offering is far less attractive when a large percentage of the proceeds is destined for the owners, because that clearly signals a lack of commitment on the part of the owners to the future success of the business.

Advantages and Disadvantages of Going Public

The principal advantage of a public offering is that it provides the offering company with a tremendous source of interest-free capital for growth and expansion, paying off debt, or product development. With the IPO comes the future option of additional offerings once the company is well known and has a positive track record. A public company has more prestige and clout in the marketplace, so it becomes easier to form alliances and negotiate deals with suppliers, customers, and creditors. It is also easier for the founders to harvest the rewards of their efforts by selling off a portion of their stock or borrowing against it. Research reveals that the median ownership percentage of officers and directors in public companies declines in the decade following an IPO, from about 68 percent to 18 percent.[2] In addition, restricted stock and stock options can be used to attract new employees and reward existing employees.

There are, however, some serious disadvantages to the public offering. Since 1980, more than 9,000 companies have completed initial public offerings, raising a total of $450 billion. Recent research conducted by Peristiani and Hong for the Federal Reserve Bank of New York found that in the two-decade period from 1980 to 2000, there was a dramatic decline in the pre-IPO financial condition of issuers, as well as a significant rise in the failure rate of issuers after the offering.[3] In general, those firms that undertook an IPO with negative earnings (many such cases occurred in the later part of the 1990s) were three times more likely to be dropped from a stock exchange than their profitable counterparts. In fact, 2001 saw an unprecedented 3.8 percent of all publicly traded stocks dropped from the major stock exchanges.[4] A public offering is a very expensive process. Whereas a private offering can cost about $100,000, a public offering can run well over $300,000, a figure that does not include a 7–10 percent commission to the underwriter, which compensates the investment bank that sells the securities. One way to prevent a financial disaster should the offering fail is to ask for stop-loss statements from lawyers, accountants, consultants, and investment bankers. The stop-loss statement is essentially a promise not to charge the full fee if the offering fails.

Going public is enormously time-consuming. Entrepreneurs report that they spend the better part of every week on issues related to the offering over a four- to six-month period.[5] Part of this time is devoted to learning about the process, which is much more complex than this chapter can express. One way many entrepreneurs deal with the knowledge gap is by spending the year prior to the offering preparing for it by talking with others who have gone through the process, reading, and putting together the team that will see the company through it. Another way to speed up the process is to start running the private corporation like a public corporation from the beginning—that is, doing audited financial statements and keeping good records.

A public offering means that everything the company does or has becomes public information subject to the scrutiny of anyone interested in the company. A shift in company control makes the CEO of a public company responsible primarily to the shareholders and only secondarily to anyone else. The entrepreneur/CEO, who before the offering probably owned the lion's share of the stock, may no longer have a controlling portion of the outstanding stock (if he or she agreed to an offering that resulted in the loss of control), and the stock that he or she does own can lose value if the company's value on the stock exchange drops, an event that can occur through no fault of the company's performance. Macro-economic events, such as world events and domestic economic policy, can adversely (or positively) affect a company's stock, regardless of what the company does.

A public company faces intense pressure to perform in the short term. An entrepreneur in a wholly owned corporation can afford the luxury of long-term goals and controlled growth, but the CEO of a public company is pressured by shareholders to show almost immediate gains in revenues and earnings, which will translate into higher stock prices and dividends to the stockholders. Last but not least of the disadvantages, the SEC reporting requirements for public companies are very strict, time-consuming, and therefore costly.

The Public Offering Process

There are several steps in the IPO process, as depicted in Figure 16.4. The first is to choose an underwriter, or investment banker. This is the firm that sells the securities and guides the corporation through the IPO process. Some of the most prestigious investment banking firms handle only well-established companies because they believe that smaller companies will not attract sufficient attention among major institutional investors. Getting a referral to a competent investment banking firm is a first step in the process.

The importance of investigating the reputation and track record of any underwriter cannot be overemphasized. Investment banking has become a very competitive industry, and the lure of large fees from IPOs has attracted some firms of questionable character. The entrepreneur should also examine the investment mix of the bank. Some underwriters focus solely on institutional investors, others on retail customers or private investors. It is often useful to have a mix of shareholders; private

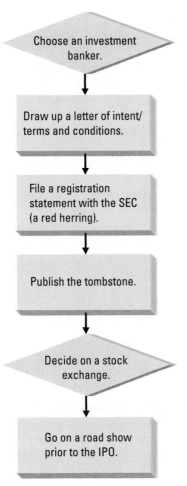

FIGURE 16.4
The IPO Process Simplified

investors tend to be less fickle than institutional investors, so their presence contributes more stability to the stock price in the market. The investment bank should also be able to support the IPO after the offering by giving financial advice, aid in buying and selling stock, and assistance in creating and maintaining interest in the stock over the long term.

Once chosen, the underwriter draws up a letter of intent, which outlines the terms and conditions of the agreement between the underwriter and the entrepreneur/selling stockholder. It normally specifies a price range for the stock, which is a tricky issue at best. Typically, underwriters estimate the price at which the stock will be sold by using a price/earnings multiple that is common for companies within the same industry as the IPO. That multiple is then applied to the IPO's earnings per share. This is only a rough estimate; the actual going-out price will not be determined until the night before the offering. If the entrepreneur is unhappy with the final price, the only choice is to cancel the offering, an action that is highly unattractive after months of work and expense.

A registration statement must be filed with the SEC. This document is known as a "red herring," or prospectus, because it discusses all the potential risks of investing in the IPO. This prospectus is given to anyone interested in investing in the IPO. After filing of the registration statement, an advertisement called a "tombstone" announces the offering in the financial press. The prospectus is valid for nine months; after that, the information becomes outdated and cannot be used without officially amending the registration statement.

Another major decision is where to list the offering—that is, on which exchange. In the past, smaller IPOs automatically listed on the American Stock Exchange (AMEX) or the National Association of Securities Dealers Automated Quotation (NASDAQ) because they couldn't meet the qualifications of the New York Stock Exchange (NYSE). Today, however, with technology companies such as Amazon.com and QUALCOMM listed there, NASDAQ is the fastest-growing exchange in the nation.

NASDAQ operates differently from the other exchanges. The NYSE and AMEX are auction markets with securities traded on the floor of the exchange, enabling investors to trade directly with one another. NASDAQ, by contrast, is a floorless exchange that trades on the National Market System through a network of broker–dealers from respected securities firms that compete for orders. In addition to these three, there are regional exchanges (such as the Boston stock exchange) that are less costly alternatives for a small, growing company.

The high point of the IPO process is the road show, generally a two-week whirl-wind tour of all the major institutional investors by the entrepreneur and the IPO team to market the offering. This is done so that once the registration statement has met all the SEC requirements and the stock is priced, the offering can be sold virtually in a day, before its value has the chance to fluctuate in the market. The coming-out price determines the amount of proceeds to the IPO company, but those holding stock prior to the IPO often see the value of their stock increase substantially immediately after the IPO.

On the other hand, many IPOs reach the final stage only to be withdrawn at the last minute. One Houston, Texas, company had revenues of $50 million in January 1998 when it decided to raise $35 million in an IPO to support its growth strategy of acquiring small companies in a highly fragmented industry. Unfortunately, the underwriter pulled the offering because of negative market conditions. The offering was launched again in the summer of 1998, and once more the underwriter pulled it for the same reason. An IPO can help a company grow much more rapidly than it otherwise might, but the market dictates whether a company can successfully execute the IPO. After the dot com bust, many companies had to pull their plans for an initial public offering because institutional investors were backing away from the public markets. An entrepreneur who is considering doing an IPO should look at the condition of the market and very carefully weigh the pros and cons of becoming a public company at that time.

Growing via Strategic Alliances

Strategic alliances with larger companies are also an excellent source of growth capital for young companies. Sometimes the partnership results in major financial and equity investments in the growing venture. Such was the case for United Parcel Service of America, which acquired Mail Boxes Etc. (MBE) for $191 million in 2001 after that company had become the industry leader.

Growing companies that link with established companies usually get a better deal than they would have gotten from a venture capitalist. In addition, they derive some associated benefits that give them more credibility in the marketplace. The large investing partner is looking for a return of the cost of capital and, in general, for a return of at least 10 percent on the investment.

Strategic alliances are every bit as tricky as partnerships, so the potential partner must be evaluated carefully, and due diligence must be conducted on the company to make sure that it is everything it claims to be. The entrepreneur should examine its business practices, talk to its customers and value chain members, and make sure that this company will make the entrepreneur's company look good. It is also crucial not to focus on one potential partner but, instead, to consider several before making a final decision. For the partnership to work best, the benefits should flow in both directions; that is, both partners should derive cost savings and/or revenue enhancement from the relationship. It probably is wise not to form a partnership that makes one of the partners (usually the smaller company) too heavily dependent on the other for a substantial portion of its revenue-generating capability. This is a dangerous position to be in and can spell disaster if the partnership dissolves for any reason.

Valuing the Business

A key component of any financial strategy is determining the value of the company, because a realistic value figure is needed no matter which avenue is taken to raise growth capital. Today the already difficult task of valuation is exacerbated by the fact that most of the valuable assets that companies hold are intangible. That is, they consist of patents, knowledge, and people instead of plant and equipment.[6]

Calculating Value

Calculating value is challenging at best, because *value* is a subjective term with many meanings. In fact, at least six different definitions of value are in common use. They can be summarized as follows:

Fair Market Value—the price at which a willing seller would sell and a willing buyer would buy in an arm's-length transaction. By this definition, every sale would ultimately constitute a fair market value sale.

Intrinsic Value—the perceived value arrived at by interpreting balance sheet and income statements through the use of ratios, discounting cash flow projections, and calculating liquidated asset value.

Investment Value—the worth of the business to an investor based on his or her individual requirements in terms of risk, return, tax benefits, and so forth.

Going-Concern Value—the current financial status of the business as measured by financial statements, debt load, and economic environmental factors (such as government regulation) that may affect its long-term continuation.

Liquidation Value—the amount that could be recovered by selling off all the company's assets.

Book Value—an accounting measure of value that reflects the difference between total assets and total liability. It is essentially equivalent to shareholders' or owners' equity.

In today's economy, those who finance ventures also use some new, nonfinancial yardsticks to measure value. These include

- The experience level of the management team
- The innovative level of the firm's distribution channels
- The nature of the company's relationships in the industry and with customers
- The company's ability to be fast and flexible
- The amount and kind of the company's intellectual property

Methods for Valuing a Business

This section examines some financial measures for business valuation. The first thing to know about valuation is that nearly all techniques rely on the analysis of the future market for the company's products. This is why neither book value nor liquidation value is a satisfactory method, except to establish a residual value to use in

Profile 16.2   WHEN A COMPANY'S VALUE GOES DOWN

From its founding in 1999–2000, CollabNet, a California-based software firm, had no trouble raising capital. Venture capital firms such as Benchmark Capital, Hewlett-Packard, and Intel Capital invested $38 million in the company. But when the technology market crashed, CollabNet CEO Bill Portelli had to consider what is known in the industry as a "down round," a round of venture funding that results in a lower company valuation. Because a down round often signals that a company is failing, he was quite naturally reluctant to pursue this path. Portelli had already closed down research projects and some product lines and had laid off about 40 people from his 120-person staff so that the company could focus its limited resources on its primary software development tool, SourceCast.

The company continued to hobble along on its internal cash flows, but Portelli knew that if the economy experienced another downturn, his company might not survive. It was not an auspicious time to seek funding, but now was better than waiting until he absolutely had to have the cash. When CollabNet received its second round of funding in 2000, its value was highly inflated

at $70 million. The new round of funding would bring that valuation down to $20 million. Thus it would significantly dilute the equity positions of the current investors and risk lawsuits from shareholders, who could not be certain that even the new money would save the company. Complicating the situation was the fact that the company had been courted for acquisition by larger companies such as Borland and Oracle, but founder Brian Behlendorf, didn't relish being part of a large corporation.

Ultimately, Behlendorf and the board decided to take a $13 million third round at the lower valuation, reasoning that although the shareholders' stock would be diluted, the company would be healthier and stronger, making the shares more valuable in the long term. One of the keys to success in a down round is to make sure that all shareholders feel they were treated fairly and were not coerced or defrauded. Another key is to not focus so heavily on the company valuation that you lose sight of what's important: building a sustainable company.

Sources: B. Gossage, "The down-round dilemma," *Inc. Magazine* (April 2003), www.inc.com; and CollabNet http://www.collab.net/.

a discounted cash flow method. Further, with more businesses—and more new businesses—relying on intangible assets, book value does not make sense.

Market multiples such as price/earnings (P/E) ratios are often used by venture capitalists, but their use is speculative because they are based on public companies in the industry and on the bet that the new company will go public in three to five years. The discounted cash flow (DCF) method is probably the technique most commonly used to account for the going-concern value of a business. The multiples technique and the DCF are discussed in the following sections.

Multiple of Earnings

A multiple of earnings is frequently used to value publicly owned companies because the technique is simple and direct. The first step is to figure normal earnings and

TABLE 16.1	Using Multiples to Calculate Value	
Net income plus depreciation		$ 2,425,000
Earnings multiple		6 X
Company value including long-term debt		$17,953,410
Less outstanding debt		1,500,000
Company value		$16,453,410

then capitalize them at some rate of return or at a multiple of earnings. The rate of return or multiple used is based on assumptions about the company's risk level and projected future earnings, so the greater the potential earnings, the higher the multiple will be. Similarly, the greater the risk, the lower the multiple. For example, Table 16.1 presents some information used to calculate the value of a hypothetical company.

Another method, which typically results in a higher valuation, is multiplying a year's worth of after-tax earnings by the industry average multiple based on the P/E ratio of public companies in the industry. This method must be used with care. To say that a young private company with earnings of $250,000 in an industry where the average P/E is 12 should be valued at $3 million is probably overstating the case. It has been suggested that public firms have a premium value of about 25–35 percent over closely held companies because they are more highly regarded by the financial community. Remember that public companies are subjected to greater scrutiny than private companies, so any P/E multiple that is used should be discounted to reflect that premium.[7] This would mean that our private company now has a value of $2,250,000 ($250,000 × 9). Even with discounting, the variation in the ways in which a company can calculate earnings and the difficulty in finding a public company that is comparable often make multiple of earnings a dubious measure for purposes of valuation.

Discounting Cash Flows

If valuing the business by its potential earning power is the goal, the most common measure—and the one that gives the most accurate results—is discounted future cash flows, because only cash or cash equivalents are used in the calculations. The method is called **discounted cash flow analysis,** or capitalization of future cash flows to the present value. This simply means calculating how much an investor would pay today to have a cash flow stream of X dollars for X number of years into the future.

There are four components of the DCF that must be addressed:[8]

1. **The assumptions.** Assumptions define the model for conducting the business and take into account sales, R&D, manufacturing costs, selling costs, and general and administrative costs. These should be benchmarked against the growth of other successful companies in the industry.

2. **Forecast period.** Typically, the forecast period is three to five years and reflects the length of time that investors intend to have a stake in the venture.
3. **Terminal value.** Terminal value is the going-concern value at the end of the projection period, assuming that the company will continue in operation into the foreseeable future (in perpetuity). It may be thought of as a perpetuity, which assumes no growth and constant earnings (annual payment divided by the cost of money), or as a growth in perpetuity, which estimates a growth rate and profitability.
4. **Discount rate.** The discount rate determines the present value of the projected cash flows and is, in reality, the expected rate of return for the investor.

For this analysis, the entrepreneur uses pro forma cash flow statements for the business and determines a forecast period. (Refer to Chapter 8 for a discussion of pro forma cash flows and methods for forecasting sales and expenses.) The entrepreneur must also understand the length and nature of business cycles in the industry in order to decide whether the forecast period goes from trough to trough or from peak to peak. In other words, the forecast period must include at least one complete business cycle in order to give a fair representation of the effect of that cycle on cash flow (see Figure 16.5).

Once the forecast period has been defined and the cash flow projections prepared, a discount rate must be chosen. This is not a purely arbitrary exercise. The buyer's or investor's point of view must be considered, and that viewpoint will often include the opportunity cost of investing in or buying this business. It has been suggested that the decision should be based on three factors:

1. The rate achievable in a risk-free investment such as U.S. Treasury notes over a comparable time period. For example, for a five-year forecast, the current rate on a five-year note is appropriate.
2. A risk factor based on the type of business and the industry, which should be added to the interest rate. Several precedents for determining what these

FIGURE 16.5   Business Cycles and the Forecast Period

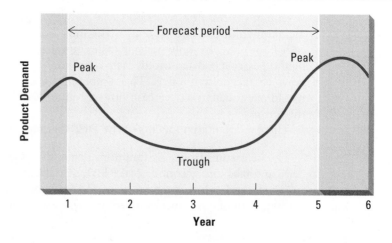

factors are have been established over years of study. One accepted standard is that offered by James H. Schilt[9] in the form of six categories of business. Note that even within each category, there is room for degrees of risk.

a. Category 1: Established businesses with good market share, excellent management, and a stable history of earnings: 6–10 percent

b. Category 2: Established businesses in more competitive industries, still with good market share, excellent management, and a stable earnings history: 11–15 percent

c. Category 3: Growing businesses in very competitive industries, with little capital investment, an average management team, and a stable earnings history: 16–20 percent

d. Category 4: Small businesses dependent on the entrepreneur or larger businesses in very volatile industries; also the lack of a predictable earnings picture: 21–25 percent

e. Category 5: Small service businesses operating as sole proprietorships: 26–30 percent

3. The life expectancy of the business. Discounting is typically based on this factor. The example in Table 16.2 illustrates this valuation method. Assuming that the current rate on a ten-year Treasury note is 6 percent and that the business is a Category 2 business with a 14 percent risk factor, the adjusted discount rate becomes 20 percent. Using a calculator or a present value table, one can calculate the present value of the five-year cash flow stream. The hypothetical business in this example will generate $1,575,000 of positive cash flow over five years. Hence, a buyer would be willing to pay $875,700 today for that business, given the discount rate.

It is possible to create three future scenarios for the firm: success, survival, and liquidation. This will give three values for the business. Then assign a probability of occurrence to each scenario based on the probability that the scenario will occur, and multiply the discounted cash flow by that probability to arrive at an adjusted present value.

TABLE 16.2	**One Method for Discounting Cash Flows**

Assume: 6% risk-free rate
        +14% risk factor (Category 2 business)
        20% discount rate

Discount the Cash Flow

END OF YEAR	CASH FLOW ($000)	FACTOR (20%)	PRESENT VALUE
1	200	.8333	166.7
2	250	.6944	173.6
3	300	.5787	173.6
4	375	.4823	180.9
5	450	.4019	180.9
Totals	$1,575		$875.7

Once a mathematical estimate of value has been achieved, other factors will come into play that are difficult to put into the equation and are more rightly points of negotiation. All the projections used in the valuation of the business are based on assumptions, and the buyer/investor is likely to question them and perhaps to discount the value of the business even further.

Another factor affecting the final valuation is the degree of legitimate control the owner has over the business. This is typically measured by the amount of stock the owner holds. Buying out an owner who holds the majority of the stock is more valuable than buying out one who does not hold a majority interest. A company in which the entrepreneur can control the majority of the stock is more valuable than one in which the entrepreneur holds only a minority interest. Finally, intangibles such as a loyal customer list, intellectual property, and the like create additional value. The "real" value or market value of the business will ultimately be determined through negotiation with investors, lenders, or underwriters. However, doing the calculations just discussed provides an excellent point of departure for the negotiations.

The Real Options Model

A relatively new approach to valuation is real options, which derive from financial options applied to securities, currencies, and commodities. In a new venture, they are applied to management options under changing circumstances.[10] The entrepreneur calculates the probability that specific events will occur and how they will affect the business. Traditional discounted cash flow analysis often yields a negative net present value for many scenarios, and the potential investor who relied on it would decide not to invest in the new venture. Under a real options approach, however, the question would be whether the future earnings of the company are greater than the cost to grow the business to a defined level. What is the probability that sufficient customers will be found to justify the market size that the entrepreneur is projecting? The higher the risk, the lower the value of the business. Using real options as a valuation method is more complicated than can be presented here. Check the resources at the end of the chapter to learn more about this method.

The Hockey Stick Approach

With this approach, the VC firm determines what return is required during the holding period it desires. It then applies a P/E ratio or multiple of earnings at the end of that period to value the company. The term *hockey stick* arises from the graph of this method, which produces a curve that represents no earnings in the early stages and then rapid growth.[11] Percentage ownership is calculated by using the following formula:

$$\frac{(\text{Initial Investment} \times \text{Expected Payoff})}{(\text{After-Tax Earnings} \times \text{Comparable P/E})} = \text{Percent Ownership}$$

For example, suppose a company required an investment of $5 million over three years. The VC wants a return of five times the initial investment and forecasts that the company's after-tax earnings in the third year will be $6.5 million. The investor sets the P/E ratio at 16 on the basis of comparables in the public market.

Using the formula above, the investor would expect to receive the following equity stake in the company:

$$\frac{(\$5M \times 5)}{(\$6.5M \times 16)} = 24\% \text{ ownership}$$

Valuation is by its very nature an incremental process of bringing together key pieces of information that give some insight into the health and future of the business. In all discussions of value, the entrepreneur should be clear about whose definition of value is being used. In general, what a willing buyer and seller can agree on under normal market conditions is the real value of the company at a particular point in time.

With a new venture, there are many financing options. However, creating a capital structure that works depends in large part on creativity and persistence in securing, at the right price, the capital needed to launch the venture successfully.

Recall from Chapter 1 that entrepreneurs work with a vision of where their companies are going and what they will look like when they get there. That vision sustains them through the ups and downs of start-up and the breathless speed of growth when the company finally takes off. It also supports them in the difficult search for capital to feed that growth and ensure that the business will remain successful. The growth period of a world-class venture can be an extraordinarily exciting time for everyone involved if the entrepreneurial team has prepared for growth by performing the following tasks:

- Network, research, and line up potential capital sources well in advance of need.

- Determine at least three years in advance whether the company will go public at the most appropriate window of opportunity. This early planning ensures that the company, if it hasn't already done so, will now begin to prepare audited financial statements regularly, using a nationally recognized accounting firm, and to put in place the financial and control systems required of a public company.

- Update the comprehensive business plan to reflect the most current information the entrepreneur has about the business.

Growing a venture requires substantial resources, but if the company has established a healthy track record and has good potential for growth, the number of resources available to the business increases substantially. Preparing for growth is the subject of Chapter 17.

New Venture Checklist

Have you:

☐ Determined how much growth capital will be needed?

☐ Developed a strategy for seeking growth capital?

☐ Considered whether and, if so, when to proceed with the IPO?

☐ Established a value for the business?

Issues to Consider

1. At what stage of venture development do venture capitalists typically become involved, and why?
2. For what kind of business would soliciting private venture capital be a logical financial strategy for growth? Why?
3. How can strategic alliances be used to help grow the business?
4. What are some things that an entrepreneur should do to prepare for a public offering before the year of "going public"?
5. In approaching a venture capitalist, how can the entrepreneurial team deal from a position of strength?
6. What are the key components in valuing a new or growing venture?

Experiencing Entrepreneurship

1. Interview a partner in a venture capital firm. Ask the partner to describe the investment that the firm most recently completed. What were the critical factors that made the firm decide to invest?
2. Locate a business that was recently sold or had an initial public offering. Talk to a principal and, if possible, to the buyer or investment banker to learn what was considered when they valued the company. How much of the decision on valuation was based on negotiation and nonmonetary factors?

Additional Sources of Information

Bartlett, J.W. (1999). *Fundamentals of Venture Capital.* New York: Madison Books.

Boer, F.P. (2002). *The Real Options Solution: Finding Total Value in a High-Risk World.* New York: Wiley.

Boer, F.P. (1999). *The Valuation of Technology.* New York: Wiley.

Koller, T., J. Murrin, T. Copeland, and W. Foote (2000). *Valuation: Measuring and Managing the Value of Companies.* 3d ed. New York: Wiley.

Tuller, L.W. (1998). *Small Business Valuation Book.* Holbrook, MA: Bob Adams.

Wilmerding, A. (2003). *Deal Terms: The Finer Points of Venture Capital Deal Structures, Valuations, Term Sheets, Stock Options, and Getting Deals Done.* Boston, MA: Aspatore Books.

Relevant Case Studies

Case 5 iRobot, p. 432

Case 6 The Crowne Inn, p. 435

17

Planning for Growth

"No great thing is created suddenly."

Epictetus, c. 60–120
Roman Stoic philosopher

LEARNING OBJECTIVES

- Decide whether to grow the venture.

- Discuss intensive growth strategies—growing within the current market.

- Explain integrative growth strategies—growing within the industry.

- Examine diversification growth strategies—growing outside the industry.

- Consider growing by going global.

Profile 17.1 **WHEN ONE BUSINESS IS NOT ENOUGH**

Karen McMasters knows how to run a three-ring circus. In 1998, she started selling "gently worn" baby clothing on eBay. Within two years, she had launched her first business (Bare Babies, based in Fountain Valley, California) on Yahoo! Stores. Bare Babies quickly grew into a $2.5 million baby products business, and in just three years, McMasters started AllCola.com with her mother as her partner. AllCola is a site dedicated to Coca-Cola memorabilia, a passion of her mother's. The goal of the business was to get her mother closer to retirement doing something she loved.

Then, in 2004, McMasters launched Ciao Bella Baby. The launch of this business came as a result of her having used the word *bare* in the name of her business, Bare Babies. She discovered that some of her customers who used computer child protection security software were having troubling accessing her site. She decided to create another company,

Ciao Bella Baby, similar in merchandising and focus, instead of changing the name of Bare Babies, because that would only confuse her loyal customer base.

Growing with multiple businesses is a rather unusual strategy, but McMasters believes that diversification is the key to long-term success—and it makes her life more interesting. McMasters is among a growing number of "parallel" entrepreneurs, those who start new businesses without exiting their previous start-up. According to McMasters, the task gets easier with each additional business, because the parallel entrepreneur can leverage existing customer relationships and diversified experience gives one realistic guidance on how to get things done.

Sources: A.P. Sherman, "Parallel Universe," *Entrepreneur,* 36 (June 2004), http://www.barebabies.com/index.html, accessed 9/1/04; http://www.ciaobellababy.com, accessed 9/1/04; and http://www.allcola.com, accessed 9/1/04.

Expansion is a natural by-product of a successful start-up. Growth helps a new business secure or maintain its competitive advantage and establish a firm foothold in the market. Growth is the result of a strong vision on the part of the entrepreneur and the founding team. The vision guides decision making and ensures that the company stays on course and meets its goals. Depending on those goals, entrepreneurs choose controlled growth that relies on building solid relationships with customers. The company then grows through referrals or word of mouth. More rapid growth occurs through leverage, acquisition, or an initial public offering.

Some entrepreneurs shy away from growth because they are afraid of losing control. That fear is not unfounded; many businesses falter during rapid growth because of the enormous demands placed on the resources of the company. Furthermore, it is unlikely that a business can consistently grow over its life without ever faltering. It is, in fact, a myth that great companies grow indefinitely.[1] Of the original Forbes 100 list in 1917, only 18 companies remained in the top 100 by 1987, and 61 had ceased to exist. Of the remaining group, only General Electric Co. and Eastman Kodak Co. outperformed the S&P 500's 7.5 percent average return over the 70-year period, and they surpassed it by only 0.3 percent.[2] A pretty dismal record overall. The truth is that all companies have periods in which they appear to stall, but the larger a company gets, the more its growth rate slows.[3] What this means to the entrepreneur is that sustaining double-digit growth over the long term is probably not possible. But with solid planning in place before growth occurs, many of the pitfalls of rapid growth can be avoided, and growth can continue for a longer time than would otherwise be possible.

It is a common misconception that to grow rapidly, a company must seek the support of formal venture capital. However, a review of the Inc. 500 Fastest Growing Private Companies for the year 2003 indicates that 98 percent of the fastest growing private companies were not venture backed; that is, they were not funded by venture capital. In fact, in 2003, only 10 companies in the Inc. 500 received venture capital. Most companies grow through their own internal resources or with private investor money or debt.[4] In fact, 48 percent of the Inc. 500 started their ventures with less than $20,000.

The Inc. 500 are representative of rapidly growing private ventures. The statistics about them reveal some interesting patterns. According to *Inc. Magazine's* annual survey, 31 percent of respondents said that winning new business has grown significantly harder, and 35 percent attributed their lack of growth to a sluggish economy. But turn those statistics around and the picture is much brighter. Over 69 percent did not find winning new business a problem, and 65 percent were not experiencing problems with growth. The top five growth companies were in the following industries: telecommunications, computer hardware, human resources, consumer products, and financial services.

High-growth companies stand out from the crowd because they display some very distinct characteristics. Typically, they are first in a niche market that they created and in which they soon become the leaders. They are often better at what they do than their competitors. They are leaner in their operations and unique in what they offer.

Being first in the market with a new product or service, if executed effectively, is one of the strongest competitive advantages. It provides a chance to establish brand recognition so that customers immediately think of the company when they think about a particular product or service. This allows the entrepreneurial venture to set the standards for those who follow. This was certainly the strategy of Samuel Adams in the microbrewed beer industry, Amazon.com in the online book industry, and Microsoft in the operations and applications software industry. By combining a pioneering strategy with innovative processes, leaner operations, and a unique, innovative product or service, companies can create formidable barriers to competition.

To Grow or Not to Grow

Some entrepreneurs make a conscious choice to control growth even in the face of extraordinary market demand. This is not to say that growth is slowed to single digits. Instead, the entrepreneur may choose to maintain a stable growth rate of 35 to 45 percent per year rather than subject the young venture to a roller coaster ride in the triple digits. In general, entrepreneurs who restrain growth do so because they are in the business for the long term; in other words, they're not in a hurry to harvest their newly created wealth by selling the business or doing a public offering. They also typically don't like to take on a lot of debt or give up equity to grow. Consequently, they don't advertise heavily, and they don't aggressively seek new customers beyond their capabilities. They also diversify their product or service line from the beginning to make themselves independent of problems that may face their customers or their industries. By offering a diversified product/service line, they maintain multiple streams of revenue that protect them from the loss of any one customer or market.

It is intoxicating for a new venture to realize that potential demand for its product or service is enormous and that the company could grow well beyond industry averages. But "hyper-growth" has destroyed many companies that did not have the capacity, skills, or systems in place to meet demand. Recall the holiday season of 1999, when all the Internet retail businesses, such as eToys, were unprepared for demand. They had inadequate or no fulfillment systems in place and no plan for handling returns. These very companies are no longer in business today. The growth phase of a new business can be one of the most exciting times for an entrepreneur. But if the entrepreneur has not prepared for growth with a coherent plan and a budget to match, it can be disastrous.

How, then, does an entrepreneur decide whether to grow or not to grow? In many cases, it may not be the entrepreneur's decision at all; demand for the product or service may compel the entrepreneur to keep up, or, by contrast, the market may not be big enough to allow the company to grow. Normally, by the time the company has reached a point where it is poised to grow to the next level, it will have a few employees and, of course, the founding team. To take that next step, some benchmarks for successful growth should be considered.

Successful growth requires leadership. When entrepreneurs start businesses, they are involved in every one of the business's activities, but as the company begins to grow, they find it necessary to delegate tasks to others. The more they delegate, the more they realize that their job has suddenly changed. Now they are not needed to do the tasks of the business; they are needed to lead the business—to make sure that the vision becomes reality. Everyone looks to the entrepreneur to ensure that the company survives. Leadership involves guiding the company and its people to achieve the company's goals. To accomplish that, the entrepreneur must have the ability to inspire people to action.

Also, employees must be given opportunities to learn and grow. A company can't successfully grow and change if its people don't grow and change with it. Employees should be encouraged to stretch beyond what they knew when they were hired in the early days of the company, to learn more aspects of the business, and to offer input into how the business is run.

The company must have a commitment to growth. With growth comes change—new ways to serve customers, new products and services, and new processes. Growing effectively requires the commitment of employees and customers. They have to see that growth is a good thing for them.

Everyone in the organization must be responsible and accountable for the success of the company. Everyone should understand what he or she contributes to the financial success of the company, and everyone should have a stake in that financial success. Rapid growth requires teamwork, and for teams to operate effectively, they must be given responsibility and accountability for what they do.

There are times, however, when saying no to growth makes sense for the business. For example, Bishop Partners' managers learned early on to say no to clients who pulled their small executive search firm away from its core values and mission. Even though the company was growing quickly, Susan Bishop, its founder, noticed that its profit margin remained low and that, even as it took on more clients, the company's earnings remained flat. Bishop pulled her team together and started asking questions. To her amazement, she discovered that everyone had a different vision of the company and where it was going. No wonder they had problems defining the right customer for the company. Once Bishop conveyed her vision to the employees, they worked together to define those customers and say no to those who didn't match their model. In the end, the company grew faster and remained healthy with a more focused strategy.

To comprehend the role of growth in a company's evolution, it is important to understand the factors that affect growth.

Market Factors That Affect Growth

The degree of growth and the rate at which a new venture grows are dependent on both the market and the management strategy. Market factors affect a firm's ability to grow.

The Size, Characteristics, and Buying Power of the Target Market

If the niche market that the company is entering is by nature small and relatively stable in terms of growth, it will of course be more difficult to achieve the spectacular growth and size of the most rapidly growing companies. On the other hand, if the product or service can expand to a global market, growth and size are more likely to be attained.

The Nature of the Competition

Entering a market dominated by large companies is not in and of itself an automatic deterrent to growth. A small, well-organized company is often able to produce its product or service at a very competitive price while maintaining high quality standards, because it doesn't have the enormous overhead and management salaries of the larger companies. Moreover, if an industry is an old, established one, a firm entering with an innovative product in a niche market in that industry can experience rapid rates of growth.

The Degree of Product Innovation in the Market

In some industries, such as the computer industry, innovation is a given, so merely offering an innovative product is not in itself enough. In highly innovative industries, the key to rapid growth is the ability to design and produce a product more quickly than competitors. By contrast, in an industry that is stable and offers products and services that could be considered commodities, entering with an innovative product or process will provide a significant competitive advantage.

The Status of Intellectual-Property (IP) Rights

Intellectual-property rights, like patents, copyrights, trademarks, and trade secrets, offer a competitive advantage to a new venture because they provide a grace period in which to introduce the product or service before anyone else can copy it. However, relying on proprietary rights alone is not wise. It is important to have a comprehensive marketing plan that enables the new business to secure a strong foothold in the market before someone attempts to reproduce the product and compete with it. True, an owner of intellectual property has the right to take someone who infringes on those proprietary rights to court, but the typical small company can ill afford this time-consuming and costly process when it needs all its excess capital for growth. See Chapter 6 for a more in-depth discussion of intellectual property.

The Volatility of the Industry

Some industries are by their very nature volatile; that is, it is difficult to predict what will happen for any length of time and with any degree of accuracy. The computer industry in the 1980s was such an industry; it has lately become somewhat more predictable as leading players have emerged. The emerging nanotechnology industry, however, is very volatile at this time. Consequently, there are opportunities for extraordinary growth in new ventures and, at the same time, a higher risk of failure. A new entry into such an industry needs to maintain a constant awareness of potential government regulations, directions that the industry is taking, and emerging competitors.

The Barriers to Entry

Some industries, simply by virtue of their size and maturity, are difficult for a new venture to enter and difficult to penetrate with sufficient market share to make a profit. Other industries prohibit new entries because the cost of participating (plant and equipment, fees, and/or compliance with regulations) is so high. Yet in the right industry, a new venture can erect barriers of its own to slow down the entry of competing companies. Patent rights on products, designs, or processes, for example, can effectively erect a temporary barrier to allow the new venture a window of opportunity to gain market share.

Management Factors That Affect Growth

Along with market factors, management factors also influence a company's growth.

The Inertia of Success

When the new company has survived and is successful, even as a small business, there is a tendency to believe that it must be doing everything right and should continue in the same way. That is a fatal error on the part of many entrepreneurs who don't recognize that change is a by-product of success. Many times it isn't until the venture is in crisis that the entrepreneur realizes the time has come to make a transition to professional management, a step that requires of the entrepreneur a fundamental change in attitudes and behaviors.[5]

The Entrepreneur's Ability to Delegate Authority and Responsibility

Rapid growth requires skills different from start-up skills. In the beginning of a new venture, the entrepreneur has more time to take part in and even control all aspects of the business. But when rapid growth begins to occur, systems must be in place to handle the increased demand without sacrificing quality and service. Unless the entrepreneur is able to bring in key professional management with experience in high-growth companies, chances are good that growth will falter, the window of opportunity will be lost, and the business may even fail needlessly. Many entrepreneurs have found that at some point in the business's growth, they must step down and allow experienced management to take over.

The Ability to Encourage Entrepreneurship in the Entire Venture Team

Growing the business does not have to mean that the entrepreneurial spirit is lost, only that the entrepreneur must become very creative about maintaining that sense of smallness and flexibility while growing. Subcontracting some aspects of the business is one way to keep the number of employees down and retain team spirit. Developing self-managing teams is another way.

Stages of Growth in a New Venture

Rates and stages of growth in a new venture vary by industry and business type; however, there appear to be some common issues that arise in the areas of strategic, administrative, and managerial problems. The importance of knowing when these issues will surface cannot be overstated, for it should be part of the entrepreneur's well-orchestrated plan to anticipate events and requirements before they occur.

Research results suggest that organizations progress sequentially through major stages in their life and development.[6] Still other studies have noted that at each stage of development, the business faces a unique set of problems.[7] For example, the start-up stage is characterized by marketing and financial problems, whereas the growth phase is associated with strategic, administrative, and managerial problems. One study corroborated these findings by learning that the number of organizations that claimed their most difficult problem was obtaining financing declined from 17 percent at start-up to 1 percent in the growth phase, and that the percentage of firms with human resource problems increased from 5 percent at start-up to 17 percent in the growth phase.[8]

The stages of growth (see Figure 17.1) can be described as four phases through which the business must pass. (1) Start-up is characterized by concerns about capital, customers, and distribution, (2) initial growth by concerns about cash flow and marketing, (3) rapid growth by concerns about resources, capital, and management, and (4) stable growth by concerns about innovation and maintaining success.

Start-up Success

During start-up, the first stage, the entrepreneur's main concerns are to ensure sufficient start-up capital, seek customers, and design a way to deliver the product or service. At this point, the entrepreneur is a jack-of-all-trades, doing everything that needs to be done to get the business up and running. This includes securing suppliers, distributors, facilities, equipment, and labor. The very complexity of start-up is one reason why many new ventures fail. Complexity also suggests that a team-based venture is better equipped to achieve a successful launch than a solo effort. If the company survives to achieve a positive cash flow from the revenues it generates, it is

| FIGURE 17.1 | Stages of Growth |

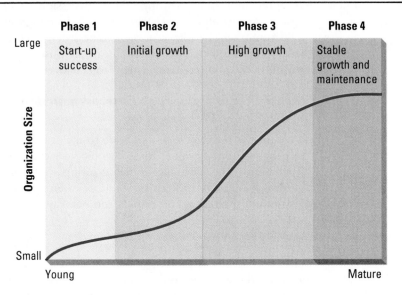

in a good position to grow and expand its market. If, however, revenues generated fail to cover company expenses, it will not be possible to grow without seeking outside capital in the form of equity or debt.

Initial Growth

If the new venture makes it through the first phase, it enters the second level of activity with a viable business that has enough customers to keep it running on the revenues it generates. Now the entrepreneur's concerns become more focused on the issue of cash flow. Can the business generate sufficient cash flow to pay all its expenses and at the same time support the growth of the company? At this point, the venture is usually relatively small, there are few employees, and the entrepreneur is still playing an integral role. This is a crucial stage, for the decisions made here will determine whether the business will remain small or move to the next level, rapid growth, which entails some significant changes in organization and strategy. The entrepreneur and the team need to decide whether they are going to grow the business to a much larger revenue level or remain stable yet profitable.

Rapid Growth

If the decision is to grow, all the resources of the business have to be gathered together to finance the growth of the company. This is a very risky stage because growth is expensive, and there are no guarantees that the entrepreneur will be successful in the attempt to reach the next level. Planning and control systems must be in place and professional management hired because there will be no time to do that during the period of rapid growth.

The problems during this stage center on maintaining control of rapid growth. They are solved by delegating control and accountability at various levels; failure usually is due to uncontrolled growth, lack of cash, and insufficient management expertise to deal with the situation. If growth is accomplished, it is at this stage that entrepreneurs often sell the company at a substantial profit. It is also at this stage that some entrepreneurs are displaced by their boards of directors, investors, or creditors because the skills that made them so important at start-up are not the same skills the company needs to grow to the next level. As a result, many entrepreneurial ventures reach their pinnacle of growth with a management team entirely different from the one that founded the company. To the extent that the entrepreneur is a vital part of the vision of the company and can identify an appropriate new role in the now larger company, he or she will remain the primary driver of the business. Bill Gates, Microsoft's co-founder, is one example of an entrepreneur who stayed at the helm and took his company from start-up to global corporate giant. Only in the past several years did he step out of the CEO position in favor of one of the founding team members, Steve Ballmer.

Stable Growth and Maintenance

Once the business has successfully passed through the phase of rapid growth and is able to manage effectively the financial gains of growth, it has reached Phase 4, stable growth and maintenance of market share. Here the business, which usually is now large, can remain in a fairly stable condition as long as it continues to be innovative, competitive, and flexible. If it does not, sooner or later it will begin to lose market share and could ultimately fail or revert to being a much smaller business. High-tech companies seem to be an exception to traditional growth patterns. Because they typically start with solid venture capital funding and a strong management team (dictated by the venture capitalists), they move out of Phases 1 and 2 very rapidly. During Phases 3 and 4, if the structure is effective and their technology is adopted in the mainstream market, they become hugely successful. If, on the other hand, the structure is weak and the technology is not readily adopted, they can fail rapidly.

Problems with Growth

It is a sad fact that many entrepreneurial ventures that start with great concepts and experience early success eventually hit a wall. Growth stalls, or the firm can even die. Studies have found that among all the factors affecting growth, the most critical in a slowdown or failure appears to be inability to understand and respond to the business's environment.[9] That is, the entrepreneur did not recognize the opportunities and challenges developing outside the company and their potential to harm it.

For example, in its first 8 years, one manufacturer's representative firm with 30 highly trained salespeople grew to $20 million in sales and came to dominate its midwestern market. But at the 8-year point, the firm stopped growing and sales hit a plateau. Its founder thought the problem was an internal one, sales effectiveness. What really happened, however, was that the firm's competitors had changed their marketing and distribution strategies. One competitor had moved into direct sales; another developed a strong telemarketing capability. The effect of these changes was to depress the sales of the entrepreneur's company in a matter of just months.[10] This entrepreneur had failed to recognize the changes in the environment and respond rapidly to them.

TABLE 17.1	A Framework for Growth

STRATEGY	TACTICS

Scan and assess the environment.	1. Analyze the environment.
	  a. Is the customer base growing or shrinking? Why?
	  b. How are competitors doing?
	  c. Is the market growing?
	  d. How does your company compare technologically with others in the industry?
	2. Do a SWOT analysis (strengths, weaknesses, opportunities, threats).

Plan the growth strategy.	3. Determine the problem.
	4. Brainstorm solutions.
	  a. Don't limit yourself to what you know and have done in the past.
	  b. Choose 2 or 3 to test.
	5. Set a major goal for significant change in the organization.
	6. Set smaller, achievable goals that will put you on the path to achieve the major goal.
	7. Dedicate resources (funding and staff) toward the achievement of these goals.

Hire for growth.	8. Put someone in charge of the growth plan. 9. Bring in key professional management with experience in growing companies. 10. Provide education and training for employees to prepare them for growth and change.
Create a growth culture.	11. Involve everyone in the organization in the growth plan. 12. Reward achievement of interim goals.
Build a strategy advisory board.	13. Invite key people from the industry who can keep you apprised of changes. 14. Make them part of the planning process. 15. Invite more outsiders than insiders.

What this suggests is that entrepreneurs must continually scan their environment and assess it for changes and emerging competitors. They must also plan for growth and hire for growth. Most important, growth must become part of the company culture. Table 17.1 provides a framework for growing the business.

For the most part, growth is a very positive thing for a new business. It does, however, raise some issues for which the entrepreneur must be prepared. For example, if the new venture is a retail business and expands by opening additional stores, it is necessary to decide whether to retain control of all functions in one main store or to delegate the day-to-day management of each store and centrally control only

| FIGURE 17.2 | Growth Strategies for Entrepreneurs |

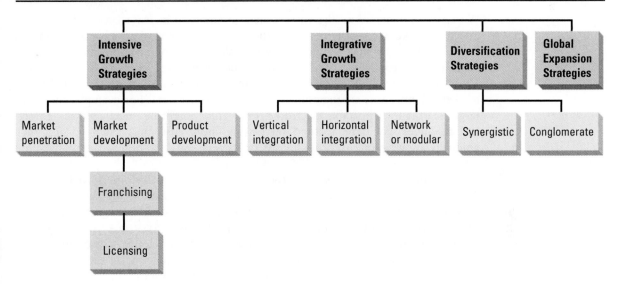

marketing, accounting, finance, and purchasing. In either case, a computer network will be necessary to keep track of sales at all locations. For a manufacturing firm, expansion may entail making a significant capital investment in additional plant and equipment or developing new strategic alliances to keep production in line with demand. It may also mean locating additional distributors and even new channels of distribution. For a service business, growth may mean taking on additional associates or employees and investing in computer systems to manage information. And, of course, for the entrepreneur, growth means giving up some control to others who have the management skills to guide the company successfully.

Growth Strategies

There are four major strategies for growing a business: (1) *Intensive growth strategies* exploit opportunity in the current market; (2) *integrative growth strategies* take advantage of growth within the industry as a whole; (3) *diversification strategies* exploit opportunities outside the current market or industry; and (4) *global strategies* take the business into the international arena. See Figure 17.2 for an overview of these strategies.

Intensive Growth Strategies — Growing Within the Current Market

Intensive growth strategies focus on exploiting the current market fully—that is, expanding the market share to the greatest extent possible. This is accomplished by increasing the volume of sales to current customers and the number of customers in the target market. There are generally three methods for implementing an intensive growth strategy: market penetration, market development, and product development.

Market Penetration

With market penetration, the entrepreneur attempts to increase sales by using more effective marketing strategies within the current target market. This is a common growth strategy for new ventures because it allows entrepreneurs to work in familiar territory and grow while they're getting their systems and controls firmly in place. Under this strategy, the company would move out gradually from the initial target market, whether it is a geographic area or a customer base. For example, the initial target market for a portable electronic travel guide might be travel agencies. Efforts and resources would be focused on getting those customers solidified and then gradually moving on to other target customers, such as hotels and convention bureaus.

Promoting additional uses for the product persuades customers to buy more. Arm & Hammer experienced that when its customers began buying baking soda not only for cooking but also for brushing their teeth and deodorizing their refrigerators. Yet another way to employ market penetration is to attract customers from competitors by advertising product qualities, service, or price that distinguishes the entrepreneur's product from others. A fourth way is to educate nonusers of the product or service about its benefits, in an effort to increase the customer base.

Market Development

Market development consists of taking the product or service to a broader geographic area. For example, a company that has been marketing on the East Coast may decide to expand across the rest of the United States. One of the most popular ways to expand a market geographically is to franchise, because this approach is generally less costly than setting up a national distribution system.

Franchising

Franchising allows the business to grow quickly in several geographic markets at once. The franchiser sells to the franchisee the right to do business under a particular name; the right to a product, process, or service; training and assistance in setting up the business; and ongoing marketing and quality control support once the business is established. The franchisee pays a fee and a royalty on sales, typically 3–8 percent. For this fee, the franchisee may get

- A product or service that has a proven market,
- Trade names and/or trademarks,
- A patented design, process, or formula,
- An accounting and financial control system,
- A marketing plan, and/or
- The benefit of volume purchasing and advertising.

Franchises generally come in three types: dealerships, service franchises, and product franchises. Dealerships allow manufacturers to distribute products without having to do the day-to-day work of retailing. Dealers benefit from combined marketing strength but are often required to meet quotas. Service franchises provide customers with services such as tax preparation, temporary employees, payroll preparation, and real estate services. Often the business is already in operation independently before it applies to become a franchise member. The most popular type of franchise is one that offers a product, a brand name, and an operating model. Examples include Great Harvest Bread Company and Golf USA.

Although it is a popular vehicle for growth, franchising a business is not without its risks. It is much like creating a whole new business, because the entrepreneur (franchiser) must carefully document all processes and procedures in a manual that will be used to train the franchisees. Potential franchisees need to be scrutinized to ensure that they are qualified to assume the responsibilities of operating a franchise. Moreover, the cost of preparing a business to franchise is considerable and includes legal, accounting, consulting, and training expenses. Then, too, it may take as long as three to five years to show a profit.

The risk to franchisees who may have purchased the franchise as an entry into business ownership is also great. Franchisees typically pay the franchiser 2–10 percent of gross sales in monthly royalties and marketing fees, which means that it is a tremendous challenge for the franchisees to control costs and get a return. One reason why so many franchises fail is that they are typically found in retail industries (35–40 percent of retail sales come from franchised businesses),[11] primarily eating and drinking establishments, which have a pattern of high risk and low return. However, other types of franchises in the recent past have been successful. For example, MinuteMan Press International has grown into one of the top full-service printing franchises, with over 850 locations. And Snap-on Tools, now a $2 billion company, is the leading global developer, manufacturer, and marketer of tool and equipment solutions.

Despite these successes, many studies have found failure rates among franchisees to range from 38.1 percent to 71.4 percent.[12] Bankruptcy of the parent company, the franchiser, should be another concern for potential franchisees, and it's not uncommon. In the past decade, dozens of franchises, including 7-Eleven, Nutri-System, American Speedy Printing, Church's Fried Chicken, and Days Inns, have experienced Chapter 11 bankruptcy. Most have emerged intact, but not without some harm to the franchisees. During the bankruptcy, the franchisees are left in limbo, without support or information, wondering whether they'll have a viable business when it's all done. The association of the franchisee with the bankrupt parent is also likely to have a negative effect, because customers assume that if the parent has financial problems, so does the offspring. Furthermore, most franchisees have invested their life's savings in their businesses. Under the arbitration clauses in most franchise agreements, franchisees don't have the option of going to court to recoup their losses. Even if the company comes out of Chapter 11, its image is tarnished. It will have to cut back somewhere, and savvy consumers know this to be true.

Not all businesses should use franchising as a means for growth. A successful franchise system will need to have the following characteristics: a successful prototype store (or preferably stores) with proven profitability and a good reputation so that the potential franchisee will begin with instant recognition; a registered trademark and a consistent image and appearance for all outlets; a business that can be systematized and easily replicated many times; a product that can be sold in a variety of geographic regions; adequate funding, because establishing a successful franchise program can cost upwards of $150,000; a well-documented prospectus that spells out the franchisee's rights, responsibilities, and risks; an operations manual that details every aspect of running the business; a training and support system for franchisees, both before they start the business and ongoing after start-up; and site selection criteria and architectural standards.

Developing a franchise program requires the assistance of an attorney and an accountant, both of whose advice should be carefully considered before undertaking the effort. One of the things that will be developed with the aid of an attorney is a franchise agreement. This document is often 40–60 pages in length and deals with a variety of legal issues. The franchise agreement should include the following: rules by which the franchisor and franchisee will have to abide during the term of the franchise; reference to the operations manual for the franchise to ensure that the franchisee adheres to the approved system for running the business; the term of the agreement (a franchise is like a lease where the franchisee is merely renting the business for the period of the franchise); renewal provisions that include when notice must be given that the franchisee wishes to renew the agreement and what fees are to be paid; first right of refusal or option to take on additional franchises offered by the franchisor; costs associated with purchasing the franchise (these may include an up-front fee, regular meeting expenses, and a percentage of the gross revenues to cover marketing and promotion costs); rules related to the premises on which the franchise will be located (the franchisor may pay some of the costs of renovation and will often lease the property and grant a sublease to the franchisee); the stock of goods and materials needed to open the business and maintain a proper level of inventory; intellectual-property rights and who owns them; whether the contract gives the franchisee the right to sell the franchise; how the franchise agreement can be terminated; and what to do in case of disputes. It is very clear why it's important to engage an attorney when structuring a franchise offering!

Licensing

Like franchising, **licensing** is a way to grow a company without investing large amounts of capital in plant, equipment, and employees. A license agreement is a grant to someone else to use the company's intellectual property and exploit it in the marketplace by manufacturing, distributing, or using it to create a new product. For example, a company may have developed a new patented process for taking rust off machinery. That process could be licensed to other companies to use on their equipment in return for paying a royalty back to the company. Conversely, an entrepreneur may have an idea for a new line of promotional products and want to license a famous name and likeness to use on them, to make them more attractive to consumers. This would entail seeking a license agreement from the owner of the trademarked name and likeness to use it commercially. An example is seeking a license from the Walt Disney Company to use Mickey Mouse on a line of products.

But licensing is much more than this, and entrepreneurs need to understand fully the value of intellectual property and how it can provide income in a variety of different ways. For the purposes of this discussion, anything that can be patented, copyrighted, or trademarked, and anything that is a trade secret, has the potential to be licensed. If a company has intellectual property that someone else might pay to use or commercialize in some way, certain steps should be taken to ensure that both parties to the transaction win. Licensor and licensee depend very much on each other for the success of the agreement, so the outcomes must be worthwhile at both ends of the deal.

The following are steps that licensors should take to ensure a successful transaction.

Step 1: Decide exactly what will be licensed. The license agreement can be for a product, the design for a product, a process, the right to market and distribute, the right to manufacture, or the right to use the licensed product in the production of yet another product. It will also be important to decide whether the licensee may only license the product as is or may modify it.

Step 2: Understand and define the benefits the buyer (licensee) will receive from the transaction. Why should the licensee license from the company? What makes the product, process, or right covered by the license unique and valuable? The licensee should be convinced that dealing with the licensor offers many advantages and will be much more profitable than dealing with someone else.

Step 3: Conduct thorough market research to make certain that the potential customer base is sufficient to ensure a good profit from the effort. Of course, the licensee will also have done market research, particularly if he or she approaches a company with a proposal for a licensing agreement. But the latter situation is typical only with intellectual property that is well recognized in the marketplace—characters, for instance (Batman, Harry Potter). A company with a new intellectual property that is unproven in the marketplace may need to seek out licensing agreements to get the product commercialized.

Step 4: Conduct due diligence on potential licensees. It's important to make certain that any potential licensee has the resources to fulfill the terms and conditions of the license agreement, can properly commercialize the intellectual property, and has a sound reputation in the market. A license agreement is essentially a partnership, and choosing partners carefully is vital.

Step 5: Determine the value of the license agreement. The value of a license agreement is determined by several factors: (1) the economic life of the intellectual property—that is, how long it will remain viable as a marketable product, process, or right; (2) the potential that someone could design around the intellectual property and compete directly; (3) the potential for government legislation or regulation that could damage the marketability of the IP; (4) any changes in market conditions that could render the IP valueless.

Once the monetary value of the license has been calculated on the basis of these four factors, the license becomes negotiable. Generally, the licensor wants some money up front, as a sign of good faith, and then a running royalty for the life of the license agreement. The amount of this royalty will vary by industry and by how much the licensee must invest in terms of plant, equipment, and marketing to commercialize the license.

Step 6: Create a license agreement. With the help of an attorney who specializes in licenses, draw up a license agreement or contract that defines the terms and conditions of the agreement between licensor and licensee.

Product Development

The third way to exploit the current market is to develop new products and services for existing customers or offer new versions of existing products. That is the tactic employed by software companies, which are constantly updating software with new versions their customers must buy if they want to enjoy all the latest features.

Savvy businesses get their best ideas for new products from their customers. These new ideas usually come in one of two forms: incremental changes in existing products or totally new products. Incremental products often come about serendipitously when engineers, sales personnel, and management spend time out in the marketplace with customers, learning more about their needs. Bringing all these team members together on a weekly basis to discuss ideas helps the business zero in quickly on those incremental products that are possible within the current operating structure and budget. The advantage of incremental products is that, because they are based on existing products, they can usually be designed and manufactured quite rapidly, and the marketing costs are less because customers are already familiar with the core product.

Brand new or breakthrough products, on the other hand, have a much longer product development cycle and are therefore more costly to undertake. Breakthrough products cannot be planned for; instead, they usually come about through brainstorming, exercises in creativity, and problem-solving sessions. In other words, if the entrepreneur creates a business environment that encourages creative, "off-the-wall" thinking, the chances are greater that the company will eventually come up with breakthrough products. The breakthrough environment, of necessity, has no budget or time constraints and does not run on a schedule. Offering a combination of incremental and breakthrough products is probably the most effective approach. The speed and cost efficiency of the incremental products keep cash flowing into the business to help fund the more costly breakthrough products.

Branding

The most successful entrepreneurs recognize the power of a brand name. They strive to gain brand name recognition for their products and services as quickly as possible, so that they can use the recognition to create a family of related products and services under that name. A company that is able to establish brand recognition will find its marketing effort that much easier and its costs reduced. A brand name that reflects quality, service, and value is an asset that ultimately can generate huge profits for the business.

To establish brand recognition, entrepreneurs should list the strengths of the company and its products. For example, does the company offer a higher-quality product, a wider range of accessories or models, or exciting new colors? The entrepreneur should also educate customers about the company's strengths. Once core strengths have been identified, they should be communicated over and over again in all marketing efforts, from brochures to signage to advertising. They should literally become a mantra for the customer. The minute customers think of this prod they should associate it with its strengths. In addition, the entrepreneur should develop a set of rules for using the brand name. If the brand name should be associated only with family values, the entrepreneur probably won't want to advertise during a television show containing violence or explicit language. Another important task is to get feedback on brand name recognition. To make sure the brand name is achieving the recognition level sought, it is important to check periodically with the target customer to determine what their favorite brands are and how often they choose a product on the basis of brand. And once brand name recognition has been established, the entrepreneur needs to take advantage of it by developing related products under the same brand name. However, this works only when the entrepreneur is offering new benefits to the target market or taking the same benefits to a new market. When a new product is taken to a new market, brand recognition does not necessarily follow.

Integrative Growth Strategies — Growing Within the Industry

There are many opportunities for entrepreneurs to pursue **integrative growth strategies**—to grow their ventures through acquisition. Acquisition is in many respects less about the financial ability of the entrepreneur to purchase another company and more about the ability to negotiate a good deal. With several research studies reporting that upwards of 75 percent of all acquisitions damage shareholder value, it is clear that this approach to growth must be taken very carefully.[13] In general, successful acquisitions target opportunities that integrate well with the core business, that can be implemented quickly, and that ensure the continuation of smooth operating processes.[14]

Traditionally, when entrepreneurs have wanted to grow their businesses within their industries, they have looked to vertical and horizontal integration strategies, but now that it is important to run leaner operations, they have been looking, more often than not, to a modular or network strategy. This section examines all three strategies—vertical, horizontal, and modular.

Vertical Integration Strategies

An entrepreneurial venture can grow by moving backward or forward within the distribution channel. This is called *vertical integration*. With a backward strategy, either the company gains control of some or all of its suppliers or it becomes its own supplier by starting another business from scratch or acquiring an existing supplier that has a successful operation. This is a common strategy for businesses that have instituted a just-in-time inventory control system. By acquiring the core supplier(s), the entrepreneur can streamline the production process and cut costs. With a forward strategy, the company attempts to control the distribution of its products by either selling directly to the customer (that is, acquiring a retail outlet) or acquiring the distributors of its products. This strategy gives the business more control over how its products are marketed. Surface Technology, Inc. (STI) is a Trenton, New Jersey–based nickel-plating shop working in a very tough business. To continue to grow, STI must find broader uses for its customers' parts, so it talked to customers to find out exactly what the various processes are that their parts go through before coming to STI for coating, and then where they go after leaving the STI plant. For example, STI found that before certain steel parts came to its shop, they were hardened in a process conducted by another vendor. STI saw a value in developing its own trademarked process and eliminating one vendor from the customer's process. A side benefit was that quality for the customer went up because STI now controlled how the two processes worked together. Similarly, STI developed downstream processes so that eventually it became more of a one-stop shop for the customer.[15]

Horizontal Integration Strategies

Another way to grow the business within the current industry is to buy up competitors or start a competing business (sell the same product under another label). This is *horizontal integration*. For example, an entrepreneur who owns a chain of sporting goods outlets could purchase a business that has complementary products, such as a batting cage business, so that customers can buy their bats, balls, helmets, and the like from the retail store and use them at the batting cage.

Another example of growing horizontally is agreeing to manufacture a product under a different label. This strategy has been used frequently in the major-appliance and grocery industries. Whirlpool, for example, produced the Sears Kenmore washers and dryers for years. Likewise, many major food producers put their brand name food items into packaging labeled with the name of a major grocery store.

Modular or Network Strategies

The latest way for a company to grow within an industry is for the entrepreneur to focus on what he or she does best and let others do the rest. If the core activities of the business include designing and developing new products for the consumer market, other companies can make the parts, assemble the products, and market and deliver them. In essence, the entrepreneur's company and its core activities become the hub of the wheel, with the best suppliers and distributors as the spokes. This **modular strategy,** or **network strategy,** helps the business grow more rapidly, keep unit costs down, and turn out new products more quickly. In addition, the capital saved by not having to invest in fixed assets can be directed to those activities that provide a competitive advantage. The electronics and apparel industries used this growth strategy long before it became trendy. Today many other industries are beginning to see the advantages of a modular approach. Even service businesses can benefit from outsourcing functions such as accounting, payroll, and data processing, which require costly labor.

Outsourcing noncore functions to strategic partners can often help a company get products to market faster and in greater quantities, while at the same time spreading risk and delivering the capabilities of a much larger company without the expense. Finding key capabilities that will help the venture grow more rapidly is another use of outsourcing. The cost to the entrepreneur is perhaps the same as that of performing the task in house, but the company acquires access to key processes and expertise that will speed its growth. In 1994 Family Christian Stores, Inc. had 120 stores and $130 million in sales. The CEO believed that with appropriate information technology systems, the company could grow more rapidly. The CEO put together a partnership with an IT provider that took over FCS's existing IT staff, added more, and replaced all the legacy hardware and software in 18 months. The provider also brought in a financial partner to fund the transformation.[16]

One study found that firms that used "transformational outsourcing" (outsourcing to facilitate rapid change, launch new strategies, and radically change the scope of the company) achieved dramatic results.[17] An example is TiVo, the personal video recorder company founded in 1997. To achieve its goal of becoming the standard in the industry, it had to bring on strategic partners who had competencies that the new company did not have so that it could quickly make a market impact. TiVo brought on board manufacturing and marketing partners such as Sony Corp. and Royal Philips Electronics. But being the first mover is no walk in the park. It is still not clear whether TiVo will ever be able to dominate the market against the deep pockets of cable operators and companies like DirecTV Group Inc.; without question, it could not have achieved its current market position without outsourcing. And 94 percent of U.S. households still don't have digital video recorders.

As with anything else, there are some drawbacks to outsourcing. If most functions are outsourced, it becomes difficult to develop any kind of corporate culture that will bind workers together and make them loyal to the company. When "employees" are no longer employees, they may find it easier to leave on a moment's notice. They also will tend to be less committed to the company's goals because they don't see a long-term role for themselves. These problems also apply to suppliers and distributors to whom an entrepreneur may outsource a capability. They must understand how they can also benefit from this relationship. That way, when the business begins to grow rapidly, they will be willing to ramp up to meet demand.

Diversification Growth Strategies—Growing Outside the Industry

When entrepreneurs expand their businesses by investing in or acquiring products or businesses outside their core competencies and industries, they are employing a **diversification growth strategy.** Generally, but not always, this strategy is used when the entrepreneur has exhausted all growth strategies within the current market and industry and now wants to make use of excess capacity or spare resources, adapt to the needs of customers, or change the direction of the company because of impending changes in the market or economy. One way to diversify is to use a synergistic strategy in which the entrepreneur attempts to locate new products or businesses that are technologically complementary. For example, a food processor may acquire a restaurant chain that can serve as a showcase for the food. Another way to diversify is to acquire products or services unrelated to the company's core products or services. For example, a manufacturer of bicycle helmets may acquire an apparel manufacturer to make clothing with the company logo on it to sell to helmet customers. A final strategy for diversifying, conglomerate diversification, entails acquiring businesses that are not related in any way to what the company is currently doing. An entrepreneur might use this strategy to gain control of a related function of doing business—for example, purchasing the building in which the business is housed and then leasing out excess space to other businesses to produce additional income and gain a depreciable asset. Many entrepreneurs whose work causes them to travel extensively find it advantageous to acquire a travel agency to reduce costs and provide greater convenience.

No matter where a business is located, there are ways to diversify to grow the business. Daffodil Harris started a tiny laundry business out of her boat in Admiralty Bay off a seven-square-mile island called Bequia near the Grenadines. She would travel from yacht to yacht picking up soiled clothing and returning it washed, dried, and folded. People loved the service. But Harris was not satisfied to be a one-person business. By 1999, she had grown the business into a multidivisional conglomerate that included a desalination plant, a marine service to rent moorings and dinghies and repair sails and equipment, a Chinese restaurant, and a grocery store. All of these businesses came out of asking customers what they wanted and then adding that product or service to her diversified offering. Today, Harris employs 23 workers for her multidivisional company, "Daffodil Marine Service."[18]

A diversification strategy for growth is not something to undertake without careful consideration of all the factors and potential outcomes, and this is particularly true of acquisition. The entrepreneur can find consultants who are experts in mergers and acquisitions to help smooth the path financially and operationally, but it is extremely difficult to predict with any degree of confidence how the cultures of the two businesses will merge. Acquisitions and mergers cannot be successful on the basis of financial and operational synergy alone. Organizational styles and the individual personalities of key managers all come into play when an acquisition or a merger takes place. As a result, the human side of the two businesses must be analyzed and a plan developed for merging two potentially distinct cultures into one that can work effectively.

 Global Insights

Surfing in China?

Picture the finest shopping street in Shanghai. Now picture a Quicksilver Boardriders Club positioned between an Adidas outlet and a Starbucks. Surfing in China? What was Quicksilver, the successful Huntington Beach, California, surf, snowboard, and skateboard apparel store, thinking? Well, it was thinking about numbers; there are more teenagers in China than there are people in the United States. That presents a very attractive market for a company whose primary customers are teenagers. Quicksilver's CEO Robert McKnight is confident that patience in this market will pay off. Of the three primary sports that Quicksilver targets, skateboarding appears to be the best one with which to enter the Chinese market.

Quicksilver already had three stores in Hong Kong when it found a partner in Glorious Sun Enterprises, a Shanghai retailer who guided McKnight to open the first Shanghai store at 9:30 a.m. on February 27. This time and day were the most auspicious according to *feng shui*. Quicksilver will also use local celebrities to wear its clothing and educate consumers. Educating customers when there is no readily apparent need to satisfy is entering a market the hard way. Quicksilver will have to create excitement and play on young people's love of having something new that no one else has. Despite the challenge that China presents for these board fanatics, the founders are steadfast in their belief that "there must be waves somewhere."

Sources: L. Earnest, "Catching a Wave of New Consumers," *Los Angeles Times Business Section* (May 16, 2004); and www .quicksilver.com.

Many researchers have attempted to determine the most effective growth strategy for a new venture. In general, it has been found that horizontal integration, vertical integration, and synergistic diversification have been more successful than unrelated diversification. This is true whether the entrepreneur acquires an existing company or starts another company to achieve the goal. That is not to say that unrelated diversification should never be chosen as a growth strategy. If the potential gains are extraordinarily high, the risk may be worth taking. It is also generally true that an acquired business has a better chance of success than a brand-new venture, for the obvious reason that it usually has already passed the crucial start-up and survival stages and is more likely to be poised to grow.

Growing By Going Global

Today the question for a growth-oriented company is not "Should we go global?" but "When should we go global?" There are many reasons why entrepreneurs must consider the global market even as early as the development of their original business plan.

For one thing, because of rapidly changing technology, product lives are growing increasingly short. With R&D so expensive, companies are forced to enter several major markets at once to gain the maximum advantage from brief windows of opportunity. Entrepreneurs who attend world trade shows know that their strongest competition may as easily come from a country in the Pacific Rim as from the company next door. Entrepreneurs also know they may have to rely on other countries for supplies, parts, and even fabrication to keep costs down and remain competitive. The United States, huge market though it is, represents less than half the total global market.[19]

Furthermore, with increasing competition and saturated markets in some industries, looking to global markets can add a new dimension to the entrepreneur's business. Many entrepreneurs have found new applications for their products in other countries or complementary products that help increase the sales of their products domestically. Several events have made exporting U.S. products to other countries more attractive than ever before. Relatively low interest rates in the United States have made it easier for businesses to finance the exporting of their products. The North American Free Trade Agreement (NAFTA) eliminated trade barriers among the United States, Mexico, and Canada, which has made exporting to those countries more attractive. Also, the opening up and growth of untapped markets such as China and Vietnam means more potential customers for U.S. products. The establishment of the first four Federal Export Assistance Centers has provided a new source of help for businesses that are considering exporting. The four centers are located in Baltimore, Long Beach, Miami, and Chicago. The Uruguay Round of GATT (General Agreement on Tariffs and Trade) reduced or eliminated tariffs among 117 countries in 1995. It also improved patent and copyright protection, which is urgently needed by businesses that export protected products to other countries where proprietary rights may not be recognized or protected. Although a global strategy should be contemplated in any business planning, a new venture may not be able to export until it is somewhat established and is offering a high-quality product or service at a competitive price. Nevertheless, more and more "global start-ups"—an example is Logitech, the Swiss manufacturer of computer mouses—take a global strategy from their very inception. Researchers have found that the number of global start-ups appears to be growing.[20] Oviatt and McDougal studied a dozen global start-ups and followed them over time. Four failed, for a variety of reasons, but those that failed tended to exhibit fewer of the "success characteristics" that Oviatt and McDougal found in those that survived. These success characteristics include

1. A global vision from the start.
2. Internationally experienced managers.
3. Strong international business networks.
4. Preemptive technology.
5. A unique intangible asset, such as know-how.
6. Closely linked product or service extensions. (The company derives new and innovative products and services from its core technology.)
7. A closely coordinated organization on a world-wide basis.[21]

However, going global is also a risky proposition. Building a customer base and a distribution network is difficult in the domestic market; it is a colossal challenge in foreign markets. Moreover, financing is more difficult in global markets.

Those concerns are not unfounded. Many small entrepreneurial companies have made their first foray into the global marketplace via a single order from a potential customer in another country. If that one transaction goes smoothly, the entrepreneur may forge ahead under the mistaken impression that doing business in another country is easy. One small computer component business learned that lesson the hard way. The company shipped a $10,000 replacement component to a customer in France. Six months later the naïve entrepreneur was billed $2,500 for value-added tax, something he knew nothing about. He had no choice but to absorb the loss.

Exporting is a long-term commitment that may not pay off for some time. In the meantime, it may be necessary to adapt the product or service somewhat to meet the requirements of the importing country and develop good relationships with agents in the country. If the entrepreneur is dealing in consumer products, it's a good idea to target countries that have disposable income and like U.S. products. If, however, the entrepreneur is dealing in basic or industrial products, it might be wise to look to developing countries that need equipment and services for building infrastructures and systems. One example is Mexico, which is taking on the enormous task of building bridges and roads as it positions itself as a major player in the world market.

Finding the Best Global Market

Finding the best market for a product or service can be a daunting task, but consulting certain sources of information can make the job easier. A good place to start is the *International Trade Statistics Yearbook of the United States,* which is available in any major library or can be purchased online. With the United Nations Standard Industrial Trade Classification (SITC) codes found in this reference book, it is possible to locate information about international demand for a product or service in specific countries. The SITC system is a way of classifying commodities used in international trade. Entrepreneurs should also be familiar with the Harmonized System of classification, which is a ten-digit system that puts the United States "in harmony" with most of the world in terms of commodity-tracking systems. If an international shipment exceeds $2,500, it must have an HS number for documentation.

The district office and the Washington, DC, office of the International Trade Administration are also excellent sources, as is the Department of Commerce (DOC). The commerce department's online database links all the DOC International Trade Administration offices and provides a wealth of valuable research information.

The successful launch of a program of global growth should include a marketing plan and a budget directed toward that goal. It is also important to bring onto the team someone who has international management experience or export experience. Depending on the budget, a consultant who specializes in this area can be hired. It is also a good idea to attend foreign trade shows to learn how businesses in countries of interest conduct business, who the major players are, and who the competition is.

Export Financing

To make a sale in the global market, a company needs funds to purchase the raw materials or inventory to fill the order. Unfortunately, many entrepreneurs assume that if they have a large enough order, getting financing to fill the order will be no problem. Nothing could be further from the truth. Export lenders, like traditional lending sources, want to know that the entrepreneur has a sound business plan and the resources to fill the orders. Entrepreneurs who want to export can look for capital from several sources, including bank financing, internal cash flow from the business, venture capital or private investor capital, and prepayment, down payment, or progress payments from the foreign company placing the order.

A commercial bank is more interested in lending money to a small exporter if the entrepreneur has secured a guarantee of payment from a governmental agency such as the Import-Export Bank, because such a guarantee limits the risk undertaken by the commercial bank. Asking buyers to pay a deposit up-front, enough to cover the purchase of raw materials, can also be a real asset to a young company with limited cash flow.

Foreign Agents, Distributors, and Trading Companies

Every country has a number of sales representatives, agents, and distributors who specialize in importing U.S. goods. It is possible to find one agent who can handle an entire country or region, but if a country has several economic centers, it may be more effective to have a different agent for each center. Sales representatives work on commission; they do not buy and hold products. Consequently, the entrepreneur is still responsible for collecting receivables, which, particularly when one is dealing with a foreign country, can be costly and time-consuming.

Using agents is a way to circumvent this problem. Agents purchase a product at a discount (generally very large) off list and then sell it and handle collections themselves. They solve the problem of cultural differences and the related difficulties inherent in these transactions. Of course, using an agent means losing control over what happens to the product once it leaves the entrepreneur's hands.

The entrepreneur has no say over what the agent actually charges customers in his or her own country. If the agent charges too much in an effort to make more money for himself or herself, the entrepreneur may lose a customer.

Entrepreneurs who are just starting to export or are exporting to areas not large enough to warrant an agent should consider putting an ad in U.S. trade journals that showcase U.S. products internationally. For products the entrepreneur is manufacturing, it may be possible to find a manufacturer in the international region being targeted that will let the entrepreneur sell his or her products through its company, thus providing instant recognition in the foreign country. Ultimately, that manufacturer could also become a source of financing for the entrepreneur's company.

Another option is to use an export trading company (ETC) that specializes in certain countries or regions where it has established a network of sales representatives. ETCs often specialize in certain types of products. What typically happens is that a sales representative may report to the ETC that a particular country is interested in a certain product. The ETC then locates a manufacturer, buys the product, and sells it in the foreign country. Trading companies are a particularly popular vehicle when a company is dealing with Japan.

Choosing an Intermediary

Before deciding on an intermediary to handle the exporting of products, entrepreneurs should undertake some due diligence. Specifically, they should check the intermediary's current listing of products to see whether there is a good match, understand the competition and question whether the intermediary also handles these competitors, and find out whether the intermediary has enough representatives in the foreign country to handle the market. They should also look at the sales volume of the intermediary, which should show a rather consistent level of growth. And they should make sure the intermediary has sufficient warehouse space and up-to-date communication systems, examine the intermediary's marketing plan, and make sure the intermediary can handle servicing of the product.

Once a decision has been made, an agreement detailing the terms and conditions of the relationship should be drafted. This is very much like a partnership agreement, so it is important to consult an attorney who specializes in overseas contracts. The most important thing to remember about the contract is that it must be based on performance, so that if the intermediary is not moving enough product, the contract can be terminated. It is best to negotiate a one- or two-year contract with an option to renew should performance goals be met. This will probably not please the intermediary, because most want a five- to ten-year contract, but it is in the best interests of the entrepreneur to avoid a longer-term contract until the intermediary proves that he or she is loyal and can perform.

Other issues should be addressed in the agreement. Retaining the ability to use another distributor is important. The entrepreneur should negotiate for a nonexclusive contract to have some flexibility and control over distribution. Another issue concerns the specific products the agent or distributor will represent. As the company grows, the entrepreneur may add or develop additional products and may not want this agent to sell those products. Specific geographic territories for which the agent or distributor will be responsible should be outlined, as well as the specific duties and responsibilities of the agent or distributor. Finally, the agreement should include a statement of agreed-upon sales quotas and should indicate the jurisdiction in which any dispute would be litigated. This will protect the entrepreneur from having to go to a foreign country to handle a dispute.

Choosing a Freight Forwarder

The job of the **freight forwarder** is to handle all aspects of delivering the product to the customer. The method by which a product is shipped has a significant impact on the product's cost or on the price to the customer, depending on how the deal is structured, so the choice of a freight forwarder should be carefully considered. Filling shipping containers to capacity is crucial to reducing costs. Freight forwarders can present shipping documents to a bank for collection. They can also prepare the shipping documents, which include a bill of lading (the contract between the shipper and the carrier) and an exporter declaration form detailing the contents of the shipment. The entrepreneur, however, is responsible for knowing whether any items being shipped require special licenses or certificates, as in the case of hazardous materials and certain food substances.

Growth can be an exciting time. And although a company's growth rate won't resemble a hockey stick for long (if ever), strong growth can be sustained over time if entrepreneurs plan for it and keep scanning the horizon for changes.

New Venture Checklist

Have you:

☐ Identified market factors that may affect the growth of the business?

☐ Determined which growth strategy is most appropriate?

☐ Identified potential international markets for the product or service?

☐ Developed a plan for globalization of the company at some point in the future?

Issues to Consider

1. What are four characteristics of high-growth companies?
2. How can both market and management factors affect the growth of a new venture?
3. What questions should you ask at each level of the new venture's growth?
4. What advantages do intensive growth strategies have over integrative and diversification strategies?
5. Why is it important to start a growth-oriented business with a plan for globalization from the beginning?
6. How do foreign agents, distributors, and export trading companies differ in the services they provide?

Experiencing Entrepreneurship

1. Visit an export center in your area and talk to a Department of Commerce trade specialist who can advise you on how to become prepared to export. What did you learn that you hadn't learned from reading this text?

2. Interview an entrepreneur whose new venture is in its early stages, and question him or her about the growth strategy for the business. Can you identify the type of strategy being used?

Additional Sources of Information

Catlin, K., and J. Matthews (2001). *Leading at the Speed of Growth: Journey from Entrepreneur to CEO.* New York: Wiley.

DePalma, D.A. (2002). *Business Without Borders.* New York: Wiley.

Hill, C.W.L. (2000). *International Business: Competing in the Global Marketplace: Postscript 2001.* New York: Irwin.

McKnight, L.W., P.M. Vaaler, and R.L. Katz (2001). *Creative Destruction: Business Survival Strategies in the Global Internet Economy.* Cambridge, MA: MIT Press.

Trade Information Center. Tel. (800) USA-TRADE or (800) 872–8723. Ask for an industry desk officer who specializes in your industry.

Woznick, A., and E.G. Hinkelman (2000). *A Basic Guide to Exporting.* 3d ed. Novato, CA: World Trade Press.

Relevant Case Studies

Case 1 Overnite Express, p. 402
Case 4 Wizards of the Coast, p. 423

Case 5 iRobot, p. 432
Case 8 Finagle a Bagel, p. 450

18

Planning for Change

"We know not yet what we have done, still less what we are doing. Wait till evening and other parts of our day's work will shine than we had thought at noon, and we shall discover the real purport of our toil."

Henry David Thoreau

LEARNING OBJECTIVES

- List the components of a contingency plan.
- Discuss the purpose of a harvest plan.
- Describe how to deal with failure: bankruptcy.

Profile 18.1 TAKING RISK IN UNCERTAIN TIMES

Ron Perry was faced with what appeared to be a golden opportunity whose downside was the potential loss of $1 million, but whose upside was at least 10 times that amount. His Montana power company, Commercial Energy, was approached by a railroad that was trying to reduce its electricity prices by generating energy at much lower cost from diesel locomotives that were not in service. The deal was that Perry's company would put up $1 million, which would pay half the cost of retrofitting the locomotives. Commercial Energy would also handle sales and the scheduling of power transmission to customers.

This was a highly risky venture from the standpoint that using trains to generate power was basically unheard of. Moreover, the energy market was extremely unstable, with "landmines" everywhere. Nevertheless, Perry could identify three reasons why this might be a good investment. If the venture succeeded, he would have a 50 percent share in the profits. He would also develop a closer relationship with his most important customer, and he would have an opportunity to begin producing his own power, a long-term goal of his company.

Understanding the nature of his industry well, Perry was a fanatic about risk management. As part of the due diligence he conducted in the course of making this investment decision, he used Crystal Ball, a software product that predicts the probability that various energy-price scenarios will occur. He supplied the computer model with every variable he could imagine and created thousands of alternative scenarios involving possible fluctuations in the price of electricity and diesel fuel. Then he had the program calculate three things: 1) the likelihood that those prices would move in opposite directions, 2) the potential customer demand, and 3) the contract prices. He discovered that the greatest probability was that his company would earn $2 million to $3 million in six months.

If opportunities depended only on business models and did not include the human element, Perry would have been correct in deciding to move forward with the investment. He clearly understood the industry and knew what he stood to lose; he also knew that he could withstand the loss. But problems emerged when neighbors complained about having a Diesel conversion plant near their homes. The neighbors' complaints attracted local environmental groups, who managed to attract *NBC Nightly News,* and soon the railroad began to backpedal on the deal. Finally, when the Federal Energy Regulatory Commission capped electricity prices at $100 a megawatt, both parties realized that the profits they predicted would not materialize. When the deal fell apart, Perry had lost about half his investment.

Perry was philosophical about the loss, calling it a reversible risk. Risks are not all equal in their severity. The important question is whether, if the deal fails, the company will recover. In Perry's case, he knew it would. He had examined the opportunity under many different assumptions, so his decision to go forward was a good one given the information he had at the time.

Sources: Commercial Energy of Montana, http://www.commercialenergy.net/; and L. Buchanan, "How to Take Risks in a Time of Anxiety," *Inc. Magazine* (May 2003), www.inc.com.

If one thing is certain about entrepreneurship, it is that change will be an inevitable part of any venture's life. There is no way to avoid change because businesses today operate in a very dynamic environment; therefore, they must be ready and willing to adapt to new conditions, new threats, and new opportunities. No crystal ball exists to tell entrepreneurs precisely what the future holds for their new ventures. Many an entrepreneur has started a business with a vision and a plan for where that business would go but has found that things changed along the way. Forces beyond the control of the entrepreneur pushed the venture in new directions, and a new set of plans had to be constructed. That was certainly the case for Commercial Energy of Montana when it considered undertaking an extremely risky venture to grow (see Profile 18.1).

Consider the highly volatile technology market during the first two years of the new millennium. How many entrepreneurs who had developed business plans for new e-commerce ventures and were seeking capital in early 2000 knew that their window of opportunity to secure those investments was about to close? In April of that year the stock market plummeted, foreshadowing an enormous shakeout in the dot com world and the end of "money for nothing." In a matter of months, hundreds of potential new e-commerce ventures failed to make it to the marketplace because they had no backup plan in place.

Some would argue that the signs were there all along, but the easy availability of venture capital inspired the notion that all an entrepreneur needed was a great idea to scale out to a huge market. In any case, most entrepreneurs were not prepared for the change and had no contingency plans in place.

Business owners everywhere knew that the war in Iraq was coming and that they would have to operate a company during what might be a protracted period of high uncertainty. No one knew what the impact of the war would be, so for a time, businesses held off on plans to expand. They stopped hiring, and their sales slowed while the economy sputtered under a constant barrage of news from the front. But those businesses that had stayed in touch with the economy, had diversified, and had made contingency plans did not feel the impact nearly as much as their less-prepared counterparts. Sam Brown, the CEO of Knight & Carver, a San Diego yacht builder, recognized that his business involved discretionary purchases and customers who, in down times, would simply stop buying yachts. His business couldn't afford to wait until times changed, so it made sense to diversify into business activities that didn't experience the same kind of response to a down economy. As early as 1996, Knight & Carver began exploring the alternative-energy business to use their expertise in composite materials to build wind turbine blades. The demand was great, and this new venture provided a strong additional stream of revenue for the company. When the war began, Brown was uncertain how much of a toll it would take on his business, but because about 70 percent of his business came from repair work, he was relieved to find that customers were still taking care of repairs on their vessels.

Brown is an example of a business owner who knows the value of contingency planning. In the absence of planning, entrepreneurs find themselves in a reactionary mode, dealing from a position of weakness.

One of the events for which entrepreneurs often fail to plan is the harvest or exit from the business. Knowing in what manner the entrepreneur wants to realize the benefits of having created a successful business guides decision making throughout the life of the business. This chapter looks at contingency planning, alternatives for harvesting the wealth of the venture, and alternatives to consider if the venture should fail.

The Components of a Contingency Plan

By compelling entrepreneurs to consider multiple outcomes and possibilities, contingency plans help a growing business deal with downturns and upturns in the economy, new regulations, changes in customer tastes and preferences, and many other events that regularly—and often without much warning—disrupt the equilibrium of the firm. The 2001 recession pointed out how many businesses fail to understand business cycles. Recessions in general are actually quite normal in the U.S. economy, but the 2001 recession displayed distinct characteristics resulting from the fact that it occurred in the middle of an industrial revolution.[1] American icons such as Bethlehem Steel, Burlington, Kmart, and United Airlines all faced bankruptcies. However, recessions do not happen overnight. There are signs, even within specific industries, that signal a slowdown. Since the government began compiling indices on the economy after World War II, some consistent trends have emerged. For example, the Leading Index of Economic Indicators, which consists of such items as the Producer Price Index, the Consumer Confidence Index, and the Manufacturers' Orders for Durable Goods, typically declines for 9 months prior to the onset of a recession. The **coincident-lagging index,** which is a ratio of the coincident index (employment, personal income, industrial production) to the lagging index (Consumer Price Index, interest rates, unemployment), declines for 13 months prior to the onset of a recession.

Recognizing the signs of recession before they affect the business gives the entrepreneur a chance to prepare in many ways, including maintaining a higher degree of liquidity. In recessionary times, it is more difficult to raise capital from either bankers or private sources, so liquidity opens up opportunities that become available only during recessions. For example, the entrepreneur may be able to purchase a building that in good economic times was beyond reach, or he or she may be able to negotiate more favorable terms from suppliers just to keep the business moving forward.

An effective contingency plan will answer several important questions:

1. In the event of a problem, which suppliers would be willing to extend the entrepreneur's repayment time and for how much?
2. What nonessential assets does the business have that can be turned into cash quickly?
3. Is there additional investment capital that could be tapped?
4. Does the business have customers who might be willing to prepay or purchase earlier than planned?
5. Has a good relationship with a banker and accountant been established? How can they help the business get through the crunch?

After answering these questions, entrepreneurs can (1) identify the potential risks associated with their venture, (2) calculate the probability that those identified risks will in fact occur, (3) assign a level of significance to the losses, and (4) calculate the overall loss risk.[2]

Identifying Potential Risks

Risk is a fact of business life, and a company's exposure to risk increases as the venture grows. Understanding where the risk lies allows the entrepreneur to respond

Socially Responsible Entrepreneurship

The Social Venture Network

What happens when a group of visionary leaders come together to make a difference in the world of entrepreneurship and investment. What happens is a nonprofit network, the Social Venture Network (SVN), whose mission is to promote "models and leadership for socially and environmentally sustainable business." SVN has created a community of practice that provides information and community forums that empower their members to achieve the vision collectively. Founded in 1987, SVN's membership stands at nearly 400 business owners, investors, and nonprofit leaders who are dedicated to making the business world a better place. One of SVN's passionate members is Judy Wicks, founder of the White Dog Café in Philadelphia. Serving a clientele that includes the University of Pennsylvania, Wicks's café is a hot spot for promoting social causes in addition to providing locally grown organic foods. In a tough industry where margins are in the 3 percent range, Wicks is posting margins of 7.4 percent. Once a year, the White Dog offers eco tours to visit a family farm or a water treatment facility. On Monday nights, traditionally a slow night in the industry, the restaurant hosts a celebrity lecture series, featuring speakers such as Eric Schlosser, author of *Fast Food Nation*. Find out more about SVN at http://www.svn.org/organization.html.

---

effectively through process improvement strategies and buffer strategies. *Process improvement strategies* involve reducing the probability that the risk will occur by forming strategic alliances with strong partners[3] or developing backup suppliers and better communication with suppliers.[4] However, even with process improvement strategies in place, it is impossible to eliminate risk completely. *Buffer strategies* are used to protect the company against potential risk that can't be prevented. Maintaining sufficient inventory and alternative sources of supply are two types of buffer strategies.

Supply Chain Risks

The common practice of outsourcing the upstream activities of the business—raw materials, manufacturing, assembly, inventory—presents advantages and risks to the entrepreneur. The advantages of outsourcing include the sharing of risk, expertise, and resources. The risks are many and significant, however. The financial health of the supplier is critical to the stability of the entrepreneur's business. When a supplier faces financial hardships and cannot provide supplies, raw materials, and so forth in a timely manner and the entrepreneur has no backup, the results can be loss of customers and, in some cases, the failure of the entrepreneur's business. Supplier capacity constraints are another source of risk for the entrepreneur. When demand fluctuates or increases precipitously, suppliers may not be able to ramp up quickly enough to meet the demand.[5] Quality-related risks and the inability of suppliers to keep up with technological change can have ramifications throughout the entire value chain, including raising the cost of producing a product.[6] Changes in customer needs can affect product design and, by extension, the types and quantities of supplies needed. When suppliers are unable to make changes in product design that are required, entrepreneurs incur a risk. Finally, risks in the form of disasters—floods, fire, earthquakes—can disrupt supply chains and affect the entrepreneur's ability to manufacture and distribute products.

Taxes and Regulations

During the life of every business, new laws, regulations, and rules will be enacted, and frequently there is no way to prepare for them. Government regulations and regulatory paperwork are severe problems for growing ventures, and the cost of compliance is rising to the point where entrepreneurs are looking for ways to avoid coming under the purview of some of the regulations. For example, the Family Leave Act now has a threshold firm size of 50 employees, which means that very small businesses are now faced with the possible protracted absence of an employee who cannot easily be replaced. As a result, many small businesses fight to stay below that important number.

The cost of employing an individual is becoming so prohibitive that many companies are solving the problem by subcontracting work and leasing employees. The U.S Department of Labor reports that employers' costs for employee compensation averaged $24.95 an hour in March 2004.[7] Of this cost, 28 percent was attributed to employee benefits, which include such things as paid vacations, holidays, sick leave, and other leave; supplemental pay (overtime and premium pay for work in addition to the regular work schedule, such as weekends and holidays); insurance benefits (life, health, short-term disability, and long-term disability insurance); retirement and savings benefits; and legally required benefits (Social Security, Medicare, federal and state unemployment insurance, and workers' compensation). Benefits, as a percentage of total compensation, have increased every year since 2001. It is no wonder that many business owners prefer to work with independent contractors. However, the government is cracking down on businesses that incorrectly categorize people as independent contractors, so IRS rules must be carefully followed. (See Chapter 7.)

Product Liability

The chances are fairly good that any company that manufactures products will face a product liability suit at some point. The states with the heaviest concentration of industry naturally have the highest number of claims, with Pennsylvania, Ohio, Texas, and New York leading the list. More and more of the risk of product-related injuries has been shifted to manufacturers, creating a legal minefield that could prove disastrous to a growing company.

Even if a company carefully designs and manufactures a product and covers it with warnings and detailed instructions, that company may still be vulnerable if misuse of the product results in injury. For a company to be legally liable, the product must be defective and an injury must have occurred. But in a litigious society, those requirements don't stop people from initiating lawsuits. Most product liability insurance covers the costs of defense, personal injury, or property damage, but not lost sales and the cost of product redesign. Moreover, if the insurance company must pay on a claim, the entrepreneur's premiums will no doubt increase.

A growing company must plan for potential litigation from the very inception of the business. One proven method is to establish a formal safety panel that includes people from all the major functional areas of the business. During the start-up phase, that panel may consist of only the entrepreneur and one or two outside advisers with experience in the area. It is the job of the safety panel to review safety requirements on a regular basis, establish new ones when necessary, and document any injuries or claims made against the product.

Prior to product introduction in the marketplace, the panel should see that careful records are maintained of all decisions regarding final product design, testing, and evaluation procedures. Advertising of the product should contain no exaggerated claims or implied promises that may give customers the impression that the company is claiming more safety features than the product actually has. Implied promises can be used against the entrepreneur in a court of law. Instruction manuals should be easy to follow and should point out potential hazards. They should also include guidelines for when and how to service the product, which components made by other manufacturers are not covered by the company's warranty (unless pass-through warranties have been negotiated), and statements that the warranty is invalidated by misuse, improper assembly, or modification and is valid only if the specified maintenance procedures are followed. Of course, the best insurance is to keep in contact with customers so that if a problem occurs, the entrepreneur will be given an opportunity to fix it before legal action is taken.

Early in the operation of the business, it is important to identify a qualified attorney familiar with the industry to handle any potential product liability claims. This attorney should handle the first case that confronts the business. Thereafter, if other suits arise in various parts of the country, the entrepreneur can save money by hiring a "local attorney" in the jurisdiction of the claim. Then the primary attorney should brief the local attorney on the precedent-setting cases related to the claim and assist while the local attorney carries the case to court. In this way, the entrepreneur does not have to send the primary attorney on the road, incurring significant travel and time expenses.

Succession Planning

Even less today than in the past can any company count on having the same management team over the life of the business—or even after the start-up phase.

The Loss of Key Employees

The demand for top-notch management personnel (particularly in some industries, such as high-tech) means that other companies will constantly be trying to woo the best people away from the best firms. Losing a CEO in times of high turnover, not to mention physical risks such as death, is not uncommon. In 2001, many companies changed CEOs, including Yahoo, Maytag, Hershey Foods, Gateway, and GE. Succession planning—identifying people who can take over key company positions in an emergency—is thus an important part of contingency planning. Ideally that person or persons will come from within the company, but in the case of a growing entrepreneurial company that has been operating in a "lean and mean" mode, promoting from within may not be possible, so outsiders must be found. To prepare for the possible loss of a key employee, the entrepreneur must have shared his or her

Pro2serve homepage

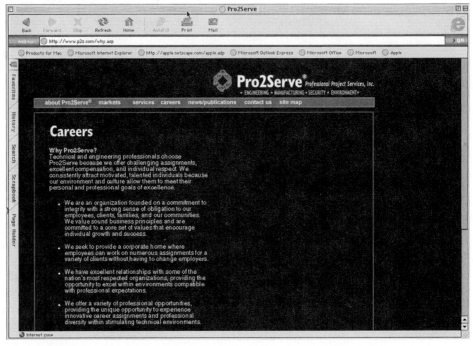

Source: http://www.p2s.com/why.asp, accessed 9/1/04.

vision for the company with others both inside and outside the company. It's also a good idea to purchase "key-person insurance" to cover the cost of suddenly having to replace someone.

Barry Goss is the owner of Pro2Serve, a 225-person engineering firm based in Oak Ridge, Tennessee. Recognizing that employee turnover is high and is a significant risk to his business, he came up with a plan to stem the tide. When the company lands a big contract, he treats all the employees to a special dinner, and every week he sends out dozens of thank-you e-mails to employees who are doing particularly good jobs. He also promotes from within the company. He doesn't want to fall, as so many businesses have, into the trap of being lulled into complacency during the last couple of years when turnover was low because jobs were scarce. Employees in general are overworked and looking for pre-recession benefits and salaries. The business environment has the makings of a "perfect storm," causing a tidal wave of employee exits.[8]

Bringing in a consultant to guide the management team in succession planning is a valuable exercise for any growing venture. Often consultants are even hired temporarily to take over a vacant position for a specified period, during which they train a permanent successor. Another solution is to cross-train people in key positions so that someone can step in, at least for the short term, in the event of an emergency. Cross training is generally an integral part of a team-based approach to organizational management.

Succession Planning in Family-Owned Businesses

Entrepreneurs who head family-owned companies face special problems because they tend to look to a son, daughter, or other family member to succeed them. Succession in a family-owned business will not happen unless it is planned for, however. In fact, over half of family-owned businesses don't continue into the second generation.[9] This is partly because the entrepreneur must deal not only with business issues related to succession—ownership, management, strategic planning—but also with the unexpected, such as a death and relationship issues with family members, a much more difficult task. Succession planning tends to expose family issues that may have been kept in the background but have been building over time. For example, the daughter whom the entrepreneur assumed would take over the business may have no interest in doing so but may never have told her entrepreneur father. Or, by contrast, the child may believe himself or herself capable of simply stepping into a managerial role with no previous experience. If the entrepreneur has created a plan for succession, a problem like this may be solved by making it a requirement that a child or potential successor work for another company for several years to gain some business savvy and to decide whether he or she wants to take over the family business. Robert Bradford is CEO of the Center for Simplified Strategic Planning in Ann Arbor, Michigan. He believes that it is important to think about succession planning very early in the growth of the business, because finding the right person to succeed the entrepreneur parent in the business is not an easy task.[10] CEOs act as visionaries and also play functional roles, balancing finance, marketing, and operations. A person whom an entrepreneur has chosen to succeed him or her must be given the time to understand the role; it's not something that will happen overnight. Bradford planned for succession by evaluating his current human resources and also the company's ability to evaluate a potential candidate. He wrote his own job description and then began looking at people inside his firm for signs of leadership skills. Once he had narrowed the field to a few potential candidates, he asked them to do a self-assessment. Then he compared the gaps between the skills they believed they had and his own job description. In fact, Bradford did this himself before he succeeded his father in the business.

To start the process of succession planning, put all the active family members on a committee to explore the options. Some of the questions to examine are the following:

- Is the next generation being sufficiently prepared to take over the business when the time comes?
- What is the second generation's expectation for the future of the business, and is it congruent with the company's vision?
- What skills and experience does the second generation need to acquire?
- What would the ideal succession plan look like?

Then, with the help of an attorney, buy–sell agreements should be developed to ensure that heirs receive a fair price for their interest in the business upon a partner's death and to protect against irreparable damage in the event of a shareholder's permanent disability by outlining provisions for buying out the disabled partner's interest. An estate planning professional can help evaluate the impact of any changes in the business on the entrepreneur's personal assets.

Given that most privately owned businesses in the United States are family-owned businesses, this succession planning strategy is useful for any business that wants to be prepared for the loss or retirement of its leader.

Decline in Sales

When sales decline and positive cash flow starts looking like a memory, entrepreneurs often go into a period of denial. They start paying their suppliers more slowly to preserve cash, they lay people off, they stop answering the phone, and they insulate themselves against the demands of their creditors. Their panic frequently causes them to make poor decisions about how to spend the precious cash they do have. They figure that if they can just hold on long enough, things will turn around. Unfortunately, this attitude only makes the problem worse, effectively propelling the business toward its ultimate demise. How can an entrepreneur lose touch with the business and the market so much that he or she puts the business at risk? What often happens is that entrepreneurs get so wrapped up in the day-to-day operations of the business that they don't have time to contemplate the "big picture" or stay in tune with their customers. Consequently, all too often they don't see a potential crisis coming until it's too late.

When sales decline, lowering prices isn't necessarily the solution. If the entrepreneur has educated the company's customers about the value of the product or service, any such sudden discounting will confuse them. When there is a decline in sales, it is especially important to look at all possible sources, not just the economy. The entrepreneur may have been lax about checking the credit status of customers and distributors, or the inventory turnover rate may have changed. The entrepreneur may have failed to notice an emerging competitor offering a product or service more in line with current tastes and preferences.

When a growing business first notices a dip in sales, it is time to find the cause and make the necessary changes. This will be easier if the business has a contingency plan in place. If, however, those changes cannot be made in time to forestall a cash-flow problem, it is time to consult a debt negotiation company, a crisis management consultant, or a bankruptcy attorney who is willing to work through the problem without going to court. These experts can help the entrepreneur work with creditors until the problem is resolved. To prepare the best defense against a cash-flow crisis, entrepreneurs must remain committed to producing exceptional-quality products; controlling the cost of overhead, particularly where that overhead does not contribute directly to revenue generation (expensive cars, travel, excessive commissions); controlling production costs through subcontracting and being frugal about facilities; making liquidity and positive cash flow the prime directive, so that the company can ride out temporary periods of declining demand; and having a contingency plan in place.

Calculating the Probability That the Risk Will Occur

It is extremely difficult to calculate the probability that a given risk will occur with any degree of accuracy.[11] Consequently, any cost/benefit analysis conducted will probably have flaws and may even cause the company to decide that the cost of protecting itself is not worth it for the return on the investment.[12] Nonetheless, it is important to gauge, based on industry and customer knowledge, the chance that a particular risk will occur. For example, an entrepreneur might want to know how many widgets to order for the summer season. He knows he can sell 50 in a day and that he makes a profit of $10 each. The average number of days in the season is 95. Thus he multiplies 4,750 widgets times $10 to get the average profit for the season. He has just committed a common error that Sam Savage, a consulting professor at Stanford University, has called the "flaw of averages."[13] The problem with averages is that they mask risk. Savage claims that average inputs don't always produce average outputs. For example, if a lower-than-average demand produces a lower-than-average revenue, then a higher-than-average demand is not possible because the company would have made only enough product to satisfy an average demand. This kind of error is quickly exposed when doing probability modeling such as Monte Carlo simulation, which models multiple uncertainties within a specified period. Decision trees are another way to decide whether to do something. Working with these types of modeling packages are a good way to get a feel for risk.

Assigning a Level of Significance to the Losses

Assigning a level of significance is again an arbitrary exercise, because the weight given to any impact of risk is based on the company's goals, core competencies, and focus. The importance of assigning a significance level lies in the need to distribute limited resources effectively. Most entrepreneurs don't do contingency planning because they have neither the time nor the resources to devote to it. Therefore, if probable risks are identified and rank-ordered, it is easier to choose where to allocate whatever resources are available.

Calculating the Overall Risk of Loss

The overall risk of loss is simply the sum of the risk times its probability of occurring times the cost of the impact to the business times the level of significance. For example, suppose an entrepreneur determines that there is a 40 percent chance that she will lose a key manager to a competitor. The financial cost of that loss is the cost of doing a search for a new manager, which she estimates at $10,000 (this does not include the nonfinancial costs, such as loss of tacit knowledge). She assigns a weight of 80 percent, on a scale of 1 percent to 100 percent to reflect the importance of this risk. Thus the overall risk of loss is approximately $3,200 [($10,000 × 0.40) × 0.80]. If the entrepreneur does this for all the identified risks, it will be easier to decide on which risks to concentrate efforts and focus resources.

The Harvest Plan

Many first-time entrepreneurs have questioned the need for an exit plan, or harvest plan, because they are more concerned with launching the business and making it a success than with thinking about how they're going to get out. But even though some entrepreneurs stay with their new ventures for the long term, the majority enjoy the challenge of start-up and the excitement of growth and abhor the custodial role of managing a stable, mature company. Consequently, exiting the business does not necessarily mean exiting the role of entrepreneur. It may in fact mean taking the financial rewards of having grown a successful business and investing them in a new venture.

There are entrepreneurs who do that very thing over and over again throughout their lives, and in the recent past we have seen more and more entrepreneurs build businesses to "flip"—that is, to take public or sell to a larger firm. In other cases, when the venture reaches a certain size, the business needs professional management skills that the entrepreneur does not possess. In fact, the entrepreneur may actually be holding the company back without realizing it. Whether or not an entrepreneur intends to exit the business at that point, there should be a plan for harvesting the rewards of having started the business in the first place.

Entrepreneurs need to think of their companies as part of an ongoing career path. So says Jerome Katz, professor of management at St. Louis University. He has been studying the career paths of entrepreneurs and finds that there are four major types:

1. **Growth entrepreneurs.** These are entrepreneurs who measure their success by the size of their company. They tend not to have an exit plan because they're always striving for bigger, better, faster.

2. **Habitual entrepreneurs.** These are people who love to start businesses and may start and run several at once. They are probably even less likely to have an exit plan because there are always new opportunities out there.

3. **Harvest entrepreneurs.** These entrepreneurs start and build a venture for the purpose of selling it. Some of these owners will start, build, and harvest many companies during a career.

4. **Spiral, or helical, entrepreneurs.** Women entrepreneurs often fall into this category. These entrepreneurs are driven by what is going on in their personal lives, so their entrepreneurial tendencies emerge in spurts. At times they may appear oblivious to the business as they deal with family issues.

Katz believes it is never too early to begin to think about an endgame strategy, so that the exit will be graceful rather than "feet first."[14] The following paragraphs examine several methods by which an entrepreneur can achieve a rewarding harvest.

Selling the Business

Selling the business outright to another company or an individual may be the goal if the entrepreneur is ready to move on to something else and wants to be financially and mentally free to do so. Unfortunately, however, selling a business is a life-changing event. For several years, the entrepreneur has probably devoted the majority of his or her time and attention to growing the business, and it played an important role in structuring the entrepreneur's life. When the business has been sold, its owner may experience a sense of loss, much like what accompanies the death of a loved one. If the owner has not prepared for this change, emotional stress could be the consequence. Therefore, planning for this enormous change will be very important. (Several alternatives to selling the business outright are discussed in the next section.)

The best way to sell a business is for the entrepreneur to know almost from the beginning that selling is what he or she wants to do. In this case, the entrepreneur will make decisions for the business that will place it in the best position for a sale several years later. For one thing, the business will need audited financial statements that give the business forecasts more credibility. The tax strategy will not be to minimize taxes by showing low profits but, rather, to show actual profits and pay the taxes on them, because the entrepreneur will probably more than make up for the expense at the time of sale. Higher recorded profits are likely to make the business worth more. Business expenses and activity should be kept totally separate from personal expenses. It will also be important to plan for the time it will take to sell the business and wait to sell until the window of opportunity has opened.

Smaller businesses for sale often use the services of business brokers; however, a high-growth venture is more likely to employ the services of an investment banking firm that has experience with the industry. Investment banks normally want a retainer to ensure the seriousness of the commitment to sell, but that retainer will be applied against the final fee on the sale, which averages 5 percent of the purchase price. It is recommended, however, that a third party with no vested interest in the sale be enlisted to judge the fair market value of the business. This "appraiser" can also prepare financial projections based on the history of the company and the appraiser's independent market research.

When a business is sold, the entrepreneur does not have to sell all the assets. For example, the building could be held out of the sale and leased back to the business purchaser, with the original owner staying on as landlord.

While the potential purchaser is conducting due diligence on the entrepreneur and the business, the entrepreneur needs to do the same with the purchaser. The purchasing firm or individual should be thoroughly checked out against a list of criteria the entrepreneur has developed. The purchaser should have the resources necessary to continue the growth of the business, be familiar with the industry and with the type of business being purchased, have a good reputation in the industry, and offer skills and contacts that will ensure that the business continues in a positive direction. In order to compare one buyer with another fairly, it is often helpful to make a complete list of criteria and then weight them to reflect their relative importance.

Cashing Out But Staying In

Sometimes entrepreneurs reach the point where they would like to take the bulk of their investment and gain out of the business but are not yet ready to cut the cord entirely. They may want to continue to run the business or at least retain a minority interest. There are several mechanisms by which this can occur.

Selling Stock

If the company is still privately owned, the remaining shareholders may want to purchase the entrepreneur's stock at current market rates so that control doesn't end up in other hands. In fact, the shareholders' agreement that was drafted when the entrepreneur set up the corporation may have specified that shareholders must offer the stock to the company before offering it to anyone else.

If the company is publicly traded, the task of selling the stock is much simpler; however, if the entrepreneur owns a substantial portion of the issued stock, strict guidelines set out by the SEC must be followed when liquidating the shareholders' interests. If the company had a successful IPO, founders' stock will have increased substantially in value, which presents a tax liability that should not be ignored. That is why many entrepreneurs in such situations cash out only what they need to support whatever goals they have. This strategy, of course, is based on the presumption that the company stock will continue its upward trend for the foreseeable future.

Restructuring

Entrepreneurs who want to cash out a significant portion of their investment and turn over the reins to a son, daughter, or other individual can do so by splitting the business into two firms, with the entrepreneur owning the firm that has all the assets (plant, equipment, vehicles) and the other person owning the operating aspect of the business while leasing the assets from the entrepreneur's company. See Figure 18.1.

A Phased Sale

Some entrepreneurs want to soften the emotional blow of selling the business, not to mention softening the tax consequences, by agreeing with the buyer—an individual or another firm—to sell in two phases. During the first phase, the entrepreneur sells a percentage of the company but remains in control of operations and can continue to grow the company to the point at which the buyer has agreed to complete the purchase. This approach gives the entrepreneur the ability to cash out a portion of his or her investment and still manage the business for an agreed-upon time, during which the new owner will probably be learning the business and phasing in. In the second phase, the business is sold at a prearranged price, usually a multiple of earnings.

This approach is fairly complex and should always be guided by an attorney experienced in acquisitions and buy–sell agreements. The buy–sell agreement,

---

FIGURE 18.1   Restructuring the Business

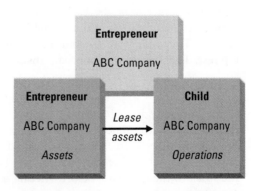

Profile 18.2 HOW DO YOU GRACEFULLY EXIT FROM ENRON?

It was 2001 and Tracy Price was on top of the world. As the co-founder/CEO of FieldCentrix Inc., an Irvine, California, software company, Price was about to sell his small company to Enron Corp, the company whose unethical and fraudulent practices in the energy industry would lead to its downfall in a matter of months. Price had negotiated this acquisition because the IPO market was, for all intents and purposes, dead, so selling to a Fortune 500 company appeared to be the next best thing. Price had conceived FieldCentrix as a producer of software and computer systems for field service technicians. Its field service system eliminates field paperwork, the critical pain of field engineers, by letting them submit time sheets, services performed, travel time, and expenses from a handheld device via a wireless Internet connection. The sale to Enron would provide FieldCentrix with a cash infusion and a richer resource base. The new entity would be called ServiceCo Holding Inc. Enron would hold a minority stake in FieldCentrix and would put it and several subsidiaries into the holding company. Price and his partners received cash and stock in the new entity. But just a few months later, when Enron filed a bankruptcy petition, FieldCentrix realized that it had to find a way to separate itself from Enron. Otherwise, it could potentially be sold to the highest bidder in liquidation with its investors losing everything.

When Enron filed for Chapter 11 reorganization, Price and his investors began to look at their options. They decided to seek an investor to provide buyout funding. The original investors had put $37.5 million into FieldCentrix and now were faced with the possibility of having to invest more to save what they had. After numerous meetings and negotiations with Enron, FieldCentrix separated from Enron and, in April 2004, announced an $8.9 million investment from existing and new partners to finance its efforts to retain its leadership position in the field.

Sources: FieldCentrix, www.fieldcentrix.com; "FieldCentrix Secures $8.9 Million from New and Existing Equity Investment Partners," *PR Newswire* (April 5, 2004); and A. Simons, "Small Company Tries to Shake Loose of Enron," *Los Angeles Business Journal* (October 14, 2002).

which spells out the terms of the purchase, specifies the amount of control the new owner can exert over the business before the sale has been completed and the amount of proprietary information that will be shared with the buyer between Phases 1 and 2.

Joining a Roll-up

In recent times, the consolidation play has become a way for many small business owners to realize the wealth they have created in their businesses. This is how it works. A large, established company finds a fragmented industry with a lot of mom-and-pop–type businesses. The consolidator buys them up and puts them under one umbrella to create economies of scale in the industry. The local management team often stays in power, while the parent company begins to build a national brand presence. The payoff for the entrepreneur comes when the consolidator takes the company public and buys out all the independent owners.

It is important to conduct due diligence on any consolidator, because one's ability to cash out will be a function of the consolidator's ability to grow the company and take it public.

Dealing with Failure: Bankruptcy

Death is certainly part of the business life cycle, and some entrepreneurs must exit their businesses through liquidation. For whatever reasons, the business could not manage a down sales cycle, find new sources of revenue, pay its obligations, or secure capital to float the business until conditions improved. Certainly no entrepreneur starts a high-growth venture with liquidation in mind as the exit strategy, but sometimes the forces working against the business are so great that the entrepreneur must have an exit vehicle so he or she can move on to do something else. What forces a corporation into bankruptcy is difficult to pinpoint. The immediately precipitating cause is the failure to pay debt; however, myriad other events contributed to that cause. They include a lack of understanding of economic and business cycles, excessive debt, surplus overhead, shifts in demand, excessive expenses, poor dividend policies, union problems, supplier problems, and poor financial management. Of course, the common denominator for all these factors is poor management.

Not all businesses can file for bankruptcy protection. Those that are exempt include savings and loan associations, banks, insurance companies, and foreign companies. Furthermore, a bankruptcy filing cannot occur where the intent has been to defraud, and a company may file only once every six years.

The Bankruptcy Reform Act of 1978 and Public Law 95–958 provide for more than just liquidation of the business. Therefore, it is important to have a clear understanding of the bankruptcy mechanisms available if the entrepreneur is faced with financial adversity. The bankruptcy code consists of several chapters, but two chapters are relevant to an entrepreneurial business: Chapter 7 discusses liquidation, and Chapter 11 handles reorganization of businesses.

Chapter 11

Chapter 11 reorganization under the bankruptcy code is really not a bankruptcy in the commonly used sense of the word. It is simply a reorganization of the finances of the business so that it can continue to operate and begin to pay its debts. Only in the case where the creditors believe the management is unable to carry out the terms of the reorganization plan is a trustee appointed to run the company until the debt has been repaid. Otherwise, the entrepreneur remains in control of the business while in a Chapter 11 position. If the entrepreneur has aggregate noncontingent liquidated secured and unsecured debts that do not exceed $2 million (11 U.S.C. Sec. §101[51C]), then she or he qualifies to be considered a small business owner, which puts the case on a fast track and doesn't require a creditors' committee. After filing for reorganization, the entrepreneur and the creditors must meet within 30 days to discuss the status and organization of the business. The court then appoints a committee, which usually consists of the seven largest unsecured creditors, to develop a plan for the business with the entrepreneur. That plan must be submitted within 120 days, and acceptance of the plan must come within 60 days of submittal. Of the total number of creditors affected by the plan, representing at least two-thirds of the total dollar amount, at least one-half must accept the plan. Once the court has approved the reorganization plan, the entrepreneur is relieved of any debts except those specified in the plan.

Chapter 7

The filing of a petition under Chapter 7 of the bankruptcy code constitutes an Order for Relief and is usually chosen when the business does not have sufficient resources to pay creditors while continuing to operate. It is essentially the liquidation of the assets of the business and the discharge of most types of debt. The debtor files a petition and several required schedules of assets and liabilities with the bankruptcy court serving the area in which he or she lives. A trustee is appointed to manage the disposition of the business, and a meeting of the creditors is held 20 to 40 days after the petition is filed. The goal of the bankruptcy is to reduce the business to cash and distribute the cash to the creditors where authorized. After exemptions, the monies derived from liquidation go first to secured creditors and then to priority claimants, such as those owed wages, salaries, and contributions to employee benefit plans.

Any surplus funds remaining after this distribution go to the entrepreneur. Prior to distribution, the entrepreneur has the right to certain exempt property. If the business is a corporation, those exemptions are minimal. They include interest in any accrued dividends up to a specified maximum; the right to social security benefits, unemployment compensation, public assistance, veterans' benefits, and disability benefits; and the right to stock bonuses, pensions, profit sharing, or a similar plan. Lest it seem as though the entrepreneur is at the mercy of the creditors in a bankruptcy situation, it should be made clear that in either type of bankruptcy petition, Chapter 7 or Chapter 11, the business owner has a great deal of power and control over the process. This power comes from the natural desire of the creditors for a quick and equitable resolution to the problem and from the protections inherent in the bankruptcy law. Often the creditors are better served by negotiating a restructuring of debt while the company is still operating and prior to Chapter 7 liquidation, where they are likely to receive a lesser portion of what is owed them, if anything. There are, however, certain things the entrepreneur will not be permitted to do within a certain period of time before the filing of a bankruptcy petition. These prohibited acts include hiding assets or liabilities, giving preferential treatment to certain creditors up to 90 days prior to the filing of the petition, and making any potentially fraudulent conveyances up to one year prior to the filing. Also the court may nullify any of the above transactions during the bankruptcy proceedings.

Entrepreneurs can take advantage of a vehicle under Chapter 11 known as a "prepackaged bankruptcy." It requires the entrepreneur to present the creditors and equity owners with a reorganization plan before the bankruptcy filing actually goes to court. If the entrepreneur can achieve the required number of votes agreeing to the plan (more than half the total creditors and two-thirds within each class of creditors), the prepackaged plan can then go forward expeditiously. This process generally takes just four to nine months to complete, rather than the typical nine months to two years.

The entrepreneur gains an obvious advantage from using this approach. Under the traditional Chapter 11 process, the creditors and everyone else learn of the company's problems only at the filing. With a prepackaged plan, by contrast, an approved plan is already in place at the point at which the public becomes aware of the problem, and the creditors thus may experience a greater sense of confidence in the entrepreneur. Moreover, the prepackaged plan ties up far less time in legal processes. For this approach to succeed, however, the statement of disclosure about the positive and negative aspects of the business must be carefully constructed to give the creditors all the information they need in order to consider the plan and protect their interests.

Before considering bankruptcy as an option to either exit a troubled business or restructure the business in an effort to survive, entrepreneurs should seek advice from an attorney and/or a specialist in turnarounds in the industry. Turnaround consultants are good at putting an unhealthy business on a diet, setting small, achievable goals, and making sure the business stays on track until it is in the black. Even when the business cannot be turned around, a bad situation can still be turned into a more positive one by heeding the following advice:

- Talk to other entrepreneurs who have been in a similar situation and listen carefully to what they learned.
- If the business is going to fail, end the business quickly before it affects the entrepreneur's personal life. The business may have failed, but the entrepreneur did not. A hard deadline should be set for when the business must be profitable or generate a positive cash flow; if it doesn't, the business should be closed. When the numbers don't add up, the entrepreneur should limit the time devoted to making the business work.
- Under no circumstances commingle personal and business funds or other assets. If the entrepreneur lends money to the corporation, she or he will simply be another creditor in line to receive funds from the bankruptcy. And, in fact, the entrepreneur may be required to return any funds received in repayment of the loan during the year prior to filing of the bankruptcy petition.
- It is important not to ignore the government. The entrepreneur may risk personal assets and accrue a debt for life if he or she borrows funds from payroll-tax and sales-tax accounts.
- Begin looking for opportunity. It is important not to wallow in failure. Sometimes the best opportunities are found when the entrepreneur is willing to leave a failing business behind.
- The entrepreneur should do whatever possible to pay back investors. While it is true that they took a calculated risk investing in the business, if there is a way to pay them back—even if it takes a long time—they will respect the entrepreneur and be there when that next opportunity comes along.

With the aid of an accountant, assets and liabilities will be audited to see whether the business can qualify for and benefit from Chapter 11 reorganization. Often, seeking help before filing a bankruptcy petition can lead to alternative, less difficult solutions that are more beneficial to the entrepreneur and creditors alike.

In the end, knowing what the goals the entrepreneur has for the business and how the entrepreneur intends to harvest the wealth the business has created can help in structuring a growth plan that will get the entrepreneur where he or she wants to go. Preparing for the unexpected—contingency planning—will go a long way toward ensuring that the business stays on the path to achieving its goals.

Some Final Thoughts

The field of entrepreneurship has been in vogue for more than 20 years. There is hardly a media source today that does not talk about entrepreneurs. In fact, the term is in real danger of becoming a cliché and losing its value because it is used to describe all kinds of ventures, from the small "mom and pop" to the Fortune 500 conglomerate. This book has focused on the birth and early growth of innovative, growth-oriented new ventures and has used the classic definition of the term *entrepreneurship:* the discovery, evaluation, and exploitation of opportunities that are innovative, growth oriented, and that create new value. These ventures face unique opportunities and challenges, but their relatively small size and lean structure make them particularly adaptable to a rapidly changing environment. They are the source of breakthrough innovation, economic growth, and job creation. Entrepreneurial ventures and the entrepreneurs who found them stand out from the crowd—they are the essence of new venture creation.

But entrepreneurship is more than just new venture creation; it is a mindset, a set of attitudes, and a skill set that can be learned. Adopting an entrepreneurial mindset is valuable for corporate venturers, small business owners, and those who want to take charge of their lives and differentiate themselves so they can realize their dreams. In that sense, entrepreneurship is for everyone who wants to experience the freedom and independence that come from knowing that opportunity and the resources to make that opportunity a reality are within their grasp.

New Venture Checklist

Have you:

☐ Identified the issues that could affect the business at various points in the future?

☐ Developed a contingency plan for all the various scenarios that may affect the business at some future date?

☐ Determined goals for the business relative to an exit strategy?

Issues to Consider

1. Contingency planning is not foolproof. How can an entrepreneur ensure that the contingency plans he or she has devised will keep the business on the path to its goals?
2. How can the entrepreneur prepare for potential product liability litigation, both to minimize the chance that such lawsuits will be brought and to give the company the best chance of prevailing against a product liability claim?
3. How can an entrepreneur prepare for a potential decline in sales?
4. Suppose an entrepreneur has built a successful business over several years and now has the opportunity to start another business compatible with the current one. How can the entrepreneur leave the original business and yet stay involved in it?
5. If an entrepreneur's business finds itself in trouble, what are the options available to the entrepreneur to attempt to remedy the situation?

Experiencing Entrepreneurship

1. Interview an entrepreneur in an industry of your choice to learn what his or her harvest strategy is. What is this entrepreneur doing to ensure that the harvest strategy will be achieved?

2. Interview a turnaround consultant about some ways to recognize problems that could lead to business failure. From this interview, devise a list of do's and don'ts that will help an entrepreneur avoid business failure.

Additional Sources of Information

Bradford, R.W., J.P. Duncan, P. Duncan, and B. Tarcy (1999). *Simplified Strategic Planning*. Worcester, MA: Chandler House Press.

Dinapoli, D. (1999). *Workouts and Turnarounds II: Global Restructuring Strategies for the Next Century*. New York: Wiley.

Hawkey, J. (2002). *Exit Strategy Planning: Grooming Your Business for Sale or Succession*. Hampshire, UK: Ashgate Publishing.

Nadeau, A. (2002). *Entrepreneurial Strategic Planning*. Bloomington, IN: Authorhouse.

Salerno, T.J., J.A. Kroop, and C.D. Hansen (2001). *The Executive Guide to Corporate Bankruptcy*. Frederick, MD: Beard Books. www.beardbooks.com.

Staubus, M., R. Bernstein, D. Binns, and M. Hyman (2001). *Transitioning Ownership in the Private Company: The ESOP Solution*. La Jolla, CA: Foundation for Enterprise Development.

Relevant Case Studies

Case Studies

Case 1

Overnite Express

The overnight-delivery parcel industry is an integral part of today's fast-paced economy. As our "instant gratification" society moves forward, being able to ship and receive documents and packages in a dependable and timely manner can make or break a crucial business deal. The biggest players in this very important industry are United Parcel Service (UPS), Federal Express (FedEx), and the U.S. Postal Service. These companies offer next-day delivery to many parts of the country.

Background

Rob Ukropina graduated from the University of Southern California in 1976. Upon graduation, Ukropina began a two-year stint in the restaurant business working for the Velvet Turtle in a management capacity. In 1977, he shifted his focus to the commercial printing industry while getting his feet wet as a salesman at Welsh Graphics in Pasadena. Ukropina spent two years at Welsh before going to work for Jeffries Banknotes Company in 1979. Jeffries specialized in printing financial documents such as prospectuses and stock certificates. It was during this period that he began laying the foundation of his network. Through his sales and managerial duties, Ukropina made numerous contacts with

This case was written by Matthew Benson, MBA University of Southern California, as a basis for class discussion rather than to illustrate either effective or ineffective handling of a business situation. Reprinted by permission.

financial institutions and law firms that would serve him well in the future.

In 1983, Ukropina took a position at Pandick Printing, the largest financial printer in the United States. He became a division president at the age of 30 and ran the Orange County division from 1983 to 1989. Although he was successful at his job—his gross income in 1989 was $300,000—Ukropina found that he was bored working for a large company and wanted to do something on his own. His first venture was to start a leasing company in which he served as the director of sales, marketing, and operations, while his partner put up the financial backing to support the endeavor. The company leased small equipment to businesses and also financed small businesses. In addition to the leasing company, Ukropina ventured into the publishing business and started his own magazine, *Business for Sale*. The publication served as an *"Auto Trader"* of sorts for buying and selling small businesses.

In order to give his businesses the best possible chance to survive, Ukropina did not draw a salary for himself from 1989 to 1992. Everything he made he reinvested in the business. Unfortunately, as a consequence of many external factors (including a recession and an unsupportive partner), Ukropina watched his net worth fall from $1.6 million in 1989 to zero in 1992. His family moved from their spacious 3000-square-foot home in Newport Beach to a 1000-square-foot apartment. In 1991, his wife went back to work to help the family pay for food and clothing (her entrepreneurial success in later years is equally impressive, but that's another story).

The Opportunity

There was little question that Ukropina would eventually run his own company again. He was brought up in an entrepreneurial family; his parents owned their own company. Furthermore, his in-laws were prominent entrepreneurs in the fields of engineering and real estate. Their influence would entice his wife, Joyce, to start a successful company in advertising. Once he hit rock bottom in 1992, Ukropina decided to explore opportunities that he had uncovered in his past.

Throughout Ukropina's career in the printing business, he had had to wrestle with the high costs of distribution. While at Pandick, Ukropina was quoted in the February 1999 issue of *Traffic World*:

> It was a 24-hour, seven-day-a-week business where 25% of our bills came from distribution costs. To get documents printed and delivered for public offerings on time, the company would routinely spend $30,000 for pick-ups after 5 p.m. and some $5 million a year on Next Flight Out courier services. We're talking about spending $1,100 per five-pound package to deliver documents nationwide, because what's $1,100 when you have a $110 million public offering that needs to be filed on time with the Securities and Exchange Commission?

He believed he could drastically cut those expenses if Pandick distributed on a regional, rather than strictly national, pattern. Ukropina's entire motivation was based on providing superior and less-costly service to his customers. He determined that UPS and FedEx did not deliver 3 percent of their packages because of making errors in sorting or having the wrong address. FedEx also stopped pickups at 7:00 p.m., even though many businesses work much later into the evening trying to make deadlines. For many of these businesses, the only alternative is to use a ground messenger at a rate of $1 per mile.

Ukropina saw an opportunity to fill a niche as a regional delivery service that was small enough to make corrections in mid-shipment if there were any logistics problems. If a package were addressed incorrectly, the driver would be able to call in and get proper directions for the destination. The larger companies would simply take such a package back to the hub and try to redeliver it the next day. There was definitely an opportunity to compete with the big boys in the terms of flexible pick-up times, quality, and service, something Ukropina took a lot of pride in.

From Opportunity to Business

The first thing that Ukropina did was to put together a five-year business plan in early 1992. Drawing from the experience of his failed leasing company and magazine, he knew that he needed a first-class advisory board to help him start the company and invest in his idea. He did not try to load his board with a bunch of buddies but started calling on business contacts he had made throughout his years in sales. Early members on the advisory board included a CEO of a health care network, an airline executive, and an executive from Peat Marwick.

In order to attract investors, Ukropina offered 10 percent of Overnite Express for $150,000 and quickly brought the net worth of the company to $1.1 million. To get his first customers, Ukropina used a network of "friends." He called on all the law firms that he had done printing for in the past and explained what he was doing. He asked them whether he could put an Overnite Express drop box in their offices and promised unparalleled service if they would use it. Because they had known Ukropina for his service in the printing business, many of them agreed to take a chance on him.

Because it did not have an established delivery system in place, Overnite would pick up the packages in the drop boxes and subcontract a route courier service to deliver them to their destinations in an area that extended from Santa Barbara to the Mexican border. Ukropina claims to have spent many a sleepless night in the beginning with crossed fingers, praying no problems would arise. Luckily, everything went well and Overnite was able to start delivering on its own.

Nine months into the venture, Overnite Express had exhausted the original capital investment, and Ukropina took on a partner, Doug Schneider. Together they managed to raise another $400,000 and, in a year, acquired another $100,000 through

SBA financing. Also, through his trials and tribulations, Ukropina never allowed his credit to be adversely affected. In year 3 of business operations, Overnite Express secured a $300,000 receivable line of credit.

As Ukropina had learned from his other jobs, the only way to maintain a high level of quality is to ensure that the people who work for you are happy and enjoy what they do. He used his entrepreneur philosophy in putting together an incentive plan that would enable him to prevent good employees from becoming complacent or, worse, leaving the company. Everyone in the company, including Ukropina, is paid a permanently fixed salary. In addition to that, everyone is paid a percentage of the gross profits, along with an incentivised bonus structure that is based on the number of packages delivered and the time they are delivered. For example, a driver can make more money by delivering the majority of his packages before 9:00 a.m. than by delivering them by 11:00 a.m.; he or she makes even less if most packages are delivered by 4:00 p.m. Thus everyone in the company is an entrepreneur in his or her own right. Ukropina attributes the fact that very few employees ever leave to the entrepreneur spirit that thrives throughout the company.

Growing the Company

For 12 years, Overnite Express has flourished in the regional southern California market in which it operates. In 1999, after constant pressure from clients to expand its delivery area to include northern California, Ukropina performed a feasibility study to establish the profitability of such a venture. It turned out that many of Overnite's existing clients tended to choose a national courier if they had more than one package going out and did not know whether Overnite delivered north of Bakersfield. Regardless of cost, it was less trouble to make one call instead of two. As Ukropina was quoted as saying in the April 20, 2000, issue of *Orange County Metro:*

> Many of our customers ship most of their packages inside California. By expanding, we have made it easier for the customer. If it is easier for the customer, it is a good business decision. . . . Now they don't have to think, since I have one package going to San Diego and another going to San Jose, I guess I will use FedEx for both. Now they can use us for both. Now it's simple—if you are shipping inside California, use Overnite Express.

Ukropina expected to get 28 percent more business by moving into northern California and, at the same time, to expand the southern California business by 30 percent. In May 2000, he borrowed $200,000 to finance the expansion and estimated the break-even point to be approximately six months. To his surprise and delight, the venture broke even in 60 days. Not only did Overnite Express get more packages from northern California, but it also started getting more shipping deals from existing customers because they could define the delivery area more clearly; it was an easier decision just to stick with Overnite for all their express needs. Still, developing the northern region has gone slowly because Overnite does not enjoy the brand recognition that it has in southern California.

Ukropina continued to expand the company's sales and marketing efforts. He acquired two airplanes to help serve the northern California region. Oakland is now the northern California hub, Irvine the southern California hub. Notably, 99 percent of Overnite's clients are previous FedEx users, generally in the professions: lawyers, advertising firms, and title companies. Its competitors are California Overnite, based in Phoenix, and Golden State, based in Alameda, California. Despite serious competition, Overnite has the highest average tariff in the industry, at $14.25, because of the quality of its service. Early on, Ukropina recognized the importance of investing in technology to remain competitive. Overnite's tracking technology sends an e-mail confirmation of delivery to both the sender and the recipient. Its computer lets Overnite know if a package is in danger of not making it on time to the customer. If the driver has not recorded the delivery 10 minutes before it is due, a message is sent to headquarters and the client is called. In the overnight industry, the primary reason for delays is a minor address discrepancy. This is also the primary reason a package is never delivered at all.

FEDEX and UPS have delivery completion rates of about 97 percent, whereas Overnite Express's completion rate is 99.9 percent because Overnite takes the time to figure out what is wrong. Its on-time rate is 99.2 percent, comparable to or better than FEDEX and UPS. Not bad for a company that ships one million pieces a year and makes 5,000 deliveries a day with 1,000 drop boxes and 110 delivery vehicles.

From 1998 to the present, the company has been growing at 25 to 30 percent a year, and the 2004 growth rate was expected to be the greatest yet thanks to a high level of client referral and excellent customer care. Ukropina has added more sales and marketing staff and is doing more direct mail. He is now looking at expanding the company's scope.

The Future

When asked what he felt his future held, Ukropina had to take a minute to answer. Then he had to qualify his answer by categorizing his future in terms of Overnite Express, his career, and his family. The growth strategy for Overnite Express is simple. He wants it to grow only in terms of being able to provide the greatest service to his clients. If the business warrants, the company will expand its operations as much as needed to maintain the current level of excellence. However, because of the niche that he enjoys and his position as the only delivery company that can boast 100 percent delivery rates while servicing only the state of California, he does not foresee the company expanding to a national level. As Ukropina likes to say, "We plan to stay humble and continue to operate below the radar screen of UPS and FEDEX. The reality is that we have to offer better service here in California in order to compete with FEDEX and UPS."

To date, Overnite Express has been in the express guaranteed-overnight service delivering primarily documents, but it is faced with a challenge going forward. As business moves rapidly toward a dependence on electronic data, document shipping is likely to slow down. Thus Ukropina is looking at ground product services with smaller packages and reliance on trucks. To prepare for that eventuality, in 2003 he built a $6 million, 50,000-square-foot building, which serves as the main sorting facility. There he and his team have developed the first "humanless" sorting system. A conveyor belt separates packages, scans and weighs them, and sends them to their ultimate delivery route. During the process, if a package falls off the belt or gets misplaced, the system stops and alerts the operator. This innovation has increased Overnite's throughput four times over. It was cost-effective the first day and eliminated the need for ten hand sorters. Curiously, industry giant FEDEX still sorts packages by hand. If Ukropina decides to go into ground product services, he will build a separate sorting system to handle those packages. He has leased 14,000 square feet of his new facility to another company, but the lease is up in a year, and that space will house the new ground delivery system.

Ukropina has not suffered the drop in cash flow that many entrepreneurs experience when they expand their businesses. The savings from the new sorting system and from owning the building have helped to keep cash flows on an even keel.

Overnite is merely a blip on the radar screen of UPS, which enjoys $40 billion in sales annually, and Ukropina likes that. He is able to provide service in a niche market wherein the larger companies do not feel the need to compete. As for his career, Ukropina considers himself a "builder" rather than a "maintainer." As long as the challenges are present to keep him motivated, he will stay with Overnite. The minute he feels that the company has achieved its full potential, he will gladly step aside and move on to a new endeavor. Hence he must also position himself and the company for the time when he might take on a new challenge. There are many ways to exit a business either in part or completely. Ukropina wonders how he should prepare for that eventuality.

Discussion Questions

1. How did Ukropina obtain his first customer and what did that tell him about his business?
2. What is Overnite's competitive advantage in an industry dominated by companies like Federal Express?
3. With the obvious move toward more electronic data transfer, what new sources of revenues should Ukropina consider developing?
4. Is it a wise decision to limit the company to California? Why or why not?
5. What is Ukropina's growth strategy?

Case 2

Craigslist: It's About Helping Others

Craig Newmark would have fit in perfectly in the 1990s Generation X movie *Revenge of the Nerds,* about a group of super-bright, but socially inept, young college students who succeed despite being constantly ridiculed by the stereotypical popular set—the football players and cheerleaders. Newmark grew up a nerd and is proud still to be considered a nerd today at 51 years of age. An introvert who describes himself as "academically intelligent and . . . socially retarded," Newmark has surprised everyone with the enormous success of his very hip website Craigslist.org. It's the place where a 24-year-old law student like Kit-Ling Mui, living in West Covina, California, can find an apartment, sell her parents' car, adopt a cat, and even meet her boyfriend. But Craigslist can do more. When 67-year-old Leonard Becker needed a kidney transplant, he decided not to wait for his number to come up on a donor list. Instead, he posted his need on Craigslist, and soon an office manager from Albany, New York, responded, offering her kidney and saving his life.

In fact, the site has become a phenomenon with over 2.5 million postings per month. Neilsen/NetRatings reports that Craigslist is ranked in the top 20 of all U.S. portals, up there with Yahoo, MSN, and AOL. By itself, this would be surprising, but when you add the fact that Craigslist has no sales force, does no advertising, and is visually as sterile as you can make a website, it is stunning. Forrester Research calls Craigslist the "most efficient job recruiting site" available, outranking multi-million dollar companies such as Monster.com and Careerbuilder.com.

The Early Years

Newmark grew up in a working-class family in Morristown, New Jersey. Losing his father to lung cancer when he was 13, Newmark and his younger brother were raised by their bookkeeper mother. At 18, he entered Case Western Reserve University in Cleveland, Ohio, where he earned bachelor's and master's degrees in computer science. Following a 17-year stint at IBM as a software programmer, he went to work in computer security at Charles Schwab in 1993, and the rest, as they say, is history. While at Schwab, Newmark met Darek Milewski, who introduced him to the Web, which at that time was in its earliest stages. Newmark immediately saw the potential for people to communicate.

In 1995, he left Schwab to become an independent contractor to companies such as Sun Microsystems and Bank of America. At that time, a lot of people were looking for technology jobs, so Newmark began sending e-mails to the people he knew in the area to advise them of art and technology parties at a local art house, the Anon Salon. The e-mails' scope included tidbits about San Francisco culture, and recipients began adding their acquaintances to the e-mail list. By the middle of 1995, Newmark's e-mail distribution list had grown to over 240 members. It was soon time to post the newsletter on the newly emerging Internet. At first he planned to call the site San Francisco Events, but since his devoted followers had dubbed it "Craig's List," he decided to use that name instead.

The Company Philosophy and Business Model

Located in San Francisco's Inner Sunset neighborhood among coffee shops and restaurants, Craigslist is basically, according to Newmark, a classified ads business. Craigslist makes money from one revenue source. Employers pay $45 a month to list job openings on the site; users pay nothing. For those employers who subscribe, Craigslist has been a godsend. In particular, casting directors for reality TV shows love the site. They often are able to staff an entire production from among the respondents to the job offerings on Craigslist. That revenue source supports a staff of 14.

Despite the mundane nature of the business, people who use Craigslist feel connected, so it has become much more than just a classified ads site. Craigslist is a for-profit business that keeps its financial information private. In 2004, however, *Fortune* magazine reported that the company generates about $7 million a year, with Newmark taking a salary in the $200,000 range. Newmark will not comment on that report, but he does reveal that his income enables him to contribute to more than 50 charitable and nonprofit organizations in the San Francisco area. Newmark's philosophy revolves around what he calls "nerd values," which includes making "enough for a comfortable living, at which point you do something fun like changing the world." According to Newmark, the only way to change the world is to do the "mundane stuff everyday." His company is about helping people, and his business model is a testament to that belief.

This sense of social responsibility carries over into his personal life as well. He lives near his office in a small flat in a 1908 Edwardian-style building—a building that wasn't wired for Internet access. He installed a wireless access point on the roof of this building to provide wireless Internet access not only to his unit but to the entire neighborhood as well. Newmark also serves on the boards of several nonprofit organizations and sponsors many activities for writers. In 2000, the company formed Craigslist Foundation, which provides the knowledge, resources, and visibility that deserving parties need to raise capital. For example, the foundation sponsors a wish list for teachers that serves as a conduit for them to get their wishes fulfilled by local businesses.

The Growth of Craigslist

Newmark could have easily chosen the route of other Internet businesses by taking one of the many buyout options that have come his way, which would have made him a multimillionaire. But it's not about the money for Newmark; it's about giving someone a break. Therefore, Craigslist has grown, for the most part, by word of mouth, talked up by users who wanted others to know that Craigslist was the best resource around. Today it serves 45 cities with 50 servers and is looking at global expansion. Even the technology that supports Craigslist reflects Newmark's "nerd values." The company runs open-source software on generic PC servers, using such open-source brands as Linux, Apache, qMail, and Squid cache. And, true to his philosophy, Newmark even turned down an offer by Microsoft Sidewalk to run banner ads on his site, something that would have brought a lot of money to the company.

Newmark spends about 40 hours a week dealing with issues related to the site—scams, community problems, and anything else that customers toss his way. Because he's an engineer, customer service is not what he's most comfortable doing, so he's determined to spend time on it. In fact, he is actually obsessed with customer service. His mantra is "ask for feedback, read all feedback and summarize, do something in response, and repeat."

Recognizing that he was not the right person to lead the organization as it grew, Newmark promoted Jim Buckmaster from his position as CTO and lead programmer to CEO. Both firmly believe that the source of innovation and change in their company must be customers and employees.

Craigslist has grown to the point where it is now getting the attention of major newspapers, which see it as a threat to their classifieds. Craigslist is pulling recruitment dollars from them with its simple text postings, while the newspapers, along with online competitors such as monster.com, continue to add features that make their sites more complex and harder to sort through. Newmark's keep-it-simple philosophy seems to be working—so well, in fact, that the Washington Post Co., and Knight-Ridder invested in a social networking site, Tribe.net, that includes listings much like those on Craigslist. So far, however, most social networks are not making money, whereas the noncommercial Craigslist is—and without doing any advertising. What makes Craigslist a success is the culture of trust it has built; when something goes wrong, the company fixes it. Time will tell whether these competitors survive. According to Newmark, they are not usually around for the long term. They are usually built to attract a lot of traffic and then get sold. In addition, their lack of community involvement is apparent to users.

Newmark is looking at international expansion, but he understands that this would require hiring translators and providing more customer service, which would make his simple business model more complex. Will he sacrifice the culture of his company for the opportunity to grow globally? Can the type of social network he created work in very different cultures?

Discussion Questions

1. What was the innovation behind the Craigslist concept?
2. What are Craigslist's competitive advantages?
3. Evaluate the challenges facing Craigslist as it grows globally. How can it overcome those challenges?

References

Davidson, I. (June 13, 2004). "The Craigslist Phenomenon." *Los Angeles Times Magazine*.

Glaser, M. (June 3, 2004). "Nerd Values Help Propel Tiny Craigslist into Classifieds Threat." *USC Annenberg Online Journalism Review*, http://ojr.org/ojr/business.

Mara, J. (August 21, 2000). "List Man—Craig Newmark—Founder of Craigslist.org." *Brandweek*, http://www.findarticles.com.

King, C., (accessed July 5, 2004). "Craig Newmark: Geek Chic? Screw It, I'm a Nerd." *Technical Entrepreneur Profile*, Sun Microsystems Developers Site. http://developers.sun.com/toolkits/articles/Newmark.html.

Beanos Ice Cream Shoppe

Terry Smith has spent the last six months preparing to purchase a Beanos Ice Cream franchise. Because his personal assets were limited, Smith needed a partner who could finance the purchase. After Smith found a prospective partner, Barney Harris, they negotiated a purchase price with Beanos. Then Harris gave Smith a partnership proposal. As the case opens, Smith is evaluating the partnership proposal. He has three choices: to accept Barney Harris's partnership proposal, to make a counterproposal, or to try to find a new partner.

Introduction

Two months ago, Terry Smith had been so confident that he would soon own his own Beanos Ice Cream franchise that he had put an "I LOVE BEANOS ICE CREAM" bumper sticker on his Honda. As he looked at it now, he noticed how faded it had become in such a short time. He *wondered* if in fact it had been a short time—or a lifetime.

Until recently, Smith had rarely second-guessed himself. After carefully researching an issue, he would base his decision on the facts and then proceed—without looking back. Now, however, he knew he had to put all of the momentum from the past six months to one side. He had to forget about the months spent investigating franchises, selecting Beanos, writing his business plan, and looking for

This case was written by Todd A. Finkle, University of Akron, as a basis for class discussion rather than to illustrate either effective or ineffective handling of a business situation. Reprinted by permission.

financing. He had to forget about the fact that he had found only one prospective partner who could finance the deal—Barney Harris—and that he and his partner had spent several more months negotiating to purchase the franchise. He had to set aside his own emotional investment in the deal now and make one more critical decision: Should he go into partnership with Harris?

If he signed the partnership proposal that Barney Harris had given him, Smith would get his franchise. If he did not sign the agreement, he might or might not ever see his dream come to life. It depended on whether he decided to make a counteroffer, to look for a new partner, or to walk away from the deal altogether. It was that simple: Sign the proposal and get all the marbles, or risk everything for the chance to get something better.

Now, as Smith looked at his faded bumper sticker, he realized that he had to evaluate the proposal in the context of the whole franchise deal. The question was not just "Is this a good partnership proposal?" The real question was "Given the potential of this particular franchise, and given my financial and managerial needs, will this proposal help me reach my goals?"

Smith's Background

In the fall of 1995, Terry Smith, a 36-year-old marketing representative for a Fortune 500 telecommunications firm in Cleveland, was among the thousands of employees who lost their jobs to downsizing.

At first, he investigated the possibility of working for other major corporations in Cleveland.

His education (a B.S. in biology and an MBA) and experience made him very marketable. During the seven years he had spent with the telecommunications firm, he had developed a solid reputation in his field. In a relatively short time, he received several job offers for about $60,000 per year.

And yet . . . Smith felt reluctant to jump back into a large corporation. He realized that as a new employee, he would be among the first to be cut if his employer experienced a downturn. Did he want to go through *that* again?

Smith had had a positive experience as an entrepreneur during the years when he was in college getting his degrees. He had started a successful mobile music company. It had not made him a millionaire, but it had paid for his education and living expenses, even though he had worked only when he could take time away from his studies.

One day, he found himself captivated by an article in *Entrepreneur* magazine. It pointed out that the number of downsized executives who were turning to entrepreneurship had doubled over the past two years. In 1993, between 6 and 8 percent started their own businesses; in 1995, over 12 percent did so.

Smith decided that he needed to explore his options as an entrepreneur. He knew the drawbacks of owning a business: the long hours, the stress, problems with employees, paperwork, and a lack of benefits. However, he felt that these could be outweighed by the opportunity to make all of the important decisions himself.

After several months of research, he decided to explore seriously the purchase of an ice cream franchise in Gainesville, Florida, called Beanos Ice Cream Shoppe, which cost $275,000 (see Exhibits 1–3 for the estimated costs and financial statements for a Beanos franchise). Smith had a net worth of $50,000 and a liquidity of $20,000, which meant that he had to obtain financing.

Background

Beanos was the brainchild of Bill Hogan, Jeff Pricer, and Annie Aubey, three former executives who had grown weary of the corporate world. In 1968, armed with a secret ice cream recipe, they founded Beanos.

Since opening its first ice cream shop, Beanos has become one of the most respected ice cream companies in the United States, selling superpremium ice cream, low-fat and non-fat frozen yogurt, and ice cream novelties. Sales and net income for Beanos have been increasing in recent years. Net sales grew from $48 million in 1989 to $120 million in 1993. Net income increased from $1.5 million to $6.7 million over the same time period. In the last quarter of 1994, net sales totaled $27,193,000, up 2 percent from $26,532,000. Overall, 1994 net sales went up from $120,328,000 to $128,802,000, an increase of 7 percent.

The company used the finest, high-quality, all-natural ingredients. It differentiated itself from the competition with: (1) superior ingredients, (2) new product development, (3) new market development, and (4) environmentally conscious behavior. These strategies have given Beanos several competitive advantages over the competition in the frozen dessert industry. Beanos has held the number-three market position in sales within the U.S. superpremium ice cream market for the past few years, behind Haagen-Dazs and Ben and Jerry's. The company has two primary growth strategies: (1) international expansion and (2) increased domestic penetration.

Beanos had 300 franchises located all over the world, with the majority located in the United States. Five percent of the franchises were company-owned, and 75 percent of the franchises were located in the Washington, D.C.–Boston corridor and southern California. More recently, the company has targeted warmer climates such as Florida, Texas, and Georgia.

The company has not had a franchise failure since 1991. Overall, only 5 percent of Beanos franchises have failed. The average franchise had $350,000 a year in sales. However, in more successful markets, average annual sales were closer to $500,000. The company's domestic franchise agreements were generally for a 10-year term with an option for renewal. The agreements granted the franchisee an exclusive area to sell bulk ice cream and frozen yogurt, which the franchisee was required to purchase directly from the company.

Beanos provided its franchisees with (1) a seven-day training seminar, (2) on-going operational support, which included access to a territory franchise consultant, (3) phone support, and (4) help with real estate and site selection. An input committee, comprising five of the most successful franchisees, was developed to assist existing franchisees. There was also an annual franchisees' meeting, which included workshops. Finally, Beanos sent field consultants to visit each franchisee four times a year.

The Industry Environment

In 1995, the U.S. Frozen Dairy Dessert Industry was in the mature stage of the industry life cycle, with the market segmented into the retail (dipping-store franchises) sector and the supermarket (take-home) sector. Estimated sales for 1998 were $12.8 billion, an increase of about 20 percent over 1993 sales. Two contrasting trends had developed in recent years: a movement toward full-fat products (which appeal to indulgent consumers) and a movement toward fat-free products (which appeal to health-conscious consumers). Brands, such as Healthy Choice, that were able to offer both rich taste and low-fat content, prospered.

Some of the consumer trends were the following: The fastest-growing age group was the 45- to 54-year-olds, there were more two-income families, the U.S. annual population growth rate was expected to average 0.9 percent per year through the remainder of the decade, the population was aging, disclosure requirements for food labeling were becoming more stringent, there were more single-occupant and single-parent households, and there was a significant trend toward health-conscious eating.

Ice cream has historically been one of the most popular dessert items. However, increased competitive pressures from entrants into supermarkets (Starbucks, Colombo, TCBY, and Swensen's) and new product development (novelty items such as Haagen-Dazs' frozen yogurt bars) made the industry fiercely competitive.

In response to this competitive environment, Baskin-Robbins, International Dairy Queen, Haagen-Dazs, and TCBY have increased their advertising. Finally, there has been a movement toward locating stores in nontraditional places, including airports, grocery stores, and other franchises (such as Baskin-Robbins and Dunkin' Donuts).

The Local Environment

Gainesville is located in north-central Florida. The city was ranked as *Money Magazine*'s "Best Place to Live" in the United States for 1995. It had been ranked among Florida's most livable cities since 1991.

Employment growth in the 1990s had averaged 6.2 percent, which was nearly double the national average. Gainesville also had a low cost of living compared to other U.S. cities of similar size. In 1994, the unemployment rate was 2.8 percent, whereas the national average was 5.9 percent. In the past three years, Florida's economy has surpassed the national average. Florida was also one of nine states without a state income tax. Some statistics descriptive of Gainesville can be seen in Exhibit 4.

Prior marketing research efforts in Gainesville showed wide acceptance for Beanos products. Beanos had two promotional events in Gainesville, in which ice cream was given to consumers. The feedback about the quality of the products was very positive, and the company had experienced success at selling products in local supermarkets.

Additionally, research showed that franchises located in college towns had sales averages that were surpassed only by resort areas. This made Gainesville very appealing, because the largest university in the South is located there. The University of Florida had an enrollment of 38,000 students and employed 15,500 people. Other institutions of higher education in Gainesville had a total enrollment of 20,000 students.

The population for Gainesville and Alachua County had increased 26 percent since 1980, an average increase of 2 percent a year (see Exhibit 5).

Exhibit 6 shows the Median Household Effective Buying Income Groups for Gainesville and Alachua County. The total effective buying income for Gainesville rose from $627,766,000 in 1981 to $1,041,191,000 in 1992, an average increase of 6 percent a year. The average household income for Gainesville was $29,073.

Local Competition

Fifteen local dipping store competitors are listed in Exhibit 7, which includes information about each store's age, number of employees, and estimated sales. It should be noted that 3 of these 15 stores have sales of $500,000 to $1,000,000.

In addition to these dipping stores, the local market also included supermarkets, convenience stores, restaurants, and an ice cream truck that parked near campus. Of these sources, three were seasonal. The ice cream truck, the campus food court, and a campus Freshen's Yogurt all operated only during the school year.

Four features were missing from the local competition. First, there were no national competitors of *superpremium* desserts in Gainesville. Second, no competitor had a place for customers to sit outside. Third, no competitor had a policy of "giving back to the community." And fourth, there were no Haagen-Dazs stores. This was significant, because Haagen-Dazs had been one of the first and strongest competitors, with sales peaking at $560,000 at one location. Then a decline in sales prompted its withdrawal from the market.

A discussion of the four largest players in the local market follows.

Lauries Café

Lauries Cafe was a locally owned competitor that served superpremium ice cream, low-fat frozen yogurt, bagels, gourmet coffee, sandwiches, and salads. Lauries had two stores and offered delivery services. The first store was located directly across from the university and had been there for three years. The second store was new and was larger than the first.

TCBY

The city had three TCBY stores. Two of the franchises had sales between $500,000 and $1,000,000. These were located in the upper-income areas of Gainesville. The other store was younger (five years old) and located near campus. The stores sold soft-serve frozen yogurt and superpremium ice cream products, along with novelty items. Currently, TCBY was marketing its "Treats" program heavily.

The Treats program featured candy mixed into their ice cream and frozen yogurt.

International Dairy Queen

Two successful Dairy Queen franchises were located in Gainesville. Dairy Queen sold hamburgers, hot dogs, barbecue, fish and chicken sandwiches, french fried potatoes, and onion rings. Their desserts consisted of cones, shakes, malts, sundaes and sodas, hard-packed products, and frozen ice cream cakes and logs.

Baskin-Robbins

Baskin-Robbins had two stores in Gainesville. One, located directly across from the main campus, had standing room only. Baskin-Robbins had recently remodeled this store and signed a ten-year lease. The other store was located one mile west of the University. Baskin-Robbins was known for its wide variety of flavors. It served both frozen yogurt and other ice cream products.

Smith's Goals and Financial Objectives

Smith saw an opportunity to obtain a franchise that had brand-name recognition and a history of success. Florida already had four Beanos franchises — in Miami, Fort Lauderdale, Jacksonville, and Orlando. However, there were ample opportunities to open other stores in Florida.

Smith's goals were as follows:

Phase I: Open one franchise in the Gainesville area in the fall of 1996. For the first two years of operation, the focus would be on the success of that store.

Phase II: Open a second store in Tallahassee in early 1998.

Phase III: Open a third, fourth, and fifth store in consecutive years (1999, 2000, and 2001) in Orlando.

The financial objectives were as follows:

Objective 1: Pay off any loans to each store by the sixth year.

Objective 2: Maintain an average return on investment of 20 percent for each store.

Objective 3: Maintain a positive cash flow starting in year 1 for each store.

Objective 4: Have sales of 2.5 million at the end
of ten years.

The Search for Investors

Because Smith had already founded one company,
he knew how difficult raising capital could be. He
developed a list of people to talk with and then pro-
ceeded as described in the following paragraphs.

SBA Consultant

The Small Business Administration (SBA) consultant, Tom Hughes, was impressed with Smith's
education, work experience, and detailed business
plan. He stated that Smith would have no problem
getting a loan of $175,000 as long as he had one-
third of the loan amount in liquid assets. For example, if Smith wanted a loan of $175,000, he would
need approximately $58,000 in liquid assets. How-
ever, over the past few months, living expenses had
eroded Smith's liquidity to $7,000. Consequently,
he needed an investor.

Mr. Hughes also informed Smith that if he got
an investor who owned 20 percent or more of the
company, the SBA required that person to sign
on the note. Smith realized that this could pose
a problem, because the investor(s) would be at risk
for the entire investment of $275,000 if they put up
$100,000. That could discourage them from invest-
ing in the venture. Mr. Hughes also explained that
Smith could not receive an SBA loan in the state of
Ohio. He would have to go through an SBA
branch office located in Florida.

Banker

Smith's banker was Mike Tork, a casual friend. Tork
was also impressed with Smith's credentials and
affirmed that he should not have a problem getting
an SBA loan for $175,000 if he got an investor
or investors to put in $100,000. Tork indicated
that the bank preferred to see the following
before granting a loan: (1) a quality management
team, (2) likelihood of success, and (3) financial
projections. Tork also stated that obtaining a loan

would be easier thanks to Beanos' successful
track record.

The bank required Smith to submit his business
plan, his tax returns for the past three years, and
a current copy of his personal financial statement.
Tork sent a copy of the business plan to Don
Pelham, the branch manager in Orlando, Florida.
Pelham told Smith that he might be willing to give
him a conventional loan, which would exclude the
SBA. Pelham stated, "We want you to be successful,
and we will do whatever it takes. The more successful you become, the more successful we become."
Pelham gave Smith two scenarios from which to
choose.

The first scenario was an SBA loan guaranteed by
the federal government. This would involve a lot of
paperwork. Pelham estimated the interest rate to be
around 9.25–9.5 percent, or 1–1.5 percent above
prime, plus a closing cost of $3,300. The terms
of the loan would be worked out later, but Smith
figured he would pay off the loan over a 6- or
7-year period.

The second scenario would be a conventional
loan from the bank. The time frame to obtain this
loan was similar to the SBA's. However, the terms
of this loan would be much more conducive to
the needs of Smith's company. The loan would be
broken down into operating and reducing lines of
credit (both using variable interest rates). The exact
interest rate percentages were not discussed. However, Smith learned through friends that these loans
were usually structured at 5 points above prime.

The operating line of credit would be oriented
toward short-term operations (working capital,
inventory, and payroll). Pelham told Smith that the
bank was very flexible on the terms. For instance,
it would allow Smith to pay only interest during
the first year. Pelham also said that he was willing to
let Smith pay only interest for up to 36 months.
However, the loan would have to be paid off over
6–8 years.

The reducing line of credit would be used for
equipment, renovation, and other fixed assets. For
this line, Pelham also stated that he would allow
Smith to pay only interest for up to 2 or 3 years,
and Smith would have to pay off the note at the
end of 6–7 years.

SCORE Counselor

Smith's last meeting was with the local Service Corps of Retired Executives (SCORE) counselor, George Willis. Willis had worked for Dupont for 30 years in various marketing positions and had owned his own executive search franchise for 14 years. Willis had also consulted with several franchisees in the frozen dessert industry.

Willis told Smith to obtain two partners with an equity interest of 20 percent or less, because having one partner with a 33 or 40 percent interest puts the entrepreneur at the mercy of that partner. What if that partner decided not to do the deal? What if something happened to that partner? Also, that partner would have too much control because he or she has the money. When you have two partners, you have much more control. If one partner drops out, then you can get another. Smith digested this information and began his search for capital.

Family, Friends, and Savings

Remembering his days in graduate school, Smith sought out the number-one source of financing for most startups: friends, family, and savings. He failed at finding resources there.

Business Professionals

Smith's next step was networking through his database of business professionals in the Cleveland area. The first person he contacted was an acquaintance, Barney Harris, whom he had met a year earlier through a friend. Harris was a very successful restaurateur. Smith called Harris to arrange a meeting. Harris agreed, but he wanted a copy of the business plan a week in advance. Smith dropped off a copy of the plan and a confidentiality agreement contract the next day.

A week later, Smith and Harris met. Harris stated, "You know Terry, most of the people who come to see me with business deals just talk. They do not have a business plan, and they expect me to invest hundreds of thousands of dollars with them. Your business plan is excellent. I like how you examined the business from broad and narrow perspectives. This is exactly what I like to see."

Harris was also impressed with Smith's intensity and ambition. Harris stated that he knew Smith had what it takes to become successful—a "fire in the belly." Harris told Smith that he was interested in becoming a potential partner, not an investor, and would be willing to put up $100,000.

After four months of hard work, Smith was excited at the opportunity of obtaining a partner. In his excitement, Smith stated that he was willing to give up 33 percent of the company in exchange for an investment infusion of $100,000. No further business professionals were contacted.

The Selection Process at Beanos

The selection process at Beanos required the potential franchisee(s) to send in an application form, psychological questionnaire, and personal financial statement. The next step was an independent phone interview that lasted an hour, followed by another half-hour for questions from the applicant. After this stage, there was a personal interview at Beanos' corporate headquarters in Phoenix, Arizona. The interview focused on the specifics of running a small business.

This process lasted approximately six weeks. After Smith and Harris passed, they received a letter containing a password that allowed them to contact any franchisee. Beanos also sent the potential franchisee a copy of its Uniform Franchise Offering Circular (UFOC), a legal document providing information on the company's history, management, finances, operations, and franchisees.

Smith quickly took advantage of this opportunity to gather more information by making a list of questions. He contacted ten franchisees and learned about sales, profitability, successful and unsuccessful marketing strategies, employees, and horror stories of partnership agreements. One of the franchisees from Tucson, Arizona, was kind enough to send Smith a copy of his financial statements from the previous year. After examining the differences between the franchisee's numbers and his projected pro formas, Smith made some changes (see Exhibit 8 for the revised expected scenario).

One of the most significant changes that Smith noticed was the cost of the franchise. Early in the negotiation process, Smith had estimated the cost of a franchise at $275,000. After talking with several franchisees in similar college towns, he estimated the cost of starting a franchise in Gainesville at $220,000, including working capital.

Smith also noticed that he initially overestimated the profitability of the business. In his original financial statements, Smith estimated the expected net income of the business at $34,400, $91,800, $116,800, $135,700, and $138,300 for the years 1997–2001. He revised his figures to $29,000, $49,000, $67,600, $87,100, and $87,800. There was a significant difference, primarily because of his failure to include employee wages in the financial statements. This was a gross oversight.

Smith realized that he needed to get the partnership agreement out of the way as soon as possible. After all, they had been negotiating with Beanos for over five months now. Beanos had given Smith and Harris the green light. Now it was time for them to fulfill their side of the deal—to produce a partnership agreement and then move forward with construction of the franchise.

Harris's Partnership Proposal

Smith went to Harris and told him that it was time for them to draw up a partnership agreement. They had previously talked about a partnership proposal wherein Harris's percentage of the business would be 33 percent for an investment infusion of $100,000. Smith offered to write up the proposal. However, Harris insisted that he would write up the initial proposal. Two weeks later, Smith received it (see Exhibit 9) in the mail.

Smith found three surprises in this proposal. First, Harris changed the structure of the deal. Second, Harris charged him for accounting services, when Smith could do the bookwork himself. Third, the buyout clause proposed three times the cash flow of the business, averaged over the number of years they were in business, divided by the ownership percentage. Cash flow was not defined.

Smith was stunned. Quickly, he sketched out the proposal that he had expected to receive, so that he could compare them side by side (see Exhibit 10).

Conclusions

Terry Smith winced as he turned away from his "I LOVE BEANOS ICE CREAM" bumper sticker. He knew he had three choices: He could take what Harris had offered in the proposal, even though it was not the proposal Smith had expected; give Harris a counterproposal that included the three changes Smith wanted, knowing that there was a chance that Harris would back away from the deal altogether; or start looking for a new partner. Smith began to walk across the parking lot, knowing it was time to make his next move.

Discussion Questions

1. What were the internal strengths and the external opportunities that Smith's franchise would face? What were the internal weaknesses and the external threats?
2. Should Smith and Harris go for an SBA loan or a conventional loan? Why? What problems will this cause for Smith?
3. Harris states that he wants 49 percent of the company for a $90,000–$95,000 loan at prime to be repaid over a five-year period of time. Does this seem like a fair deal for Smith?
4. For the buyout arrangement, Harris wants three times the cash flow from the business averaged over the number of years the business has been open. This figure would then be divided by the ownership percentage of the person who is being bought out. On the basis of the financial material in the case, does this seem like a fair buyout clause? Why or why not? If not, how would you devise a fair buyout clause based on the financial projections in this case?
5. After the franchiser approved Harris and Smith as partners, Smith began to work on the partnership agreement. Is this the correct time to do this? Why or why not? Is there anything Smith should have done to protect himself?
6. Smith states that one of the primary reasons why he wants to go into business for himself was the financial rewards. Judging on the basis of the figures in the case study, do you think that Smith has made the correct decision to forgo his

corporate job at $60,000 a year in exchange for a Beanos franchise?

7. Overall, do you think it would be wise for Smith to become a partner with Harris in this venture? Why or why not?

References

Answers to Frequently Asked Questions About Franchising. *Franchising in the Economy.* International Franchise Association (IFA), 1995.

Hill, T. and Jacobs, M. (1995). "Franchise Turnover Ratio Below Nine Percent." Frandata Corp. for the International Franchise Association's Education Foundation.

Top 50 Franchisers Ranked by System-Wide Sales. *Restaurant Business,* November 1, 1995.

Vaughn, B. (1976). "The International Expansion of U.S. Franchise Systems: Status and Strategies." *Journal of International Business* (Spring), pp. 65–72.

EXHIBIT 1	Investment Breakdown of Beanos Ice Cream Shoppe Franchise

EXPENDITURE	DOLLARS
Franchise Fee	$ 30,000
Design & Architecture Fees	$ 15,000
Real Estate & Improvements	$ 80,000
Professional Fees	$ 2,000
Equipment	$ 40,000
Signage & Graphics	$ 15,000
Miscellaneous Opening Costs	$ 7,000
Initial Inventory	$ 11,000
Working Capital	$ 75,000
Total:	$275,000

EXHIBIT 2 Pro Forma Income Statement/Cash Flow Summary for the Years 1997–2001, Expected Scenario (in 000's)

	1997 $	1997 % SALES	1998 $	1998 % SALES	1999 $	1999 % SALES	2000 $	2000 % SALES	2001 $	2001 % SALES
Sales	$300.0	100.0%	$400.0	100.0%	$450.0	100.0%	$490.0	100.0%	$500.0	100.0%
Cost of Sales	105.0	35.0	140.0	35.0	157.5	35.0	171.5	35.0	175.0	35.0
Gross Profit	195.0	65.0	260.0	65.0	292.5	65.0	318.5	65.0	325.0	65.0
Operational Expenses										
Employee Wages	21.0	7.0	28.0	7.0	31.5	7.0	34.3	7.0	35.0	7.0
Management Wages	30.0	10.0	31.5	7.9	33.1	7.4	34.8	7.1	36.5	7.3
Health Insurance	3.0	1.0	3.3	0.8	3.6	0.8	3.9	0.8	4.2	0.8
Rent	37.5	12.5	39.3	9.8	41.4	9.2	43.5	8.9	45.6	9.1
Utilities	5.3	1.8	5.4	1.3	5.6	1.2	6.2	1.3	6.5	1.3
Prop/Liability Insurance	4.5	1.5	5.2	1.3	5.1	1.1	5.5	1.1	5.9	1.2
Marketing	13.6	4.5	15.4	3.9	17.4	3.9	19.6	4.0	20.0	4.0
Accounting/Legal	2.0	0.7	2.4	0.6	2.6	0.6	2.8	0.6	2.9	0.6
Supplies	4.2	1.4	0.7	0.2	1.0	0.2	1.0	0.2	1.2	0.2
Repairs/Maintenance	1.4	0.5	1.8	0.5	2.1	0.5	2.4	0.5	2.8	0.6
Telephone	1.8	0.6	2.1	0.5	2.4	0.5	2.7	0.6	2.7	0.5
Bank Charges	0.3	0.1	0.3	0.1	0.6	0.1	0.7	0.1	0.8	0.2
Association/Chamber Dues	0.5	0.2	0.5	0.1	0.5	0.1	0.5	0.1	0.5	0.1
Auto	—	0.0	4.5	1.1	4.5	1.0	5.0	1.0	5.0	1.0
Depreciation	12.0	4.0	12.0	3.0	12.0	2.7	12.0	2.4	12.0	2.4
Miscellaneous Expenses	8.0	2.7	3.0	0.8	4.8	1.1	5.0	1.0	5.5	1.1
Total Operating Expenses	145.0	48.3	157.3	39.3	168.2	37.4	179.8	36.7	186.6	37.3
EBIT	50.0	16.7	102.7	25.7	124.7	27.7	138.7	28.3	138.4	27.7
Interest Income	0.6	0.2	1.2	0.3	1.2	0.3	2.0	0.4	2.0	0.4
Interest Expense	15.0	5.0	12.1	3.0	9.1	2.0	5.7	1.2	2.1	0.4
Earnings before Taxes	34.4	11.5	91.8	23.0	116.8	26.0	135.7	27.7	138.3	27.7
Add: Depreciation Expense	12.0	4.0	12.0	3.0	12.0	2.7	12.0	2.4	12.0	2.4
Cash From Operations	46.4	15.5	103.8	26.0	128.8	28.6	147.7	30.1	150.3	30.1
Debt Service	0	0.0	31.7	7.9	34.7	7.7	38.1	7.8	41.7	8.3
DISTRIBUTIONS	$46.4	15.5%	$72.1	18.0%	$94.1	20.9%	$109.6	22.4%	$108.6	21.7%

EXHIBIT 3	Pro Forma Financial Statement Assumptions 1997–2001

General: Projections are made on one store location in Gainesville, FL. The projections do not include additional store openings projected in the business plan. It appears that cash flow from first store operation is adequate for additional store(s) after Year 3. The timing of first store opening would affect the timing of the projections but would not adversely affect the revenues and expenses used in the forecast, only the timing.

Depreciation: Equipment purchased of $40,000 is depreciated over a five year life. Real Estate improvements and expenditures of $80,000 are depreciated over 31.5 years consistent with IRS tax depreciation laws.

Charitable/Advertising: Four Percent of sales after sales tax.

EBIT: Earning Before Interest and Taxes

Interest Expense: Estimated at 9.25% applied to average outstanding debt balance.

Fixed Assets: Recorded at Historical Cost.

Debt Services: Initial borrowings of $275,000 at assumed rate of 9.25%. Payoff of debt service assumed to be made from internally generated funds and is forecasted to conclude in 2002. Extra funds will be used to pay off debt early.

EXHIBIT 4	Statistics for Gainesville, Florida

Gainesville (excluding students)	91,000
Area Population (Alachua County)	191,000
Total Labor Force	114,346
Cost of a Three Bedroom House	$82,000
Property Tax	$ 1,618
Retail Sales Tax (excluding food and medicine)	6%
State Personal Income Tax	0%
Franchise and Inventory Tax	0%
Unemployment	2.8%
Robberies/100,000	301
Annual Sunny Days	242
Mean Temperature (degrees F)	70.1
Average Sunshine/Day (hrs)	7.8
Annual Rainfall (inches)	49.9
Percent of population over 65	9.3%

Source: *Gainesville/Alachua County Community Overview 1994,* produced by The Council for Economic Outreach, Gainesville, Florida.

| EXHIBIT 5 | Area Population Trends

YEAR	GAINESVILLE	ALACHUA COUNTY
1970	64,510	107,764
1980	81,370	151,369
1990	84,770	181,596
1995	91,000	191,000
2000	NA	208,900
2005	NA	221,600
2010	NA	233,900
2015	NA	245,200
2020	NA	256,200

Source: *Gainesville/Alachua County Demographics 1994*, produced by The Council for Economic Outreach, Gainesville, Florida.

EXHIBIT 6 Median Household Effective Buying Income Groups

GROUP	GAINESVILLE (%)	ALACHUA COUNTY (%)	FLORIDA (%)
Under $10,000	21.8	20.7	12.6
$10,000–19,999	20.6	19.7	18.0
$20,000–34,999	22.1	22.7	25.4
$35,000–49,999	14.2	15.1	18.8
$50,000–Over	21.3	21.8	25.2

Source: *Gainesville/Alachua County Demographics 1994*, produced by The Council for Economic Outreach, Gainesville, Florida.

EXHIBIT 7 Dipping Store Competitors in Gainesville

STORE	AGE	EMPLOYEES	SALES
Dairy Queen	5 years	10–19	$500–1M
Dairy Queen	1	Unknown	Unknown
Baskin-Robbins	Pre 85	10–19	Less $500K
Baskin-Robbins	7	Unknown	Unknown
TCBY	10	5–9	$500–1M
TCBY	9	5–9	$500–1M
TCBY	5	5–9	Less $500K
Bresler's	5	5–9	Less $500K
Doug's Dairy Twirl	5	5–9	Less $500K
Fast Eddie's	7	1–4	Less $500K
Lauries Cafe	3	10–19	Less $500K
Lauries Cafe	2 months	Unknown	Unknown
Gator Ice Cream	1	5–9	Less $500K
Ice Cream Club	1	5–9	Less $500K
Real Italian Ice	Unknown	Unknown	Unknown

EXHIBIT 8 Revised Pro Forma Income Statement/Cash Flow Summary for the Years 1997–2001, Expected Scenario (in 000's)

	1997 $	1997 % SALES	1998 $	1998 % SALES	1999 $	1999 % SALES	2000 $	2000 % SALES	2001 $	2001 % SALES
Sales	$340.0	100.0%	$385.0	100.0%	$435.0	100.0%	$490.0	100.0%	$500.0	100.0%
Cost of Sales	119.0	35.0	134.8	35.0	152.3	35.0	171.5	35.0	175.0	35.0
Gross Profit	221.0	65.0	250.3	65.0	282.8	65.0	318.5	65.0	325.0	65.0
Operational Expenses										
Employee Wages	46.9	13.8	52.0	13.5	57.6	13.3	64.9	13.3	66.8	13.4
Management Wages	30.0	8.8	31.5	8.2	33.1	7.6	34.8	7.1	36.5	7.3
Payroll Taxes	10.0	2.9	11.2	2.9	12.4	2.9	14.0	2.9	14.9	2.9
Worker Compensation	1.2	0.4	1.5	0.4	1.5	0.4	1.7	0.4	1.8	0.4
Health Insurance	3.0	0.9	3.3	0.9	3.6	0.8	3.9	0.8	4.2	0.8
Rent	37.5	11.0	39.3	10.2	41.4	9.5	43.5	8.9	45.6	9.1
Utilities	5.3	1.6	5.4	1.4	5.6	1.3	6.2	1.3	6.5	1.3
Prop/Liability Insurance	4.5	1.3	5.2	1.4	5.1	1.2	5.5	1.1	5.9	1.2
Marketing	13.6	4.0	50.4	4.0	17.4	4.0	19.6	4.0	20.0	4.0
Accounting/Legal	2.0	0.6	2.4	0.6	2.6	0.6	2.8	0.6	2.9	0.6
Supplies	4.2	1.2	0.7	0.2	1.0	0.2	1.0	0.2	1.2	0.2
Repairs/Maintenance	1.4	0.4	1.8	0.5	2.1	0.5	2.4	0.5	2.8	0.6
Telephone	1.8	0.5	2.1	0.5	2.4	0.6	2.7	0.6	2.7	0.5
Bank Charges	0.3	0.1	0.3	0.1	0.6	0.1	0.7	0.1	0.8	0.2
Association/Chamber Dues	0.5	0.1	0.5	0.1	0.5	0.1	0.5	0.1	0.5	0.1
Auto	—	0.0	4.5	1.2	4.5	1.0	5.0	1.0	5.0	1.0
Depreciation	12.0	3.5	12.0	3.1	12.0	2.8	12.0	2.4	12.0	2.4
Miscellaneous Expenses	8.0	2.4	3.0	0.8	4.8	1.1	5.0	1.0	5.5	1.1
Total Operating Expenses	181.5	53.4	192.9	50.1	217.7	50.0	226.6	46.2	234.3	46.9
EBIT	39.5	11.6	57.4	14.9	74.6	17.1	91.8	18.7	90.7	18.1
Interest Income	0.6	0.2	1.2	0.3	1.2	0.3	2.0	0.4	2.0	0.4
Interest Expense	10.9	3.2	9.6	2.5	8.2	1.9	6.7	1.4	5.0	1.0
Earnings before Taxes	29.0	8.5	49.0	12.7	67.6	15.5	87.1	17.8	87.8	17.6
Add: Depreciation Expenses	12.0	3.5	12.0	3.1	12.0	2.8	12.0	2.4	12.0	2.4
Cash From Operations	41.0	12.1	61.0	15.8	79.6	18.3	99.1	20.2	99.8	20.0
Debt Service	0	0.0	12.7	3.3	13.9	3.2	15.3	3.1	16.8	3.4
DISTRIBUTIONS	$41.0	12.1%	$48.3	12.5%	$65.7	15.1%	$83.8	17.1%	$83.0	16.6%

EXHIBIT 9 Barney Harris's Partnership Proposal

Short-term goal:	1 Store by Fall 1996
Long-term goal:	5 Stores
Incorporation:	Limited Liability Corporation
My Investment:	$100,000 with $5,000 going to equity in the company and $95,000 as a loan to the company. The loan would be repaid off in the next five years. I would receive quarterly interest at the prime rate for the loan. Also I would like to increase my equity position to 49% of the company.
Scoop Shop Operations:	Terry Smith agrees to spend 100% of his time operating the store.
Book Work:	I would like to have my accountant do all of the book work. Her fees are as follows: $2,000 to set up the books and $600/month thereafter, not including franchise reports, budgets, and forecasts.
Buyout Arrangement:	I would like to propose three times the cash flow of the business, averaged over the number of years we are in business. This figure would then be divided by our ownership percentages. For example, if our partnership developed cash flows of $100,000/year and you wanted to purchase my interest, we would multiply the $100,000 times three for $300,000 times my ownership percentage of .49, meaning the purchase price would be $147,000.

EXHIBIT 10 Expected Proposal from Harris

Short-term goal:	1 Store by fall 1996
Long-term goal:	5 Stores
Incorporation:	Limited Liability Corporation
Your Investment:	Harris's investment would be $100,000 with $100,000 going towards a 33% equity position. The other $120,000 will be obtained through an SBA loan. All debt service must be current prior to distributions paid out to partners. The expansion of future stores will occur at a later date.
Scoop Shop Operations:	All day-to-day operations will be performed by Smith.
Book Work:	Smith will do the book work and have a payroll service do the taxes.
Buyout Arrangement:	Two formulas will be used to estimate the value of the company: Price-to-Sales Discounted Cash Flow Purchase price will be repaid over a five year period while the seller holds the note to the debt. The loan will be repaid on a quarterly basis at the current prime rate for that quarter (as quoted in the *Wall Street Journal*). I also propose that we each have a first right of refusal of our stock and neither party has the right to sell until after three years.

Case 4

Wizards of the Coast

he excitement was high among the top managers of Wizards of the Coast, the world's leading adventure gaming company, as they sat down to review the company's progress during the first half of 1997. The company had just completed the acquisition of a major competitor, and with the opening of its first gaming entertainment center, it was pioneering a new retail concept. Fueled by one hit product, three years of tremendous growth had been followed by an unexpected downturn in revenues in 1996. Wizards now looked to be on the rebound, but everyone knew that the company still had to prove it had a sustainable-growth strategy for the future.

Creating the Magic

Wizards of the Coast was a privately held company best known for creating the world's leading adventure trading-card game, Magic: The Gathering. Since its release in 1993, over five million consumers worldwide had embraced the game, which was available in nine languages and played in over fifty countries. See Exhibit 1 for a brief description of Magic.

The Genesis

Wizards of the Coast was founded by Peter Adkison and a group of other young professionals in 1990 to develop role-playing games. Adkison had been

This case was prepared by Charles W. L. Hill, Suresh Kotha, and Richard Moxon, all of the University of Washington, and Frank Rothaermel of Michigan State University. Used with permission.

intrigued by strategy and role-playing games ever since he was eleven, and in high school he had developed a passion for the Dungeons & Dragons adventure role-playing game. He was working for Boeing as a computer systems analyst but was eager to start his own venture. Recalls Adkison, "I was a small cog in a huge machine that itself was a small cog in a huge machine." He and his friends kept their jobs but began developing role-playing games in their spare time.

In 1991, Adkison was introduced to Richard Garfield, a doctoral student in combinational mathematics at the University of Pennsylvania and an avid game player who had been designing his own games since he was a teenager. When the two got together at a game convention, the concept for Magic was born. Adkison had the idea that there was a need for a fantasy role-playing game that was portable and could be played anywhere in no more than an hour. He thought that it could be a card game. Garfield had also been interested in fantasy games since playing a game called Cosmic Encounter in the 1980s. One of the pieces in Cosmic Encounter had special powers. By invoking these powers, a player could change the rules of the game. This intrigued Garfield, and he wondered what would happen if all the pieces were magic, each one altering the game in some unique way. He believed that this idea could lead to a fantasy board game, but Adkison persuaded him to focus on cards instead and to think about a format in which players could trade cards, buying and selling collectible cards similar to those showcasing their sports heroes.

Garfield came back a few weeks later with a prototype of Magic: The Gathering. The idea was to combine trading cards and a fantasy game in which players controlled the acts of mystical characters. Recalls Garfield, "The concept of a trading-card game was one of the only 'Eureka!' experiences I've had."

Operating out of the basement of Adkison's home, Wizards of the Coast released Magic: The Gathering in August 1993. The game became an overnight success. The first printing of ten million cards, which was expected to last a year, sold out in six weeks. According to one game-store owner, "My initial was for 24 units, my second was for 572, and my third was, 'Send everything you've got in the warehouse.'" With sales success also came critical acclaim, with Magic winning several game and toy industry awards. Soon, Adkison left Boeing, and Garfield a new teaching job, to work full-time on Wizards of the Coast.

Products and Customers

Magic cards were sold in starter decks of 60 randomly selected cards for about $8.95 and booster packs of 8 or 15 cards for about $2.95. Even though these were the recommended retail prices, it was not uncommon for retailers to unbundle decks and mark up the prices of cards in great demand. Because the cards also had original artwork that appealed to fantasy-game players and collectors, they were both collected and traded, their price determined by their strategic role and collector value. Each deck was unique, so no two players had identical sets of cards. Players traded cards in order to create a deck with desired characteristics.

According to the chief game developer for Wizards of the Coast, the typical Magic player was a person with a good education, a high household income, and an interest in computers. Although the game was most popular with males in their teens or twenties, it had also caught on with younger teens and older men and women. College dormitories had been a breeding ground for new "gamers." Compared to the typical players of a board game such as Monopoly, the players of Magic saw the game more as a hobby—something on which they spent a significant amount of time and money.

Manufacturing and Distribution

Wizards contracted out the design, manufacturing, and packaging of its cards and other products. Most of its cards were designed by independent artists, who earned royalties from their Wizards sales. In the beginning, the company relied on one supplier, Carta Mundi in Belgium, because no other firm could deliver the quality needed and do the sophisticated card sorting required. During the first two years of booming popularity, manufacturing capacity was the single biggest constraint on the growth of Wizards. Carta Mundi remained the largest supplier, but other suppliers were contracted as the game grew and they were able to meet Wizards' standards.

Wizards had built a widespread retail network to market its cards. Most adventure games were sold through small game, comic, or hobby shops, often mom-and-pop stores supplied by relatively small distributors. These shops were critical to reaching the serious gamers and accounted for about 75 percent of the company's sales. Wizards allocated new card series to these stores, and there was often a feeding frenzy as consumers rushed to get an advantage by buying the cards. With the popularity of Magic, Wizards was able to enter such national chains as Toys 'R' Us, Barnes & Noble, and Target. These stores did not have the special atmosphere of the small retailers but were more effective for reaching the mass market.

Growth Problems

The success of Magic put Wizards on an explosive growth trajectory. Sales of about $200,000 in 1993 rocketed to $57 million in 1994 and $127 million in 1995. Wizards and Adkison became entrepreneurial superstars. The company grew to about 500 employees, moved in 1994 to new corporate offices, and opened several international sales offices.

Growth also brought problems. Many of the gamers who started with the company were not ready to move into managerial roles, and some managers who had been brought in could not work well with the gamers. In one case, Adkison found that someone who had been on the payroll for several months had never been hired by or reported to anybody. As Adkison said, "I've made so many mistakes, it's not even funny."

But growth came to a sudden halt in 1996, when sales fell off to $117 million. Moving quickly to control costs, Wizards had its first layoffs. According to Adkison, one cause was the inevitable leveling off of Magic's customer base, and another was the fragmentation of the retail game stores. The success of Magic had drawn too many entrepreneurs into the game-store business, and the resulting shakeout caused some distributors to go under, affecting Wizards too.

While sales in 1997 were expected to be about at the 1996 level, Adkison was aiming at future growth. "We certainly can operate in a slow-growth mode and make nice profits," he said. "But we are focused on growing the company more rapidly in the future." Part of the pressure for growth was coming from its original investors. Many of them were friends of the original entrepreneurs, came from modest backgrounds, and had become rich from their investment in Wizards. But this wealth was all on paper, and many wanted to cash out part of their investments. To take the company public at an attractive price, Wizards would need to have a good growth plan. Coming up with a sustainable-growth strategy was therefore critical.

The Wizards Culture

While developing the systems needed to manage a much larger enterprise, Adkison tried to preserve the creative culture in which the company had been formed. For many years, he refused to have his own office or even a cubicle. On his business cards and memos, his position and title were given as "CEO and janitor." He saw the company as a kind of small software firm with a casual, creative atmosphere that tolerated individualism and creativity—expressed, for example, in eccentric clothing, body piercing, and frequent nerf wars among the employees. Over the years, however, the atmosphere became more reserved, and Adkison even acquired a corner office.

Wizards executives and employees tended to be very committed to the gaming concept. Richard Garfield, the inventor of Magic, saw adventure games as the "intellectual counterpart of sports: they keep you mentally fit." He believed that with playing Magic came "a lot of stealth education," whether it was art appreciation because of the beautiful cards or enhanced literacy because of the occasional quote from Shakespeare. Garfield also believed that Magic was a strategic game that could be played successfully only when the player had a good understanding of strategy, probability, and chance.

However, Adkison recognized that devoted gamers did not always make good executives. "There's nobody in the company who's ever managed a company this size, including me," he said. "We're trying to balance the desire for top-notch people to take us to the next level with the desire to stay true to people who founded the company." The firm had hired experienced managers from established toy companies, used consultants on strategic and operational issues, and brought outsiders onto its board of directors. Adkison himself obtained a master's degree from the University of Washington Business School, knowing that he would need to continue strengthening the organization and help it develop a strategy for sustainable growth.

The Adventure Gaming Industry

Wizards executives defined the company as part of the adventure gaming industry, which was itself part of the much larger toy industry. They followed publications of the Toy Manufacturers of America, as well as the more specialized *Comics Retailer*, a monthly publication with in-depth reports on gaming developments. Total U.S. toy industry sales in 1996 were estimated at over $17 billion, of which the biggest single category was video games. The games and puzzles category accounted for approximately $1.4 billion in sales. Role-playing, trading-card, and war games—the segments in which Wizards competed most directly—accounted for about $350 million to $500 million in 1996 sales, according to *Comics Retailer*. The Game Manufacturers Association estimated gaming sales at $750 million.

The adventure gaming industry began in the 1960s with the development of a number of war games. The industry was revolutionized in the early 1970s with the introduction of Dungeons & Dragons, the first popular role-playing game. The game attracted players by being complex and by giving players the opportunity to exercise their creativity. The industry was revolutionized once again in the early 1990s with the introduction of Magic. By 1997, Dungeons & Dragons and Magic were still the top-selling role-playing and trading-card games. Wizards' acquisition in 1977 of TSR, the developer of Dungeons & Dragons, brought the two largest game manufacturers under one roof. The rest of the industry consisted of companies that were much smaller. Industry observers predicted that the most serious competition would come from companies in other industries invading adventure games.

Although there was no clear distinction between adventure and family games, people pursued adventure games as a serious hobby, sometimes dedicating many hours a week to playing a certain game. This led some critics to characterize players of Dungeons & Dragons and Magic as members of a "cult." Industry executives felt that this was an unfair image and saw most "gamers" as devoted to the games' intellectual and creative challenges. According to a survey by the Game Manufacturers Association, adventure game enthusiasts were young and literate and did well in school.

One issue facing the gaming industry was the rise of the Internet and computer-based games. Although most people in the industry considered typical video games to represent either lonely quests through fantasy worlds or "shoot-'em-up" arcade-like games, the Internet offered the possibility of role-playing and trading cards in a virtual world. Whether or not gamers would prefer this to the face-to-face experiences of Dungeons and Magic was of concern to Wizards executives.

Growing the Magic

As the dominant adventure trading-card game, Magic did not have much potential for increasing its share of this market. Wizards focused instead on extending the Magic brand name into other products and targeting the mass market to increase the size of the adventure trading-card industry. At the same time, the company had begun promoting Magic tournaments in an effort to increase the game's legitimacy and defend it from its competition.

Extending the Brand

Adkison was now attempting, through licensing, to leverage the Magic brand name into books, computer games, and other products. With the popularity of Magic, Wizards was able to pick and choose its opportunities.

Magic also appeared as a book series by Harper-Collins, selling over half a million copies, and came out as part of two CD-ROM computer games. Wizards executives felt that bookstores were a logical market for its products because Magic players tended to be heavy readers, and the game was often played in bookstores.

Also through licensing agreements, Magic merchandise had been extended into prepaid phone cards, clothing, card albums and protectors, a Magic strategy guide and encyclopedia, and calendars. Wizards had also reached an agreement with an Internet development and design company to produce interactive CD-ROM products that would serve as guides to the fantasy worlds created by Wizards. The company also received movie and television offers, but no agreements were reached. Licensing revenues were estimated to be about $1 million a year.

Going for the Mass Market

The dream of Wizards and other adventure game developers was the mass-market role-playing game. Selling a typical board game brought a company less than $10 a game in revenue, but customers could spend up to $500 per year on a role-playing game. A mass-market hit could easily generate a billion dollars.

Wizards introduced a more mainstream version of Magic named Portal, which was targeted at a broader audience (younger teens and families) and was launched with a media campaign costing nearly $5 million. This new game used card decks based on a variety of popular TV characters—such as Xena the Warrior Princess—and allowed these decks to be intermingled. The aim was to interest a consumer other than the gamer who had made Magic a success. Portal was to be distributed through mass-market retailers such as Toys 'R' Us and Target.

But Wizards saw risks with the mass market also. Magic gamers were attracted to the atmosphere of game stores and to the experience of the game, not just to the game itself. Mass-market retailers, on the other hand, saw games as "boxes." And with retailers' tremendous buying power, Wizards would not enjoy the same margins as it did on its Magic sales.

Developing Tournaments

To increase Magic sales, Wizards attempted to professionalize the activity of playing Magic, transforming it into a legitimate sport. Noted Adkison, "It's been proven that sports are very sustainable. They hold people's attention for a long time." One part of the strategy was to create players who had celebrity standing and who could popularize the game in the mass market.

Tournaments had been organized informally in the first years of Magic, many held in and sponsored by stores selling the game. Hundreds of these were held each year. In 1996, the company organized a six-city professional tournament series that offered $1 million in prizes and scholarships. Wizards also created a global ranking system for all professional players that was accessible at its home page (www.wizards.com). In the United States, over 50,000 tournament players competed in 30 leagues.

The Magic world championship series generated such interest that in 1997 it was carried on television by ESPN. Players from over 40 countries competed for individual and team titles and for $250,000 in prize money. Wizards was able to attract a corporate partner, MCI Telecommunications, to sponsor the series. According to one news analysis, the partnership gave legitimacy to Wizards and provided the game with a mass audience, while MCI was able to tap an attractive audience by associating itself with a "cool" event. According to the company that brokered the deal, Magic players were considered a good market because of their passion for the game and their desire to collect everything associated with it. "You've never seen loyalty like this. It's unrivaled across any other product or service category." MCI agreed to sponsor Wizards' Magic tournaments in exchange for exclusive worldwide rights to produce and distribute Magic prepaid telephone cards featuring the artwork of Magic cards.

Wizards also published a variety of magazines connected with its games. *The Duelist* contained articles, tips from celebrity players, and information on upcoming Magic tournaments. *Dragon* magazine, which came to Wizards with the acquisition of the Dungeons & Dragons game, had been published since the 1970s.

Defending the Brand

In addition to aggressively promoting Magic, Wizards of the Coast had applied for a patent covering not the design of the cards but the method of play. Entry barriers to the game industry were relatively low, and Wizards estimated that there were over one hundred games trying to compete with Magic. The company was set on collecting royalty payments from imitators.

Beyond Magic

The success of Magic had not blinded the Wizards executives to the need to seek new sources of revenue. As the leading trading-card game company, it was the target of game developers constantly looking for the next hit. Wizards's response was to develop new games and to acquire other game companies.

Product Development

Wizards developed and marketed what were considered to be great games, but none was able to replicate Magic. Adkison remained optimistic, but he realized that repeating that success would be difficult. "We have several things we're working on in R&D that could turn out to be like Magic," he said. "But in the gaming business, you can't bank on past success. We have to learn to make money with smaller releases."

The adventure game industry had developed largely as a result of two runaway hits: Dungeons & Dragons and then Magic. Adkison expected that another hit would again revolutionize the industry one day. But it seemed unlikely that the same company would be responsible. Wizards needed to position itself to succeed even if it was not the one to develop the next hit.

Acquisitions

After completing two major acquisitions, Wizards was considering others. One of these two acquisitions was Five Rings Publishing, developer of the Legends of the Five Rings trading-card game; the other was TSR Inc., creator of Dungeons & Dragons. Integrating these acquisitions had been a major challenge for Wizards. TSR had serious financial difficulties that Wizards had to sort out, and the company was in the process of moving TSR operations and many of TSR's staff from Wisconsin to its Seattle headquarters.

Wizards confirmed reports that it had held discussions with Westend Games, which had the licenses to a Star Wars role-playing game and a DC Comics role-playing game. Other small game companies also looked like attractive acquisition candidates.

Global Magic

Wizards estimated that Magic was played in over 50 countries by more than 5 million players. The company had international offices in Antwerp, London, Milan, and Paris and planned to open offices in Asia. Adkison noted that international sales had been very important to sustaining the company during the downturn in U.S. sales in 1996 and that there was still a lot of expansion potential in the international market.

Game Centers

In May 1997, Wizards of the Coast opened its first retail and gaming store, a 34,000-square-foot Wizards of the Coast Game Center, located in Seattle close to the campus of the University of Washington. Designed as the first entertainment center for adventure gamers, it offered an extensive array of arcade video games, sold games and associated merchandise, offered food and beverages, and provided a place for trading-card gamers to meet and compete with others. It was also intended to be a site for tournaments.

According to Adkison, the game center was "sort of like Niketown or Planet Hollywood. We have the opportunity to create the ultimate gaming atmosphere. This is a club, a hangout, a place for the devoted game players to go and play anytime." Wizards hoped that game centers would create an even stronger game-playing community by encouraging people to consider games an entertainment choice, like going to the movies or dining out. Just as the cineplex concept broadened the movie-going public, Wizards hoped that "gameplexes" would encourage the growth of the game-playing community. The Seattle Game Center carried many competitive games, but Wizards games were featured most prominently.

Another function of the game centers was to improve the retail distribution of the Wizards product line. The company was disappointed with the support that traditional retailers gave the games and felt that it knew better than retailers how to sell and support its games.

Wizards also knew that the success of game centers was not a sure thing. Companies such as Gameworks had introduced family entertainment centers with very limited success. Wizards was encouraged, however, by the success of Games Workshop—the developer of the popular Warhammer game—with a similar concept.

Lightning Strikes Twice: Pokemon

In 1998, Adkison recognized that Wizards of the Coast was still a one-product company whose future was tightly linked to the success of Magic. He said, "Magic provides over 90 percent of our cash flow. It is obviously our primary focus. The big strategic issue with Magic is to develop its potential to become a 'classic game' that yields steady profits year after year. I wouldn't mind being a $500 million to $1 billion company. We want to make games as big as the movies." As he thought about the company's future strategy, it seemed highly unlikely that Wizards would have another hit like Magic.[1] How wrong he was! Within a year Wizards would be riding a wave much bigger than that generated by Magic.

Named after the endearing set of characters invented by Nintendo, Pokemon had begun life in Japan as a game for Nintendo's N64 and Game Boy

---

[1] Charles Hill assisted in the facilitation of strategic planning sessions at Wizards that helped produce this strategy.

video game platforms. In 1997, one of Nintendo's employees developed the Pokemon trading-card game. The Nintendo employee was an avid player of Magic, and he had simply taken the underlying structure of the game—referred to in the industry as the "game mechanic"—and inserted a new set of characters: those of the Pokemon world. The resulting trading-card game was a sensation in Japan.

Seeing the potential, Nintendo decided to sell the trading-card game in the rest of the world. However, it faced two problems in selling Pokemon outside of Japan. First, it lacked the distribution required to sell the game, and second, Wizards of the Coast had applied for and received a patent on the game mechanic underlying Magic. Since the Pokemon trading-card game used the same game mechanic, Nintendo might be in violation of this patent. The obvious solution to this dilemma was for Nintendo to license the ex-Japanese rights to the Pokemon game to the company with the patent on the underlying game mechanic and with an established distribution system, brand name, and industry expertise: Wizards of the Coast.

The results of the deal soon exceeded the expectations of both companies. Pokemon quickly became a global phenomenon among the 6- to 12-year-old set. Sales of the trading cards rocketed, along with sales of the video games, and the growing popularity of an associated TV series. For Wizards, the result was an unexpected bonanza. The company's sales surged from $150 million in 1998 to an estimated $400 million in 1999. The popularity of Pokemon trading cards accounted for some $225 million of this increase.[2] As with Magic, Wizards quickly issued expansion sets that emphasized new themes and generated incremental sales revenues. The collectible aspect of Pokemon trading cards was, if anything, greater than that of Magic. Kids competed with each other to collect a full set of trading cards, including highly valued rare cards.

Another appealing aspect of the Pokemon phenomenon was that it broadened Wizards's appeal to a demographic that it had not been able to reach with Magic: 6- to 12-year-old kids. The "dark themes" of Magic had put off many parents, but they appealed to 14- to 25-year-olds with a passion for strategy games. At Wizards, the hope emerged that kids would cut their teeth on Pokemon and, when they grew older, move on to Magic. Moreover, Pokemon allowed Wizards to widen its distribution system, selling in mainstream locations that had not sold Magic.

The Hasbro Acquisition

With Pokemon emerging as *the* theme of the 1999/2000 Christmas season, the success of Wizards attracted the attention of major players in the toy industry, including, most notably, Hasbro. In September 1999, Hasbro made a $325 million bid to acquire Wizards, which the company quickly accepted.[3] Under the terms of the deal, Peter Adkison would continue as CEO of Wizards for at least four years, the company would remain at its current location, and it would be granted a high degree of operating autonomy. Hasbro was looking to Wizards to broaden its offering of Pokemon toys and games in advance of the holiday season. In addition, the growing presence of Wizards in the hobby niche of the gaming industry, along with its growing retail presence, appealed to Hasbro, which was suffering from stagnating sales of many of its traditional toy offerings.

From Wizards's perspective, the bid from Hasbro had a number of attractive features. Wizards had long planned to take the company public, but it recognized that executing an initial public offering (IPO) might be very difficult, given the skeptical view of the hobby gaming industry held on Wall Street. Many of Wizards's key employees had significant stock holdings in the company, but in the absence of an IPO, this stock was not very liquid. The market was thin because there were only about 300 stockholders. The Hasbro bid allowed these employees to turn their illiquid Wizards stock into cash—a very appealing option to many. Moreover,

[2] J. Milliot. "Hasbro to Acquire Wizards of the Coast." *Publishers Weekly* (September 20, 1999), p. 12.

[3] J. Pereira and D. Golden. "Games: With Wizards and Dragons, Hasbro Expands Its Reach." *Wall Street Journal* (September 10, 1999), p. B1.

an acquisition by Hasbro gave Wizards the opportunity to use Hasbro's brand name to open certain doors, such as those of mass-market retailers who had traditionally been reluctant to stock the products of the hobby gaming industry. Hasbro's financial muscle could also help Wizards to accelerate its retail store strategy, to make further acquisitions in the industry, and to fund the advertising required to strengthen its brand.

Strategy Going Forward

The acquisition by Hasbro did not signal any big change in strategy at Wizards. The company continued to take steps to build its Magic and Pokemon trading-card games, hoping that, like Monopoly and Risk, these games would become "classics." These steps included an extension of the organized-play concept to the Pokemon game, the issuing of more expansion packs and new editions for Magic and Pokemon, television advertising campaigns, and a broadening of the distribution for Magic. In addition, the company continued to look for other opportunities to add to its franchise in the trading-card arena. In February 2000, Wizards announced that it had reached an agreement with Warner publishing to create a Harry Potter trading-card game that would employ a game mechanic similar to that of Magic and Pokemon and would be marketed to 10- to 14-year-olds, the prime demographic for the best-selling Harry Potter books.[4] The game was scheduled to be released in late 2000. In February 2000, the company also announced that it had reached an agreement with the Major League Baseball Association and the Major League Baseball Players Association to create a trading-card game with a baseball theme, using league players as its central characters.

Wizards also continued to pursue its retail strategy aggressively, making a major strategic move prior to the Hasbro acquisition. In May 1999, Wizards acquired The Game Keeper Inc., which owned a chain of 53 retail stores that sold chess, puzzles, backgammon, dominoes, and family board games. Most of the stores were located in malls on the West Coast. The plan was to sell the full range of Wizards games in these stores and gradually convert them over to the Wizards brand name.[5] The company also continued to expand the bigger game centers. In mid-1999, it had 6 game centers. By April 2000, the number had risen to 18, and the company announced plans to open another 34 that year. Six of these 34 would be converted from Game Keeper stores; the remaining game centers would be net additions. Not all of the game centers would be as large as the one in Seattle, but the average size would remain around 2,700 square feet, encompassing a retail store, an area for game play, and a section dedicated to coin-operated video games. The combination seemed to be a winning formula; the video game and game-playing areas drew in customers (and money, in the case of the video games), who would make purchases from the retail store.[6]

Discussion Questions

1. How was Wizards of the Coast able to "re-create" the adventure game market?
2. How important was the early international expansion of Wizards? What strategy did the firm pursue? What are the opportunities and threats in international growth in the future?
3. What were the sources of capital for Wizards of the Coast? What implications does this have for the future strategy of the company?
4. What were some of the challenges Wizards experienced as a result of its tremendous growth?
5. What would you do given the situation in mid-1997 described in this case? If you chose to end the game, how would you go about it? What path would you pursue? Why?

---

[4] S. P. Chan. "Wizards to Make Harry Potter Cards." *Seattle Times* (February 12, 2000), p. B1.

[5] B. Ramsey. "Wizards Buys Chain of Stores." *Seattle Post Intelligencer* (May 6, 1999), p. D2.
[6] D. Scheraga. "Would You Like to Play a Game?" *Chain Store Age* (April 2000), pp. 50–51.

| EXHIBIT 1 | Magic: The Gathering |

The game Magic: The Gathering combines elements of chess, bridge, and the role-playing game of Dungeons & Dragons. Magic is a trading-card game in which two players are rival wizards dueling for control of a magical "multiverse" called Dominia. Each player starts out with 20 life points. The goal is to reduce the opponent's life points to zero before the opponent can do the same — that is, to kill the opponent.

Before starting the game, each player builds a deck of at least 40 cards from his or her collection. Each player begins by shuffling the deck and drawing 7 cards. Players alternate turns, with each turn a series of actions, such as attacking and defending. There are several types of illustrated cards. Lands are the most basic, providing the magical energy a player needs to play other cards. Others represent creatures, and still others represent spells that a player can cast. The basic strategy lies in choosing when to play what card and when to use what creatures for what purposes. Games usually last 15 to 30 minutes, but some can last for hours.

One of the key features of Magic is that each game played is unique: Each player starts out with a deck of 40 cards selected from among the more than 4,000 sold. It is not uncommon for a player to own several hundred cards. This encourages players to buy or trade cards to enhance their powers and increase their strategic options.

The game is in perpetual evolution because new cards are released periodically and older ones retired by Wizards of the Coast. Retired cards gained instant status as collectibles and can be bought, sold, and traded between individuals, in hobby stores, and on the Internet. New cards are issued in different sets and limited editions. These expansions have kept the game novel and thus have contributed to its phenomenal growth. Because the basic strategy in Magic is assembling the unassailable deck, serious players invest heavily in their collections.

In addition, the fantasy multiverse expands with each edition of new cards. Magic has undergone many extensions, and further expansion is limited only by the players' willingness to remain bewitched.

Case 5

iROBOT: Robots for the Home

R obots have been around for a long time. Detroit has used robots for four decades to build cars, and manufacturers of all kinds of goods use some form of robotics to achieve efficiencies and productivity. But until iRobot brought its battery-powered vacuum cleaner to the market, no one had successfully used robots in the home as an appliance. The issue was not whether it was possible to use robots in the home but whether they could be produced at a price customers would pay. Until the introduction of Roomba, iRobot's intelligent vacuum cleaner, robots for the home cost tens of thousands of dollars. At Roomba's price point of $199, it was now possible to afford to have a robot clean the house. That in itself is an interesting story, but even more interesting is the entrepreneurial journey of Colin Angle and his company, iRobot.

Background

Colin Angle was raised in Schenectady, New York, by his mother and stepfather. He and his three stepbrothers all became engineers, but Angle was the inventor/builder of the group. Beginning in his earliest years, he built pinball machines and constructed complex pulley systems in the trees of his back yard. While attending MIT in the 1980s, he was drawn to the innovative work of Rodney Brooks, director of the university's artificial intelligence lab. Brooks was a controversial figure in the robotics field, but he served as the inspiration for what would become some of Angle's most practical inventions. As a student, Angle was part of a group that succeeded in building insect-like robots that

could perform simple tasks on reflex. In fact, Angle's creation, Genghis, appeared on the cover of *Popular Science*. It was clear by then that his future lay in inventions.

The Opportunity

In 1990 Brooks and Angle, who by then had become close working partners, borrowed from their credit cards and used bank debt to found iRobot in a tiny apartment in Somerville, Massachusetts. The goal of the company was to build robots that would affect how people lived their lives. At that time, no one could conceive of a way to bring robots into domestic life in an affordable manner, and iRobot was still years away from discovering the one application that would launch it into the consumer market. To stay alive, the company sought government and corporate contracts for new product development. Over the next decade, iRobot designed and built a vast array of products from nuclear waste detectors to toy robots. Angle and his team believed that diversifying their product development skills would insulate them from the risk of any one customer killing a project, something that happened frequently in their industry. Angle also had no idea which of the many products they developed would be the one that would propel the company into rapid growth, so he did not want to focus too narrowly too soon.

Diversification in those first years enabled the company to stockpile a range of patents that would become the basis for the product for which they became most famous. Angle reasoned that he had to make certain that customers did not end up owning technology that his company might need in future product development. For example, in 1992 he sold the rights to the underlying technology on a robot called Grendel to separate it from technology that would be used to take the company in new directions. Prior to this, iRobot did not control the patents for products it developed for large customers, as is typical with smaller businesses. However, after selling the Grendel rights, Angle decided that henceforth the company would retain all rights to the technologies it developed. As it turned out, a cleaning technology that iRobot had developed for Johnson Wax Professional and tiny processors developed for Hasbro, the toy company, were critical components of Roomba.

Shall We Dance?

iRobot had secured two parts of the three components of its growth strategy. It had become a flexible company that could develop products in a broad area, and it had built up a strong base of intellectual capital. Now, the only thing missing was a way to bring robots to the domestic market economically, and that was no easy task. Angle had already experienced the agony of defeat on a proposal for Hasbro. In 1996, iRobot developed a storytelling machine with characters that moved and gestured while they talked. It seemed to everyone at iRobot that this could be the next big toy until they showed Hasbro management what it looked like inside. It was a masterpiece of engineering, but the microprocessors cost $60 each, the flash card cost $400, and the parts all totaled ran about $3,000. Hardly a likely candidate for the next Christmas season! But Angle had learned a lot about the consumer products industry from this experience and now had a good idea what it would take to develop successful products for the toy industry. It was all about cost—saving pennies so that the toy company could meet its competitive price point in the market. iRobot became an exclusive partner with Hasbro and, over the next two years, proposed dozens of new toy projects, most of which were turned down because they were too expensive to make. Finally, in 2000, iRobot saw one if its creations, My Real Baby, hit the store shelves.

It was, in fact, this new understanding of the consumer products business that inspired the idea for Roomba. Originally, iRobot had considered partnering with a large vacuum cleaner company such as Hoover, but one of the reasons why a smaller company partners with a large, established company is to take advantage of the latter's access to suppliers. The iRobot team had become experts in sourcing product components efficiently, so they chose to do it on their own.

Developing Roomba

The engineers at iRobot were unaccustomed to building mundane products for domestic use, so to avoid wasting the talents of his most brilliant engineers, Angle created a new division in the company that would design and launch these domestic products. Technologies developed from contract work now found a home in Roomba. For example, the crop circle algorithm it uses came from a technology used to sweep minefields. The company worked its way through 20 iterations of Roomba, bringing each version home to spouses and relatives to test. One thing was clear: This device had to be easy to use. Generally speaking, consumers won't tolerate a steep learning curve, so iRobot's engineers pictured something as simple as a large button labeled "clean." In fact, they ended up with a button that provided a choice of S, M, or L for small, medium or large room size. The customer puts Roomba on the floor, turns it on, and presses the size button. Then the robot plays a tune and starts sweeping the floor in ever-widening circles. When it runs into something, it heads off in a different direction. The circle algorithm alternates with a wall-and-furniture-hugging algorithm and straight lines. Sometimes, at random, it simply goes in one direction until it runs into something. It runs on a nickel-metal-hydride battery that gets recharged on an overnight charger. It also comes with an invisible wall that projects an infrared beam if you need to keep the robot confined to a particular area. It even has three different backup systems to keep it from falling down stairs.

From its experience with Hasbro, iRobot had learned to be extremely stingy on costs, right down to the penny, so it knew that a price tag of $199 would keep competitors at bay.

Market Entry

iRobot's shrewd entry strategy saw Roomba hitting the market just in time for the Christmas season through such gift outlets as Sharper Image and Brookstone. These stores are willing to demonstrate products, something that is critical with a new product. Although Roomba was the first product from iRobot, it sold $15 million in 2002 and soared to $50 million in sales in 2003. This was accomplished on five rounds of venture funding totaling $27.5 million.

IRobot also hired a Boston PR firm to conduct a media blitz to create customer awareness. Stories appeared in the *Wall Street Journal* and *Time* and on TV shows such as *Live with Regis and Kelly*. Women's magazines were another popular media venue. But not all advertising is good advertising. Angle had to be careful to ensure that Roomba would not be perceived as a novelty—a toy—but rather as an everyday appliance. Therefore, the company chose not to refer to Roomba as a robot in any of its advertising or promotional materials. Instead, it was described as an "intelligent floorvac system." These high-tech engineers left their techie egos at the door and resorted to consumer terms. But the market dictates what companies should do, and once iRobot found out that 60 percent of its customers were naming their Roombas, the company began using the term *robot* on its packaging. Angle knew that once competition entered the market and achieved a lower price point, it would be important to customers to know that their robot vacuum came from a robot company rather than a vacuum cleaner company.

The Future

iRobot continues to do contract research. The Federal Defense Advanced Research Projects Agency (DARPA) has funded its Robot's Swarm project, in which it is working on getting robots to coordinate among themselves. Angle can see a future for this technology in the home as well. Picture robot appliances deciding among themselves what should be cleaned first! But are consumers willing to go that far with domestic robots? Are they willing to give them decision-making power in the home? That remains to be seen.

Discussion Questions

1. What are the unique challenges facing a new product development company?
2. What role did patents play in iRobot's strategic plan?
3. Evaluate iRobot's approach to the consumer market. Was it effective? Would you have done anything differently?

References

Buchanan, L. (July 2003). "Death to Cool." *Inc. Magazine,* www.inc.com.

Pennington, A.Y. (2003). "Mechanically Inclined: These Entrepreneurial Robophiles Take Their Business Where No Man Has Gone Before." *Entrepreneur Media,* www.finarticles.com.

Garfinkel, S. (October 9, 2002), "iRobot Roomba." *MIT Technology Review,* www.technologyreview.com.

Case 6

The Crowne Inn: A Classic Case of a Family Business in Turmoil

Introduction

It was on a clear, cool fall day in late 2000 that Barbara Johnston, a retired nurse, was confronted with one of the biggest challenges of her life. Her son Bruce entered her dilapidated house, threw down his keys, and blurted out the following:

> You are all plotting behind my back. You are trying to bankrupt and steal the bar away from me. Well, you can have the keys to my house, car, and the lousy bar. But you will lose your son and two grandchildren forever.
>
> No one wanted the bar. I made the bar what it is today. If I leave, the business will collapse and then you will have nothing. I have already talked to the employees and they will all walk out. After this is over, I am going to disown this whole family. I have had it with all of you!!

Barbara's family was on the verge of being torn apart over the family's largest asset, a bar called The Crowne Inn located in Kansas City, Missouri. Since the death of her husband Harvey in 1997, Barbara had had problems with Bruce's inability to honor his previously agreed upon oral agreement to take care of her. On the day of his father's retirement in 1995, Bruce made an oral agreement to pay off the second mortgage on his parents' house ($23,500),

give them $500 in *cash* per month, and pay their health insurance and medical bills for the rest of their lives. He made this oral agreement in front of his parents and their attorney, Bobby Free. However, despite repeated warnings from Free, Harvey refused to execute a formal written contract. As a result of the oral agreement, Bruce received all of the proceeds from the bar.

After five years, Bruce had not lived up to his agreement with his parents. The family was trying to work out a deal with Bruce's lawyer and accountant to sell him the business. The family's attorney, Bobby Free, devised three possible solutions to the problem: (1) Have Bruce pay a lump sum, (2) have Bruce pay a smaller lump sum and $500 per month, or (3) sell the bar outright to an outside party.

Bruce stated that he would pay a lump sum of not more than $60,000 to his mother. The family was unsure whether this was a fair offer. And if not, what was a fair offer? Also, was the lump-sum method the best way to handle the problem? Furthermore, would Bruce be willing and/or able to pay a higher lump sum? Previously, he had told his older brother Karl that he refused to pay $75,000, stating that he would be better off going into business with someone else.

The real challenge was solving the family crisis without alienating Bruce and his family. Furthermore, Bruce only had a good relationship with only one of his four brothers (Karl). Barbara was looking to her sons and her attorney for an answer to this complicated, nerve-racking family crisis.

This case was written by Todd A. Finkle, the University of Akron, as a basis for class discussion rather than to illustrate either effective or ineffective handling of a business situation. Reprinted by permission.

435

The Johnston Family

Born in Kansas City in 1934, Barbara Johnston grew up in a lower-middle-class Lutheran family, and many of her attitudes were shaped by the Depression. But despite her challenging upbringing, Barbara was a gregarious, warm, friendly, family-oriented woman.

During her junior year in high school, she fell in love with a senior named Harvey Johnston. Harvey married Barbara four years after she graduated from high school. The marriage was very tumultuous but produced five healthy boys and six grandchildren. Most of the boys had personality characteristics similar to those of their father, which included a very high need for independence, an extremely strong work ethic, and an entrepreneurial flair. The oldest son, Karl, a twice-divorced 47-year old, was currently married (Caren). Karl was a street-smart, successful entrepreneur who owned a 3M dealership in Seattle, Washington. He had grown the business to over $1.5 million in sales in four years. His salary, not including the profits from the business, was around $85,000 a year.

Barbara's second son, Cal, had been married to Jessica for 22 years. His marriage produced three children: Jason, Jennifer, and Jim. Cal was a religious and optimistic 45-year-old cardiologist who lived in Kansas City. Of the five brothers, Cal was the most financially successful. His independent medical practice had sales of $1,000,000 with an annual net income of $250,000.

The middle child, Bruce had been married to Sharon since 1985 and had two children, Albert and Bob. Bruce and Sharon were currently running the family business, The Crowne Inn. Bruce enjoyed partying with his friends from the bar. Bruce and Sharon worked at the bar and made a combined salary of $84,000 (1999), not including the profits from the bar. See Exhibit 1.

The fourth son, Tyler, was a single (never married), 40-year-old dentist living in Las Vegas, Nevada. He was a hard-working free spirit who enjoyed his freedom and convertibles. His dental practice was very successful, and he made approximately $100,000 a year.

Danny, the last son, was also single (37 years old). He was extremely creative and enjoyed working with his hands. He had just started his own entertainment company that specialized in decorations for holidays and special events.

The Crowne Inn

Harvey and Barbara Johnston were married in 1952. Before their marriage, Johnston's father, Norm, realized that his son needed a profession to support his new wife. Norm approached his 22-year-old son and asked him what profession he wanted to enter. After some thought, Johnston stated that he wanted to start his own bar. The loose, free lifestyle appealed to him.

Before opening the bar, Johnston asked his best friend, Leo Smith, if he wanted to be his partner. Smith had been bartending with Johnston for the past two years and enjoyed it, so he agreed. Smith also had more experience in the bar business, so it was a good match. He was a warm, friendly man who was married with one daughter.

In 1952, Johnston and Smith took out a $10,000 loan and started a bar called Leo and Harvey's in downtown Kansas City. The bar was structured as an S-Corporation, where both Johnston and Smith owned 50 percent of the stock in the company.

After seven years of moderately successful business, they made a decision to move the business to the northeast part of Kansas City. The downtown area had become increasingly dangerous; crime had burgeoned, as had the number of homeless people. The new location had fewer competitors, less crime, and a better clientele. The partners purchased the land and building and moved into the new location in 1959, renaming the bar The Crowne Inn.

The Crowne Inn was unique in that it was patterned after the Old West. Old wooden barrels lined the front of the building. The building itself was made of wood boards, and signs mounted all over the front of the building ranged from "Dance Girls Wanted" to "Whisky Served Here" to "Coldest Beer in Town." On the top of the building was a 7Up sign.

Near the entrance of the smoke-filled bar there was a shiny, dark-stained, wooden bar with ten stools for customers. A pair of small swinging doors led to the back of the bar, where a small cooler held mugs, cans, and bottles of beer and wine. There were five taps: one each for Champagne, Cold

Duck, and Miller High Life and two for Budweiser (their best-selling beer). On the other side of the bar were a small grill, refrigerator, office, and cooler for kegs and cases of beer. A limited supply of hard alcohol and food items was also for sale behind the bar.

The Crowne Inn differentiated itself from other bars in a number of ways. First, the bar had a very homey atmosphere, with approximately 15 tables and a total capacity of 70 people. This gave customers the ability to converse without all the hassles (such as fights and loud music) of a typical bar. The bar also served lunch (hamburgers, hot dogs, chili dogs, and chips) and snacks (Slim Jims, beef jerky, and bags of peanuts). The bar initially had a pool table and color TV, but the pool table was dropped after several fights over games occurred.

The historic ambiance of the bar was enhanced by historic newspaper clippings shellacked on the walls. Actual articles on the Japanese surprise attack at Pearl Harbor, the sinking of the Lusitania, and the D-Day invasion were all exhibited on the wall. The bar was full of historic relics, which included old menus, beer trays, political buttons, and beer cans. Jim Bean bottles (novelty bottles filled with whiskey) were also located all over the bar.

The Crowne Inn's busiest times were weekdays for lunch (11–1 p.m.), happy hour (5–7 p.m.), and weekend evenings (8–1 a.m.). Business professionals made up the largest segment of customers at lunch. During the late afternoon and evening, the customers were primarily local blue-collar workers.

Johnston and Smith worked alternating, two-week shifts: day (10 a.m. to 6 p.m.) and evening (6 p.m. to 2 a.m.). As their business slowly grew, so did their families. Smith eventually had four girls and moved into a beautiful four-bedroom house, and Johnston had five boys, moved into a small three-bedroom house, and struggled to pay his bills.

Transitional Years

In 1981, Harvey Johnston bought out Smith's stock in the company for $50,000 cash. At the age of 28, Karl joined the business full-time. Karl brought a new ambiance to the bar. He had a high level of energy, creativity, and numerous innovative ideas to enhance the sales of the bar. One of the

first things that he did was add a large cooler that contained over 80 imported beers from all over the world. He also created an advertising campaign in the local entertainment papers, and he bought a popcorn machine, a stereo system, and a VCR to play movies. These ideas, along with Karl's jovial personality, bolstered sales and changed the culture of the bar from a primarily neighborhood blue-collar establishment to a spot frequented by a younger, trendier 25–40-year-old crowd.

By late 1982, Karl had grown weary of the long hours, drunks, and low pay. Furthermore, he had recently been married, and his wife, Jessica, wanted him to leave the bar business. Despite the rise in sales of the bar to $125,000, he was not making as much money as he had hoped. He quit the bar and moved to San Diego, California.

Turnaround

By late 1982, Johnston's middle son, Bruce, started working part-time for the bar; however, Harvey still worked the majority of the hours. In 1984, Karl returned from San Diego as a divorcee and started working at the bar again. Karl and Bruce came up with some innovative ideas to increase sales. They started selling warm roasted peanuts at $.75 a bowl and ice-cold pints of imported beer (such as Guinness, Heineken, and Bass Ale) on tap. They also started selling pickles and added video games, a pinball machine, a jukebox CD player, and a big-screen television.

After two years, sales had increased to $185,000, but despite the increased success of the bar, Karl again decided to quit. He had been robbed twice at gunpoint, including one occasion when the robbers took all of the money and jewelry from the customers. He had also remarried, and his second wife, Judy, was pushing him to get out of the bar business. Karl and Judy moved to San Diego at the end of 1986.

By the end of 1986, Bruce was working full-time with his father. Bruce refined his entrepreneurial flair over the next 10 years. One of his most innovative moves was a strategic alliance with an Italian restaurant across the street, called Pappa's Pizza. This take-out or dine-in restaurant offered tasty Italian food. Since the bar did not serve food (besides snacks) in the evenings, it was an ideal strategy to allow people to order food from Pappa's Pizza and bring it into the bar. This strategy beefed up sales for both businesses.

Bruce also arranged promotional events where guest DJs would come in and play music. One of his most innovative special events was Crownewood. Crownewood was held every year on the night of the Oscars. Customers would vote on which stars would win. Those who guessed correctly won prizes. Other events focused on sports. For example, free chili was served during Monday Night Football.

These activities, combined with advertising in the local entertainment paper, *Rebel*, attracted two new market segments, the college crowd and young urban professionals. The Crowne Inn had transformed itself from a primarily blue-collar neighborhood bar into one of the most progressive bars in Kansas City. As a result, the Johnstons increased their prices and sales. Under Harvey and Bruce's tenure, the sales of the bar increased from $145,000 in 1984 to $200,000 in 1994 (an increase in sales of 4 percent a year). See Exhibit 2.

One of the keys to Bruce's success in turning the bar around was his girlfriend, Sharon, whom he eventually married in 1985. Sharon was a very savvy businessperson with a strict, authoritarian management style with tight controls. This was in contrast to Harvey and Bruce's laid-back personalities, which led Sharon to take control of the bar.

Failure of the Oral Agreement

In 1994, after running the bar for 42 years, Harvey was ready to retire. Harvey had emphysema, suffered from diabetes, and was obese. He approached his sons to see who wanted the bar. Bruce was the logical person to purchase the bar, because he had been running it successfully for the past 11 years.

On the day of his father's retirement, Bruce entered into an oral agreement with his parents. In exchange for the future proceeds from the bar, Bruce agreed to pay off the $23,500 that remained of the second mortgage on his parent's house, to give them $500 in cash each month, and to pay for their health insurance and medical costs for the rest of their lives. Harvey refused to have a written contract.

Harvey remained president of the company and owned all of the stock. If he passed away, the stock would move into his wife's name. After they had both passed away, the stock would pass on to Bruce. The remainder of the estate's assets would then be divided among the other four siblings. The estimated amount of the remainder of the estate in 2001 was $50,000 (house), $80,000 (cash and securities), automobile ($10,000), and miscellaneous ($5,000).

Bruce paid his parents' health care premiums for the most inexpensive policy up until his father's death in 1997. But beginning in 1998, when Barbara became eligible for Medicare, Bruce did not pay for any of her health care costs, which included Medicare ($46 per month) and medications ($300 per month). Cal ended up paying for the medications, which caused resentment from Cal and his wife. Barbara paid for her Medicare.

From 1994 to 1998, Bruce paid his mother $500 per month. However, he treated her as an employee. Therefore, taxes were deducted from her paycheck of $500, which resulted in a final sum of approximately $400. Bruce did pay $500 cash for one year, but in 2000 he treated his mother as an employee again. Furthermore, Barbara often complained that Bruce did not pay her on time (the 5th of the month). However, Barbara stated that after a phone call to Bruce, he always paid her by the end of the month. She insisted that he never missed a payment.

To make matters worse, the bar's accountant was also Bruce and Barbara's personal accountant. In April 2000, Bruce told his mother that she owed $10,000 in taxes for the tax year 1999. He stated that she owed this because she cashed in $15,000 in stock (initial cost basis of $1,352 in 1965) to refurbish parts of her house. Barbara's total income and taxes paid for 1999 can be seen in Exhibit 3.

Bruce and Sharon recommended that Barbara take out a $10,000 loan for the taxes that she owed, which she did within 24 hours. When Barbara informed her sons about this, they were suspicious. They decided to obtain a copy of the financial statements of the bar from 1997 to 1999. In October 2000, Danny requested a copy of the financial statements from Bruce. Bruce vehemently refused, stating that because Danny was not a shareholder in the bar, he could not receive a copy of the financials. The next day Danny and Barbara visited Bruce's accountant and demanded a copy of the financial statements for the past three years. The accountant reluctantly gave copies to Barbara. See Exhibits 4, 5, and 6.

The next day the accountant called Barbara to inform her that she would be receiving a refund of approximately $6,482 from her taxes. Bruce and Sharon both went ballistic. They charged over to Barbara's house and threatened to disown her and the family,

> You have no right looking into our personal financial situation. You are trying to steal the bar away from us! You are taking away my kids' education money.

The following day Bruce and Sharon showed up unannounced at Barbara's house with an unsigned contract (see Exhibit 7). Under duress, they took Barbara to see their attorney and pressured her to sign the contract. After this, they quickly went to see Barbara's attorney, Bobby Free. There was a sense of urgency on the part of Bruce and Sharon to get the contract signed immediately. Free could tell by the look on Barbara's face that she was under duress. Danny showed up at Free's office, and they stated that they needed time to examine the contract before they would allow her to sign anything. See Exhibit 7.

Everyone left, but the turmoil continued. Danny updated the brothers, and they determined that something had to be done about the situation. This had gone on for too long.

The Bar Industry in 2001

In 2001, the bar industry was in its mature stage of the industry life cycle. The sales of alcoholic beverages in the United States had increased from $90.5 billion in 1998 to $96.1 billion in 1999. Consumption of packaged alcohol had increased from $44.7 to $48.7 billion, and that of alcoholic drinks from $45.8 to $47.4 billion, during the same time period. A recent survey of 434 colleges polled by the Higher Education Research Institute found that beer drinking in 2000 had decreased from the previous year by half a percentage point (Dees, 2001).

Over the past few years the industry has seen numerous changes. One of the more popular trends was the increasing demand for liquors and beers imported from all over the world. Another trend was the increase in sales of micro-brewed beer. Many bars have also increased the number of movies/videos, video games, and billiards available to customers.

Technology has also had an effect on the bar industry. Leisure time has been down 25 percent over the past 10 years because of the introduction of the Internet, digital television, and game consoles. Sixty percent of the bars in the United States currently offer access to the Internet. Finally, implementation of the .08 alcohol intoxication limit in most states has increased the liability associated with owning a bar.

Local Environment and Competition in 2001

Kansas City was the home of pro baseball's Kansas City Royals and pro football's Kansas City Chiefs. The city was split in two by the Missouri River. There was a Kansas City, Kansas and a Kansas City, Missouri. Two million people currently live in the metropolitan Kansas City area.

The cost-of-living index for Kansas City was 98.6 on a U.S. scale = 100. This was significantly lower than other high-cost areas such as San Francisco, which had an index of 179.8. Wages for most occupations were close to the U.S. national average. Furthermore, out of 180 metropolitan areas surveyed by the National Association of Home Builders, Kansas City ranked fourteenth in housing affordability during the fourth quarter of 2000.

The Crowne Inn was located on the northeast side of Kansas City (Clay County) about five miles from downtown. The surrounding area was a combination of residential and commercial properties.

The total number of households in the surrounding area with the same zip code was 12,800, with a population of 31,500. The median age, household income, and household size were 43, $37,786, and 2.3, respectively. Most of the people owned their house, and only 30 percent of the households had children.

The primary competitive advantage for The Crowne Inn was its location. Several businesses, two major universities, a medical school, and two major hospitals were located within a five-mile radius. This added 30,000 people to the bar's customer base, over and above the local residential market.

There were five competitors located within a one-mile radius. However, the Crowne Inn had its niche. It was known as a homey place where customers could relax, get good food and drinks, and have quiet conversations.

The Decision

Barbara and her sons had to come to a final resolution with Bruce. It was quite evident that Bruce was unable to meet his oral obligations. Their attorney came up with three alternatives. First, they could sell the bar outright to Bruce and receive a lump sum. This would allow Bruce to pay off all of his future financial obligations to his mother in one lump sum. Second, they could have Bruce pay a smaller sum and continue making payments of $500 per month. Third, they could sell the bar to a third party.

Karl and Bruce discussed an appropriate way to deal with the problem. Karl communicated to his family that Bruce wanted to pay a lump sum of not more than $60,000. It became increasingly evident that Karl was now on Bruce's side and was not looking at the situation objectively. Karl insinuated that Bruce had done nothing wrong. Bruce stated to Karl that

> I am not willing to go above $60,000. If you want me to pay more than that I will go into business with the owner of Pappa's Pizza. We have been talking about opening a new pizza/bar in one of the fastest-growing segments of the city, the East. This area is dangerous. We have been robbed three times in the last three years. If we move, this would put The Crowne Inn out of business.

The family, excluding Karl, Bruce, and Sharon, met over Christmas and discussed their next move. They were unsure whether the $60,000 was a fair offer. They were also uncertain how to go about determining a fair lump sum. Bruce had previously sent Karl a letter outlining all of the money that he had spent on his parents over the years and stating

that he had given his parents $98,275 over the past five years. He insinuated that he had already paid for the bar. See Exhibit 8.

Danny asserted that $60,000 was a ridiculously low offer. In 1999, the bar had sales of $346,000, and Bruce and Sharon made $84,000 plus the profits from the bar. Danny stated that they should pay $175,000. Danny also pointed out that

> We need to determine the average life expectancy for a person in Barbara's age group. Once we do this, we can determine a fair offer.

See Exhibit 9. According to the tables, Barbara had a life expectancy of 17.5 years; however, her history of health problems (such as a heart condition) reduced her life expectancy to 14.5 years.

As the holidays came to an end, Karl, Cal, Tyler, and Danny had a number of questions. Was the lump-sum method the best way to handle the problem? If so, was the $60,000 offer fair? If this was not a fair offer, what *was* fair? Furthermore, would Bruce be willing and/or able to pay a higher lump sum? He had earlier told Karl that he was unwilling to pay $75,000. As they sat around pondering the situation, their mother was thinking,

> I do not want to lose my son and grandchildren over this bar. It is not worth it. However, Bruce made an oral agreement to take care of me.

Discussion Questions

Describe the historical transgression of The Crowne Inn? What has made the business successful?

1. What mistakes did Harvey make during the succession process? As a result of having no written succession plan, what happened?
2. Why were the brothers so mad? Were they justified?
3. Bruce attempted to get his mother to sign a contract under duress (see Case Exhibit 7). Do you think this was a fair contract? If not, what was wrong with the contract?
4. Bruce gave the brothers a detailed analysis of all of the money that he had given to their mother since 1995. What role should this play in determining your final recommendation to the family?

5. Based on the financial information in the case, place a value on the business using the following methodologies: Balance Sheet, Income Statement, and Discounted Cash Flow Methods.
6. Based on the financial and statistical information in the case, what would you recommend to the Johnston family? Why?
7. How do you think the culture of the family will change in the future?

References

Dees, J. (2001). "Fighting Back," http:/www.nightclub .com/magazine/July01/fight.html.

Health Care Financing Administration (HCFA). *State Medical Manual 1999*, # 3258.9 (HCFA Transmittal No. 64).

EXHIBIT 1	Annual Salaries for Bruce and Sharon Johnston and The Crowne Inn's Net Income (Pretax) from 1997 to 2000

YEAR	BRUCE	SHARON	BAR'S NET INCOME (PRETAX)	TOTALS
1997	53,500	20,000	(500)	73,000
1998	60,000	20,000	3,440	83,440
1999	62,000	22,000	6,450	90,450
2000	64,000	24,000	6,500	94,950

EXHIBIT 2	The Crowne Inn Sales from 1982 to 2000

YEAR	SALES ($)
1982	$125,000
1983	135,000
1984	145,000
1985	165,000
1986	185,000
1987	170,000
1988	175,000
1989	180,000
1990	185,000
1991	190,000
1992	192,500
1993	197,500
1994	200,000
1995	225,000
1996	250,000
1997	295,000
1998	326,000
1999	346,000
2000	366,000

| EXHIBIT 3 | Barbara Johnston's Sources of Income and Tax Summary for the Tax Year 1999 |

SOURCE OF INCOME	AMOUNT($)
Taxable Interest	2,294
Dividends	2,752
Cashed in Stock (Capital Gain)	13,648
Taxable Pension	5,778
Taxable S-Corp Income (Bar)	2,299
Total Income	26,771
Adjusted Gross Income	26,771
Standard Deduction	5,350
Personal Exemptions	2,750
Taxable Income	18,671
Total Federal Tax	**2,576**
Total State Tax	**942**
Total Tax	**$3,518**

| EXHIBIT 4 | Income Statement: The Crowne Inn, 1997–1999 |

	1997		1998		1999	
	$	%SALES	$	%SALES	$	%SALES
Sales	$295,621	100.00%	$326,352	100.00%	$345,669	100.00%
Cost of Goods Sold	$156,100	52.80%	$157,231	48.18%	$174,139	50.38%
Gross Profit	$139,521	47.20%	$169,121	51.82%	$171,530	49.62%
OPERATIONAL EXPENSES						
Advertising	$8,318	2.81%	$8,277	2.54%	$5,777	1.67%
Bank Charges	$892	0.30%	$1,094	0.34%	$1,592	0.46%
Insurance — General	$9,762	3.30%	$7,024	2.15%	$11,555	3.34%
Payroll — General	$94,951	32.12%	$96,027	29.42%	$98,383	28.46%
Professional Expense	$1,083	0.37%	$1,424	0.44%	$2,341	0.68%
Repairs and Maintenance	$2,096	0.71%	$9,211	2.82%	$1,687	0.49%
Taxes — Other	$7,813	2.64%	$23,312	7.14%	$27,308	7.90%
Utilities	$7,011	2.37%	$7,689	2.36%	$6,883	1.99%
Other	$5,678	1.92%	$7,882	2.42%	$6,369	1.84%
Total SG&A Expense	$137,604	46.55%	$161,940	49.62%	$161,895	46.84%
Operating Profit	$1,917	0.65%	$7,181	2.43%	$9,632	2.79%
Depreciation Expense	$1,753	0.59%	$2,353	0.72%	$2,086	0.60%
Interest Expense	$664	0.22%	$1,387	0.43%	$1,096	0.32%
Pretax Profit (Loss)	($500)	−0.17%	$3,441	1.05%	$6,451	1.87%

EXHIBIT 5 The Crowne Inn: Balance Sheet, 1997–1999

	1997	1998	1999
Current Assets			
Cash & Marketable Securities	$ 6,280	$ 5,359	$ 8,118
Inventory	$ 6,250	$ 7,325	$ 6,785
Total Current Assets	$ 12,530	$ 12,684	$ 14,903
Property, Plant, & Equipment	$ 80,790	$ 82,315	$ 86,467
Less: Accumulated Depreciation	$ 60,791	$ 63,144	$ 69,384
Total Net Fixed Assets	$ 19,999	$ 19,171	$ 17,083
Total Assets	$ 35,529	$ 31,855	$ 31,986
Current Liabilities			
Accounts Payable	$ 5,146	$ 3,183	$ 3,456
Sales & Income Tax Payable	$ 1,460	$ 1,481	$ 1,827
Total Current Liabilities	$ 6,606	$ 4,664	$ 5,283
Long-Term Liabilities	$ 14,045	$ 11,872	$ 9,085
Total Liabilities	$ 20,651	$ 16,536	$ 14,368
Common Stock or Owner's Equity	$ 6,000	$ 6,000	$ 6,000
Retained Earnings	$ 5,878	$ 9,319	$ 11,618
Total Equity	$ 11,878	$ 15,319	$ 17,618
Total Liabilities and Owner's Equity	**$ 32,529**	**$ 31,855**	**$ 31,986**

EXHIBIT 6 The Crowne Inn Cash Flow Summary, 1997–1999

	1997	1998	1999
Total Sales	$ 295,621	$ 326,352	$ 345,669
Total Cash Available	$ 295,621	$ 326,352	$ 345,669
Total Purchases	$ 156,100	$ 157,231	$ 174,139
Increase (Decrease) in Inventory	$ 820	$ 1,075	($ 540)
Cash Available After Purchase	$ 156,920	$ 158,306	$ 173,599
Uses of Cash:			
Operating Expenses:			
Total per Income Statement	$ 137,604	$ 161,940	$ 161,896
Financing Activities:			
Interest Expense	$ 664	$ 1,387	$ 1,096
Principal Payments (Loan Additions)	($ 14,045)	$ 2,173	$ 2,787
Assets Additions	$ 16,917	$ 1,525	
Other Decreases (Increases)	$ 2,282	($ 1,942)	($ 3,532)
Cash Flow	($ 157)	($ 921)	$ 2,759
Beginning Cash	$ 6,437	$ 6,280	$ 5,359
Ending Cash	$ 6,280	$ 5,359	$ 8,118
Cash Flow Increase (Decrease)	($ 157)	($ 921)	$ 2,759

EXHIBIT 7   Contract Proposed by Bruce

AGREEMENT

This agreement made and entered into this 11th day of November, 2000, by and between Barbara A. Johnston, hereinafter referred to as Seller and Bruce S. Johnston, hereinafter referred to as Buyer:

WITNESSETH:

WHEREAS, Seller is the owner of a majority of the stock in The Crowne Inn, Inc; and

WHEREAS, Buyer desires to buy the Seller's stock, and to purchase all of the Seller's interest in the real and personal property where The Crowne Inn conducts business; and

WHEREAS, the parties had previously agreed to a monthly payment for the purchase of Seller's stock which agreement the parties wish to codify herein.

NOW THEREFORE, in consideration of the mutual promises and convenants contained herein, the parties agree as follows:

1. That Seller shall sell to Buyer, and the Buyer shall buy from Seller, the real and personal property where The Crowne Inn, Inc. conducts its business. The parties agree that subsequent to this Agreement, all of the documents will be prepared, to effectuate said transfer, including a deed to the real property and bill of sale to all personal property, and both parties shall execute such necessary documents. The consideration for this transfer shall be the sum of $50,000.00, which the Buyer shall pay forthwith even though the transfer documents shall not be prepared until after the date of this Agreement.

2. That Buyer shall continue to pay to Seller the sum of $500.00 per month, for the remainder of her life, said payment being the consideration for the present transfer of all of the Seller's stock in The Crowne Inn, Inc. Seller shall, immediately upon receipt of said funds, execute any and all documents necessary to transfer all of Seller's interest in the stock in The Crowne Inn to Buyer.

IN WITNESS WHEREOF, the parties hereto have entered in this Agreement the day and date first above written.

_____   _____
Barbara A. Johnston, Seller   Bruce S. Johnston, Buyer

State of Missouri   :
                : SS.
County of Jackson   :

On this ____ day of _____ , 2000, before me, the undersigned, a notary public, duly commissioned and qualified for said state, personally came Barbara A. Johnston, to me known to be the identical person whose name is subscribed to the foregoing instrument, and acknowledged the execution thereof to be her voluntary act and deed.

WITNESS my hand and notarial seal the day and year last above written.

_____
Notary Public

State of Missouri   :
                : SS.
County of Jackson   :

On this ____ day of _____ , 2000, before me, the undersigned, a notary public, duly commissioned and qualified for said state, personally came Bruce S. Johnston, to me known to be the identical person whose name is subscribed to the foregoing instrument, and acknowledged the execution thereof to be his voluntary act and deed.

WITNESS my hand and notarial seal the day and year last above written.

_____
Notary Public

| EXHIBIT 8 | Money Bruce Spent on His Parents Since 1995 |

TYPE OF PAYMENT	AMOUNT ($)
5 Years at $500 per Month	$30,000
Mortgage on House	23,500
Extra Money Given at Christmas for 5 Years	4,000
Cost of Insurance	30,000
Lawn and Snow Care at House	3,000
Repair Bills Paid	2,000
New Furnace and Air Conditioner	4,800
Personal Tax CPA Costs	975
TOTALS	$98,275

| EXHIBIT 9 | Life Expectancy Table for Females |

AGE	LIFE EXPECTANCY (YEARS)
10	68.6
20	59.8
30	50.2
40	40.6
50	31.4
60	22.9
65	19.0
66	18.2
67	17.5
68	16.8
69	16.0
70	15.4
80	9.1
90	4.7
100	2.5
110	1.3
120	.6

Source: Health Care Financing Administration (HCFA), *State Medical Manual 1999,* No. 3258.9 (HCFA Transmittal No. 64).

Case 7

Linksys: The Essence of Opportunity Recognition

Once upon a time there were two immigrant entrepreneurs who founded a company in the garage of their Orange County, California, home. After years of bootstrapping the company along, the founders achieved a seven-year run on the Inc. 500 Fastest Growing Companies list, and in the spring of 2003, they sold the company to a large technology firm for $500 million. Sound like a fairytale? It's not. Victor and Janie Tsao represent the spirit of entrepreneurship, and theirs is a story that inspires and teaches what it takes to survive and grow in the dynamic world of high technology.

The Opportunity

Victor and Janie Tsao met at Tamkang University in Taiwan. With the goal of becoming independent before the age of 40, they immigrated to the United States, where Janie worked in information technology at Carter Hawley Hale and Victor did the same at Taco Bell, while also earning an MBA from Pepperdine University. Both were known for their frugality (until the sale of the company, they drove a 12-year-old Mercedes), their drive, and their tireless ability to work day and night.

When Janie was 35 and Victor 37, they decided to test their entrepreneurial skills by forming a consulting company they called DEW International that would match U.S. technology vendors with Taiwanese manufacturers who could do the work significantly more cheaply. From the garage of their Irvine home, they worked and developed good relationships with Taiwanese manufacturers. One day,

one of the manufacturers brought a new product idea to the Tsaos. At that time, the cables that connected printers to computers could not be more than 15 feet long, because beyond that length the data would degrade. The manufacturer had invented a way to use telephone wire to extend that length to 100 feet, but he had no knowledge of markets and distribution and wanted the Tsaos to take this product to the U.S. market. The Tsaos agreed. Within a short time, this manufacturer also invented products that connected multiple PCs to multiple printers. The Tsaos immediately saw the opportunity to develop a new company, so they renamed their existing company Linksys and invested $7,000 in it. Over the next two years, Victor left his job, and the company moved twice, ending up in a 2,000-square-foot office. By means of technology catalogues, they were selling 8,000 units a month of their new device, which they dubbed Multishare.

At the launch of Linksys, Victor began working 100 hours a week, surviving only with naps on the floor of his modest office, because he felt the need to be involved in every part of the business. During the day he immersed himself in the operations of the business; at night he was on the phone to his Taiwanese manufacturers until the early hours of the morning. Janie's job was marketing and bringing in revenues, and Victor's was making sure they spent as little money as possible. By then their family had grown to four, with two little boys, and they lived on the salary of $2,000 a month that Janie drew from the company. Victor did not take a salary until the mid-1990s, and even then he wasn't the highest-paid employee and never took a raise.

The Linksys Culture

The Linksys culture is clearly one of frugality and making sure that everyone "fits right" in the organization. The Tsaos have been known to let great talent walk away if they didn't have the right mindset to fit into the culture at Linksys. The Tsaos run a lean and fast-moving operation with a payscale that is middling at best. Because they don't have to pay top dollar for their talent, they tend to have young workers who are highly productive, generating about $1.8 million in revenue per full-time employee, compared with about $560,000 for Cisco. Their turnover rate is 5 percent, significantly below the industry average of 9 percent. Linksys saves money anywhere it can. It even produces its own graphics by photographing its products, scanning the photos, sending them to the printer, and even pasting the labels on the boxes.

Linksys also believes in fast product development. When one Taiwanese partner came to Victor with an idea for a product, they were able to move through product development in an astounding three weeks. Victor believes that he's not doing anything original—he just knows how to execute, and that's the secret to success in a rapidly changing environment.

Linksys Grows

A key moment in Linksys's growth came when Microsoft introduced Windows 95 with built-in network functions. Now businesses and homes could network just like big business. To take advantage of the opportunity, Linksys had to get shelf space in the major retail chains. By 1995, Janie had pushed her way into Fry's Electronics, and Linksys's revenue had doubled to $10.7 million, but Janie had her sights set on a national chain. It is rare that a company the size of Linksys wins a national account, but Janie was determined to get Linksys into Best Buy. In April 1996, she attended the RetailVision trade show but was unable to secure an appointment with the buyer for Best Buy. Determined not to go home without a sale, she boldly tracked him to his hotel room and there presented the Linksys product line. The result was an order for $2 million.

From printer-to-PC connectors, Linksys expanded to Ethernet hubs, cards, and cords—everything small businesses and home owners needed to connect their computers and share data and hardware. In 1994 this was a niche market, and the Tsaos' company grew slowly and organically through internal cash flows until 2000, in part because the Tsaos refused to take on debt or investors. But getting into Best Buy helped them boost their revenue to $21.5 million in 1996, $21.1 million in 1997, and $65.6 million in 1998. At that time, Linksys moved from its 2,000-square-foot office space to 20,000 square feet.

In the late 1990s, the home broadband Internet sector began to thrive despite significantly higher costs than the user paid for dial-up connections. Victor again foresaw that people might want to link their home computers or small business computers to a single broadband line. To do this, they would need a router. Large corporations were already using routers to link computers and other hardware, but those routers were very expensive and difficult to configure. Victor saw this dilemma as an opportunity to solve a pain in the market. He developed a low-cost router for consumers and small businesses that ended up being a significant turning point for Linksys. It cost only $199 and had a wizard that walked people through the setup process. Linksys introduced the product in 1999 and succeeded in being the first low-cost router in the market. Curiously, the Tsaos' first big success occurred in Canada, a market that their competitors had avoided because of hardware compatibility problems. That success increased Linksys's market share from 10.8 percent to 18.6 percent in one year. Revenue increased from $107.6 million to $206.5 million. Victor attributes his ability to foresee a potential market to listening to manufacturers and customers rather than doing traditional market research.

Victor continued to introduce a stream of new products around his broadband router, such as cards that let laptops connect to routers. And then he discovered the next milestone in Linksys's growth—wireless networking. What could be better than giving customers a way to connect without wires? Again applying his strategy of being first with a low-cost version, he plunged into the 802.11g wireless standard. At that time, the industry, which was still

FIGURE 1 Linksys: Growth in Revenue, Employees, and Market Share

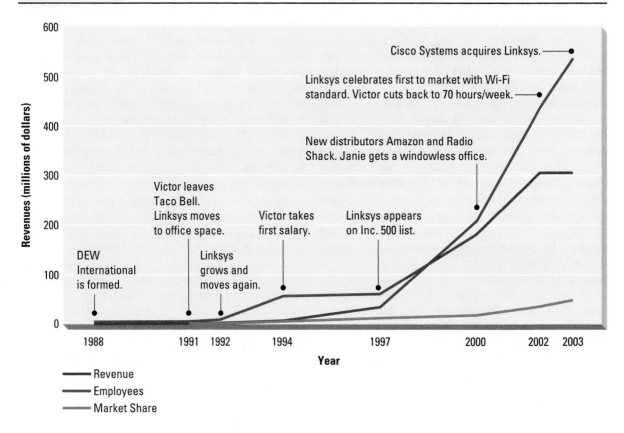

FIGURE 1 Linksys: Growth in Revenue, Employees, and Market Share

arguing over aspects of the standard, expected the standard to be finalized in June 2003, but until then, changes in it were very likely. Victor wanted to take advantage of Christmas sales and bring his new product out early, so the only way to avoid the possibility of the product being made obsolete because of a last-minute change in the standard was to allocate as many parameters as possible to the software. He calculated the risk and charged ahead. Fortunately for Linksys, Victor had covered all the bases, and the demand for the 802.11g access points was phenomenal. In the first quarter of 2003, Linksys had half a million orders. Its market share increased to 34.2 percent. Victor's ability to spot an opportunity

and act on it quickly is precisely what attracted the attention of networking giant Cisco. See Figure 1 for Linksys's growth profile from 1988 to 2003.

The Cisco Opportunity

It was never the Tsaos' intention to sell their business. When the Cisco opportunity came along, it was a matter of what was best for the company. The Tsaos had wanted to expand globally, but they didn't have the cash to do it. They also knew that huge potential competitors—Dell, Microsoft, and HP—were all studying their market, and every one of them had much deeper pockets than Linksys.

Cisco was interested in Linksys because it wanted to diversify into the small business and home office products sector. It saw Linksys as the "premium-priced player with lean operating costs."[1] Conversations with the Tsaos began in 2002, and by March 2003, they announced that Cisco would pay $500 million in stock for Linksys and that the Tsaos would stay on in their current positions for two years. This was the first time that Cisco had ever acquired a company and let it remain a separate firm. At the time of the acquisition, the president of one of Linksys's main competitors, D-Link Systems, stated, "For Cisco to reach out to the consumer at large and come into the field of home networking in retail at this time means that it perceives the massive growth potential in the market, right where our market focus has been."[2]

Victor is happy with the way the company is operating, but if it ever stops being the Linksys he created and becomes more like Cisco, he will quit. Right now, things are moving as quickly and flexibly as ever. Victor is positioning Linksys in the emerging multimedia streaming and wireless console gaming market, as well as exploring the previously unsuccessful Internet telephone market. Prior to the acquisition, about 95 percent of Linksys's revenue came from the United States and Canada. In October of 2003, Linksys launched its products in China.

Victor attributes Linksys' success to five factors: 1) speed to market; 2) the right products with a customer focus; 3) the right attitude about making it easy for customers to do business with Linksys; 4) internal efficiencies through a lean organization and low-cost manufacturing; and 5) external advantages in the breadth and strength of their sales channels and brand. The question is how long Cisco will allow the company to operate independently. What will happen to the culture of Linksys if Cisco moves the offices to something grander and plays a stronger role in how Linksys operates?

Discussion Questions

1. How did the Tsaos' background and previous experience contribute to their ability to recognize the Linksys opportunity?
2. Evaluate the Linksys company culture. How does it contribute to the firm's success? Would you do anything differently? If so, why?
3. Evaluate the Taos' financial strategy. Could they have done anything more effectively?
4. How did the acquisition of Linksys by Cisco benefit each of the companies? What new challenges did it create?

References

Chai, W. (April 21, 2004). "Linksys Finds Its Voice." *CNET News.com,* www.news.com.

"Early Wi-Fi Payoff for Linksys," accessed July 9, 2004, *Goldsea Asian-American,* www.goldsea.com/Business.

Mount, I. (January, 2004). "Entrepreneurs of the Year." *Inc. Magazine,* www.inc.com.

---

[1] Benicek, K. "Cisco Snags Linksys, But Just Who Does It Help?" *Tech-edge,* www.homepage.mac.com/techedgeezine.
[2] Ibid.

Case 8

Finagle a Bagel: Managing the Pace of Rapid Growth in a Family Business

Background

There are many paths to entrepreneurship. Sometimes starting from scratch is not the best way to own a business, especially one in an industry about which you know nothing, other than that you like the products. Laura Beth Trust and Alan Litchman loved bagels, but they had no idea how the bagel business worked. All they knew was that they wanted a business where they would be in direct contact with customers who would then help them decide which products to offer. As a husband-and-wife team, they also longed for an opportunity to start a family business.

Opportunity

Trust and Litchman, both MBA graduates of the Sloan School of Management at MIT, were well schooled in the art of recognizing a profitable opportunity. While in Hong Kong, they noticed a lot of American fast-food restaurants, including Starbucks, but what they did not see were bagel shops. It seemed to them that the sophisticated and multicultural Hong Kong would be enthusiastic about New York–style bagels, and so, with a great deal of optimism, they formed a corporation, found a partner, and then began to do some research back in the United States.

Meanwhile, thousands of miles to the east, Larry Smith was busy operating six very successful bagel stores in Boston. Smith was a serial entrepreneur who in 1982 co-founded a cheesecake store, Julian's Cheesecakes, in historic Quincy Market. Faced with the problem of finding a use for leftover cream cheese, he decided to try his hand at making and selling bagels and cream cheese. The bagels were such a hit that Smith and his partners decided to refocus the store on bagels. They even renamed it Finagle a Bagel. The demand at the first store led to the opening of several other stores in the Boston area, and sales rose to $10 million annually. In 1998, Smith was looking for capital to grow additional stores.

A Meeting of the Minds

Back from Hong Kong, Trust and Litchman met with Larry Smith to seek advice about the bagel business. They were attracted to Finagle a Bagel's strong brand recognition and loyal following in the Boston area. An added bonus was that both Trust and Litchman had family in the Boston area. In late 1998, after much research and many meetings with Smith, they purchased a majority stake in Finagle a Bagel and began to plan an aggressive growth strategy for the company. The plan worked so well that within just a few years, Trust and Litchman were able to buy out the original founder and become the sole owners.

Growing the Company

The foundation of the company's growth strategy was to model itself after the strategies of the Cheesecake Factory and In-and-Out Burger, two successful California-based chains that remained primarily in one state for many years before venturing beyond. In fact, up to the time of this writing, In-and-Out Burger has never left California. Similarly, Trust and Litchman want to dominate their geographic region first before even considering geographic expansion.

One way for small companies to grow their current market is to diversify their product lines, so Trust and Litchman began introducing different kinds of bagels, sandwiches, and salads, all in one way or another linked to the core product, the bagel. The company is known for the freshness of everything it makes and also for customization, which requires a lot of interaction between employees and customers. To get ideas for new products, Finagle a Bagel does informal research with customers and employees in addition to exploring food magazines and cookbooks for new flavors. Once the staff comes up with a new idea, they begin developing a recipe and going through many iterations to find exactly the right combination of ingredients. Then they do a lot of taste-testing, especially by giving the product away to customers with a coupon to come back and buy it. This is all part of one of Finagle a Bagel's fundamental principles: Spend no money on advertising. Trust and Litchman believe that the best way to attract customers to a new product is to whet their appetites by giving them a sample. They have come up with a number of new products that give customers reason to come back after breakfast and even lunch. One new offering that turned out to be a success was the bagel pizza.

Another way for small businesses to grow within their current market is find new customers for their current products. Finagle a Bagel began wholesaling bagels to universities, hospitals, and corporate cafeterias, as well as selling packaged bagels under its brand name to the Shaw's grocery chain. This move into the Shaw's supermarkets opened other opportunities for growth. If their bagels did well in a particular market, Trust and Litchman would open a store near the market to capture the supermarket customers who wanted to have a fresh bagel and coffee.

Another tenet of Trust and Litchman's philosophy about business is that they want to stay in control. Thus franchising was not an option, because although the company would receive a large infusion of capital, the owners would not be able to control the "people component" of the business or the product and service quality. Raising money through an initial public offering (IPO) was also a possibility, but it was not likely to be very successful in the food business, and again, the owners would not be able to control the timing of growth. It appeared that slow growth through internal cash flows might be the most appropriate strategy.

Building on the Brand

Having acquired a company with a loyal customer base and a good deal of brand recognition, it was Trust and Litchman's job to build on that base and give customers more opportunities to give input to the company. To reinforce their relationship with the customer, they began offering a Finagle a Bagel Frequent Finagler card, which gave cardholders one point for every dollar they spent at the store. The points could be redeemed for food items, including a baker's dozen of bagels. They launched this concept on their website (www.finagleabagel.com) and made it possible for customers to check the status of their points at the website and also to receive free gifts by mail. Using the website was also a way to drive new traffic to their stores.

In Trust and Litchman's view, to build a successful brand, you must have consistency to reinforce the brand image. Their stores have a similar look and feel to assure customers that they won't be surprised at what they get. But they also recognize that the suburban stores serve a different clientele than the downtown stores. To recognize that, some of the suburban stores have furniture for children, free weekly concerts, and a family-friendly atmosphere. By contrast, the Harvard Square store, which services a large university crowd, has a trendier, more urban feel and even has a liquor license.

One thing Finagle a Bagel will never do, no matter what, is compromise quality. When Trust and Litchman price a new product, they start by figuring in the cost of the finest ingredients. Then they calculate a retail price that they think the customer will pay and test it against competitors' pricing and what customers say is a great value for the price. The owners do not vary the pricing by store because they believe it is important to treat every customer fairly.

Competition

Finagle a Bagel competes not only with other bagel shops in the Boston area but also with other types of food establishments. Because people typically have limited disposable income for eating out, it is Finagle a Bagel's job to convince them that their money is best spent at this store. Much larger competitors, Bruegger's and Einstein, are expanding and revamping their bagel menus to include muffins and soups in addition to entrée salads and new sandwiches. Bruegger's is also looking at an upscale dining design with enhanced beverage options. The fast-food industry is a dynamic one where a company such as Finagle a Bagel can survive if it innovates and capitalizes on its regional prominence.

The Company Culture

If you drew an organizational chart of Finagle a Bagel, you would see the co-presidents, Trust and Litchman, at the top and then the middle management, store managers, and other employees beneath. But Heather Robertson, who wears many hats as Finagle a Bagel's director of marketing, human resources, and product development, enjoys turning that org chart upside down to point out that the co-presidents' role is to support everyone else, general managers support-store managers, and so on down the chain. General managers are given the authority to do whatever it takes to alleviate problems in their stores or to increase sales. Because Finagle a Bagel supports its employees, its turnover

rate is very low compared to the rest of the industry, so the company spends less time and money training new employees. In fact, a large number of employees have been with this 400-employee company for many years, because they like the warm and caring atmosphere that the owners have fostered.

When choosing managers for their stores, Trust and Litchman have an easier time with the downtown stores because they are close enough to manage more carefully. For the suburban stores, they look for people who have an owner mentality and want to build a regional business. To encourage that, the company splits the profits with a store that has achieved more than a specified level of sales or profits. Historically, the best managers have come from the ranks of the company, working their way up.

Many of Finagle a Bagel's employees come from other regions of the world: Latin America, Europe, and western Africa, among many others. The company often sponsors new Americans who need government-issued work permits to remain in the United States legally. There are many benefits to this multicultural workforce—new ideas and the ability to reach out to a broader customer base, to name two—but there are challenges as well. For example, to prevent communication problems and avoid confusion, Finagle a Bagel requires that all its employees speak English when working with customers.

Technology

The company uses technology to create efficiencies, to interact with customers, and to learn which products should be kept and which should be dropped. Because every dollar counts, Trust and Litchman invest only in technology that directly supports their business by making it more efficient or saving it money. For example, their new point-of-sale system makes it easier to track points on customer loyalty cards and to determine which products are doing well and which are not. This new capability saves the company money by reducing inventory that doesn't turn over quickly and by focusing production on products that customers really want.

Social Responsibility

Finagle a Bagel believes in social responsibility. For example, no bagel is ever thrown away at the end of the day. Leftover bagels are donated to schools, shelters, and other nonprofits. Bagels are also donated to fundraisers to feed the volunteers.

The Future

Today Finagle a Bagel is a 17-store chain with a corporate support center and a dough-making factory. Eight of its stores are in downtown Boston and nine in suburban areas. Revenues are at $25 million a year, which is remarkable considering that the owners never sought outside capital or sold stock in the company. They did, however, manage to get a bank to provide them an unsecured line of credit of nearly $4 million on the basis of the company's proven record of success with multiple stores and a well-documented business plan.

Their success so far has not gone unrecognized. They have twice been voted the best in Boston by *Boston Magazine,* and they have received the Best Small Business Award from the Massachusetts Chamber of Commerce in 1998, among several other awards.

The owners plan to continue opening new stores, but it is clear that one day they might receive an acquisition offer that they can't refuse because it will give them the ability to expand more rapidly. At that point, what will happen to the culture Trust and Litchman have built? Will the founders be able to give up control?

Discussion Questions

1. As potential entrepreneurs, what did Trust and Litchman bring to the new venture they were considering? What factors affected their decision about going into the bagel business?
2. Describe Finagle a Bagel's initial market strategy? What are the company's options for further growth?
3. Describe the culture of Finagle a Bagel. How does that culture affect the firm's business strategy?

References

Pride, William M., Robert J. Hughes, and Jack R. Kapoor, *Business,* 8th ed. (Boston: Houghton Mifflin, 2005), 100–101, 192–193.
http://www.finagleabagel.com.

Aegis Performance Apparel

Business Plan
David Dobkin
Annemarie Dillard

The University of Southern California

Executive Summary

Getting hurt on the slopes is no fun. Not only is the injury bad, but also the pain, doctor's visits, ruined vacations, loss of job productivity, and above all, no more skiing or snowboarding that season. People go to the mountains to have fun, not to get hurt. The success of the X games and the desire to "go big" are sending more snowriders to the mountains—and to the hospital. Even though snowsports participants are increasingly aware of the possibility of injury, outside of a helmet, injury protection is not widely available. Aegis Performance Apparel ("Aegis" or the "Company") will answer the call.

Company Concept

Aegis will provide integrated snowsports apparel that combines fashion, function, and protection to the risk-conscious snowsports participant, allowing for feelings of security, freedom, and peace of mind. Targeted direct customers for the line include specialty snowsports apparel retailers, and the targeted end consumers will be Generation X and Y, intermediate to advanced snowsports enthusiasts who are weary of injury and seek a viable medium of protection. Distribution will occur on an annual basis, products being shipped directly to retailers who will then be responsible for selling goods to end consumers.

Industry and Market Potential

The Snowsports Industry—High Growth:

As the fastest-growing segment of the sports entertainment industry, the action sports industry accounts for over $12 billion in annual sales.[1] Over the last 20 years, the participation in and growth of the action sports industry have skyrocketed. Of the action sports, snowsports (more specifically, skiing and snowboarding) are growing at nearly 13% annually, accounting for $2.1 billion in sales in 2003.[2] Today, the snowsports apparel industry alone is a $1.2 billion dollar industry, not including the accessories market, consisting of helmets, eyewear, and protective gear. Current snowsports apparel manufacturers are not focused on injury prevention and, as a result, have not been able to launch such a product line successfully.

Aegis has identified the primary target market to be specialty retail stores catering to generation X and Y (ages 12–34) skiers and snowboarders in the United States. Currently, the market size is $650 million. After considering the responses to Aegis's surveys and the current market for helmets, Aegis estimates the demand for Aegis's products to be $325 million.[3]

Management

Entrepreneurs

The entrepreneurs behind Aegis Performance Apparel include Annemarie Dillard and David Dobkin. Annemarie comes to Aegis with years of experience in the fashion industry (including Dillard's Inc., BCBG Maxazria and Left Coast Style), as well as a business degree in entrepre-

---

[1] Sporting Goods Manufacturer Association, 2003 *Superstudy of Sports Participation.*
[2] Sporting Goods Manufacturer Association, 2003 *Superstudy of Sports Participation.*
[3] The demand is calculated to be the mean of affirmatives survey interest (60%) and helmet users (37%) times 2003 apparel sales.

neurship from the University of Southern California. David Dobkin, a Ph.D. candidate in bio-medical engineering from USC, was a health care investment banker at Wasserstein Perella in New York, completing deals in biotechnology, medical devices, and services. David was founder of Dealprovider.com, a Web-based deal-finder, and managed a staff of over 100 for Versity.com, an online-notes company. David also brings his experience as a competitive skier and ski instructor at Breckenridge and Mammoth Mountains.

Board of Directors
The board of directors advising Aegis has considerable experience in retail apparel, action sports, and the snowsports industry. Board members include Alex Dillard, president of Dillard's Inc.; Matthew Levenson, CEO of 9star; and Rusty Gregory, CEO of Mammoth Mountain.

Operations
As a start-up entity, Aegis will outsource most of the workflow to third parties. A trading company will oversee the manufacturing of the product line and shipping to the United States. A third party will be used for warehousing and distribution to retailers. Aegis will hire independent designers to produce the initial designs of Aegis. The founding members will perform sales and marketing duties.

After the initial roll-out of the product line, a sales team and back office support will be hired. Support duties will include customer service, order fulfillment, and office management. Other possible hires include a design team and general manager.

Marketing
Aegis's marketing initiatives will raise awareness of Aegis products, work to establish a viable need for protection, and inspire purchases from both direct and end consumers. Aegis will target both retailers and end users through directed marketing campaigns, tradeshows, and grassroots approaches.

Financials
Aegis believes that a targeted marketing campaign and end-user demand will lead to rapid sales and margin growth from 2006 onward. The projected results are dependent on the successful implementation of management's strategies and are based on industry research.

Table 1: Summary of Financials

	2005	2006	2007	2008	2009	2010	2011
Revenue	$0.0	$2,271,524.3	$3,407,286.4	$5,110,929.7	$6,133,115.6	$7,359,738.7	$8,463,699.5
% Growth	*NA*	*NA*	*50%*	*50%*	*20%*	*20%*	*15%*
Gross Margin	$0	$1,135,762	$1,703,643	$2,811,011	$3,373,214	$4,047,856	$4,655,035
% of Revenue	*NA*	*50%*	*50%*	*55%*	*55%*	*55%*	*55%*
EBITDA	($127,561.9)	$823,118.5	$1,215,062.2	$2,088,681.5	$2,513,575.2	$3,023,510.5	$3,475,797.1
% of Revenue	*NA*	*36%*	*36%*	*41%*	*41%*	*41%*	*41%*
Net Income	($118,594.67)	$545,937.48	$696,924.43	$1,265,624.06	$1,629,530.29	$1,978,228.18	$2,299,109.31
% of Revenue	*NA*	*24%*	*20%*	*25%*	*27%*	*27%*	*27%*

Table of Contents

Business Concept

Concept Statement

Aegis Performance Apparel will provide integrative snowsports apparel that combines fashion, function, and protection to the risk-conscious snowsports participant, allowing for feelings of security, freedom, and peace of mind. Targeted direct customers for the line include specialty snowsports apparel retailers, and the targeted end consumers will be Generation X and Y, intermediate to advanced snowsports enthusiasts who are weary of injury and seek a viable medium of protection. Independently contracted designers, who will work with management to source goods from fabric producers, will design the product line. Actual goods production will be subcontracted through an independent trading company to factories in China and India in order to take advantage of manufacturing superiority and price competitiveness. Distribution will occur on an annual basis, products being shipped directly to retailers who will then be responsible for selling goods to end consumers.

Company Culture

Mission

Aegis Performance Apparel seeks to provide high-quality, protective apparel that offers an integrated and unique combination of fashion, function, and protection, allowing for the ultimate snowsports experience.

Core Values
- Integrity
- Responsibility
- Passion for product
- Commitment to quality
- Dedication to customers

Product

Initially, the primary focus will be on jackets and pants that offer a removable fitted protective padding layer incorporated into a fashionable shell, as well as integrated knee braces. Key focuses of protective features will include support and protection for areas of the body identified as being at high risk of injury during participation in snowsports.

Design for protective measures of Aegis products has been undertaken. Aegis is in the preliminary stages of obtaining intellectual-property rights for the designs: working with patent lawyers to establish patentable material, determining appropriate protective materials, and seeking a designer for the development of prototypes.

Benefits:

The products of Aegis will provide undisputable benefits for its consumers.
- *Security:* The protective aspects of the products provide snowsports participants a feeling of security while participating in their sport.
- *Freedom:* The products offer security and protection while integrating a comfort that allows wearers the feeling of freedom of activity.

1

- *Peace of Mind:* Through the comprehensive integration of fashion, protection, and comfort, Aegis is able to provide consumers with peace of mind while they participate in snowsports.

Customers

Aegis will target retailers who are actively looking to offer bundled products that increase profit margins and who, due to industry seasonality, participate in a narrow window of time for turning inventory, requiring timely delivery of goods with impeccable products that will promote sales for the store. Aegis seeks to target end consumers in Generation X and Y, upper-middle class, price-conscious, moderately risk-averse, avid snowsports enthusiasts who are intermediate to advanced skiers and snowboarders. They are impressionable by sports and entertainment and to some degree follow the various aspects of the extreme-sports market. They are social and enjoy participating in snowsports in groups. Often on top of the latest fashion trends, they wish to portray that quality to others in their social circle, while at the same time having functional gear that offers a nearly uninhibited freedom of movement.

Market Opportunity

The Snowsports apparel industry is in the midst of significant growth. Given the increased acceptance of freestyle snowriding popularized by mainstream media in the form of the X Games on ABC/ESPN and the Gravity Games on NBC, the number of snowriders participating in the sport has never been higher. Consequently, the number of snowrider injuries has far outstripped the increased number of participants. Currently, there are limited preventive orthopedic products available in the market, and no brand has been able to successfully launch a protective layer integrated into a fashionable shell. In survey research, Aegis was able to establish a relatively high demand for such a product in the current marketplace.

Growth Opportunity

Due to the nature of Aegis's products, there are many possible outlets for growth:
- Aegis brand product extensions
- Expansion into new demographics
- Expansion into new markets
- Direct sales to end consumers

Distribution

Distribution will occur primarily through snowsports retailers. Guerilla marketing tactics, coupled with various publicity stunts and grassroots word of mouth, will be the primary means for marketing the line in order to keep costs down. Because Aegis's target demographic is young and impressionable by celebrities, snowsports "heroes," and current market trends, Aegis will endorse various celebrities and competitions in order to establish the line as "all the rage." While marketing methods aimed at consumers will double to gain retailer attention, marketing to retailers will occur primarily through the use of advertisements in leading industry trade journals, press and public relations packets, and presence and advertisement at industry trade show events.

Entrepreneurs

The entrepreneurs behind Aegis Performance Apparel are Annemarie Dillard and David Dobkin. Annemarie comes to Aegis with an "entrepreneurship emphasis" business degree from the University of Southern California, as well as years of experience in the fashion industry, including internships with the Los Angeles-based consumer and product research company Left Coast Style, BCBG Maxazria (including visual merchandising and sales departments), and Dillard's, Inc., as well as experience working on a live marketing project for the JWT agency in Los Angeles. David Dobkin comes to Aegis with a degree in biomedical engineering from Columbia University and is in the process of obtaining a Ph.D. in biomedical engineering from USC, conducting his research on tendon and ligament tissue engineering. Prior to pursuing his doctorate, David was a health care investment banker at Wasserstein Perella in New York, completing deals in biotechnology, medical devices, and services. David was founder of Deal-provider.com, a Web-based deal-finder, and managed a staff of over 100 for Versity.com, an online-notes company. David also brings his experience as a competitive skier and ski instructor at Breckenridge and Mammoth Mountains.

Business Model

The Aegis business model consists of manufacturers, wholesalers, and retailers. Aegis, the wholesaler, will design and order snowsports apparel from the manufacturers and sell directly to specialty retailers. The retailer will then sell direct to the consumers. Although individually, snowsports apparel and protective gear are not unique, the combination of the two can be widely patented. In addition to the primary retail revenue source, Aegis will aggressively market directly to ski resorts as an option for staff uniforms. In an effort to keep worker compensation costs low, an injury-preventive uniform would be in high demand. Associated costs of the business include designer fees, intellectual-property and legal fees, inventory float, labor, marketing and advertising, and insurance. Due to the nature of the business, the initial investment will target the 2006-2007 season, with the initial orders coming in spring of 2006. The critical success factors for Aegis include verification of the target market and of demand, and creating awareness.

The Snowsports Industry and Market Analysis

The Snowsports apparel industry is in the midst of significant growth. Given the increased acceptance of the freestyle snowriding popularized by mainstream media in the form of the X Games on ABC/ESPN and the Gravity Games on NBC, the number of snowriders participating in the sport has never been higher. Consequently, the number of snowrider injuries has far outstripped the increased number of participants.

Today, the snowrider apparel industry is highly fragmented, with many apparel lines vying for market share. Among all brands, only a few companies have been able to acquire sizable market share. Established ski apparel companies have specialized and differentiated to appeal to niche demographics including ski racing (Spyder and Phoenix), high fashion (Nils and Bogner), and backcountry technical (The North Face and Mountain Hardware). Most of the other companies, including 686, Sessions, and Volcom, especially in the snowboard segment, are unorganized and have not aggressively entered the industry. This industry is in the growth stage, allowing for significant market penetration given proper execution.

Industry Background:
The Snowsports Industry - High Growth
The action sports industry, the fastest-growing segment of the sports entertainment industry, accounts for over $12 billion in annual sales.[4] Over the last 20 years, the participation in and growth of the action sports industry have skyrocketed. Of the action sports, snowsports (more specifically, skiing and snowboarding) are growing at nearly 13% annually, accounting for $2.1 billion in sales in 2003.[5] Snowrider visits totaled 57.6 million during the 2002-2003 season, the highest ever: a 5.8% increase over the previous high in 2000-2001 and 11.3% above the running average from 1978 to 1979.[6] Given the superior snowfall this season, the number of snowrider days is expected to grow even further.[7] Ski resorts are embracing additional snowsports, offering terrain parks, tubing parks, upgrading, and first-time skier/children's facilities that are drawing more long-term participants.

Snowsports Evolution
With the advent of easy-turning shaped skis, the boom in the market for female-specific equipment, and the explosive growth of the X Games in the youth market, former diehard snowboarders are turning to skiing as an alternative to sliding down the mountain. The advent of twin-tip skis has allowed the sport to "progress" in unexpected directions, catching a new wave of growth for the entire snowsports industry.[8] More important, the line between skiing and snowboarding is beginning to blur, with increased numbers of skiers in the terrain parks and fashion trends worn by all snowsports riders.

Orthopedic Products Industry
The non-operative orthopedics industry is currently focused on post-injury products designed for patients with slight to moderate injuries. Due to the curative rather than preventive nature of the health care industry, knee bracing has not been widely marketed as a preventive measure despite studies indicating the beneficial effects.[9] In this $1.6 billion industry, DJ Orthopedics and Biomet are the major competitors. These companies manufacture and sell both functional (post-injury) and prophylactic (preventive) knee braces directly to doctors and require a prescription.[10] Functional knee braces are custom fit, whereas prophylactic braces can be adjusted for multiple people. Current research indicates that these two braces do not differ in ef-

---

[4] Sporting Goods Manufacturer Association, 2003 *Superstudy of Sports Participation.*
[5] Sporting Goods Manufacturer Association, 2003 *Superstudy of Sports Participation.*
[6] Robert A. Schless & Co. Inc., 2004, *Sports Incident Management Report.*
[7] Cnn.com, *U.S. Ski Resorts could see record year,* 1/12/05.
[8] SnowSports Industries America, Press Release, 2004.
[9] D. Rod Walters, "Prophylactic Bracing of the Collegiate Football Knee: A Review of Custom Fitted Functional versus Lateral Braces in Offensive Lineman." University of South Carolina, 1999.
[10] Biomet 10-K, 2004.

fectiveness on subjects whose ligaments are intact.[11] These prescribed knee braces can cost up to $1000. As a result, there is little purpose in investing in a custom- fit brace for injury prevention.

Increase in Injuries
From the 1970s to the early 1990s the absolute incidence of snowsports injuries decreased by 50%.[12] Recently, however, injuries have been on the increase. With the addition of terrain features and popularization of the X Games, snowsports injuries are rapidly on the rise. Mountain High, based in Big Bear Lake, California, in January 2005 had surpassed its previous record 2003-2004 injury total by over 500 on-mountain injuries.[13]

Statistically, snowsports are safer than full-contact sports, but as the slopes become more crowded, snowsports enthusiasts are becoming more aware about the severity and increased incidence of injury. Unlike participants in contact sports, most snowsports enthusiasts approach the sport for recreation, rather than for competition, and cannot risk injury.[14] The snow industry as a whole has made a recent push to educate participants about the inherit dangers of snowsports. In 2004, the American Association of Snowboard Instructors, along with the National Ski Patrol and the Professional Ski Instructors of America, produced public service announcements that aired on ESPN, Outdoor Life Network, Resort Sports Network, MTV, and major and local stations near ski areas from December to March.[15] As a result, participant consciousness of potential injuries has increased, resulting in higher sales of protective wear.[16]

Protective Gear
The introduction of the ski helmet has presented a new revenue stream to the once stale ski industry. More skiers and riders are aware of the inherent dangers associated with snowriding and are actively taking precautionary measures. Other current protection measures include using motocross body armor, wrist guards, impact shorts, and kneepads. According to the National Ski Areas Association, more than 654,000 helmets were sold last season, ten times the number sold in the past six years combined.[17]

Please see appendix for Helmets Sold.

Snowsports Apparel Industry Overview
Today, the snowsports apparel industry alone is a $1.2 billion industry. This number does not include the accessories market, consisting of helmets, eyewear, and protective gear. Two key characteristics of the industry are seasonality and dynamism.

[11] Beynnon B, Pope M, Wertheimer C, et al. The effect of functional knee-braces on strain on the anterior cruciate ligament in vivo. J Bone Joint Surg. 74-A (9): 1298-1312, 1992.
[12] http://www.ski-injury.com/alpine.htm.
[13] Mountain High Ski Patrol.
[14] "Growing concern over skiing injuries." BBC News. 12/31/02.
[15] "Snow Buzz: Public Service Announcements on Snowboarding Safety." *Transworld Business*. Jan 2005.
[16] SnowSports Industries America News, Intelligence Report, 2004.
[17] "Ski helmets gain acceptance on the slopes." Colorado Springs Outdoors. 5/18/05.

- *Seasonality:*
  - The snowsports apparel industry is highly seasonal, with the vast majority of sales occurring between August and February each year, coinciding with the snowsports season. This creates a cyclical effect in which inventory is renewed on a yearly basis. Products are sold at an industry-wide standard margin of 50%.

- *Dynamism:*
  - Snowsports apparel is moving away from the mountaineering motif, with snowriders opting instead for fashion and style. Urban trends are a big influence in snowrider looks, as is versatility-the ability to go from the slopes to the bar or town.[18]
  - Snowboarding has matured from a fringe sport with counter-culture styles to adopt the warmth, functionality, and comfort normally associated with ski apparel.
  - Outerwear technology has greatly increased. New fabrics have enabled designers to make lighter outfits with more flexibility and less noise, allowing the snowrider to stay more comfortable in a greater range of conditions. According to Bill Post, president of Sport Obermeyer, a leading skiwear manufacturer based in Aspen, Colorado, "technology sells." He strongly believes that any new form of technology drives trends in the marketplace and is nearly always a huge hit for his company.[19]
  - 2004-2005 early-season sales figures from specialty stores indicate a 3% increase in year-on-year sales with a 1% increase in unit growth. Ski apparel shot up 12% for tops and 4% for bottoms, while snowboard apparel declined 22%. This trend indicated a blurring of the line between skiers and snowboarders with more crossover between sports and a resurgence of skiing.

- *Future Trends:*
  - Increasingly, more snowriders are more aware of the inherent dangers of injury in the sport created by the new extreme style of the sport. As the number of injuries increases, there will be a sizable need for effective whole-body protection.
  - The segmentation style of the industry between skiing and snowboarding will disappear, and all snowriders will consider themselves part of the same fraternity.[20]
  - Addressing the greatest barrier to growth in the industry, retaining first-time skiers, ski resorts are going to considerable effort to lower the cost of lifts, rentals, and lessons, creating "First Timer" packages and building "I can do it" centers focused on making the process of getting on snow as easy as possible. These efforts will lead to a larger snowrider base and to overall growth of the industry.

[18] SnowSports Industries America News, 2004.
[19] Post, Bill. Interview. Jan 24, 2005.
[20] "This Motorcycle Event Is No Snow Job". *Los Angeles Times,* 1/31/05, D11.

Market Analysis

Aegis has identified the primary target market to be specialty retail stores catering to generation X and Y (ages 12-34) skiers and snowboarders in the United States. Currently the market size is $650 million, with over 8,500 retailers in the United States. The demand for Aegis products, taking into account the responses to Aegis's surveys and the current market for helmets, is considered to be $325 million.[21]

Key Factors: Snowsport Participants

There are approximately 15 million snowriders in the United States: 8 million skiers and 7 million snowboarders.[22] Of this population, 53% of skiers and 93% of snowboarders fall into the Gen XY demographic. Almost 80% of skiers and 65% of snowboarders have a combined household income greater than $50,000.

Target Market Analysis

The snowsports apparel retail market can be segmented into chain retailers and specialty retailers.

- *Specialty retailers* account for 80% of snowsports sales annually.[23] These retailers tend to appeal to various niche markets within the snowsports industry: snowboarding, high fashion, outdoor sports, etc.
- *Chain retailers* tend to appeal to multiple sports and carry lower-end products for each sport.

Customer Profile: Specialty Retailers

A specialty retailer has intimate knowledge of the snowsports industry and the year-on-year trends. These retailers want to increase their profits and turn their inventory faster. They understand that the Gen XY market is the driving force in the industry and that their desires drive demand. These retailers look to achieve higher margins through the bundling of products, as exemplified by the integration of the ski and binding systems.

Primary Research

Consumer Test

In order to establish a need for the product, as well as to obtain information about Aegis's targeted end consumers, 150 surveys of snowsports participants were collected at mountain resort sites, including Steamboat, Aspen/Snowmass, and Mammoth Mountain, as well as through the USC ski and snowboard club.

Please refer to the appendix sections "Consumer Test Methodology," "Survey," and "Survey Results."

Results of the test suggested a high demand for Aegis's product, with 80% of those surveyed replying either yes or maybe when asked whether they would be interested in purchasing the product. The test identified the percentage of helmet wearers or users of other protective gear.

---

[21] The demand is calculated to be the mean of affirmative survey interest (60%) and helmet users (37%) times 2003 apparel sales.
[22] SnowSports Industries America News, Intelligence Report, 2004.
[23] SnowSports Industries America News, Intelligence Report, 2004.

This group accounted for over one-third of all surveyed. Aegis plans to target this group because they already recognize the need for safety precautions while participating in snowsports. *(Please refer to the appendix section "Product Interest.")*

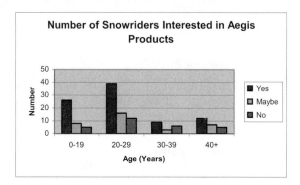

Investigation of Aegis's primary research reveals that there is a wide interest among snowriders in Aegis products. Futher analysis shows that snowboarders tend to have a greater interest than skiers, with 86% of snowboarder interested and 75% of skiers interested. The only demographic to show only moderate interest was male skiers aged 20-29, with 55% interest.

Market Entry

Aegis plans to enter the market with a specialized line targeted toward both male and female snowboarders to be sold to specialty retailers. Because larger chain retailers are less likely to take risk on a new product line, Aegis will introduce its products through specialized retailers with intimate knowledge of the space.

Aegis will seek intellectual-property protection on its designs to prevent competitors from infringing on Aegis's ideas.

Aegis will initially target the U.S. retail snowsports market. After a successful launch and achievement of brand awareness, the underlying Aegis technology can be applied to other markets and industries. Aegis will build upon the current base of snowriders and increase the market for apparel by bringing into the sport people who are fearful of falling and getting injured.

Barriers to Entry

The barriers to entry in the snowsports apparel industry are relatively high, given the seasonality of the business, and the need to achieve economies of scale with one turn of the inventory a season, requiring sizable market penetration. Brand loyalty is also a significant barrier, requiring large efforts in marketing in order to gain market penetration.

Value Chain Analysis

| Suppliers | Manufacturers | Wholesalers | Retailers |

- Margins: approx. 50%   50%   50%   50%
- Location: Asia   Asia   USA   USA

The value chain for the snowsports apparel industry is highly linear, with margins steady throughout. Although snowsports account for significant sales, the fragmentation of the retailers, distribution of products to the consumer, and the seasonal nature of the industry have limited the cost efficiencies that can be acquired through value chain integration.

Competitor Analysis

As of today, no snow wear provider has been able to successfully integrate a removable protective layer into a fashionable outer shell. However, Aegis will be still faced with competition. Competition for Aegis can be broken down into the following categories: mass sporting goods manufacturers, snowboard-specific, ski-specific, gender-specific, and protective wear providers (please refer to the appendix). Although there are numerous companies specializing in various areas, few have established any significant market share. The industry is in the growth stage, so significant market penetration is possible given proper execution.

Direct Competition
There are a number of snowsports apparel companies in the market. These companies, however, do not actively manufacture products for injury prevention. Aegis believes that it has discovered an underserved niche.

Indirect Competition
Currently, snowriders who wish to buy protective apparel are forced to buy products made for other industries, including motocross and hockey. These companies present a direct threat to Aegis if they decided to enter the snowsports apparel market.
(Please see the appendix section "Competition.")

Competitive Advantage

Aegis is well prepared to enter the protective apparel market. In addition to Aegis's expertise in retail manufacturing and sales, Aegis has intimate biomedical knowledge that will create patented product designs for Aegis's products. Consumers will be drawn to the functionality and fashion of the product line, unmatched by other available products. Aegis's unique capability to incorporate protective elements into a fashionable shell provides benefits not currently available to the snowsports market.

Management

Both David Dobkin and Annemarie Dillard will share duties during the start-up phase of Aegis. After the initial launch, Aegis will outsource a designer, manufacturing, and distribution and eventually a sales team. Initial oversight of each entrepreneur will be as follows:

- David Dobkin will be responsible for aspects related to overall operations and to product sales and distribution of goods. Using his background in finance, Mr. Dobkin will oversee the financial aspects of Aegis. Using his biomedical engineering experience, Mr. Dobkin will also work closely with the designer to help devise protective aspects for the apparel.
- Annemarie Dillard will be responsible for oversight of all product development and production and will use her background in fashion in working closely with the designer to ensure quality products for Aegis. Ms. Dillard will also use her experience in marketing to effectively promote Aegis.

All other tasks will be shared equally by Mr. Dobkin and Ms. Dillard.

Company Organization

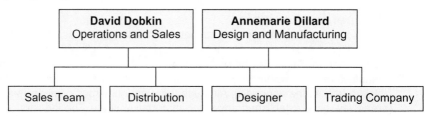

Management Team
David Dobkin
David Dobkin brings ski industry experience, biomedical engineering experience, and financial and operations expertise to the Aegis team. Currently, Mr. Dobkin is a Ph.D. candidate at the University of Southern California in biomedical engineering. His research focuses on tendon and ligament tissue engineering at Childrens Hospital Los Angeles. Mr. Dobkin is currently a ski instructor for Mammoth Mountain, California, and previously worked in that capacity for Breckenridge, Colorado. He has competed in both collegiate racing and professional ski competitions. Recently, Mr. Dobkin was an investment-banking analyst at Wasserstein Perella, as a member of the heath care group where he was working on deals in biotech, medical devices, and health care services. Before that, Mr. Dobkin founded Dealprovider.com, a Web-based deal finder service. Mr. Dobkin also served as Campus Operations Manager for Versity.com, a collegiate note-taking business where he managed a staff of over 100 people. Mr. Dobkin graduated from Columbia University with a Bachelor of Science Degree in biomedical engineering.

Annemarie Dillard
Annemarie Dillard will come to Aegis upon graduation from the Marshall School of Business at the University of Southern California with an emphasis in entrepreneurship. Having been on the Dean's List for five semesters in college, Ms. Dillard brings hard work and diligence, as well as a background in both entrepreneurship and the fashion retail industry. As the president of

her sorority, Ms. Dillard has experience in leadership positions and will be able not only to aid in the foundation of Aegis but also to assist in the day to day running of the business. Ms. Dillard comes with many in-depth experiences in the fashion industry. With internships at one of the most successful contemporary women's fashion houses, BCBG, the research and buying offices of Left Coast Style, and the second largest upscale department store chain in the United States, Dillard's, Inc, Ms. Dillard brings a working knowledge of the apparel-manufacturing process. Ms. Dillard has been an avid skier since the age of three and spends a significant amount of the winter season on the mountain.

Note: Please refer to the appendix section "Résumés" for more information.

Board of Directors

A board of directors of experienced industry leaders will help to guide the progress of Aegis while also serving as mentors for the entrepreneurs and as expert references. Board members to date include

- *Rusty Gregory:* CEO of Mammoth Mountain, California. Mr. Gregory brings overall expertise in the snowsports industry.
- *Alex Dillard:* Currently president and board member of the retail department store chain Dillard's, Inc., based in Little Rock, Arkansas. Mr. Dillard brings extensive knowledge of the retail and manufacturing industry, as well as a background in snowsports as an avid enthusiast for over 30 years.
- *Matthew Levenson:* The current CEO and president of 9star, Inc., an Action Sports "category killer" retailer located in Los Angeles, California. Mr. Levenson brings to Aegis strong familiarity with action sports and retailing.

Note: Please refer to appendix section "Board Member Profiles" for more information.

Management Philosophy

The Aegis management aims to create a company that promotes innovation while maintaining a reliable, efficient, and enjoyable work environment. Aegis understands the importance of happy employees and will work to ensure employee happiness while maintaining a successful company.

Mission

Aegis Performance Apparel seeks to provide high-quality, protective apparel that offers an integrated and unique combination of fashion, function, and protection, allowing for the ultimate snowsports experience.

Core Values
- Integrity
- Responsibility
- Passion for product
- Commitment to quality
- Dedication to customers

Legal Structure and Ownership

Aegis will file for incorporation as an S-Corp. The initial allotment of shares will be 49% to Mr. Dobkin and 49% to Ms. Dillard, with 2% for the board of directors. In the event of a disagreement that cannot be resolved by the owners, the board of directors will settle the dispute. A vested employee incentive plan will be established and determined, details depending on the position.

Production and Operations

Organization

As a start-up entity, Aegis will outsource most of the workflow to third parties. A trading company will oversee the manufacturing of the product line and shipping to the United States. Third parties will be used for warehousing and distribution to retailers. Aegis will hire independent designers to produce the initial designs of Aegis. The founding members will perform sales and marketing duties.

After the initial roll-out of the product line, a sales team and back office support, including customer service, order fulfillment, and office management, will be hired. The office space for headquarters will be leased in Los Angeles to oversee all functions of Aegis.

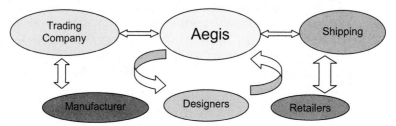

(Please see the appendix section "Production and Distribution Cycle.")

Production Plan

The production of Aegis's products can be summarized in the following graph:

Materials Sourcing
Materials will be sourced through fabric sourcing companies directed at supplying fabric to outdoorwear providers. The materials will initially be accessed by the designers and will be purchased in minimal amounts for the construction of samples. Bulk quantities will then be purchased and shipped to the factories for production.

Sample Production

Production begins with an apparel sample. Samples will be made from the designs of free-lance, independently contracted designers. Patterns will then be produced, and samples will be manufactured on an as-needed basis domestically. Upon approval of samples, an independently contracted designer will work with the factory to produce production patterns that meet the specifications of the sample garments.

Goods Manufacturing

Aegis will subcontract all manufacturing, through the trading company William E. Connors and Associates, to independent factories in China and India in order to take advantage of the lower manufacturing costs and high-quality production. Aegis will use an independent trading company to help monitor the manufacturing process and ensure that factories adhere to all international standards of manufacturing as well as to ensure the quality and timing of production. Shipping from the factories will be conducted through the trading company. Goods will be inspected for quality and stored through a third-party independent warehousing service. Goods that do not meet minimum standards of production will be shipped back to the factories to be corrected.

Pricing/Cost Model for Product

Aegis will benchmark the costs and pricing for its products to compete with high-end quality apparel. Aegis will target a 20% premium over existing prices, with a majority of the price increase passed on to retailers through the MSRP. Current cost estimates are $75 per jacket and $50 per pant. Priced at 50% margins, jackets will be sold to retailers for $150 and pants for $100. Suggested MSRP for retailers will be $330 for jackets and $225 for pants.

Distribution Plan

Goods will be shipped from the warehouse directly to retailers via parcel services through small-business accounts that will be set up through major service providers, including United Parcel Service and Federal Express.

Operations and Controls

Systems for maintaining and controlling the various operational systems of Aegis will be implemented to help manage Aegis.

Goods Quality and Inventory Control

Standards of acceptable deviances in measurements will be established for each SKU of every garment that Aegis will produce. Upon receipt of goods from factories, an in-house quality control will be performed on 20% of each item type of all incoming goods. If any items fall outside the acceptable range, all SKUs of that item in the delivery will be checked for accuracy. All items not meeting requirements will be sent back to the factory to be corrected. Each item measured will go directly into a computer system to facilitate monitoring the efficiency and number of mistakes at each factory. An evaluation of the efficiency of each factory will be conducted and used in the determination of future relationships with that factory. The system will also work to maintain an inventory of all goods and their location throughout the system.

Retailer Relationship Observance
The success of Aegis's goods relies heavily on the success of retailers. As a result, a computer observance system will be implemented to keep track of relationships with retailers. The system will be set up in separate segments in order to keep track of all aspects of the relationships.

- *Orders.* Customer orders will be entered for each retailer into a system, which will also work to track the order throughout Aegis's system, from the point of order, to manufacturing, to overseas shipping, warehousing, and retail shipping. Orders returned by retailers for various reasons will be categorized and reviewed. Retail percentage sell-through will be tracked as well, to the best of Aegis's ability. This will not only enable Aegis to determine which retailers are most successful with Aegis's goods, but will also show which geographic areas are most profitable, offer insight into future customer targets, and allow for an annual evaluation of retailers.
- *Year-End Evaluation of Retailers.* Just as customers are inevitably important to the success of Aegis, the reputation and profitability of retailers are likewise vital to the success of Aegis products. Aegis seeks to retail its goods through outlets that may best represent Aegis. Thus, information gathered from information provided by the IT system will allow for an annual review of the retailers and will be used to determine the future of Aegis's relationships with them.
- *Customer Feedback.* Also, at the end of every selling season, Aegis will obtain feedback on the overall service provided by Aegis in an effort to identify areas for improvement.

Cash Control
In order to ensure the accuracy of Aegis's financial statements, a CPA will be used to balance the books. Also, reviews and approvals by both entrepreneurs will be required to finalize any financial statements. In an effort to control cash exits from Aegis, all cash withdrawals from Aegis will require the signatures of both entrepreneurs.

Action Plan and Schedule *(Please see the appendix section "Timeline.")*
Patents and Trademarks
Measures are currently being taken to secure and trademark Aegis's name and symbol. The designs, which are considered vital to Aegis's innovative and contemporary product development, have begun to be developed, and Aegis is currently working with lawyers to establish patentable material. Patents are expected to be applied for by April 2005. Aegis shall also be established as a legal entity by that time.

Product Development
Product development will begin with the hiring of a designer by May 2005. At this point, negotiation with manufacturers will begin along with product development. Samples will be approved and produced by December 2005. Attending trade shows and selling will begin toward the end of December 2005 and extend until April 2006. The line will be in production until June 2006 and will be shipped to retailers beginning in July 2006. Development of the 2007 product line

will begin in January 2006. The reason why product development for the 2006 line will begin later than industry average is based on the time of the establishment of Aegis. Aegis believes there will be ample time to develop a first line during this time because the limited number of products that will be available for the first delivery. Beginning with the 2007 line, Aegis will follow the more popular industry product development schedule.

Other
Office Space: Office space will be located by June 2005. Until this point, business will be conducted at third-party venues and in the residences of the entrepreneurs.
Warehouse Space: Warehouse space will not have to be secured until February 2006, which will give ample time to ready the area for the first delivery, which will be received in June 2006. Goods will then be shipped during the subsequent month.

Contingency Plan

Several plans will be implemented to allow Aegis to continue in the event that certain circumstances occur.

Drastic Declines In Snowsports Participation: According to Bill Post, CEO of *Sport Obermeyer,* one of the largest challenges facing the snowsports industry in the future is keeping participant levels growing, given the trends toward warm-weather vacations. As a result, Aegis will attempt to keep its designs versatile so that they may be adapted to other sports. This will allow Aegis to continue its growth if a significant decline in the snowsports industry occurs.

Poor Snow Years: Given the seasonality of the snowsports industry, a poor snow season can have drastic effects on all aspects of the industry. In the event that a poor snow year does occur, and Aegis's retailers are unable to pay for their product orders, Aegis will actively work with the retailers to reallocate the inventory at minimal cost to other retailers in better snow environments.

Forecast Demand for Aegis Products Is Too Low: In the event that retailers aggressively order from Aegis, Aegis will hire additional staff, in both sales and order fulfillment, to meet demand.

Forecast Demand for Aegis Products Is Too High: In the event that there is lackluster interest from retailers, Aegis will target individual retailers to test-run the product to accurately gauge end-user demand. If deemed successful, a wide scale launch will be undertaken in the subsequent year.

Interest Rates Significantly Increase: Although Aegis plans to rely on private investment, a loan will be taken out to cover working capital needed for the manufacturing and delivery cycle. In the event that interest rates make the cost of capital too great, subsequent private investment will be used to float the inventory.

Patent Protection Is Not Sufficient: Once Aegis is established, there is considerable chance that competitors will copy Aegis designs and enter into the protective apparel market. Aegis will aggressively pursue litigation to block such action based on its patents. In the event that Aegis cannot protect its interests, Aegis will rely on first-mover advantage and marketing to compete.

Future growth and direction

Future growth of Aegis will come through an extended product development. Although initial extensions will target the U.S. retail snowsports market, after a successful launch and heightened brand awareness, the underlying technology can be applied to other markets and industries. Aegis will build upon the current base of snowriders and increase the market for apparel by bringing into the sport people who are fearful of falling and getting injured. The following are possible means of expansion:

Snowsports Product Extensions
- Goggles and Sunglasses
- Gloves
- Helmets
- Integrated fleece
- Stand-alone knee brace

New Demographics
- Children's Snowsports Apparel
- *Snow Industry Uniforms:* The high and rapidly increasing workers' compensation liability that ski resorts currently assume makes the adoption of the Aegis line for uniformed employees a natural fit, leading to a reduction in on-the-job injuries.

New Markets
- *International Markets:* After Aegis has been able to establish itself in the United States, there will be opportunity to expand, offering Aegis products to international markets.
- *Other Action Sports Apparel:* The patented protection aspects can probably be easily integrated into apparel for other sports, including football, motocross, skateboarding, horseback riding, BMX, etc.
- *Military Fatigues:* There may be opportunities to adapt Aegis's protective technology to the vast market of military needs.

Direct Sales
After Aegis has been established and has become familiar with the manufacturing process, independent flagship stores and an Aegis website may establish a method for Aegis to sell goods directly to end consumers.

Exit Strategy

It is the goal of the founders to build up Aegis and the brand and then to divest themselves of Aegis once the brand has been established. Considerable consolidation within the industry is currently occurring, driven by publicly held companies looking for growth. In 2004, K2 acquired

Volkl, Marmot, and The Marker Group, while VF Corp. purchased Vans, Kipling, and Napapijri. Aegis looks to create brand awareness and position Aegis for sale.
- Sale to a competitor—Aegis will look for a sale to a competitor or larger conglomerate.
- IPO—Depending on the state of the IPO market, the founders may choose to enter the public market.

Sales and Marketing

Selling Safety

As previously mentioned, the American Association of Snowboard Instructors has teamed up with the National Ski Patrol and the Professional Ski Instructors of American to launch a safety awareness campaign through local and national television and radio stations near ski areas. This campaign supports the uses of helmets and other protective gear. Aegis plans to piggy-back this influence on the snowsports population. In selling safety to retailers, the Company will rely on statistical demand for such products in conjunction with independent research conducted by Aegis that has established a need for such a product. The technical superiority, high-quality designs, and proven demand of Aegis products will appeal to retailers. When comparing Aegis products to existing products, end consumers will see the "Aegis advantage": In buying Aegis products, they will be acquiring protection and functionality without having to sacrifice style.

Sales

Sales emphasis will be placed on reaching retailers though major trade show events, including
- *Nation's Best Sports Winter Sports Specialty Market*
- *Action Sports Retailer Trade Expo*
- *SIA Snowsports Show*
- *Outdoor Retailer Winter Market*

On-site sample line presentations will also be conducted upon identification of necessity. Retail buyers will place orders based on the sample line and on product information catalogs that will be presented during the trade show events.

Sales presentations will initially be conducted by Mr. Dobkin and Ms. Dillard. After the first year of operations, Aegis plans to hire reputable independent representatives in the areas in which there is a significant demand for the product. Sales representatives will be responsible for showing and selling the product line at trade show events.

Initial sales emphasis will be placed on specialty and boutique ski and snowboarding stores throughout the United States. This will give Aegis an opportunity to nail down distribution aspects before approaching large-scale sporting goods retailers. A secondary focus will be on securing a sales outlet through sports catalogs such as Athleta, as well as through ski and sporting goods websites.

After Aegis has been established and has become familiar with the manufacturing process, independent flagship stores may also be established, allowing Aegis to sell goods directly to end consumers.

Marketing

Aegis marketing initiatives will raise awareness of Aegis's products, work to establish a viable need for protection, and inspire purchases from both direct and end consumers.

Target Market: Customer Profile

Retailers

The snowsports apparel retail market can be segmented into chain retailers and specialty retailers.

- *Specialty Retailers:* Specialty retailers account for 80% of snowsports sales annually.[24] These retailers tend to appeal to various niche markets within the snowsports industry: snowboarding, high-fashion, outdoor sports, etc.
- *Chain Retailers:* Chain retailers tend to appeal to multiple sports and carry lower-end products for each sport with a more limited interest in premium quality goods.

Because larger chain retailers are less likely to take the risk of stocking a new product line, Aegis will introduce its products through specialized retailers with intimate knowledge of the space. Specialty retailers have intimate knowledge of the snowsports industry and the year-on-year trends, wanting to increase profits and turn inventory faster. They understand that the Gen XY market is the driving force in the industry and that their desires drive demand. These retailers look to achieve higher margins through the bundling of products, as exemplified by the integration of the ski and binding systems.

End Consumers

Aegis seeks to target intermediate to advanced female and male snowsports enthusiasts, who are concerned with all aspects of their gear, from fashion to function, while at the same time desiring some protection.

Marketing and Promotions

Marketing of Aegis's goods will come in two forms:
- Retail-directed
- End-consumer-directed

Retail-directed promotions will come through an emphasis on public relations marketing and advertising through major trade publications, including
- *SBC Business*
- *Transworld Business*
- *Ski Press*
- *Outdoor Business*
- *Snowboard Trade News*

---

[24] SnowSports Industries America News, Intelligence Report, 2004.

Marketing to develop buzz about the product prior to its premier at the 2006 SIA Industry Trade Event will occur through the sending of information packets complete with brochures *(please see the appendix section "Brochure")* and press releases regarding the release of the product line to targeted retailers in the months prior to the show.

Aegis will provide product information seminars to specialty retailers in order to educate them about the technological aspects of Aegis, allowing them to better sell the merchandise. Seminars will be presented by Mr. Dobkin and Ms. Dillard until independent representatives are hired.

End-consumer-directed marketing will come in numerous forms:

- Sponsorship of local contests
- Guerilla marketing initiatives both on-mountain and in cities with high populations of snowsports participants (such as Los Angeles, San Francisco, Denver, Dallas, and New York)
- Company website promotion
- Supplying professional skiers and snowboarders with free gear
- Free media plugs, using in-house public relations to get the idea to the press in the mainstream media, including news, morning shows, specialty shows, specialty magazines, and lifestyle magazines
- Sponsorship of National Ski Association programs to promote the inherent dangers of snowsports

Budget

In order to illustrate the need for Aegis products to both customers and end users, Aegis will focus considerable effort on marketing and branding its products. Approximately 67% of all expenses in 2006 and 64% in 2007 will go toward marketing. The single largest cost component of marketing is the trade show and preparation for it. The remaining funds will be used for end-user and consumer marketing.

Table 2: Annual Marketing Expense *(in 000's)*

	2005	2006	2007
Marketing	$41	$213	$320
% of Total Costs	33%	67%	64%
% of Revenue	NA	9%	9%

The Aegis Product Line

Aegis's products will consist of one product line per season, tailored to injury- conscious snowriders. The product selection will start with integrative outer layers and later evolve to include protective accessories.

The initial collection will include designs specifically tailored to men and women. There will be approximately 6 jackets and 4 pants, available in women's sizes 0-12 and men"s sizes small-

XXL. Items will also be available in various color combinations, accounting for approximately 40 total SKUs.

Jackets: Jackets will consist of soft-shell parkas, whose new lighter and warmer technologies allow for a more stylish, less bulky look. The protective aspects target areas that are considered high-risk while the wearer is participating in snowsports and include integrated
- Clavicle pads
- Shoulder protection
- Rib protection
- Elbow pads

Pants: Pants will integrate a patented injury-preventive knee brace and protective padding into a stylish and functional snow pant. The brace is designed specifically to reduce the incidence of ACL injury, the most common injury in snowsports. Other padding features protect areas at high risk of injury. Features include integrated
- ACL support brace
- Jib protection
- Impact shorts

Note: Please see the appendix for product designs and designer profile.

Product Benefits
The products of Aegis will provide undisputable benefits for its consumers, including
- *Security:* The protective aspects of the products give snowsports participants a feeling of security while participating in their sport.
- *Freedom:* The products offer security and protection while integrating a comfort that allows wearers freedom of activity.
- *Peace of Mind:* Through the comprehensive integration of fashion, protection, and comfort, Aegis is able to provide consumers with peace of mind while they are participating in snowsports.

Note: Please refer to the appendix for force diagrams.

Product Warranties
All products will have a 30-day retailer return period in which goods deemed inaccurate (inconsistent with order) may be returned to Aegis. An end-consumer warranty will provide consumers with a period of one year in which any malfunctioning of the garment (torn seams, broken zippers, etc.) will be repaired by Aegis free of charge.

Pricing Strategy
Aegis will seek to price its products competitively with the established apparel companies. However, due to the technological aspects of the products, price points will probably be 10-20% higher than current outerwear providers. However, the bundling of protection with a durable shell provides a value-added product, which consumers will recognize. Goods will range in retail price from $200 to $400.

Summary of Financials

Aegis is projecting sales of $2.3 million for 2006 and $3.4 million for 2007, increasing to $8.5 million in 2011, in the United States. The compound annual growth rate ("CAGR") for the five-year period is 30%. Growth in sales will be driven by a number of factors, including a full-market launch in the United States during the 2006 season and a significant increase in sales force in 2007; greater market acceptance by snowriders, especially after the initial launch in 2006; and greater acceptance by snowsports retailers.

The sales projections take into account only sales derived from the primary product lines for Aegis (jackets and pants) and do not incorporate potential sales resulting from Aegis's entry into other markets and applications.

Gross margins are expected to rise from 50% in 2006 to 55% in 2008 as Aegis is able to realize greater cost efficiencies. The largest driver of the increasing margins is increased order size, followed by negotiating better deals with both suppliers and manufacturers. As the total sales volume for Aegis increases, Aegis plans to achieve economies of scale with both logistics and sourcing.

The financial projections summarized on the following pages reflect Aegis's assessment of the potential opportunity if the business were to operate as an independent entity targeting a single product line.

Aegis is projecting EBITDA of $823,118 in 2006 and $1.2 million in 2007, increasing to $3.5 million in 2011. The increase in EBITDA is expected to be a result of increasing product sales and an improving gross margin.

Financial Assumptions

The demand for Aegis products is assumed to be 3.3 million units annually. This number is derived from the number of snowsports helmet wearers, 37%, and the survey results of affirmative interest, 60%. These values were averaged and applied to the number of units sold in 2003, 6.8 million. Of the initial demand for the product, Aegis assumes moderate market penetration and predicts 16,520 units, or 0.5% of the market demand, to be sold in 2006. 16,520 units is comparable to start-up sales figures for Cold-As-Ice, a female-specific snowboard apparel wholesaler.

Using the industry standard, Aegis assumes that 75% of units sold will be jackets and 25% will be pants.

Initial start-up costs are assumed to be $450,000, with marketing, trade show, and sample costs accounting for $125,000. Other start-up costs include office and warehouse space, inventory systems, designer and employee costs, insurance, utilities, other fixed costs, and a safety net of 18 months, the time when Aegis will receive initial revenues and break even.

Note: Please refer to the appendix section "Financials."

Appendices

Table of Appendices
Financials
- Monthly Cash Flow and Income Statement
- Consolidated Yearly Income Statement
- Balance Sheet
- Capitalization
- Working Capital
- Breakeven Analysis
- Start-up Requirements

United States Helmet Sales
Consumer Test Methodology
Survey
Survey Results
Product Interest
Brochure
Competition
Resumes
Board Member Profiles
Production and Distribution Cycle
Product Designs
Designer Profile
Force Diagrams
Timeline
References

Financials

Monthly Cash Flow and Income Statement

	Start-up	May-05	Jun-05	Jul-05	Aug-05	Sep-05	Oct-05	Nov-05	Dec-05	2005	Jan-06	Feb-06
Revenue Received	$0	$0	$0	$0	$0	$0	$0	$0	$0	$0	$0	$0
Inventory Expense	$0	$0	$0	$0	$0	$0	$0	$0	$0	$0	$0	$0
Gross Profit:												
Research and Development	$0	$0	$0	$0	$0	$0	$0	$0	$0	$0	$0	$0
G&A	$8,727	$8,727	$8,727	$8,727	$8,727	$8,727	$8,727	$8,727	$8,727	$78,545	$8,727	$8,727
Marketing:	$0	$0	$0	$0	$0	$0	$0	$0	$41,667	$41,667	$41,667	$41,667
Start-up Cost	$7,350	$0	$0	$0	$0	$0	$0	$0	$0	$7,350	$0	$0
Total Costs	$16,077	$8,727	$8,727	$8,727	$8,727	$8,727	$8,727	$8,727	$50,394	$127,562	$50,394	$50,394
EBIT	($16,077)	($8,727)	($8,727)	($8,727)	($8,727)	($8,727)	($8,727)	($8,727)	($50,394)	($127,562)	($50,394)	($50,394)
Cash at Beginning of Period	$450,000	$435,008	$427,346	$419,665	$411,965	$404,246	$396,508	$388,750	$380,973	$450,000	$331,405	$280,272
Cash on Hand:	$433,923	$426,280	$418,619	$410,938	$403,238	$395,519	$387,781	$380,023	$330,579	$322,438	$281,011	$229,878
Interest Income (3%)	$1,085	$1,066	$1,047	$1,027	$1,008	$989	$969	$950	$826	$8,967	$703	$575
Line of Credit for Inventory	$0	$0	$0	$0	$0	$0	$0	$0	$0	$0	$0	$0
Cash available for Debt Repayment	($66,077)	($73,720)	($81,381)	($89,062)	($96,762)	($104,481)	($112,219)	($119,977)	($169,421)	($177,562)	($218,989)	($270,122)
Current Debt	$0	$0	$0	$0	$0	$0	$0	$0	$0	$0	$0	$0
Repayment	$0	$0	$0	$0	$0	$0	$0	$0	$0	$0	$0	$0
Ending Debt	$0	$0	$0	$0	$0	$0	$0	$0	$0	$0	$0	$0
Interest Expense (10%)	$0	$0	$0	$0	$0	$0	$0	$0	$0	$0	$0	$0
Cash After Loan	$435,008	$427,346	$419,665	$411,965	$404,246	$396,508	$388,750	$380,973	$331,405	$331,405	$281,714	$230,453
EBT	($14,992)	($7,662)	($7,681)	($7,700)	($7,719)	($7,738)	($7,758)	($7,777)	($49,567)	($118,595)	($49,691)	($49,819)
Carry Forward Profit/ Loss	($14,992)	($22,654)	($30,335)	($38,035)	($45,754)	($53,492)	($61,250)	($69,027)	($118,595)	($118,595)	($168,286)	($218,105)
Taxable income	$0	$0	$0	$0	$0	$0	$0	$0	$0	$0	$0	$0
Tax (35%)	$0	$0	$0	$0	$0	$0	$0	$0	$0	$0	$0	$0
Net Income	($14,992)	($7,662)	($7,681)	($7,700)	($7,719)	($7,738)	($7,758)	($7,777)	($49,567)	($118,595)	($49,691)	($49,819)
Cash after Tax Payment	$435,008	$427,346	$419,665	$411,965	$404,246	$396,508	$388,750	$380,973	$331,405	$331,405	$281,714	$230,453

	Mar-06	Apr-06	May-06	Jun-06	Jul-06	Aug-06	Sep-06	Oct-06	Nov-06	Dec-06	2006
Revenue Received	$0	$0	$0	$0	$0	$0	$0	$378,587	$378,587	$378,587	$1,135,762
Inventory Expense	$0	$0	$0	$0	$1,135,762	$0	$0	$0	$0	$0	$1,135,762
Gross Profit:											
Research and Development	$0	$0	$0	$0	$0	$0	$0	$0	$0	$0	$0
G&A	$8,727	$8,727	$8,727	$8,727	$8,727	$8,727	$8,727	$8,727	$8,727	$8,727	$104,727
Marketing:	$0	$0	$0	$0	$0	$10,000	$10,000	$10,000	$50,000	$50,000	$213,333
Start-up Cost	$0	$0	$0	$0	$0	$0	$0	$0	$0	$0	$0
Total Costs	$8,727	$8,727	$8,727	$8,727	$1,144,489	$18,727	$18,727	$18,727	$58,727	$58,727	$318,060
EBIT	($8,727)	($8,727)	($8,727)	($8,727)	($1,144,489)	($18,727)	($18,727)	$359,860	$319,860	$319,860	$817,702
Cash at Beginning of Period	$229,012	$219,394	$209,751	$200,085	$190,395	$170,761	$141,508	$112,181	$452,960	$383,189	$331,405
Cash on Hand:	$220,284	$210,666	$201,024	$191,358	($954,095)	$152,034	$122,781	$472,042	$772,820	$703,049	$1,149,107
Interest Income (3%)	$551	$527	$503	$478	$0	$380	$307	$1,180	$1,932	$1,758	$8,892
Line of Credit for Inventory	$0	$0	$0	$0	$1,135,762	$0	$0	$0	$0	$0	$1,135,762
Cash available for Debt Repayment	($279,716)	($289,334)	($298,976)	($308,642)	($1,454,095)	($347,966)	($377,219)	($27,958)	$272,820	$203,049	$649,107
Current Debt	$0	$0	$0	$0	$1,135,762	$1,135,762	$1,135,762	$1,135,762	$1,135,762	$862,942	$1,135,762
Repayment	$0	$0	$0	$0	$0	$0	$0	$0	$272,820	$203,049	$475,869
Ending Debt	$0	$0	$0	$0	$1,135,762	$1,135,762	$1,135,762	$1,135,762	$862,942	$659,893	$659,893
Interest Expense (10%)	$0	$0	$0	$0	$9,465	$9,465	$9,465	$9,465	$7,191	$5,499	$50,549
Cash After Loan	$220,835	$211,193	$201,527	$191,836	$172,203	$142,949	$113,623	$463,757	$494,741	$496,259	$631,582
EBT	($8,177)	($8,201)	($8,225)	($8,249)	($18,192)	($27,812)	($27,885)	$351,576	$314,601	$316,119	$776,045
Carry Forward Profit/ Loss	($226,282)	($234,482)	($242,707)	($250,956)	($269,148)	($296,960)	($324,845)	$26,731	$341,332	$657,450	$657,450
Taxable income	$0	$0	$0	$0	$0	$0	$0	$26,731	$314,601	$316,119	$657,450
Tax (35%)	$0	$0	$0	$0	$0	$0	$0	$9,356	$110,110	$110,642	$230,108
Net Income	($8,177)	($8,201)	($8,225)	($8,249)	($18,192)	($27,812)	($27,885)	$342,220	$204,491	$205,477	$545,937
Cash after Tax Payment	$220,835	$211,193	$201,527	$191,836	$172,203	$142,949	$113,623	$454,401	$384,631	$385,617	$401,474

Note: These details can be viewed on the student website at http://college.hmco.business/allen/launching/4e/students.

	Jan-07	Feb-07	Mar-07	Apr-07	May-07	Jun-07	Jul-07	Aug-07	Sep-07	Oct-07	Nov-07
Revenue Received	$0	$0	$0	$0	$0	$0	$0	$0	$0	$567,881	$567,881
Inventory Expense	$0	$0	$0	$0	$0	$0	$1,703,643	$0	$0	$0	$0
Gross Profit:											
Research and Development	$1,667	$1,667	$1,667	$1,667	$1,667	$1,667	$1,667	$1,667	$1,667	$1,667	$1,667
G&A	$13,091	$13,091	$13,091	$13,091	$13,091	$13,091	$13,091	$13,091	$13,091	$13,091	$13,091
Marketing:	$50,000	$50,000	$0	$0	$0	$0	$0	$20,000	$20,000	$20,000	$80,000
Start-up Cost	$0	$0	$0	$0	$0	$0	$0	$0	$0	$0	$0
Total Costs	$64,758	$64,758	$14,758	$14,758	$14,758	$14,758	$1,718,401	$34,758	$34,758	$34,758	$94,758
EBIT	($64,758)	($64,758)	($14,758)	($14,758)	($14,758)	($14,758)	($1,718,401)	($34,758)	($34,758)	$533,124	$473,124
Cash at Beginning of Period	$384,175	$312,587	$240,820	$218,998	$197,122	$175,191	$153,205	$116,621	$60,241	$3,721	$299,546
Cash on Hand:	$319,418	$247,830	$226,062	$204,240	$182,364	$160,433	($1,565,196)	$81,863	$25,484	$536,845	$772,669
Interest Income (3%)	$799	$620	$565	$511	$456	$401	$0	$205	$64	$1,342	$1,932
Line of Credit for Inventory	$0	$0	$0	$0	$0	$0	$1,703,643	$0	$0	$0	$0
Cash available for Debt Repayment	($180,582)	($252,170)	($273,938)	($295,760)	($317,636)	($339,567)	($2,065,196)	($418,137)	($474,516)	$36,845	$272,669
Current Debt	$659,893	$659,893	$659,893	$659,893	$659,893	$659,893	$2,363,537	$2,363,537	$2,363,537	$2,363,537	$2,326,692
Repayment	$0	$0	$0	$0	$0	$0	$0	$0	$0	$36,845	$272,669
Ending Debt	$659,893	$659,893	$659,893	$659,893	$659,893	$659,893	$2,363,537	$2,363,537	$2,363,537	$2,326,692	$2,054,022
Interest Expense (10%)	$5,499	$5,499	$5,499	$5,499	$5,499	$5,499	$19,696	$19,696	$19,696	$19,389	$17,117
Cash After Loan	$314,717	$242,950	$221,128	$199,252	$177,321	$155,335	$118,751	$62,372	$5,851	$481,953	$484,815
EBT	($69,458)	($69,637)	($19,691)	($19,746)	($19,801)	($19,856)	($34,454)	($54,249)	($54,390)	$515,077	$457,938
Carry Forward Profit/ Loss	$587,992	$518,355	$498,664	$478,918	$459,117	$439,261	$404,808	$350,559	$296,169	$811,245	$1,269,184
Taxable income	$0	$0	$0	$0	$0	$0	$0	$0	$0	$515,077	$457,938
Tax (35%)	$0	$0	$0	$0	$0	$0	$0	$0	$0	$180,277	$160,278
Net Income	($69,458)	($69,637)	($19,691)	($19,746)	($19,801)	($19,856)	($34,454)	($54,249)	($54,390)	$334,800	$297,660
Cash after Tax Payment	$314,717	$242,950	$221,128	$199,252	$177,321	$155,335	$118,751	$62,372	$5,851	$301,676	$324,536

	Dec-07	2007
Revenue Received	$567,881	$1,703,643
Inventory Expense	$0	$1,703,643
Gross Profit:		
Research and Development	$1,667	$20,000
G&A	$13,091	$157,091
Marketing:	$80,000	$320,000
Start-up Cost	$0	$0
Total Costs	$94,758	$497,091
EBIT	$473,124	$1,206,553
Cash at Beginning of Period	$322,406	$384,175
Cash on Hand:	$795,530	$1,590,728
Interest Income (3%)	$1,989	$8,882
Line of Credit for Inventory	$0	$1,703,643
Cash available for Debt Repayment	$295,530	$1,090,728
Current Debt	$2,054,022	$2,363,537
Repayment	$295,530	$605,044
Ending Debt	$1,758,493	$1,758,493
Interest Expense (10%)	$14,654	$143,243
Cash After Loan	$487,335	$851,323
EBT	$460,458	$1,072,191
Carry Forward Profit/ Loss	$1,729,642	$1,729,642
Taxable income	$460,458	$1,072,191
Tax (35%)	$161,160	$375,267
Net Income	$299,298	$696,924
Cash after Tax Payment	$326,174	$476,056

Note: These details can be viewed on the student website at http://college.hmco.business/allen/launching/4e/students.

Consolidated Yearly Income Statement

	2005	2006	2007	2008	2009	2010	2011
Revenue:							
Operating	$0.0	$2,271,524.3	$3,407,286.4	$5,110,929.7	$6,133,115.6	$7,359,738.7	$8,463,699.5
COGS (50% of Revenues)	0.0	1,135,762.1	1,703,643.2	2,299,918.3	2,759,902.0	3,311,882.4	3,808,664.8
Gross Margin	$0	$1,135,762	$1,703,643	$2,811,011	$3,373,214	$4,047,856	$4,655,035
Gross Margin %	*NA*	*50.0%*	*50.0%*	*55.0%*	*55.0%*	*55.0%*	*55.0%*
Expenses:							
Research and Development	$0	$0	$20,000	$20,000	$20,000	$20,000	$20,000
Sales and Marketing	$41,667	$213,333	$320,000	$480,000	$576,000	$691,200	$794,880
General and Administrative	$78,545	$104,727	$157,091	$235,636	$282,763	$339,315	$390,213
Other Expense, net	$7,350	$0	$0	$0	$0	$0	$0
EBIT	($127,561.9)	$817,701.8	$1,206,552.7	$2,075,375.6	$2,494,450.7	$2,997,340.8	$3,449,941.9
Depreciation and Amortization	0.0	5,416.7	8,509.5	13,305.9	19,124.5	26,169.7	25,855.2
EBITDA	($127,561.9)	$823,118.5	$1,215,062.2	$2,088,681.5	$2,513,575.2	$3,023,510.5	$3,475,797.1
Interest Income	8,967.2	8,892.4	8,881.8	47,587.6	12,519.0	46,087.2	87,149.3
Interest Expense	0.0	50,549.0	143,243.1	175,849.3	0.0	0.0	0.0
Income Before Income Taxes	(118,594.7)	776,045.1	1,072,191.4	1,947,113.9	2,506,969.7	3,043,428.0	3,537,091.2
Carry Forward Loss	(118,594.7)	(118,594.7)	0.0	0.0	0.0	0.0	0.0
Taxable Income	0.0	657,450.5	1,072,191.4	1,947,113.9	2,506,969.7	3,043,428.0	3,537,091.2
Income Taxes	$0	$230,108	$375,267	$681,490	$877,439	$1,065,200	$1,237,982
Net Income	($118,594.67)	$545,937.48	$696,924.43	$1,265,624.06	$1,629,530.29	$1,978,228.18	$2,299,109.31

Balance Sheet – As of December 31

Assets	2005	2006	2007
Current Assets:			
Cash	$331,405.3	$384,175.4	$1,586,254.8
Receivables	0.0	186,700.6	280,050.9
Inventories	0.0	1,135,762.1	1,703,643.2
Total Current Assets	331,405.3	1,706,638.2	3,569,949.0
PP & E	0.0	17,298.5	42,861.9
Total Assets	331,405.3	1,723,936.7	3,612,810.9

Liabilities	2005	2006	2007
Current Liabilities:			
Accounts Payable	0.0	186,700.6	280,050.9
Total Current Liabilities	0.0	186,700.6	280,050.9
Total Debt	0.0	659,893.3	1,758,492.7
Retained Earnings	(118,594.7)	427,342.8	1,124,267.2
Paid-In Equity	$450,000.0	$450,000.0	$450,000.0
Total Liab. and equity	$331,405.3	$1,723,936.7	$3,612,810.9

Capitalization

Aegis plans to initially fund Aegis with private investment. A line of credit will be used to cover initial working capital expenses.

Working Capital

Given the nature of the snowsports industry, where inventory gets only one turn per year, a line of credit will be required to purchase the inventory. The initial estimated line of credit is estimated to be $2.0 million, with $1.1 used in 2006. The facility will be paid back once cash flows are great enough to cover ongoing costs.

Breakeven Analysis

Aegis will break even in October 2006 when the first revenues are received.

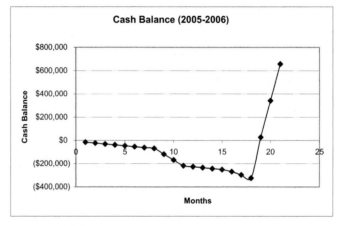

Start-up Capital Requirements

Aegis requires $450,000 in start-up capital. This figure includes 18 months of a safety cushion needed until the initial revenues are received in October 2006. The start-up capital breakout is as follows:

Table 4: Start-up Capital Requirements

Fixed Costs	$7,350
Designing Costs	$20,000
Insurance Expense	$19,505
Supplies	$1,942
Legal	$20,000
Utilities	$4,080
Trade Shows	$50,000
Other Marketing Costs	$60,000
Total	**$182,887**
18-Month Cushion	$267,391
Total Start-up	**$450,278**

Start-up Costs
Itemized start-up costs and other expenses expected for the Company during initial operations.

Start-up Costs:

Item	Cost per unit	Units	Subtotal:
Warehouse (psf)	$1	5000	$3,750
Computer	$500	2	$1,000
Desks	$50	3	$150
Telephone System	$200	1	$200
Inventory System	$2,000	1	$2,000
Chairs	$50	5	$250
			$7,350

Insurance Expense	Amount	Freq.	Total
Inventory Insurance	$4,500	1	$4,500
Liability Insurance	$11,405	1	$11,405
Health Insurance	$300	12	$3,600
		Per Year:	$19,505
		Per Month	$1,625

G&A Calculation:

Items	Amount	Quantity	Total/Year	Total/Month
Water	$45	18	$810	$68
Toilet Paper	$10	12	$120	$10
Paper Towels	$10	12	$120	$10
Cleaning Supplies	$20	6	$120	$10
Paper	$25	4	$100	$8
Toner	$100	4	$400	$33
Cups	$7	6	$42	$4
Pens/Pencils	$10	4	$40	$3
Web Domain	$10	1	$10	$1
Web Hosting	$15	12	$180	$15
	$252		$1,942	$162

Utilities	
Electricity	$200
Gas	$40
Water	included in rent
Trash	included in rent
Telephone	$100
Total	$340

Marketing and Trade Show Costs

Trade Show Rent	$50,000
Marketing	$50,000
Traveling Costs	$10,000
Sample Costs	$20,000
	$130,000

United States Helmet Sales:

Helmets Sold in the United States[25]		
2001–02	**2002–03**	**2003–04**
653,959	880,510	680,896

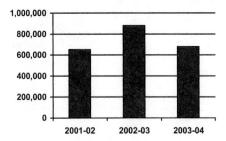

Although helmets were once a hot item, growth in helmet sales appears to have leveled off. Unlike apparel or equipment sales, snowsports participants tend not to replace their helmet frequently. Nonetheless, the acceptance of helmets and desire to prevent injuries has not waned.

---

[25] SnowSports Industries America News, Intelligence Report, 2004.

Consumer Test Methodology

The process of clearly identifying a target end consumer for Aegis involved the use of a survey, which served as the primary tool for gathering data about the demographics and types of products that interest prospective customers.

In order to establish a need for the product as well as obtain information about Aegis's targeted end consumers, 150 surveys of snowsports participants were collected at mountain resort sites, including Steamboat, Aspen/Snowmass, and Mammoth Mountain, as well as through the USC ski and snowboard club throughout the winter season. The areas were chosen in an attempt to obtain information from a variety of snowsports enthusiast demographics from around the United States and world.

The surveys focused on discovering what types of goods potential end customers are currently purchasing, determining injury statistics, establishing which demographic segments are most interested in the product, and finding out about how much money they would be willing to spend. Results of the test revealed a high demand for Aegis's product, with 80% of those surveyed replying either yes or maybe when questioned whether they would be interested in purchasing the product. The test also established the percentage of people who were wearing helmets, or other protective gear, who accounted for over one-third of all surveyed, as one group to target aggressively; they already recognize the need for safety precautions while participating in snowsports.

UNIVERSITY OF SOUTHERN CALIFORNIA
Department of Biomedical Engineering
Snow Sports Survey

How long have you been skiing/snowboarding?

How often do you ski/snowboard? (days/season)

Do you compete at skiing/snowboarding? If so, on what level?

When skiing/snowboarding, where do you spend the majority of your time (please rank)?
On easiest slopes
On intermediate slopes
On advanced slopes
On expert only slopes
In terrain parks
Other_____

What brand of ski/snowboard clothing do you most often purchase?

What do you look for in ski/snowboard clothing? (warmth, comfort, potential for mobility, protection, fashion, etc.)

Where do you currently purchase your ski/snowboard clothing? (ski shops, online, catalog, etc.)

Have you ever had any injuries due to skiing/snowboarding that have required a visit to a doctor? If so, please describe.

Have you ever had any minor injuries due to skiing/snowboarding that prevented you from skiing/riding for any period of time? If so, please describe. (Injury did not necessitate a visit to a doctor.)

What do you use to protect yourself against injuries?

30

How effective do you believe your current methods of protection are?

Are there any changes you would like made in these items?

Would you be interested in integrative protective wear especially configured for skiing/snow-boarding?

How much money per year, on average, do you spend on snow sports equipment?
$0 - $250
$250 - $500
$500 - $1000
$1000 - $5000
over $5000

Age:

Hometown:

Gender:

Sport:
Skiing
Snowboarding
Both
Other

Level of Skier/Boarder:
Beginner
Beginner-Intermediate
Intermediate
Intermediate-Advanced
Advanced
Expert

Survey Results

How long have you been skiing/snowboarding?

      14.74 years

How often do you ski/snowboard (days/year)?

      24.44 days/season

Do you compete at skiing/snowboarding?

      Compete: 27

      Do Not Compete: 123

When skiing/snowboarding, where do you spend the majority of your time?

      Average rankings:

            Intermediate

            Advanced

            Expert Only

            Terrain Parks

            Easiest

            Backcountry

            Trees

What brand of ski/snowboard clothing do you most often purchase (top fifteen)?

Burton	26	Patagonia	5	Spyder	4	Obermeyer	3
Northface	26	Salomon	5	Volki	4	Quicksilver	3
Columbia	15	686	4	32	3	Rossignol	3
Volcom	9	Nordica	4	Bonfire	3		
K2	7	Ride	4	Forum	3		
Oakley	7	Roxy	4	Mountain Hardware	3		

What do you look for in ski/snowboard clothing?

Warmth	109	Mobility	36	Durability	4	Quality	2
Fashion	86	Price	9	Pockets	3	Safety	1
Comfort	79	Functionality	7	Performance	2		
Protection	39	Fit	4	Breatheability	2		

Where do you currently purchase your ski/snowboarding clothing?

Ski shops	93	Skate/snow/surf shops	7	Sales	1
Sporting goods stores	27	Catalog	7	Discount ski shops	1
Online	24	Department stores	3	Oakley	1
Manufacturers	7	Outlets	2	Thrift stores	1

Have you ever had any injuries due to skiing/snowboarding that have required a visit to a doctor? If so, please describe.

Total: 57 people

Knee	29	Neck and back	9	Stitches	3	Spleen	1
Wrist	10	Thumb	5	Collar bone	2	Calf muscle	1
Ribs	10	Ankle	5	Kidney	2		
Shoulder	9	Leg	4	Tendons	2		
Head	9	Arm	3	Frostbite	1		

Have you ever had any minor injuries due to skiing/snowboarding that prevented you from skiing/riding for any period of time? (Injury did not necessitate a visit to a doctor.)

Total: 40

Knee	15	Neck and back	3	Shoulder	2	Bruises	1
Head	7	Toe	2	Bone chip	1	Frostbite	1
Thumb	4	Tail bone	2	Bruised bones	1	Ice burn	1
Wrist	3	Hip	2	Leg	1	Calf muscle	1
Shin	3	Cuts	2	Rib	1	Ripped muscles	1

What do you do to protect yourself from injury?

Avoidance/caution	50	Back support/guard	1
Helmet	45	Tape up knee	1
Stretching	11	Hand/shin guards	1
Staying fit	9	A lot of padding	1
Wrist guards	8	Long sleeve shirt	1
Good clothing/equipment	6	Advil	1
Knee brace	5	Snow	1
Knee pads	5	Impact shorts	1
Cup	2		
Beer	2		
Butt pads	1		

How effective do you believe your current methods of protection are?
INCONCLUSIVE
Are there any changes that you would like made in these items?
INCONCLUSIVE

Would you be interested in an integrative protective wear especially configured for skiing/snowboarding?

Yes	86
Maybe	34
No	28

Money on average spent per year on equipment

$0–$250	45
$250–$500	50
$500–$1000	37
$1000–$5000	15

Age: average 26.31

Hometown:

California	80	Australia	2	Indiana	1	Oklahoma	1
Colorado	17	New Jersey	2	Kentucky	1	Pennsylvania	1
Arkansas	6	North Carolina	2	London	1	Vermont	1
Connecticut	4	Texas	2	Maine	1	Virginia	1
Illinois	4	Alaska	1	Michigan	1	Washington	1
New York	5	Canada	1	Missouri	1	Wisconsin	1
Florida	3	Finland	1	Montana	1		
New Zealand	3	Idaho	1	Netherlands	1		
Venezuela	3						

Gender:

Male:	79
Female:	69

Sport:

Skiing	75
Snowboarding	43
Both	29

Level of Skier/Boarder:

Beginner	10
Beginner-Intermediate/Intermediate	1
Beginner-Intermediate	12
Intermediate	25
Intermediate-Advanced	36
Intermediate-Advanced/Advanced	1
Advanced	28
Advanced-Expert	9
Expert	29

Product Interest

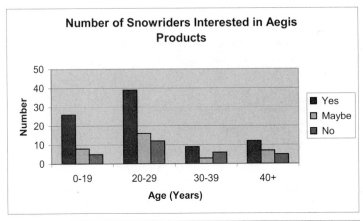

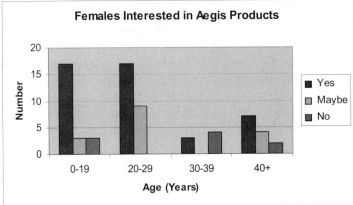

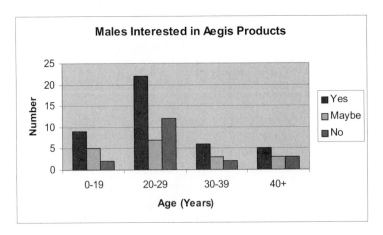

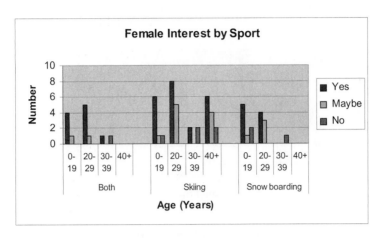

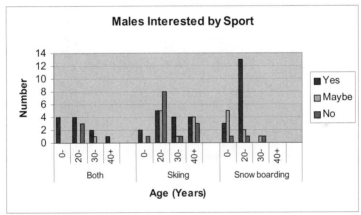

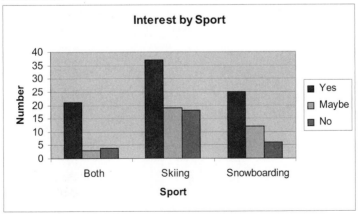

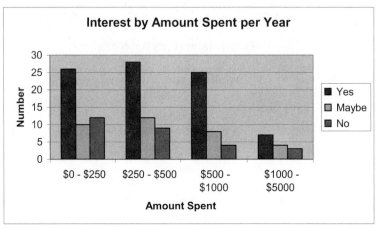

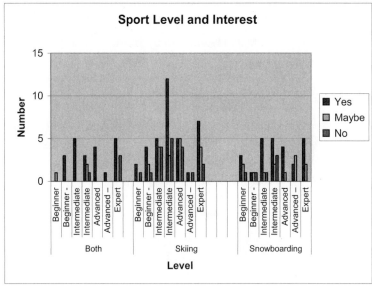

Brochure

Aegis Performance Apparel

Aegis Performance Apparel seeks to provide high quality, protective snowsports apparel that offers an integrative and unique combination of fashion, function, and protection. Our one of a kind combination of a removable protective inner layer paired with a well designed high quality outer shell allows participants protection as well as fashion all rolled into one.

Aegis
Performance Apparel

667 West 28th Street
Los Angeles, California 90007

Phone: 213-361-8822

Email: information@aegis.com

Aegis
Performance Apparel

667 West 28th Street
Los Angeles, California 90007
Phone: 213-361-8822
Email: information@aegis.com

Of the action sports industry, the fastest growing segment of the sports entertainment industry is in snowsports with over 270 million participants in the world today. However, almost 30% have experienced some form of injury related to the sport. According to ski experts, the most common injuries involve:

- Knee joints and ankles
- Shoulder and clavicle
- Wrists and thumbs

Aegis Performance Apparel has recognized this fact and in turn come up with a fully unique product line that provides protection aimed at helping to prevent these specific injuries. Through state of the art engineering we have been able to integrate such protection into fully functional skiwear apparel.

Our Products
Outerwear:

Pants:

As the flagship product for Aegis Performance Apparel our pants integrate a patented preventative knee brace into a stylish and functional snow pant. The brace is designed specifically to reduce the incidence of ACL injury, the single most common injury in snowsports.

- Integrated ACL support brace
- Integrated jib protection
- Integrated impact shorts

Tops:

Aegis Performance Apparel tops consist of soft shell parkas, which are constructed of the latest technology providing for a lighter, less bulky look yet a warmer experience. Features of our top line include:

- Integrated clavicle pads
- Integrated shoulder protection
- Integrated rib protection

Protective Accessories:

Gloves:

Designed specifically for either a skier or a boarder to help prevent common injuries associated with the sport, our glove line like out outwear integrates high protection with a stylish appearance. Focuses of protection for our glove line include:

- Integrated thumb protector for ski gloves
- Integrated wrist guard for snowboard gloves

Aegis, the Greek word for shield, provides just that: a protective layer for you against the dangers of the mountain, while allowing a comfortable restriction free freedom of mobility to let you push your limits and ski to the extreme.

We are the only integrative protective snow apparel line on the market today.

Contact us today for more information.

667 West 28th Street
Los Angeles, California 90007

Phone: 213-361-8822

Email: information@aegis.com

Competition

Table 3: Competitor Profiles

Outerwear

	Ownership	Annual Sales	Snow Apparel Retail	Distribution Channels
Mass Sporting Good				
Northface	VF Corporation	NA	Approx $100 - $300	Department, Specialty, Sporting Goods, Online, Catalog, Flagship
Columbia	Columbia Sportswear	$1.1 billion	Approx $100 - $300	Department, Specialty, Sporting Goods, Online, Catalog
Patagonia	Patagonia	$150 million	Approx $100 - $300	Department, Specialty, Sporting Goods, Online, Catalog, Flagship
Ski Specific				
Spyder	Spyder Active Sports	$7.8 million	Approx $150 - $450	Sporting Goods, Specialty, Online
Rossignol	Skis Rossignol S.A.	$602.7 million	Approx $150 - $450	Sporting Goods, Specialty, Online
K2	K2 Inc	$718.5 million	Approx $150 - $450	Sporting Goods, Specialty, Online
Snowboard Specific				
Burton	Burton Snowboards	$140 million	Approx $100 - $400	Sporting Goods, Specialty, Online, Catalog
Quicksilver	Quicksilver, Inc	$1.3 billion	Approx $100 - $400	Department, Specialty, Sporting Goods, Online, Catalog, Flagship
Cold As Ice	CAI Brands, Inc	$2.2 million	Approx $100 - $400	Sporting Goods, Specialty, Online, Catalog

* Please note that the above is not meant to be a comprehensive list but simply a representation of the various types of competition the company will face

Protective Wear

	Ownership	Location	Annual Company Sales	Protective Snowsports Goods
Asterisk	Asterisk Llc	United States	$890,000	Injury-preventative knee braces
Crash Pads	Crash Pads	United States	$600,000	Padded top and bottom under layers
Steletools	Skeletools	United States	NA	Torso, elbow, knee pads, impact shorts
Dainese	Dainese S.B.A.	Italy	$102 million	Integrative jackets, pants, helmets
North Peak	North Peak	Japan	NA	Torso, elbow, knee pads, impact shorts, knee and elbow pads
RED	Burton Snowboards	United States	NA	Helmets, impact shorts, rail guards, wrist guards, skull cap
Pro-Tec	Mosa Extreme Inc	United States	NA	Helmets, knee, elbow, wrist, hips, back pads
Market	Marker USA	United States	NA	Helmets
Boeri	Boeri Ski & Snowboard	United States	$230,000	Helmets
Giro	Bell Sports, Inc	United States	NA	Helmets
Leedom	Endorphin Enterprises	United States	$580,000	Helmets
Briko	Luxottica Group S.B.A.	Italy	$4.37 billion	Helmets
K2	K2 Inc	United States	$718.5 million	Helmets
Salamon	Adidas-Salamon	United States	$7.87 billion	Helmets
UVEX	UVEX Sports Inc	United States	$2.4 million	Helmets
Carrera	Carrera Sport	United States	$97,000	Helmets
Team Wendy	Team Wendy, LLC	United States	$690,000	Helmets
Acerbis	Acerbis Plastica USA	United States	$2.2 million	Helmets

David Dobkin

Relevant Experience:
July 2001 – September 2002

Wasserstein Perella & Co. *(now Dresdner Kleinwort Wasserstein)*   New York, NY
Analyst, Mergers and Acquisition - Healthcare
Perform valuations and build financial models with projections for companies in the healthcare industry, specifically in the medical device, pharmaceuticals, services and biotechnology sectors. Research, analyze and prepare comprehensive strategic analyses, including discounted cash flow, comparable company, comparable acquisition and relative contribution analysis, for clients and senior management. Conducted strategic valuation and analysis assignments for foreign medical device companies which entailed valuing an entire market and forming the company's internal development, market entry and distribution strategies. Advised on multiple buy and sell side cross-border transactions with significant client, buyer and seller contact. Participated in high yield and secondary equity offerings.
 Deal Experience:
 • January 2002 - Advised Biocompatibles plc on the sale of its Eye Care Division to The Cooper Companies for $100MM
 • February 2002 – Advised Draegerwerk AG on its attempted purchase of Spacelabs Medical
 • March 2002 – Performed a strategic market analysis for Paul Hartmann AG
 • May 2002 – Advised Biocompatibles plc on the sale of its cardiovascular stent business to Abbott Laboratories for $235MM
 • June 2002 – Advised Nexan plc on its sale to Welch Allyn, Inc. for an undisclosed amount

April 2000 – May 2001

DealProvider.com   New York, NY and Los Angeles, CA
Co-founder, Chief Financial Officer, and Director
Created a new Internet technology that allows for personalized real-time eCommerce deal finding. Prepared business and marketing plans, cash flow analysis, and 52-week user profiles for years one through five. Acquired first round of venture capital in August 2000. Implemented national viral marketing campaign. Managed company accounts.

August 1999 –
December 1999

Versity.com   New York, NY
Campus Operations Manager
Launched the education supplement-based web site at Columbia University and managed the regional effort. Hired and managed a staff of 60 people. Managed a $24,000 budget. Produced campus and regional marketing campaign. Increased operations by 600% to become the number two operation in the Nation.

Additional Experience:
November 2002 – April 2003

Breckenridge Ski and Ride School   Breckenridge, CO
Certified Adult Ski Instructor
Instructed and coached adults in skiing technique at all skill levels. Participated in the Bombers, children's winter ski camp instructing a level 5 group.

May 1999 – February 2000

Koenigsberg Engineering   New York, NY
Structural Engineering Consultant
Performed physical safety inspections of buildings in New York City. Prepared fifteen to twenty page comprehensive safety reports on a building's status to be filed with the city.

Education:
2003 - present

University of Southern California   Los Angeles, CA
School of Engineering and Applied Science
Ph.D. candidate in Biomedical Engineering - Tissue Engineering
Research in Heart Valve Tissue Engineering at Children's Hospital of Los Angeles

1997-2001

Columbia University   New York, NY
School of Engineering and Applied Science
B.S. in Biomedical Engineering, GPA: 3.7/4.0

Honors:

Dean's List (eight semesters); Howard Cagel Leadership Scholar
National Merit Scholar (1997)
University of California, Santa Barbara, Creative Sciences Biology Award Recipient (1997)

Leadership Activities:

Captain, **Columbia University Ski Team**   2000 – 2001
Secretary, **Biomedical Engineering Society, Columbia University**   2000 – 2001
Congressional Intern, **United States House of Representatives**   Summer 1996

Annemarie Dillard

<u>**EDUCATION**</u>

University of Southern California – Los Angeles, CA
- Marshall School of Business, Entrepreneur emphasis
  Business Scholar
  BA in Business
  3.51 GPA
  Expected Date of Graduation 5/2005

Pulaski Academy – Little Rock, AR
- Cum Laude Graduate
- Headmaster's List 1998-2001

<u>**EXPERIENCE**</u>

Left Coast Style – *Market Researcher,* January 2004 – April 2004, September 2004 - present
- Division of Dillard's Department Stores Inc.
- Researched and compiled reports on shopping centers throughout the greater Los Angeles area

BCBGMaxazria – *Assistant Visual Merchandising Manager,* April 2004 – July 2004
- Published visual merchandising standards information for all BCBGMaxazria stores
- Worked in retail stores to show employees how to properly follow merchandising materials
- Compiled presentations for annual meetings for visual managers
- Assisted buyers in New York market week

Got It Right, LLC. – *Administrator Lucky Brand Jeans Philanthropic Sale*, January 2004
- Developed selling team
- Ensured associates understood productivity and job performance standards
- Administered on the job training
- Managed sale

BCBGMaxazria – *Intern,* April 2003 – July 2003
- Prepared periodic inventories of showroom for account executives
- Maintained visual merchandising and selling floor standards
- Strategized and managed sale setup for sales representatives
- Sold to various accounts at Los Angeles market

Left Coast Style – *Intern,* Jan. 2003 - April 2003
- Division of Dillard's Department Stores Inc.
- Researched and comprised buying/selling reorder recaps for Dillard's buyers
- Assisted executives in general office duties
- Met with vendors and presented new lines to Dillard's buyers and executives
- Shopped retail stores for new trends and compiled reports based on findings

Dillard's Department Stores – *Intern,* On and Off Fall 1998 - Present
- Assisted in setting up BCBG shop-in-shops in Dillard's stores
- Participated in product development for Dillard's private labels Copper Key, Antonio Melani, Gianni Bini, Michelle D, Sole Choice
- Met markets in Dallas, Los Angeles, and New York

J.E.P – Joint Educational Project - *Student Tutor,* January 2003 – May 2003
- Non-Profit Organization aimed to assist youth in Inner City Los Angeles
- Tutored students on the fundamentals of Geology

Centers for Youth and Family Clothing Drive – *Founder and Administrator,* 2001
- Administered Clothing Drive for abandoned and abused children in Little Rock, Arkansas

<u>**SKILLS AND INTERESTS**</u>
- Pi Beta Phi Sorority – *President and Vice President*
- Horseback Riding – 7th in the Nation: American Horse Shows Association
- President of Interact/Rotary and Spanish Clubs 2000-2001
- Vice President of YWCA Y-Teens 2000-2001
- Proficient in Word, Excel and PowerPoint

Board Member Profiles

Rusty Gregory

Rusty Gregory brings considerable ski industry experience and expertise to Aegis. Mr. Gregory currently serves as CEO of Mammoth Mountain Resort. During his tenure, he has transformed the resort from a Southern California commuter destination into a world-class ski resort, competing with Vail and Breckenridge as the most visited resort in the United States. Mr. Gregory is on the board of directors for the National Ski Areas Association. Mr. Gregory holds a Bachelor of Science degree in Business Administration from UCLA.

Alex Dillard

Alex Dillard brings a skill set to Aegis that is rare. Having been exposed to the industry since birth, Alex has been an employee of the fashion retail industry for over thirty years. Alex was the top graduate of the University of Arkansas with a degree in accounting, as well as the valedictorian award at the University of Texas School of Law. Currently, he serves at the president of Dillard's, Inc., and as a member of the board. As the largest single-name upscale department store chain in the United States, Alex has in-depth experience in all aspects of the retail, wholesale, and manufacturing industries. Alex has been an avid skier for over thirty years and has skied throughout the world.

Matthew Levenson

Matthew Levenson brings years of teen marketing experience and operations expertise to the Aegis team. Currently, Mr. Levenson is the CEO and president of 9star, Inc., an Action Sports Center and "category-killer" multichannel retailer for the currently fragmented Action Sports industry. Most recently, Mr. Levenson ran the day-to-day operations serving as chief operating officer for Liquidseats Inc., now known as Stubhub.com, a secondary ticketing solutions provider to the professional sports and entertainment industries. Before that, Mr. Levenson served as the head of field operations for Versity.com, a collegiate note-taking business, where he built the business from 7 branch locations in 1999 to 165 branch locations and 10,000 field employees in 2000. Prior to that Mr. Levenson served as executive vice president at General Meters, servicing over 500 colleges and universities with proprietary card key systems. Before joining General Meters, Mr. Levenson was CEO of a marketing company, Campus Card, providing a debit card to college students whereby their parents could budget spending. Mr. Levenson graduated from the Wharton School of Business with a Bachelor of Science degree, with dual concentrations in Finance and Entrepreneurial Management.

Production and Distribution Cycle

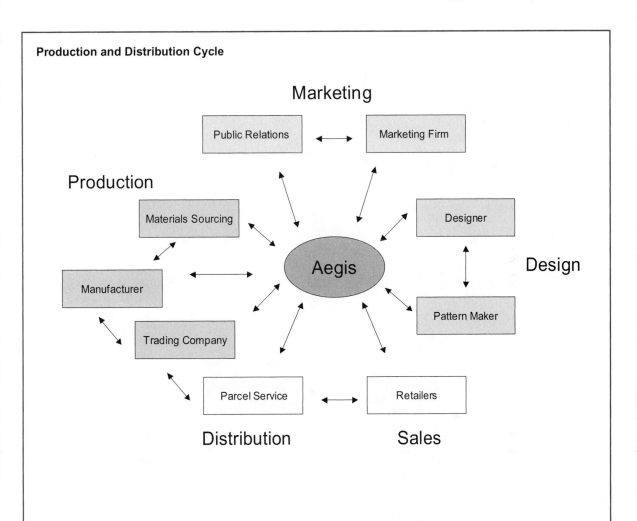

Product Designs

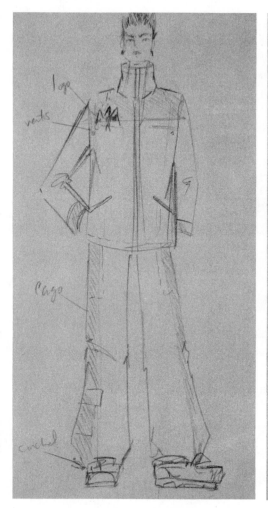 

Aegis product designs with integrative protective wear. Knee braces and pads are hidden underneath the jacket and pants.

Designer Profile

Shannon Figgins
Fashion Institute of Design and Merchandising, class of 2005
    Advanced Associate of the Arts degree in Fashion Design
    Top graduate in class of 2,000 students

Scholarship Winner of:
- Robert Nelson (full year's tuition)
- TALA of Los Angeles
- Ebell fo Los Angeles
- Steven Dodd shoewear Design scholarship
- DreamWorks Home Entertainment
- Instituto Di Koefia Full-year scholarship to study couture in Rome, Italy October 2005

Experience:
Designed, produced patterns for, and constructed a 32-piece women's sportswear collection and had a runway show "Debut Show 2005" in Santa Monica, California, in February of 2005.

Designed, produced patterns for, and constructed a 22-piece women's sportswear collection for runway show at Mercedes-Benz LA fashion week show on March 19, 2005.

Press Accolades:
LA Times - January 16, 2005
California Apparel News - February 2005 & March 2005
WWD - Twice in March 2005
Zinc Magazine - Article to come out May 2005
Elle Magazine - Article to come out May 2005

Freelance work:
- Susan Sarandon Celebrity Charity Corset auction with R.A.I.N.
- DreamWorks SKG/Home Entertainment
- LA Chamber of Commerce
- Frederick's of Hollywood
- FIDM
- Yaras, Inc.
- McKinney Studios

Force Diagrams

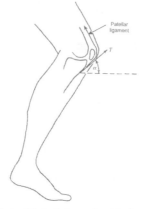

Figure 2.15. Diagram of the tensile force on the patellar ligament during squatting. The tension T is very large when a person is in a low squat.

The forces generated in the knee are considerably larger than just the effect of a person's weight. During activity, the combination of mass and velocity can increase the forces generated by over one hundred times a person's weight. In order to decrease the chance of injury, both support and increasing flex duration can mitigate the occurrence.

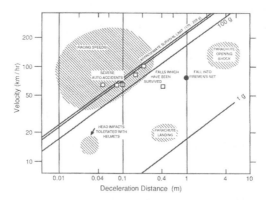

Figure 2.17. A compilation of documented cases of impact results on humans shown as a log-log plot of the velocity on impact versus the deceleration distance during impact. The diagonal lines show the deceleration in terms of acceleration of gravity g. (One g is equal to your body weight.) The hollow squares represent data from documented free-fall survivors. The shaded areas represent guestimates for the other situations. (After R. G. Snyder, *Bioastronautics Data Book,* Second Ed., p. 228 (1973).

Despite the increased force placed on the body, it is not the force, but rather rapid acceleration or deceleration, that causes injury. By increasing the deceleration time, the resultant force (F = Δmv/Δt) can be reduced. In snowsports, participant speeds typically are greater than 50 km/hr and can increase to over 200 km/hr. The use of protection devices can increase the stopping time, thus lowering force and preventing injury.

Timeline

Project	2005											2006											
	Feb.	Mar.	Apr.	May	Jun.	Jul.	Aug.	Sep.	Oct.	Nov.	Dec.	Jan.	Feb.	Mar.	Apr.	May	Jun.	Jul.	Aug.	Sep.	Oct.	Nov.	Dec.
File for trademark	■	■																					
Obtain legal documents		■	■																				
Incorporate		■	■																				
File patent papers			■																				
Hire designer			■	■																			
Locate office space				■	■																		
Negotiate with manufacturers					■	■																	
2006 apparel development						■	■																
2006 apparel samples							■	■															
Marketing emphasis - retailer								■	■			■	■	■									
Hire sales team									■														
Attend trade shows									■	■													
Take 2006 orders										■	■	■	■	■									
2007 apparel development												■	■	■									
Locate warehouse space												■	■										
2007 apparel samples														■	■								
Warehouse preparation															■	■	■						
2006 manufacturer production																■	■	■					
Ship 2006 orders																		■	■				
Marketing - end consumers																				■	■	■	■

References

Interviews:

Boshart, Mike. Interview. VP of Purchasing, REI. February 7, 2005.

Franklin, Andy. Interview. Director of Manufacturing. March 3, 2005.

Fujas, Pep. Interview. Pro Skier and X Games participant. April 18, 2005.

Gregorton, Colin. Interview. Director of Research, DJ Orthopedic. February 17, 2005.

Gregory, Rusty. Interview. CEO, Mammoth Mountain. February 3, 2005.

Lazirus, Lisa. Interview. Designer, Reef Apparel. February 23, 2005.

Levenson, Matthew. Interview. CEO, 9star. January 17, 2005.

Post, Bill. Interview. President, Obermeyer Sport Inc. January 24, 2005.

Post, Darcy Lee. Interview. CEO/owner, CAI Brands, Inc. February 17, 2005.

Post, Tina. Interview. Head of Customer Service, CAI Brands, Inc. February 17, 2005.

Saunders, Steve. Interview. Mountain High Ski Patrol. January 29, 2005.

Trade Events:

Action Sports Retailers, Annual Trade Show. San Diego, CA. January 17, 2005.

SnowSports Industries America, Annual Trade Show. Las Vegas, NV. January 24, 2005.

Sources Referred To That Are Not Otherwise Cited:

Biomet, Inc. Annual Report, 10-K, 2003.

Columbia, Inc. Annual Report, 10-K, 2003.

DJ Orthopedic, Inc. Annual Report, 10-K, 2003.

"Growing Concern over Skiing Injuries." BBC News. December 31, 2002.

"Head Moves into Protection Category." *Transworld Business.* December 21, 2004.

"Outwear Technology 2005." *Transworld Business.* October 1, 2004.

Pennington, Bill. "Doctors See a Big Rise in Injuries for Young Athletes." *New York Times.* February 22, 2005.

Ryan, Thomas J. "Eaten Alive-Mergers and Acquisitions Continue to Change the Face of the Sporting Goods Industry." *SGB.* January 2005.

"Skiing Evolving into a New Wave of Growth and Versatile Products." *SAI News.* 2005.

"Snowsports People Urged to Take Care." www.acc.co.az. July 2003.

SnowSports Industries America News, Intelligence Report, 2004.

"Urban Trends Influence Snowboard Apparel Styles." SIA News. 2005

"U.S. Ski Resorts Could See Record Year." Cnn.com. January 12, 2005.

"Women's Skiing Apparel Manufacturers." Skisite.com. December 25, 2005.

RadioNOW

A Feasibility Study for Digital Audio Recording Technology

Daniel Bohm
Samit Varma

The University of Southern California

Executive Summary

Introduction

RadioNow has witnessed the revolution started by digital video recorders and realizes that consumers are demanding greater control over their media experiences. The focus on improving the viewing experience of television audiences has left no one focused on improving the listening experience of radio audiences. Advances in microchip technologies have made it possible for RadioNow to create a solution that fills this gap. RadioNow has developed a Digital Audio Recorder (DAR) that allows radio listeners to record, playback, or pause any radio program at the touch of a button, all while in the car. No longer will not being near a radio mean forever missing the program. No longer will a cell phone call mean missing out on one's favorite song. No longer will commuters be subject to programming they are not interested in. RadioNow is the first company to offer a compelling, digital solution that car stereo manufacturers and automobile manufacturers can seamlessly integrate into their products.

Business Concept

RadioNow creates Digital Audio Recorder (DAR) technology that enables anytime-recording and on-demand-playback of radio programming. The technology will be licensed to stereo manufacturers wanting to offer more sophisticated functionality to attract customers in the competitive car audio industry.

Industry Analysis

Trends in the car stereo industry show that fewer consumers are upgrading their car stereos to after-market ones and are, therefore, increasingly keeping the stereo installed by the dealer. Upgrades to higher-end car audio systems are occurring at the automobile dealership at the point of sale and include premium sound systems as an option (or standard on high-end models).

Market Analysis

Market demand for the product was arrived at by using market research, surveys, and interviews with various potential customers. A survey was conducted that included 89 customers with varying demographics. In the survey it was determined that 75% of them would pay extra for DAR functionality on their car stereos. The end-user profile of the target market was males and females under the age of 37 primarily. The primary research also confirmed that most customers are not inclined to purchase after-market car stereos. Discussions with Alpine USA and with Pioneer supported this finding.

Product

The DAR technology takes a plurality of incoming AM/FM analog signals and converts them to a digital signal. This signal is then stored on several non-volatile memory units. A microprocessor then controls user inputs to recall and play back the recorded signals. This essentially allows for a car stereo to have VCR-like function on real-time radio.

Founding Team

RadioNow was co-founded by Daniel Bohm and Samit Varma. The technology is in the process of being provisionally patented with the help of Kleinberg and Lerner, LP. Samit Varma will oversee the prototyping and development of the product, and Daniel Bohm will conduct business development and marketing.

Financial Plan

Using sales assumptions and demand estimations attained from primary market research, RadioNow will show positive cash flow in year 3. A cumulative cash balance of $706,600 will result at the end of year 3. EBIT for the first three years will be ($63,600), ($90,450) and $847,100, respectively. This is largely because the first sale is not made until year 2, and typically adoption has taken several months for this type of technology. Initial start-up capital required will be $150,000, which includes a $60,000 safety buffer. The break-even point will be 18 months after launch, in June of 2006, after 15,000 units have been sold. DAR will be introduced in a single automobile line first and then will gradually be adopted by other automobile lines.

Timeline to Launch

A timeline has been formed, and RadioNow has been on schedule thus far. A period of 4 months has been allotted for final design and prototyping, with prototype completion scheduled for March of 2005 and the first sale coming a year after launch.

Feasibility Decision

Based on the market research that was conducted and the interviews with industry experts, RadioNow has a feasible product that has significant market potential. Plans to move forward with the final design and prototype are in place, and the company will file for a provisional patent of the technology. In search of its first customer, RadioNow has secured open invitations with Alpine Stereo and Pioneer to demonstrate its technology.

Table of Contents

Feasibility Decision

Based on research that strongly suggests that the market is ready for digital audio recorder technology, RadioNow believes that developing and licensing its technology will result in a significant profit opportunity and high returns for investors. The founding team will execute on the feasibility analysis and formally form RadioNow, Inc.

Business Concept

Summary

RadioNow creates Digital Audio Recorder (DAR) technology that enables anytime-recording and on-demand-playback of radio programming. The technology will be licensed to stereo manufacturers wanting to offer more sophisticated functionality to attract customers in the competitive car audio industry.

Customer Identification

All car stereo manufacturers are potential RadioNow customers, and certainly none will be turned away. RadioNow's target market, based on primary and secondary industry research, is made up of car stereo manufacturers that have existing relationships with automobile manufacturers – see Table 1. Some of the car stereo manufacturers listed in Table 1 have entered Original Equipment Manufacturer (OEM) relationships with the auto makers, whereas others have maintained their car stereo's brand in the automobile.

Table 1[1]

Stereo Manufacturer	Automobile Manufacturer—Non-Luxury	Car Manufacturer—Luxury
Bose	Chevrolet, Mazda, Nissan	Acura, Audi, Cadillac, Infiniti, Porsche
Boston Acoustics	Chrysler	
Mach	Ford	
Monsoon	Volkswagen	
Panasonic	Toyota	Acura
JBL	Toyota	
Harman Kardon		BMW, Saab, Land Rover
Alpine	Honda	Jaguar
Mark Levinson		Lexus
THX-certified		Lincoln
Dolby Pro-Logic		Volvo
Visteon	Ford, Dodge	

Customer Benefits

Car stereo manufacturers are increasingly pressured to come up with compelling products and features that entice consumers to purchase.[2] RadioNow's system allows car stereo manufacturers to easily incorporate a digital audio recorder into their products to give their customers more power over radio content. Table 2 describes the benefits to the parties in the car audio value chain.

1

Table 2—Digital Audio Recorder Benefits Throughout Value Chain

Stereo Manufacturer	Automobile Manufacturer	End User (purchaser of premium audio package)
• Attract consumers seeking new technology. • Possibly recognized as innovator.	• Possibly recognized as innovator. • Attract consumers seeking new technology.	• Save time by skipping commercials. • Increased entertainment value. • More pleasant in-car experience.

Differentiation

RadioNow has an advantage over competing products and technologies because of two primary differentiators. First, the non-volatile memory bank system allows for multiple recorded files to exist simultaneously without requiring writing the content to disk. This architecture requires less power, which makes the technology ideal for mobile devices and also makes it easier for content-demanding consumers to expand the unit's storage capacity. Second, RadioNow's distribution strategy is unlike that of any other company that has digital audio recorder technology, because it focuses on a licensing model applied to the automotive industry. Table 3 in the competitor analysis section showcases RadioNow's unique position.

Business Model

After its intellectual property is sufficiently protected by patents, RadioNow will demonstrate its digital audio recorder technology to stereo and automobile manufacturers by leveraging its contacts in these industries. It will generate revenue by licensing its technology to car stereo manufacturers, who will ultimately acquire the necessary components, build the DAR-equipped car stereo, and sell it to partner auto makers. RadioNow will receive a royalty of 10% based on the car stereo manufacturer's revenues from the selling of stereos containing RadioNow's digital audio recorder technology.[3]

Future designs for the DAR technology include full integration with satellite radio. Additionally, the team will focus on developing components that are highly interoperable with personal computers and other handheld devices, primarily through USB, infrared, or wireless (802. 11B/G) connections. The next product iteration will include increased support for various file formats, such as WAV, WMA, and even video formats containing audio. On-the-fly burning capabilities and recording to memory cards are other enhancements for future products.

RadioNow will also have the opportunity to add new revenue streams by expanding into the home stereo segment of the industry. This could be done by licensing its technology to major consumer electronics manufacturers, such as Sony and Panasonic, who make stereo receivers and radios that can be used either at home or at work.

Industry Analysis

Industry Summary

Innovations in microprocessor technology and advances in car stereo design have led to today's state-of-the-art audio systems. In this highly competitive sector of consumer electronics, missing out on the next big trend can be a fatal mistake.[4] Car audio technologies that contribute to drivers' and passengers' in-car entertainment experience are growing in demand. The

2

industry has seen a rise in new in-car technologies, such as DVD and MP3 players, but no company to date has offered digital audio recording functionality in any of its product lines.

Industry Overview

The car entertainment industry is a multi-billion dollar industry that, after much stagnation, is in the midst of a revival.[5] Based on the total number of new-car sales in 2003, 8,103,000,[6] RadioNow estimates the premium audio segment of this industry at about $1.2 billion.[7] The after-market car stereo industry, a subset of the car entertainment industry, has been shrinking. Revenue during the 12-month period that ended in March 2004 was about $460 million, down from $490 million during the same period in 2002 and 2003. Revenue from March 2001 to March 2002 was $540 million.[8] Car manufacturers are largely to blame because the stereos they pack into cars are more integrated into the rest of the car than ever before. Many recent models, for example, incorporate the stereo's controls (volume, tuner, source-select) into the steering wheel for safe, one-touch control of the stereo. Owners of such cars rarely purchase an after-market stereo because it would jeopardize the dash's structural integrity and aesthetic fluidity.

Users who once demanded only loud, good-quality sound from their systems are now demanding feature-rich products that provide a more compelling in-car entertainment experience.[9] That is, consumers now focus less on after-market car stereos and more on products that increase the joy of being in the car. This can be seen by the rise in DVDs and video game consoles being installed in automobiles.[10] As cities become more crowded, the traffic worsens, thereby increasing commute times and subsequently the amount of time spent in the car.

Consumers are starting to favor more advanced features, such as MP3 players and satellite radio. Although MP3 playback capability and satellite radio currently have limited market share in the automotive industry, the technologies are poised for significant growth in the near future, a JD Power and Associates survey said. The report found that although only 3% of consumers currently have MP3 playback capability in their current vehicle, 75% of those consumers indicate that they "definitely" or "probably" want the technology in their next vehicle. Similarly, only 11% of consumers currently have satellite radio, but 73% of those consumers want the feature in their next vehicle. The AM/FM/single-CD player is the most popular audio system configuration on the market today, representing 34% of all factory-installed audio systems in 2004. AM/FM/cassette/single-CD players, the most popular system in 2003, with 32% market share, dropped to 26% in 2004. AM/FM/multi-CD changers, which took just 1% of the market in 1998, are now the third-most-popular system, with 18% market penetration.[11]

Future Trends in Car Audio

Industry experts predict that the demand for car electronics will grow. The MP3 revolution has manufacturers scrambling to incorporate MP3 playback into its components (BMW has recently partnered with Apple to support iPod).[12] Meanwhile, no products have attempted to reproduce the Digital Video Recorder phenomenon, launched by TiVo and ReplayTV. Until recently, the technology to produce such a product economically did not exist. Modern digital audio compression and decompression algorithms, more commonly referred to as codecs, and microprocessors are able to provide stereo head units with more computational power than ever before. RadioNow believes this will lead to the introduction of more advanced car stereos that provide higher levels of interoperability with other electronic components and seamless file transferring.

Competitor Analysis

Competition to RadioNow exists in two forms: direct competition from companies planning on producing a product similar to what RadioNow will produce; secondary competition from hand-held devices and computer software that have integrated digital audio recording capabilities.

On-Demand Audio: On-Demand Radio is a car stereo that gives listeners the ability to tune to, record, and listen to content from AM or FM radio stations. Additionally, with On-Demand Audio's patent-pending SongSurfer technology, recorded radio content behaves as a CD does, allowing users to skip from song to song or to skip past ads. This company has an exclusive license to produce products based on the patent owned by Pause Technology. This product is not yet on the market but will be available to consumers in the first quarter of 2005.[13]

Radio Your Way: Radio Your Way by Pogo Products is a handheld digital radio and MP3 player that incorporates VCR-like technology, but cannot pause and continue live broadcasts. It has a USB interface that allows users to connect with their computers for transferring digital files.[14]

RadioSHARK: RadioSHARK by Griffin Technology adds an AM/FM radio to Macs or PCs and can record any AM or FM radio broadcast in real time. It can record a scheduled show or "pause" live radio through Time-Shift Recording. RadioSHARK includes an application that controls all radio and recording functions. Any recorded broadcast can be transferred to an iPod or another AIFF-compatible digital music player for replay.[15]

Table 3—Feature Comparison[16]

Company	Product	Head Unit Replacement	Supports Computer File Transfers	Time-Shift Capability	VCR-Like Control
Gotuit Audio	On-Demand Audio	X	X	X	X
Griffin Technology	RadioSHARK		X		X
Pogo Products!	Radio Your Way		X		X
RadioNow	RadioNow Recorder		X	X	X

Despite this competition, RadioNow is uniquely positioned in the industry because it is the only company that sells its technology as a building-block component. RadioNow believes its product is sufficiently different from those of Pogo and Griffin Technology and will, therefore, serve a different market.

There are no digital audio recorders for the automobile currently on the market. RadioNow and On-Demand Audio, the greatest source of competition to RadioNow, are the only two companies that are actively developing products to be used in automobiles. Barriers to entry, however, are low because advances in technology have made storage, memory, and analog-to-digital processors readily available and affordable. New entrants or established car stereo manufacturers could develop unique, competing technology.

Market Analysis

Market Summary

Any car stereo manufacturer who believes that giving consumers more control over radio content will result in higher unit sales is a potential RadioNow customer. RadioNow's target market, however, is car stereo companies that have strong and mature relationships with large automobile manufacturers, such as Toyota, GM, and Nissan. The first customers will be achieved by leveraging industry contacts that RadioNow has established at Toyota and Alpine-USA.

Target Market Analysis

RadioNow's reason for targeting car stereo manufacturers with strong ties to the automotive industry is twofold. First, the market for car stereos that are bundled with automobiles is far greater than the after-market car stereo market, as shown in Figure 1. This includes either stereos purchased through OEM channels or premium audio package upgrades. Second, RadioNow's research showed that sales of after-market stereos are declining and are not expected to return to sales highs of the 1990s. Today's automobile purchasers are less likely to remove the stereo that originally came with the car and replace it with an after-market brand. Little marketing emphasis will be given to car stereo manufacturers, such as Clarion and Kenwood, that cater solely to the after-market industry.

Figure 1 – Premium Branded Audio Purchase Preference[17]

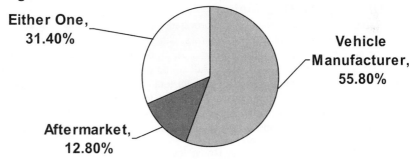

Either One, 31.40%

Vehicle Manufacturer, 55.80%

Aftermarket, 12.80%

RadioNow can further segment its target market by focusing on those car stereo manufacturers that supply premium stereos, which come standard in luxury cars and are typically included in premium audio packages for non-luxury cars. Table 1 above lists the target customers and matches them with their automotive partners. These players in the car audio market are highly interested in offering feature-rich packages that go beyond simply offering better sound. The premium audio packages available today include traditional upgrades such as better speakers and more sophisticated head units (e.g., multiple CD changers or DVD players), but many car manufacturers have requested that their audio partners include newer technologies, such as MP3 players and audio hard drives, in next-generation products as demanded by consumers. No premium packages on the market today offer digital audio recorder technology.

Primary Research – Methodology and Results

RadioNow's primary research first targeted its direct customer, car stereo manufacturers. Specifically, two car stereo manufacturers, Alpine and Pioneer, were approached to learn their opinion on the value added by DAR technology. The product development managers from both firms stated that they were interested in seeing the results of the research and gave RadioNow invitations to demonstrate the technology.

To be successful, however, RadioNow will also have to convince automobile and car stereo manufacturers that consumers find value in, and would pay extra for, a system enhanced by digital audio recorder technology. RadioNow addressed this by administering a product survey that polled a random audience for their opinions of this technology. All other contacts in the founders' personal and business address books were selected to receive the survey. Of the

127 people who were solicited for input, 96 responded. The survey consisted of eight questions that gradually moved from questions about demographic data to questions related to learning the value of the technology to the consumer. This was done intentionally to minimize bias. SurveyMonkey was used to administer the survey online. The favorable results justified digital audio recorder technology as a compelling feature desired by consumers. A summary of the survey's findings follows.

- 71% of the respondents would listen more frequently to certain radio programs if they were in the car more often during the broadcast.
- 71% would like "TiVo-like" or "VCR-like" control over the radio.
- 93% would use the technology to skip commercials
- 83% would pay a premium to have RadioNow's technology as part of the car stereo.
- Participants under the age of 37 make up RadioNow's customer profile, with males slightly more likely to purchase a DAR-equipped stereo than females.

Distribution Channels

RadioNow will execute on a two-pronged, push-pull distribution strategy that targets both car stereo and automobile manufacturers. Sales efforts will primarily focus on approaching car stereo manufacturers and convincing them to enter into licensing agreements for the use and resale of RadioNow's technology. Additionally, auto makers will be engaged to help RadioNow understand the consumer desire for its technology and how this desire will translate into increased sales of premium audio packages to the manufacturers. The auto makers have the buyer power and, if sufficiently compelled by RadioNow's technology, can easily commission its stereo suppliers to produce a head unit equipped with digital audio recorder technology.[18]

The licensing model chosen by RadioNow minimizes capital outlay and financial risk and allows it to operate with low fixed and operating costs. On-Demand Audio, RadioNow's largest competitor, has chosen to vertically integrate and produce a complete car stereo head unit. This significantly increases the amount of capital required to fund their operation, it but opens the door to larger profits if there are substantial unit sales. Furthermore, RadioNow believes that consumers are less likely to switch to an unknown head unit brand, such as On-Demand Audio, that has DAR technology, than to a known brand, such as Alpine, that is equipped with DAR.

Entry Strategy

Backed by patents to protect its intellectual property, RadioNow will directly market to a niche market of car stereo and automobile manufacturers to gain customers in its target market. RadioNow will first pursue Toyota and Lexus in order to secure licensing agreements with their audio component partners, Panasonic, JBL, and Marc Levinson. The choice to go after Toyota and Lexus first was based on where the industry contacts were strongest. RadioNow will demonstrate to Toyota the value proposition of DAR technology and the ease with which the technology can be integrated into car stereos and, in turn, Toyota's automobiles.

Table 4—Pricing[19]

Company	Product	Price
Gotuit Audio	On-Demand Audio	NA
Griffin Technology	RadioSHARK	$69.99
Pogo Products!	Radio Your Way	$149.99
RadioNow	RadioNow Recorder	Licensing fee = $10 per unit sold

6

Product Analysis

Product Summary

DAR technology is the future of radio listening. It allows users to have complete control over their radio listening, enabling them to skip portions of broadcasts they do not like, pause the broadcast and play it later, and replay their favorite programs or songs.[20]

Product Description and Features

The digital audio recorder, developed by RadioNow, Inc., consists of a series of off-the-shelf components. These include a power supply, microprocessor, analog-to-digital converter, and non-volatile memory system (flash memory cards).[21] The DAR continuously records AM/FM radio signals from one or more broadcasts and stores them in the associated memory banks. The microprocessor then accesses the stored media according to user preferences. In effect, this system allows the on-demand playback of any radio station or signal at any time, giving the user VCR-like control over his or her radio.[22] Figures 1 and 2 of Appendix A depict the flow of audio traffic to a car stereo listener.

Technology Assessment

This technology showcases the convergence of mobile technologies with component interoperability.[23] Digital recording allows users to record programs from a live source to a storage medium for on-demand playback. A DAR is a device that converts a radio feed to a digital audio file that is then stored on a hard drive. Users interface with their catalog of recordings through software that has been written onto read-only memory, otherwise known as *firmware*.[24]

Many radio programs have set schedules and program times. For example, National Public Radio has a program called "Marketplace" that airs every day at 2:00 p.m.[25] This program is of interest to many listeners who normally would be at work during this time. With the DAR, listeners could very easily have the program automatically recorded and play it back on their way home from work.

An added benefit of the DAR is that it allows users to skip commercial breaks and programs or songs that are not of interest. The skip intervals will be such that they skip in "commercial" increments (60 seconds), "song" increments (2–3 minutes), or "program" increments (30 or 60 minutes). These skip options will be complemented by a general set of standard review options such as fast-forward, rewind, and pause.

Design and Prototyping Plan

Design of the DAR has been completed on a rudimentary level, and electrical engineers will begin work on an actual prototype starting in January 2005. Functional specifications will be completed first, and the subsequent timeline is included as Appendix E. A block diagram of the components and their interactions is included as Figure 1 of Appendix A. A simple design of the on-demand audio interface is provided as Figure 2 of Appendix A. A working prototype is expected to be completed by March 2005. The prototype will consist of an actual head unit equipped with DAR technology that can be displayed to potential customers.

RadioNow is currently seeking engineering consultants from the University of Southern California faculty to aid in the development process.

7

Timeline to Completion

Prototype completion is expected to occur in January of 2005. A complete timeline of product launch is provided in Appendix E.

Intellectual-Property Acquisition

The team has consulted with two patent attorneys, Marshall Lerner and Fin Simmensen of Kleinberg and Lerner, LP, an intellectual-property attorney firm. A provisional patent will be applied for, and existing patents will be researched further. Currently, the most notable patent, the Pause patent (RE 36,801), is being evaluated as a similar patent but with different premises of DAR.[26] The tray of memory banks concept developed by RadioNow significantly differentiates its technology from the technology described in the Pause patent. The team expects to apply for a full patent within one year of issuance of the provisional patent.[27]

The team will also explore the possibility of trademarking the name "RadioNow."

Founding Team

Qualifications

The team is highly qualified to pursue this project. Both Daniel Bohm and Samit Varma are attending the USC Marshall School of Business MBA program, where they have learned all aspects of business administration, including operations, finance, and marketing. Additionally, Daniel Bohm has worked in five successful start-up companies and has the management and experience to lead RadioNow, Inc. He also has a significant computer programming and research-and-development background that allows him to fully manage the development of a cost-effective and powerful microprocessor that controls all functions of the DAR. Daniel Bohm's résumé is included as Appendix C. Samit Varma has an extensive engineering background that includes electrical, mechanical, and nuclear. He has led and managed a 2 billion dollar nuclear submarine as the fifth most senior man and has since founded and managed a start-up technology company. Samit Varma's résumé is included as Appendix D.

Critical Task Assignments

Daniel Bohm will be responsible for marketing and business development. He has several contacts at Toyota USA and will be using them to get access to OEMs and others in the car stereo business. Samit Varma will be managing the product development as well as conducting business development. He teaches undergraduate engineering classes and will have access to USC staff and faculty to help develop the working prototype. Samit also has a contact at Alpine USA that has currently agreed to consider the DAR as an additional feature to their existing in dash components.

Gap Analysis

The team is actively seeking an electrical engineer to aid in the development of a working prototype. The team also has been consulting with Marshall Lerner, Esq. for intellectual-property issues.

8

Financial Plan

Financial Summary

Using sales assumptions and demand estimates obtained from primary market research, RadioNow will show positive cash flow in year 3. A cumulative cash balance of $706,600 will result at the end of year 3. EBIT for the first three years will be ($63,600), ($90,450) and $847,100, respectively. This is largely because the first sale is not made until year 2. Initial start-up capital required will be $150,000, which includes a $60,000 safety buffer. The break-even point will be 18 months after launch, in June of 2006, after 15,000 units have been sold. DAR will be introduced in a single model line first and then will gradually be adopted by other automobile lines.

The financial plan for RadioNow is predicated on several key points. First is that no new sales are expected to be made until January of 2006. Due to the nature of the industry, changes to premium sound packages will not be online until the 2007 model lines are available. With a prototype not ready until March, RadioNow estimates that it will be an additional six to nine months before the first sale can be finalized. The delay in the first sale adds significantly to the maximum negative cash balance, as shown in Appendix E. Next, the adoption of DAR technology is expected to mimic that of other, similar technologies. Typically, the introduction of a new technology, such as DAR, begins with one vehicle model and spreads to others if adoption is high or consumer reaction to the new technology is favorable. This phenomenon is modeled in the pro forma income statements shown in Appendix D.

Assumptions

Line Item
1. Units Sold—As an industry standard, royalties are charged on a per-unit basis, and therefore it is necessary to track total unit sales. The technology is to be adopted by one model line in the beginning, the Lexus SC430. This model was chosen because, based on consumer preferences, it has the highest likelihood of adopting DAR technology. To attain unit sales, RadioNow first took the total number of sales for the Lexus SC430 and multiplied it by 55%, which reflects the number of consumers who purchased the premium audio package.[28] This number was then allocated over the yearly cycle based on historical cyclicality consistent with the SC430 sales.[29] This first sale is predicted to occur in January of 2006. The next model line to adopt DAR is the Lexus GS300, which happens in the second quarter of 2006. Again the same methodology was used to calculate unit sales. RadioNow predicts that in January of 2007, the entire Lexus line, as well as a new Infiniti sports line, will have DAR included in their premium sound package. The number of Lexus premium audio packages sold equals the number of royalty payouts RadioNow will receive from Mark Levinson. Similarly, RadioNow will receive royalties from Bose based on the number of premium audio packages sold by Infiniti.
2. Total Units—A numerical summary of all unit sales from individual model lines.
3. Total Revenue—This was calculated by taking the total unit sales and multiplying it by the licensing fee charged by RadioNow of $10.00. $10.00 was arrived at by conducting a survey of end-users. 25% of the average car stereo price of $200 was

$50, which is $50 more than could be charged for the premium sound package. Industry standards allow a 20% margin for the licensing fee, which equals $10.00.

4. Patent—A numerical sum of line items 5 and 6.

5. Filing—Included in filing is all the time required to prepare the paperwork that needs to be filed with the USPTO. This is estimated to be $3000 a quarter, with an initial write-up fee of $5000. The $3000 covers continual amending and "tightening" of the patent. The filing fee increases to $5000 in January 2006, because this is when the actual patent file is submitted to replace the provisional patent, which only lasts one year.[30]

6. Legal—It has been determined that this industry is highly litigious among competitors including Tivo, Pause Technology, and iPod, as well as in other industries such as radio broadcasting, satellite radio, and others.[31] To provide RadioNow with security, an attorney will be retained. Estimated costs for the attorney include an initial charge of $10,000 as well as $2000 a month increasing by $2000 a month every year as the patents and technology get further developed.

7. Development—An initial charge of $15,000 is provided for building the first prototype of the technology. Thereafter, Research and Development is given as 20% of sales on a continuing basis.

8. Sales—A numerical sum of line items 9 and 10.

9. Travel—The travel expenses incurred by the founders will not be much because we are targeting Toyota, which is located in Torrance, and Alpine USA, which is also located in Torrance, CA. The travel budget is maintained at $1000 a month.

10. Commissions—Commissions are the only way that sales staff is compensated for the first three years. Commissions are therefore a hefty 15% of sales.

11. General and Administration - A numerical sum of line items 12, 13, and 14.

12. Equipment—$5000 at the beginning of every year, to include two computers for the founders/sales staff as well as office supplies.

13. Rent—No rent will be charged because the company plans to use home offices to begin with. In July 2005, as the prototype is completed and the sales effort increases, a 1000-square-foot office space will be leased for $2000 a month.

14. Utilities—This includes high-speed Internet access, phone bills, etc. This expense will be $200 a month for the home office and then jumps to $400 a month once the office space is leased.

Cash Needs Assessment and Break-Even Analysis

In order to start RadioNow, Inc., an initial investment of $150,000 will be needed. The highest negative cash balance will occur in year 2 at (90,000). To this a $60,000 safety factor is added. The safety factor is two-thirds of the maximum negative cash balance to provide a buffer to handle any unexpected additional legal costs that may arise in this highly litigious industry.

Monthly pro forma income statements for the first three years are provided as Appendix F, and the yearly cash flow statement until the time when cash flow is positive is provided as Appendix G.

10

In order to break even, the firm will need to overcome the initial investment of $150,000. RadioNow earns a 10% royalty on an average price of $100 ($10 per unit sold) and thus will need to sell 15,000 units to break even. This occurs in June of 2006.

Timeline to Launch

The complete timeline of activities leading up to RadioNow's launch is given in Appendix E. The company intends to begin aggressive sale of its digital audio recorder technology in August of 2006 after the prototype is complete.

Endnotes

1. Novak, Anthony (October 2004), Toyota Motor Sales. Product and Planning Division.
2. Lamm, Greg (June 25, 2004). Car Toys Sees After-market Electronics Demand Shrink. *Business Journal* from http://www.bizjournals.com/seattle/stories/2004/06/28/focus3.html?jst=s_rs_hl.
3. The 10% royalty rate was calculated based on standard industry margins in the car audio space as observed and reported to us by Toyota Motor Sales.
4. Macpherson, Sholto (August 31, 2004). *Hard-drive hi-fi.* Australian IT from http://australianit.news.com.au/articles/0,7204,10594483%5E15841%5E%5Enbv%5E,00.html.
5. Staff (2004). *The Basics of Factory-Installed Sound Systems.* MSN Autos from http://autos.msn.com/advice/article.aspx?contentid=4021174&src=News.
6. http://www.bts.gov/publications/national_transportation_statistics//2003/html/table_01_16.html.
7. Market size computation: Total number of new-car sales in 2003 was 8,103,000. Based on market research, the average number of new cars sold with premium sound packages was 30%, and the average price for a premium sound package was $500.00. Using the equation 8,103,000 * .30 * $500 yields a total market size of 1.2 billion.
8. Lamm, Greg (June 25, 2004). Car Toys Sees After-market Electronics Demand Shrink. *Business Journal* from http://www.bizjournals.com/seattle/stories/2004/06/28/focus3.html?jst=s_rs_hl.
9. Buckley, Patrick (10/28/2003). Market Getting Serious About Interfaces. *Car Audio Resources* from http://www.caraudioresources.com/content/audio_news/45/1.
10. Hallauer, Thomas (2004). Telematics Update from http://www.telematicsupdate.com/ces2005.
11. just-auto.com (11/19/2004). *USA: Significant Growth Predicted for MP3 Players and Satellite Radio.*
12. Apple (2004). Retrieved on 10/1/2004 from http://www.apple.com/ipod/bmw.
13. On-Demand Audio (2004). Retrieved on 11/05/2004 from http://www.gotuit.com/audio.
14. PogoProducts (2004). Retrieved on 10/7/2004 from http://www.pogoproducts.com/radio_yourway.html.
15. Griffin Technology (2004). Retrieved on 10/7/2004 from http://www.griffintechnology.com/products/radioshark.
16. Features matrix compiling using information from respective vendors' websites.
17. Toyota Motor Sales (October 15, 2004). Premium Audio Research.
18. Chan, Emily (2004). Toyota Motor Sales. 10/11/2004.
19. Prices, when available, were taken from respective vendors' websites.
20. Batista, Elisa (May 2003). A TiVo Player for the Radio. Wired News from http://www.wired.com/news.

21. Salkever, Alex (November 2004). The Word on the Next iPod: Flash. *Business Week Online,* Retrieved November 14, 2004 from http://www.macnewsworld .com/story/38051.html.

22. Buckley, Patrick (2003). Market Getting Serious About Interfaces. *Car Audio Resources.* Retrieved on September 28, 2004 from http://www.caraudioresources .com/content/audio_news/45/1/.

23. Memmer, Scott (n.d.). Retrieved on September 28, 2004, from, MSN News and Advice at http://autos.msn.com/advice/article.aspx?contentid=4021174&src=News.

24. Indiana University Knowledge Base (June 2004). Retrieved November 2, 2004, from http://kb.indiana.edu/data/ahtw.html?cust=4.

25. NPR schedule of programming (November 2004). Retrieved November 18, 2004, from http://www.npr.org/audiohelp/progstream.html.

26. Logan, James (1996). Time delayed digital video system using concurrent recording and playback. US patent number RE36,801 granted August 1, 2000.

27. United States Patent and Trademark Office (USPTO: October 2004). Provisional Patent Application received on November 6, 2004, from http://www.uspto.gov/ web/offices/pac/provapp.htm.

28. Novak, Anthony (October 2004). Toyota Motor Sales. Premium Audio Information ppt. October 14, 2004.

29. AutoFan (2004). New Toyota and Lexus Products Fuel Strong October Sales. Autofan.com Explorer of the auto world. Retrieved on November 3, 2003, from http://www.autofan.com/newsdetail.asp?id=807&mn=11&yr=2003.

30. United States Patent and Trademark Office (USPTO October 2004). Provisional Patent Application received on November 6, 2004, from http://www.uspto.gov/ web/offices/pac/provapp.htm.

31. Haley, Colin (October 4, 2001). Pause Sues TiVo Over Patent. Boston Internet.com, Retrieved on November 1, 2004, from http://boston.internet.com/ news/article.php/2001_897481.

Appendix A – Digital Audio Recorder Technology and Prototype

Figure 1. Digital Audio Recorder Schematic

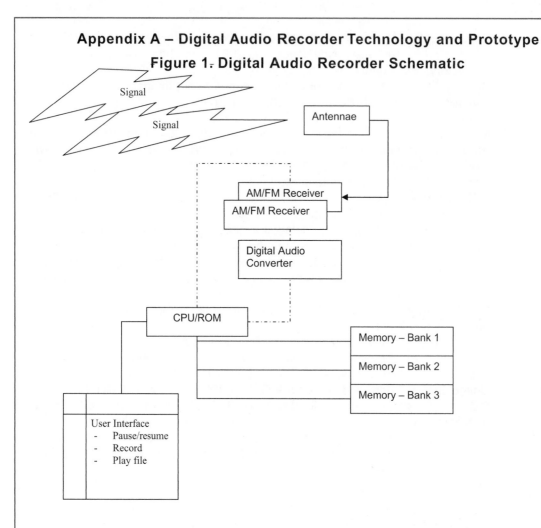

Figure 2. Prototype Car stereo head unit with Digital Audio Recorder

Appendix B—Questions Used in Customer Survey

What is your sex?

Male	36	37.50%
Female	60	62.50%

Are you older or younger than 37?

Older than 37	17	17.71%
Younger than 37	79	82.29%

Have you ever purchased an after-market car audio system?

Yes	42	44.21%
No	53	55.79%

If you have purchased an after-market car audio system, how much did you spend for the head unit only? (Do not include the cost of installation, speakers, or amplifiers.)

Does not apply	45	53.57%
< $99	1	1.19%
$100–$150	8	9.52%
$151–$200	11	13.10%
$201–$300	12	14.29%
> $301	7	8.33%

Are there radio programs (talk or morning shows, sporting event broadcasts, etc.) you would listen but often miss because you are not in the car while the program is broadcasted?

Yes	68	70.83%
No	28	29.17%

Would you like to have "TiVo-like" control over the radio?

Yes	67	70.53%
No	28	29.47%

If you had the ability to fast-forward or skip within a radio program, would you use this feature primarily to skip commercials?

Yes	89	92.71%
No	7	7.29%

Consider two car stereos that generally look and function the same except for the fact that one stereo has "Tivo-like" functionality (record, on-demand playback, skip/fast forward/rewind/pause) built into it. What is the most you would be willing to pay for the stereo equipped with Digital Audio Recorder technology?

I would not pay extra for this feature	16	17.39%
1%–10% extra	21	22.83%
11%–20% extra	34	36.96%
21%–30% extra	14	15.22%
31%– 50% extra	4	4.35%
more than 51% extra	3	3.26%

Appendix C—Résumé of Daniel Bohm

DANIEL BOHM

Experience

2003–Present   **FRONTBRIDGE TECHNOLOGIES**, Marina Del Rey, CA
Senior Sales Engineer
Lead sales engineer in all enterprise deals, providing expertise in message management, e-mail security, and regulation compliance.
- Closed 2-year, $1.5 million deal, the largest of 2004. Organized response to largest, most detailed RFP/RFQ in company's history.
- Grew sales of the VeriSign OEM partnership by $85K in monthly reoccurring revenue in 6 months, faster than any other channel.
- Lead product review and requirement meetings with customers.
- Host monthly training for sales team of 24 on industry trends and new product and service enhancements.

2002–2003   **WILTEL COMMUNICATIONS**, Tulsa, OK
Senior Manager, Project Management
Led the combined operations teams of 26 people after the iBeam acquisition to consolidate both WilTel and iBeam's products and services, saving $10 million annually.
- Managed key accounts during transition, such as BellSouth and MTV, and attained post-merger client retention goals by hosting technology review sessions for top 15 customers.
- Migrated iBeam's core web applications to the J2EE platform, adopting the Rational Unified Process for new software development efforts.
- Improved operational performance by increasing the number of metrics tracked from 12 to 63. Authored escalation, outage resolution, and disaster recovery documents.

1999–2002   **IBEAM BROADCASTING** (acquired by WilTel Communications—2001), Sunnyvale, CA
Director, Operations
Directed 22 people with a $3.2 million budget and led the team managing an $8 million infrastructure budget. Complete ownership of industry's largest content delivery network of over 200 servers and network devices, delivering 2.2 Gbps of data from 5 data centers.
- Led technology and network architecture discussions with WilTel, resulting in their decision to first invest in and, ultimately, acquire iBeam.
- Improved network reliability from 96% to 99.92%, exceeding the highest customer service level agreement by 0.2%, during 45% traffic increase and customer expansion.
- Spearheaded pre-sales and account management of large accounts, such as Viacom, NFL, and Sony.
- Introduced "Daily Dashboard" to deliver key operational metrics to executive staff.

Senior Manager, Network Administration
Managed an operations team of 10 to administer content delivery network.
- Decreased the number of escalations to engineering and empowering the team to handle 90% of all customer-affecting issues.

1997–1999   **INTERVU, INC.** (acquired by Akamai Technologies), San Diego, CA
Manager, Research and Development
Focused group of 7 on software development, QA, documentation, and deployment.
* Developed 5 new automation utilities, including the industry's first stream monitoring and Windows Media server administration software, based on Visual Basic, IIS, SQL, and ASP.

Senior Web Developer
Integrated client's web applications with Intervu's distributed content delivery network.

Education
2003–2005   **UNIVERSITY OF SOUTHERN CALIFORNIA, MARSHALL SCHOOL OF BUSINESS,** Los Angeles, CA
Master of Business Administration. Dean's list.

1992–1997   **UNIVERSITY OF CALIFORNIA, SAN DIEGO,** La Jolla, CA
Bachelor of Science in Cognitive Science. Minors in Psychology and Music. Dean's list.
Ski and Snowboard Club Officer of Recruitment.

Additional Information

Awards and Bonuses: Retention Bonus (WilTel), Transition Bonus (iBeam), Leadership Award (Intervu). Taught competitive swimming and water polo to 7th and 8th graders. Conversational Romanian and basic Spanish. Enjoy freshwater fishing, golf, surfing, and free-diving for lobsters.

Appendix D—Résumé of Samit Varma

SAMIT K. VARMA

EXPERIENCE

UNIVERSITY OF SOUTHERN CALIFORNIA	**Los Angeles, CA**
ASSISTANT PROFESSOR OF NAVAL SCIENCE/	**2003–Present**
RECRUITING OFFICER	

- Revamped and completely turned around the Nuclear Officer recruiting program. Exceeded goal by over 400% per year. 100% success rate in preparing new candidates for passing interviews.
- Negotiated and achieved several new incentives to aid in the recruitment of top Nuclear candidates.

LIEUTENANT, UNITED STATES NAVY	**Kings Bay, GA**
NUCLEAR SUBMARINE OFFICER	**2000–2003**
USS NEBRASKA SSBN-739	

Analysis and Process Improvement
- Identified, evaluated and corrected areas that needed improvement in the submarine's radiological controls program which allowed NEBRASKA to meet increasingly strict environmental requirements. This program was implemented as the model for the entire Atlantic Submarine Fleet.
- Redesigned shipboard firefighting plan, which increased efficiency of personnel and saved money in equipment maintenance and labor hours.

Leadership and Project Management
- Served as Assistant Engineer and supervised the operation of all mechanical, electrical, nuclear, and chemical activities of the S8G Pressurized Water Reactor Plant.
- Led 40-person cross-functional team in daily operation of $2.0 billion nuclear submarine.
- Directed a team of 25 technicians through an intense engineering overhaul and dry dock period to complete maintenance 10% ahead of schedule and in full compliance with strict Environmental Protection Agency guidelines. Performed flawlessly on EPA, unannounced, inspection.
- Made critical technical decisions under pressure as the 5th most senior man on board to ensure safety of ship and its 160 crewmembers.

AWARDS/CERTIFICATIONS
- Selected Junior Officer of the Year, 2002, from over two hundred officers based on excellent leadership, planning, management, initiative, personal moral and ethical standards, and attention to detail.
- Ranked #1 of 110 junior officers in Submarine Squadron Sixteen and #1 of 11 junior officers on USS NEBRASKA.
- Described by the Commanding Officer with over 20 years experience, as "the finest Junior Officer with whom I have ever served."
- Awarded three Navy Achievement Medals for technical and leadership excellence.
- Qualified Engineer Officer on Naval Nuclear Power Plants.

EDUCATION

UNIVERSITY OF SOUTHERN CALIFORNIA   **Los Angeles, CA**
Masters in Business Administration, Candidate, 3.74 GPA   **August 2003–Present**

NAVY NUCLEAR PROPULSION PROGRAM   **Charleston, SC**
Master of Science Equivalent, Nuclear Engineering 3.1 GPA   **January 2000**

UNITED STATES NAVAL ACADEMY   **Annapolis, MD**
Bachelor of Science, Mechanical Engineering 3.1 GPA   **May 1998**
- Graduated with Merit (top 15%)
- Innovative Senior Project on Drag Reduction researched by the Naval Warfare Research Center.

Appendix E – Timeline to Launch

	Jan	Feb	Mar	Apr	May	Jun	Jul	Aug
Feasibility Analysis	██							
Funding								
Prospect investors	██	██	██					
Negotiate terms of contract			░░					
Sign contract				░░				
Business Plan								
Research	██	██						
Data analysis		░░	░░					
Prepare and review			░░					
Execute business plan				██				
Incorporate RadioNow								
File incorporation application				██				
Operating agreement				░░				
Articles of incorporation				░░				
Establish Virtual Office								
Secure 800 number				██				
Route number to cell				░░				
Obtain PO box				░░				
Marketing Materials								
Create collateral				██	██			
Register domain name					░░			
Develop website					░░	░░	░░	
Prototype Development								
Functional specifications	██	██						
Hire engineers			░░					
Design specifications			░░					
Review specifications				██	██			
Develop prototype					░░	░░	░░	
Prototype QA						██	██	
Provisional Patent								
Circuit and timing diagrams		██						
Retain IP lawyer		░░						
File patent application			██					
	Jan	Feb	Mar	Apr	May	Jun	Jul	Aug

Appendix F—Income Statement, Monthly for 3 Years

INCOME STATEMENT—Monthly for 3 Years

Line Item	Month	Startup	Jan-05	Feb-05	Mar-05	Apr-05	May-05	Jun-05	Jul-05	Aug-05	Sep-05	Oct-05	Nov-05	Dec-05	Jan-06	Feb-06	Mar-06	Apr-06	May-06	Jun-06
Sales																				
1	Units Sold																			
	Lexus SC430														1100	400	2000	2000	3000	2000
	Lexus GS300 + SC430																	1000	500	4000
	Entire Lexus Line																			
	Infiniti Sports																			
2	Total Units		0	0	0	0	0	0	0	0	0	0	0	0	1100	400	2000	3000	3500	6000
3	Total Revenue	$0.00	$0.00	$0.00	$0.00	$0.00	$0.00	$0.00	$0.00	$0.00	$0.00	$0.00	$0.00	$0.00	$11,000.00	$4,000.00	$20,000.00	$30,000.00	$35,000.00	$60,000.00
Expenses																				
4	Patent	$15,000.00	$5,000.00	$2,000.00	$2,000.00	$5,000.00	$2,000.00	$2,000.00	$5,000.00	$2,000.00	$2,000.00	$5,000.00	$2,000.00	$2,000.00	$9,000.00	$5,000.00	$4,000.00	$4,000.00	$4,000.00	$4,000.00
5	filing	$5,000.00	$3,000.00	$0.00	$0.00	$3,000.00	$0.00	$0.00	$3,000.00	$0.00	$0.00	$3,000.00	$0.00	$0.00	$5,000.00	$800.00	$4,000.00	$6,000.00	$7,000.00	$12,000.00
6	legal	$10,000.00	$2,000.00	$2,000.00	$2,000.00	$2,000.00	$2,000.00	$2,000.00	$2,000.00	$2,000.00	$2,000.00	$2,000.00	$2,000.00	$2,000.00	$4,000.00	$1,000.00	$4,000.00	$5,500.00	$6,250.00	$10,000.00
7	Development	$15,000.00	$1,000.00	$1,000.00	$1,000.00	$1,000.00	$1,000.00	$1,000.00	$1,000.00	$1,000.00	$1,000.00	$1,000.00	$1,000.00	$1,000.00	$1,000.00	$1,000.00	$1,000.00	$1,000.00	$1,000.00	$1,000.00
8	Sales	$3,000.00	$1,000.00	$1,000.00	$1,000.00	$1,000.00	$1,000.00	$1,000.00	$1,000.00	$1,000.00	$1,000.00	$1,000.00	$1,000.00	$1,000.00	$1,650.00	$600.00	$2,500.00	$4,500.00	$5,250.00	$9,000.00
9	Travel	$3,000.00	$0.00	$0.00	$0.00	$0.00	$0.00	$0.00	$0.00	$0.00	$0.00	$0.00	$0.00	$0.00	$7,500.00	$2,500.00	$2,500.00	$2,500.00	$3,000.00	$2,500.00
10	Commissions	$5,400.00	$200.00	$200.00	$200.00	$200.00	$200.00	$200.00	$2,400.00	$2,400.00	$2,400.00	$2,400.00	$2,400.00	$2,400.00	$5,000.00	$5,000.00	$2,000.00	$2,000.00	$2,000.00	$2,500.00
11	General and Admin	$5,000.00	$0.00	$0.00	$0.00	$0.00	$0.00	$0.00	$0.00	$0.00	$0.00	$0.00	$0.00	$0.00	$5,000.00				$2,000.00	$2,000.00
12	Equipment	$0.00	$200.00	$200.00	$200.00	$200.00	$200.00	$200.00	$400.00	$400.00	$400.00	$400.00	$400.00	$400.00	$2,000.00	$2,000.00	$2,000.00	$2,000.00	$2,000.00	$2,000.00
13	Plant	$0.00																		
14	Utilities	$200.00	$200.00	$200.00	$200.00	$200.00	$200.00	$200.00	$400.00	$400.00	$400.00	$400.00	$400.00	$400.00	$500.00	$500.00	$500.00	$500.00	$500.00	$500.00
	Startup Cost	$38,400.00																		
	Net Income Before Tax	$38,400.00	$6,200.00	$3,200.00	$3,200.00	$6,200.00	$3,200.00	$3,200.00	$8,400.00	$5,400.00	$5,400.00	$8,400.00	$5,400.00	$5,400.00	$10,350.00	$4,900.00	$5,500.00	$12,000.00	$15,250.00	$31,500.00
	Tax(40%)																$2,200.00	$4,800.00	$6,100.00	$12,600.00
	Net Income After Tax	$38,400.00	$6,200.00	$3,200.00	$3,200.00	$6,200.00	$3,200.00	$3,200.00	$8,400.00	$5,400.00	$5,400.00	$8,400.00	$5,400.00	$5,400.00	$10,350.00	$4,900.00	$3,300.00	$7,200.00	$9,150.00	$18,900.00

Note: These details can be viewed on the student website at http://college.hmco.business/allen/launching/4e/students.

Appendix F – Income Statement, Monthly for 3 Years (Continued)

	Jul-06	Aug-06	Sep-06	Oct-06	Nov-06	Dec-06	Jan-07	Feb-07	Mar-07	Apr-07	May-07	Jun-07	Jul-07	Aug-07	Sep-07	Oct-07	Nov-07	Dec-07
	1000	1100	1100	1000	500	500	8000	8000	7000	12000	12000	13000	10000	10000	10000	10000	10000	10000
	2000	2000	1500	1000	800	800	2000	1400	2300	1700	3000	2400	3100	3100	3500	2400	2200	2300
	3000	3100	2600	2000	1300	1300	10000	9400	9300	13700	15000	15400	13100	13100	13500	12400	12200	12300
	$30,000.00	$31,000.00	$26,000.00	$20,000.00	$13,000.00	$13,000.00	$100,000.00	$94,000.00	$93,000.00	$137,000.00	$150,000.00	$154,000.00	$131,000.00	$131,000.00	$135,000.00	$124,000.00	$122,000.00	$123,000.00
	$4,000.00	$4,000.00	$4,000.00	$4,000.00	$4,000.00	$4,000.00	$11,000.00	$6,000.00	$6,000.00	$6,000.00	$6,000.00	$6,000.00	$6,000.00	$6,000.00	$6,000.00	$6,000.00	$6,000.00	$6,000.00
							$5,000.00											
	$4,000.00	$4,000.00	$4,000.00	$4,000.00	$4,000.00	$4,000.00	$6,000.00	$6,000.00	$6,000.00	$6,000.00	$6,000.00	$6,000.00	$6,000.00	$6,000.00	$6,000.00	$6,000.00	$6,000.00	$6,000.00
	$6,000.00	$6,200.00	$5,200.00	$4,000.00	$2,600.00	$2,600.00	$20,000.00	$18,800.00	$18,600.00	$27,400.00	$30,000.00	$30,800.00	$26,200.00	$26,200.00	$27,000.00	$24,800.00	$24,400.00	$24,600.00
	$5,500.00	$5,650.00	$4,900.00	$2,950.00	$2,950.00	$2,950.00	$16,000.00	$15,100.00	$14,950.00	$21,550.00	$23,500.00	$24,100.00	$20,650.00	$20,650.00	$21,250.00	$19,600.00	$19,300.00	$19,450.00
	$1,000.00	$1,000.00	$1,000.00	$1,000.00	$1,000.00	$1,000.00	$1,000.00	$1,000.00	$1,000.00	$1,000.00	$1,000.00	$1,000.00	$1,000.00	$1,000.00	$1,000.00	$1,000.00	$1,000.00	$1,000.00
	$4,500.00	$4,650.00	$3,900.00	$3,000.00	$1,950.00	$1,950.00	$15,000.00	$14,100.00	$13,950.00	$20,550.00	$22,500.00	$23,100.00	$19,650.00	$19,650.00	$20,250.00	$18,600.00	$18,300.00	$18,450.00
	$2,500.00	$2,500.00	$2,500.00	$2,500.00	$2,500.00	$2,500.00	$7,500.00	$2,500.00	$2,500.00	$2,500.00	$2,500.00	$2,500.00	$2,500.00	$2,500.00	$2,500.00	$2,500.00	$2,500.00	$2,500.00
							$5,000.00											
	$2,000.00	$2,000.00	$2,000.00	$2,000.00	$2,000.00	$2,000.00	$2,000.00	$2,000.00	$2,000.00	$2,000.00	$2,000.00	$2,000.00	$2,000.00	$2,000.00	$2,000.00	$2,000.00	$2,000.00	$2,000.00
	$500.00	$500.00	$500.00	$500.00	$500.00	$500.00	$500.00	$500.00	$500.00	$500.00	$500.00	$500.00	$500.00	$500.00	$500.00	$500.00	$500.00	$500.00
	$12,000.00	$12,650.00	$9,400.00	$5,500.00	$950.00	$950.00	$45,500.00	$51,600.00	$50,950.00	$79,550.00	$88,000.00	$90,600.00	$75,650.00	$75,650.00	$78,250.00	$71,100.00	$69,800.00	$70,450.00
	$4,800.00	$5,060.00	$3,760.00	$2,200.00	$380.00	$380.00	$18,200.00	$20,640.00	$20,380.00	$31,820.00	$35,200.00	$36,240.00	$30,260.00	$30,260.00	$31,300.00	$28,440.00	$27,920.00	$28,180.00
	$7,200.00	$7,590.00	$5,640.00	$3,300.00	$570.00	$570.00	$27,300.00	$30,960.00	$30,570.00	$47,730.00	$52,800.00	$54,360.00	$45,390.00	$45,390.00	$46,950.00	$42,660.00	$41,880.00	$42,270.00
							$847,100.00											

Note: These details can be viewed on the student website at http://college.hmco.business/allen/launching/4e/students.

Appendix G – Cash Flow Statement, Year 1 to Positive Cash Flow

Year Number	0	1	2	3
Operating Cash Inflows				
Sales	0	0	293000	1494000
AR	0	0	73250	373500
Operating Cash Outflows				
G+A	400	15600	30000	30000
Sales	3000	$12,000	$55,950	$236,100
Patent Fees	15000	$24,000	$48,000	$72,000
Discretionary Outflows				
R and D	15000	$0	$58,600	$3,000
Equipment	5000	$0	$5,000	$5,000
Total Cash Outflows	38400	51600	197550	346100
Total Cash Inflows	0	0	219750	1120500
Net Change in Cash	−38400	−51600	22200	774400
Cumulative Cash Balance	−38400	−90000	−67800	706600

Notes

Chapter 1

1. Lumpkin, G.T., and G.G. Dess (1996). "Clarifying the Entrepreneurial Orientation Construct and Linking It to Performance." *Academy of Management Review,* 21(1): 135.
2. Schumpeter, J. (1934). *The Theory of Economic Development.* Cambridge, MA: Harvard University Press; Solow, R.M. (2000). *Growth Theory: An Exposition.* New York: Oxford University Press; and Grossman, G.M. & E. Helpman (1994). "Endogenous Innovation in the Theory of Growth." *Journal of Economic Perspectives,* 8(1): 23–44.
3. Romer, Paul (1986). "Increasing Returns and Long-Run Growth." *Journal of Political Economy,* 94: 1002–1037.
4. Allen, K.R. (2003). *Bringing New Technology to Market.* Upper Saddle River, NJ: Prentice-Hall.
5. Gongloff, Mark (2002). "U.S. Productivity Soars." *CNNMoney,* May 7.
6. Thesmar, D., and M. Thoenig (2000). "Creative Destruction and Firm Organization Choice." *Quarterly Journal of Economics,* 115(4): 1201–1237; and Thomis, M. (1993). *The Luddites: Machine-Breaking in Regency England.* Hampshire, England: Ashgate Publishing.
7. Caballero, R., and M. Hammour (2000). "Creative Destruction and Development: Institutions, Crises, and Restructuring." Paper presented at the Annual World Bank Conference on Development Economics, Washington, DC.
8. *The Economist* (2002). "Self-Doomed to Failure," 6 July: 24–26.
9. Jovanovic, B., and G. MacDonald (1994). "The Life-Cycle of a Competitive Industry." *Journal of Political Economy,* 102(2): 322–347.
10. U.S. Bureau of the Census; Advocacy-funded research by Joel Popkin and Company (Research Summary #211); Federal Procurement Data System; Advocacy-funded research by CHI Research, Inc. (Research Summary #225); Bureau of Labor Statistics, Current Population Survey; and U.S. Department of Commerce, International Trade Administration (2003).
11. U.S. Bureau of the Census; Administrative Office of the U.S. Courts; *Endogenous Growth and Entrepreneurial Activities.*
12. Reynolds, P.D. (1995). "Family Firms in the Start-up Process: Preliminary Explorations." Paper presented at the 1995 annual meetings of the International Family Business Program Association, Nashville, Tennessee, July.
13. Shane, S., and S. Venkataraman (2000). "The Promise of Entrepreneurship as a Field of Research." *The Academy of Management Review,* 25(1): 217–226; and Begley, T., and D. Boyd (1987). "Psychological Characteristics Associated with Performance in Entrepreneurial Firms and Smaller Businesses." *Journal of Business Venturing,* 2: 79–93.
14. Bhave, M.P. (1994). "A Process Model of Entrepreneurial Venture Creation." *Journal of Business Venturing,* 9: 223–242; and Reynolds, P.D., and B. Miller (1992). "New Firm Gestation: Conception, Birth, and Implications for Research." *Journal of Business Venturing,* 7: 405–417.
15. Block, Z., and I.C. MacMillan (1985). "Milestones for Successful Venture Planning." *Harvard Business Review,* 85(5): 184–188.
16. Carter, N., W.B. Gartner, and P.D. Reynolds (1996). "Exploring Start-up Events Sequences." *Journal of Business Venturing,* 11: 151–166.
17. Donald G. Reinertsen (1999). "Taking the Fuzziness Out of the Fuzzy Front End." *Industrial Research Institute, Inc.* (November/December): 25–31.
18. Birley, S., and P. Westhead (1993). "A Comparison of New Businesses Established by Novice and Habitual Founders in Great Britain." *International Small Business Journal,* 12(1): 38–60.
19. Small Business Administration (2004). "Small Business Economic Indicators for 2003." *Small Business Administration, Office of Advocacy,* www.sba.gov.
20. Small Business Administration (1999). "Small Business Economic Indicators for 1999." *Small Business Administration,* Office of Advocacy, www.sba.gov.
21. *Factors Leading to Surviving and Closing Successfully* by Brian Headd, Center for Economic Studies, U.S. Bureau of the Census, Working Paper #CES-WP-01–01, January 2001; Advocacy-funded research by Richard J. Boden (Research Summary #204).
22. Ibid. Provided by U.S. Department of Labor, Bureau of Statistics.
23. Lynch, M., and K. Post (1996). "What Glass Ceiling?" *Public Interest,* 27–36.
24. "Women in Business," www.sba.gov/advo.
25. Neck, H., A.L. Zacharakis, W. Bygrave, and P. Reynolds (Eds.) (2002). *Global Entrepreneurship Monitor 2002 Executive Report,* p. 14.
26. Buttner, H.E., and D.P. Moore (January1997). "Women's Organizational Exodus to Entrepreneurship: Self-Reported Motivations and Correlates with Success." *Journal of Small Business Management,* 34–36.
27. *2000 Statistical Abstract of the United States.* Washington, DC: U.S. Department of Commerce, Bureau of the Census. www.census.gov/cds/mwb.

28. Center for Women's Business Research. "Top Facts," www.nfwbo.org/topfacts.html, accessed September 2004.

29. Advocacy publications—Women in Business, 2001; Dynamics of Women-Operated Sole Proprietorships, 1990–1998; Minorities in Business, 2001; veteran self-employment data from a special tabulation of the Current Population Survey.

30. Carlson, E. (1992). "Battling Bias." *Wall Street Journal* (April 3): R1.

31. Pitta, J. (1998). "Silicon Valley South." *Forbes* (November 16): 214–216.

32. "Minority Vintners Call Attention to Growth Market." (August 15, 2003). HispanicBusiness.com.

33. Brockhaus, R.H. (1980). "Risk-taking Propensity of Entrepreneurs." *Academy of Management Journal*, 23: 509–520; and Drucker, P.F. (1985). *Innovation and Entrepreneurship*. New York: Harper & Row.

34. McClelland, D.C. (1965). "N-Achievement and Entrepreneurship: A Longitudinal Study." *Journal of Personality and Social Psychology*, 1: 389–392.

35. Teal, E.J., and A.B. Carroll (1999). "Moral Reasoning Skills: Are Entrepreneurs Different?" *Journal of Business Ethics*, 19(3): 229–240.

36. Lumpkin and Dess, 1996.

37. Greenberger, D.B., and D.L. Sexton (1988). "An Interactive Model of New Venture Initiation." *Journal of Small Business Management*, 1–7; Brockhaus, R., and P. Horowitz (1986). "The Psychology of the Entrepreneur." In *The Art and Science of Entrepreneurship*, ed. D. Sexton and R. Smilor. Cambridge, MA: Ballinger.

38. Begley, T., and D. Boyd (1987). "Psychological Characteristics Associated with Performance in Entrepreneurial Firms and Smaller Businesses." *Journal of Business Venturing*, 2: 79–93.

39. Shane, S., and S. Venkataraman. (2000). "The Promise of Entrepreneurship as a Field of Research." *Academy of Management Review*, 25(1): 217–226; and Begley, T., and D. Boyd (1987). "Psychological Characteristics Associated with Performance in Entrepreneurial Firms and Smaller Businesses." *Journal of Business Venturing*, 2: 79–93.

40. Gartner, W.B. (1988). "Who Is an Entrepreneur Is the Wrong Question." *American Journal of Small Business*, 11–31.

41. Gartner, W.B., and C.B. Brush (1997). "Entrepreneurship: Emergence, Newness, and Transformation." Paper presented at the Academy of Management Entrepreneurship Division Doctoral Consortium, Boston, August.

42. Hofman, M. (September 2002). "The Bad Boy." *Inc. Magazine*, www.inc.com.

43. American Association of Home-Based Businesses, www.jbsba.com/, accessed September 2004.

44. Buchanan, L. (December 2002). "The Absolutist." *Inc. Magazine*, www.inc.com.

45. Buchanan, L. (December 2002). "A Sharper Image." *Inc. Magazine*, www.inc.com, http://www.premiumknives.com.

46. Gross, N., P.C. Judge, O. Port, and S.H. Wildstrom (1998). "Let's Talk: Speech Technology Is the Next Big Thing in Computing." *BusinessWeek* (February 23): 61–80. www.businessweek.com.

47. Op.cit., Shane and Venkataraman (2000).

48. Cohen, W., and R. Levin (1989). "Empirical Studies of Innovation and Market Structure." In *Handbook of Industrial Organization, II*, ed. R. Schmalensee and R. Willig. New York: Elsevier.

49. Case, J. (1992). *From the Ground Up*. New York: Belknap Press, p. 44.

50. Ibid., 46.

51. Ibid., 64.

52. Gupta, U. (1989). "Small Firms Aren't Waiting to Grow Up to Go Global." *Wall Street Journal*, (December 5): B2.

53. McDougall, P.O., S. Shane, and B.M. Oviatt (1994). "Explaining the Formation of International New Ventures: The Limits of Theories from International Business Research." *Journal of Business Venturing*, 9: 469–487.

54. Reuber, A.R., and E. Fischer (1997). "The Influence of the Management Team's International Experience on the Internationalization Behaviors of SMEs." *Journal of International Business Studies*, 28: 807–825.

55. Drucker, P.F. (1993). *Innovation and Entrepreneurship*. New York: HarperBusiness.

56. Finkle, T.A., and D. Deeds (2001). "Trends in the Market for Entrepreneurship Faculty During the Period 1989–1998." *Journal of Business Venturing*, 16(6): 613.

57. Ibid.

58. Venkataraman, S. (1997). "The Distinctive Domain of Entrepreneurship Research: An Editor's Perspective." In *Advances in Entrepreneurship, Firm Emergence, and Growth*, ed. J. Katz and R. Brockhaus. Greenwich, CT: JAI Press.

59. Op. cit., Shane and Venkataraman (2000).

60. Amit, R., L. Glosten, and E. Muller (1993). "Challenges to Theory Development in Entrepreneurship Research." *Journal of Management Studies*, 30(5): 815–834.

61. Kirzner, I. (1997). "Entrepreneurial Discovery and the Competitive Market Process: An Austrian Approach." *Journal of Economic Literature*, 35(1): 60–85.

62. Kaish, S., and B. Gilad (1991). "Characteristics of Opportunities Search of Entrepreneurs versus Executives: Sources, Interests, and General Alertness." *Journal of Business Venturing*, 6: 45–61.

63. Baumol, W. (1993). "Formal Entrepreneurship Theory in Economics: Existence and Bounds." *Journal of Business Venturing*, 8: 197–210.

64. Kirzner, I. (1978). *Competition and Entrepreneurship*. Chicago: University of Chicago Press.

65. Evans, D., and L. Leighton (1989). "Some Empirical Aspects of Entrepreneurship." *American Economic Review*, 79(3): 519–535; and Aldrich, H., and C. Zimmer (1986). "Entrepreneurship Through Social Networks." In *The Art and Science of Entrepreneurship*, ed. D. Sexton and R. Smilor. Cambridge, MA: Ballinger.

66. Cooper, A., C. Woo, and W. Dunkelberg (1989). "Entrepreneurship and the Initial Size of Firms." *Journal of Business Venturing*, 4: 317–332; and Carrol, G., and E. Mosakowski (1987). "The Career Dynamics of Self-Employment." *Administrative Science Quarterly*, 32(4): 570–589.

67. Khaneman, D., and D. Lovallo (1994). "Timid Choices and Bold Forecasts: A Cognitive Perspective on Risk Taking." In *Fundamental Issues in Strategy: A Research Agenda,* ed. R.P. Rumelt, D.E. Schendel, and D. Teece. Boston: Harvard Business School Press, pp. 71–96.

68. Busenitz, L.W., and J.B. Barney (1997). "Differences Between Entrepreneurs and Managers in Large Organizations: Biases and Heuristics in Strategic Decision-Making." *Journal of Business Venturing,* 12(1): 9–30.

69. Aldrich, H., and C. Zimmer (1986). Entrepreneurship Through Social Networks." In *The Art and Science of Entrepreneurship,* ed. D.L. Sexton and R.W. Smilor. Cambridge, MA: Ballinger.

70. Granovetter, M. (1982). "The Strength of Weak Ties: A Network Theory Revisited." In *Social Structure and Network Analysis,* ed. P.V. Marsden and N. Lin. Beverly Hills, CA: Sage.

71. Fisher, D., and S. Vilas (2000). *Power Networking: 59 Secrets for Personal and Professional Success.* Marietta, GA: Bard Press.

Chapter 2

1. Matthews, J. and J. Dennis, with P. Economy (2003). *Lessons from the Edge.* New York: Oxford University Press.

2. Eng, S. (July 10, 2001). "Impress Investors with Your Firm's Endgame." *Wall Street Journal Startup Journal,* www.startupjournal.com.

3. Barker, E. (July 2000). "Rambling for Gems." *Inc. Magazine,* www.inc.com.

4. Breeden, R. (2002). "Older Can Be Better for Small Businesses." *Wall Street Journal Startup Journal,* www.startupjournal.com.

5. Miller, K.D. (1992). "A Framework for Integrated Risk Management in International Business." *Journal of International Business Studies,* 23: 311–331.

6. Leavy, B. (2003). "Understanding the Triad of Great Leadership—Context, Conviction and Credibility." *Strategy & Leadership,* 31(1): 56–61.

7. Hopkins, M.S. (June 2003). "Why Leadership Is the Most Dangerous Idea in American Business." *Inc. Magazine,* www.inc.com.

8. Barnett, William P., Henrich R. Greve, and Douglas Y. Park (1994). "An Evolutionary Model of Organizational Performance." *Strategic Management Journal,* 15 (Winter special issue): 11–28.

9. Baum, Joel A.C., and Christine Oliver (1991). "Institutional Linkages and Organizational Mortality." *Administrative Science Quarterly,* 36: 187–218.

Chapter 3

1. Gryskiewicz, S.S. (September 2000). "Cashing In on Creativity at Work." *Psychology Today,* www.findarticles.com.

2. Drazin, R.D. (1999). "Multilevel Theorizing About Creativity in Organizations: A Sensemaking Perspective." *Academy of Management Review,* 24(2): 286; Drazin, R. (1990). "Professionals and Innovation: Structural-Functional versus Radical-Structural Perspectives." *Journal of Management Studies,* 27(3): 245–263; and Amabile, T.M. (1988). "A Model of Creativity and Innovation in Organizations." In *Research in Organizational Behavior,* Vol. 10, ed. B.M. Staw and L.L. Cummings. Greenwich, CT: JAI Press, pp. 123–167.

3. Ibid. Drazin (1999); Woodman, R.W., J.E. Sawyer, and R.W. Griffin (1993). "Toward a Theory of Organizational Creativity." *Academy of Management Review,* 18(2): 293–321.

4. Singh, B. (1986). "Role of Personality versus Biographical Factors in Creativity." *Psychological Studies,* 31: 90–92; Barron, F., and D.M. Harrington (1981). "Creativity, Intelligence, and Personality." *Annual Review of Psychology,* 32: 439–476; and Gardner, H. (1993). *Frames of Mind.* New York: Basic Books.

5. Amabile, T.M. (1988). "A Model of Creativity and Innovation in Organizations." In *Research in Organizational Behavior,* Vol. 10, ed. B.M. Staw and L.L. Cummings. Greenwich, CT: JAI Press, pp. 123–167; Oldham, G.R., and A. Cummings (1996). "Employee Creativity: Personal and Contextual Factors at Work." *Academy of Management Journal,* 39: 607–634; Mumford, M.D., and S.B. Gustafson (1988). "Creativity Syndrome: Integration, Application, and Innovation." *Psychological Bulletin,* 103: 27–43; and Payne, R. (1990). "The Effectiveness of Research Teams: A Review." *In Innovation and Creativity at Work,* ed. M.A. West and J.L. Farr. Chichester, England: Wiley, pp. 101–122.

6. Woodman, R W., J.E. Sawyer, and R.W. Griffin (1993). "Toward a Theory of Organizational Creativity." *Academy of Management Review,* 18(2): 293–321.

7. Klein, K.J., F. Dansereau, and R.J. Hall (1994). "Levels Issues in Theory Development, Data Collection, and Analysis." *Academy of Management Review,* 19(2): 195–229.

8. Giddens, A. (1994). *Central Problems in Social Theory: Action, Structure and Contradiction in Social Analysis.* Berkeley, CA: University of California Press; Kazanjian, R.K. (1988). "Relation of Dominant Problems to Stages of Growth in Technology-based New Ventures." *Academy of Management Journal,* 31: 257–279; and Peterson, M.F. (1998). "Embedded Organizational Event: The Units of Process in Organizational Science." *Organization Science,* 9: 16–33.

9. Siler, T. (1999). *Think Like a Genius.* New York: Bantam Books.

10. Ibid.

11. Hills, G.E. (1985). "Market Analysis in the Business Plan: Venture Capitalists' Perceptions." *Journal of Small Business Management* (January): 38–46.

Chapter 4

1. Javers, E. (March 2003). "Case Study: Spy in the Sky." *Inc. Magazine,* www.inc.com.
2. Thanks to Dr. Gerald Loeb, Nicholas Sachs, Hilton Kaplan, and the rest of the BION team for providing this example.
3. Tucker, R.B. (2001). "Strategy Innovation Takes Imagination." *Journal of Business Strategy,* 22(3): 23–27.
4. Magretta, J. (May 2002). "Why Business Models Matter." *Harvard Business Review,* 80(5): 86–92, 133.
5. Ibid.
6. Stuart, A. (December 2002). "This Year's Model." *Inc. Magazine,* www.inc.com.
7. Downes L., and C. Mui (1998). *Unleashing the Killer App.* Boston: Harvard Business School Press.
8. Rayport, J.F., and J.J. Sviokla (1994). "Managing in the Market-space." *Harvard Business Review* (Nov.-Dec.): 141–150.
9. Slywotzky, A.J. (1996). *Value Migration.* Boston: Harvard Business School Press.
10. Munson, C.L., M.J. Rosenblatt, and Z. Rosenblatt (1999). "The Use and Abuse of Power in Supply Chains." *Business Horizons* (Jan.-Feb.), www.findarticles.com.
11. Stern, L.W., and A.I. El-Ansary (1996). *Marketing Channels.* 5th ed. Englewood Cliffs, NJ: Prentice-Hall.

Chapter 5

1. Starbuck, W.H. (1992). "Organizations and Their Environments." In *Handbook of Industrial and Organization Psychology,* ed. M.D. Dunnette. Palo Alto, CA: Consulting Psychologists Press; and Pfeffer, J., and G.R. Salancik (2003). *The External Control of Organizations.* Stanford, CA: Stanford University Press.
2. Porter, M.E. (1980). *Competitive Strategy: Techniques for Analyzing Industries and Competitors.* New York: Free Press, p. 3.
3. Dees, J.G., J. Emerson, and P. Economy (2001). *Enterprising Nonprofits.* New York: Wiley.
4. Hall, J.A. (1991). *Bringing New Products to Market.* New York: AMACOM.
5. Gray, R. (2000). "The Relentless Rise of Online Research." *Marketing* (May 18).
6. Capell, P. "Five Owners Describe How They Got Started." *Wall Street Journal Startup Journal.* www.startupjournal.com, accessed September 2004.

Chapter 6

1. Pine II, B.J. (1993). *Mass Customization.* Boston: Harvard Business School Press.
2. von Braun, C. (1990). "The Acceleration Trap." *Sloan Management Review,* 32(1): 49.

3. Wolff, M.F. (2003). "Innovation Is Top Priority Again." *Research Technology Management,* 46(4): 7.
4. Cooper, R.G., and S.J. Edgett (2003). "Overcoming the Crunch in Resources for New Product Development." *Research Technology Management,* 46(3): 48.
5. Cooper, R.G. (2001). *Winning at New Products: Accelerating the Process from Idea to Launch.* 3d ed. Boston: Perseus Publishing.
6. Crawford, C.M. (1992). "The Hidden Costs of Accelerated Product Development." *Journal of Product Innovation Management,* 9(3):188–199.
7. Stevens, G.A. and J. Burley (2003). "Piloting the Rocket of Radical Innovation." *Research Technology Management,* 46(2): 16–26.
8. Ibid.
9. Quinn, J.B. (2000). "Outsourcing Innovation: The New Engine of Growth." *Sloan Management Review,* 41(4): 13–29.
10. *Diamond v. Chakrabarty,* 447 U.S. 303 (1980).
11. "Qualifying for a Patent." NOLO Law for All. www.nolo.com/encyclopedia/articles/pts/pct3.html #FAQ-294.
12. U.S. Patent and Trademark Office: Design Patents. www.uspto.gov/web/offices/pac/doc/general/design.html.
13. Bonisteel, S. (2001). "Bounty Hunters Get Bonus for Effort on Amazon Patent." *Newsbytes* (March 14).
14. *State Street Bank & Trust v. Signature Financial Group Inc.,* 149 F.3d 1368, 47 USPQ2d 1596 (Fed. Cir. 1998).
15. Love, J.J., and W.W. Coggins (2001). "Successfully Preparing and Prosecuting a Business Method Patent Application." Presented at AIPLA, Spring 2001, www.uspto.gov/web/menu/pbmethod/aiplapaper.rtf.
16. U.S. Patent and Trademark Office: Disclosure Document Program, www.uspto.gov/web/offices/com/pac/disdo.html, accessed September 2004.
17. U.S. Patent and Trademark Office, www.uspto.gov/web/offices/pac/disdo.html.
18. Ibid.
19. Oddi, A.S. (1996). "Un-unified Economic Theories of Patents: The Not-Quite-Holy Grail." *Notre Dame Law Review,* 71: 267–327.
20. Trademark Act of 1946, 15 U.S.C. § 1127.
21. Brown, J.D., and J.E. Prescott (2000). "Product of the Mind: Assessment and Protection of Intellectual Property." *Competitive Intelligence Review,* 11(3): 60.
22. *Whelan v. Jaslow,* 797 F.2d 1222; 21 Fed. R. Evid. Serv. (Callaghan) 571: U.S. Court of Appeals for the Third Circuit (1986).

Chapter 7

1. Gartner, W.B., K.G. Shaver, E. Gatewood, and J.A. Katz (1994). "Finding the Entrepreneur in Entrepreneurship." *Entrepreneurship: Theory and Practice,* 18(3): 5–10.

2. Van de Ven, A.H., R. Hudson, and D.M. Schroeder (1984). "Designing New Business Start-ups." *Journal of Management*, 10(1): 87–108.

3. Ruef, M. (2002). "Strong Ties, Weak Ties, and Islands: Structural and Cultural Predictors of Organizational Innovation." *Industrial and Corporate Change*, 11: 427–429.

4. Bird, B.J. (1989). *Entrepreneurial Behavior.* Glenview, IL: Scott, Foresman; and Kamm, J.B., J.C. Shuman, J.A. Seeger, and A.J. Nurick (1990). "Entrepreneurial Teams in New Venture Creation: A Research Agenda." *Entrepreneurship Theory and Practice*, 14(4): 7–17.

5. Ensley, M.D., J.W. Carland, and J.C. Carland (2000). "Investigating the Existence of the Lead Entrepreneur." *Journal of Small Business Management*, 38(4): 59–88.

6. Aldrich, H., and C. Zimmer (1986). "Entrepreneurship through Social Networks." In *The Art and Science of Entrepreneurship,* ed. D.L. Sexton and R.W. Smilor. Cambridge, MA: Ballinger, pp. 3–23.

7. Moss Kanter, R. (2001). "A More Perfect Union," *Inc. Magazine* (February): 93–98, www.inc.com.

8. Dubini, P., and H. Aldrich (1991). "Personal and Extended Networks Are Central to the Entrepreneurial Process." *Journal of Business Venturing*, 6(5): 305–313.

9. Ibid.

10. Roure, J.B., and M.A. Madique (1986). "Linking Prefunding Factors and High-Technology Venture Success: An Exploratory Study." *Journal of Business Venturing*, 1(3): 295–306.

11. Murray, A.I. (1989). "Top Management Group Heterogeneity and Firm Performance." *Strategic Management Journal*, 10: 125–141.

12. Kamm, J.B., J.C. Shuman, J.A. Seeger, and A.J. Nurick (1990). "Entrepreneurial Teams in New Venture Creation: A Research Agenda." *Entrepreneurship Theory and Practice*, 14(4), 7–17.

13. Eisenhardt, K., and C.B. Schoonhoven (1990). "Organizational Growth: Linking Founding Team, Strategy, Environment, and Growth Among U.S. Semiconductor Ventures, 1978–1988." *Administrative Science Quarterly*, 35: 504–529.

14. Ancona, D. and D. Caldwell (1992). "Demography and Design: Predictors of New Product Team Performance." *Organization Science*, 3: 321–341.

15. Aldrich, H.E., A. Elam, and P.R. Reese (1996). "Strong Ties, Weak Ties, and Strangers: Do Women Business Owners Differ from Men in Their Use of Networking to Obtain Assistance?" In *Entrepreneurship in a Global Context*, ed. S. Birley and I. MacMillan. London: Routledge, pp. 1–25.

16. Carroll, G., and M. Hannan (2000). *The Demography of Corporations and Industries*. Princeton, NJ: Princeton University Press.

17. Blau, P. (1980). "A Fable About Social Structure." *Social Forces*, 58: 777–788.

18. Anonymous (2002). "Making Virtual Collaborations Work." *Research Technology Management*, 45(2): 6–7.

19. Gersick, C.J.G., and Hackman, J.R. (1990). "Habitual Routines in Task-Performing Groups." *Organizational Behavior and Human Decision Processes*, 47: 65–97.

20. Kozlowski, S.W.J., S.M. Gully, P.P. McHugh, E. Salas, and J.A. Cannon-Bowers (1996). "A Dynamic Theory of Leadership and Team Effectiveness: Developmental and Task Contingent Leader Roles." In *Research in Personnel and Human Resource Management*, ed. G.R. Ferris. Greenwich, CT: JAI, pp. 253–305.

21. McDougall, P., S. Shane, and B. Oviatt (1994). "Explaining the Formation of International New Ventures: The Limits of Theories from International Business Research." *Journal of Business Venturing*, 9 (November): 469–487.

22. Oviatt, B., and P. McDougall (1994). "Toward a Theory of International New Ventures." *Journal of International Business Studies*, 25(1): 45–64.

23. Miesenbock, K.J. (1988). "Small Business and Exporting: A Literature Review." *International Small Business Journal*, 6(2): 42–61.

24. Eisenhardt, K. M. and C.B. Schoonhoven (1996). "Resource-based View of Strategic Alliance Formation: Strategic and Social Effects in Entrepreneurial Firms." *Organization Science*, 7(2): 136–150.

25. Kidwell, R.E., and N. Bennett (1993). "Employee Propensity to Withhold Effort: A Conceptual Model to Intersect Three Avenues of Research." *Academy of Management Review*, 18(3): 429–456.

26. Goodstein, J., K. Gautam, and W. Boeker (1994). "The Effects of Board Size and Diversity on Strategic Change." *Strategic Management Journal*, 15(3): 241–250.

27. Jonovic, D.J. "Professionalizing: The Key to Long-Term Shareholder Value, Part 1." Baylor University. http://hsb.baylor.edu/html/cel/ifb/legacies/jonovic.htm.

28. Ibid.

29. Lawton, J. (2000). "Mentors for Life." EntreWorld. www.entreworld.org.

30. Michael F. Corbett & Associates (1999). *The 1999 Outsourcing Trends Report*. New York: Michael F. Corbett & Associates Ltd. The company surveyed the opinions of U.S. private- and public-sector executives and industry experts.

31. Barthelemy, J. (2001). "The Hidden Costs of Outsourcing." *MIT Sloan Management Review,* 42(3) (Spring): 60–69.

32. Sovereign, K.L. (1999). *Personnel Law*. 4th ed. Upper Saddle River, NJ: Prentice-Hall.

Chapter 8

1. McGrath, R.M. (1999). "Falling Forward: Real Options Reasoning and Entrepreneurial Failure." *Academy of Management Review*, 24: 1, 13–31.

2. Collis, D., and C. Montgomery (1995). "Competing on Resources: Strategy in the 1990's." *Harvard Business Review* (July-August): 118–128; and Wernerfelt, B. (1984). "A Resource-Based View of the Firm." *Strategic Management Journal*, 5: 171–180.

3. Covin, J., and D. Slevin (1990). "Content and Performance of Growth-Seeking Strategies: A Comparison of Small Firms in High and Low Technology Industries." *Journal of Business Venturing*, 5(6): 391–412.

4. Brush, C.G., P.G. Greene, M.M. Hart, and H.S. Haller (2001). "From Initial Idea to Unique Advantage: The Entrepreneurial Challenge of Constructing a Resource Base." *Academy of Management Executive*, 15(1) (February): 64–78.

5. Amit, R., and P. Shoemaker (1993). "Strategic Assets and Organizational Rent." *Strategic Management Journal*, 14: 33–46.

Chapter 9

1. Lawton, J. (1999). "The Just-Right Business Plan." *Entrepreneur's Byline* (March 1), www.entreworld.org/Content/Entrebyline.cfm?ColumnID=75.

2. Gumpert, D.E. (2002). *Burn Your Business Plan! What Investors Really Want from Entrepreneurs.* Needham, MA: Lauson Publishing.

3. Rich, S.R., and D.E. Gumpert (1992). "How to Write a Winning Business Plan." In *The Entrepreneurial Venture*, ed. W.A. Sahlman and H.H. Stevenson. Boston: Harvard Business School Publishing.

4. Kelly, P., and M. Hay (2000). "The Private Investor–Entrepreneur Contractual Relationship: Understanding the Influence of Context." In *Frontiers of Entrepreneurship Research*, ed. E. Autio et al. Wellesley, MA: Babson College.

5. Ibid., 65.

6. Lawton, J. (1999). "The Just-Right Business Plan." *Entrepreneur's Byline* (March 1), www.entreworld.org/Content/Entrebyline.cfm?ColumnID=75.

7. Hankin, R.N. "Creating and Realizing the Value of a Business." *Entrepreneur's Byline*, EntreWorld.org, www.entreworld.org/Content/EntreByline.cfm?ColumnID=198.

8. Block, Z., and I.C. Macmillan (1992). "Milestones for Successful Venture Planning." In *The Entrepreneurial Venture*, ed. W.A. Sahlman and H.H. Stevenson. Boston: Harvard Business School Publishing, pp. 138–148.

9. Mason, C.M., and R.T. Harrison (2000). "Investing in Technology Ventures: What Do Business Angels Look for at the Initial Screening Stage?" In *Frontiers of Entrepreneurship Research*, ed. E. Autio et al. Wellesley, MA: Babson College, p. 293.

Chapter 10

1. Statistics of Income Division, Internal Revenue Service, www.sba.gov/advo/stats/rbwosp_03.pdf.

2. Greco, S. (2001). "Balancing Act." *Inc. Magazine* (January): 56–60, www.inc.com.

3. "Partnership Basics." NOLO Law for All, www.nolo.com/encyclopedia/articles/sb/partnerships.html.

4. "Partnership Basics." NOLO Law for All, www.nolo.com/encyclopedia/articles/sb/buy_sell.html.

5. United States Department of Health and Human Services, http://www.hhs.gov/ocr/hipaa/.

Chapter 11

1. Barrier, M. (1988). "Doing the Right Thing." *Nation's Business* (March), http://www.findarticles.com/p/articles/mi_m1154/is_n3_v86/ai_20401415, accessed September 2004.

2. Anderson, D., and K. Perine (2000). "Marketing the DoubleClick Way." *The Industry Standard Magazine* (March 6), www.thestandard.com.

3. Fenn, D. (2001) "Rescue at cc:," *Inc. Magazine*, February 27.

4. Freeman, R.E. (1984). *Strategic Management: A Stakeholder Approach.* Englewood Cliffs, NJ: Prentice-Hall.

5. Evan, W., and R.E. Freeman (1996). "A Stakeholder Theory of the Modern Corporation: Kantian Capitalism." In *Ethical Theory and Business,* ed. T. Beauchamp and N. Bowie. Englewood Cliffs, NJ: Prentice-Hall.

6. Longenecker, J.G., J.A. McKinney, and C.W. Moore (1989). "Ethics in Small Business." *Journal of Small Business,* 27: 27–31.

7. McDonald, G.M., and R.A. Zepp (1989). "Business Ethics: Practical Proposals." *Journal of Business Ethics*, 81: 55–56.

8. McNamara, C. *Complete Guide to Ethics Management: An Ethics Toolkit for Managers.* Free Management Library, www.mapnp.org/library/topics.htm.

9. Josephson Institute for Ethics, http://www.charactercounts.org/defsix.htm.

10. Cavanaugh, G.F., D.J. Moberg, and M. Valasquez (1981). "The Ethics of Organizational Politics." *Academy of Management Review*, 6(3): 363–374.

11. Dees, J.G., H.J. Emerson, and P. Economy (2001). *Enterprising Nonprofits: A Toolkit for Social Entrepreneurs.* New York: Wiley.

12. The Nature Conservancy's website, www.nature.org, accessed September 2004.

13. "Introduction to Corporate Social Responsibility," *Business for Social Responsibility Report*, www.bsr.org.

14. Greco, S. (1997). "Volunteering: The New Employee Perk." *Inc. Magazine* (September 1), www.inc.com.

15. Ibid.

16. Muoio, A. "Ways to Give Back," *Fast Company*, 12 (December 1997–June 1998), p. 113.

17. Collins, J., and J. Porras (1997). *Built to Last: Successful Habits of Visionary Companies.* New York: HarperBusiness.

18. www.nortelnetworks.com/corporate/community/ethics/guide.html#living. Reprinted with permission of Nortel Networks.

19. Ibid., 76.
20. Nash, L. (1988). "Mission Statements—Mirrors and Windows." *Harvard Business Review* (March-April): 155–156; and Schermerhorn Jr., J.R., and D.S. Chappell (2000). *Introducing Management.* New York: Wiley.
21. "Drucker Foundation Self-Assessment Tool: Content— How to Develop a Mission Statement," Leader to Leader Institute, www.pfdf.org/leaderbooks/sat/mission.html, accessed January 1, 2004.
22. Boyd, D.P., and D.E. Gumpert (1983). "Coping with Entrepreneurial Stress." *Harvard Business Review* (March-April): 44–64.
23. Bird, B.J. (1989). *Entrepreneurial Behavior.* Glenview, IL: Scott, Foresman.

Chapter 12

1. Barth, H. (2003). "Fit among Competitive Strategy, Administrative Mechanisms, and Performance: A Comparative Study of Small Firms in Mature and New Industries." *Journal of Small Business Management,* 4(2): 133–148.
2. Hanks, S.H., and G.N. Chandler (1994). "Patterns of Functional Specialization in Emerging High Tech Firms." *Journal of Small Business Management,* 32(2): 22–37; and Jennings, P., and G. Beaver (1997). "The Performance and Competitive Advantage of Small Firms: A Management Perspective." *International Small Business Journal,* 15(2): 6375.
3. Ibid.
4. Stone, M.M., and C.G. Brush (1996). "Planning in Ambiguous Contexts: The Dilemma of Meeting Needs for Commitment and Demands for Legitimacy." *Strategic Management Journal,* 17(8): 633–653.
5. Churchill, N., and V. Lewis (1983). "The Five States of Business Growth." *Harvard Business Review,* 61: 30–50.
6. Reed, M.I., and M. Hughes, eds. (1996). *Rethinking Organizations: New Directions in Organization Theory and Analysis.* London: Sage; Hassard, J., and M. Parker (1993). *Postmodernism and Organizations.* London: Sage; and Boje, D.M. (1996). *Postmodern Management and Organization Theory.* Thousand Oaks, CA: Sage.
7. Osborne, R.L. (1992). "Minority Ownership for Key Employees: Dividend or Disaster?" *Business Horizons,* 35(1): 76.

Chapter 13

1. Chang, M. (1995). "Turning Raw Materials into Finished Products." *Laser Focus World,* November, http://lfw.pennnet.com.
2. Trebilcock, B. (2001). "E-Manufacturing Gets Started." *Modern Materials Handling* (May 15), www.manufacuring.net.
3. Ibid.

4. Anderson, E., and B. Weitz (1992). "The Use of Pledges to Build and Sustain Commitment in Distribution Channels." *Journal of Marketing Research,* 29 (February): 18–34; and Doney, P.M., and J.P. Cannon (1997). "An Examination of the Nature of Trust in Buyer–Seller Relationships." *Journal of Marketing,* 61 (April): 35–51.
5. Anderson, E., and A.T. Coughlan (1987). "International Market Entry and Expansion via Independent or Integrated Channels of Distribution." *Journal of Marketing,* 51 (January): 71–82.
6. Lusch, R.F., and J.R. Brown (1996). "Interdependency, Contracting, and Relational Behavior in Marketing Channels." *Journal of Marketing,* 60 (October): 19–38; and Noordewier, T.G., G. John, and J.R. Nevin (1990). "Performance Outcomes of Purchasing Arrangements in Industrial Buyer–Vendor Relationships." *Journal of Marketing,* 54 (October): 80–93.
7. Emshwiller, J.R. (1991). "Suppliers Struggle to Improve Quality as Big Firms Slash Their Vendor Rolls." *Wall Street Journal* (August 16): B1, B2.
8. Magnet, M. (1994). "The New Golden Rule of Business." *Fortune* (February 21): 60–64.
9. Cannon, J.P. (1999). "Buyer–Seller Relationships in Business Markets." *Journal of Marketing Research,* 36(4): 439–461.
10. "Feigenbaum's 40 Steps to Quality Improvement." In *Federal Quality Management Handbook,* Appendix IA: "How to Get Started," June 1990, http://deming.eng.clemson.edu/pub/tqmbbs/prin-pract/feig40.txt.
11. Ibid.
12. Hopper, K. (1982). "Creating Japan's New Industrial Management: The Americans as Teachers." *Human Resource Management,* 21(2–3): 13–34.
13. Bartholomew, D. (2001). "Cost v. Quality." *Industry Week* (September), www.industryweek.com.
14. Terry, R. (2002). "Training Toys." *Washington Techway* (July 23), www.washtech.com.
15. Op. cit. Feigenbaum (1990), 1.
16. Challener, C. (2001). "Six Sigma: Can the GE Model Work in the Chemical Industry?" *Chemical Market Reporter* (July 16), www.findarticles.com.
17. Boswell, C. (2001). "Technically, Inc. Boosts Process Development with Six Sigma." *Chemical Market Reporter* (July 16), www.findarticles.com.

Chapter 14

1. Wind, J. (1999). "Marketing Strategy in the Global Information Age." *Knowledge@Wharton* (October 13), http://knowledge.wharton.upenn.edu.
2. Peppers, D., and M. Rogers (1993). *The One to One Future: Building Relationships One Customer at a Time.* New York: Currency/Doubleday.
3. Ibid., 36.

4. "Big-Time Marketing on a Small Budget." (2000). *Inc. Magazine* (October 11), www.inc.com.

5. Levinson, J.C. (1993). *Guerrilla Marketing*. Boston: Houghton Mifflin.

6. Pennington, A.Y. (2003). "Food for Thought." *Entrepreneur Magazine* (July), www.entrepreneur.com.

7. McConnell, B., and J. Huba (2002). "Top 6 Tips to Understanding Customer Evangelism." *MarketingProfs.com* (November 26).

8. Cannon, J.P. (1999). "Buyer–Seller Relationships in Business Markets." *Journal of Marketing Research,* 36(4): 439–461.

9. Bartholomew, D. (2001). "Cost v. Quality." *Industry Week* (September), www.industryweek.com.

10. Gupta, S. and Lehmann, D.R. (2002). "What are Your Customers Worth?" *Optimize*, Issue 22. http://www.optimizemag.com/article/showArticle.jhtml?articleId=17700715&pgno=2.

11. Terry, R. (2002). "Training Toys." *Washington Techway* (July 23), www.washtech.com.

Chapter 15

1. Venkataraman, S. (1997). "The Distinctive Domain of Entrepreneurship Research." *Advances in Entrepreneurship Research: Firm Emergence and Growth*, 3: 119–138; and Gompers, P. (1997). "An Examination of Convertible Securities in Venture Capital Investments." Working Paper, Harvard University.

2. Barney, J. (1991). "Firm Resources and Sustained Competitive Advantage." *Journal of Management,* 17(2), 99–120.

3. Brush, C.G., P.G. Greene, M.M. Hart, and H.S. Haller (2001). "From Initial Idea to Unique Advantage: The Entrepreneurial Challenge of Constructing a Resource Base." *The Academy of Management Executive,* 15(1): 64–78.

4. Ibid.

5. Ibid.

6. Kirchhoff, B.A. (2003). "Entrepreneurship Economics." In *The Portable MBA in Entrepreneurship*. ed. W.D. Bygrave. 3d ed. New York: Wiley.

7. Global Entrepreneurship Monitor 2003, www.gemconsortium.org, accessed September 2004.

8. Moore, G. (2002). *Crossing the Chasm*. New York: HarperBusiness.

9. Bhide, A. (1992). "Bootstrapping Finance: The Art of Start-Ups." *Harvard Business Review,* 70(6): 109–117.

10. Fenn, D. (August 2000). "The Classic Bootstrapper." *Inc. Magazine*, www.inc.com.

11. Clifford, S. (February 2005). "Fast-Growth Firms Sidestep Bank Loans," *Inc. Magazine,* www.inc.com.

12. "Brief Profiles of 2004 Inc. 500 Companies," *Inc. Magazine* (October 2003), www.inc.com.

13. Ibid.

14. Wellner, A.S. (2003). "Blood Money." *Inc. Magazine* (December), www.inc.com.

15. Mayer, M. (2003). "Taking the Fear Out of Factoring." *Inc. Magazine* (December), pp. 90–97.

16. Brinsley, J. (2000). "Incubator Becoming Dirty Word in Net Business." *Los Angeles Business Journal* (May), http://www.labusinessjournal.com/.

Chapter 16

1. Hoffman, H., and J. Blakely (1987). "You Can Negotiate with Venture Capitalists." *Harvard Business Review* (March-April), pp. 6–24.

2. Mikkelson, W.H., M. Partch, and K. Shah (1997). "Ownership and Operating Performance of Companies That Go Public." *Journal of Financial Economics,* 44: 281–308.

3. Peristiani, S. and G. Hong (2004). "Current Issues in Economics and Finance." *Federal Reserve Bank of New York,* 10(2), www.newyorkfed.org/research/current_issues, accessed September 2004.

4. Ibid.

5. Brokaw, L. (1992). "The First Day of the Rest of Your Life." *Inc. Magazine,* 15(5): 144.

6. Birchard, B. (1999). "Intangible Assets Plus Hard Numbers Equals Soft Finance." *Fast Company,* (28): 316, www.fastcompany.com, accessed September 2004.

7. Ibid.

8. White, M.C. "The Valuation of Newly-Formed Technology Companies." White and Lee, www.whiteandlee.com/valuatn.htm.

9. Tuller, L.W. (1994). *Small Business Valuation Book*. Holbrook, MA: Bob Adams, p. 43.

10. Boer, F.P. (2000). "Valuation of Technology Using Real Options," www.boer.org/files/RTMOptions2.doc, accessed September 2004.

11. Allen, K.R. (2003). *Bringing New Technology to Market*. Upper Saddle River, NJ: Prentice-Hall.

Chapter 17

1. Kaplan, S., and R. Foster (2001). *Creative Destruction: Why Companies That Are Built to Last Underperform the Market—and How to Successfully Transform Them*. New York: Doubleday/Currency.

2. Mackey, J., and L. Valinkangas (2004). "The Myth of Unbounded Growth." *MIT Sloan Management Review* (Winter), pp. 89–92.

3. Stanley, M.H.R., L.A.N. Amaral, S.V. Buldyrev, S. Havlin, H. Leschhorn, P. Maass, M.A. Slainger, and H.E. Stanley (1996). "Scaling Behaviour in the Growth of Companies." *Nature*, 379: 804–806.

4. Hofman, M. (2003). "Inc. 500: The Big Picture." *Inc. Magazine* (Fall), www.inc.com.

5. Bishop, S. (1999). "The Strategic Power of Saying No." *Harvard Business Review* (November/December).

6. Roberts, M.J. (1999). "Managing Growth." *New Business Venture and the Entrepreneurs.* New York: Irwin/McGraw-Hill.

7. Hannan, M., and J. Freeman (1984). "Structural Inertia and Organizational Change." *American Sociological Review,* 49: 149–164; and McKelvey, B., and H. Aldrich (1983). "Populations, Natural Selection, and Applied Organizational Science." *Administrative Science Quarterly,* 28(1): 101–128.

8. Kuratko, D.F., and R.M. Hodgetts (1989). *Entrepreneurship: A Contemporary Approach.* Chicago: Dryden Press.

9. Terpstra, D.E., and P.D. Olson (1993). "Entrepreneurial Start-up and Growth: A Classification of Problems." *Entrepreneurship Theory & Practice* (Spring), pp. 5–20.

10. Osborne, R.L. (1994). "Second Phase Entrepreneurship: Breaking Through the Growth Wall." *Business Horizons* (January-February), pp. 80–86.

11. Lafontaine, F. (1998). "Franchising Growth and Franchisor Entry and Exit in the U.S. Market: Myth and Reality." *Journal of Business Venturing,* 13: 95–112.

12. Bates, T. (1999). Franchising Testimony of Dr. Timothy Bates to the U.S. House of Representatives Judiciary Committee's Subcommittee in Commercial and Administrative Law, U.S. Government Printing Office; Shane, S. (1996). "Hybrid Organizational Arrangements and Their Implication for Firm Growth and Survival: A Study of New Franchisors." *Academy of Management Journal* (February), 216–231; and Op. cit. Lafontaine (1998).

13. Mannion, M.J. (2003). "Advice on Acquisition Advisors." *Inc. Magazine* (July), www.inc.com.

14. Ibid.

15. Kline, S.R. (accessed 6/20/2004). "Growth and Diversification Through Vertical Integration." *PF Online,* www.pfonline.com.

16. Linder, J.C. (2004). "Transformational Outsourcing." *MIT Sloan Management Review* (Winter), pp. 52–58.

17. Ibid, 52.

18. Austin, N.K. (1999). "Sailor's Delight." *Inc. Magazine* (November), www.inc.com; and "Bequia's Queen of Clean Has Caribbean Sailors All Washed Up." *BoatTalk News* (April 2000). http://www.boattalk.com/boattalknews/042800.htm.

19. U.S. Department of Commerce (2000). *U.S. Export Statistics,* www.census.gov/foreign-trade/www/, accessed September 2004.

20. Oviatt, B.M., and P. McDougall (1995). "Global Start-ups: Entrepreneurs on a Worldwide Stage." *The Academy of Management Executive,* 9(2): 30–44.

21. Ibid.

Chapter 18

1. Thurow, L. (2004). "Help Wanted: A Chief Knowledge Officer." *Fast Company* (January), pp. 78, 91.

2. Yates, J.F., and E.R. Stone (1992). "Risk Appraisal." In *Risk-Taking Behavior,* ed. J.F. Yates. New York: Wiley.

3. Smeltzer, L.R., and S.P. Siferd (1998). "Proactive Supply Management: The Management of Risk." *International Journal of Purchasing and Materials Management,* 34(1): 38–45.

4. Krause, D.R. (1999). "The Antecedents of Buying Firms' Efforts to Improve Suppliers." *Journal of Operations Management,* 17(2): 205–224.

5. Lee, H.L., V. Padmanabhan, and S. Whang (1997). "The Bullwhip Effect in Supply Chains." *Sloan Management Review,* 43(4): 93–102.

6. Robertson, T.S., and H. Gatignon (1998). "Technology Development Mode: A Transaction Cost Conceptualization." *Strategic Management Journal,* 19(1): 515–531.

7. U.S. Department of Labor's Bureau of Labor Statistics (March 2004), http://www.bls.gov/news.release/ecec.nr0.htm.

8. McCuan, J. (2004). "Guard Your Exits!" *Inc. Magazine* (April), p. 44.

9. Kahn, A.D. (1999). "Facing the Reality of Succession Planning." *The CPA Journal* 69(9): 66–67.

10. Matthews, C. (2001). "Planning for Succession." *Inc. Magazine* (October 17), www.inc.com.

11. Yates, J.F., and E.R. Stone (1992). "The Risk Construct." In *Risk-Taking Behavior,* ed. J.F. Yates. New York: Wiley.

12. Zsidisn, G.A., and A. Panelli (2000). "Purchasing Organization Involvement in Risk Assessments, Contingency Plans, and Risk Management: An Exploratory Study." *Supply Chain Management,* 5(4): 187.

13. Buchanan, L. (2003). "How to Take Risks in a Time of Anxiety." *Inc. Magazine* (May), www.inc.com.

14. Katz, J.A. (1995) "Which Track Are You On?" *Inc. Magazine* (October), p. 27.

Index

Note: *f* indicates *figure,* *p* indicates *profile,* and *t* indicates *table.*